LETTS GUIDE TO

ORCHIDS

of the

WORLD

MARGARET HODGSON   ROLAND PAINE
NEVILLE ANDERSON

CHARLES LETTS · *Letts* · FOUNDED 1796

First published in the United Kingdom in 1991
by Charles Letts & Co Ltd
Diary House, Borough Road,
London SE1 1DW
England

by arrangement with CollinsAngus&Robertson
Publishers Pty Limited (ACN 009 913 517)
A division of HarperCollinsPublishers
Unit 4, Eden Park Industrial Estate
31 Waterloo Road
North Ryde
New South Wales 2113
Australia

British Library Cataloguing in Publication Data:
  Hodgson, Margaret
  Letts guide to orchids of the world.
  1. Orchids
  I. Title
  584.15

  ISBN 1 - 85238 - 113 - 2

'Letts' is a registered trademark of Charles Letts (Scotland) Ltd

Cover photograph: Laelia tenebrosa *(front),*
Trichoglottis philippinensis *(back) by Roland Paine*

Printed in Australia by Griffin Press

CONTENTS

PREFACE

Orchidaceae is one of the largest, most diverse and exciting families of the flowering plant kingdom, comprising more than 700 genera and some 35 000 species of orchids scattered throughout the world. Their diversity in shape, size, colour, habitat and perfume, seem to be of unknown combinations and range.

A Guide to Orchids of the World has been designed for the keen amateur and exacting professional grower alike. We intend this book also to be a useful buyers' guide. Throughout the world there is renewed interest in species for hybridisation, since more orchid enthusiasts have begun doing their own hybridising and breeding. This book provides information to assist them.

As a book for both the novice and the professional *A Guide to Orchids of the World* has a wealth of information ranging from an introduction to what an orchid is, to details of cultivation, and a selection of illustrated botanical terms showing orchid plant structures from one species to the other. The book examines pollination, breeding, propagation, tissue culture, pests and diseases and provides a detailed glossary. Each section contains illustrations and photographs. A comprehensive range of genera are described in detail. The genera are fully illustrated and are accompanied by distribution maps and a selection of 458 species, each photographed in colour and described. The species include epiphytic, lithophytic and terrestrial orchids from around the world.

ACKNOWLEDGMENTS

In the preparation of a book, authors depend on many people for their assistance in gathering information and supplying plant specimens for photography and illustrations. We wish to acknowledge the contributions of individuals throughout the world.

Thank you to the staff of the Royal Botanic Gardens, Sydney, Australia, especially John Firlonger, and the staff of the National Parks and Wildlife Services in Australia and Borneo.

In Australia, we thank John Reipon, Sydney; Ross Whittle, Copmanhurst; Peter and Anne Schardin in assisting with our overseas travel, and film processing; and Michael Healy also of Murwillumbah; Lorrie Friar, Grafton; Steve Clemesha, Coffs Harbour; Graham Gamble, Lismore; York Meredith and Barney Greer, Sydney and Neville Fenton, Port Macquarie. A special thanks to Alan Englert of Tucabia for his assistance. We extend an extra special thanks to Alanah Anderson, also 'Sandy' and Ollie Anderson, of Woolgoolga, Australia, for their long hours of help and for making many specimens available.

We express our deep appreciation to Tony Ila, Member of Parliament for Lae, and Michael Coutts, both of Port Moresby, Papua New Guinea; Jeff Dennis, Government Botanist Honiara, from the Solomon Islands; Kevin Weinert, Peter Makuyike and Simon Daka, all of Madang, Papua New Guinea; Dick Phillips, Suva, Fiji; Som Sakdi, Bangkok, Thailand; and Elias and Alicia Javier, Manila, Philippines.

We extend our appreciation to our guides who assisted us while we were in the Malay Peninsula; Maijol Kakut, our guide while at Mount Kinabalu, Borneo; James Enjah, guide from the Iban tribe, Miri, Borneo; Laurence Lye of Kuching, Borneo; and Masi, our guide in Fiji.

Thanks to Margaret Hodgson's and Roland Paine's son Naradarn Hodgson Paine for the many hours he put into typing the manuscript. Last but not least thank you to Margaret Hodgson's mother, Thelma Hodgson, for keeping the home fires burning.

CLIMATE KEY

Hot—Minimum 15 degrees Celsius (59°F)

Warm—Minimum 10 degrees Celsius (50°F)

Intermediate—Minimum 5 degrees Celsius (41°F)

Cool—Minimum 1 degree Celsius (33.8°F)

This key is for tropical to sub-tropical climates where daytime temperatures rise some 15 to 20 degrees Celsius above the night-time minimum. In cold climates this factor should be taken into consideration and minimums set higher.

ABBREVIATIONS

aff.—Akin to, close to forma form: a taxonomic level below subspecies.

Gk—Greek.

Lat.—Latin (including Neo-Latin and botanical Latin).

sp.—Species.

ssp.—Subspecies: a taxonomic level below species and above variety.

syn.—Synonym: indicates an older name that applies to the same species.

var.—Variety: a taxonomic level below subspecies, but often in almost the same way as subspecies.

X—Natural native hybrid cross; indicates the name given to the resultant plant, or is used to link the names of the two parents.

INTRODUCTION

Orchidaceae is the largest family of the flowering plant kingdom, comprising some 35 000 species, and possibly there are the same number of hybrids produced both by natural cross and artificial pollination.

The flowers of the world are divided into two basic groups:
• The *regular flowers* are symmetrical—when viewed face on they can be cut through the centre along any plane to produce identical halves.
• The *irregular flowers* have segments of different shape and size, and when viewed face on cannot be cut along any plane to produce identical halves.

The orchid is an irregular flower, but it is special—view it face on, and in one plane only can it be cut to produce identical halves. A line drawn from the apex of the dorsal sepal through the centre of the column to the apex of the labellum will produce halves, one a mirror image of the other. This type of flower is said to be *zygomorphic*, from the Gk *zygot* (occurring in pairs) and *morph* (shape or form) with reference to the one form but with identical halves.

The Orchidaceae family has to be the most diverse in the world for colour, size, shape, habitat and perfume. Orchids vary in height from the minute Australian species *Bulbophyllum minutissimum*, approximately 3mm (1/16″) high, to the tallest (also an Australian species) *Galeola foliata*, which climbs to heights of 30m (100′) or more.

Orchid flowers are beautiful and, at times, bizarre. Many of the exquisite species belong to the *Dendrobium* (epiphytes) and *Paphiopedilum* (terrestrials) genera, such as *Dendrobium nobile* from Asia and *Paphiopedilum insigne* from India. One of the more bizarre is the Australian terrestrial, *Arthrochilus irritabilis*. While the pollinating wasp attempts to pseudocopulate with the flower, the irritable claw which attaches the labellum to the column is activated by the weight of the insect, causing the hammer-shaped lamina of the labellum, to which the wasp clings, to hammer the pollinator against the column, thus transferring any pollinium the wasp may be carrying on to the stigma. The result is the fertilisation of the flower.

Perfumes of the orchid flowers may be sweetly fragrant or may have the foul smell of something dead. Many species of *Dendrobiums*, *Cymbidiums*, *Phaius* and *Zygopetalums* produce exquisite, almost intoxicating, perfumes. In contrast, many species of *Bulbophyllums*, *Oncidiums* and *Coelogynes* carry overpowering offensive smells.

The structure of the flowers varies greatly, from simple *Cymbidiums* and *Cattleyas* to complex *Gongoras*, *Catasetums* and *Coryanthes*. By design, the shape of the flowers is determined by the way they are pollinated; often the labellum resembles a moth, bee, fly, wasp or spider, such as in the following genera: *Phalaenopsis* from the Philippines, *Ophrys* from Europe, *Cryptostylis* and *Caladenia* from Australia and *Oncidium* from South America.

In spite of their diverse shapes, all orchids have the same basic structure. Six basic floral segments make up the arrangement of an orchid flower; three sepals and three petals, alternating around the column which holds the reproductive parts of the plant. The sepal at the top of the flower is called the dorsal sepal and is usually different from the lateral sepals and may vary in shape and size.

The petal opposite the dorsal sepal is known as the labellum, from the Latin *labium*, meaning 'a lip'; it is different from the other petals and is generally trilobed. The labellum is often the most beautiful segment of the orchid flower. In some genera the flowers are inverted, with the labellum superior and the dorsal sepal at the bottom. The *Prasophyllums* are typical. With this species the lateral sepals are connate, or joined (refer to botanical illustrations).

Like most other flowers, orchids are bisexual, having both female and male parts. But orchids are special because the female and male parts—the stamens, the style and stigma— are united in one structure, called the column. This feature separates the orchid from other flowers, although in some species the flowers are unisexual e.g. *Catasetums*.

Orchid hunting will take the enthusiast through a diverse range of habitats in most parts of the world, except arid and frozen regions. Orchids also grow from sea level to an altitude of 4200m (14 000′).

Life-forms of orchids are usually divided into two main groups: epiphytes and terrestrials. Epiphytes (Lat. *epi*—upon, and *phyt*—plant, meaning on another plant or tree-dweller) use trees as their host. The majority of epiphytic orchids are confined to rainforest regions, wet sclerophyll forests, coastal tree belts, Paper Bark (*Melaleuca*) swamps and mangroves. Their long aerial roots not only hold them to their hosts but draw nutriments from leaf mould collected around their root systems and moisture from the air.

Terrestrials (Lat. *terrestris*—growing on the ground) are earth dwellers growing in the ground. They have fleshy rhizomes, fibrous roots or small tubers. Terrestrials range from rainforest, grasslands, savannah and open woodlands to coastal wetlands, but the habitat for most terrestrials is forests and woodlands of both northern and southern hemispheres. Many terrestrials have a five- or seven-year flowering cycle.

There are also orchids which are lithophytes (Gk *litho*— a stone). These orchids grow on moist rocks or cliff faces. From time to time epiphytes and terrestrials become lithophytic if growing conditions are right.

Saprophytes (Gk *sapros*—rotten, putrid) are plants that grow and derive most of their nourishment from decaying organic matter, often apparently lacking chlorophyll, and are mostly leafless. These plants live on the by-products of fungi which break down leaf mould and other vegetative matter. Saprophytes include *Corallorrhiza maculata* from Canada, U.S.A., Mexico and Guatemala. *Dipodium punctatum* is a representative Australian saprophyte.

SYMPODIAL AND MONOPODIAL GROUPS

Orchid growth can be classified into two main groups: sympodial and monopodial.

Sympodial (from Gk *sym*—united, and *podo*—a foot) refers to the pseudobulbs or stems being joined by a rhizome which is not always visible between them. The rhizome is the woody part of the root stock which varies in length and which joins one pseudobulb to the next.

The majority of orchids have a sympodial growth pattern. Sympodial orchids have pseudobulbs, so called because they are not true bulbs but thickened bulb-like stems. These stems are a storehouse of moisture and food, enabling the plant to survive dry periods. The main stem growth stops at the end of each season, and the new growth is produced at the base of the previous season's growth, similar to most perennial herbaceous plants. There is enormous diversity in the shapes of pseudobulbs; they range from minute to large in size and from round to egg-shape, and have club to thick cane stems. Some examples of genera belonging to this group are: *Cattleya, Dendrobium, Lycaste, Oncidium, Cymbidium, Odontoglossum, Encyclia, Epidendrum, Coelogyne* and *Phaius.*

Some sympodial orchids, within the terrestrial group, are without pseudobulbs. However their natural habitat maintains a constant seasonal supply of moisture to keep their root system or rhizome alive, so they are ready to produce new growth from the base of the last season's growth (for example, *Paphiopedilum* and its close relative *Phragmipedium*).

Monopodial (from the Gk *mono*—one, and *podo*—a foot) with reference to the plant having a single shoot which continues to grow from its terminal bud. The monopodial orchid's growth pattern is principally an upward direction extending the growth of previous years. The main stem produces alternating leaves on each side. Pseudobulbs are not present with monopodial growth. Monopodials may be described as climbing orchids; *Arachnis* is a good example, climbing to heights up to 20m (66'). Other examples in the monopodial group are *Vanda, Angraecum* and *Aerides.* Less vigorous growing monopodials are *Doritis* and *Phalaenopsis*; their growth is slow and compact.

SYMPODIAL

MONOPODIAL

    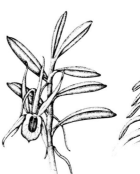

Cattleya labiata   *Dendrobium canaliculatum*   *Coelogyne speciosa*   *Phalaenopsis amabilis*   *Angraecum infundibulare*   *Vanda tricolor*

Parts of an Orchid

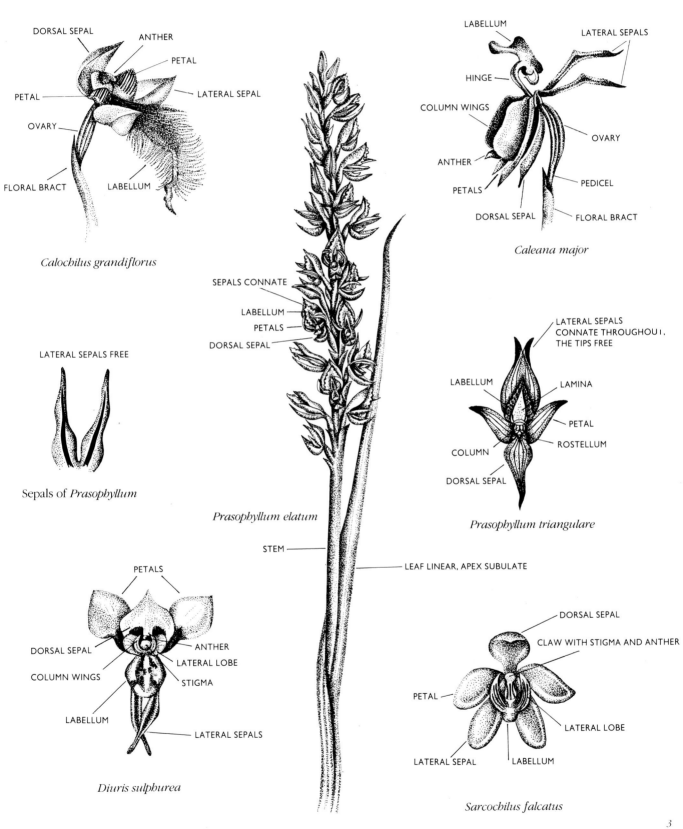

DORSAL SEPAL
ANTHER
PETAL
PETAL
LATERAL SEPAL
OVARY
FLORAL BRACT
LABELLUM

Calochilus grandiflorus

LABELLUM
LATERAL SEPALS
HINGE
COLUMN WINGS
OVARY
ANTHER
PETALS
PEDICEL
DORSAL SEPAL
FLORAL BRACT

Caleana major

SEPALS CONNATE
LABELLUM
PETALS
DORSAL SEPAL

LATERAL SEPALS FREE

Sepals of *Prasophyllum*

LATERAL SEPALS
CONNATE THROUGHOUT,
THE TIPS FREE
LABELLUM
LAMINA
PETAL
ROSTELLUM
COLUMN
DORSAL SEPAL

Prasophyllum triangulare

Prasophyllum elatum

STEM
LEAF LINEAR, APEX SUBULATE

PETALS
DORSAL SEPAL
ANTHER
LATERAL LOBE
COLUMN WINGS
STIGMA
LABELLUM
LATERAL SEPALS

Diuris sulphurea

DORSAL SEPAL
CLAW WITH STIGMA AND ANTHER
PETAL
LATERAL LOBE
LATERAL SEPAL
LABELLUM

Sarcochilus falcatus

3

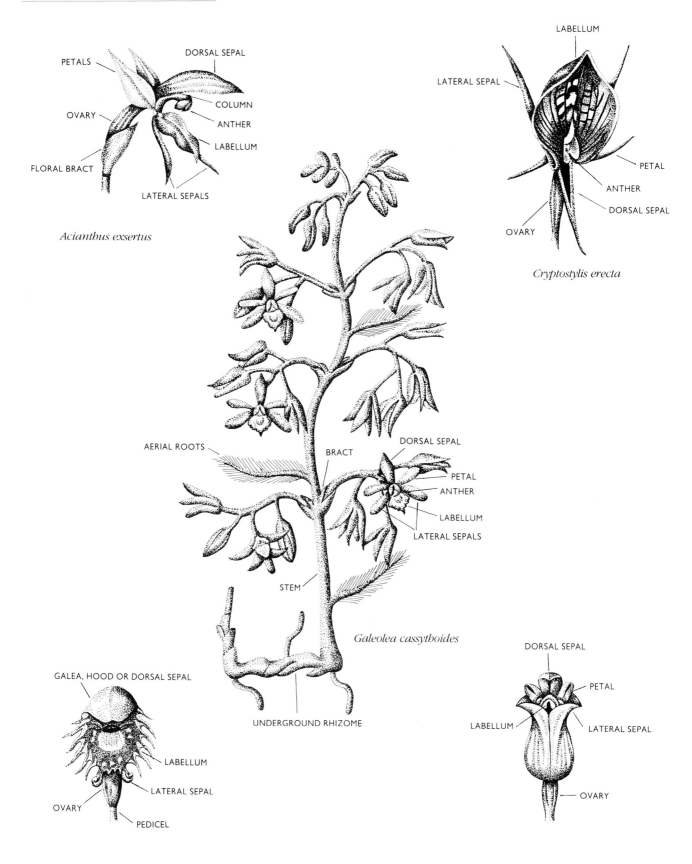

PETALS

DORSAL SEPAL

OVARY

COLUMN

ANTHER

LABELLUM

FLORAL BRACT

LATERAL SEPALS

Acianthus exsertus

LABELLUM

LATERAL SEPAL

PETAL

ANTHER

DORSAL SEPAL

OVARY

Cryptostylis erecta

AERIAL ROOTS

BRACT

DORSAL SEPAL

PETAL

ANTHER

LABELLUM

LATERAL SEPALS

STEM

Galeolea cassythoides

UNDERGROUND RHIZOME

GALEA, HOOD OR DORSAL SEPAL

LABELLUM

LATERAL SEPAL

OVARY

PEDICEL

Corybas undulatus

DORSAL SEPAL

PETAL

LABELLUM

LATERAL SEPAL

OVARY

Gastrodia sesamoides

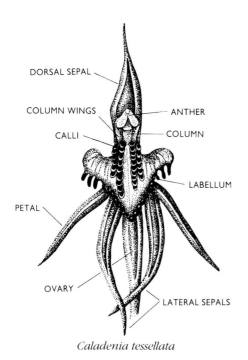

DORSAL SEPAL

COLUMN WINGS — ANTHER

CALLI — COLUMN

LABELLUM

PETAL

OVARY — LATERAL SEPALS

Caladenia tessellata

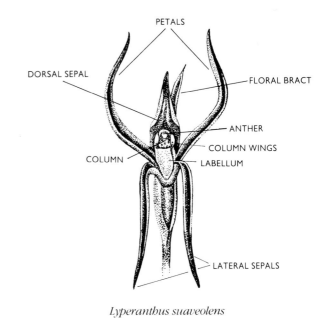

PETALS

DORSAL SEPAL — FLORAL BRACT

ANTHER

COLUMN WINGS

COLUMN — LABELLUM

LATERAL SEPALS

Lyperanthus suaveolens

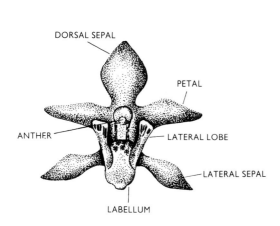

DORSAL SEPAL

PETAL

ANTHER — LATERAL LOBE

LATERAL SEPAL

LABELLUM

Pterocaras spathulatus

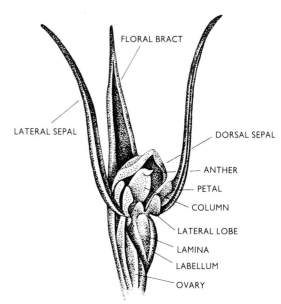

FLORAL BRACT

LATERAL SEPAL — DORSAL SEPAL

ANTHER

PETAL

COLUMN

LATERAL LOBE

LAMINA

LABELLUM

OVARY

Orthoceras strictum

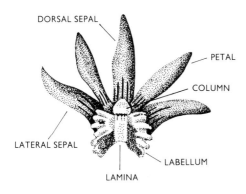

DORSAL SEPAL

PETAL

COLUMN

LATERAL SEPAL — LABELLUM

LAMINA

Dendrobium pugioniforme

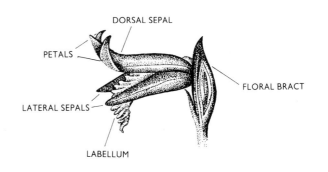

DORSAL SEPAL

PETALS

FLORAL BRACT

LATERAL SEPALS

LABELLUM

Spiranthes sinensis

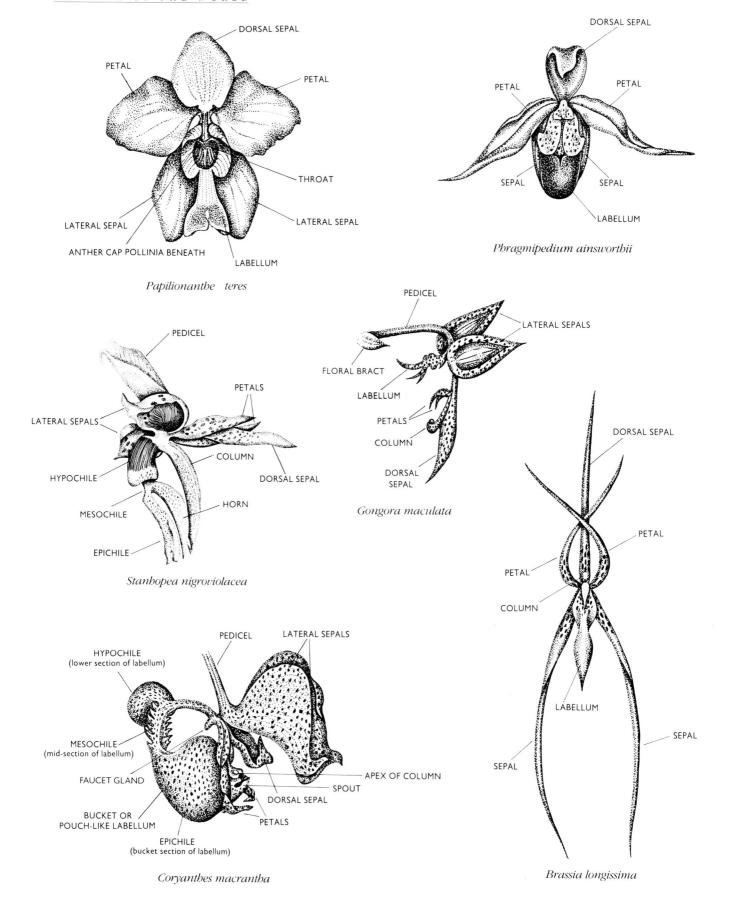

DORSAL SEPAL

PETAL

PETAL

THROAT

LATERAL SEPAL

LATERAL SEPAL

ANTHER CAP POLLINIA BENEATH

LABELLUM

Papilionanthe teres

DORSAL SEPAL

PETAL

PETAL

SEPAL

SEPAL

LABELLUM

Phragmipedium ainsworthii

PEDICEL

PETALS

LATERAL SEPALS

COLUMN

HYPOCHILE

DORSAL SEPAL

MESOCHILE

HORN

EPICHILE

Stanhopea nigroviolacea

PEDICEL

LATERAL SEPALS

FLORAL BRACT

LABELLUM

PETALS

COLUMN

DORSAL SEPAL

Gongora maculata

DORSAL SEPAL

PETAL

PETAL

COLUMN

LABELLUM

SEPAL

SEPAL

Brassia longissima

HYPOCHILE
(lower section of labellum)

PEDICEL

LATERAL SEPALS

MESOCHILE
(mid-section of labellum)

FAUCET GLAND

APEX OF COLUMN

SPOUT

DORSAL SEPAL

BUCKET OR
POUCH-LIKE LABELLUM

PETALS

EPICHILE
(bucket section of labellum)

Coryanthes macrantha

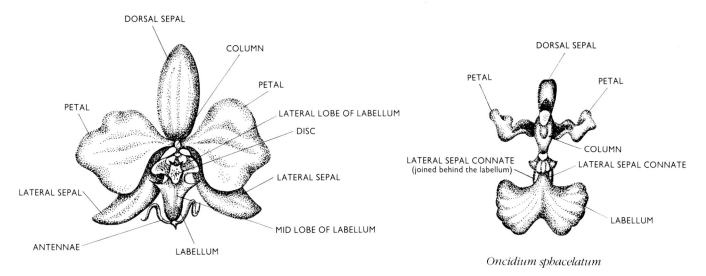

DORSAL SEPAL

COLUMN

PETAL

LATERAL LOBE OF LABELLUM

DISC

PETAL

LATERAL SEPAL

LATERAL SEPAL

MID LOBE OF LABELLUM

ANTENNAE

LABELLUM

Phalaenopsis sanderiana

DORSAL SEPAL

PETAL

PETAL

COLUMN

LATERAL SEPAL CONNATE
(joined behind the labellum)

LATERAL SEPAL CONNATE

LABELLUM

Oncidium sphacelatum

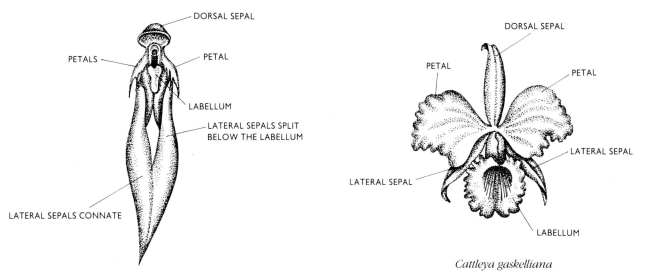

DORSAL SEPAL

PETALS

PETAL

LABELLUM

LATERAL SEPALS SPLIT
BELOW THE LABELLUM

LATERAL SEPALS CONNATE

Bulbophyllum picturatum

DORSAL SEPAL

PETAL

PETAL

LATERAL SEPAL

LATERAL SEPAL

LABELLUM

Cattleya gaskelliana

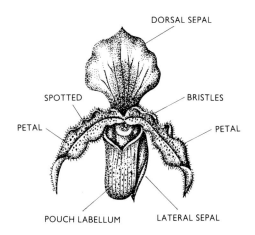

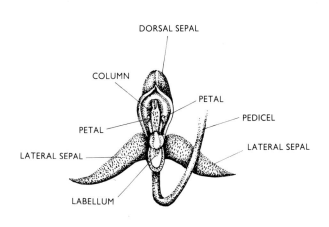

DORSAL SEPAL

SPOTTED

BRISTLES

PETAL

PETAL

POUCH LABELLUM

LATERAL SEPAL

Paphiopedilum hirsutissimum

DORSAL SEPAL

COLUMN

PETAL

PETAL

PEDICEL

LATERAL SEPAL

LATERAL SEPAL

LABELLUM

Gongora galeata

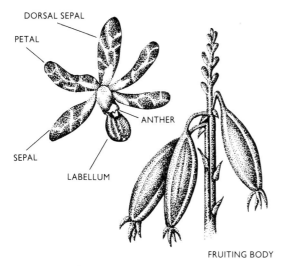

DORSAL SEPAL

PETAL

ANTHER

SEPAL

LABELLUM

FRUITING BODY

Dipodium punctatum

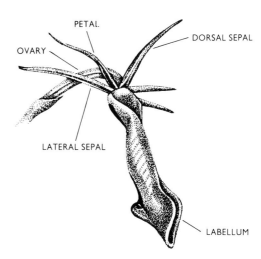

DORSAL SEPAL

ANTHER

PETAL

LATERAL SEPAL

LABELLUM

Dendrobium bigibbum

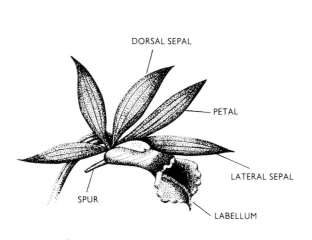

DORSAL SEPAL

PETAL

LATERAL SEPAL

SPUR

LABELLUM

Phaius australis

PETAL

OVARY

DORSAL SEPAL

LATERAL SEPAL

LABELLUM

Cryptostylis subulata

GLANDS

HINGE

COLUMN

CLAW

ANTHER

DORSAL SEPAL

LABELLUM

PETALS

LATERAL SEPALS

BRACT

Drakea elastica

LABELLUM

HINGE

GLANDS

CLAW

ANTHER

COLUMN WINGS

LATERAL SEPALS

OVARY

DORSAL SEPAL

PETALS

Arthrochilus irritabilis

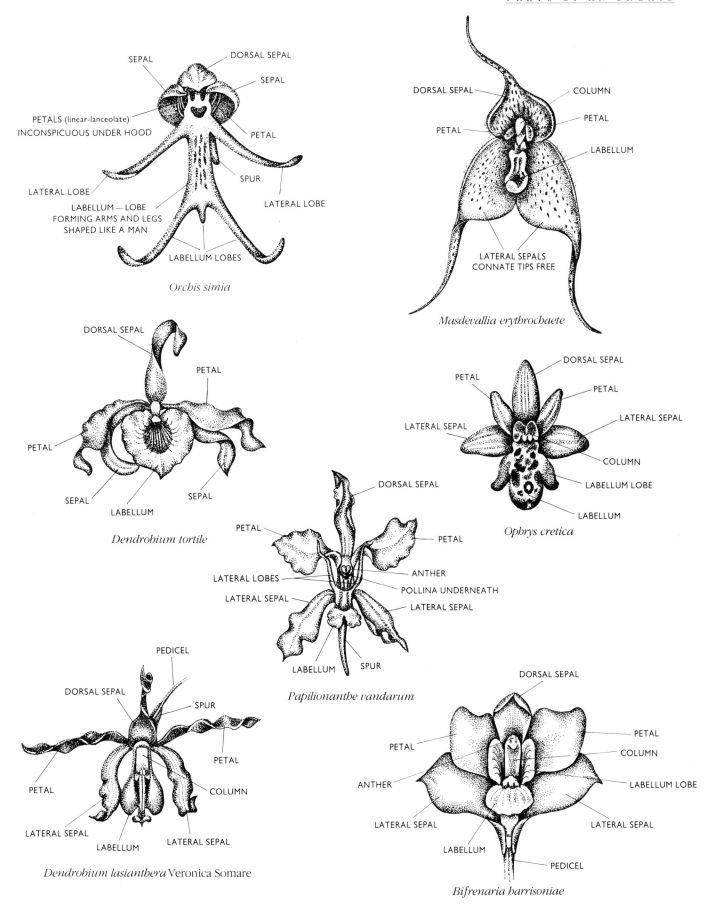

Orchis simia

Masdevallia erythrochaete

Dendrobium tortile

Ophrys cretica

Papilionanthe vandarum

Dendrobium lasianthera Veronica Somare

Bifrenaria harrisoniae

LEAF AND PSEUDOBULBS ILLUSTRATED

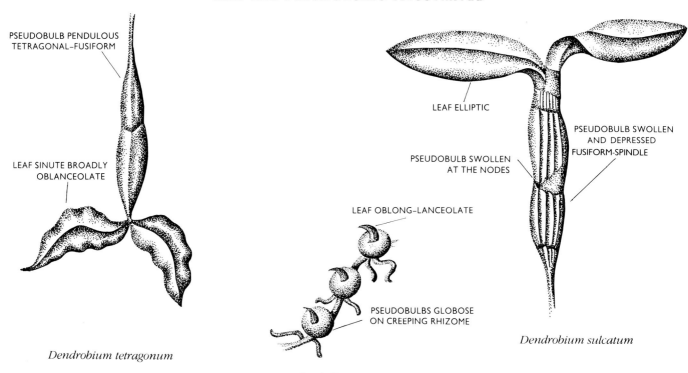

PSEUDOBULB PENDULOUS
TETRAGONAL–FUSIFORM

LEAF SINUTE BROADLY
OBLANCEOLATE

Dendrobium tetragonum

LEAF ELLIPTIC

PSEUDOBULB SWOLLEN
AND DEPRESSED
FUSIFORM-SPINDLE

PSEUDOBULB SWOLLEN
AT THE NODES

LEAF OBLONG–LANCEOLATE

PSEUDOBULBS GLOBOSE
ON CREEPING RHIZOME

Dendrobium sulcatum

Bulbophyllum minutissimum

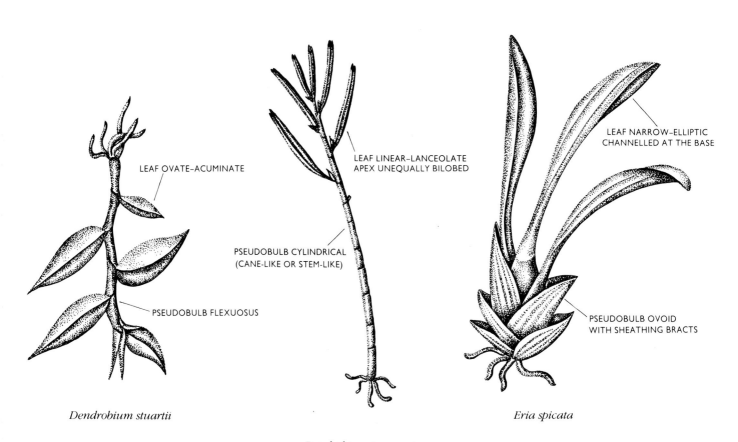

LEAF OVATE–ACUMINATE

PSEUDOBULB FLEXUOSUS

LEAF LINEAR–LANCEOLATE
APEX UNEQUALLY BILOBED

PSEUDOBULB CYLINDRICAL
(CANE-LIKE OR STEM-LIKE)

LEAF NARROW–ELLIPTIC
CHANNELLED AT THE BASE

PSEUDOBULB OVOID
WITH SHEATHING BRACTS

Dendrobium stuartii

Eria spicata

Dendrobium tozerensis

LEAF AND PSEUDOBULBS ILLUSTRATED

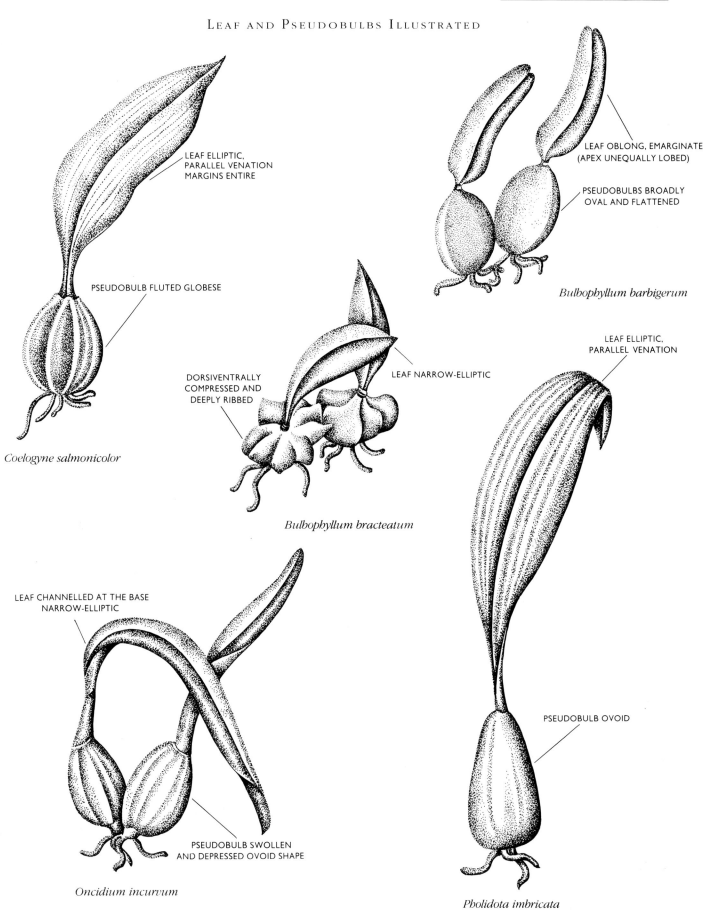

LEAF ELLIPTIC,
PARALLEL VENATION
MARGINS ENTIRE

PSEUDOBULB FLUTED GLOBESE

Coelogyne salmonicolor

LEAF OBLONG, EMARGINATE
(APEX UNEQUALLY LOBED)

PSEUDOBULBS BROADLY
OVAL AND FLATTENED

Bulbophyllum barbigerum

DORSIVENTRALLY
COMPRESSED AND
DEEPLY RIBBED

LEAF NARROW-ELLIPTIC

Bulbophyllum bracteatum

LEAF ELLIPTIC,
PARALLEL VENATION

LEAF CHANNELLED AT THE BASE
NARROW-ELLIPTIC

PSEUDOBULB SWOLLEN
AND DEPRESSED OVOID SHAPE

Oncidium incurvum

PSEUDOBULB OVOID

Pholidota imbricata

Leaf and Pseudobulbs Illustrated

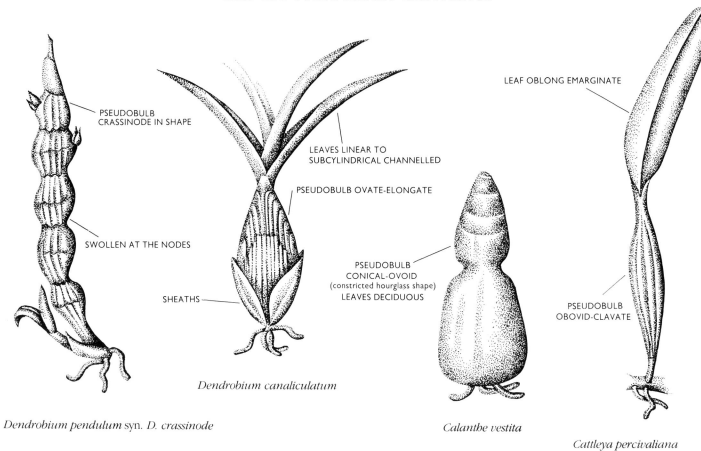

PSEUDOBULB
CRASSINODE IN SHAPE

SWOLLEN AT THE NODES

SHEATHS

LEAVES LINEAR TO
SUBCYLINDRICAL CHANNELLED

PSEUDOBULB OVATE-ELONGATE

LEAF OBLONG EMARGINATE

PSEUDOBULB
CONICAL-OVOID
(constricted hourglass shape)
LEAVES DECIDUOUS

PSEUDOBULB
OBOVID-CLAVATE

Dendrobium pendulum syn. *D. crassinode*

Dendrobium canaliculatum

Calanthe vestita

Cattleya percivaliana

Dendrobium Group Showing Variants Within a Genus

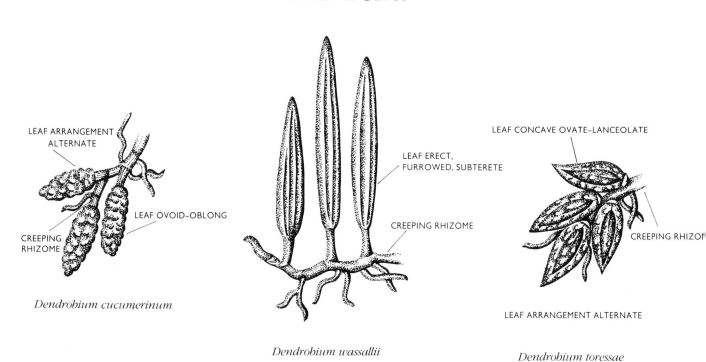

LEAF ARRANGEMENT
ALTERNATE

CREEPING
RHIZOME

LEAF OVOID–OBLONG

LEAF ERECT,
FURROWED, SUBTERETE

CREEPING RHIZOME

LEAF CONCAVE OVATE–LANCEOLATE

CREEPING RHIZOI

LEAF ARRANGEMENT ALTERNATE

Dendrobium cucumerinum

Dendrobium wassallii

Dendrobium toressae

DENDROBIUM GROUP SHOWING VARIANTS
WITHIN A GENUS

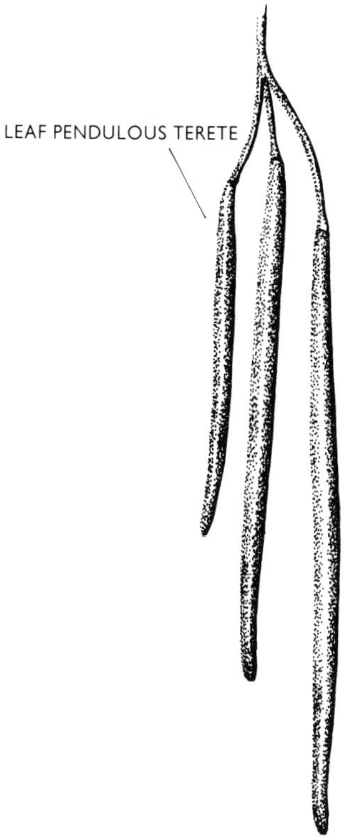

LEAF PENDULOUS TERETE

CREEPING RHIZOME

LEAF RIBBED OVATE

CREEPING RHIZOME

LEAF ARRANGEMENT
ALTERNATE

LEAF OVATE TO
LANCEOLATE

LEAF ALTERNATE

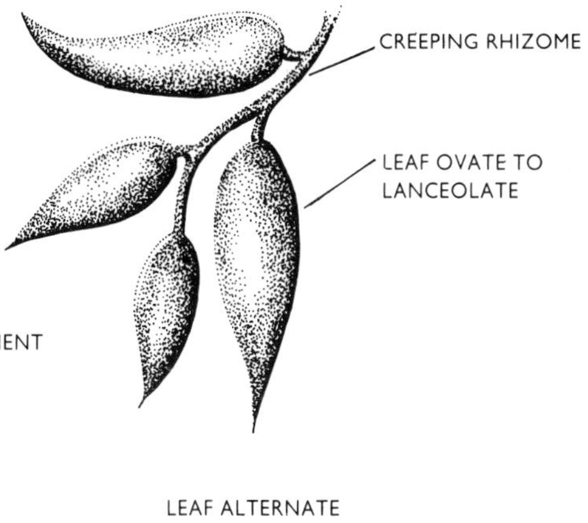

Dendrobium pugioniforme

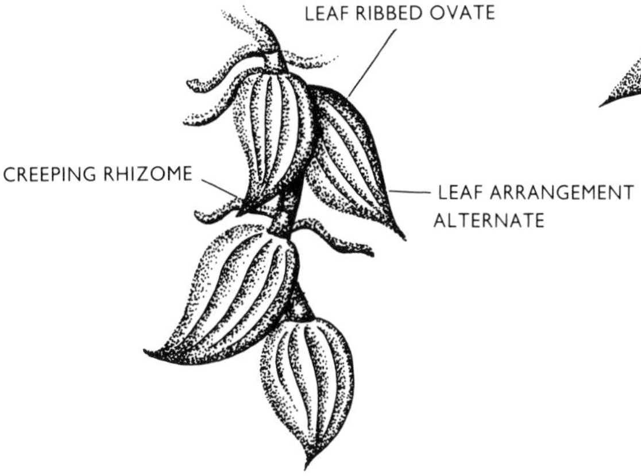

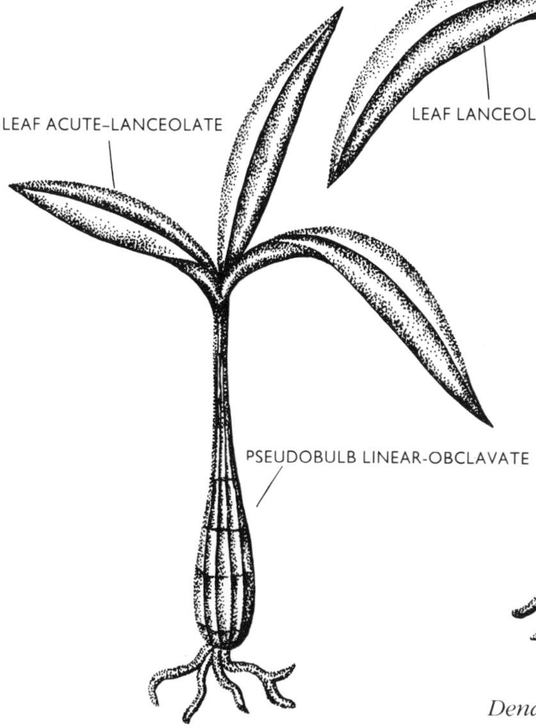

Dendrobium linguiforme

Dendrobium tenuissimum

LEAF LANCEOLATE

LEAF ACUTE-LANCEOLATE

LEAF OVATE-OBLONG

PSEUDOBULB CYLINDRICAL

PSEUDOBULB LINEAR-OBCLAVATE

PSEUDOBULB FUSIFORM

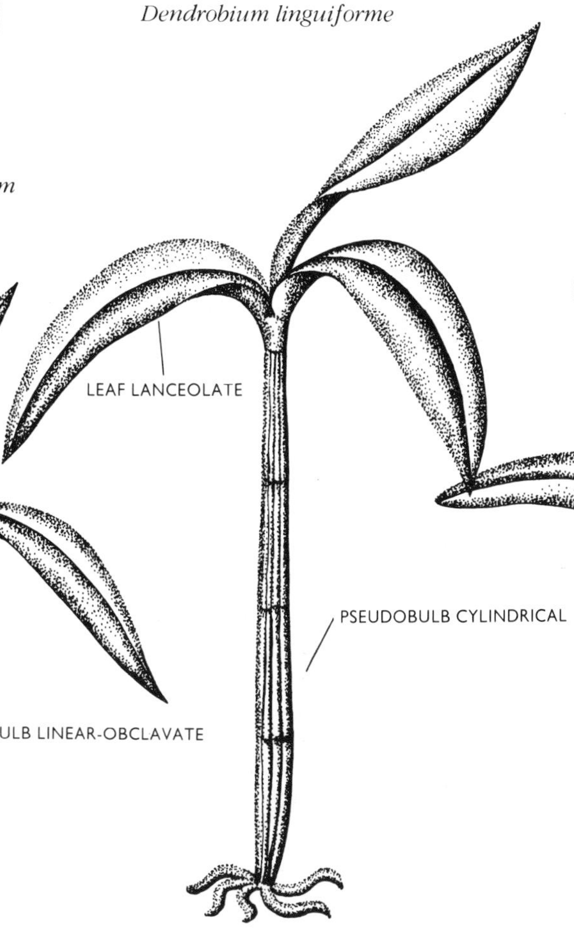

Dendrobium gracilicaule

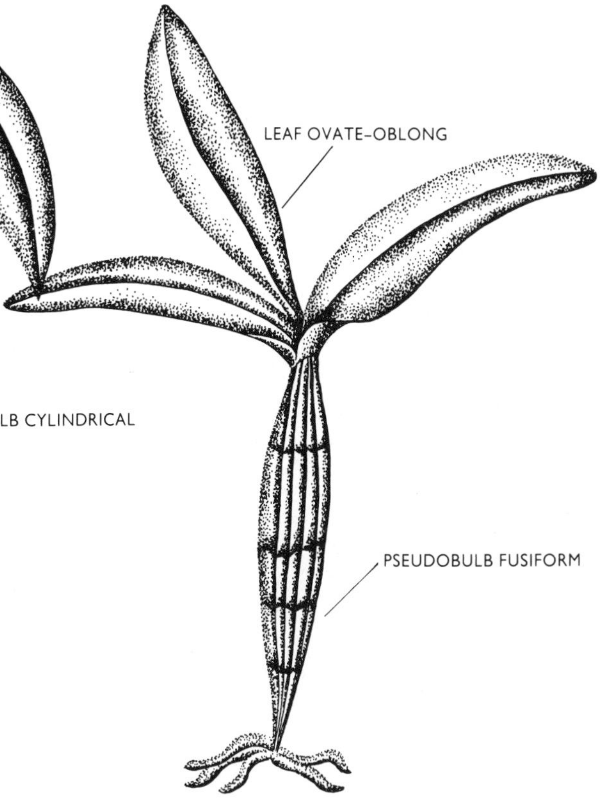

Dendrobium kingianum

Dendrobium ruppianum

LEAF AND PETAL SHAPES

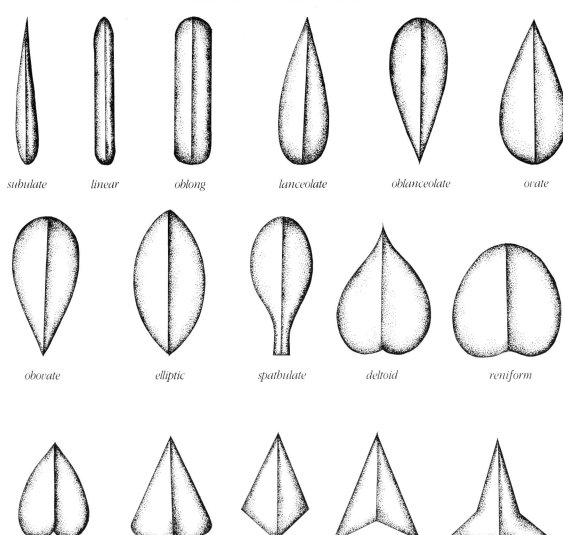

subulate   *linear*   *oblong*   *lanceolate*   *oblanceolate*   *ovate*

obovate   *elliptic*   *spathulate*   *deltoid*   *reniform*

cordate   *triangular*   *trullate*   *sagittate*   *hastate*

LEAF AND PETAL TIPS

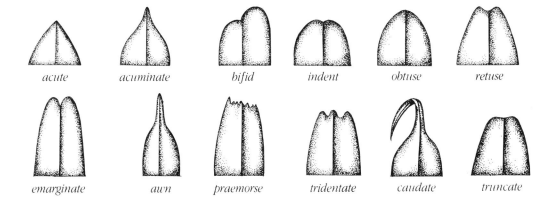

acute   *acuminate*   *bifid*   *indent*   *obtuse*   *retuse*

emarginate   *awn*   *praemorse*   *tridentate*   *caudate*   *truncate*

CLASSIFICATION OF ORCHIDS

Orchidaceae is one of the largest of the flowering plant families. It is an exceedingly rich and diverse group of more than 35 000 species, and this number increases with the discovery of new specimens by both amateur and professional collectors.

One of the first botanists to attempt to classify orchids into genera was the botanist L. Fuchs in 1542. In 1583 Dosloneus set about a further reclassification of the expanding orchid family. Orchid collections were growing in size as well, with more and more collections appearing throughout Europe as the rich indulged in a new found hobby.

Caspar Bauhin published his work on the classification of orchids in 1620. In 1753, Carl Von Linne' (Linnaeus), the father of modern taxonomy, published a detailed description of 69 species of 8 genera.

In America between 1788 and 1800, O. Swartz recognised the difference between species with one anther and those with two anthers.

A further development occurred in 1810 when R. Brown recognised the importance of the anther and pollinia character and habit of the species.

By 1825 the famous taxonomist John Lindley started the first major classification of orchids, and for the next forty years he worked continuously on revising his classification. Lindley's work was revised with the advent of a number of younger research taxonomists—Ames, Pfitzer, Rolfe and others.

In the early 1900s Rudolf Schlecter began to be known as 'a splitter'. He based his research on the works of Pfitzer, but first increased the number of subtribes in Pfitzer's classification. Where most taxonomists were content to recognise variations of a species, Schlecter split the variations off into new species, thus expanding the number of species in a genus. Often he placed them into a new genus, thus expanding the number of genera. This process became known as the Schlecter System and remained unchanged until about 1930. Since then the system has been under continual review and modification. Today taxonomists fall into one of two schools and are classified as either a 'splitter' or 'lumper'.

The Orchidaceae family is growing day by day as field workers, amateurs and professionals alike find new specimens. When describing these new arrivals, taxonomists often need to create a new genus; sometimes in doing so, they find a new home for a well known, but problematic species, hence a new name is bestowed on an old favourite and another synonym is born.

Even with all this splitting, lumping and reclassification, the Orchidaceae family remains in the sub-division of Angiospermae of the Spermataphyta division of the plant kingdom, in the Monocotyledonae class under the Microspermae order. The Orchidaceae family is divided into subfamilies, then into tribes and subtribes, these again into genera and species before our beloved orchid is finally given a name. From time to time an orchid may be found to be a subspecies or variety of the species.

When describing and naming orchids, taxonomists use Greek and Latin names. Usually, Greek is used for the genus and Latin for the species part of the name; for example, the *Ascoglossum* genus name comes from the Greek *asos* meaning a bag and *glossa* meaning a tongue, with reference to the shape of the labellum; and *leucanthus* the species name is from the Latin *leuco* meaning white and *anthus* meaning a flower. So the full name meaning is: a white flower with baggy labellum.

The taxonomist must follow the International Rules of Nomenclature when naming the orchid.

- All family names end with 'aceae,' e.g. Orchidaceae.
- Subfamily names end with 'oideae,' e.g. Orchidioideae.
- Tribe names end with 'eae,' e.g. Vandeae.
- Subtribe names end with 'inae,' e.g. Vandinae.
- Only genera and species names are printed in italics.
- Genera names end with 'a, e, as, is, um, us' e.g. *Vanda*.
- The species name ending should agree with the generic ending, e.g. *Vanda denisoniana*.
- Likewise subspecies and variety name endings should agree with the species and generic ending, e.g. var. *herbarica*.

Hence the taxonomic relationship of *Vanda denisoniana* var. *herbarica*:

Family:	Orchidaceae.
Subfamily:	Orchidioideae.
Tribe:	Vandeae.
Subtribe:	Vandinae.
Genus:	*Vanda*
Species:	*denisoniana* var. *herbarica*.

In the condensed classification chart overleaf, the Orchidaceae family is divided into 3 subfamilies, 12 tribes, 45 subtribes and 186 genera. While an expanded classification could contain up to 6 or more subfamilies with a tribal and subtribal increase of up to 800 genera, you should be able to find the place of your favourite orchid on the chart overleaf.

CLASSIFICATION CHART

Family: Orchidaceae

 I. Subfamily: Apostasioideae
  Tribe: Apostasieae
   Genera: *Apostasia, Adactylus, Neuwiedia*

 II. Subfamily: Cypripedioideae
  Tribe: Cypripedieae
   Genera: *Cypripedium, Paphiopedilum,*
    Phragmipedium, Selenipedium

 III. Subfamily: Orchidioideae (Neottioideae)

 A. Tribe: Neottieae
  1. Subtribe: Limodorinae
   Genera: *Cephalanthera, Epipactis,*
    Limodorum
  2. Subtribe: Rhizanthellinae
   Genera: *Cryptanthemis, Rhizanthella*
  3. Subtribe: Pterostylidinae
   Genera: *Caleana, Pterostylis*
  4. Subtribe: Listerinae
   Genera: *Listera, Neottia*

 B. Tribe: Diurideae
  1. Subtribe: Chloraeinae
   Genera: *Bipinnula, Caladenia,*
    Chloraea, Codonorchis,
    Gavilea, Geoblasta
  2. Subtribe: Diuridinae
   Genera: *Diuris, Orthoceras*
  3. Subtribe: Cryptostylidinae
   Genera: *Coilochilus, Cryptostylis*
  4. Subtribe: Prasophyllinae
   Genera: *Microtis, Prasophyllum*

 C. Tribe: Cranichideae
  1. Subtribe: Tropidiinae
   Genera: *Corymborchis, Tropidia*
  2. Subtribe: Spiranthinae
   Genera: *Centrogenium, Lankesterella,*
    Pelexia, Sarcoglottis, Spiranthes
  3. Subtribe: Pachyplectrinae
   Genera: *Erythrodes, Goodyera*
  4. Subtribe: Cranichidinae
   Genera: *Altenstenia, Cranichis,*
    Pontheiva, Prescottia,
    Pseudocentrum, Stenoptera

 D. Tribe: Orchideae
  1. Subtribe: Epipogiinae
   Genera: *Epipogium, Stereosandra*
  2. Subtribe: Orchidinae
   Genera: *Bonatea, Dactylorchis,*
    Galeorchis, Habenaria,
    Ophrys, Orchis, Platanthera,
    Stenoglottis

  3. Subtribe: Disinae
   Genera: *Disa, Satyrium*
  4. Subtribe: Coryciinae
   Genera: *Ceratandra, Corycium*

 E. Tribe: Gastrodieae
  1. Subtribe: Vanillinae
   Genera: *Duckeella, Epistephium,*
    Eriaxis, Galeola, Vanilla
  2. Subtribe: Gastrodiinae
   Genera: *Didymoplexis, Gastrodia*
  3. Subtribe: Pogoniinae
   Genera: *Cleistes, Isotria,*
    Monophyllorchis, Nervilia,
    Pogonia, Triophora

 F. Tribe: Arethuseae
  1. Subtribe: Arethusinae
   Genera: *Arethusa, Calopogon, Bletilla*
  2. Subtribe: Bletiinae
   Genera: *Acanthephippium, Bletia,*
    Calanthe, Chysis, Coelia,
    Hexalectus, Phaius,
    Spathoglottis
  3. Subtribe: Sobraliinae
   Genera: *Arpophyllum, Elleanthus,*
    Isochilus, Palmorchis,
    Sertifera, Sobralia
  4. Subtribe: Thuniinae
   Genera: *Arundina, Thunia*
  5. Subtribe: Collabiinae
   Genera: *Chrysoglossum, Collabium,*
    Nephelaphyllum, Tainia
  6. Subtribe: Coelogyninae
   Genera: *Coelogyne, Dendrochilum,*
    Panisea, Pholidota, Pleione

 G. Tribe: Epidendreae
  1. Subtribe: Laeliinae
   Genera: *Alamania, Barkeria,*
    Brassavola, Broughtonia,
    Cattleya, Epidendrum,
    Hexisia, Laelia,
    Schomburgkia, Sophronitis,
    Tetramicra
  2. Subtribe: Eriinae
   Genera: *Appendicula, Eria, Glomera,*
    Neobenthamia, Podochilus,
    Polystachya
  3. Subtribe: Meiracylliinae
   Genus: *Meiracyllium*
  4. Subtribe: Pleurothallidinae
   Genus: *Lepanthes, Masdevallia,*
    Pleurothallis, Restrepia, Stelis

5. Subtribe: Adrorhizinae
   Genera: *Adrorhizon, Josephia*
6. Subtribe: Thelasiinae
   Genera: *Phreatia, Thelasis*
7. Subtribe: Ridleyellinae
   Genera: *Ridleyella*

H. Tribe: Dendrobieae
1. Subtribe: Bulbophyllinae
   Genera: *Bulbophyllum, Dendrobium*

I. Tribe: Malaxideae
1. Subtribe: Liparidinae
   Genera: *Liparis, Malaxis, Oberonia*
2. Subtribe: Genyorchidinae
   Genera: *Drymoda, Genyorchis, Ione*
3. Subtribe: Thecostelinae
   Genera: *Thecostele*

J. Tribe: Vandeae
1. Subtribe: Cymbidiinae
   Genera: *Ansellia, Aplectrum,*
   Corallorhiza, Cymbidiella,
   Cymbidium, Cyrtopodium,
   Eulophia, Galeandra,
   Grammatophyllum, Tipularia
2. Subtribe: Catasetinae
   Genera: *Catasetum, Cycnoches,*
   Mormodes

3. Subtribe: Vandinae
   Genera: *Aerangis, Aerides,*
   Angraecum, Phalaenopsis,
   Renanthera, Trichoglottis,
   Vanda
4. Subtribe: Maxillariinae
   Genera: *Maxillaria, Trigonidium,*
   Xylobium
5. Subtribe: Lycastinae
   Genera: *Anguloa, Bifrenaria, Lycaste*
6. Subtribe: Zygopetalinae
   Genera: *Chondrorhyncha, Huntleya,*
   Pescatorea, Zygopetalum
7. Subtribe: Stanhopeinae
   Genera: *Acineta, Coryanthes,*
   Gongora, Peristeria,
   Stanhopea
8. Subtribe: Ornithocephalinae
   Genera: *Dichea, Ornithocephalus,*
   Telipogon, Trichoceros
9. Subtribe: Oncidiinae
   Genera: *Aspasia, Brassia,*
   Comparettia, Gomesa,
   Ionopsis, Lockhartia,
   Miltonia, Odontoglossum,
   Oncidium, Rodriguezia,
   Trichocentrum, Trichopilia

Classification is ongoing. Research botanists consider that always 'there is room for improvement and modification of the present classification'. In 1981, Dressler and Dodson published a taxonomic key that they use in updating and revising their research. A copy of that key is available from the American Orchid Society.

HABITATS

Orchid habitats are diverse, ranging from the arctic regions to the tropics, from sea level to elevations as high as 3800m (12 500′); but the most preferred regions are the warmer areas of the globe. Orchid species in tropical, sub-tropical, warm and cool temperate rainforest conditions are largely epiphytic or lithophytic, growing on trees or rocks. Of the numerous epiphytic orchids, none is parasitic. In the arctic and temperate regions the orchids are by and large terrestrials.

In the early days of orchid collection, it was generally believed that orchids in the wild grew in the steamy impenetrable tropical jungles where the most extraordinary and mysterious plants thrive—the myth still lingers. It is partly true, for 'jungle' is applied in a general way to all rainforests and the larger concentration of orchid species do occur in the equatorial girdle of tropical rainforests.

But orchids are found in all of the following habitats: rainforests, monsoon forests, cloud forests, wet sclerophyll forests, dry sclerophyll forests, savannah, woodlands, mangrove swamps. These tree habitats are vital for the existence of orchids. Other essential orchid habitats include: coastal lowlands, littoral forests, *Melaleuca* (Paper Bark) forests, water meadows, bogs, swamps, sand dunes, grasslands, moist rocks, sheltered cliff faces, creeks and mountain streams, and edges of waterfalls.

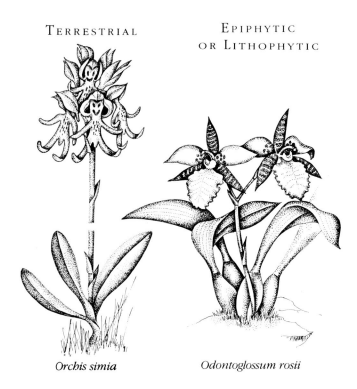

TERRESTRIAL

EPIPHYTIC OR LITHOPHYTIC

Orchis simia

Odontoglossum rosii

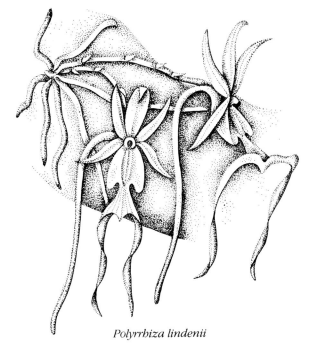

LEAFLESS EPIPHYTIC

Polyrrhiza lindenii

Paper Barks (Melaleuca)

Heathlands

Tropical lowlands (Papua New Guinea)

Swamp and rocks in woodlands

Rock garden of Dendrobium kingianum

RAINFOREST HABITATS

More than half of the world's rainforests is in the neo-tropic group: central America, Amazon and Orinoco Rivers and Brazil, and more than one quarter is in India, Malaysia, Borneo, Indonesia and Papua New Guinea. A little less than one fifth of the world's rainforest is in eastern Africa, central Africa, western Africa and Madagascar. Embedded in the tropical rainforests are monsoon forests. Unlike tropical rainforests which receive rain all year round, monsoon rainforests receive their rain during the monsoonal season which is then followed by a dry period. The sub-tropical rainforests are above and below the tropics to latitudes of 35° north and south, while the temperate and cool temperate zones with their rainforests extend to latitudes 45° north and south.

Orchids growing in tropical rainforests tend to festoon the higher branches of tall, lofty trees together with ferns,

bromeliads, mosses, and other epiphytic plants, where sufficient light and air movement penetrates the thick canopy for their growth. Their roots are exposed to the air or lie in leaf litter in the grooves of rough bark. So numerous does the concentration of plants become as these plants reach for light and air flow that the branches often break under the weight. The genera *Phalaenopsis*, *Robiquetias*, *Epidendrums* and *Stanhopeas* are among the orchids found at this altitude.

In the monsoon rainforests the base of the stems of the epiphytic orchids are swollen and bulb-like in formation. These pseudobulbs hold a supply of moisture to save the plant from dehydration and death during the dry season between the monsoonal rains. These epiphytic orchids include: *Coelogyne*, *Bulbophyllum* and *Dendrobium*.

In the sub-tropics, rain is seasonal. In these rainforests

the trees are not so tall, nor is the vegetation so close; there is an understorey of shorter trees with tree-ferns and on the forest floor lamandras grow. The canopy above is more open and the vines are not so thick. Epiphytes such as *Catasetum* and *Gongoras* grow in the upper limbs, while *Sarcochilus* grow on the tree trunks and lower branches.

In the cool, temperate rainforest the trees are not tall, their branches are adorned with hanging moss, the understorey is thicker and the lianas fewer. As in the wet sclerophyll forests, the terrestrial orchids are plentiful— orchids such as *Vandas, Oncidiums, Epidendrums, Encyclias, Maxillarias* and *Paphiopedilum.*

In all these forests along creeks, by waterfalls, and on rock faces where there are moderate amounts of shade, orchids such as *Calanthe, Phaius, Dendrobiums* and *Sarcochilus ceciliae* grow in abundance.

Above 750m (2500′), the lowland rainforests give way to montane forests. Here the trees are much shorter than in other rainforests and are of different species. The understorey is thicker. Orchids grow along the moss covered branches and on the forest floor are a great number of

terrestrials in large groups. Often matting large areas are orchids such as *Bulbophyllum, Coelogyne, Lycaste, Maxillaria* and *Phragmipedium.*

At 1500m (5000′) the growth ceiling of many plants is reached. There are no lofty trees and the trees diminish in height the higher one climbs. *Oncidium* and *Odontoglossum* grow here.

A complete change of vegetation seems to occur close to 2100m (7000′). Different species thrive in the damp, humid cloud forest. Every tree is covered with epiphytic growth, among which are orchids, such as *Bulbophyllums* and *Dendrobiums. Coelogyne* grow among the ferns, vines and plants that carpet the ground and which are almost impenetrable. At this altitude the canopy is more open allowing light to penetrate the forest, and here orchids grow and flourish.

Above 3300m (11 000′), on the edge of the tree line, the vegetation is stunted and sparse. At 3800m (12 500′) the eye-catching pure white Mountain Necklace Orchid (*Coelogyne papillosa*) on Mount Kinabalu, in Sabah, grows in the rock crevices like cascading snow drifts.

Rainforest

Rainforest

Rainforest

Rainforest

Waterfalls

Cloud forest (Mt Kinabalu, Borneo)

NON-RAINFOREST HABITATS

In the coastal lowlands, terrestrials grow in open grasslands, forest areas or are partly buried underneath leaf mould on the forest floor at the base of trees and in rock crevices. Genera such as *Corybas, Orchis, Sobralia, Spiranthes* and *Thelymitra* grow here.

A small group of terrestrial orchids are leafless and are known as saprophytes. They grow in association with fungi and depend entirely on absorbing organic compounds produced from decaying matter. In the lowland forests in the south-eastern region of Western Australia there grows a subterranean saprophytic species. This amazing orchid, *Rhizanthella gardneri*, grows and flowers underground. The inflorescence rises to just below the surface. When the flower is ready to open, the floral bracts force open the soil allowing the rosette of flowers to open at ground level ready for

UNDERGROUND ORCHID
(SUBTERRANEAN)

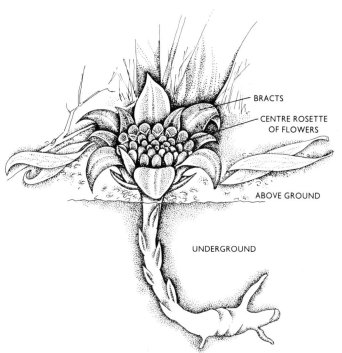

Rhizanthella gardneri

pollination. This plant is rare. In the eastern parts of Australia, *Cryptanthemis slarateri* is the only known allied species and it is even more rare. First recorded in 1931 and again in 1975, rewards are now being offered to finders as government botanists are eager to conduct research work on these rare species.

Swamplands

Orchids grow at a lower level and usually in great numbers along the edges of rainforests, and near logging roads or tracks where sunlight and air can penetrate. Interestingly, beyond about 7.5m (25′) in from the edge of the rainforest or the forest logging roads the orchids become less numerous.

In the coastal lowland many orchid-growing habitats are found, including sand dunes, heathlands, bog or water meadows, mangrove swamps and grasslands. Open grasslands or grassy meadows together with heathlands, swamps and rock areas occur on the tablelands.

Among the various plants used to stabilise sand dunes are species of the *Epipactic* genus (such as *E. helleborine* in Europe and *E. gigantea* in South America) and *Geodorum densiflorum* in Australia and Papua New Guinea. These orchids have deep-seated root systems which penetrate the dunes.

Many species of orchids grow specifically in mangrove swamps, orchids such as *Epidendrum boothianum* in the Florida Keys and *Dendrobium mirbelianum* in the Pacific region.

Open grasslands are the home of thousands of species of terrestrial orchids. *Pterostylis* and *Diuris* in Australia, *Spiranthes* in southern Asia, *Neobenthamia* in Africa and *Orchis* in European regions.

Water meadows and wetlands are characterised by swamps and bogs and are the habitats for thousands of species, such as *Spathoglottis, Cypripediums, Habenaria, Calopogon, Prasophyllum, Orthoceras, Calochilus* and *Thelymitra*.

In rock habitats lithophytes abound. Some of the world's

Coastal

most beautiful orchids, such as *Rupicolia, Laelias, Cattleya* and *Dendrobium*, are lithophytic.

Of all orchid-growing areas of the world, Mount Kinabalu in Sabah, Borneo, must be the richest, with over 1500 known species. Mount Kinabalu is 4101m (13 455′) high, and comprises granite rock with sandstone surrounds. Orchids grow from sea level to 4000m (13 000′). At the higher altitude *Coelogyne papillosa* grows and is believed to be the highest growing orchid in the world.

Orchid habitats are extremely diverse so to grow any orchid species successfully it is most important to emulate as far as possible the growing conditions of that species' natural habitat.

POLLINATION

Cross-pollination is an important factor in the orchid flower's development. Cross-pollination results in cross-fertilisation which ensures the recycling of numerous genes throughout the entire species population. This redistribution of genes gives variety and strength to the species.

Self-pollination, or 'selfing', occurs towards the end of the life of the flower if cross-pollination by a pollinator does not take place. The rostellum is important in this selfing process. The rostellum is the beak-like cell which separates the pollinia at the top of the column beneath the anther cap from the stigma lower down the column. As the flower ages and begins to fade, the rostellum withers completely and the pollinia reaches the stigma, thus fertilising the ovaries. If selfing continues over many generations, the colony becomes weak, losing vigour.

Those features which attract us to the fascinating family of orchids—the tremendous variety of colour, shape, size and perfume—are designed by nature for one purpose: to attract a suitable pollinator. Insects, such as bees, wasps, butterflies, moths and flies, are the largest group of pollinators. Birds, such as honeyeaters and humming birds, together with small possums, fruit bats, and the like also play their part in the pollination process.

In their search for food (pollen or nectar) insects become agents in pollinating. A great number of orchids store nectar in the hollow of the spur. The spur is an extension at the back of the labellum. When the insect, bird or animal uses its long proboscis or tongue to reach down for the liquid it pushes up the anther cap, allowing the pollinia to be deposited on the head or body. When the nectar is exhausted the insect flies off in search of another orchid where the process is repeated, but this time the insect deposits pollinia on the stigma of the orchid as it reaches for the nectar.

POLLINATION BY HONEYEATER BIRDS

CRIMSON TOPAZ HUMMING BIRD
TOPAZA PELLA

CATTLEYA

TRAP METHOD OF POLLINATION

Many orchids employ what is termed the trap mechanism for pollination. *Pterostylis*, an Australian genus, attracts mosquitoes and gnats to nectar at the base of the labellum. The sensitive labellum is attached by a moveable irritable claw to the foot of the column which acts like a trapdoor. Once the insect lands on the labellum, the claw prompts the labellum to snap shut. The insect can escape only by tunnelling its way between the labellum and the column, unwittingly collecting pollinia in the process. Once free, the insect carries the pollinia to the next flower it visits. (Refer to illustration of *Pterostylis nutans* on page 24.)

Orchids such as *Arthrochilus*, *Drakaea*, and *Spiculaea* in Australia, use what may be termed the *hammering process*.

The labellum is anvil- or hammer-like in shape, and is attached to the base of the column by a long, irritable, hinged claw. The male insect is attracted to the orchid by the deceptive scent of a female of its species. When it lands on the sensitive labellum with intent to copulate, the moveable claw swings, hammering the insect against the column, and pollinia is released onto the insect's back.

Another interesting orchid, the *Gongora* genus, presents its pollinator with the waxy surface of the labellum as a landing pad. On landing, the insect loses its grip, slides on its back, passing the column, dislodging the anther cap, and so gathering pollinia on its abdomen.

TRAP METHOD OF POLLINATION

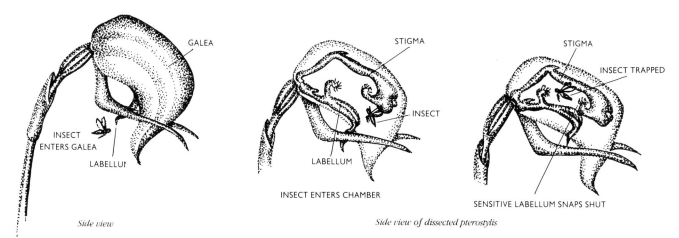

Side view

Side view of dissected pterostylis

Pterostylis nutans

One of the most interesting traps is used by the *Coryanthes* genus (see illustration top of page 25). The trap utilises the complex organ of the pouch or bucket-like labellum. Bees are attracted by the large, brightly coloured flower and by the strong fragrant secretion on the inner margins of the epichile. Above this waxy cup-like labellum two fleshy 'faucet glands' secrete a clear liquid drop-by-drop, filling the cup to the level of an apical spout-like channel. On the inner margin or rim of this waxy cup the bees gather to gnaw on the secretion. Inevitably, a bee falls into the liquid. Its only exit is through the narrow channel just below the anther and the stigma of the column. Thus the bee leaves with the pollinia firmly attached to its back and ready to be transferred to the stigma of the next flower the bee visits. This is a perfect example of a plant in complete harmony with its pollinator. This cross-pollination by bees through the trap method is used by numerous other orchids, such as the *Stanhopea*, *Paphiopedilum* and *Cypripedium* genera groups.

The use of fragrance and colour to attract insects, such as moths, is common (see illustration at right). For example, the African genus *Angraecum* has perfected the selection of moths. The perfume is all but absent during the day; insects, birds and other moths pass the flowers by. With the onset of evening the night air is almost intoxicating with their scent. At night, a particular moth, attracted by the unusual perfume, locates the gleaming white flower which yields its nectar in return for fertilisation.

There are also orchids that attract flies as pollinators, such as *Bulbophyllums*, a large genera widespread throughout the world. Many species of *Bulbophyllums* give off a foul-smelling and most offensive odour, like something putrid or dead. Carrion flies are attracted to these orchids. Some *Oncidiums*, *Coelogyne* and *Himantoglossums* possess and give off such foul smelling odours.

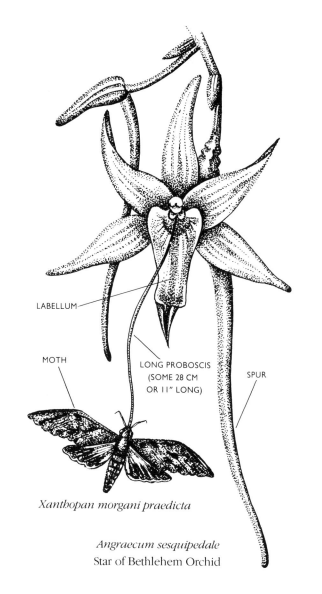

Xanthopan morgani praedicta

Angraecum sesquipedale
Star of Bethlehem Orchid

THE BUCKET ORCHID TRAP

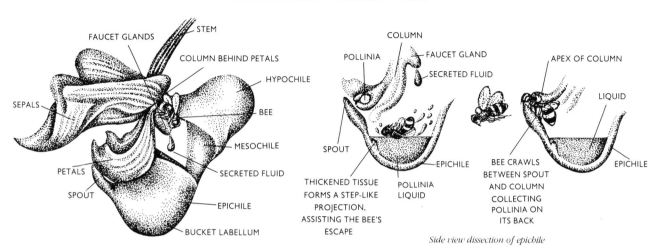

Side view dissection of epichile

Pollination of Coryanthes *by bees*

Pseudocopulation is another fascinating means of pollination. The *Ophrys* from Europe, northern Africa and the Middle East, *Cryptostylis* from Australia, *Trichoceros parviflorus* from Ecuador and *Oncidium henekenii* from the West Indies are examples.

These orchids practise a sexual deception on the males of many species of insects. Rather than produce a sweet nectar, the orchid produces a volatile secretion, the aroma of which is similar to that of a particular female wasp or insect. The flowering time of these orchids coincides with the emergence of the male of the species. By nature the female is a week or two later emerging from pupation, so leaving the male without a mate. The males are attracted to the source of the sexual aroma. Often the shape of an orchid's labellum resembles that of the body of a female wasp or insect. This similarity, together with the sexual aroma, prompts the male to approach the orchid, head first or injecting its tail under the base of the labellum, to try to copulate.

In Australia along the east coast and nearby mountains, late November and early December witness the common male Ichneumon Wasp *Lissopimpla semipunctata* frustratingly trying to copulate with the various species of the genus *Cryptostylis*. Not so noticeable is its cousin *L. excelsa*. During this period the male frantically seeks his mate and is deceived into believing that the flowers are the female of his species. During this pseudocopulation the pollinia is firmly attached to the wasp and carried to the next flower.

POLLINATION BY PSEUDOCOPULATION

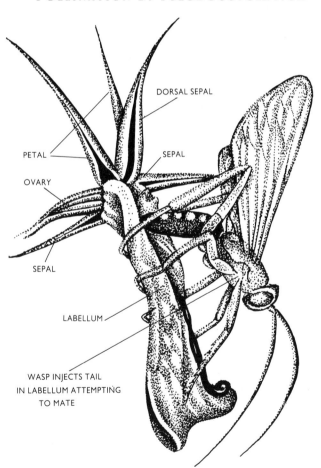

Cryptostylis subulata
LISSOPIMPLA SEMIPUNCTATA ICHNEUMON WASP (MALE)

ARTIFICIAL POLLINATION

Although there are some 35 000 species and hybrids occurring naturally around the world, orchidists are always looking for something new. To satisfy this appetite, breeders are continually producing more hybrids by artificially cross-pollinating species, not only within a genus but inter-genetically. The results of such propagation experiments have produced some extraordinarily beautiful flowers.

Most orchids produce bisexual flowers, and can be either self-pollinated or cross-pollinated using another plant that is genetically compatible. In the wild, a pollinating agent, usually an insect, collects the pollinia from a flower and deposits it on the stigma of another flower, thus pollinating the second flower. Should the second flower be a species different from the first flower from which the pollinia has been removed, and be compatible, the result is a natural hybrid. Fortunately, compatible species do not always occur in close proximity in the wild.

The artificial pollination of an orchid flower is a relatively simple procedure. With artificial propagation the orchidist carries out the same procedure as the insect. Taking a tooth-pick or sharpened matchstick the pollinia is removed from under the anther cap on the column of the flower chosen to be the female parent plant, and is discarded. Then, with another matchstick, the pollinia is removed from the flower chosen to be the male parent and is introduced to the stigma of the first flower, the female parent. (See diagram.) It is important to check the pollinia to see that no fungus is present.

On contact, the pollinia will adhere to the stigma. The pollen grains will grow, extending down the column tubes to the ovary, fertilising the ovules and forming the seed. On a typical orchid flower the ovary is below the flower segments with the sexual parts enclosed on the column. Once the ovary is fully swollen, after pollination, the seeds can be germinated using the 'green seed method'; the 'dry seed method' takes a little longer because the capsule must be mature. The resultant plant is a hybrid and there seems to be no end to the number of hybrids that can be propagated this way.

Possibly the world's best known hybrid is the *Vanda* X *Miss Joaquim* (*Vanda hookerana* X *Vanda teres*). This hybrid was the beginning of almost a century of *Vanda* hybridisation. First developed for the Singapore cut-flower market, *Vanda* X *Miss Joaquim* is possibly now the hybrid orchid of Hawaiian trade.

POLLINATION BY MAN

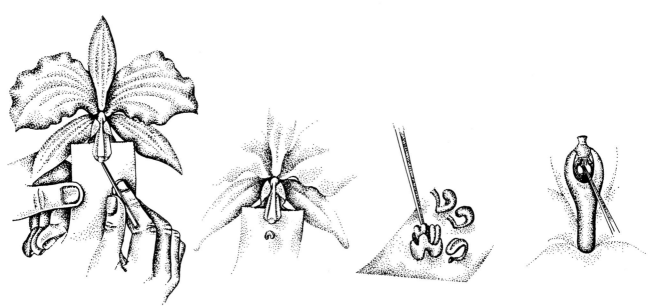

1 *Using a toothpick, remove anther from the flower selected as the parent. Shake anther onto clean paper.*

2 *Separate anther from column.*

3 *Separate the pollinia from the anther.*

4 *Pick up a pollinium. Bring its tip in contact with the sticky fluid of the stigma and touch the caudicle of a pollinium. Place pollinium on the stigma. Now pollination is complete.*

PROPAGATION

DIVISION AND TOP CUTTING

Mention propagation to most orchid fanciers and they will almost invariably think of laboratories with flasks, lamina-flow cabinets and culture mediums. But the most common form of propagation is by simple division. Most growers have split a plant of *Cymbidiums*, *Cattleyas* or *Dendrobiums* into two or more plants for repotting, and thus propagating more plants.

For many years this division was the only way to increase the number of plants of a particular clone: a clone is a group of individuals, each a ramet, produced asexually from a single parent, whether it is produced vegetatively (for example by division or a cutting or by apomixis) or is derived from a single seed, no matter how often it has been divided or multiplied. In fact, with *Paphiopedilums* division is still the main method of propagation because they are not

Having cut the rhizome, break apart.

If needed, the two divisions may be further divided.

Rootbound pot plant in need of division and repotting.

Select suitable position for separation.

Or the divisions can be repotted.

amenable to tissue culture. Propagation by division is suitable for all sympodial orchids, that is orchids whose main stem grows horizontally with new growth rising from and along the rhizome.

However, monopodial orchids cannot be divided in this way. Monopodial orchids have one foot; the plants grow perpendicular and their branches are lateral. Examples include *Ascocentrum*, *Vandas* and *Phalaenopsis*. Monopodial orchids are propagated by 'top cutting'. When the plants grow to a considerable length roots will emerge well up the stem. Once the roots have attained a reasonable length, cut off the top of the orchid below one or more roots and plant the top section. The stump will quickly send up one or more suckers and these will develop into flowering plants.

Cutting the top section of the monopodial. Cut below the aerial root second from the top and pot.

KEIKIS

Some orchids reproduce by means of keikis. The term *keiki* comes from the Hawaiian language and means 'baby'. It refers to the plantlets that grow from the nodes of pseudobulbs above the level of the potting material, sometimes on flower spikes, and rarely from the roots. Keikis develop in quite a number of genera including *Catasetum*, *Epidendrum*, *Lycaste*, *Zygopetalum* and especially *Dendrobiums*. It seems that all species of *Dendrobiums* are capable of reproduction in this manner, in particular the *Eugananthe* section and notably the species *nobile*. Some nurseries rely on this method for most of their plant reproduction.

Often if old back pseudobulbs are cut and placed in a plastic bag with a small amount of moist sphagnum moss, some of the unflowered nodes will start to grow and produce plantlets. Often each node at the bottom of a flower spike can be the source of a keiki if correctly treated. After flowering cut the spike into short sections with a node in the middle of each piece. Submerge vertically in sphagnum moss and enclose in a clear plastic bag. Once the keikis are of sufficient size, plant them out. Rare and endangered species, such as *Phaius tancarvilliae*, can be increased more rapidly using this method, than by the division of backbulbs. Keikis from time to time do develop along the roots of various *Phalaenopsis* species, such as *schilleriana* and *leuchorroda*. Keikis also develop along the flowering spikes of these species.

A keiki growing on a Dendrobium *cane.*

Cut the cane two nodes below the keiki.

Keiki on root of Phalaenopsis leuchorroda.

Keiki on root of Phalaenopsis schilleriana.

Though most orchidists claim to know all about root keikis, exceptionally few growers have ever seen them or had any experience with their growth. The photograph above left shows the root system of a *Phalaenopsis leuchorroda* which had escaped over the side of the pot and had grown along the bench. At the time of repotting, the roots were torn from the plant. Within weeks the roots developed several eyes, from which keikis grew and which quickly resulted in several healthy plants. The photograph above shows a keiki growing from an eye on the root of a *Phalaenopsis schilleriana.* Naturally, the results are perfect clones of the parent plant.

SEED CULTURE

Orchid plants can be propagated in many different ways. Every orchid in cultivation today started life from a tiny seed. So small are they that as many as 72 000 seeds may be in a single seed pod. In the wild the naked seed (so called because it has no endosperm, that is stored carbohydrates needed for growth) is incapable of germination and depends upon the aid of a fungus. Should a plantlet emerge directly from the seed, it would not survive. The plantlet must first grow into a protocorm, many times the size of the seed, before developing a root or shoot. To do this it is dependent on a special association with several species of fungi growing within the vicinity of the parent orchid species.

Particular orchid species have associations with particular species of fungi. This fact accounts to some extent for the isolated distribution of many orchid species. It is very simple: if a fungus species does not grow or occur in an area, then the associated orchid species seed cannot germinate.

Early workers propagating with orchid seed used this knowledge to germinate not only species seed but also the seed of their attempted hybrids. To simplify somewhat, the method involved the following procedures: seed was sown onto a culture kept moist with distilled water, and a few cut-up pieces of the parent orchid's roots were scattered amongst the seed. In the moist conditions, the fungus on the roots grew and spread rapidly and allowed the seeds to germinate and develop into protocorms—then, in a short time into small plantlets.

Today, these crude but reasonably successful methods are no longer used. In the 1920s, Lewis Knudson, a plant physiologist, developed the asymbiotic method of germinating orchid seed.

First a sterilised agar-agar culture gel is prepared in a sterilised vessel or flask. This gel contains all the nutriments the seed will need to develop into a strong plantlet once germinated.

Growers today use one of two methods of seed preparation:

(a) The dry mature seed is taken from the seed pod and treated with a chlorine bleach solution to kill any fungi spores attached to the seed. The dry seed is then introduced onto the surface of the culture gel and the vessel or flask is immediately sealed.

(b) In the green seed method, the chlorine bleach is applied to the green fruiting body or pod containing the seed. On opening the pod the green seed (which because of its enclosure in the green pod is in a naturally sterilised condition) is introduced onto the surface of the culture gel, and the vessel or flask is immediately sealed.

This entire procedure—the sterilisation of vessels or flasks, the preparation of the gel-culture, and the chlorine treatment of the seed—is conducted in a sterile, clean-air chamber, known as a Lamina-Flow Cabinet, to reduce the risk of contamination by airborne fungi spores.

The green seed culture is the more popular method. The risk of damage to the seed by the harsh chlorine bleach is avoided using this method because only the capsule comes in contact with the bleach and the pod is harvested before the seed is mature. Once the pod is open and the seed sprinkled on the culture surface, the seed continues to mature.

Once the seed germinates and swells into a protocorm it takes approximately six weeks, depending on species, for the shoots (roots and leaf) to appear. The plantlets continue to grow in the flask until ready to be potted.

For those interested in germinating orchid seed the Knudson formula (C) is included below. It is simple to prepare.

KC – MEDIUM			KNUDSON C MEDIUM (1946)			
COMPOUND	ml STOCK PER LITRE OF MEDIUM	AMOUNT PER LITRE OF MEDIUM	COMPOUND	AMOUNT PER LITRE		
					MASS	MOLE
(a) KH_2PO_4	20	2.0 mmol	(a) KH_2PO_4	250 mg	1.84 mmol
$Ca(NO_3)_2$	40	4.0 "	$Ca(NO_3)_24H_2O$	1000 "	4.23 "
$(NH_4)_2SO_4$	40	4.0 "	$(NH_4)_2SO_4$	500 "	3.78 "
$MgSO_4$	10	1.0 "	$MgSO_4.7H_2O$	250 "	1.01 "
(b) $MnSO_4$	3.5	35 μmol	(b) $MnSO_4$ $4H_2O$	7.5 "	33.6 μmol
(c) $FeSO_4$	} 9	90 "	(c) $FeSO_4.7H_2O$	25 "	89.9 "
Na_2EDTA	}	90 "	——	——	——
(d) SUCROSE	20.5386 g	60 mmol	(d) SUCROSE	20 g	58.4 "
(i) * AGAR	17.5 g	17.5 g	(i) * AGAR	17.5 g	17.5 g

* 17.5g AGAR is a relatively high concentration; it is possible that a less highly purified agar, such as *Difco Bacto–Agar*, might be used.

TISSUE CULTURE (Mericloning)

The term *mericlone* was coined by orchid growers, from *meristem* and *clone*, and refers to plants that have been propagated in the laboratory by the tissue culture technique. The first workers in this field believed they were producing plants from the *meristematic* tissue (particularly tips of roots and/or apex of vegetative or floral shoots), but later it was revealed that a much larger piece of tissue was used to form a protocorm, the tissue used contained one or more leaf axils and should have been termed *shoot-tip*. However *mericlone* has stuck.

The tissue culture technique involves taking a new growing shoot from the orchid plant; excise the tip together with any axillary shoots and introduce them onto a previously prepared sterile nutrient medium in laboratory glass culture dishes. (Refer to illustrations 1 to 10 on following pages.) On excision, the tissue or shoot is thoroughly cleansed and sterilised, as explained in the diagrams and instructions. Place the culture dishes into a lamina-flow, or a clean-air cabinet. With the aid of a microscope and using a sterilised scalpel, cut from the tiny growing tip 0.5cm squares and sow them onto a pre-prepared solid agar gel medium or place into a solution of the same nutriments.

This completed, place covers over the glass dishes and put them on a slowly revolving wheel (like a potter's wheel) or a shaker. Whether you use the wheel or shaker depends on the genus of the mericlone. It is only from experience that tissue culturists learn which genus is best suited to either the wheel or the shaker, and which genus does best on agar gel or in the nutrient solution. The principle is the same in both media forms.

The tiny tissue squares enlarge, forming protocorm-like bodies known as PLBs. The nutriments used in the medium are designed to produce PLBs—plantlets *do not* form at this stage. From these PLBs the excision process can be repeated as many times as is required. While the PLBs remain in the nutriment they continue to grow. The larger the PLBs grow, the more excisions can be made to produce more tiny PLBs to thus repeat the process. At any stage during this process PLBs can be transferred onto a culture medium, the ingredients of which will encourage shoots and roots to develop, and so new plantlets to form.

This method enables the nursery workers to produce particularly good, if not perfect, clones quite quickly. Thousands, if not millions, of plants can be propagated quite cheaply, hence accelerating the distribution of plants that will flower exactly the same as the original. Unfortunately, some genera cannot be propagated by this method, notably *Paphiopedilum*. Undoubtedly researchers are continuing to work on the problem.

1 *Select a new growing shoot, preferably before the young terminal leaf has split and opened.*

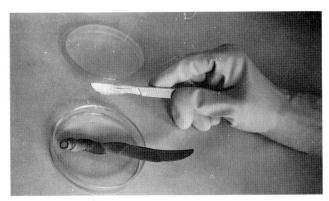

2 *Wash in clean running water for twenty minutes, then place in glass dish.*

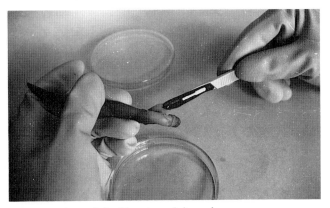

3 *Remove the node bud bracts and discard.*

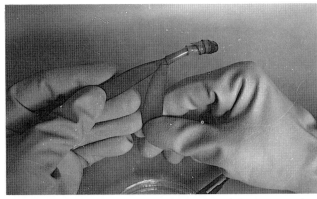

4 *Remove the terminal exposing the sterile tip of the new growth.*

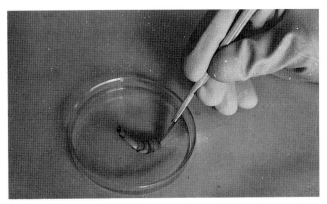

5 *Wash again for five minutes. Now let soak fully submerged in a solution of sugar and cold boiled water (a teaspoon of sugar to a cup of water) for up to four hours. The solution encourages any fungi spores to germinate. The shoot or tissue is sterilised in chlorine bleach for five minutes as compared with half an hour or more without the sugar solution treatment. The chlorine bleach is very hard on the tender tissue, so the less time the tissue is bleached the better. Wash the shoot in distilled water.*

6 *In a lamina-flow sterile cabinet excise the tip of the shoot, about a quarter of a square centimetre, and place in a sterile glass dish.*

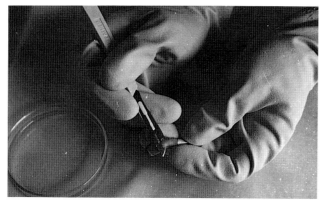

7 *Now excise the node buds which were under the node bracts and place in the sterile glass dish. Discard the rest of the shoot.*

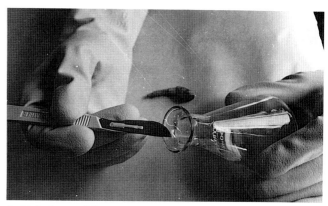

8 *With the tip of the scalpel, place the excised tissues in the pre-prepared nutrient solution or on nutrient agar-agar gel. Agitate slowly for an hour before placing on the 'light' shelf.*

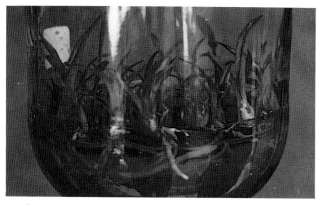

9 *The tissues develop into protocorm-like bodies. When large enough they may be divided again and again until you have the required number. These are then transferred on to a growing gel, and within weeks plantlets develop.*

10 *When the plantlets are large enough and at a healthy growing stage they are transferred to communal pots and can be placed in a nursery.*

POTTING

Orchidists today pot most if not all their plants. At first, all orchids were potted in the same way as terrestrials. Although the plants flourished at first they soon died. Botanists quickly realised that orchids were not all the same. Those that grew in the ground (terrestrials) could be potted, while those that grew in trees (epiphytes) must be treated differently.

With the advent of different potting mediums, horticulturists were soon achieving better results. Potting mediums vary considerably from country to country and in differing climates. In the tropics, volcanic and igneous rock are very popular ingredients in potting mix. In cooler climates, rock is often too cold for the plant's root system, and bark is used instead.

Consider the individual plant's needs when determining potting mixes and procedures. Epiphytic plants in the forest do not require composted organic material as their roots

are aerial feeders, but they do require support. The modern day horticulturist adopts a regular fertilising program to supply the plant's nutrients so the potting mix doesn't need to include compost humus for epiphytes.

The size of the potting ingredients is very important. Epiphytic orchids require adequate ventilation and drainage around their roots. The primary purpose of the potting mix is to support the epiphyte. Newly potted epiphytes must be staked to give support until the root system can grow to give sufficient self support. For mature plants of the *Cattleya, Dendrobium, Phalenopsis* and *Vanda* species, use chunks of material approximately 2.5cm (1″) thick and 10 to 15cm (4 to 6″) pots. The mixture should include five parts sterilised pine bark, one part rock and one part charcoal. For smaller pots the chunks of potting medium need to be smaller. Likewise for larger plants, the pots should be larger and the chunks relatively larger: 3 to 4cm (1½ to

2″) thick. A mixture of rock and fibre chunks allows air movement and the retention of sufficient moisture. As the plant grows, roots will escape and surround the pot.

Terrestrial species require much more moisture around the roots. Here the potting media is much heavier. A mixture of sterilised conifer bark or artificial coarse composite medium, sphagnum and rice hulls or fine grade bark gives excellent results.

Epiphytic and or lithophytic species comprise the majority of cultivated orchids. With these species great care should be taken to ensure that the base, or rhizome, of the plant is not buried in the potting mixture or medium. The new growth rising from an eye at the base of the pseudobulb needs to elongate the rhizome along the surface of the potting medium before rising up to form a new pseudobulb.

When potting terrestrial species of orchids, the pseudobulbs need to be potted to a depth sufficient to cover the base or the crown of the roots. Species such as *Phaius*, *Calanthe* and *Spathoglottis* normally grow around the edges of swamps, along creeks or in the litter of the rainforests. Their roots are surface feeders, spreading out just beneath the surface of the soil or, in forests, beneath the leaf litter and debris on the forest floor. Support is needed for these newly potted plants until the root system develops through the mix to give the plant stability and support.

A firmly staked plant will establish itself more quickly and growth will be much faster than an unstaked or loosely potted plant, for the root system is easily damaged and new root tips will break off if allowed to move in the pots.

METHOD OF POTTING EPIPHYTES

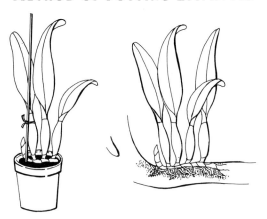

METHOD OF POTTING TERRESTRIALS

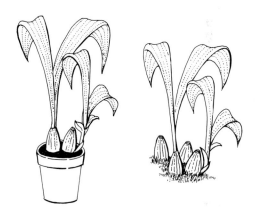

FERTILISING

There is an increasing move away from using composted organic mixtures, and towards using an inert or partly inert medium. Fertiliser should be viewed as a complete nutrient source similar to that used in hydroponic situations, rather than as an additive to a compost. For this reason many orchid fertilisers marketed as 'complete' were developed as additives and have insufficient quantities of some elements, such as calcium, whereas these are found in generous quantities in hydroponic formulations.

Possibly adding extra phosphorus before flowering on more floriferous species would be an advantage, as phosphorus levels in flowers are approximately six times that in the vegetative plant, and hydroponic formulations are generally based on plant growth rather than flower production. Therefore a recommended formula would consist of a 10:10:10 N.P.K. ratio with added calcium and trace elements.

AIR MOVEMENT

The majority of cultivated orchid species are either epiphytic or lithophytic, and these plants in the wild are often exposed to the extremes of climatic conditions. Many are exposed to typhoons, cyclones or tropical storms. Almost all orchid species receive constant air movement in their natural environment. One need only watch the wind in the trees in the areas where epiphytes are plentiful to be reminded

of the movement of air required; wind tends to gust rather than be of a constant velocity.

When orchidists house plants under artificial conditions, the addition of increased air movement is crucial to the well-being of the plants. Therefore, in glasshouse growing conditions, oscillating fans could be beneficial.

ORCHID GENERA

ACAMPE
(ah-kam-pee)

Acampe from the Gk *akampes* (rigid) possibly refers to the brittle flowers. This genus has about a dozen species, several previously known as *Vanda* or *Saccolobium*, spread across South-east Asia, China, India and the African tropics. The plants are monopodial, robust *Vanda*-like in appearance; the leaves are fleshy and coriaceous. Inflorescence may be few or many-flowered in dense cylindrical racemes or tight heads. Flowers are small to medium-sized, fleshy, fragile and fragrant. Sepals and petals are free, spreading and subsimilar; the lateral sepals are adnate to labellum spur. The labellum is spurred or saccate. This is an interesting plant, but rare in collections. Hybridisation with the various allied genera is possible. *Acampe* crossed with *Vanda* produces *Vancampe*.

Culture: Compost, in large well-drained pots or baskets. Requirements are similar to those of the *Vanda*. Grow in baskets or on cork or tree-fern fibre to allow ample aeration of the fleshy roots.

Acampe longifolia

Acampe longifolia

Acampe longifolia

COMMON NAME: None.
COLOUR: Flowers yellow with orange-brown markings. Labellum mostly cream with some purple spots at the base.
SIZE: Growing up to 1.2m (4′) high.
CLIMATE: Intermediate.
DISTRIBUTION: Native to Himalayas, Peninsula Malaysia and Langkawi Island.
FLOWERING TIME: Summer.
DESCRIPTION: Leaves fleshy, sheathing, lanceolate. Inflorescence short. Flowers 2cm (¾″) across. Some botanists consider *A. longifolia* as syn. with *A. rigida* which occurs from tropical to eastern Africa, but we consider it as sufficiently different to remain under *A. longifolia*.

ACANTHEPHIPPIUM
(ah-kan-the-fip-ee-um)

Acanthephippium from the Gk *akantha* (thorn) *ephippion* (saddle) with reference to the shape of the labellum blade which somewhat resembles a saddle. This genus of about fifteen species of terrestrial orchids is found in the tropics from southern China through Java, Papua New Guinea to Fiji. It is a large terrestrial herb with epiphytic-type roots. Pseudobulbs are long and furrowed with epiphytic-type roots. The leaves are large and plicate. Inflorescence is a stout erect raceme. There are few flowers; they are large, cup- to bottle-shaped, fleshy, showy and very fragrant. Sepals enclose the petals and labellum in a swollen fleshy tube. The petals are narrow and the labellum is tri-lobed and saddle-shaped.

Culture: Coarse compost in perfectly drained pots as for *Phaius.* Place in a shady, humid situation with plenty of water and frequent application of fertiliser. Do not allow roots to become too wet. Once pseudobulbs are fully grown, keep plants almost dry in a cooler place.

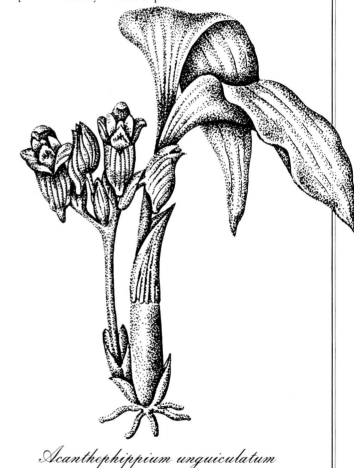

Acanthephippium unguiculatum

Acanthephippium vitiense

COMMON NAME: None.
COLOUR: Flowers yellow to pale pink, with maroon veining.
SIZE: Grows up to 45cm (18″) high.
CLIMATE: Warm to hot.
DISTRIBUTION: Native to Fiji. Grows in moist hot jungles in well-shaded areas.
FLOWERING TIME: Summer.
DESCRIPTION: Terrestrial herb. Pseudobulbs elongate, conical 15cm (6″) high. Leaves apical, plicate, broad-elliptic, 30cm (12″) long, petiole. It has few flowers, about 5cm (2″) long.

Acanthephippium vitiense

AERANTHES

(ah-er-an-theez)

*A*eranthes from the Gk *aer* (air, mist) *anthos* (flower) with reference to the epiphytic habit or the delicate flower (air-flower), or misty habitat (mist flower).This genus of some thirty species originates from Madagascar and the adjacent islands and has one genus in Africa. This is a most unusual epiphytic or lithophytic herb. It is typically stemless, the leaves are fleshy-coriaceous and distichous when a stem is present. Inflorescence is wire-like or branching, racemose and pendulous. The flowers are mostly large, green or white and fragrant. The sepals are long, attenuate and adnate to the column foot; the petals are similar, but smaller. The labellum is articulate, broad and the apex long-attenuate.

Culture: Compost as for *Angraecum* or *Vanda*; preferably mount it on a tree-fern fibre slab or in a basket with shredded tree-fern fibre or sphagnum moss; remember the inflorescence is pendulous. *Aeranthes* requires plenty of water and heat at all times. If grown in pots, the compost must have perfect drainage. The plants are rare in collections.

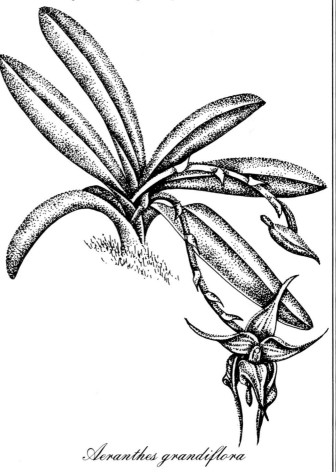

Aeranthes grandiflora

Aeranthes arachnitis

COMMON NAME: None.
COLOUR: Flowers green to lemon.
SIZE: Grows up to 20cm (8″).
CLIMATE: Intermediate to warm.
DISTRIBUTION: Native to Madagascar.
FLOWERING TIME: Summer to autumn.
DESCRIPTION: Leaves long and leathery, up to 20cm (8″) long. Flower spikes bear a few flowers which are fragrant and 5cm (2″) across. The labellum is complex.

Aeranthes arachnitis

AERIDES
(ah-er-i-dee)

*A*erides comes from the Gk *aer* (air) *eides* (resembling). The implied meaning is 'children of the air' which refers to the epiphytic habit. A genus of some seventy species, *Aerides* occurs in the tropics in the Himalayas, Burma, China, Japan, the Philippines, Borneo, Indonesia and Papua New Guinea. It is often known as the Fox-Tail Orchid. The epiphytic herbs fall into two groups: *Planifoliae* and *Teretifolia*. In the former, the leaves are flat, leathery and spreading, and in the latter the leaves are cylindrical and fleshy. Stems are leafy. The plant lacks pseudobulbs. The leaves are coriaceous. Inflorescence is long, dense, decurved with pendulous racemes. The flowers are waxen, fragrant and all open at the same time. Sepals and petals are broad and spreading; lateral sepals are adnate at base to column foot. The labellum is tri-lobed, complex with basal spur; lateral lobes range from obscure to large; the mid-lobe is variable in size, incurved, with margins beautifully fringed. It has variable colour shades of magenta and green in various combinations with white.

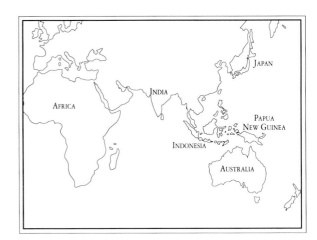

Culture: Plant in loose, chunky compost in hanging baskets, allowing the numerous long rampant roots to grow and hang outside; disturb as little as possible. It needs a humid, shady situation. *Aerides* is a willing parent when crossing with allied groups.

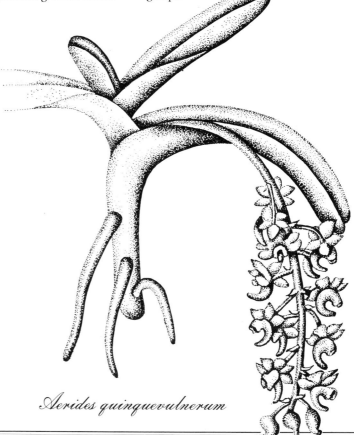

Aerides quinquevulnerum

Aerides fieldingii

COMMON NAME: Fox Brush Orchid.
COLOUR: Flowers pink or mauve, and may be white on the margins.
SIZE: A robust epiphytic species growing up to 25cm (10″) high.
CLIMATE: Intermediate.
DISTRIBUTION: Native to Thailand, and Assam and Sikkim in India.
FLOWERING TIME: Spring and summer.
DESCRIPTION: Flower scape about 45cm (18″) in length, resembles a fox tail, numerous blooms, about a hundred flowers to a stem, 2.5cm (1″) across.

Aerides fieldingii

Aerides krabiensis

Aerides krabiensis

COMMON NAME: None.
COLOUR: Flowers white to pink and marked with dark pink.
SIZE: Growing up to 15cm (6″) high.
CLIMATE: Warm.
DISTRIBUTION: Native to Thailand (Isthmus of Kra—Gulf of Krabi).
FLOWERING TIME: Spring to summer.
DESCRIPTION: A small epiphytic plant. Leaves linear-oblong, up to 10cm (4″) long. Inflorescence arching and pendulous, up to 15cm (6″) long. Flowers up to 1cm (½″) across.

Aerides multiflorum

COMMON NAME: Fox-Tail Orchid
COLOUR: Flowers white or rose-purple and may be spotted.
SIZE: A large epiphyte species growing erect or pendulous, up to 25cm (10″) long.
CLIMATE: Intermediate.
DISTRIBUTION: Native to Indo-China, Tenasserim (Burma), India and south to Thailand, and tropical Himalayas.
FLOWERING TIME: Summer
DESCRIPTION: Leaves strap-like, channelled and keeled, 35 cm (14″) long. Inflorescence up to 30cm (12″) long. Flowers numerous, up to 3.2 cm (1¼″) across.

Aerides multiflorum

Aerides odoratum

COMMON NAME: None.
COLOUR: Flowers purple or mauve, may be spotted and tipped with purple. Apex of spur is green-yellow.
SIZE: A variable epiphytic species, up to 90cm (3') high.
CLIMATE: Intermediate.
DISTRIBUTION: Native to tropical Himalayas of India and Nepal, South-east Asia, southern China, Java and the Philippines.
FLOWERING TIME: Late summer and autumn.
DESCRIPTION: Leaves incurved, oblong strap-like apex lobed up to 30cm (12") long. Inflorescence pendulous, flowers numerous, fragrant, and about 4cm (1½") across.

Aerides odoratum

Aerides odoratum var. *alba*

COMMON NAME: None.
COLOUR: Alba flower is white.
SIZE: Same as the type.
CLIMATE: Intermediate.
DISTRIBUTION: Native to Philippines, and from India to Thailand.
FLOWERING TIME: Same as the type.
DESCRIPTION: Same as the type, except for colour.

Aerides quinquevulnerum

Aerides odoratum var. *alba*

Aerides quinquevulnerum

COMMON NAME: None.
COLOUR: Flowers white, tipped and spotted with amethyst purple.
SIZE: Growing up to 40cm (16") high.
CLIMATE: Warm.
DISTRIBUTION: Native to the Philippines (Luzon).
FLOWERING TIME: Late summer to autumn.
DESCRIPTION: A robust plant, often branching stems up to 40cm (16") long. Leaves oblong-lanceolate, up to 30cm (12") long. Inflorescence up to 40cm (16") long; blooms densely numerous. Flowers fragrant, up to 2.5cm (1") long. Labellum trilobed.

ANGRAECUM
(an-gry-kum)

Angraecum comes from the Malayan word *angurek*, given to a group of epiphytic orchids resembling the appearance of the *Vandas*. This genus has over two hundred species and is widely distributed throughout tropical Africa and Madagascar, with several species in Sri Lanka. Because of differing and complex descriptions by various botanists in the past, recent work restricts the once very large genus to those species in which the labellum is deeply concave with the base enveloping the column, the apex of which is deeply divided in front. These small to large epiphytic or lithophytic herbs have monopodial stems, not pseudobulbous, and are usually leafy along the full length. The leaves are fleshy and distichous. Inflorescence has short to elongated racemes. Flowers are small to large, fleshy, star-shaped, white, yellow or green and often very beautiful. The sepals and petals are very similar. The labellum is larger than the sepals and petals; it is concave with the base enveloping the column. The spur has a wide mouth, often exceedingly long, as with *A. sesquipedale*, the spur of which is up to 30cm (12″) long. The column is short with the apex deeply cleft in front.

Culture: Compost in pot or basket for the lithophytic species and for the epiphytic, mount on a tree-fern slab or other suitable support. Smaller species, such as *A. distichum*, are best in small pots packed in shredded tree-fern fibre or sphagnum moss. Water well during the growing period. Place the plant in shady positions.

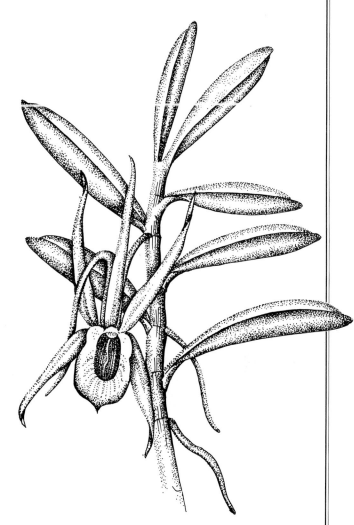

Angraecum infundibulare

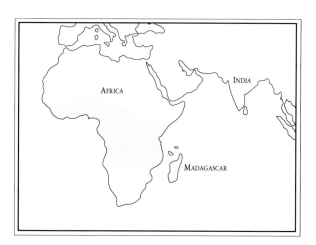

Angraecum compactum

COMMON NAME: None.
COLOUR: Flowers white. Spur greenish.
SIZE: Growing up to 20cm (8″) high.
CLIMATE: Intermediate.
DISTRIBUTION: Native to Madagascar. Growing at altitudes of 800 to 2000m (2500 to 6000′).
FLOWERING TIME: Spring to summer.
DESCRIPTION: Leaves green, thick, succulent, oblong, up to 12.5cm (5″) long. Flowers up to 7.5cm (3″) across.

Angraecum didieri

COMMON NAME: None.
COLOUR: Flower white.
SIZE: Growing up to 10cm (4″) high.
CLIMATE: Intermediate.
DISTRIBUTION: Native to Madagascar, grows at elevations of 1000m (3300′).
FLOWERING TIME: Spring to summer.
DESCRIPTION: A small angraecoid plant, epiphytic. Leaves alternate linear-oblong, up to 5cm (2″) long. Inflorescence short, flowers solitary, large, showy, 7.5cm (3″) across. Spur up to 17.5cm (7″) long.

Angraecum compactum

Angraecum didieri

Angraecum eburneum

COMMON NAME: None.
COLOUR: Flowers white and green, and yellow.
SIZE: A large epiphytic, terrestrial or lithophytic species up to 90cm (3′) high.
CLIMATE: Intermediate.
DISTRIBUTION: Native to Madagascar, eastern Africa, Mascarene Islands, Comoro Island.
FLOWERING TIME: Autumn to early winter.
DESCRIPTION: Leaves strap-like, unequally emarginate, 30cm (12″) long. Flowers inverted, showy, up to 8cm (3½″) across. Spur long and elegant up to 10cm (4″) long.

Angraecum eburneum

Angraecum sesquipedale

COMMON NAME: Star of Bethlehem or Comet Orchid.
COLOUR: Flowers white, spur greenish.
SIZE: Generally solitary stem, about 90cm (3′) high.
CLIMATE: Intermediate.
DISTRIBUTION: Native to Madagascar. Growing at sea level to 100m (330′) altitude.
FLOWERING TIME: Summer.
DESCRIPTION: Leaves oblong, strap-like, sheathing at the base, about 30cm (12″) long. Inflorescence horizontal to arching. Flowers few, fragrant, star-shaped, long-lived, up to 17.5cm (7″) across. Spur long, about 30cm (12″) long.

Angraecum sesquipedale

ANSELLIA

(an-sel-ee-ah)

*A*nsellia is named after John Ansell, who collected the first species on Fernando Poo Island (Macias Nguema), West Coast Africa. This genus has highly variable species. This is a large epiphytic, often terrestrial, herb. The pseudobulbs are tall, 30 to 50cm (12 to 20″) long, cane-like, tufted, with many aerial roots. It has 6 to 7 plicate leaves. Inflorescences are erect, paniculate, up to 50cm (20″) long, with many flowers. These flowers are variable in shape, are showy, yellow, and the sepals and petals are deeply blotched with brown or maroon; they are sub-similar, free and spreading. The labellum is tri-lobed, with side lobes erect and mid-lobe subacute. The column is slender and about 1cm (⅓″) long.

Culture: Easy to grow; use compost in a large well-drained pot as the roots grow vigorously. Water carefully until the roots are well established, then use plenty of water. Once fully grown, the plants require less water. The plant requires light, shady conditions.

Ansellia gigantea var. *azanica*

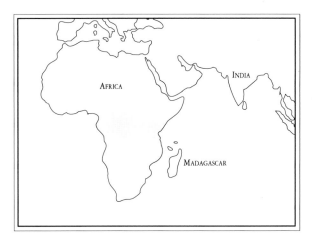

Ansellia africana

COMMON NAME: African Leopard Orchid.
COLOUR: Flowers yellow, blotched with chocolate brown.
SIZE: Grows up to 60cm (24″) high.
CLIMATE: Cool to intermediate.
DISTRIBUTION: Native to Madagascar and eastern Africa.
FLOWERING TIME: Spring.
DESCRIPTION: Pseudobulbs cylindrical, joined, up to 60cm (24″) high. Leaves lanceolate, ribbed. Inflorescence spreading, branching. Flowers numerous, 6.3cm (2½″) across.

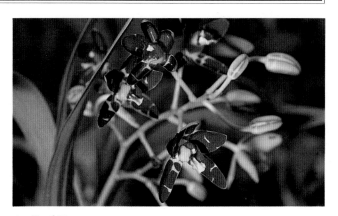

Ansellia africana

ARMODORUM
(ar-mo-doe-rum)

*A*rmodorum is a diminutive of Lat. *armata* (to be armed) and *ornare* (ornament) which refers to the pronounced horn-like spur at the base of the labellum. This genus of at least three epiphytic species is widespread from Assam, through Burma, to Sumatra and Java. It is classified as a 'very rare orchid'. It is a robust plant with climbing vine-like stems, at times up to about a metre (3′) in length. Leaves are distichous or at distinct intervals, coriaceous, dark green, and are 16 to 25cm (7 to 10″) long. Inflorescence is horizontal or ascending, to 20cm (8″) long. The three to eight flowers are fleshy or waxen, long-lasting and fragrant. Sepals and petals are sub-similar, free, spreading, blotched yellow or greenish with red-brown margins. The labellum is tri-lobed, erect, fleshy, convex, white or yellowish or streaked with brown, with a cylindrical spur, curved forward.

Culture: As for *Vanda*. Compost. Use large well-drained pots or baskets. Plants have strong aerial root growth, so pots and benches soon become overgrown. *Armodorum* will do well on large tree-fern slabs or on trees in the open garden.

Armodorum stavachilus

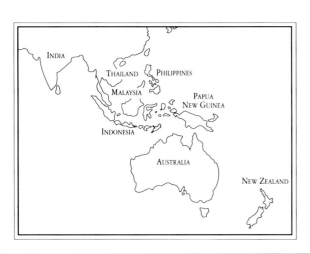

Armodorum stavachilus

Armodorum stavachilus

COMMON NAME: None.
COLOUR: Flowers cream to white, marked brown. Labellum white, blotched purple.
SIZE: Climbing up to 60cm (24″) high.
CLIMATE: Warm.
DISTRIBUTION: Native to Java and Sumatra.
FLOWERING TIME: Autumn.
DESCRIPTION: A climbing, branching epiphyte. Leaves fleshy, linear-oblong, acute, up to 20cm (8″) long. Inflorescence pendulous. Flowers numerous, small, 5mm (¼″) across.

ARPOPHYLLUM
(ar-poe-fil-um)

Arpophyllum from the Gk *hape* (sickle) *phyllon* (leaf) with reference to the shape of the leaf of the type species *A. spicatum*. The genus is widespread from Mexico to Costa Rica, through Guatemala and Honduras. The genus has about five species of exceedingly spectacular, epiphytic or terrestrial herbs. The rhizomes are simple and branching. The stems are slender, pseudobulb-like, and grow to 75cm (30″) long. Leaves are fleshy with a leathery texture. The inflorescence is very showy, terminal, erect, densely flowered, with a cylindrical raceme. The flowers are purple. The sepals and petals are similar and spreading. Labellum is upper and is saccate at the base. The column is erect.

Culture: Compost in well-drained pots. Plants need plenty of water while growing, but once growth is complete water just sufficiently to avoid shrivelling. Plant requires shade, but also plenty of light and also humidity. Treat as for *Cattleya*.

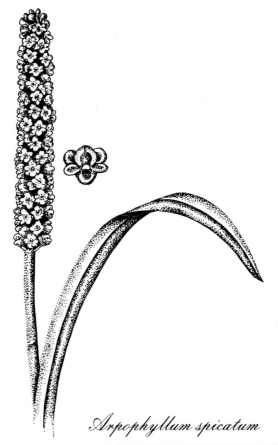

Arpophyllum spicatum

Arpophyllum spicatum

COMMON NAME: None.
COLOUR: Flowers pink to purple.
SIZE: Up to 1.2m (4′) high.
CLIMATE: Intermediate.
DISTRIBUTION: Native to Jamaica, Mexico, Guatemala, Honduras, Costa Rica and Colombia.
FLOWERING TIME: Spring.
DESCRIPTION: Pseudobulbs, stem-like, up to 1.2m (4′) high. Leaves long, narrow, channelled and leathery. Flower spike dense forming a cylindrical shape. Flowers 10mm (¼″) across.

Arpophyllum spicatum

ARTHROCHILUS
(ar-thro-ki-lus)

Arthrochilus from the Gk *arthros* (a joint) *chilus* (labellum) and referring to the irritable hinged labellum. This genus of four species extends through southern Papua New Guinea and the following parts of Australia: tropical Northern Territory, Queensland, and along the east coast of New South Wales and Victoria. *Arthrochilus* differs from *Spiculaea*, from which it was separated, in that the labellum is superior over the column. It is a glabrous terrestrial plant. The leaves form a prostrate rosette, unattached to the flowering stem and not present at time of flowering. Inflorescence is in the form of a terminal raceme up to 40cm (16″) high. Flowers are few or many. Sepals and petals are more or less similar, either spreading or deflexed. The dorsal sepal is erect. The labellum is superior to the column, and is articulate on a highly moveable claw; the blade or lamina is peltate, hammer-shaped or large insectiform callus.

Culture: Place in a pot or garden plot. Apply a liberal dressing of leaf compost and disturb as little as possible.

Arthrochilus huntiana

Arthrochilus irritabilis syn. *Spiculaea irritabilis*

Arthrochilus irritabilis syn. *Spiculaea irritabilis*

COMMON NAME: Leafy Elbow Orchid.
COLOUR: Flowers green with red markings.
SIZE: Growing up to 40cm (16″) high.
CLIMATE: Cool.
DISTRIBUTION: Native to coastal eastern Australia.
FLOWERING TIME: Summer to autumn.
DESCRIPTION: Slender terrestrial. Leaves basal, ovate-lanceolate, up to 10cm (4″) long. Flowers 15mm (¾″) long. Labellum hammer shaped.

ARUNDINA
(ah-run-dee-na)

*A*rundina from the Gk *arundo* (reed-like) referring to the reed-like stems. This is a small genus and possibly consists of only one highly variable species. It is widespread, extending from the Himalayas across Burma, to southern China down through Indonesia to the Pacific Islands. It is a tall terrestrial herb. Stems are 1.3 to 2.5m (4 to 8') high. The distichous, grass-like leaves are 10 to 30cm (4 to 12") long. Inflorescence is terminal, erect and produces a succession of blooms. The flowers are large, showy and resemble a *Cattleya*. Sepals and petals are free, spreading, acuminate, white, flesh-coloured, purple-red to pastel rose-mauve, and are up to 10cm (4") long. The labellum is tubular at the base, the throat is pale-rose veined with purple, the tip is bright rose-purple, the disc is yellow with three lamellate nerves, margins are crisped, and the apex emarginate. The very rare *A.* sp. var. *alba* is white with a yellow throat.

Culture: As for *Sobralia*. Compost in well-drained pots. Plants require lots of careful watering and moderate shade. From northern Queensland, Fiji and the Hawaiian Islands come reports of plants naturalising and growing wild in domestic gardens.

Arundina graminifolia

Arundina graminifolia syn. *A. bambusifolia*

COMMON NAME: Bamboo Orchid.

COLOUR: Flowers are white to pale lilac. Labellum generally a deeper pink to purple.

SIZE: Growing up to 3.6m (12') high.

CLIMATE: Warm to hot.

DISTRIBUTION: Native to southern China, the Himalayas, Malaysia, Indonesia and the Pacific Islands.

FLOWERING TIME: Throughout the year.

DESCRIPTION: Leafy, erect stems growing up to 3.6m (12') high. Leaves are grass-like and linear and grow up to 30cm (12") long. Flowers are terminal, resembling small *Cattleya*, and measure up to 7.5cm (3") across. Labellum is tubular with apex spreading.

Arundina graminifolia syn. *A. bambusifolia*

ASCOCENTRUM
(as-koe-sen-trum)

Ascocentrum from the Gk *ascos* (bag) *kentron* (spur) with reference to the spur of the labellum. This genus of about nine or more species is allied to *Vanda* and *Ascoglossum*. It extends from the Himalayas, through Southeast Asia to Formosa, the Philippines, Borneo and Java. It is a small epiphytic monopodial plant. The stems are fleshy, densely leafy, less than 25cm (10″) high, with cord-like roots. Leaves are distichous, bifid or truncate, falling with age. Inflorescence is erect, densely flowered, showy, facing in all directions. The flowers are small, scarlet, rose-red, orange or yellow. Sepals and petals are similar. The labellum is tri-lobed, adnate at base to column, side-lobes erect, mid-lobe tongue-shaped porrect or recurved. The spur is cylindrical and shorter than the lamina.

Culture: As for *Vanda*. Being a small plant, it is best grown in pans or in a basket. Use loose compost. It needs humid conditions at all times, with plenty of light. Water often during the growing period and drain well.

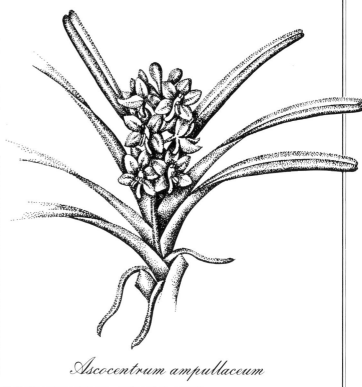

Ascocentrum ampullaceum

Ascocentrum miniatum (orange form)

Ascocentrum miniatum

COMMON NAME: None.
COLOUR: Flower colour is variable, from orange-yellow, orange to red.
SIZE: Growing up to 25cm (10″) high.
CLIMATE: Warm.
DISTRIBUTION: Native to Borneo, the Himalayas to the Peninsula Malaysia and Java.
FLOWERING TIME: Spring to early summer.
DESCRIPTION: An erect epiphytic herb. Stems are thick, woody and grow up to 20cm (8″) long. Leaves are fleshy, keeled underneath, linear, unequally emarginate, up to 20cm (8″) long. Inflorescence erect, up to 25cm (10″) high. Flowers are numerous, measuring up to 1.5cm (½″) across.

ASPASIA
(as-paz-ee-ah)

*A*spasia derives from either the Gk *aspasios* (glad, delightful) with reference to the delightful flower, or is named in honour of Aspasia, the delightful Athenian wife of Pericles. The genus is allied to *Brassia, Miltonia, Helcia* and *Trichopilia,* but differs in that the margins of the labellum are joined to the base of the column for half its length, the lamina then bends at right angles to the column. The genus has about nine species found in the tropics of Central America, from Guatemala, Nicaragua to Brazil, up to 1000m (3000′) altitude. This epiphytic herb is often found on the branches of trees overhanging streams or rivers, and is 40cm (16″) or more tall. Pseudobulbs are short, erect and are covered by leaf-like bracts. Leaves are coriaceous, spreading, up to 30cm (12″) long. Inflorescence is an erect raceme with one to a few flowers. Flowers are showy and faintly fragrant. Sepals and petals are sub-similar, free, spreading, up to 7cm (3″) long, and are variable in colour, being dull-white or pink, or greenish with spots or blotches. The labellum is adnate at base to column; lamina free, perpendicular to column, pandurate, spreading.

Culture: Grow in compost using shredded or very small chunks of tree-fern in pots. They thrive when mounted on slabs of tree-fern. They require warm, moist temperatures, and bright light.

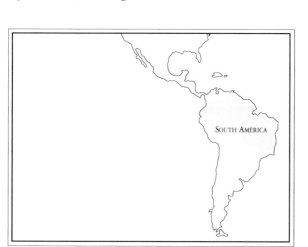

SOUTH AMERICA

Aspasia epidendroides

Aspasia lunata

COMMON NAME: None.
COLOUR: Flowers cream and spotted green, barred with brown. Labellum white blotched with violet.
SIZE: Growing to 25cm (10″) high.
CLIMATE: Intermediate.
DISTRIBUTION: Native to Brazil.
FLOWERING TIME: Spring.
DESCRIPTION: Pseudobulbs oval, compressed, up to 5cm (2″) high. Leaves strap-like, acute, up to 20cm (8″) long. Flowers about 4cm (1½″) long.

Aspasia lunata

BAPTISTONIA
(bap-tis-ton-ee-ah)

*B*aptistonia is named after Jean Baptiste Antoine Guillemin. Originally it was known as *Oncidium brunleesianum*. It comes from Rio de Janeiro and Sao Paulo, Brazil. For a time, botanists moved the plant between both old and new genera until renamed *Baptistonia* by Dr Joao Barrbosa-Rodrigues, author of *Orchidearum Novarum, Brazil* (1877–82). This genus of a single species was little known until about 1970 when it began to appear more frequently in collections. Pseudobulbs are compressed, oblong, and narrowing upwards. Leaves are coriaceous. Inflorescence is erect or arching and is densely flowered. Flowers are 2cm (¾″) across. Sepals and petals curve forward. Petals have markings on the apical half. The labellum is tri-lobed; lateral lobes incurved to column; mid-lobe smaller, reflexed, almost black in colour; disc or crest shallow, dark purple with two erect white teeth. The column is terete with broad round wings and the anther is hooded.

Culture: As for *Oncidium*. Compost in well-drained pots. The plant requires humid conditions. Water frequently. Care must be taken with fragile new growth; don't let water lie around the new growing tips as rotting may occur. The plant cannot tolerate stale conditions.

SOUTH AMERICA

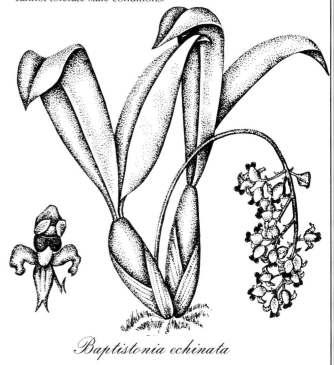

Baptistonia echinata

Baptistonia echinata syn. *Oncidium brunleesianum*

Baptistonia echinata syn. *Oncidium brunleesianum*

COMMON NAME: None.
COLOUR: Flowers yellow. Labellum maroon.
SIZE: Growing up to 20cm (8″) high.
CLIMATE: Intermediate to warm.
DISTRIBUTION: Native to Brazil.
FLOWERING TIME: Early spring.
DESCRIPTION: Pseudobulbs elongate, covered in papery bracts, up to 7.5cm (3″) high. Leaf is solitary, apical, lanceolate and grows up to 12.5cm (5″) long. Inflorescence up to 30cm (12″) long, paniculate. Flowers numerous, shy openers, cup-shaped, nodding, about 1.5cm (½″) across.

BIFRENARIA
(bi-fre-nah-ree-ah)

Bifrenaria comes from the Lat. *bi* (two) *frenum* (strap, rein) with reference to the two strap-like stalks between the viscidium and the pollinia. This feature distinguishes the genus from *Maxillaria*. *Bifrenaria* is a genus of about thirty species and spreads from Panama to Brazil. The genus *Stenocoryne* is considered a synonym. This is a small epiphytic, often terrestrial herb. Pseudobulbs are four-cornered, 5 to 7cm (2 to 3″) tall. Leaves are erect coriaceous or papyraceous, plicate, glossy, and are up to 30cm (12″) long. Inflorescence is basal, erect and racemose with one to five flowers. These flowers are showy, often fragrant, large, up to 7.5cm (3″) across, and come in various combinations or shades of purple, yellow and white. Sepals and petals are sub-similar coriaceous, free, spreading, up to 5cm (2″) long; lateral sepals are adnate to column base, dorsal sepal is concave. Labellum is clawed, articulate to column-base, tri-lobed, with side-lobes erect, mid-lobe reflexed, fleshy, crisp, margin undulate, pubescent; the spur is sub-cylindrical. **Culture:** The plant is easily grown, even by the novice hobbyist. Compost, in well-drained pots. It requires intermediate warmth and shade, as much humidity as possible, and plenty of water while growing.

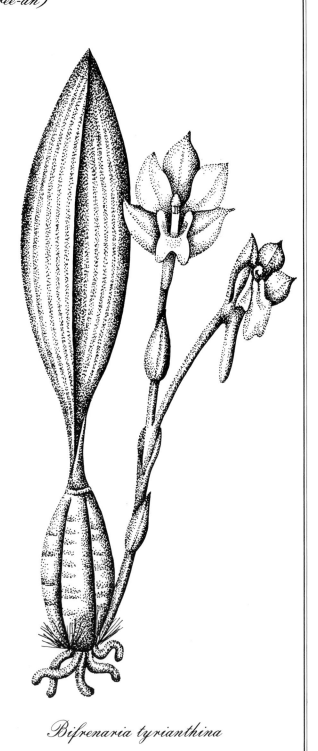

Bifrenaria tyrianthina

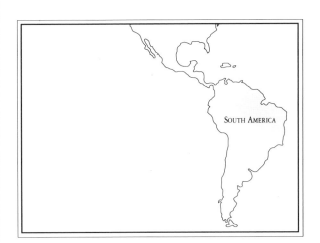

SOUTH AMERICA

Bifrenaria harrisoniae

COMMON NAME: None.
COLOUR: Variable, white or yellow-green with purple labellum.
SIZE: Up to 37.5cm (15″) high.
CLIMATE: Cool to intermediate.
DISTRIBUTION: Native from Panama to Brazil.
FLOWERING TIME: Spring to early summer.
DESCRIPTION: Pseudobulbs angular ovoid, clustered, up to 7.5cm (3″) high. Leaf solitary, broad, oblong-elliptic, acute, rigid, up to 30cm (12″) long. Flowers are large, growing singly or in pairs, fragrant, with a waxy labellum.

Bifrenaria harrisoniae

Bifrenaria tetragona

COMMON NAME: None.
COLOUR: Flowers olive-green streaked maroon. Labellum white, blotched purple underneath. Dark maroon purple throat.
SIZE: Growing up to 45cm (18″) high.
CLIMATE: Intermediate.
DISTRIBUTION: Native to Brazil.
FLOWERING TIME: Spring to early summer.
DESCRIPTION: Pseudobulbs tetragonal, tapering to the apex, up to 12.5cm (5″) high. Leaf broad-lanceolate, up to 35cm (14″) long. Inflorescence short, produced from base of pseudobulbs, bearing three to four blooms. Flowers up to 5cm (2″) across. Lateral sepals fused to foot of the column.

Bifrenaria tyrianthina

COMMON NAME: None.
COLOUR: Flowers purple, darker at the base. Labellum darker purple.
SIZE: Grows up to 37cm (15″) high.
CLIMATE: Intermediate.
DISTRIBUTION: Native to Brazil.
FLOWERING TIME: Spring to early summer.
DESCRIPTION: Pseudobulbs, ovoid, angled, up to 12.5cm (5″) high. Leaves solitary, elliptic-oblong, acute, up to 30cm (12″) long. Flowers up to 7.5cm (3″) across. Labellum tri-lobed; throat white, mid-lobed and hairy.

Bifrenaria tetragona

Bifrenaria tyrianthina

BRASSAVOLA

(bra-sah-voe-la)

Brassavola is named after Sr Antonio Musa Brassavola, botanist and Professor of Logic, Physics and Medicine at Ferrara, Italy. *Brassavola* is a genus of about fifteen species extending from Mexico, Central America, Jamaica to Bolivia, Argentina and Peru. This polymorphic genus of epiphytic or terrestrial orchids is allied to *Laelia*, differing in that the lamina of the labellum of *Brassavola* widens abruptly. It has primary stems or rhizomes. Stems are erect or pendulous, up to 50cm (20″) long with secondary stems developing into pseudobulbs. Leaves at summit, plicate to flat, fleshy or coriaceous. Inflorescence is erect with a one- to many-flowered raceme. Flowers are small to large, showy, and are green, yellow or white in colour. Sepals and petals are sub-equal, spreading, linear up to 12.5cm (5″) long; lateral sepals are adnate to column-foot. The labellum is clawed and joined to the column, is tubular at base, and margins are entire, lacerate, retuse or bifid.

Culture: Compost. *Brassavola* are very easily grown. They are best in a hanging basket. They require high humidity and plenty of light. Do not allow leaves to shrivel during the resting period.

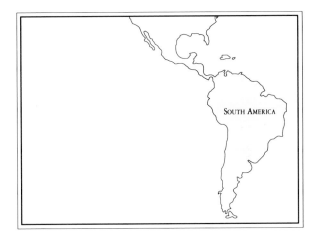

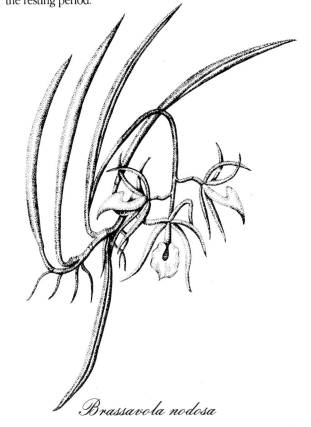

Brassavola nodosa

Brassavola nodosa

COMMON NAME: None.
COLOUR: Flowers green. Labellum white, spotted purple.
SIZE: Epiphytic or lithophytic species up to 45cm (18″) high.
CLIMATE: Warm.
DISTRIBUTION: Native to Mexico, Panama and Venezuela. Altitude: sea level to 500m (1640′). Often found growing in xerophytic conditions on cacti and roots of mangroves.
FLOWERING TIME: Throughout the year.
DESCRIPTION: Leaves linear to almost terete, up to 20cm (8″) long. Inflorescence terminal. Flowers large and showy, up to 10cm (4″) across.

Brassavola nodosa

BRASSIA
(bras-ee-ah)

Brassia is named after William Brass, botanical illustrator and plant collector for Sir Joseph Banks in western and southern Africa. This is a confusing genus of about twenty-five species of small to large plants. They are found throughout tropical America from southern Florida and Mexico to Peru and Brazil. Rhizomes are creeping and stout. Pseudobulbs are rather flat with sheathing leaf-like bracts. Leaves are large, coriaceous, usually three at apex of pseudobulb. Inflorescence is a spike from base of pseudo-bulb, a raceme with few to many flowers. Flowers are small to large and are showy. Sepals and petals are sub-equal, free-spreading, narrow-linear, up to 20cm (8″) long. The labellum is sessile, shorter and wider than other segments, spreading and pandurate. The column is very short, footless and wingless.

Culture: Compost in well-drained pots as for *Cattleya*. Water often up to flowering or during the growing period. Do not disturb for several years. Roots will leave the pot; this is usually a good sign of a healthy plant. Avoid shrivelling during the rest period.

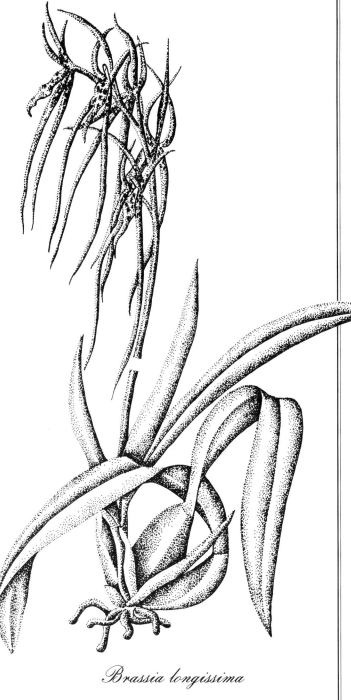

Brassia longissima

SOUTH AMERICA

Brassia gireoudiana

COMMON NAME: None.

COLOUR: Flowers green to yellow and spotted and blotched red-brown at the base.

SIZE: Up to 50cm (20″) high.

CLIMATE: Intermediate to warm.

DISTRIBUTION: Native to Panama and Costa Rica.

FLOWERING TIME: Late spring to summer.

DESCRIPTION: Pseudobulbs, compressed, ovate-oblong, up to 10cm (4″) high. Leaves oblong-oblanceolate, up to 40cm (16″) long. Inflorescence spreading. Flowers about 30cm (12″) long.

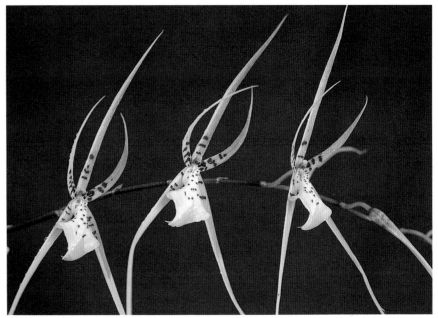

Brassia gireoudiana

Brassia longissima

Brassia longissima

COMMON NAME: None.

COLOUR: Flowers orange or yellow-green with maroon blotches. Labellum cream, spotted purple.

SIZE: Up to 60cm (2′) high.

CLIMATE: Intermediate to warm.

DISTRIBUTION: Native to Peru, Panama, Ecuador and Costa Rica.

FLOWERING TIME: Spring.

DESCRIPTION: A large, variable species with a creeping rhizome. Pseudobulbs compressed, ovoid, up to 18cm (7″) high. Leaves oblong-elliptic, 55cm (22″) long. Flowers numerous, large, up to 25cm (10″).

Brassia verrucosa

COMMON NAME: Spider Orchid.

COLOUR: Flowers yellow to green. Labellum white spotted, with green at the centre margin.

SIZE: Up to 47.5cm (19″) high.

CLIMATE: Intermediate.

DISTRIBUTION: Native to central America and Mexico.

FLOWERING TIME: Spring and summer.

DESCRIPTION: Pseudobulbs compressed, ovoid, up to 10cm (4″) high. Leaves in pairs oblong-elliptic, up to 37.5cm (15″) long. Flower scape bears eight to ten flowers on an arching inflorescence. Flower long and elegant. Entire length of flower is 17 to 20cm (7 to 8″). Petals and sepals long and linear. Labellum broad.

Brassia verrucosa

BULBOPHYLLUM
(bul-bow-fil-um)

Bulbophyllum from the Gk *bulbos* (bulb) *phyllum* (leaf) with reference to the leafy pseudobulbs. This is the largest collection of species in one genus of Orchidaceae. The genus spreads throughout tropical and sub-tropical areas of the world. Recent estimates suggest about 2000 species with Papua New Guinea the possible dissemination centre, having more than 600 species. The genus has from very tiny to large epiphytic herbs. Rhizomes are creeping. Pseudobulbs are very small to medium, spherical to conical, spreading or clustered along the rhizomes. It has one or two leaves terminal on pseudobulb, fleshy, coriaceous, erect or pendulous. Inflorescence rising from rhizome at base of pseudobulb, one to many-flowered. Flowers are tiny to medium, with colours ranging from white, green, yellow to near black with various shades and hues in-between. The dorsal sepal is free. Lateral sepals are connate at base, with petals free, often complicated, and smaller than sepals; the labellum is tri-lobed, fleshy and often pubescent. The flower often has a foul smell.

Culture: Compost. Mount the plant on tree-fern or platyserium slabs. It requires high humidity and shade. Species from mist forests must be kept moist. Leave the plant undisturbed for as long as possible.

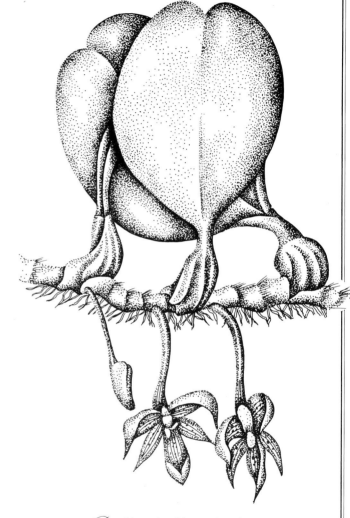

Bulbophyllum baileyi

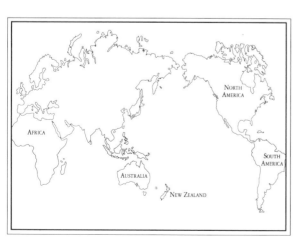

Bulbophyllum affine

COMMON NAME: None.
COLOUR: Flower yellow to green, veined red to purple. Labellum yellow to orange.
SIZE: Growing up to 15cm (6″) high.
CLIMATE: Intermediate to warm.
DISTRIBUTION: Native to Thailand, North Vietnam and India, growing at altitudes of 800 to 1300m (2600 to 4250′).
FLOWERING TIME: Summer.
DESCRIPTION: Pseudobulbs elongate on a creeping rhizome, up to 4cm (1½″) or higher. Leaves apical from pseudobulb, linear-lanceolate, up to 15cm (6″) long. Inflorescence basal from pseudobulb. Flower solitary and measures up to 2.5cm (1″) across.

Bulbophyllum affine

Bulbophyllum baileyi

COMMON NAME: Spotted Bulbophyllum.
COLOUR: Flowers lemon and spotted purple.
SIZE: Up to 20cm (8″) high.
CLIMATE: Warm to hot.
DISTRIBUTION: Native to north-eastern Australian and Papua New Guinean rainforests. Altitude up to 900m (3000′).
FLOWERING TIME: Summer.
DESCRIPTION: An epiphytic or lithophytic plant on creeping rhizome. Pseudobulbs short and angular. Leaves single channelled, emarginate up to 20cm (8″) long. Flowers 4cm (1½″) across.

Bulbophyllum baileyi

Bulbophyllum aurantiacum

COMMON NAME: None.
COLOUR: Flowers pale to dark apricot.
SIZE: Pendulous to 45cm (18″) long.
CLIMATE: Cool.
DISTRIBUTION: Native to eastern Australia.
FLOWERING TIME: Mainly summer.
DESCRIPTION: Pseudobulbs small and ovoid on creeping pendulous rhizomes. Leaves thick, oblong-linear, up to 10cm (4″) long. Numerous flowers 6mm (¼″) long.

Bulbophyllum aurantiacum

Bulbophyllum careyanum

Bulbophyllum careyanum

COMMON NAME: Carrion Orchid.
COLOUR: Flowers orange-yellow or green, spotted and suffused red-brown. Labellum purple or orange-yellow.
SIZE: Growing up to 30cm (12″) high.
CLIMATE: Intermediate.
DISTRIBUTION: Native to Nepal, India, Kasia Hills, Burma and China.
FLOWERING TIME: Autumn.
DESCRIPTION: An epiphytic plant on a creeping rhizome. Pseudobulbs globose-ovoid, up to 5cm (2″) high. Leaves linear-oblong, up to 25cm (10″) long. Flowers small, densely-imbricate. Has an unpleasant odour of rotting meat, hence its common name.

Bulbophyllum concinnum

Bulbophyllum concinnum

COMMON NAME: None.
COLOUR: Flowers yellow, with tip of sepals orange. Labellum orange.
SIZE: Growing up to 10cm (4″) high.
CLIMATE: Intermediate to warm.
DISTRIBUTION: Native to Singapore, Johore, Thailand and Sumatra, growing along rivers and estuaries, and using mangroves as its host.
FLOWERING TIME: Summer to autumn.
DESCRIPTION: Pseudobulbs borne on elongated creeping rhizome, cylindrical, up to 2.5cm (1″) high. Leaves solitary, broad-lanceolate, up to 4cm (1½″) long. Inflorescence basal, up to 10cm (4″) long. Flowers produced in a terminal cluster, up to 4cm (1½″) long. Flowers are small, up to 5mm (¼″) long.

Bulbophyllum elisae

COMMON NAME: None.
COLOUR: Flowers green. Labellum red to purple.
SIZE: Growing up to 12.5cm (5″) high.
CLIMATE: Cool.
DISTRIBUTION: Native to Australia, central east coast and mountain ranges, up to an altitude of 1100m (3500′).
FLOWERING TIME: Winter to late spring.
DESCRIPTION: Lithophytic on granite boulders or occasionally epiphytic. Pseudobulbs ovoid, knobbly, up to 3cm (1¼″) high. Leaf solitary, lanceolate, up to 10cm (4″) long. Flowers small, delicate, wing-like.

Bulbophyllum macranthum

Bulbophyllum macranthum

COMMON NAME: None.
COLOUR: Flower white-cream, densely spotted red-purple. Labellum yellow-cream.
SIZE: Up to 32.5cm (13″) long.
CLIMATE: Warm to hot.
DISTRIBUTION: Native to Papua New Guinea, Borneo, Java, Sumatra, Peninsula Malaysia, Celebes and Thailand. Altitude up to 1200m (4000′).
FLOWERING TIME: Spring.
DESCRIPTION: Pseudobulbs ovoid about 2.5cm (1″) high. Leaves lanceolate up to 30cm (12″) long. Flowers solitary.

Bulbophyllum scabratum

COMMON NAME: None.
COLOUR: Flower ochre to yellow.
SIZE: A dwarf epiphytic plant, 12.5cm (5″) high.
CLIMATE: Intermediate.
DISTRIBUTION: Native to Nepal, Sikkim, Meghalaya and east Bengal, growing at elevations of 1000 to 2000m (3280 to 6550′).
FLOWERING TIME: Spring.
DESCRIPTION: Pseudobulbs clustered, small, ovoid up to 1.5cm (½″) high. Leaves solitary, linear-lanceolate, up to 10cm (4″) long. Flower scape up to 4cm (1½″) high. Flower 1.5cm (½″) long. Lateral sepal connate, tips free.

Bulbophyllum elisae

Bulbophyllum scabratum

Bulbophyllum longiflorum

COMMON NAME: None.
COLOUR: Flowers white to cream. Dorsal sepal, petals and labellum marked golden crimson.
SIZE: Growing up to 25cm (10″) high.
CLIMATE: Warm.
DISTRIBUTION: Native to Australia and extending from Uganda to Fiji, Madagascar and Mascarene Islands. Growing in shady, humid areas, usually in rainforest.
FLOWERING TIME: Autumn to spring.
DESCRIPTION: Pseudobulbs borne along a creeping rhizome, ovoid, tetragonal, 4cm (1½″) high. Leaf solitary, erect, oblong, up to 20cm (8″) long. Inflorescences usually erect, 25cm (10″) long, up to twelve blooms in a hanging umbel. Flowers 5cm (2″) long.

Bulbophyllum longiflorum

CALADENIA
(kal-a-den-ee-ah)

Caladenia from the Gk *kalos* (beautiful) *aden* (a gland) and possibly referring to the calli or glands on the labellum. This genus, little known to orchidists, has about seventy species of terrestrial plants and is found mainly in Australia with many species in Indonesia, New Caledonia and New Zealand. It is a terrestrial herb growing up to 30cm (12″) high, and is often hairy. Tubers are small and globular; the leaf is basal, solitary, ranging from linear to linear-lanceolate, is hairy and is up to 20cm (8″) long. Flowers are solitary or in a loose raceme, and are erect, complex, very variable within species, and of various colours. The dorsal sepal is incurved over the column, the lateral sepals are flat, spreading and often reflexed. Petals are erect and spreading; sepals and petals grow up to 12cm (5″) long. The labellum is erect on a freely moveable claw, is tri-lobed or entire,

with side-lobes erect; lamina calli arranged in longitudinal rows or scattered or crowded, in bright attractive hues.

Culture: *Caladenia* is not easy to grow. It requires rich, well-drained, free-moving compost. In pots, use broken crock, granulated or crushed brick, topped with equal parts of shredded tree-fern, leaf mould, crumbled loam, sharp gritty sand and sphagnum moss. Slightly bury the tubers, feed with liquid fertiliser as plants rapidly exhaust the compost. The plants are spectacular with large flowers; they make a very admirable addition to collections.

Caladenia patersonii

Caladenia recticulata

COMMON NAME: Veined Spider Orchid.
COLOUR: Flowers dark red and green.
SIZE: Slender terrestrial up to 30cm (12″) high.
CLIMATE: Cool.
DISTRIBUTION: Native to eastern Australia (widespread).
FLOWERING TIME: Late winter to spring.
DESCRIPTION: Leaf solitary, radical, linear-lanceolate. Flowers usually solitary.

Caladenia recticulata

CALANTHE
(ka-lan-thee)

Calanthe from the Gk *kalos* (beautiful) *anthe* (flower), refers to the pretty flowers. This genus of about 150 species is distributed throughout tropical Asia, Indonesia, Papua New Guinea, Australia, extending across India to Madagascar and Africa. This medium to large terrestrial herb is divided into two groups, those with corm-like insignificant pseudobulbs, and those with short or long stems with several leaves. Leaves are large, petiolate, plicate and grow up to 60cm (2′) long. Inflorescence is terminal or grows from the side of the pseudobulb and is erect, racemose, densely-flowered, and up to 90cm (3′) long. Flowers are small to medium in size and are showy. Sepals are sub-equal and spreading; petals are similar to sepals. Labellum is adnate to base of column, tri-lobed, with the mid-lobe often bifid. The genus is allied to *Phaius*.

Culture: Compost. Deciduous species need moderate shade, warmth and moisture while growing. After leaf fall they need to be kept cool and dry. Flowering will occur from the base of the pseudobulbs. The evergreen species need more shade. Never let the roots become dry. Less water is required once flowering and growth are completed. This is a very popular plant with growers.

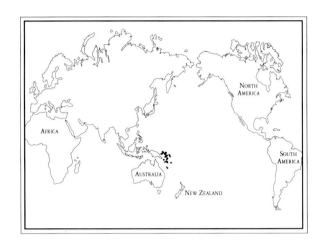

Calanthe veratrifolia

Calanthe rubens

COMMON NAME: None.
COLOUR: Flowers pink and rarely white. Labellum pink, flushed with crimson.
SIZE: Up to 55cm (22″) high.
CLIMATE: Intermediate.
DISTRIBUTION: Native to Thailand and north Malaysia. Limestone habitat.
FLOWERING TIME: Autumn.
DESCRIPTION: Pseudobulbs grooved, ovoid, up to 15cm (6″) high. Leaves elliptic petiolate, up to 40cm (16″) long. Inflorescence 50cm (20″) long. Flowers 3cm (1¼″) across.

Calanthe rubens

Calanthe triplicata

Calanthe triplicata

COMMON NAME: Christmas Orchid or Scrub Lily.
COLOUR: Flower white.
SIZE: Tall perennial terrestrial up to 90cm (3′) high.
CLIMATE: Cool, intermediate to warm.
DISTRIBUTION: Native to southern India, Southeast Asia, Japan, Thailand, Malaysia, Indonesia, Papua New Guinea, Australia and Fiji. Growing in leaf litter in shaded gullies.
FLOWERING TIME: Summer.
DESCRIPTION: Pseudobulbs are small ovoid. Leaves large, broad 90cm (3′) long. Flower scape up to 1.5m (5′) long. Basal inflorescence, with the flower 3cm (1¼″) across. Plant resembles *Phaius*.

Calanthe vestita

Calanthe vestita

COMMON NAME: None.
COLOUR: Flower colour is highly variable; may be white, yellow, or orange to red. Labellum may be pink.
SIZE: Growing up to 45cm (18″) high.
CLIMATE: Intermediate.
DISTRIBUTION: Native to Burma, Thailand, Vietnam, Peninsula Malaysia, Borneo and Celebes.
FLOWERING TIME: Winter.
DESCRIPTION: Pseudobulbs conical, ovoid, angled, up to 20cm (8″) high. Leaves deciduous lanceolate, acute, folded, up to fifteen blooms. Flowers up to 7.5cm (3″) long. The photograph shows the alba form.

CALEANA
(kal-ee-ah-na)

Caleana is named after George Caley, a collector of Australian plants in the nineteenth century. The genus comprises about five species found in Australia and New Zealand. They are terrestrial glabrous herbs. Two elongated tubers form the root system. The leaf is solitary. The raceme is a slender pedicel with one to eight flowers. The dorsal sepal is usually recurved, and lateral sepals spread with the petals erect and incurved. These plants are rare in collections.

Culture: As for *Caladenia.* When grouped in smaller beds or pots, they make a spectacular display.

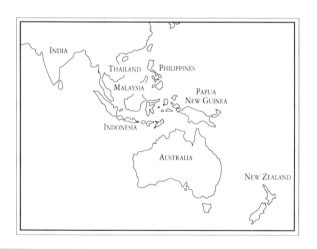

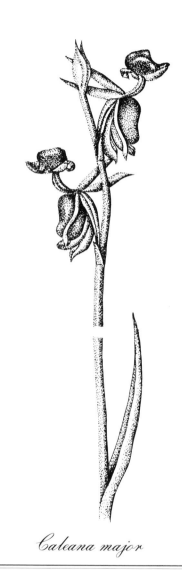

Caleana major

Caleana major

Caleana major

COMMON NAME: Flying Duck Orchid.
COLOUR: Flower perianth dark red-brown, and rarely green.
SIZE: Slender terrestrial up to 50cm (20″) high.
CLIMATE: Cool.
DISTRIBUTION: Native to eastern Australia. Occurs in swampy areas.
FLOWERING TIME: Summer.
DESCRIPTION: Leaves lanceolate to oblong and grow up to 10cm (4″) long. Up to four flowers, 25mm (1″) long. Flower resembles a flying duck, thus the common name.

CALOCHILUS
(kal-ok-i-lis)

Calochilus from the Gk *kolos* (beautiful) *chilos* (a lip) 'a beautiful lip' with reference to the labellum. It is commonly known as the Bearded Orchid. This genus of about twelve unusually beautiful terrestrial orchids is found in Australia, Papua New Guinea, New Caledonia and New Zealand. This is a tall terrestrial herb up to 60cm (2') high, rising from ovoid subterranean tubers. The leaf is basal, solitary and channelled. Inflorescence is terminal, with the raceme up to 60cm (2') long and having as many as sixteen blooms. The flowers are complex and beautiful. Sepals and petals are green, brown, rusty or yellow-green with coloured stripes. The labellum's upper surface is clothed with rather long hairs of copper-red, red-blue or purple hues of metallic lustre; its lip is up to 36mm (1½") long. The complex column gives the illusion of the nose and eyes of an old man with a beard.

Culture: As for *Caladenia*. This genus is common in collections.

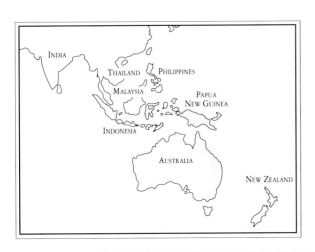

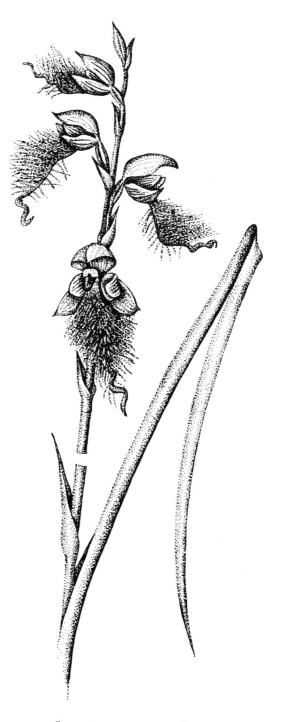

Calochilus grandiflorus

Calochilus campestris

COMMON NAME: Copper Bearded Orchid.
COLOUR: Flowers yellow-green with red-brown or purple markings.
SIZE: A glabrous terrestrial herb up to 60cm (24″) high.
CLIMATE: Cool.
DISTRIBUTION: Native to eastern Australia and New Zealand. Growing from high rainfall areas to montane areas and mallee sandhills.
FLOWERING TIME: Spring to summer.
DESCRIPTION: Solitary leaf up to 30cm (12″) long. Two to fifteen flowers.

Calochilus robertsonii

Calochilus robertsonii

COMMON NAME: Purple Bearded Orchid.
COLOUR: Flowers green. Labellum has violet-red hairs.
SIZE: Small terrestrial up to 45cm (18″) high.
CLIMATE: Cool.
DISTRIBUTION: Native to coast and nearby mountains of Australia except in the Northern Territory.
FLOWERING TIME: Spring.
DESCRIPTION: Leaf basal, channelled, linear-lanceolate, up to 40cm (16″) long. One to nine flowers. Labellum hairy, up to 3cm (1¼″) long.

Calochilus campestris

Calochilus grandiflorus

COMMON NAME: Bearded Orchid.
COLOUR: Flower golden-yellow and red-purple.
SIZE: Slender glabrous herb, up to 60cm (24″) high.
CLIMATE: Cool.
DISTRIBUTION: Native to eastern Australia.
FLOWERING TIME: Spring.
DESCRIPTION: Leaf erect, filiform, channelled, 20 to 50cm (8 to 20″) long. Flower can be solitary or up to ten. Labellum fringed. Flower resembles face of an old man with a beard.

Calochilus grandiflorus

CATASETUM
(kat-a-see-tum)

Catasetum from the Gk *kata* (down) Lat. *seta* (bristle) with reference to the two antenna-like appendages at the base of the column of the male flowers. This genus comprises about one hundred species found in tropical and central South America and the West Indies, from Mexico to Peru, with Brazil the centre of dissemination. *Catasetum* includes some of the most complex, unusual and interesting orchids. It is a truly epiphytic plant. Pseudobulbs are fleshy, ovoid, conical or fusiform, losing leaf-sheaths with age. Stems are short. Leaves are large, plicate and deciduous. Inflorescence from base of pseudobulb, erect, arching or pendulous.

The genus is divided into two groups. Group (a): (*Clowesia*) bearing perfect flowers (hermaphroditic). Group (b): (*Ortho-catasetum*) producing unisexual flowers or very rarely perfect flowers. The male (staminate) and female (pistillate) flowers of this group are not alike and may produce on separate inflorescences at the same time or at different times. In the male (staminate) flower, the labellum is concave, saccate or helmet shaped; margins are fimbriate, dentate, crenulate or entire. The column has two sensitive antennae at the base which explosively release the pollinia on touch. The female (pistillate) flowers are less numerous. The labellum is helmet-shaped or saccate, and the column is very short, anther-less and antennae-less.

Bees of the *Euglossa*, *Eulaema* and *Euplusia* genera are believed to be agents in the pollination of the *Catasetum* species. The male (staminate) flower emits a musty odour which attracts the bees. While attempting to reach the source of the odour at the base of the column, the bees touch the antennae, thus triggering the rostellum, releasing the viscidium which is thrown on to the back of the bee. The sticky secretion on the viscidium sets rapidly. The stipe hangs along the abdomen of the bee. The anther cap falls off exposing the large pollinia in the correct position to make contact with the stigmata surface of the female (pistillate) flower, resulting in the pollination of the ovary.

Culture: Grows well in a variety of composts in well-drained pots or baskets. Requires humidity and plenty of water while growing. Once new shoots appear water with caution to prevent rotting. Temperature control is vital—between 12 and 15 degrees Celsius (54-59°F) while resting, and between 15 and 18 degrees Celsius (59-64°F) during the growth period.

SOUTH AMERICA

Catasetum viridiflavum

Catasetum barbatum (male)

COMMON NAME: None.

COLOUR: Male flowers dark green, spotted brown. Labellum deep pink. Female flowers green.

SIZE: Growing up to 60cm (24″) high.

CLIMATE: Intermediate to warm.

DISTRIBUTION: Native to Guyana, Brazil and Peru.

FLOWERING TIME: Summer.

DESCRIPTION: This large epiphytic species has two sexual flower forms. Both male and female flowers may be produced on the one plant on different inflorescences, but they usually occur on different plants. The male flower is photographed here. Pseudobulbs fusiform, up to 15cm (6″) high. Leaves oblong-lanceolate, up to 45cm (18″) long. Inflorescence borne from the base, longer than the leaves. Flowers are numerous, up to 4cm (1½″) long. Female flowers are smaller than male flowers.

Catasetum barbatum (male)

Catasetum saccatum var. *incurvum* syn. *C. cruciatum, C. stupendum* (*male*)

Catasetum saccatum var. *incurvum* syn. *C. cruciatum, C. stupendum* (male)

COMMON NAME: None.

COLOUR: A blend of purple-black, green, red-brown, pink and white. Stem purplish. (Male flower illustrated.)

SIZE: Up to 60cm (24″) high.

CLIMATE: Intermediate to warm.

DISTRIBUTION: Native to Guyana, Peru and Brazil.

FLOWERING TIME: Summer.

DESCRIPTION: A large variable plant. Pseudobulbs somewhat compressed, sub-conical, up to 20cm (8″) long. Leaves lanceolate acuminate up to 40cm (16″) long. Male flower about 10cm (4″) long.

Catasetum expansum (male)

COMMON NAME: None.

COLOUR: Flowers green. Labellum cream-yellow.

SIZE: Growing up to 45cm (18″) high.

CLIMATE: Intermediate to warm.

DISTRIBUTION: Native to Venezuela and Brazil.

FLOWERING TIME: Summer.

DESCRIPTION: Pseudobulbs elongate, up to 15cm (6″) high. Leaves basal, sheathing, ribbed, broad-lanceolate, up to 35cm (14″) long. Inflorescence basal, up to 35cm (14″) long, erect or arching. Flowers 4cm (1½″) across. Both male and female flowers may be produced on the one plant, but occur more often on separate plants. The male flower is photographed here.

Catasetum expansum (male)

CATTLEYA
(kat-lee-ya)

Cattleya is named after William Cattley, the first horticulturist to grow epiphytic orchids successfully in England. This genus of over sixty species has untold varieties and forms together with a myriad of natural and artificial hybrids. It is found in tropical Central and northern South America from Mexico to Brazil. It is an epiphytic plant with pseudobulb-like stems. Leaves are thick, fleshy or coriaceous. Inflorescence is terminal, and has one or more racemes. Flowers are both solitary and several, are large and very showy. Sepals are free and wide. Petals are crisped or frilled, and spreading. The labellum is large, ornate, sessile, free, tri-lobed, with side-lobes folding and rather tube-shaped. The genus is divided into two groups: group (a) has pseudobulbs with a single apical leaf; and group (b) has pseudobulbs with two apical leaves. Flowers simulate *Laelia* and *Sobralia*.

Culture: This is one of the easiest orchids to grow. Compost in well-drained pots. It requires shade, but plenty of light, humidity, and plenty of water while growing. Once the new pseudobulbs form, reduce the water. This is possibly the most popular orchid in cultivated collections.

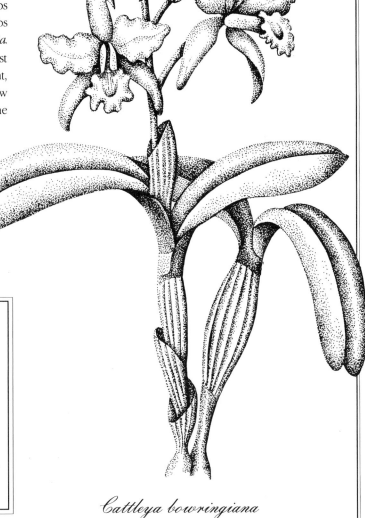

SOUTH AMERICA

Cattleya bowringiana

Cattleya amethystoglossa

COMMON NAME: None.
COLOUR: Flowers pale pink, spotted dark purple. Sepals pale pink. Labellum purple inside.
SIZE: Growing up to 60cm (24″) high.
CLIMATE: Intermediate.
DISTRIBUTION: Native to Brazil.
FLOWERING TIME: Autumn to winter.
DESCRIPTION: Pseudobulbs stem-like. Leaves in pairs, elliptic-oblong, up to 20cm (8″) long. Flowers clustered, up to 10cm (4″) across.

Cattleya amethystoglossa

Cattleya aurantiaca

COMMON NAME: None.
COLOUR: Flowers scarlet, orange or orange-yellow, may have brown or purple spots or streaks.
SIZE: Up to 55cm (22″) high.
CLIMATE: Intermediate.
DISTRIBUTION: Native to El Salvador, Mexico, Guatemala, Honduras and Nicaragua.
FLOWERING TIME: Summer to autumn.
DESCRIPTION: Pseudobulbs, cylindrical, spindly up to 37.5cm (15″) high. Leaves in pairs, broad-ovate, up to 18cm (7″) long. Flowers about 4cm (1½″) across.

Cattleya aurantiaca

Cattleya bicolor ssp. *minasgeriasensis* syn. *C. bicolor* var. *grossii*

Cattleya bicolor ssp. minasgeriasensis syn. C. bicolor var. grossii

COMMON NAME: None.
COLOUR: Flower red-brown. Labellum white and pinkish-lilac.
SIZE: Grows up to 30cm (12″) high.
CLIMATE: Intermediate.
DISTRIBUTION: Native to Brazil.
FLOWERING TIME: Summer.
DESCRIPTION: A tetraploid species and much more vigorous than the type species; pseudobulbs cylindrical up to 30cm (12″) tall. Leaves paired broad-lanceolate, apical, up to 20cm (8″) long. Inflorescence short with up to four blooms. Flowers are fragrant and grow up to 10cm (4″) across.

Cattleya bowringiana var. *coerulea*

Cattleya bowringiana

COMMON NAME: None.
COLOUR: Petals and sepals pink to purple with white throat.
SIZE: Growing up to 60cm (24″) high.
CLIMATE: Intermediate.
DISTRIBUTION: Native to British Honduras. Rare in Guatemala and Belize. Grows on rocks along streams.
FLOWERING TIME: Autumn.
DESCRIPTION: The canes have a flat bulbous swelling at the base. Leaves linear-oblong, up to 20cm (8″) long. Flower spike may produce up to fifteen blooms. Flowers 8cm (3″) across.

Cattleya bowringiana

Cattleya bowringiana var. coerulea

COMMON NAME: None.
COLOUR: Flowers blue-lilac. Labellum throat lemon, veined and edged with purple.
SIZE: Grows up to 60cm (24″) high.
CLIMATE: Intermediate.
DISTRIBUTION: Native to Guatemala and Honduras. Growing in exposed positions on rocks in ravines and along streams.
FLOWERING TIME: Autumn.
DESCRIPTION: A rare plant. Pseudobulbs clavate, up to 35cm (14″) high. Leaves linear-oblong, up to 20cm (8″) long. Inflorescence up to 25cm (10″) long, producing about three to ten blooms. Flowers showy, up to 7cm (2¾″) across. Similar to its type but blue-lilac in colour, and fewer flowers with a slender growth.

Cattleya chocoensis syn. *C. labiata* var. *quadricolor*

COMMON NAME: None.
COLOUR: Flowers white and may be tinted lilac. Labellum throat amethyst-purple, disc yellow-orange, with a purple blotch.
SIZE: Up to 50cm (20″) high.
CLIMATE: Intermediate.
DISTRIBUTION: Native to Colombia.
FLOWERING TIME: Summer.
DESCRIPTION: Pseudobulbs clavate, up to 25cm (10″) high. Leaf solitary, oblong, up to 25cm (10″) high. Flower doesn't open fully, giving it a bell-shaped appearance; fragrant.

Cattleya chocoensis syn. *C. labiata* var. *quadricolor*

Cattleya dormaniana

COMMON NAME: None.
COLOUR: Flowers dark olive-brown. Labellum bright pink.
SIZE: Grows up to 90cm (36″) high.
CLIMATE: Intermediate.
DISTRIBUTION: Native to Brazil.
FLOWERING TIME: Autumn.
DESCRIPTION: A closely allied species to *C. guttata* and *C. leopoldii*. Pseudobulbs elongate, cylindrical, up to 70cm (28″) high. Leaves borne in pairs at the apex of the pseudobulbs, oblong-elliptic, up to 20cm (8″) long. Inflorescence terminal up to 20cm (8″) long. Flowers up to 10cm (4″) across.

Cattleya dormaniana

Cattleya forbesii

Cattleya forbesii

COMMON NAME: None.
COLOUR: Flower colour variable, typical form olive-green. Labellum off-white, outside flushed with deep pink, inside yellow, throat veined red.
SIZE: Up to 45cm (18″) high.
CLIMATE: Intermediate.
DISTRIBUTION: Native to Brazil. An epiphyte growing near streams and the coast.
FLOWERING TIME: Summer to autumn.
DESCRIPTION: Pseudobulbs cylindrical; furrowing when mature, up to 30cm (12″) high. Leaves in pairs, narrow-elliptic up to 15cm (6″) long. Flowers fragrant, up to 10cm (4″) across.

Cattleya granulosa var. *schofieldiana*

Cattleya gaskelliana

COMMON NAME: None.
COLOUR: Flower colour variable, white to pale amethyst-purple. Labellum throat yellow, may be blushed pink.
SIZE: Up to 42.5cm (17″) high.
CLIMATE: Intermediate.
DISTRIBUTION: Native to Venezuela. Altitude 750 to 1000m (3500 to 3280′).
FLOWERING TIME: Summer.
DESCRIPTION: Pseudobulbs compressed, grooved, clavate, up to 20cm (8″) long. Leaf apical, elliptic-ovate, about 23cm (9″) long. Flowers large, showy, up to 17cm (6¾″) across.

Cattleya gaskelliana

Cattleya granulosa var. *schofieldiana*

COMMON NAME: None.
COLOUR: Flowers olive-green, speckled with maroon. Labellum white, marked with purple.
SIZE: Growing up to 60cm (24″) high.
CLIMATE: Intermediate.
DISTRIBUTION: Native to Brazil.
FLOWERING TIME: Autumn to early winter.
DESCRIPTION: Pseudobulbs compressed, elongate, up to 60cm (24″) high. Leaves oblong-lanceolate, up to 18cm (7″) long. Inflorescence short, terminal. Flower large, showy, fragrant, up to 15cm (6″) across. Labellum tri-lobed.

Cattleya intermedia var. *acquinii*

Cattleya labiata

COMMON NAME: None.
COLOUR: Flowers pale to rose pink. Labellum purple-magenta, throat yellow.
SIZE: Growing up to 55cm (22″) high.
CLIMATE: Intermediate.
DISTRIBUTION: Native to eastern Brazil.
FLOWERING TIME: Spring to summer.
DESCRIPTION: Pseudobulbs club-shaped, up to 30cm (12″) high. Leaf solitary, up to 25cm (10″) long. Flowers up to 12.5cm (5″) across. A highly variable species, comprising of some seventeen variants; but horticulturally these varieties are treated as species: *C. dowiana, C. eldorado, C. gaskelliana, C. lueddemanniana, C. mendelii, C. mossiae, C. percivaliana, C. quadricolor, C. rex, C. trianaei, C. wageneri, C. warneri, C. warscewiczii.*

Cattleya labiata

Cattleya intermedia var. *acquinii*

COMMON NAME: None.
COLOUR: Flowers pale mauve to white. Labellum and petal tips splashed purple.
SIZE: Growing up to 40cm (16″) high.
CLIMATE: Intermediate.
DISTRIBUTION: Native to Brazil, Paraguay and Uruguay. An epiphyte or lithophyte growing by streams or the sea.
FLOWERING TIME: Spring to summer.
DESCRIPTION: Pseudobulbs cylindrical up to 40cm (16″) high. Leaves ovate-oblong up to 15cm (6″) long. Inflorescence terminal up to 25cm (10″) long. Flowers up to 12.5cm (5″) across.

Cattleya loddigesii

Cattleya intermedia var. *alba*

Cattleya intermedia var. *alba*

COMMON NAME: None.
COLOUR: Flower is pure white.
SIZE: Growing up to 40cm (16″) high.
CLIMATE: Intermediate.
DISTRIBUTION: Native to Paraguay. Similar in habitat to the type form.
FLOWERING TIME: Spring to summer.
DESCRIPTION: Same as *C. intermedia* var. *acquinii* except for white colour.

Cattleya loddigesii

COMMON NAME: None.
COLOUR: Flowers lilac-pink. Labellum purple.
SIZE: Thickened stems up to 30cm (12″) high.
CLIMATE: Intermediate.
DISTRIBUTION: Native to southern Brazil and Paraguay.
FLOWERING TIME: Autumn to early spring.
DESCRIPTION: An epiphytic or lithophytic species. Pseudobulbs cylindrical, up to 30cm (11¾″) high. Leaves oblong-elliptic up to 12.5cm (5″) long. Flowers up to 10cm (4″) across.

Cattleya loddigesii var. *harrisoniana*

COMMON NAME: None.
COLOUR: Labellum disc yellow to yellow-orange.
SIZE: Growing up to 40cm (16″).
CLIMATE: Intermediate.
DISTRIBUTION: Native to Brazil.
FLOWERING TIME: Autumn to early spring.
DESCRIPTION: The variety differs from the type by having longer, slender canes. Labellum disc corrugated, mid-lobe side margins are reflexed.

Cattleya luteola

Cattleya luteola

COMMON NAME: None.
COLOUR: Flowers yellow to yellow-green. Labellum marked and spotted dark red.
SIZE: Growing up to 30cm (12″) high.
CLIMATE: Intermediate.
DISTRIBUTION: Native to Peru (Amazon Basin), Bolivia, Brazil and Ecuador.
FLOWERING TIME: Summer.
DESCRIPTION: A dwarf epiphyte. Pseudobulbs clavate, ellipsoid, up to 15cm (6″) high. Leaves oblong-elliptic, emarginate, up to 17.5cm (7″) long. Inflorescence terminal. Flowers small.

Cattleya loddigesii var. *harrisoniana*

Cattleya maxima

COMMON NAME: None.
COLOUR: Flowers rose-lilac. Labellum pink, purple veined.
SIZE: Growing up to 60cm (24″) high.
CLIMATE: Intermediate.
DISTRIBUTION: Native to Peru, Ecuador and Colombia.
FLOWERING TIME: Autumn to winter.
DESCRIPTION: Pseudobulbs almost cylindrical, up to 40cm (16″) high. Leaves solitary, oblong, strap-like, up to 25cm (10″) long. Inflorescence terminal. Flowers large and showy.

Cattleya maxima

Cattleya skinneri

COMMON NAME: None.
COLOUR: Flowers rose-purple. Labellum throat cream.
SIZE: Growing up to 55cm (22″) high.
CLIMATE: Intermediate.
DISTRIBUTION: Native to Costa Rica, Mexico, Belize, Guatemala, Honduras and Panama. An epiphyte or lithophyte, growing in forest and on granite slopes. Altitude 1250m (4100′).
FLOWERING TIME: Early spring.
DESCRIPTION: The national flower of Costa Rica. Pseudobulbs compressed, clavate, up to 35cm (14″) high. Leaves oblong-elliptic, up to 20cm (8″) long. Flowers large and showy.

Cattleya skinneri

Cattleya skinneri var. *alba*

COMMON NAME: None.
COLOUR: Flowers white.
SIZE: As type form.
CLIMATE: Intermediate.
DISTRIBUTION: Native to Costa Rica. Habitat as type form.
FLOWERING TIME: As type form.
DESCRIPTION: As type form, except for flower colour.

Cattleya skinneri (alba form)

Cattleya trianaei

COMMON NAME: None.
COLOUR: Flower colour variable from white,
pink-white to amethyst-purple. Mid-lobe of
labellum unusually purple-crimson, but may be
as pale as the rest of the floral segments. Disc
orange-yellow, may be veined with white or
lilac.
SIZE: Growing up to 50cm (20″) high.
CLIMATE: Intermediate.
DISTRIBUTION: Native to Colombia.
FLOWERING TIME: Summer.
DESCRIPTION: Pseudobulbs clavate, up to 25cm
(10″) high. Leaf solitary, oblong, up to 25cm
(10″) long. Flowers 20cm (8″) across.

Cattleya violacea

COMMON NAME: None.
COLOUR: Flowers red-purple, may be fused with
white. Labellum red-purple, disc white,
blotched and streaked white on both sides.
SIZE: Growing up to 40cm (16″) high.
CLIMATE: Intermediate.
DISTRIBUTION: Native to Colombia, Venezuela,
Guyana, Peru and Brazil.
FLOWERING TIME: Winter.
DESCRIPTION: Pseudobulbs clavate, furrowed with
age, up to 25cm (10″) long. Leaves oblong-
ovate, sometimes flushed red, up to 15cm (6″)
long. Fragrant flowers up to 12.5cm (5″) across.

Cattleya walkeriana

Cattleya walkeriana var. alba

COMMON NAME: None.
COLOUR: Flowers white.
SIZE: Growing up to 20cm (8″) high.
CLIMATE: Intermediate.
DISTRIBUTION: Native to Brazil. Habitat similar to
the type form.
FLOWERING TIME: Spring.
DESCRIPTION: As for type form, except for flower
colour.

Cattleya trianaei

Cattleya violacea

Cattleya walkeriana (alba form)

Cattleya walkeriana

COMMON NAME: None.
COLOUR: Flowers rose-purple to pale hues.
SIZE: Growing up to 20cm (8″) high.
CLIMATE: Intermediate.
DISTRIBUTION: Native to Brazil. Growing on trees
or rocks by streams.
FLOWERING TIME: Spring.
DESCRIPTION: Small creeping epiphyte or
lithophyte. Pseudobulbs short, bulbous, 12.5cm
(5″) high. Leaves elliptic or ovate up to 12.5cm
(5″) long. Flowers up to 10cm (4″) across.

CERATOSTYLIS

(se-rat-oh-sty-lis)

Ceratostylis from the Gk *keras* or *kerato* (horn) *stylis* (style) with reference to the fleshy horn-like appearance of the column. This is a genus of about sixty species distributed through India, South-east Asia, the Philippines, Indonesia and the Pacific Islands. A small epiphytic herb, many species resemble a small or large tuft of grass. The roots are fibrous. Leaves are fleshy or coriaceous or sub-terete. Flowers are small and solitary. Sepals are erect. Petals are narrower. The labellum is short, erect, fleshy, and is joined to the column by a long claw.

Culture: Compost in a shallow basket. It requires moderate shade, frequent watering and humid conditions. Plants must never be left dry for too long. Plants flower frequently.

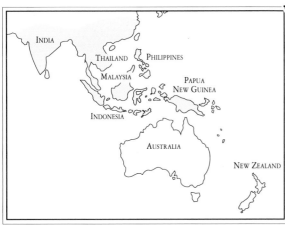

Ceratostylis rubra

Ceratostylis rubra

COMMON NAME: None.
COLOUR: Flowers red-brown. Labellum yellow-cream.
SIZE: Growing up to 12.5cm (5″) high.
CLIMATE: Warm.
DISTRIBUTION: Native to the Philippines.
FLOWERING TIME: Throughout the year.
DESCRIPTION: Stems are clustered and clothed by papery bracts. Leaves are grooved, semi-terete, up to 12.5cm (5″) long. Flowers measure approximately 2.5cm (1″) across.

Ceratostylis rubra

CHYSIS

(kye-sis)

*C*hysis from the Gk *chysis* (melting) with reference to the appearance of the pollinia after self-fertilisation. This small genus of about six species is spread throughout tropical America from Mexico, south to Venezuela and Peru. It is an epiphytic herb. Pseudobulbs are prominent, fleshy, club-shaped, pendulous and are covered by scarious sheaths. It has several leaves near apex, which are distichous, folded and eventually deciduous. Inflorescence has short raceme from nodes of old pseudobulbs produced with new growth. Flowers are showy, large, long-lived, and highly fragrant or aromatic. Sepals and petals are sub-equal, concave, large, free and spreading. The labellum is tri-lobed, erect and complexly excavated. Disc nervous with red-tipped calli. Column is erect and two winged; eight waxy pollinia.

Culture: Compost and grow in baskets. Plants require shade, humidity, warmth and water. When leaves fall at the end of growth, keep cooler and almost dry.

Chysis aurea

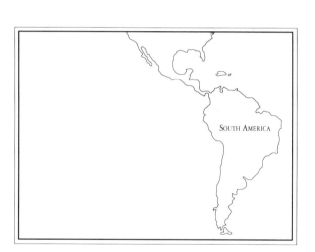

SOUTH AMERICA

Chysis aurea

Chysis aurea

COMMON NAME: None.
COLOUR: Flowers lemon, marked with brown-maroon.
SIZE: An arching to pendulous epiphyte 75cm (30″) long.
CLIMATE: Intermediate to warm.
DISTRIBUTION: Native to Venezuela, Colombia, Peru, Mexico to Panama. Up to 1700m (5777′) in altitude.
FLOWERING TIME: Mostly summer.
DESCRIPTION: Pseudobulbs are compressed, clavate, fusiform, up to 45cm (18″) long. Leaves are undulate, oblong-lanceolate, up to 45cm (18″) long. Flowers measure 7.5cm (3″) across.

CIRRHOPETALUM

(see-row-pet-a-lum)

Cirrhopetalum possibly from the Gk *kirrhos* (tawny-orange or pale yellow) *petalon* (petal) with reference to the flower colour; more likely it originates from the Latin *cirrus* (tendril or fringe) and refers to the curled sepals and petal fringe of some species. This genus of about thirty species spreads from India across tropical South-east Asia to Papua New Guinea and Pacific Islands, also to Africa and Madagascar. The genus is easily recognised by the articulate labellum on the column foot. The genus comprises creeping epiphytes of various sized plants. Pseudobulbs are spaced along creeping rhizomes. The leaf is apical and solitary. Inflorescence is erect and umbellate. Flowers one to many and are showy. The dorsal sepal is much shorter than the lateral sepals; the sepals converge. Petals are often fringed with hairs. The labellum is very small and mobile on stipe.

Culture: As for *Bulbophyllum*. Compost. Best grown in a basket or shallow pan. The plant has a creeping habit, so will spread while growing. It requires plenty of water, but less once the pseudobulbs have developed. The plant needs a shady, humid situation.

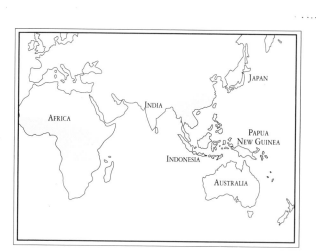

Cirrhopetalum picturatum

Cirrhopetalum fascinator

COMMON NAME: None.

COLOUR: Flower is a blend of green to red, spotted purple. Lateral sepal has numerous basal red warts.

SIZE: Growing up to 12.5cm (5″) high.

CLIMATE: Intermediate to warm.

DISTRIBUTION: Native to Vietnam and Laos.

FLOWERING TIME: Autumn.

DESCRIPTION: Pseudobulbs glabrous, shiny and 2.5cm (1″) high. Solitary leaf is narrow-elliptic, up to 10cm (4″) long. Solitary flower is 23cm (9″) long. Lateral sepals are connate.

Cirrhopetalum ornatissimum

Cirrhopetalum fascinator

Cirrhopetalum ornatissimum

COMMON NAME: None.

COLOUR: Flowers and labellum are maroon.

SIZE: Growing up to 17.5cm (7″) high.

CLIMATE: Intermediate to warm.

DISTRIBUTION: Native to Borneo, Sumatra and Peninsula Malaysia.

FLOWERING TIME: Autumn to early winter.

DESCRIPTION: Pseudobulbs tetragonal, ovoid, 3.5cm (1½″) high on creeping rhizome, about 5cm (2″) apart. Leaf solitary, oblong, up to 15cm (6″) long. Inflorescence apical, fan-shape, umbel, with three to five blooms. Flowers are fragrant. Lateral sepals connate, tips free.

Cirrhopetalum pulchrum

Cirrhopetalum graveolens syn. Bulbophyllum graveolens

COMMON NAME: None.

COLOUR: Flowers are olive-green. Labellum scarlet.

SIZE: Growing up to 30cm (12″) high.

CLIMATE: Hot.

DISTRIBUTION: Native to Papua New Guinea.

FLOWERING TIME: Spring.

DESCRIPTION: Pseudobulbs borne on creeping rhizome, tetragonal, up to 10cm (4″) high. Leaves lanceolate-spathulate, up to 25cm (10″) long. Flower scape 17cm (7″) long. Flowers terminal in carousel arrangement, showy, up to 10cm (4″) long.

Cirrhopetalum graveolens syn. *Bulbophyllum graveolens*

Cirrhopetalum pulchrum

COMMON NAME: None.

COLOUR: Flowers are white, veined with deep maroon.

SIZE: Growing up to 15cm (6″) high.

CLIMATE: Intermediate.

DISTRIBUTION: Native to India.

FLOWERING TIME: Autumn.

DESCRIPTION: Pseudobulbs are tetragonal, clustered on a creeping rhizome, 2.5cm (1″) high. Leaves apical, solitary, lanceolate to oblong, up to 15cm (6″) long. Inflorescence basal, up to 15cm (6″) long, flowers umbels. Flowers grow up to 5cm (2″) across.

COCHLEANTHES
(kok-lee-an-theez)

Cochleanthes from the Gk *kochlias* (spiral shell) *anthos* (flower) with reference to the appearance of the flower. This is a genus of about ten species widely spread throughout the tropical Americas. This genus is placed by many authors in the *Zygopetalum* genera. We feel it is readily distinguishable by the structure of the column foot and the semi-circular plate-like callus at the base of the column. It is a pseudobulbless epiphytic orchid with numerous distichous leaves. The inflorescence is short. Flowers are large, showy, fleshy, coloured white to blue, and are very aromatic. Sepals and petals are free, spreading, similar, with lateral sepals joined to base of column. The labellum is tri-lobed or entire, the claw is very short, with transverse semi-circular plate-like fleshy callus, lateral lobes surrounding column.

Culture: Compost. As for *Zygopetalum* and *Chondrorhyncha*. Treat as a terrestrial. Plant in large, well-drained pots. It requires humid conditions, shade, plenty of water while growing, but much less water required once bulbs are fully grown.

SOUTH AMERICA

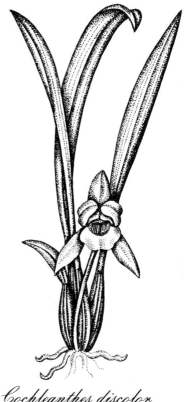

Cochleanthes discolor

Cochleanthes candida

COMMON NAME: None.
COLOUR: Flower white. Labellum veined purple.
SIZE: Growing up to 20cm (8″) long.
CLIMATE: Intermediate to warm.
DISTRIBUTION: Native to Cuba, Honduras, Panama and Venezuela.
FLOWERING TIME: Winter.
DESCRIPTION: A tufted epiphytic plant. Leaves are strap-shaped, up to 20cm (8″) long. Inflorescence short, 7.5cm (3″) long. Flowers solitary, 3.5cm (1½″) across.

Cochleanthes candida

COELEOPSIS
(see-lee-op-sis)

*C*oeleopsis from the Gk *koilos* (hollow) *opsis* (likened to) with reference to the flowers not opening fully. This single species genus from Costa Rica and Panama was first described by Reinhenbach in 1872, who placed it in the subtribe Gongorinae. Though closely allied to *Eriopsis*, *Coeliopsis* is easily distinguished by the noticeable difference in vegetation appearance.

Coeliopsis is rare in the field and very rare in collections. Very little is known of its genetic compatibility with allied genera as very few breeders have taken *Coeliopsis* in hand. It is very similar in vegetative habit to *Stanhopea*. It is epiphytic. Flower spike turns downward, inflorescences are pendulous, with a cluster of small white flowers.

Culture: Use a moisture-retaining compost in a hanging basket. As for *Stanhopea*. Water frequently. Use 1:1:1 ratio fertiliser monthly. It requires high humidity and shade.

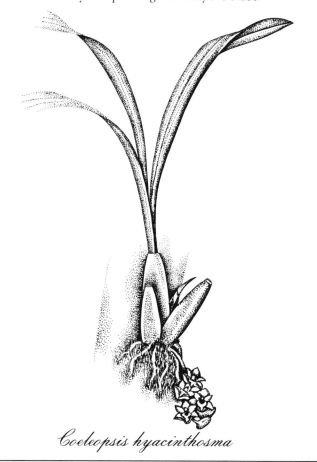

Coeleopsis hyacinthosma

SOUTH AMERICA

Coeleopsis hyacinthosma

COMMON NAME: None.
COLOUR: Flowers white. Labellum throat yellow.
SIZE: Growing up to 60cm (24″) high.
CLIMATE: Intermediate to warm.
DISTRIBUTION: Native to Panama and Costa Rica.
FLOWERING TIME: Spring.
DESCRIPTION: A rare epiphytic plant. Pseudobulbs elongate-ovoid, may be wrinkled, up to 10cm (4″) high. Leaves plicate, ribbed, narrow-lanceolate, up to 60cm (2′) long. Inflorescence 8cm (3″) long, basal, borne from the pseudobulbs, pushing through the compost, in habit of *Stanhopea*. Flowers are borne in a cluster, are fragrant, waxy, and grow up to 2.5cm (1″) across.

Coeleopsis hyacinthosma

COELOGYNE

(see-loj-in-ee)

Coelogyne from the Gk *koilos* (hollow) *gyne* (female) with reference to the deep stigmatic cavity. This genus of about 120 species extends from the Himalayas, through China, the Philippines, Indonesia, Papua New Guinea to the Pacific Islands. It is an epiphytic plant. Pseudobulbs are often angular on creeping rhizomes, clustered or at intervals, with one to four apical leaves. Leaves are erect, rigid, coriaceous, and often plicate. Inflorescence is erect, with an arching or pendulous raceme, and either one to two or multiflorous. Flowers are large, fragrant, in various colours, white-brown, yellow or green with blotching of yellow, brown and/or to almost black. Sepals are free, concave, larger than petals, spreading and joined to column foot. Petals are free, and either similar in shape to the sepals or much narrower. The labellum is tri-lobed, with lateral lobes erect, guarding the column; the mid-lobe is concave at base with lamina spreading. The disc has longitudinal veins.

Culture: Compost. Plant in basket or on tree-fern fibre slabs. Because of the great variance of temperature requirements of the various species, the genus can be divided in three groups of species: (a) Those that require warm conditions at all times. These grow continuously and do not need a rest period; (b) Those needing a more intermediate temperature, and requiring a short rest period, and; (c) Those from high altitudes which thrive in cooler climates require cool greenhouse conditions. Difficulties do arise with this group, but with attention to details of culture most problems can be overcome.

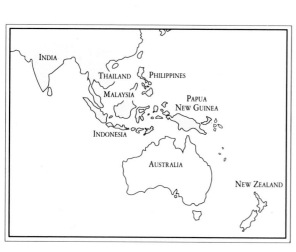

Coelogyne virescens

Coelogyne confusa

COMMON NAME: None.
COLOUR: Flowers yellowish-green. Labellum whitish-green with orange markings.
SIZE: Growing up to 25cm (10″) high.
CLIMATE: Intermediate to warm.
DISTRIBUTION: Native to the Himalayas, Java, the Philippines and found rarely on the Camigiun Island.
FLOWERING TIME: Spring.
DESCRIPTION: An epiphytic or lithophytic plant. Pseudobulbs conical, up to 7.5cm (3″) high. Leaves in pairs, elliptic-lanceolate, acuminate, up to 22cm (9″) long. Inflorescence up to 25cm (10″) long. Flowers about 4cm (1½″) across.

Coelogyne confusa

Coelogyne dayana

COMMON NAME: None.
COLOUR: Flowers pale yellow. Labellum marked with brown fringed ridges. Lateral lobes brown.
SIZE: Growing up to 1.2m (4′) high.
CLIMATE: Warm.
DISTRIBUTION: Native to Borneo.
FLOWERING TIME: Spring and summer.
DESCRIPTION: Pseudobulbs 12 to 25cm (5 to 10″) long. Leaves 60 to 108cm (24 to 43″) long. Flower scape pendulous, long with numerous blooms.

Coelogyne elata

Coelogyne cristata

COMMON NAME: None.
COLOUR: Flowers white. Labellum keel yellow.
SIZE: Growing up to 35cm (14″) high.
CLIMATE: Cool.
DISTRIBUTION: Native to the Himalayas. Altitude 1500 to 2100m (4921 to 7000′).
FLOWERING TIME: Winter to spring.
DESCRIPTION: Pseudobulbs oblong, up to 6.3cm (2½″) high. Leaves linear-lanceolate, undulate, up to 30cm (12″) long. Inflorescence arching or pendulous. Flowers fragrant, up to 10cm (4″) across.

Coelogyne dayana

Coelogyne elata

COMMON NAME: None.
COLOUR: Flowers white. Labellum central band yellow.
SIZE: Growing up to 45cm (18″) high.
CLIMATE: Cool to intermediate.
DISTRIBUTION: Native to the Himalayas. Grows at high altitudes.
FLOWERING TIME: Spring.
DESCRIPTION: Pseudobulbs cylindrical, angular, up to 15cm (6″) high. Leaves narrow-lanceolate, up to 30cm (12″) long. Inflorescence terminal, arching 60cm (24″) high. Flowers fragrant, 3.5cm (1½″) across.

Coelogyne cristata

Coelogyne lamellata

COMMON NAME: None.
COLOUR: Flowers green. Labellum white heavily marked orange to brown.
SIZE: Growing up to 30cm (12″) high.
CLIMATE: Warm.
DISTRIBUTION: Native to New Hebrides and Fiji.
FLOWERING TIME: Summer.
DESCRIPTION: Pseudobulbs elongate-conical, furrowed when mature. Leaves broad-lanceolate, plicate, up to 30cm (12″) long. Inflorescence short and produced from immature growth. Flowers are shy openers, up to 5cm (2″) across.

Coelogyne lamellata

Coelogyne marmorata syn. *C. zahlbructnerae*

Coelogyne marmorata syn. C. zahlbructnerae

COMMON NAME: None.
COLOUR: Flowers white and yellow. Labellum spotted brown.
SIZE: Grows up to 50cm (20″) high.
CLIMATE: Intermediate.
DISTRIBUTION: Native to the Philippines, Himalayas; growing in mountain areas.
FLOWERING TIME: Spring.
DESCRIPTION: Pseudobulbs clustered elongate up to 10cm (4″) high. Leaves lanceolate-oblong, up to 40cm (16″) long. Inflorescence shorter than the leaves, bearing three to eight flowers. Flowers up to 6.5cm (2½″) across.

Coelogyne ochracea

Coelogyne merrillii

COMMON NAME: None.
COLOUR: Flowers white to cream. Labellum throat white, heavily marked red-brown.
SIZE: Growing up to 40cm (16″) high.
CLIMATE: Intermediate.
DISTRIBUTION: Native to the Philippines.
FLOWERING TIME: Autumn.
DESCRIPTION: Pseudobulbs oblong-ovoid, up to 12.5cm (5″) high, deeply furrowed with age. Leaves ribbed, lanceolate, up to 20cm (12″) long. Inflorescence produced from immature growth, flattened arching to 30cm (12″) long. Flowers spreading up to 10cm (4″) across.

Coelogyne merrillii

Coelogyne ochracea

COMMON NAME: None.
COLOUR: Flowers white with yellow, orange and brown markings.
SIZE: Growing up to 25cm (10″) high.
CLIMATE: Cool to intermediate.
DISTRIBUTION: Native to the Himalayas. High elevations.
FLOWERING TIME: Autumn.
DESCRIPTION: Pseudobulbs small and cylindrical. Leaves in pairs, narrow-lanceolate, up to 20cm (8″) long. Numerous flowers.

Coelogyne pandurata

Coelogyne ovalis

Coelogyne ovalis

COMMON NAME: None.
COLOUR: Flowers soft buff-brown. Labellum with darker brown markings.
SIZE: Growing up to 25cm (10″) high.
CLIMATE: Cool.
DISTRIBUTION: Native to the Himalayas, Thailand, Tibet, China, Assam and Burma. Medium altitudes.
FLOWERING TIME: Summer.
DESCRIPTION: Pseudobulbs borne on a creeping elongated rhizome, ovoid-fusiform, up to 15cm (6″) high. Leaves narrow-elliptic, up to 15cm (6″) long. Flowers up to 5cm (2″) across.

Coelogyne pandurata

COMMON NAME: Black orchid.
COLOUR: Petals and sepals emerald green. Labellum veined with black markings on green background. Mid-lobe fringed with black warts.
SIZE: Growing up to 90cm (36″) high.
CLIMATE: Warm to hot.
DISTRIBUTION: This tropical species is native to the Philippines, Sumatra, Burma, China, northern India, Malaysia, Borneo and Indonesia.
FLOWERING TIME: Summer.
DESCRIPTION: Pseudobulbs compressed, oblong or sub-orbicular, 7.5 to 12.5cm (3 to 5″) long, well spaced on short rhizome. Leaves lanceolate, up to 20 to 45cm (8 to 18″) long. Inflorescence few-flowered, 15 to 30cm (6 to 12″) long. Flowers fragrant, bright green, 10 to 12.5cm (4 to 5″) across. Labellum tri-lobed, side lobes small, mid-lobe panduriform, cordate at base, with two high ridges, margins crisp-undulate.

Coelogyne rochussenii

COMMON NAME: None.
COLOUR: Flowers lemon-green. Labellum marked with yellow and brown.
SIZE: Growing up to 50cm (20″) high.
CLIMATE: Warm.
DISTRIBUTION: Native to Borneo, the Philippines, Thailand Peninsula, Peninsula Malaysia, Sumatra and Java.
FLOWERING TIME: Autumn.
DESCRIPTION: Pseudobulbs cylindrical ribbed, up to 20cm (8″) high. Leaves oval-elliptic, up to 30cm (12″) long. Numerous fragrant flowers, up to 3.7cm (1½″) across, borne on a pendulous inflorescence.

Coelogyne rochussenii

Coelogyne rossiana

COMMON NAME: None.
COLOUR: Flowers white. Labellum yellow with brown markings.
SIZE: Growing up to 30cm (12″) high.
CLIMATE: Intermediate.
DISTRIBUTION: Native to Burma.
FLOWERING TIME: Autumn.
DESCRIPTION: Pseudobulbs ovoid, about 10cm (4″) high. Leaves oval-elliptic, up to 30cm (12″) long. Flowers about 2.5cm (1″) across.

Coelogyne rossiana

Coelogyne speciosa

COMMON NAME: None.
COLOUR: Flowers yellowish brown. Labellum marked with dark brown-black.
SIZE: Growing up to 32.5cm (13″) high.
CLIMATE: Intermediate to warm.
DISTRIBUTION: Native to Borneo, Java, Malaysia, Sumatra and Lesser Sunda Islands.
FLOWERING TIME: Throughout the year.
DESCRIPTION: Pseudobulbs ovoid up to 7.5cm (3″) high. Leaves elliptic, 25cm (10″) long. Flowers have a musk fragrance, grow about 7.5cm (3″) across. Labellum mid-lobe margins fringed.

Coelogyne tomentosa

Coelogyne tomentosa

COMMON NAME: None.
COLOUR: Flowers light orange or salmon. Labellum yellow streaked with brown.
SIZE: Growing up to 30cm (12″) high.
CLIMATE: Intermediate to warm.
DISTRIBUTION: Native to Borneo, Malaysia, Thailand, Sumatra and Java.
FLOWERING TIME: Spring.
DESCRIPTION: Pseudobulbs ovoid-conical, up to 5cm (2″) high. Leaves lanceolate, up to 30cm (12″) long. Flowers have musk fragrance and are about 5cm (2″) across.

Coelogyne speciosa

Coelogyne virescens

COMMON NAME: None.
COLOUR: Flower colour variable from cream to light green. Labellum cream to light green with black-brown markings.
SIZE: Epiphytic plant, up to 25cm (10″) high.
CLIMATE: Cool.
DISTRIBUTION: Native to India, Burma, Northern Thailand and Indo-China; growing at elevations up to 1000m (3300′).
FLOWERING TIME: Spring.
DESCRIPTION: Pseudobulbs grooved, oblong-tetragonal, borne on a creeping stem, up to 10cm (4″) high. Leaves in pairs, linear-lanceolate, up to 20cm (8″) long. Inflorescence borne from the apex of the immature pseudobulbs, up to 15cm (6″) long. Flowers up to 4cm (1½″) across.

Coelogyne virescens

CORYANTHES

(ko-ree-an-theez)

Coryanthes from the Gk *cory(s)* (a helmet or cap), *anthos* (a flower) meaning helmet flower with reference to the labellum. It is often referred to as the Bucket Orchid. This small genus of about twenty species is an extraordinary and fascinating epiphytic orchid; it ranges from British Honduras and Guatemala to Peru and Brazil. The stems are truncate, thickened into fleshy deeply-grooved pseudobulbs. Leaves are apical, plicate, acuminate or acute, with the base narrowed into the petiole. Inflorescence is pendulous, rising from the base of the pseudobulb; it is loosely racemose. The fleshy flowers are medium to large, with segments spreading. They are unusual in their complexity of formation, and remarkable for their most unusual pollination mechanism. Sepals are free or adnate to column, and are fragile. The dorsal sepal is small, and lateral sepals are larger and oblique. Petals are narrower than the sepals. The labellum cannot be explained in a few words (refer to illustration on page 25 for detail). The whole flower is of a most complicated structure and design.

In 1916, Rudolf Schlechter attempted to subdivide *Coryanthes* into two groups (a) *Eu-coryanthes*: those with a smooth mesochile and (b) *Lamellunguis*: those with a corrugated mesochile. However, with the discovery of new species it was noted that variations occurred within species; for example, *Coryanthes boyi* from Rio Nanay in Peru has forms with both smooth and corrugated mesochiles.

Coryanthes are exceedingly rare in orchid collections; their amazing appearance makes them most desirable, but their ecology makes cultivation difficult.

Coryanthes usually occurs as a major partner in the myrmecophilous habitat, in the nests of ants of *Camponotus* and *Azteca* genera, and often in association with orange- or purple-coloured tufted *Epidendrum*. It is not uncommon to find in the wild as many as four or five species of *Coryanthes* in flower growing in different parts of the same large ant nest. Interbreeding does not occur since each species is exceedingly pollinator-specific. The pollinator of *Coryanthes macrantha* is the *Eulaema signulata*. *Coryanthes trifoliata's* pollinator is the bee *Englossa ignita*; *Coryanthes rodrigurezii* (*C. boyi*) is pollinated by the bee *Englossa superba*; *Coryanthes maculata* is pollinated by bees of *Englossa azureoviridis*. *Coryanthes leucocorys* attracts bees of *Englossa ignita* and bees of *Eulaema marianna*, but *Englossa ignita* is too small and passes under the anther without dislodging the pollen. Possibly the specific pollinators are attracted by the different odors of the various species of *Coryanthes*.

The *Coryanthes* genus is possibly the most complex of Orchidaceae. The flower is profoundly structured to attract insects and assure pollination. The flowers last but several days. *Hymenopterous* insects are attracted to the large brightly coloured flowers by a strong fragrant secretion on the inner margins of the epichile. The large sepals soon wither leaving an unobstructed path to the intricate and marvellous labellum, unique in Orchidaceae. The apex of the apical-lobe or epichile resembles a waxy cup or a helmet inverted, the front of which is prolonged into a spout-like channel just below the sharply reflexed apex of the column, with its anther and stigma exposed to any insect making its way out of the labellum before taking flight. Above the cup, at the base of the column are two fleshy glands, these secrete a clear liquid, drop-by-drop filling the cup to the level of the apical spout-like channel. On the fully open flower, bees gather to feed on the secretions of the inner margins of the cup. Any bee losing its footing plunges into the liquid. Because of wet wings, the bee's only exit is through the narrow channel just below the stigma and the anther; thus the first bee through, leaves with the pollinia firmly attached to its back and ready to be inserted in the stigma of another flower.

Coryanthes maculata of Panama is reported to grow in

SOUTH AMERICA

ant nests at the top of trees in association with *Epidendrum imatophyllum,* protected by belligerent ants capable of inflicting burning painful bites, making collection and transportation a very painful project. *Coryanthes* do not thrive long in cultivation without the essential element supplied in their natural association with ants and *Epidendrum* sp. in the wild.

Dr J.A. Fowlic collected ant nests along the Rio Nanay in Peru on which *Coryanthes* grow and found that they were loaded with formic acid. He then soaked material from these ants' nests and found that the water squeezed from them had a pH of 3; therefore, an exceedingly acid medium is essential for successful cultivation of *Coryanthes.* He also found that *Coryanthes* thrive when potted in 'Palco' wool and kept exceedingly wet. 'Palco' wool is manufactured from the bark of Redwood trees and has a pH of 3.

On the Rio Nanay in Peru where the Amazon floods its banks regularly, the trees stand for part of the year in about a metre (a few feet) of water. In the 'dry' the Amazon falls by about 6 metres (20 feet) leaving the trees standing in mud with a constant humidity close to 100 per cent and a temperature above 32°C (90°F). Unfortunately, these conditions of high temperature, high humidity and excessive moisture do not necessarily guarantee success in private cultivation.

Culture: Compost, in baskets. The plants require humidity, shade, with special attention to the essential element, formic acid which is supplied by ants.

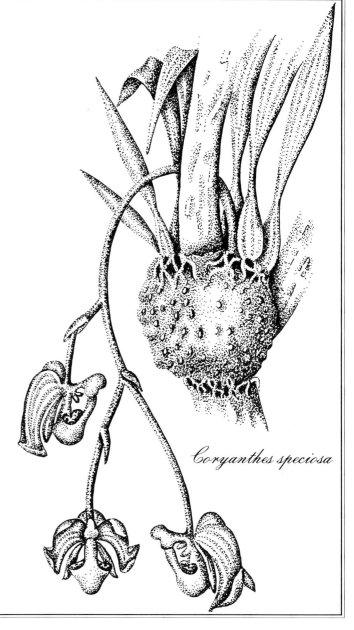

Coryanthes speciosa

Coryanthes leucocorys

Coryanthes leucocorys

COMMON NAME: Bucket Orchid.

COLOUR: Flower sepals yellow-green to cream, marked and spotted pink-brown. Petals cream. Labellum, the hypochile white, and the bucket-like epichile pink-brown.

SIZE: Growing up to 30cm (12″) high.

CLIMATE: Warm to hot.

DISTRIBUTION: Native to Peru. Growing at elevations of up to 900m (3000′) in conditions of high humidity usually near water.

FLOWERING TIME: Autumn.

DESCRIPTION: Pseudobulbs oblong or ovoid, furrowed, up to 7.5cm (3″) high. Leaves lanceolate-elliptic, 25cm (10″) long. Flowers large. The fluid released by the faucet glands has a smell similar to liniment.

CORYBAS
(ko-rye-bas)

Corybas is named after one of the dancing priests of Phrygia. This genus of over forty species spreads over an area bounded by the Himalayas in the west, the Philippines in the north, the Polynesian Islands and New Zealand in the east and by eight Australian species in the south. This is a small terrestrial plant of great interest and unusual beauty. It has one or more small subterranean globular tubers. The solitary cordate leaf lies flat on the ground, the underside having a frost-like appearance, and often with a coloured stripe. Flowers are solitary, proportionately large—about 25mm (1″) diameter—fleshy and almost sessile. The dorsal sepal forms a helmet-like hood over the large labellum and the minute sepals and petals; this appearance gives rise to the common genus name—Helmet Orchids. The labellum is large, complex with various degrees of fringing.

Culture: As for *Caladenia*. Use light dressings of a mixture of damp forest leaf litter and forest humus. The plant requires plenty of shade and normal watering. With care, these plants can be maintained well beyond three or four years and with an increase in the size of the colony.

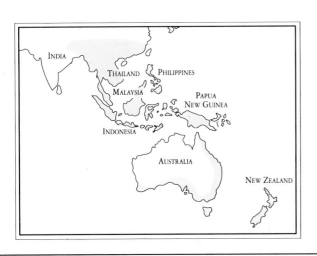

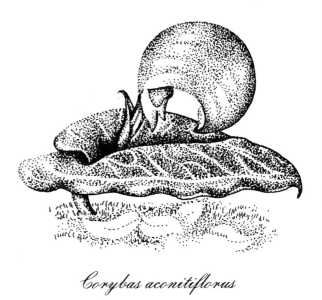

Corybas aconitiflorus

Corybas unguiculatus

Corybas unguiculatus

COMMON NAME: Small Helmet Orchid.
COLOUR: Flower red to purple to black.
SIZE: Small terrestrial plant up to 3cm (1¼″) high.
CLIMATE: Cool.
DISTRIBUTION: Native to the Australian southern coast and nearby mountains.
FLOWERING TIME: Autumn to spring.
DESCRIPTION: Leaf ovate-lanceolate, up to 4cm (1½″) long. Flower solitary about 2.5cm (1″) across. Lamina hooded. Flower resembles a helmet.

CRYPTOSTYLIS

(krip-toe-sty-lis)

Cryptostylis from the Gk *krypto* (covered, hidden), *stylo* (column) with reference to the inconspicuous style (filamentous connection) between stigma and ovary. This is a small genus of about twenty species of unusually attractive and seldom cultivated terrestrial orchids. It is distributed across the tropical lowlands of northern India, Sri Lanka, southern China, Taiwan, Indonesia, Papua New Guinea, the Pacific Islands, Fiji and Australia.

This is a terrestrial herb with a thick, fleshy, subterranean rhizome. Leaves are either absent, few or many, and may be spotted or darky veined. Flowers are many and terminal on a tall slender stem. Sepals and petals are spreading, with sepals longer than petals. The labellum is entire, broad, concave or convex. The column is short. The genus has a remarkable plant–insect relationship in which pseudocopulation occurs between the male Ichneumon Wasp (*Lissopimpla semi-punctata*) and various species of the genus.

Culture: As for *Phaius*. Use a coarse compost in perfectly drained pots. Roots need to be kept moist, but not wet. It requires shade, cool conditions, and less water once growth is complete.

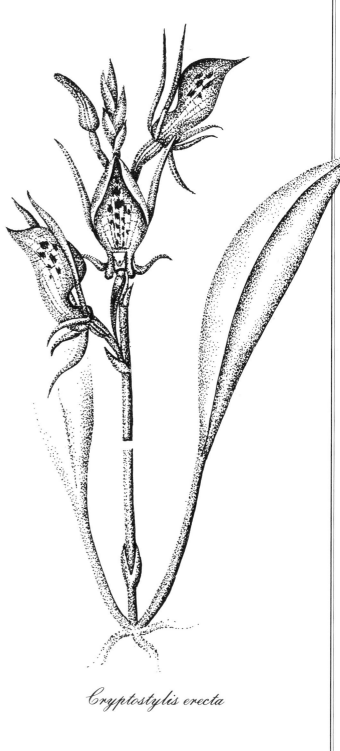

Cryptostylis erecta

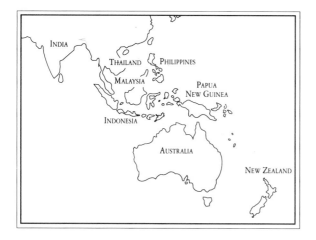

Cryptostylis erecta

COMMON NAME: Striped Hood Orchid.
COLOUR: Green petals and sepals. Labellum white, purple-veined.
SIZE: Small herbaceous terrestrial up to 45cm (18″) high.
CLIMATE: Cool.
DISTRIBUTION: Native to the Australian eastern coast and nearby mountains; found in moist areas.
FLOWERING TIME: Summer.
DESCRIPTION: Leaves fleshy, broad to lanceolate, up to 15cm (6″) long. Labellum forms a large striped hood.

Cryptostylis leptochila

Cryptostylis leptochila

COMMON NAME: Small Tongue Orchid.
COLOUR: Sepals and petals green. Labellum red-pink with white and brown markings.
SIZE: An erect terrestrial, up to 40cm (16″) high.
CLIMATE: Cool.
DISTRIBUTION: Native to Australian eastern highland forests.
FLOWERING TIME: Summer.
DESCRIPTION: Leaves few, radical, lanceolate, up to 10cm (4″) long. Three to twelve flowers. Labellum red-pink, oblong, contracted at centre, covered with minute hairs, three rows of dome-shaped calli extend almost the full length.

Cryptostylis erecta

Cryptostylis subulata

Cryptostylis subulata

COMMON NAME: Slipper Orchid or Wasp Orchid.
COLOUR: Petals and sepals green. Labellum red with black stripe.
SIZE: Small terrestrial up to 45cm (18″) high.
CLIMATE: Cool.
DISTRIBUTION: Native to eastern half of Australia; coastal mountains and swampy areas.
FLOWERING TIME: Spring to summer.
DESCRIPTION: Leaves broad-lanceolate. Labellum oblong, up to 3cm (1¼″) long, margins rolled upwards.

CYMBIDIUM

(sim-bid-ee-um)

*C*ymbidium from the Gk *kymbion* (boat-shaped) with reference to the boat-like shape of the labellum. This is a large genus of about three hundred species of which forty-nine species occur in China alone. The genus occurs throughout South-east Asia from Korea and Japan in the north, to Madagascar and the Himalayas in the west, across to the Philippines in the east and south to Indonesia, Papua New Guinea, the Pacific Islands and eastern Australia. *Cymbidium* is possibly the oldest recorded orchid. The species, *Cymbidium ensifolium*, was first discussed in the herbal section of an ancient Chinese botanical manuscript written during the Chin dynasty (221–202 BC): 'the thickened root, when boiled in water and mixed with fermented glutinous rice, is said to be good for curing stomach ache'. Confucius (551–479 BC) referred to *Cymbidium* as 'the king of fragrant flowers'.

Cymbidium can be either an epiphytic, lithophytic or, rarely, a terrestrial herb. Stems are short, reduced to pseudobulbs covered with sheathing bracts or leaves. Leaves are long, coriaceous and channelled. Inflorescence is either erect, arching or pendulous, with one to many flowers, and the raceme grows up to 1.2m (4′) long. Sepals and petals are almost equal, free, spreading or erect. The labellum is tri-lobed, attached to the base of the column; side-lobes are erect around the column, the mid-lobe is concave above, and the lamina is recurved. The disc has ridges or pubescent lamellae. The column is erect, incurved or semi-terete.

Culture: Compost. *Cymbidium* species can roughly be divided into two groups: (a) Those from the tropics which require warm conditions; and (b) Those from highlands or temperate climates which require cooler conditions, specifically cool nights, but not below 3°C (36°F). Much contradictory information has been written about the requirements of the genus. Most growers treat *Cymbidiums* as semi-terrestrials, so use a quick-draining, porous compost mixture of 3 to 5cm (1 to 2″) cubes of tree-fern fibre, sphagnum moss, dust-free sterilised bark and washed shell grit; and when fertilised monthly, plants give excellent results.

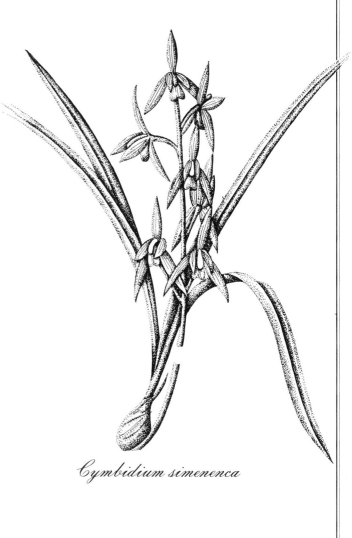

Cymbidium simenenca

AFRICA

INDIA

JAPAN

PAPUA NEW GUINEA

INDONESIA

AUSTRALIA

Cymbidium canaliculatum

COMMON NAME: White Tongued Cymbidium.
COLOUR: Flower colour variable, usually brown to green.
SIZE: An epiphytic plant, growing as high as 60cm (24″).
CLIMATE: Cool to hot.
DISTRIBUTION: Native to Australia. Sclerophyll forests, especially hollows of dead branches.
FLOWERING TIME: Spring.
DESCRIPTION: Pseudobulbs crowded, up to 20cm (8″) high. Leaves elongated, channelled, keeled, up to 60cm (24″) long. Inflorescence arching or pendulous. Numerous flowers, 3.5cm (1½″) across.

Cymbidium canaliculatum

Cymbidium canaliculatum var. *sparksii*

Cymbidium canaliculatum var. sparksii

COMMON NAME: Black orchid.
COLOUR: Dark purple to chocolate-red.
SIZE: Grows up to 60cm (2′) high.
CLIMATE: Warm.
DISTRIBUTION: Native to Australia (north-eastern Queensland only).
FLOWERING TIME: Spring.
DESCRIPTION: Same as type, except this colour variety gives a black appearance from a distance.

Cymbidium devonianum

COMMON NAME: None.
COLOUR: Flowers variable, olive-green, spotted and streaked with red-brown and purple. Labellum purple with darker blotches.
SIZE: Growing up to 40cm (16″) high.
CLIMATE: Cool.
DISTRIBUTION: Native to Himalayas, Khasia Hills, India. Altitude up to 1600m (5249′).
FLOWERING TIME: Summer.
DESCRIPTION: An epiphytic or lithophytic plant. Pseudobulbs obscure, ovoid, 4cm (1½″) high. Leaves oblong to oblanceolate, up to 35cm (14″) long. Inflorescence pendulous, flowers numerous.

Cymbidium devonianum

Cymbidium eburneum

Cymbidium eburneum

COMMON NAME: Ivory Orchid.
COLOUR: Flowers white. Labellum marked with yellow.
SIZE: Growing up to 60cm (24″) high.
CLIMATE: Cool.
DISTRIBUTION: Native to the Himalayas, Sikkim, Khasi Hills, Nepal, Bhutan, China and Burma. Altitudes 300 to 1600m (1000 to 5250′).
FLOWERING TIME: Autumn.
DESCRIPTION: Pseudobulbs obscure, covered by leaf-bracts. Leaves linear strap-shaped, up to 60cm (24″) long. One to two fragrant flowers, 7.5cm (3″) across.

Cymbidium grandiflorum

Cymbidium grandiflorum

COMMON NAME: None.
COLOUR: Flowers green. Labellum yellow with lines and spots of red-purple.
SIZE: Growing up to 60cm (24″) high.
CLIMATE: Cool.
DISTRIBUTION: Native to Nepal, Sikkim, Bhutan.
FLOWERING TIME: Early winter.
DESCRIPTION: Pseudobulbs ovoid. Leaves strap-like, acute, approximately 60cm (2′) long. Inflorescence arching, up to 75cm (30″) long. Flowers fragrant, up to 12.5cm (5″) across.

Cymbidium siamensis

COMMON NAME: None.
COLOUR: Flowers cream to green with longitudinal lines. Labellum pale yellow to green with red blotches, column yellow.
SIZE: Growing up to 35cm (14″) high.
CLIMATE: Cool to intermediate.
DISTRIBUTION: Native to Thailand; growing at elevations of 300 to 750m (1000 to 2500′).
FLOWERING TIME: Autumn to winter.
DESCRIPTION: Leaves strap-shaped, up to 35cm (14″) long. Inflorescence basal, erect, up to 30cm (12″) high, few blooms. Flowers up to 5cm (2″) across.

Cymbidium siamensis

Cymbidium suave

Cymbidium suave

COMMON NAME: None.
COLOUR: Flowers variable in colour from yellow to green. Labellum with brown markings.
SIZE: Grows up to 90cm (36″) high.
CLIMATE: Cool.
DISTRIBUTION: Native to coastal eastern Australia.
FLOWERING TIME: Spring to early summer.
DESCRIPTION: Grass-like epiphyte growing in dead trees. Leaves long and slender. Arching to pendulous and showy raceme. Small flowers with a sweet fragrance.

Cymbidium tracyanum

COMMON NAME: None.
COLOUR: Flowers greenish-yellow, veined with red-brown. Labellum yellowish-cream, veined and spotted red-purple.
SIZE: Growing up to 90cm (36″) high.
CLIMATE: Cool.
DISTRIBUTION: Native to Burma.
FLOWERING TIME: Autumn.
DESCRIPTION: A showy epiphyte. Pseudobulbs compressed, up to 15cm (6″) high. Leaves linear, strap-shaped, up to 75cm (30″) long. Inflorescence up to 1.2m (4′) long, pendulous. Flowers up to 12.5cm (5″) across.

Cymbidium tracyanum

DENDROBIUM
(den-droe-be-um)

Dendrobium from the Gk *dendron* (a tree) *biss* ('life) with reference to the aerial existence of the species (life in a tree). This genus of some 1500 species is the second-largest genus in Orchidaceae, excelled in species numbers only by *Bulbophyllum*. The genus extends from Korea and Japan south through South-east Asia, west to the Himalayas, east into the Philippines, and south through Indonesia, the Pacific Islands, New Zealand and Australia, with the highest concentration of more than 150 species in Papua New Guinea. *Dendrobium* habitats range from the steaming tropical coastal jungles of Malaya to the wind- and snow-swept mountains of the Himalayas, with a tremendous diversity of both plant and flower structure. *Dendrobiums* may be divided into four groups: those whose stems are: (a) rhizomatous; (b) erect having many nodes; (c) erect having one or two nodes with rhizomes of many nodes, and (d) without rhizomes, the new stem growing from the base of the old stem and having many nodes.

This is a genus of sympodial epiphytes having an immense variation in vegetative characteristics. Rhizomes may be tufted or creeping. Stems are either tall, erect to 3m (10′), creeping, pendulous or reduced to small roundish pseudobulbs of 2.5mm (1″). The leaves are of various shapes and sizes, and are either apical or distichous along the stem, flat, thin, thick, terete, papery or coriaceous. Inflorescence is erect, arching or pendulous. The flowers are usually showy, but can be either small or large. Sepals are sub-equal, with lateral sepals obliquely dilated at base and joined to foot of column to form spur under labellum. Petals are similar to sepals and are as long or longer. The labellum is articulate at end of column foot, tri-lobed or entire, erect, concave near base, with margins extending into lateral lobes to embrace the column; the mid-lobe is recurved or spreading, and the lamina has longitudinal ridges. The column is winged or toothed.

Culture: Depends on the species you intend to grow. Grow according to natural habitat. Compost in pots for upright species, and in a basket or on a tree-fern fibre slab for the pendulous variety. Consult your local orchid society about the care and treatment of the particular species you are growing.

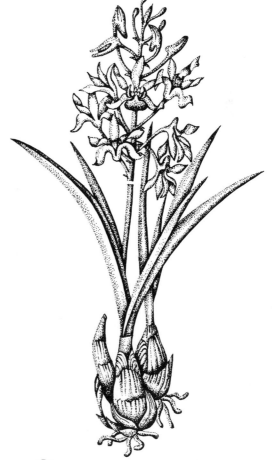

Dendrobium canaliculatum

Dendrobium aemulum

COMMON NAME: Iron Bark Orchid, Brush Box Orchid.
COLOUR: Flowers white. Labellum marked with purple.
SIZE: Growing up to 25cm (10″) high.
CLIMATE: Cool.
DISTRIBUTION: Native to eastern Australian coast and nearby mountains. Growing on Iron Bark (*Eucalyptus sideroxylon*) or Brush Box Trees (*Lophostemon confertus*).
FLOWERING TIME: Spring.
DESCRIPTION: Pseudobulbs up to 25cm (10″) long. Leaves two, terminal, oval. Flowers fragrant and showy, up to 3.5cm (1½″) across. This species has two vegetative forms: (a) those growing on Iron Bark have stout cigar-shaped pseudobulbs; (b) those growing on Brush Box have slender pencil-shaped pseudobulbs. The flowers of both forms appear to be identical.

Dendrobium aemulum

Dendrobium agrostophyllum

COMMON NAME: None.
COLOUR: Flowers bright yellow.
SIZE: Growing up to 70cm (28″) high.
CLIMATE: Cool to intermediate.
DISTRIBUTION: Native to far north-eastern Australia. Altitudes 1000m (3250′), cloud forest.
FLOWERING TIME: Late winter to spring.
DESCRIPTION: Pseudobulbs cylindrical, stem-like, slender fusiform canes up to 60cm (24″) long. Leaves narrow-ovate, emarginate, up to 10cm (4″) long. Racemes short. Flowers up to 2cm (¾″) across.

Dendrobium agrostyophyllum

Dendrobium aggregatum

COMMON NAME: None.
COLOUR: Flowers deep yellow. Labellum orange-yellow.
SIZE: Growing up to 20cm (8″) high.
CLIMATE: Intermediate.
DISTRIBUTION: Native to India, Burma, east to southern China and south to Malaysia, Indo-China, Thailand and Laos.
FLOWERING TIME: Spring.
DESCRIPTION: Pseudobulbs somewhat fusiform, angled, up to 7.5cm (3″) high. Leaf solitary, oblong, obtuse, up to 15cm (6″) long. Inflorescence borne apical. Flowers honey-scented, 3.5cm (1½″) across.

Dendrobium aggregatum

Dendrobium albosanguineum

COMMON NAME: None.
COLOUR: Flowers white, cream or lemon. Labellum has a crimson-purple spot each side of base.
SIZE: Growing up to 40cm (16″) high.
CLIMATE: Intermediate.
DISTRIBUTION: Native to Burma.
FLOWERING TIME: Spring.
DESCRIPTION: Stems pseudobulbous, cylindrical, stout and swollen at the base, up to 28cm (11″) high. Leaves deciduous, linear-lanceolate up to 15cm (6″) long. Short inflorescences borne from upper nodes of stem. Flowers fragrant, 9cm (3½″) across.

Dendrobium albosanguineum

Dendrobium amethystoglossum

COMMON NAME: None.
COLOUR: Flowers white. Labellum lilac, amethyst colour.
SIZE: Growing up to 75cm (30″) high.
CLIMATE: Intermediate to warm.
DISTRIBUTION: Native to the Philippines, Luzon; growing at high elevation.
FLOWERING TIME: Autumn to winter.
DESCRIPTION: Pseudobulbs cylindrical, stem-like, often flexuose up to 75cm (30″) high. Leaves lanceolate, deciduous, up to 10cm (4″) long. Flowers fragrant, 3.5cm (1½″) across. Labellum lobed.

Dendrobium amethystoglossum

Dendrobium amoenum

Dendrobium amoenum

COMMON NAME: None.
COLOUR: Flower colour variable, usually white
with floral segments tipped red-purple.
Labellum white, marked and veined with purple
and yellow.
SIZE: Growing up to 75cm (30″) long.
CLIMATE: Intermediate.
DISTRIBUTION: Native to the Himalayas to Burma.
FLOWERING TIME: Spring.
DESCRIPTION: Pseudobulbs slender, stem-like,
slightly swollen at the nodes, arching to
pendulous, up to 75cm (30″) long. Leaves
linear-lanceolate, acuminate, up to 12.5cm (5″)
long; margins undulate. Inflorescences borne
from leafless pseudobulbs. Flowers have a violet
perfume. Labellum velvety.

Dendrobium antennatum

Dendrobium anosmum syn. D. superbum

COMMON NAME: None.
COLOUR: Flowers pink-purple, darker blotches in
throat. Several colour varieties are to be found.
The pure white variant is rare.
SIZE: Growing up to 150cm (5′) in length.
CLIMATE: Warm.
DISTRIBUTION: Native to Malay Peninsula, Laos,
Vietnam, Philippines, Indonesia and Papua New
Guinea.
FLOWERING TIME: Late winter to spring.
DESCRIPTION: Stem-like pseudobulbs, pendulous
up to 150cm (5′) long (usually shorter). Leaves
deciduous, linear-lanceolate, up to 18cm (7″)
long. Flowers borne from leafless stems, up to
10cm (4″) across.

Dendrobium aphrodite syn. *D. nodatum*

Dendrobium antennatum

COMMON NAME: Antelope Orchid.
COLOUR: Sepals white with petals light green.
Labellum white marked with red-purple.
SIZE: Growing up to 67.5cm (27″) high.
CLIMATE: Hot.
DISTRIBUTION: Native to Papua New Guinea, New
Ireland, Solomon Islands and Australia (Cape
York Peninsula). Altitude up to 800m (2600′).
FLOWERING TIME: Summer.
DESCRIPTION: Pseudobulbs up to 60cm (24″)
high. Leaves fleshy. Flower up to 7.5cm (3″)
long, erect, twisted.

Dendrobium atroviolaceum

Dendrobium anosmum syn. *D. superbum*

Dendrobium aphrodite syn. D. nodatum

COMMON NAME: None.
COLOUR: Flower white. Labellum white, may be
blotched with purple and orange.
SIZE: Growing up to 30cm (12″) high.
CLIMATE: Intermediate.
DISTRIBUTION: Native to Thailand and Burma.
FLOWERING TIME: Spring.
DESCRIPTION: Pseudobulbs branching, swollen at
the nodes, up to 30cm (12″) high. Leaves
deciduous, oblong, obtuse, up to 7.5cm (3″)
long. Flower solitary, borne from nodes of
leafless pseudobulbs, fragrant, 7.5cm (3″)
across.

Dendrobium atroviolaceum

COMMON NAME: None.
COLOUR: Flowers cream-white or yellow, spotted
purple. Labellum green and purple.
SIZE: Growing up to 40cm (16″) high.
CLIMATE: Warm.
DISTRIBUTION: Native to Papua New Guinea.
FLOWERING TIME: Spring.
DESCRIPTION: Pseudobulbs clavate-fusiform,
about 20cm (8″) high. Leaves apical, elliptic, up
to 18cm (7″) long. Flowers fragrant, 6.5cm
(2½″) across.

Dendrobium beckleri

COMMON NAME: Pencil Orchid.
COLOUR: White flowers tinged with green.
Labellum white, marginal fringed and streaked with purple.
SIZE: An epiphyte growing to 2m (6'6") long.
CLIMATE: Cool.
DISTRIBUTION: Native to eastern Australia, growing along coastal rivers and nearby mountains. Altitude to 500m (1650').
FLOWERING TIME: Late spring.
DESCRIPTION: Leaves terete (pencil-like), from a branched cane, tending to grow upwards, but becoming pendulous to 15cm (6") long. Plant bearing a mass of white flowers.

dendrobium bigibbum

Dendrobium bifalce

COMMON NAME: None.
COLOUR: Flowers yellow-green, may be marked with purple-brown. Labellum yellow-brown.
SIZE: Growing up to 45cm (18") high.
CLIMATE: Warm.
DISTRIBUTION: Native to Australia, Papua New Guinea, Solomon Islands, Timor and New Britain.
FLOWERING TIME: Usually summer.
DESCRIPTION: Pseudobulbs base stalked, fusiform, up to 30cm (12") high. Leaves oblong, obtuse, apical, up to 15cm (6") long. Inflorescence borne from leaf axils. Flowers 4cm (¾") across.

Dendrobium beckleri

Dendrobium bigibbum

COMMON NAME: Cooktown Orchid.
COLOUR: Flowers lilac-purple with dark purple labellum.
SIZE: Growing up to 135cm (4'6") high.
CLIMATE: Warm.
DISTRIBUTION: Native to far north-eastern Australia, Torres Strait Islands and Papua New Guinea. Epiphytic plant growing on trees and rocks often in exposed areas and monsoon vine scrub.
FLOWERING TIME: Late summer to winter.
DESCRIPTION: Flower scape bears up to twenty flowers, 8cm (3½") across. Pseudobulbs narrow, cylindrical fusiform, to 120cm (48") long. Leaves ovate-lanceolate, to 15cm (6") long.

Dendrobium bigibbum var. *alba*

Dendrobium bigibbum var. alba

COMMON NAME: White Cooktown Orchid.
COLOUR: Flower white.
SIZE: Similar to type form.
CLIMATE: Warm.
DISTRIBUTION: Same as type form. Australia.
FLOWERING TIME: Similar to type form.
DESCRIPTION: A showy slender ephiphyte or lithophyte. Similar to type form, except for flower colour.

Dendrobium bifalce

Dendrobium bigibbum ssp. laratensis syn. D. biggibum var. phalaenopsis

COMMON NAME: None.
COLOUR: Flowers purple, rose-purple or white.
SIZE: Similar to type form.
CLIMATE: Warm to hot.
DISTRIBUTION: Native to Tanimbar Islands (north of Australia).
FLOWERING TIME: Autumn.
DESCRIPTION: Similar habit to type form, but more robust, flower larger and more variable than in type form.

Dendrobium bigibbum ssp. *laratensis* syn.,
D. bigibbum var. *phalaenopsis*

Dendrobium bracteosum

COMMON NAME: None.
COLOUR: Flowers white, pink or purple.
SIZE: Growing up to 40cm (16") high.
CLIMATE: Warm.
DISTRIBUTION: Native to Papua New Guinea, New Ireland and Rossel Island. Epiphyte growing from sea level to altitudes of 500m (1600'), in lowland rainforest and often on mangrove trees.
FLOWERING TIME: Spring.
DESCRIPTION: Stems slender, terete, erect or pendulous, up to 40cm (16") long. Leaves oblong, up to 7.5cm (3") long. Inflorescences dense. Flowers fragrant, up to 2.5cm (1") across.

Dendrobium bracteosum

Dendrobium bullenianum syn. D. topaziacum

COMMON NAME: None.
COLOUR: Flowers yellow to orange, with purple and red striations.
SIZE: Growing up to 60cm (2') high.
CLIMATE: Warm.
DISTRIBUTION: Native to the Philippines.
FLOWERING TIME: Spring.
DESCRIPTION: Stems up to 60cm (2') long. Leaves oblong, up to 7.5cm (3"). Inflorescence borne at the nodes on leafless stems. Flowers numerous, up to 2cm (¾") across.

Dendrobium bullenianum syn. *D. topaziacum*

Dendrobium canaliculatum

COMMON NAME: Tea-Tree Orchid, Onion Orchid.
COLOUR: Flower white tipped with yellow. Labellum marked with purple.
SIZE: Growing up to 20cm (8") high.
CLIMATE: Warm.
DISTRIBUTION: Native to north-eastern Australia and Papua New Guinea. An epiphyte, whose host is the Melaleuca species (Paper Bark trees).
FLOWERING TIME: Spring.
DESCRIPTION: Pseudobulbs ovate-elongate, up to 12.5cm (5") high, with sheathing bract. Leaves, linear, channelled, acute up to 20cm (8"). Flower up to 2.5cm (1") across.

Dendrobium chrysanthum syn. *D. paxonii*

Dendrobium chrysanthum syn. D. paxonii

COMMON NAME: None.
COLOUR: Flowers deep yellow. Labellum blotched red-brown.
SIZE: Growing up to 2m (6'6") high.
CLIMATE: Intermediate.
DISTRIBUTION: Native to upper Burma, Thailand, Himalayas, India and Nepal.
FLOWERING TIME: Spring and occasionally throughout the year.
DESCRIPTION: Fragrant flowers about 4cm (1½") across. Leaves ovate-lanceolate, acuminate, to 20cm (8") long. Pendulous stems to 2m (6'6") long with many nodes.

Dendrobium canaliculatum

Dendrobium chrysotoxum

COMMON NAME: None.
COLOUR: Flowers golden yellow. labellum throat has an orange band.
SIZE: Growing up to 32.5cm (13") high.
CLIMATE: Intermediate.
DISTRIBUTION: Native to Thailand, China (Yunnan), Laos, Burma and India (Assam).
FLOWERING TIME: Autumn to spring.
DESCRIPTION: Pseudobulbs clavate or fusiform, furrowed with age, clustered up to 20cm (8") high. Leaves apical oblong, up to 12.5cm (5") long. Flowers fragrant 4cm (1½") across. Labellum margins fringed.

Dendrobium chrysotoxum

Dendrobium chrysotoxum var. *suavissimum*

Dendrobium chrysotoxum var. suavissimum

COMMON NAME: None.
COLOUR: Flower golden yellow. Labellum throat has a large maroon blotch or band.
SIZE: Same as type form.
CLIMATE: Intermediate.
DISTRIBUTION: Same as type form.
FLOWERING TIME: Same as type form.
DESCRIPTION: Same as type form, except for flower colour.

Dendrobium conanthum

COMMON NAME: None.
COLOUR: Flowers yellow-brown, tinted and veined brown. Labellum red-purple, veined brown.
SIZE: An epiphytic plant, up to 90cm (3') high.
CLIMATE: Warm to hot.
DISTRIBUTION: Native to Papua New Guinea, Bougainville, Solomon Islands; growing on trees in lowland forest.
FLOWERING TIME: Autumn to winter.
DESCRIPTION: Pseudobulbs, cane-like stems, up to 2m (6'6") high. Leaves alternate, broad-lanceolate, 15cm (6") long. Inflorescence up to 40cm (16") long, flowers numerous. Flowers 5cm (2") across.

Dendrobium cruentum

COMMON NAME: None.
COLOUR: Flowers pale green. Labellum crimson and green.
SIZE: Growing up to 42.5cm (17") high.
CLIMATE: Warm.
DISTRIBUTION: Native to Burma, Thailand and northern Peninsula Malaysia.
FLOWERING TIME: Autumn.
DESCRIPTION: Erect stem-like pseudobulbs, cylindrical, up to 30cm (12") high. Leaves oblong, emarginate, deciduous, up to 12.5cm (5") long. Flowers up to 6.5cm (2½") across.

Dendrobium cruentum

Dendrobium cruttwellii

COMMON NAME: None.
COLOUR: Flowers whitish cream to whitish green, sepals flecked and spotted, maroon-purple on the outside. Labellum markings variable, green to white, spotted purple.
SIZE: Growing up to 25cm (10") high.
CLIMATE: Intermediate.
DISTRIBUTION: Native to Papua New Guinea, at elevations of 1800 to 2400m (5100 to 7850'). Growing on slopes in shaded forest, usually about 3m (10') above ground.
FLOWERING TIME: Throughout the year.
DESCRIPTION: An epiphytic plant. Pseudobulbs ovoid to fusiform, up to 12.5cm (5") high. Leaves borne at the apex of pseudobulbs, petiolate elliptic-lanceolate, acute up to 15cm (6") long. Inflorescence terminal and pendulous, up to 12.5cm (5") long. Flowers about 3cm (1½") across.

Dendrobium cruttwellii

Dendrobium crystallinum

COMMON NAME: None.
COLOUR: Flowers white, tipped with red-purple. Labellum orange.
SIZE: Growing up to 60cm (2') high.
CLIMATE: Intermediate.
DISTRIBUTION: Native to Himalayas, Burma, Thailand, Laos, Cambodia and Vietnam.
FLOWERING TIME: Summer.
DESCRIPTION: Pseudobulbs terete, 60cm (2') long. Leaves deciduous, falcate-lanceolate, 15cm (6") long.

Dendrobium crystallinum

Dendrobium conanthum

Dendrobium cucumerinum

COMMON NAME: Cucumber Ochid.
COLOUR: Flowers cream, streaked with maroon-purple.
SIZE: Creeping, mat forming.
CLIMATE: Cool.
DISTRIBUTION: Native to Australian eastern coast and mountains, growing along rivers and creeks on She Oaks (*Casuarina cunninghamiana*).
FLOWERING TIME: Erratic, summer to autumn.
DESCRIPTION: Epiphytic or lithophytic. Lacks pseudobulbs. Leaves gherkin-like, oblong-ovoid 4cm (1½″) long. Flowers up to 2.5cm (1″) across, borne in clusters.

Dendrobium cucumerinum

Dendrobium dearei

COMMON NAME: None.
COLOUR: Flowers white, throat green.
SIZE: Growing up to 1m (40″) high.
CLIMATE: Warm.
DISTRIBUTION: Native to the Philippines.
FLOWERING TIME: Spring to summer.
DESCRIPTION: Stem-like pseudobulbs, up to 1m (40″) high. Leaves lanceolate, acute, deciduous, up to 15cm (6″) long. Flowers to 7.5cm (3″) across.

Dendrobium dearei

Dendrobium delacourii syn. D. ciliatum

COMMON NAME: None.
COLOUR: Flower cream. Labellum apricot–cream; side lobes veined red-brown.
SIZE: Stems up to 45cm (18″) high.
CLIMATE: Intermediate.
DISTRIBUTION: Native to Thailand and lower Burma. Elevations 800 to 1300m (2600 to 4250′).
FLOWERING TIME: Late winter to spring.
DESCRIPTION: Stems fusiform, up to 46cm (16″) long. Leaves linear-elliptic, up to 10cm (4″) long. Flower 3cm (1¼″) across. Labellum front margins are fringed cavate in shape.

Dendrobium cuthbertsonii syn. *D. sophronites*

Dendrobium cuthbertsonii syn. D. sophronites

COMMON NAME: None.
COLOUR: Flower colour is variable—red, white, orange, yellow or purple.
SIZE: A diminutive plant up to 3cm (1¼″) high.
CLIMATE: Intermediate.
DISTRIBUTION: Native to Papua New Guinea in cloud forest above 2000m (6500′).
FLOWERING TIME: Throughout the year.
DESCRIPTION: Pseudobulbs small and oval. Leaves borne in pairs, linear, about 2cm (¾″) long, dark green, purple underneath. Flowers up to 2.5cm (1″) across. In this dwarf species, flowers can last up to nine months and sometimes longer. The new season's buds can appear before the last season's blooms fade.

Dendrobium X delicatum

COMMON NAME: Dainty Dendrobium.
COLOUR: Raceme erect, white or cream, often tinted pink. Labellum white marked with purple, callus yellow.
SIZE: Growing up to 45cm (18″) high.
CLIMATE: Cool.
DISTRIBUTION: Native to eastern Australia.
FLOWERING TIME: Spring.
DESCRIPTION: A natural hybrid between *D. kingianum* and *D. speciosum*. Pseudobulbs obclavate up to 45cm (18″) high. Leaves apical, lanceolate. Raceme erect.

Dendrobium X delicatum

Dendrobium delacourii syn. *D. ciliatum*

Dendrobium densiflorum

COMMON NAME: None.
COLOUR: Flowers yellow. Labellum orange-yellow.
SIZE: Growing up to 60cm (2′) high.
CLIMATE: Intermediate.
DISTRIBUTION: Native to India, the Himalayas, Nepal, Burma, Sikkim and Assam. Altitude up to 1500m (5000′).
FLOWERING TIME: Spring.
DESCRIPTION: Pseudobulbs tetragonal-fusiform, up to 50cm (20″) high. Leaves elliptic, up to 15cm (6″) long. Inflorescence pendulous, flowers dense and numerous. Flowers showy, up to 5cm (2″) across. Labellum hairy.

Dendrobium devonianum syn. *D. pictum*

Dendrobium devonianum syn. *D. pictum*

COMMON NAME: None.
COLOUR: Sepals white-cream, suffusions pink, rarely tipped with red-purple. Petals lemon or white with orange blotch each side of disc.
SIZE: Growing up to 1.5m (5′) high.
CLIMATE: Intermediate.
DISTRIBUTION: Native to the Himalayas, Burma, Thailand, China and Vietnam.
FLOWERING TIME: Spring to early summer.
DESCRIPTION: Pendulous, stem-like pseudobulbs, up to 1.5m (5′) long. Leaves linear-lanceolate, acuminate, deciduous, up to 13cm (5″) long. Flowers fragrant, 7.5cm (3″) across. Petal margins fimbriate.

Dendrobium densiflorum

Dendrobium dicuphum

COMMON NAME: None.
COLOUR: Flowers white or with pinkish tinge.
SIZE: Up to 30cm (1′).
CLIMATE: Intermediate to warm.
DISTRIBUTION: Top end of northern Australia.
FLOWERING TIME: Autumn to spring.
DESCRIPTION: Epiphyte. Pseudobulbs up to 30cm (1′) long. Leaves 3 to 15cm (1 to 6″) long on distal half of stem, deciduous. Inflorescence up to 50cm (20″) long, arching, with as many as twenty flowers. Flowers are 2.5 to 5cm (1 to 2″) across.

Dendrobium dicuphum

Dendrobium discolor syn. *D. undulatum.*

COMMON NAME: Golden Orchid.
COLOUR: Flowers usually yellow to brown.
SIZE: Growing up to 3m (10′) high.
CLIMATE: Warm.
DISTRIBUTION: Native to north-eastern Australia, Papua New Guinea, Torres Strait Islands and Solomon Islands.
FLOWERING TIME: Throughout the year.
DESCRIPTION: Pseudobulbs cylindrical, up to 5m (15′) high. Leaves oblong-lanceolate, 10cm (4″) long. Inflorescence 60 cm (24″) long, flowers numerous, 75cm (3″) across.

Dendrobium discolor syn. *D. undulatum*

Dendrobium discolor var. *broomfieldii*

Dendrobium discolor var. broomfieldii

COMMON NAME: None.
COLOUR: Flowers vary from a pale yellow to golden yellow with a white keel on the labellum.
SIZE: Same as type form.
CLIMATE: Warm.
DISTRIBUTION: Same as type form.
FLOWERING TIME: Throughout the year.
DESCRIPTION: This plant differs from the type form in that the flowers vary from a pale yellow to golden yellow with a white keel on the labellum.

Dendrobium dixanthum

Dendrobium dixanthum

COMMON NAME: None.
COLOUR: Flowers yellow; streaked with red either side of labellum base.
SIZE: Erect stems, terete up to 1m (40″) high.
CLIMATE: Intermediate.
DISTRIBUTION: Native to Burma.
FLOWERING TIME: Spring.
DESCRIPTION: Leaves lanceolate or strap-shape, up to 17cm (6½″) long. Inflorescence short, borne at the nodes. Flowers up to 4cm (1½″) across.

Dendrobium farmeri

COMMON NAME: None.
COLOUR: Flowers white, flushed mauve-pink. Labellum yellow.
SIZE: Growing up to 30cm (12″) high.
CLIMATE: Intermediate.
DISTRIBUTION: Native to India, the Himalayas, Thailand and the Peninsula Malaysia.
FLOWERING TIME: Mostly spring.
DESCRIPTION: Pseudobulbs tetragonal, up to 30cm (12″) long. Leaves apical, three or four, up to 15cm (6″) long. Inflorescence arching to pendulous with numerous flowers. Flowers up to 5cm (2″) across. Labellum hairy.

Dendrobium farmeri var. *albaflorum*

Dendrobium farmeri var. albaflorum

COMMON NAME: None.
COLOUR: Flowers white. Labellum yellow.
SIZE: Same as type.
CLIMATE: Same as type.
DISTRIBUTION: Same as type.
FLOWERING TIME: Same as type.
DESCRIPTION: Same as type, except petals and sepals pure white.

Dendrobium farmeri

Dendrobium fimbriatum

COMMON NAME: None.
COLOUR: Flowers yellow.
SIZE: Growing up to 1.2m (4′) high.
CLIMATE: Cool to intermediate.
DISTRIBUTION: Native to India, the Himalayas, Nepal, Burma, Thailand, Indo-China, Vietnam and Malaysia.
FLOWERING TIME: Spring.
DESCRIPTION: Pseudobulbs terete, 1.2m (4′) high. Leaves acuminate, lanceolate. Flowers 7cm (3″) across. Labellum fringed.

Dendrobium fimbriatum

Dendrobium fimbriatum var. *oculatum*

Dendrobium fimbriatum var. oculatum

COMMON NAME: None.
COLOUR: Flowers cream-apricot. Labellum yellow-orange, blotched with crimson.
SIZE: Stems long, 1.2m (4') high.
CLIMATE: Cool to intermediate.
DISTRIBUTION: Native to India, Burma and China.
FLOWERING TIME: Spring.
DESCRIPTION: Leaves oblong-lanceolate, acuminate, up to 20cm (8") long. Flowers clustered, large, petals wider than typical form and margins untoothed.

Dendrobium findlayanum

COMMON NAME: None.
COLOUR: Petals and sepals are white with a lilac tint. Labellum has yellow throat, tipped with pink.
SIZE: Growing up to 60cm (24") high.
CLIMATE: Intermediate.
DISTRIBUTION: Native to Burma and Thailand in a mountain climate.
FLOWERING TIME: Late summer.
DESCRIPTION: Canes swollen at the nodes, up to 60cm (24") high. Leaves deciduous, oblong-lanceolate, unequally toothed, up to 10cm (4") long. Flowers in pairs, 7.5cm (3") across. Labellum heart-shaped.

Dendrobium flaviflorum

COMMON NAME: None.
COLOUR: Flower rich golden yellow.
SIZE: Growing up to 60cm (24") high.
CLIMATE: Intermediate.
DISTRIBUTION: Native to Taiwan.
FLOWERING TIME: Summer.
DESCRIPTION: Cane-like pseudobulbs, up to 60cm (24") high. Leaves oblong-lanceolate, up to 10cm (4") long, alternating from top third of pseudobulb. Flower up to 5cm (2") across, fimbriate.

Dendrobium flaviflorum

Dendrobium fleckeri

COMMON NAME: Yellow Moth Orchid.
COLOUR: Flowers apricot. Labellum marked with white and crimson.
SIZE: Growing up to 50cm (20") high.
CLIMATE: Cool to intermediate.
DISTRIBUTION: Native to north-eastern Australia up to an altitude of 1000m (3300').
FLOWERING TIME: Late winter to summer.
DESCRIPTION: Pseudobulbs slender, furrowed, cylindrical, up to 40cm (16") high. Leaves terminal, two or three, lanceolate, up to 10cm (4") long. Flowers large and terminal.

Dendrobium findlayanum

Dendrobium formosum

Dendrobium formosum

COMMON NAME: None.
COLOUR: Flower white. Throat of labellum yellow.
SIZE: Growing up to 50cm (20") high.
CLIMATE: Intermediate to warm.
DISTRIBUTION: Native to the Himalayas, Burma and Thailand Peninsula.
FLOWERING TIME: Winter to early spring.
DESCRIPTION: Pseudobulbs ribbed, slightly fusiform, up to 37.5cm (15") high. Leaves oblong-ovate, 12.5cm (5") long. Flower size variable up to 13cm (5") across.

Dendrobium fleckeri

Dendrobium friedericksianum var. *oculatum*

COMMON NAME: None.
COLOUR: Flowers pale yellow. Labellum marked with a medium purple blotch.
SIZE: Growing up to 1.2m (4′) high.
CLIMATE: Cool to intermediate.
DISTRIBUTION: Native to Thailand.
FLOWERING TIME: Spring.
DESCRIPTION: Pseudobulbs stem-like. Leaves linear and deciduous. Flowers up to 6cm (2½″) across.

Dendrobium friedericksianum var. *oculatum*

Dendrobium gibsoni syn. D. fuscatum.

COMMON NAME: None.
COLOUR: Flowers deep yellow. Labellum marked with two brown blotches.
SIZE: Growing up to 1.2m (4′) high.
CLIMATE: Cool.
DISTRIBUTION: Native to the Himalayas, Burma, southern China and Yunnan.
FLOWERING TIME: Summer.
DESCRIPTION: Pseudobulbs cylindrical, 1.2m (4′) long. Leaves lanceolate 15cm (6″) long. Inflorescence apical and pendulous. Flowers 5cm (2″) across.

Dendrobium gonzalesii

COMMON NAME: None.
COLOUR: Flowers white to mauve. Labellum marked with purple.
SIZE: Growing up to 50cm (20″) high.
CLIMATE: Intermediate to warm.
DISTRIBUTION: Native to the Philippines, growing at an altitude of 860m (2800′).
FLOWERING TIME: Spring.
DESCRIPTION: An epiphytic plant. Cane stems pendulous, clustered up to 50cm (20″) long, may be branched. Leaves lanceolate, oblong, acute, up to 10cm (4″) long. Flowers showy, about 5cm (2″) across.

Dendrobium gordonii

COMMON NAME: None.
COLOUR: Flowers yellow to green, veined brown.
SIZE: Growing up to 45cm (18″) high.
CLIMATE: Warm to hot.
DISTRIBUTION: Native to Fiji.
FLOWERING TIME: Winter.
DESCRIPTION: An epiphyte. Pseudobulbs fusiform, furrowed when matured, up to 30cm (12″) high. Two to three apical leaves, broad-lanceolate, up to 20cm (8″) long. Inflorescence terminal. Flowers 3.5cm (1½″) across. Some botanists consider it syn. *D. macrophyllum.*

Dendrobium gibsoni syn. *D. fuscatum*

Dendrobium gordonii

Dendrobium gouldii

COMMON NAME: Guadalcanal Gold Orchid.
COLOUR: Flower colour variable, mauve to yellow-brown with mauve veins. Labellum streaked red-brown. White to mauve colour forms readily found in Papua New Guinea, while yellow and brown forms are readily found on Guadalcanal Island. (Colour form in this photograph is Guadalcanal Gold.)
SIZE: Growing up to 1.2m (4′) high.
CLIMATE: Warm to hot.
DISTRIBUTION: Native to Solomon Islands, northern and eastern coasts of Papua New Guinea, and Pacific Islands. Grows at sea level.
FLOWERING TIME: Autumn.
DESCRIPTION: Pseudobulbs stout, stem-like, canes up to 1.2m (4′) and sometimes to 2.1m (7′). Leaves elliptic-ovate, distichous up to 15cm (6″) long. Inflorescence apical, up to 60cm (24″) long, six to twenty-five blooms. Flowers 6cm (2½″) across.

Dendrobium gouldii

Dendrobium gonzalesii

Dendrobium gracilicaule

Dendrobium gracilicaule

COMMON NAME: None.
COLOUR: Flowers are yellow and blotched with maroon.
SIZE: Growing up to 75cm (30″) high.
CLIMATE: Cool.
DISTRIBUTION: Native to Australia (north-eastern coast and mountains).
FLOWERING TIME: Spring.
DESCRIPTION: An epiphytic plant. Pseudobulbs erect, cylindrical, up to 75cm (30″) long. Three to six apical leaves, lanceolate to narrow-elliptic, slightly sinuate, up to 14cm (5½″) long. Five to sixteen flowers on raceme. Flowers 2cm (¾″) across.

Dendrobium gratiosissimum syn. D. boxallii

Dendrobium gratiosissimum syn. D. boxalii and D. bullerianum

COMMON NAME: None.
COLOUR: Flower white or mauve, floral segments tipped with pink-purple. Labellum white tipped with pink-purple; disc yellow marked with orange.
SIZE: Growing up to 1m (40″) high.
CLIMATE: Cool to intermediate.
DISTRIBUTION: Native to Burma and Thailand.
FLOWERING TIME: Spring.
DESCRIPTION: Pseudobulbs stem-like, canes cylindrical, generally 1m (40″) long. Leaves strap-like, deciduous, up to 10cm (4″) long. Inflorescence borne from leafless pseudobulbs. Flower 6cm (2½″) across.

Dendrobium griffithianum

COMMON NAME: None.
COLOUR: Flowers white. Labellum yellow.
SIZE: Growing up to 30cm (12″) high.
CLIMATE: Intermediate.
DISTRIBUTION: Native to Thailand and Burma.
FLOWERING TIME: Late spring to summer.
DESCRIPTION: Pseudobulbs tetragonal, up to 30cm (12″) high. Leaves oblong or ovate, up to 12.5cm (5″) long. Inflorescence erect to pendulous, numerous flowers, up to 4cm (1½″) across. Labellum margins ciliate.

Dendrobium griffithianum

Dendrobium guerreroi

COMMON NAME: None.
COLOUR: Flowers yellow to brown.
SIZE: Grows up to 75cm (30″) high.
CLIMATE: Intermediate to warm.
DISTRIBUTION: Native to the Philippines (Mindoro and Dinagat Islands).
FLOWERING TIME: Summer.
DESCRIPTION: An epiphytic plant. Canes long and generally leafless, clustered, elongate. Leaves deciduous, lanceolate-oblong, up to 10cm (4″) long. Inflorescence pendulous, loose raceme, bearing few flowers, up to 10cm (4″) long. Flowers about 2cm (¾″) across, bracts pink to purple.

Dendrobium hercoglossum syn. D. linguella

Dendrobium hercoglossum syn. D. linguella

COMMON NAME: None.
COLOUR: Flowers pinkish-mauve. Labellum white with a bright red-purple blotch at the apex.
SIZE: Growing up to 35cm (14″) high.
CLIMATE: Cool to intermediate.
DISTRIBUTION: Native to Thailand and Indo-China.
FLOWERING TIME: Spring to summer.
DESCRIPTION: Stems slender, clustered, up to 35cm (14″) high, almost hidden by leaf-sheaths. Leaves linear-lanceolate, unequally emarginate, distichous, up to 10cm (4″) long. Inflorescence flexuose. Flowers showy. Closely allied to *D. aduncum*; the separation of the two species is due mainly to differences in the labellum.

Dendrobium guerreroi

Dendrobium heterocarpum
syn. *D. aureum*

COMMON NAME: None.
COLOUR: Flowers creamy yellow. Labellum orange-yellow, veined with maroon.
SIZE: Growing up to 90cm (36″) high.
CLIMATE: Cool to intermediate.
DISTRIBUTION: Native to India, Nepal, Burma, Assam, Sikkim, Sri Lanka, South-east Asia, Indonesia, the Philippines and Moluccas.
FLOWERING TIME: Spring to autumn.
DESCRIPTION: A variable plant. Pseudobulbs cylindrical, tapered at base, up to 90cm (3′) high. Leaves deciduous, oblong-lanceolate, 12.5cm (5″) long. Flowers fragrant, borne from the nodes, and up to 6cm (2½″) across.

Dendrobium heterocarpum syn. *D. aureum*

Dendrobium infundibulum syn. *D. moulmeinense*

Dendrobium infundibulum
syn. *D. moulmeinense*

COMMON NAME: None.
COLOUR: Flowers white. Labellum throat blotched yellow.
SIZE: Growing up to 100cm (40″) high.
CLIMATE: Cool to intermediate.
DISTRIBUTION: Native to Thailand and Burma. Elevation 1100 to 2300m (3608 to 7000′).
FLOWERING TIME: Spring to early summer.
DESCRIPTION: Pseudobulbs stem-like up to 100cm (40″) high. Leaves linear-lanceolate, 8.5cm (3¼″) long. Flowers up to 8.5cm (3¼″) across. Closely allied species *D. formosum*, the main difference is in the sepals and spur.

Dendrobium infundibulum
var. *jamesianum*, syn.
D. jamesianum

COMMON NAME: None.
COLOUR: As for type, with differences listed below.
SIZE: As for type.
CLIMATE: As for type.
DISTRIBUTION: Native to Burma.
FLOWERING TIME: Spring.
DESCRIPTION: Differing from the type in the following: pseudobulbs shorter; in shape of the labellum, lateral lobes and colour of the labellum throat, deeper yellow.

Dendrobium infundibulum var. *jamesianum*

Dendrobium kingianum

COMMON NAME: Pink Rock Orchid.
COLOUR: Flowers pinkish-mauve and rarely white.
SIZE: Growing up to 40cm (16″) high.
CLIMATE: Cool.
DISTRIBUTION: Native to eastern half of Australia, coast and mountains.
FLOWERING TIME: Spring.
DESCRIPTION: A lithophytic orchid growing on rocks and cliff faces forming a mat-like growth. Very variable in colour and growth habit. Pseudobulbs clustered, clavate up to 40cm (16″) high. Leaves terminal, lanceolate up to 10cm (4″) long. Two to nine flowers per raceme.

Dendrobium kingianum

Dendrobium kingianum var.
silcockii

COMMON NAME: None.
COLOUR: Flowers white. Labellum purple.
SIZE: Growing up to 40cm (16″) high.
CLIMATE: Cool.
DISTRIBUTION: Native to eastern Australia, coastal mountains.
FLOWERING TIME: Spring.
DESCRIPTION: Same as type, except flower colour.

Dendrobium kingianum var. *silcockii*

Dendrobium lasianthera 'May River Red'

Dendrobium lasianthera

COMMON NAME: May River Red.
COLOUR: Flowers red-bronze-brown, with yellow margins. Petal apex yellow. Labellum red-purple.
SIZE: Growing up to 3m (10') high.
CLIMATE: Hot.
DISTRIBUTION: Native to Papua New Guinea (along the May River), low altitudes.
FLOWERING TIME: Summer.
DESCRIPTION: Pseudobulbs terete, erect canes, up to 3m (10') high. Leaves up to 18cm (7") long, elliptic, alternate, emarginate. Inflorescence up to 60cm (24") long. Flowers large and showy. Petals erect and twisted.

Dendrobium lasianthera 'Veronica Somare'

Dendrobium lasianthera

COMMON NAME: Veronica Somare.
COLOUR: Flowers red-brown. Labellum white at base, pink-purple, apex yellow, yellow tint throughout flower.
SIZE: Canes up to 3m (10') high.
CLIMATE: Hot.
DISTRIBUTION: Native to Papua New Guinea; low altitudes, swamps.
FLOWERING TIME: Summer.
DESCRIPTION: Habit same as type. Flowers large, showy, petals somewhat erect and twisted.

Dendrobium lineale

COMMON NAME: Bougainville White.
COLOUR: Flowers white. Labellum flushed with mauve.
SIZE: Growing up to 1m (40") high.
CLIMATE: Hot.
DISTRIBUTION: Native to Papua New Guinea, New Ireland and Solomon Islands. Commonly growing in coastal trees and festooning the beech trees in many areas.
FLOWERING TIME: Autumn to winter.
DESCRIPTION: Pseudobulbs somewhat fusiform, slender, canes up to 1m (40") long. Flowers numerous, to about 5cm (2") across, petals quite erect and twisted.

Dendrobium linguiforme

Dendrobium linguiforme

COMMON NAME: Tongue Orchid.
COLOUR: Flower white. Labellum marked lemon.
SIZE: Creeping, mat forming.
CLIMATE: Cool.
DISTRIBUTION: Native to eastern Australia. Lithophytic growing on rock, or epiphytic on trees, especially growing on Paper Bark (*Melaleuca alternifolia*).
FLOWERING TIME: Late winter to spring.
DESCRIPTION: Creeping rhizomes, stem prostrate. Leaves numerous, thick, flattened, grooved, ovate or ovate-lanceolate, tongue-like, and up to 5cm (2") long. Raceme up to 12.5cm (5") long.

Dendrobium lineale

Dendrobium loddigesii

COMMON NAME: None.
COLOUR: Flower pastel, mauve to pink. Labellum white, fringed centre orange to yellow.
SIZE: A dwarf epiphyte with creeping, branching, soft canes to 20cm (8") long.
CLIMATE: Intermediate.
DISTRIBUTION: Native to Laos, China and Hainan Island.
FLOWERING TIME: Mid winter to spring.
DESCRIPTION: Stems bear small, ovate-elliptic, alternate, deciduous leaves. Flowers are fragrant, solitary, up to 2.5cm (1") across.

Dendrobium loddigesii

Dendrobium macrophyllum

COMMON NAME: None.
COLOUR: Flower yellow to yellow-green. Petals spotted with purple. Labellum green or yellow-green, veined purple.
SIZE: Growing up to 45cm (18") high.
CLIMATE: Warm to hot.
DISTRIBUTION: Native to Papua New Guinea, the Philippines, Malaysia and Java.
FLOWERING TIME: Spring to early summer.
DESCRIPTION: Pseudobulbs clavate, often compressed, ribbed, 45cm (18") high. Leaves up to 25cm (10") long, elliptic, acute, shiny. Flower colour variable, grows to 5cm (2") across.

Dendrobium macrophyllum

Dendrobium malbrownii

COMMON NAME: Mal Brown's Cane Orchid.
COLOUR: Flower fleshy apricot to creamy white. Labellum maroon or dark glossy purple.
SIZE: Growing up to 25cm (10") high.
CLIMATE: Intermediate to warm.
DISTRIBUTION: Native to far north-eastern Australia and Papua New Guinea.
FLOWERING TIME: Late summer to autumn.
DESCRIPTION: Pseudobulbs grass-like, up to 25cm (10") high. Leaves up to 6cm (2½") long. Flowers solitary, about 8mm (under ½").

Dendrobium malbrownii

Dendrobium margaritaceum

Dendrobium margaritaceum

COMMON NAME: None.
COLOUR: Flowers white. Labellum yellow and red.
SIZE: Stems subclavate, 5cm (2") high.
CLIMATE: Warm.
DISTRIBUTION: Native to Thailand and Vietnam, Assam.
FLOWERING TIME: Spring.
DESCRIPTION: Leaves apical, lanceolate, 4cm (1½") long. One to two flowers up to 3cm (1¼") across.

Dendrobium mirbelianum syn. *D. wilkianum*

Dendrobium mirbelianum syn. D. wilkianum

COMMON NAME: None.
COLOUR: Flowers usually yellow-green, veined and may be finely spotted with purple-brown.
SIZE: Growing up to 50cm (20") high.
CLIMATE: Warm to hot.
DISTRIBUTION: Native to Australia (Cape York Peninsula), Papua New Guinea, New Britain, Alor Islands, Hamahera, Timor and Moluccas.
FLOWERING TIME: Throughout the year, often more than once annually.
DESCRIPTION: Epiphytic growing in lowland forest. A variable plant in both vegetation and floral segments, resulting in many forms. Pseudobulbs fusiform, up to 40cm (16") high. Leaves unusually oval obtuse, up to 10cm (4") long. Flowers up to 5cm (2") across.

Dendrobium miyakei

Dendrobium miyakei

COMMON NAME: None.
COLOUR: Flowers purple.
SIZE: Growing up to 1m (40") high.
CLIMATE: Intermediate to warm.
DISTRIBUTION: Native to the Philippines (Bataan Island) and Taiwan in mountain areas.
FLOWERING TIME: Winter.
DESCRIPTION: Stems pendulous, clustered, terete, swollen at the nodes, up to 1m (40") long. Leaves linear-lanceolate, acute, up to 10cm (4") long. Inflorescence borne from leafless stems, in short raceme, four to eight blooms. Flowers about 2cm (¾") across.

Dendrobium mohlianum

Dendrobium mohlianum

COMMON NAME: None.
COLOUR: Flowers orange.
SIZE: Growing up to 45cm (18″) high.
CLIMATE: Warm.
DISTRIBUTION: Native to Fiji, growing at altitudes above 800m (2500′).
FLOWERING TIME: Autumn.
DESCRIPTION: Epiphyte of the cloud forests with cane-like pseudobulbs to 45cm (18″) high, slightly hirsute. Leaves oblong-lanceolate to 10cm (4″) long. Flowers 1.5cm (½″) across, clustered on short inflorescence.

Dendrobium monophyllum

Dendrobium monophyllum

COMMON NAME: Lily of the Valley.
COLOUR: Flowers yellow-green.
SIZE: Growing up to 20cm (8″) high.
CLIMATE: Cool.
DISTRIBUTION: Native to Australia (north-eastern coast and nearby ranges) growing at altitudes of up to 900m (3000′).
FLOWERING TIME: Mainly spring.
DESCRIPTION: Pseudobulbs thick, narrow-conical, up to 10cm (4″) high, mature bulbs often furrowed. Leaf solitary, terminal, oblong to lanceolate, up to 10cm (4″) long. Raceme solitary, terminal, about as long as the leaf. Flowers on drooping pedicel, fragrant, up to 6mm (¼″) long.

Dendrobium moschatum

COMMON NAME: None.
COLOUR: Flowers pale apricot. Labellum inside orange with two red-brown blotches.
SIZE: Canes terete, erect or pendulous, up to 2.5m (8′6″) long.
CLIMATE: Cool to intermediate.
DISTRIBUTION: Native to the Himalayas, Burma, Thailand and Laos.
FLOWERING TIME: Spring to summer.
DESCRIPTION: Leaves oblong-ovate 20cm (8″) long. Flowers up to 10cm (4″) across, musk-scented. Labellum pouch shaped.

Dendrobium moschatum

Dendrobium moschatum var. colorum

COMMON NAME: None.
COLOUR: Flower apricot, tinged purple.
SIZE: Same as type.
CLIMATE: Same as type.
DISTRIBUTION: Native to India and Burma.
FLOWERING TIME: Spring to early summer.
DESCRIPTION: Same as type, except for colour variation.

Dendrobium moschatum var. *colorum*

Dendrobium nobile

COMMON NAME: None.
COLOUR: Flowers mauve. Labellum mauve and cream, throat crimson-purple.
SIZE: Growing up to 70cm (28″) high.
CLIMATE: Cool to intermediate.
DISTRIBUTION: Native to Nepal, Sikkim, Bhutan, Upper Burma, Assam, China, Laos, Vietnam and Taiwan.
FLOWERING TIME: Spring.
DESCRIPTION: Pseudobulbs clustered, terete, somewhat compressed, up to 60cm (24″) high. Leaves deciduous, oblong, slightly emarginate, up to 10cm (4″) long. Flowers borne from the nodes in short racemes; flowers are large, up to 7.5cm (3″) across. This plant is popular as a parent for hybridisation, and also for certain medicinal properties.

Dendrobium nobile

Dendrobium nobile var. *virginale*

COMMON NAME: None.
COLOUR: Flowers white.
SIZE: Same as type.
CLIMATE: Same as type.
DISTRIBUTION: Native to Burma, growing at high altitudes, liking sunny position.
FLOWERING TIME: Spring.
DESCRIPTION: This soft cane species is an alba variety of *D. nobile*. Habit same as type *D. nobile*, differing in that flowers are white.

Dendrobium nobile var. *virginale*

Dendrobium ochreatum syn. *D. cambridgeanum*

COMMON NAME: None.
COLOUR: Flowers deep yellow. Labellum yellow with maroon blotch.
SIZE: Growing up to 30cm (12″) high.
CLIMATE: Cool to intermediate.
DISTRIBUTION: Native to Thailand, India and the Himalayas; grows generally at high elevations.
FLOWERING TIME: Spring.
DESCRIPTION: Pseudobulbs pendulous, cylindrical, stout, 30cm (12″) long, swollen at the nodes. Leaves ovate-lanceolate, acute, deciduous, 5 to 10cm (2 to 4″) long. Inflorescence short, borne from the nodes. Flowers are 5cm (2″) across.

Dendrobium ochreatum syn. *D. cambridgeanum*

Dendrobium parishii

Dendrobium pendulum syn. *D. crassinode.*

COMMON NAME: None.
COLOUR: Flowers usually white, tipped with red-purple. Labellum carries yellow-orange blotches.
SIZE: Growing up to 45cm (18″) high.
CLIMATE: Intermediate.
DISTRIBUTION: Native to India, Burma and Thailand.
FLOWERING TIME: Spring.
DESCRIPTION: Pseudobulbs crassinode in shape, usually erect, swollen at the nodes, up to 45cm (18″) long. Leaves deciduous, linear-lanceolate 12.5cm (5″) long. Flowers borne on leafless pseudobulbs, 5 to 6cm (2 to 2½″) across.

Dendrobium petiolatum

Dendrobium parishii

COMMON NAME: None.
COLOUR: Flowers purple. Labellum throat blotched with two maroon spots.
SIZE: Growing up to 20cm (8″) high.
CLIMATE: Cool to intermediate.
DISTRIBUTION: Native to Burma, Thailand, Laos, Cambodia, Vietnam and China.
FLOWERING TIME: Spring.
DESCRIPTION: Pseudobulbs cylindrical; pendulous or prostrate canes up to 20cm (8″) long. Leaves oblong-lanceolate and deciduous. Flowers borne from the nodes along the canes, and are 5cm (2″) across.

Dendrobium pendulum syn. *D. crassinode*

Dendrobium petiolatum

COMMON NAME: None.
COLOUR: Flowers are pink. Labellum marked yellow.
SIZE: Growing up to 25cm (10″) high.
CLIMATE: Intermediate to warm.
DISTRIBUTION: Native to Papua New Guinea.
FLOWERING TIME: Spring.
DESCRIPTION: Pseudobulbs are cane-like, swollen at the nodes, up to 25cm (10″) high. Leaves oblong-lanceolate, sheathing at the base, up to 10cm (4″) long. Inflorescence short, flowers clustered, up to 2.5cm (1″) across.

Dendrobium pierardii

Dendrobium pierardii

COMMON NAME: None.
COLOUR: Flowers mauve. Labellum pale yellow, veined purple.
SIZE: Growing up to 1m (40″) long.
CLIMATE: Cool to intermediate.
DISTRIBUTION: Native to India, Himalayas, Burma, China, Thailand and Peninsula Malaysia.
FLOWERING TIME: Spring to early summer.
DESCRIPTION: Pseudobulbs are stem-like, slender, pendulous, up to 1m (40″) long. Leaves are deciduous, sessile lanceolate, up to 10cm (4″) long. Flowers are fragrant, semi-translucent, and grow up to 5cm (2″) across.

Dendrobium pierardii var. *alba*

Dendrobium pierardii var. alba

COMMON NAME: None.
COLOUR: Flowers are white.
SIZE: Same as type.
CLIMATE: Same as type.
FLOWERING TIME: Same as type.
DESCRIPTION: Same as type, but for white flower.

Dendrobium polysema

COMMON NAME: None.
COLOUR: Flower whitish cream, heavily spotted with maroon. Labellum warm yellow marked with maroon.
SIZE: Growing up to 45cm (18″) high.
CLIMATE: Hot.
DISTRIBUTION: Native to Papua New Guinea.
FLOWERING TIME: Spring.
DESCRIPTION: Pseudobulbs clavate, ribbed up to 40cm (16″) high. Leaves elliptic, acute, shiny, up to 20cm (8″) long. *D. polysema* is not a synonym of *D. macrophyllum*, differing in all floral segments, especially the narrow lateral lobes of the labellum. The column is also different.

Dendrobium prasinum

Dendrobium prasinum

COMMON NAME: None.
COLOUR: Flowers white.
SIZE: Growing up to 15cm (6″) long.
CLIMATE: Warm.
DISTRIBUTION: Native to Fiji; common in forest over 600m (2000′) in altitude.
FLOWERING TIME: Early spring.
DESCRIPTION: Pseudobulbs clavate, up to 7.5cm (3″) high. Leaves linear-oblong, up to 12.5cm (5″) long. Inflorescence short, four to five, clustered. Flowers inverted, and are up to 4cm (1½″) across.

Dendrobium polysema

Dendrobium pugioniforme

COMMON NAME: Dagger Orchid.
COLOUR: Flowers green to cream with purple marks.
SIZE: Growing to 2m (6′6″) long.
CLIMATE: Cool.
DISTRIBUTION: Native to Australia (central eastern coast and nearby mountains).
FLOWERING TIME: Spring.
DESCRIPTION: Pendulous epiphyte. Leaves ovate to lanceolate, tapering to a dagger-like point, up to 7.5cm (3″) long. Flowers up to 2.5cm (1″) across.

Dendrobium pugioniforme ·

Dendrobium pulchellum syn. *D. dalhousieanum*

Dendrobium pulchellum syn. *D. dalhousieanum*

COMMON NAME: None.
COLOUR: Flowers creamy yellow to pinkish yellow. Labellum creamy white with maroon blotch on each side of disc.
SIZE: Growing up to 1.5m (5′) high.
CLIMATE: Intermediate to warm.
DISTRIBUTION: Native to Thailand, Vietnam, Himalayas to Burma and Peninsula Malaysia.
FLOWERING TIME: Spring.
DESCRIPTION: Pseudobulbs terete, canes up to 1.5m (5′) or more high. Leaves linear-oblong, up to 20cm (8″) long. Basal leaves are heart-shaped. Flowers have a musk scent, up to 10cm (4″) across.

Dendrobium revolutum

Dendrobium revolutum

COMMON NAME: None.
COLOUR: Flower white. Labellum orange.
SIZE: Growing up to 60cm (24″) high.
CLIMATE: Warm to hot.
DISTRIBUTION: Native to Burma, Thailand, Laos, Vietnam, Peninsula Malaysia and Papua New Guinea.
FLOWERING TIME: Early summer.
DESCRIPTION: Pseudobulbs are cylindrical, up to 60cm (24″) high. Leaves are oblong. Solitary flower, 2.5cm (1″) long.

Dendrobium rhodopterygium syn. *D. polyphlebium*

COMMON NAME: None.
COLOUR: Flowers pale pink to purple, may be blotched white. Labellum throat blotched with purple.
SIZE: Growing up to 20cm (8″) high.
CLIMATE: Intermediate.
DISTRIBUTION: Native to Burma.
FLOWERING TIME: Spring.
DESCRIPTION: Pseudobulbs are long, cylindrical canes up to 20cm (8″) high. Inflorescence borne from leafless canes. Flowers are fragrant and 7.5cm (3″) across. Labellum fringed.

Dendrobium rhodopterygium syn. *D. polyphlebium*

Dendrobium rhodostictum

COMMON NAME: None.
COLOUR: Flowers white. Labellum throat veined and speckled with mauve.
SIZE: Growing up to 25cm (10″) high.
CLIMATE: Warm.
DISTRIBUTION: Native to Papua New Guinea in rainforest above 1500m (5000′).
FLOWERING TIME: Spring to early summer.
DESCRIPTION: Pseudobulbs are slender clavate, up to 20cm (8″) high. Leaves are apical oval, obtuse, up to 6.5cm (2½″) long. Flowers are waxy and fragrant.

Dendrobium rhodostictum

Dendrobium ruginosum

Dendrobium ruginosum

COMMON NAME: None.
COLOUR: Flowers white. Labellum veined purple-red.
SIZE: Growing up to 37cm (14½″) high.
CLIMATE: Hot.
DISTRIBUTION: Native to Solomon Islands and Bougainville, growing in montane forests.
FLOWERING TIME: Summer.
DESCRIPTION: An epiphytic or lithophytic plant. Pseudobulbs clustered, tetragonal, clavate, up to 25cm (10″) high. Leaves broad-lanceolate, acute, up to 12cm (4½″) long. Inflorescence up to 20cm (8″) long. Flowers grow up to 4cm (1½″) across.

Dendrobium ruppianum

COMMON NAME: None.
COLOUR: Flowers white. Labellum marked with purple lines.
SIZE: Growing up to 45cm (18″) high.
CLIMATE: Cool to warm.
DISTRIBUTION: Native to Australia (far north-east); common in rainforest.
FLOWERING TIME: Late winter to spring.
DESCRIPTION: Pseudobulbs fusiform, furrowed, up to 30cm (12″). Two to seven leaves, up to 15cm (6″) long, ovate-oblong, and apical margins may be undulate. Raceme erect; flowers numerous and fragrant.

Dendrobium ruppianum

Dendrobium sanderae

COMMON NAME: None.
COLOUR: Flowers white. Labellum marked with purple and green.
SIZE: Stems erect up to 80cm (32″) high.
CLIMATE: Warm.
DISTRIBUTION: Native to the Philippines and Luzon.
FLOWERING TIME: Usually autumn to winter.
DESCRIPTION: Leaves ovate to linear-ovate, 12.5cm (5″) long. Flowers are large, showy, and 10cm (4″) across.

Dendrobium sanderae

Dendrobium sanderae var. major

COMMON NAME: None.
COLOUR: Flowers white. Labellum veined light purple.
SIZE: Growing up to 70cm (28″) or more high.
CLIMATE: Warm.
DISTRIBUTION: Native to the Philippines (Baguio).
FLOWERING TIME: Spring to summer.
DESCRIPTION: Stems clustered, elongate, up to 70cm (28″) long. Leaves lanceolate, slightly notched at the apex, up to 10cm (4″) or more long. Flowers are large and showy, about 10cm (4″) across. Labellum tri-lobed. *Dendrobium Sanderae* var. *major* is similar in habit to *D. sanderae*, but is much longer in every aspect.

Dendrobium schuetzei

COMMON NAME: None.
COLOUR: Flowers white. Labellum green, spotted at the base.
SIZE: Ephiphytic plant, 35cm (14″) high.
CLIMATE: Warm.
DISTRIBUTION: Native to the Philippines (Mindanao).
FLOWERING TIME: Autumn. It has a long flower life.
DESCRIPTION: Pseudobulbs are robust and stem-like. Flowers are large, borne in clusters of four or more, white, up to 7.5cm (3″) across and are fragrant. Labellum tri-lobed.

Dendrobium secundum

Dendrobium schuleri

COMMON NAME: None.
COLOUR: Flowers green-yellow. Labellum green-white with purple markings.
SIZE: Growing up to 1.2m (4′) high.
CLIMATE: Hot.
DISTRIBUTION: Native to northern Papua New Guinea; growing alongside swamps, creeks and lagoons.
FLOWERING TIME: Usually autumn.
DESCRIPTION: Pseudobulbs cylindrical, swollen near the base, up to 1.2m (4′) high. Leaves lanceolate, alternate, up to 17cm (6¾″) long. Inflorescence long, flowers are numerous and grow up to 6cm (2½″) across.

Dendrobium schuleri

Dendrobium sanderae var. *major*

Dendrobium secundum

COMMON NAME: Toothbrush Orchid.
COLOUR: Flowers pink. Labellum orange.
SIZE: Growing up to 1m (40″) high.
CLIMATE: Warm.
DISTRIBUTION: Native to Burma, Thailand, Vietnam, Malaysia, the Philippines, Java, Sumatra and Borneo.
FLOWERING TIME: Spring to early summer.
DESCRIPTION: Pseudobulbs erect or semi-pendulous, fusiform, 1m (40″) long or more. Leaves oblong-lanceolate, unequally emarginate, up to 10cm (4″) long. Inflorescence borne from upper nodes, with numerous, small and waxy flowers.

Dendrobium schuetzei

Dendrobium smilliae

COMMON NAME: Bottle Brush Orchid.
COLOUR: Flower colour varies from pink-mauve at the base to green-white. Labellum dark shining green.
SIZE: Growing up to 1m (40″) high.
CLIMATE: Warm to hot.
DISTRIBUTION: Native to Australia (northern Queensland), Papua New Guinea; mainly coastal and lowland forest.
FLOWERING TIME: Late winter to spring.
DESCRIPTION: Pseudobulbs cylindrical, furrowed when mature, up to 90cm (3′) high. Leaves ovate or oblong-lanceolate, up to 15cm (6″) long. Flowers dense in short raceme.

Dendrobium speciosum var. *hillii*

Dendrobium speciosum var. *hillii*

COMMON NAME: King Rock Orchid
COLOUR: Flowers creamy white, yellow.
SIZE: Growing up to 1.2m (4′) high.
CLIMATE: Cool.
DISTRIBUTION: Native to Australia (eastern rainforests).
FLOWERING TIME: Spring.
DESCRIPTION: Pseudobulbs up to 1.2m (4′) high. Leaves apical, thick, ovate to oblong 30cm (12″) long. Long raceme with numerous flowers and strongly perfumed. This giant epiphytic and lithophytic plant gives a showy display.

Dendrobium smilliae

Dendrobium spectabile syn. D. tigrinum

COMMON NAME: None.
COLOUR: Flowers cream, margin pale green-cream, veined and mottled purple-red.
SIZE: Growing up to 60cm (2′) high.
CLIMATE: Warm to hot.
DISTRIBUTION: Native to Papua New Guinea and Solomon Islands.
FLOWERING TIME: Winter to early spring.
DESCRIPTION: Pseudobulbs clavate, up to 60cm (2′) high. Leaves lanceolate to ovate, up to 20cm (8″) long. Floral segments margins crinkled.

Dendrobium spectabile syn. *D. tigrinum*

Dendrobium X superbiens

COMMON NAME: None.
COLOUR: Flowers purple to rose, mottled with purple.
SIZE: Growing up to 1.2m (4′) high.
CLIMATE: Warm.
DISTRIBUTION: Native to Australia (north-east, and Torres Strait Islands)
FLOWERING TIME: Autumn to early winter.
DESCRIPTION: A natural hybrid between *D. bigibbum* and *D. discolor.* Pseudobulbs up to 1.2m (4′) high. Flowering scape up to 93cm (3′) long. Flowers are 7.5cm (3″) across.

Dendrobium sutepense

COMMON NAME: Ueang Mali.
COLOUR: Flowers white. Labellum marked with yellow and veined orange.
SIZE: Growing up to 30cm (12″) high.
CLIMATE: Intermediate.
DISTRIBUTION: Native to Burma, Thailand and Indo-China, growing at elevations from 1500 to 1700m (5000 to 5600′).
FLOWERING TIME: Spring.
DESCRIPTION: A common epiphytic plant. Pseudobulbs cane-like, stems linear, cylindrical, narrow at the base, becoming flexuose, about 30cm (12″) high. Leaves alternate, borne at nodes, lanceolate, unequally emarginate at the apex, about 7.5cm (3″) long. Inflorescence short. Flowers borne at the leaf axis, and grow up to 3cm (1¼″) across.

Dendrobium sutepense

Dendrobium X superbiens

Dendrobium tangerinum

COMMON NAME: Tangerine Dendrobium.
COLOUR: Petals tangerine, sepals and labellum are cream marked and veined red-purple.
SIZE: Growing up to 2m (6′6″) high.
CLIMATE: Warm to hot.
DISTRIBUTION: Native to Papua New Guinea.
FLOWERING TIME: Winter.
DESCRIPTION: Pseudobulbs cane-like stems, up to 2m (6′6″). Leaves alternate, broad-lanceolate. Inflorescence erect arching up to 60cm (2′) high. Flowers to 10cm (4″) across.

Dendrobium tangerinum

Dendrobium taurinum

Dendrobium taurinum

COMMON NAME: None.
COLOUR: Sepals yellow-green. Petals purple. Labellum white to purple.
SIZE: Growing up to 1.2m (4′) high.
CLIMATE: Warm.
DISTRIBUTION: Native to the Philippines.
FLOWERING TIME: Autumn to winter.
DESCRIPTION: Pseudobulbs fusiform to cylindrical, up to 1.2m (4′) high. Leaves oblong or elliptic, emarginate, up to 15cm (6″) long. Flowers are waxy and 6cm (2½″) across. Labellum margins wavy.

Dendrobium teretifolium

COMMON NAME: Bridal Veil or Pencil Orchid.
COLOUR: Flowers white to cream with purple-brown markings.
SIZE: Pendulous epiphyte hanging to 2m (6′6″) long.
CLIMATE: Cool.
DISTRIBUTION: Native to Australia (on east coast) and Papua New Guinea.
FLOWERING TIME: Spring.
DESCRIPTION: Leaves are pencil-like and grow up to 60cm (2′) long. Flowers are about 5cm (2″) across.

Dendrobium teretifolium

Dendrobium tetragonum

COMMON NAME: Spider Orchid.
COLOUR: Flowers yellow-cream margined maroon.
SIZE: Pendulous to 60cm (2′) long.
CLIMATE: Cool to intermediate.
DISTRIBUTION: Native to Australia (eastern coast).
FLOWERING TIME: Mostly spring.
DESCRIPTION: Pseudobulbs pendulous, tetragonal, fusiform. Leaves sinuate, apical, broadly oblanceolate, 10cm (4″) long. Flowers are variable, 5cm (2″) long, and borne in clusters.

Dendrobium tetragonum (Island form)

Dendrobium tetragonum (Island form)

COMMON NAME: None.
COLOUR: Flower colour yellow-brown, barred maroon.
SIZE: Same as type.
CLIMATE: Cool.
DISTRIBUTION: Native to Australia (eastern coast lowlands), growing on Paper Barks (*Melaleuca* sp.) along rivers, creeks and on estuarine islands.
FLOWERING TIME: Late winter to spring.
DESCRIPTION: Same as its type, but a superior form. Flowers much larger. Raceme terminal, densely flowered, up to fifteen blooms. Known to many botanists as *D. melaleucaphilum*.

Dendrobium tetragonum

Dendrobium tetragonum var. gigantum

COMMON NAME: Large Spider Orchid.
COLOUR: Flowers marked maroon. Labellum white.
SIZE: Same as type.
CLIMATE: Intermediate.
DISTRIBUTION: Native to Australia (north-eastern).
FLOWERING TIME: Late autumn to spring.
DESCRIPTION: Same as type, except flowers much larger.

Dendrobium tokai

Dendrobium thyrsiflorum

COMMON NAME: None.
COLOUR: Flowers white. Labellum yellow-orange.
SIZE: Growing up to 50cm (20″) high.
CLIMATE: Intermediate.
DISTRIBUTION: Native to Himalayas, Thailand and Burma.
FLOWERING TIME: Spring.
DESCRIPTION: Pseudobulbs tetragonal-fusiform to 50cm (20″) high. Inflorescence arching to pendulous. Flowers numerous and approximately 5cm (2″) across, fragrant.

Dendrobium thyrsiflorum

Dendrobium tetragonum var. *gigantum*

Dendrobium tokai

COMMON NAME: None.
COLOUR: Flowers yellow to brown.
SIZE: Up to 1.2m (4′) high.
CLIMATE: Warm to hot.
DISTRIBUTION: Native to Fiji.
FLOWERING TIME: Late autumn to spring.
DESCRIPTION: A large, common epiphyte, with cane-like pseudobulbs to 1.2m (4′) high, leaves alternating on upper one-third of cane, to 10cm (4″) long. Flowers to 6cm (2.5″) across, sepals. and petals slightly twisted.

Dendrobium transparens

Dendrobium tortile

COMMON NAME: None.
COLOUR: Flowers mauve to purple. Labellum white or cream, veined mauve.
SIZE: Growing up to 30cm (12″) high.
CLIMATE: Intermediate to warm.
DISTRIBUTION: Native to Thailand, Burma, Vietnam and Peninsula Malaysia.
FLOWERING TIME: Spring.
DESCRIPTION: Pseudobulbs fusiform-cylindrical, erect, furrowed when matured, up to 30cm (12″) high. Leaves linear-oblong, deciduous, up to 10cm (4″) long. Inflorescence short, borne from the nodes of leafless pseudobulbs. Flowers are fragrant and up to 7.5cm (3″) across.

Dendrobium tortile

Dendrobium transparens

COMMON NAME: None.
COLOUR: Flowers lilac to pink with a transparent look. Labellum veined and blotched purple.
SIZE: Growing up to 70cm (28″) high.
CLIMATE: Intermediate.
DISTRIBUTION: Native to the Himalayas through to Burma; common in Nepal, Sikkim and Assam. Grows at an altitude of 1300m (4265′).
FLOWERING TIME: Spring to early summer.
DESCRIPTION: Pseudobulbs up to 70cm (28″) high. Leaves linear-lanceolate, acute, up to 10cm (4″) long. Inflorescence short, borne from leafless pseudobulbs. Flowers are 4cm (1½″) across.

Dendrobium trigonopsis

COMMON NAME: None.

COLOUR: Flowers are golden yellow. Labellum often has red transverse lines on both sides with greenish centre.

SIZE: Growing up to 30cm (1') high.

CLIMATE: Intermediate to warm.

DISTRIBUTION: Native to Burma, China (Yunnan), Thailand and Laos.

FLOWERING TIME: Spring.

DESCRIPTION: Pseudobulbs are clustered, fusiform, up to 20cm (8") high. Leaves are oblong or strap-like, acute, up to 10cm (4") long. Flowers are up to 5cm (2") across.

Dendrobium trigonopsis

Dendrobium victoriae-reginae

Dendrobium victoriae-reginae

COMMON NAME: None.

COLOUR: Flowers white, apical blotched and veined blue-mauve.

SIZE: Growing up to 60cm (2') high.

CLIMATE: Intermediate.

DISTRIBUTION: Native to the Philippines. Grows in damp mossy forests at altitudes of 1800 to 2400m, (3300 to 8000'().

FLOWERING TIME: Throughout the year.

DESCRIPTION: Pseudobulbs pendulous, cylindrical, stem-like, swollen at the nodes, up to 60cm (24") high. Leaves oblong-lanceolate, up to 8cm (3½") long. Inflorescence short, borne from leafless pseudobulbs.

Dendrobium wassallii

COMMON NAME: None.

COLOUR: Flowers white. Labellum marked with yellow.

SIZE: Grows up to 10cm (4") high.

CLIMATE: Intermediate.

DISTRIBUTION: Native to Australia (far north-east).

FLOWERING TIME: Late autumn to winter and sometimes late summer.

DESCRIPTION: Leaves semi-terete on creeping rhizomes. Mat-forming epiphyte or lithophyte. Raceme densely flowered. Flowers are spidery and about 2.5cm (1") across.

Dendrobium wassallii

DIMORPHORCHIS
(dye-morf-or-kis)

Dimorphorchis from the Gk *dimorphus* (having two forms) *orchi(s)*, *orchid(eus)* (orchid-like), with reference to the two distinct forms of flowers on the same inflorescence spike. This is a genus of two extraordinary epiphytic species from Borneo. Stems multiply from the roots, erect or arching, up to 2m (7') tall, and are densely leafy. Leaves are up to 1m (3') long, unequally lobed at apex. Inflorescence is pendulous and many-flowered. The flowers have two distinct forms: basal flowers are usually more fleshy than remaining flowers. The labellum is identical in structure in both forms, and is slipper-shaped. *Dimorphorchis lowii* is much more spectacular than *D. rohaniana*. This is one of the most sought after orchidaceous plants and is found in choice collections.

Culture: Compost as for tropical *Vandas*. The plant requires support on maturing. Use well-drained pots, water regularly, and provide humidity and moderate shade.

Dimorphorchis lowii

Dimorphorchis lowii

Dimorphorchis lowii

COMMON NAME: None.
COLOUR: Flowers yellow with red-brown blotches. Labellum yellow spotted with purple.
SIZE: Growing up to 2.3m (7') high.
CLIMATE: Hot.
DISTRIBUTION: Native to Borneo.
FLOWERING TIME: Autumn to early winter.
DESCRIPTION: Stems unusually erect, up to 2.1m (7') high in mature plants. Leaves strap-shaped, apical, unequally emarginate up to 90cm (3') long. Inflorescence long, pendulous, carrying two forms of flowers: basal one third, sepals and petals are broad, yellow and speckled with maroon; distal two thirds flowers, sepals and petals are yellow and heavily blotched with maroon. Flowers are numerous and grow up to 7.5cm (3") across.

DIPODIUM
(due-poe-dee-um)

Dipodium from the Gk *di* (two) *podion* (foot as in a vase) with possible reference to the two stipes of the pollinia. This genus of over twenty species is widely distributed from China through South-east Asia, the Philippines, Malaysia, Indonesia, Papua New Guinea to New Caledonia and Australia. It is a genus of extremely diverse growing habits. Some species are leafless terrestrial herbs, some are leafy terrestrial, and others start as terrestrials and develop a long, climbing epiphytic stem which continues to grow from the apex producing roots and branching. With the decay of the primary roots, the plant simulates the monopodial habit of the *Vanda*. The leafless species have a *mycorrhizal* association with Honey Fungus. The fungus is attached to both the roots of the orchid and another plant; thus, the fungus feeds the orchid on food obtained from the other plant. Flowers occur in a terminal raceme on a long stem. Sepals and petals are equal. The labellum is tri-lobed and is attached to the column foot.

Culture: The leafy terrestrial species grow as for *Phaius*, i.e. coarse compost, good drainage, shade, cool conditions and less water when growth is complete. The species with the monopodial habit grow as *Arachnis*. The leafless saprophytic species are very difficult to cultivate. Treat as for *Galeola*.

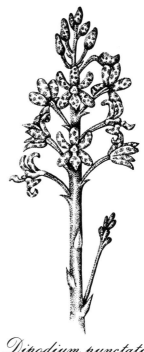

Dipodium punctatum

Dipodium punctatum

COMMON NAME: Hyacinth Orchid.
COLOUR: Flowers are pink to dark mauve with red spots.
SIZE: Leafless, rhizomeous. Inflorescence to 1.5m (5′) high.
CLIMATE: Cool.
DISTRIBUTION: Native to eastern Australia.
FLOWERING TIME: Spring.
DESCRIPTION: A variable saprophytic terrestrial living off subterranean fungi. The leafless stem carries a raceme of up to sixty flowers. Flowers are 1 to 3.1cm (½ to 1¼″) across.

Dipodium punctatum

DIURIS
(dye-yewr-is)

*D*iuris from the Gk *di* (two) *ura* (a tail) with reference to the two tail-like lateral sepals. This genus of about forty delightful species is found mainly in Australia extending to Timor and Java. It is a glabrous terrestrial herb with ovoid tubers. Leaves are few to numerous, and are linear. There are several flowers in a terminal raceme. The dorsal sepal is erect or reflexed, and broad; lateral sepals are more or less deflexed, linear or petaloid, and long. Petals are broad. The labellum is deeply tri-lobed, with the mid-lobe often longer and broader than lateral lobes. The column comprises a separate style and stamen.

Culture: As for *Caladenia.*

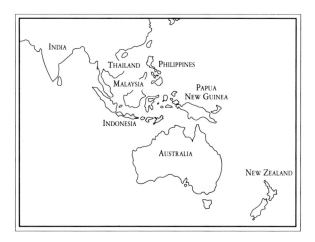

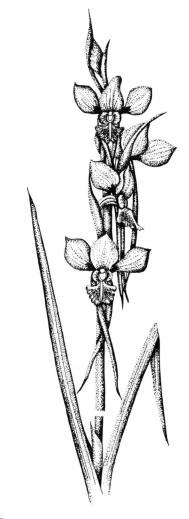

Diuris punctata forma *blakneyae*

Diuris sulphurea

Diuris sulphurea

Common Name: Donkey Orchid or Clown Orchid.
Colour: Flowers yellow with brown markings.
Size: Growing up to 60cm (2′) high.
Climate: Cool.
Distribution: Native to eastern Australia.
Flowering Time: Spring.
Description: A terrestrial plant up to 60cm (2′) high. Leaves long and flat. Labellum 15mm (½″) long, tri-lobed. Dorsal sepal shorter and broader than the petals. Flowers to 6cm (2½″) across.

DORITIS
(doh-rye-tis)

*D*oritis The derivation of the name is obscure, possibly it is from the Gk *dory* (a spear) with reference to the shape of the labellum, or after Doritis, one of the names of Aphrodite the goddess of love and beauty in Greek mythology. This is a genus of several species, or variants of a single species, and occurs from India, Burma, Sri Lanka, Thailand, Malaysia to Sumatra. This epiphytic or terrestrial monopodial herb with a clump forming habit, continuously grows then blooms, reaching ever upwards producing beautiful mauve-purple blossoms all the year round. It is pseudobulbless, with leafy stems. Leaves are distichous and coriaceous. Inflorescence is erect and up to 90cm (3') long, and has many flowers in a dense raceme. Flowers are variable in size and colour, and grow up to 5cm (2") across; they are showy and blooms remain open for long periods. Sepals and petals are free, and spreading; lateral sepals form a spur-like mentum with column foot. The labellum is tri-lobed, adnate to column foot and clawed; side-lobes are erect; mid-lobe is veined with white lines, geniculate about the middle, with two antennae behind the lateral lobes at base of the labellum; the disc has a forked callus.

Culture: Compost in pots or baskets. It shoots from the base forming clumps. Roots will grow over the side of the pots or baskets. The plant requires plenty of shade, humidity in well-drained pots, and plenty of water. Do not allow the plants to become dry, but reduce the watering when plant is not growing.

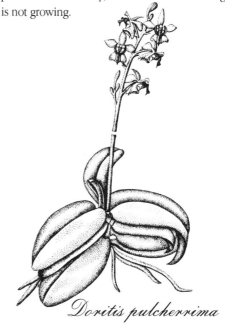

Doritis pulcherrima

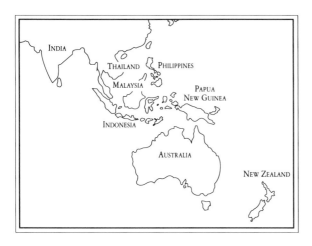

Doritis pulcherrima

COMMON NAME: None.
COLOUR: Flowers light pink-purple. Labellum darker.
SIZE: Growing up to 25cm (10") wide.
CLIMATE: Warm.
DISTRIBUTION: Native to Burma, Thailand, Laos, Cambodia, Vietnam, Peninsula Malaysia and Sumatra.
FLOWERING TIME: Mainly autumn to winter or throughout the year.
DESCRIPTION: Leaves spreading 15cm (6") long. Inflorescence about 90cm (3') high, raceme dense. Flowers vary from 1 to 5cm (½ to 2") across.

Doritis pulcherrima

DRACULA

(dray-cula)

Dracula Gk *draco* (dragon). The whimsical name dracula means 'little dragon', having reference to the monster-like appearance of some of the hairy flowers with their bizarre markings and long tails; they are often described as grotesque. In 1978 Dr C. A. Luer separated species from the genus *Masdevallia* to form a new genus, *Dracula. Dracula* differs from *Masdevallia* in having keeled leaves, and it has a mobile labellum hinged to the foot of the column and partitioned into epichile and hypochile; the petals are divided at the apex with knob-like nodules.

Culture: Plant in hanging baskets of well-drained, good moisture-retaining compost. It requires frequent watering. The leaves are prone to spotting, known as apical necrosis. Treat the disfiguration with fungicidal spray. Check the air movement and hygiene of your orchid house.

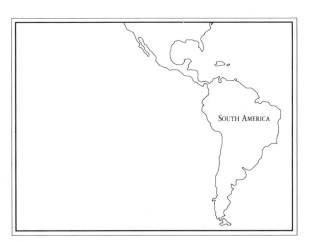

SOUTH AMERICA

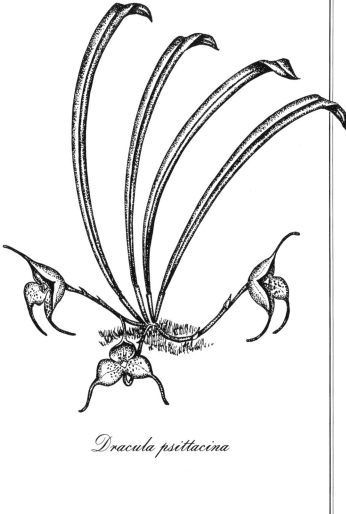

Dracula psittacina

Dracula sibundoyensis syn. *Masdevallia sibundoyensis*

Dracula sibundoyensis syn. *Masdevallia sibundoyensis*

COMMON NAME: None.
COLOUR: Flower cream, speckled maroon and tips maroon. Labellum cream.
SIZE: Growing to 16cm (6″) or more high.
CLIMATE: Warm.
DISTRIBUTION: Native to Colombia (Andes), growing in cloud forests.
FLOWERING TIME: Spring.
DESCRIPTION: A tufted epiphytic or lithophytic herb. Leaves are narrow-lanceolate, keeled, acute, up to 15cm (6″) high. Flower scape shorter than the leaves. Solitary flower grows to 10cm (4″) or more long, spreading to 3.5cm (1¼″) across.

DRYADELLA
(dry-ad-ella)

Dryadella is named after the dryads (wood nymphs), the mythological semi-divine maidens inhabiting the forests and trees. This genus comprises four species from Brazil and one from Central America; it was removed from genus *Masdevallia* by Dr C. A. Luer. *Dryadella* differ from *Masdevallia* in that their leaves are narrow, fleshy with longitudinal grooves. The flowers differ from *Masdevallia* in having a thick fold near the base of the lateral sepals; the sepals are joined forming a mentum below the column foot. The labellum is long and tongue-like.

Culture: As for *Masdevallia*. Compost, in well-drained pots. Water carefully and do not overwater.

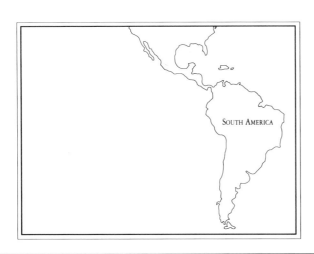

SOUTH AMERICA

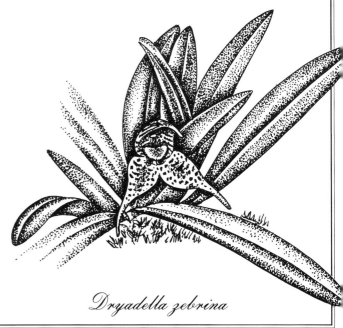

Dryadella zebrina

Dryadella zebrina syn.
Masdevallia zebrina

COMMON NAME: Partridge in the Grass Orchids.
COLOUR: Flowers yellow, spotted maroon. Labellum orange-brown.
SIZE: Growing up to 6cm (2¼″) high.
CLIMATE: Intermediate.
DISTRIBUTION: Native to Brazil.
FLOWERING TIME: Spring.
DESCRIPTION: Leaves are lanceolate, green with purple tinges, up to 6cm (2¼″) long. Flowers are small, 4.5cm (1¾″) long.

Dryadella zebrina syn. *Masdevallia zebrina*

ENCYCLIA
(en-sik-lee-ah)

Encyclia from the Gk *enkyklin* (to encircle) with reference to side lobes of the labellum encircling the column. This genus of about 150 species is found in Mexico, West Indies and the tropics of South America. It is an epiphytic and occasionally lithophytic herb. Stems form pseudobulbs and are ovoid-conical, pyriform, ellipsoid or fusiform, clustered or spaced along creeping rhizomes. Leaves are coriaceous, fleshy, lanceolate, lingulate, broad or ovate. Inflorescence panicles or racemose, erect, arching or pendulous. Flowers are showy and often delightfully fragrant. Sepals and petals are free, spreading and sub-similar. The labellum is tri-lobed or entire, free from the column, may be part adnate but never completely adnate. The genus *Encyclia* was first described in 1828, but continued to be included in *Epidendrum* by many taxonomists until 1961. *Encyclia's* features distinguishing it from *Epidendrum* are the presence of pseudobulbs and the labellum being only partially adnate to the column.

Culture: Use compost in well-drained pots or pans. Plants require moderate shade, humidity and water. Watch carefully for over watering in plants with soft stems.

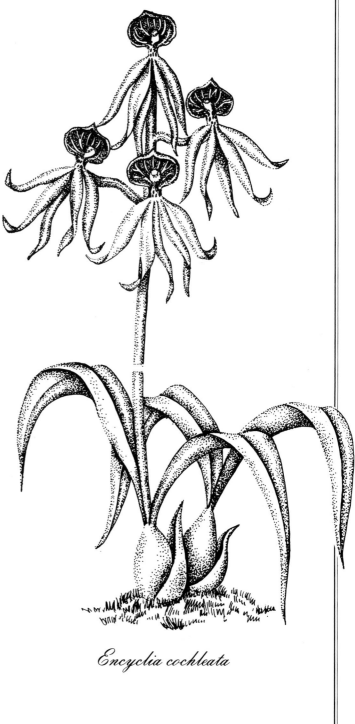

Encyclia cochleata

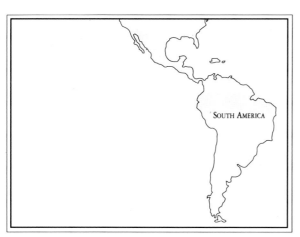

SOUTH AMERICA

Encyclia baculus syn. Epidendrum baculus

COMMON NAME: None.
COLOUR: Flowers are whitish cream. Labellum veined with purple.
SIZE: Growing up to 60cm (2′) high.
CLIMATE: Warm.
DISTRIBUTION: Native to Mexico, found as far south as Colombia.
FLOWERING TIME: Spring.
DESCRIPTION: Pseudobulbs borne on rhizome, somewhat compressed, fusiform, up to 30cm (1′) high. Leaves lanceolate or strap-shape, up to 30cm (1′) long. Inflorescence short. Flowers usually grow in pairs, borne back to back, and are up to 9cm (3½″) across.

Encyclia baculus syn. *Epidendrum baculus*

Encyclia bractescens syn. E. acicularis

COMMON NAME: None.
COLOUR: Flowers greenish yellow. Nerves red-brown. Labellum white with maroon-brown throat.
SIZE: Growing up to 20cm (8″) high.
CLIMATE: Intermediate to warm.
DISTRIBUTION: Native to Mexico, Bahamas, British Honduras and Guatemala.
FLOWERING TIME: Spring.
DESCRIPTION: Pseudobulbs clustered, up to 2.5cm (1″) high. Leaves linear-lanceolate, 20cm (8″) long. Inflorescence five to twenty flowers, 15cm (6″) long. Fragrant flowers are 2.5cm (1″) across.

Encyclia bractescens syn. *E. acicularis*

Encyclia chacaoensis syn. Epidendrum chacaoense

COMMON NAME: None.
COLOUR: Flowers greenish yellow. Labellum marked with purple.
SIZE: Growing up to 37.5cm (15″) high.
CLIMATE: Intermediate to warm.
DISTRIBUTION: Native to Panama and Mexico.
FLOWERING TIME: Winter to spring.
DESCRIPTION: Pseudobulbs are compressed, ovoid to fusiform, 7.5cm (3″) long. Leaves are narrow-obtuse, 30cm (12″) long. Short inflorescence. Flowers are fragrant, inverted and 5cm (2″) across.

Encyclia chacaoensis syn. *Epidendrum chacaoense*

Encyclia chondylobulbon

COMMON NAME: None.
COLOUR: Flowers whitish cream. Labellum white or pale green, with purple veins.
SIZE: Grows up to 1.2m (4′) high.
CLIMATE: Intermediate to warm.
DISTRIBUTION: Native to Mexico.
FLOWERING TIME: Spring.
DESCRIPTION: Pseudobulbs up to 25cm (10″) high, 3cm (1″) apart. The three to five leaves are narrow-lanceolate and up to 1m (40″) long. Four or more flowers grow on a long peduncle and are up to 7.5cm (3″) wide.

Encyclia citrina syn. Epidendrum citrinum, Cattleya citrina

COMMON NAME: None.
COLOUR: Flowers yellow.
SIZE: Growing pendulous to 30cm (12″) long.
CLIMATE: Intermediate.
DISTRIBUTION: Native to Mexico at an altitude of 1300 to 2200m (4265 to 7200′) and growing in pine and oak forests.
FLOWERING TIME: Spring.
DESCRIPTION: Pseudobulbs are pendulous in clusters, often hanging in tufts, conical ovoid or fusiform, up to 6cm (2½″) long. Leaves are pendulous, elliptic to 25cm (10″) long. Inflorescence 10cm (4″) long. The fragrant flowers grow up to 7.5cm (3″) long.

Encyclia citrina syn. *Epidendrum citrinum, Cattleya citrina*

Encyclia chondylobulbon

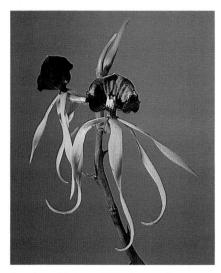

Encyclia cochleata syn. *Epidendrum cochleatum*

Encyclia cochleata syn. *Epidendrum cochleatum*

COMMON NAME: Cockleshell Orchid.
COLOUR: Flower petals lemon-green. Labellum has purple markings.
SIZE: Growing up to 50cm (20″) high.
CLIMATE: Intermediate.
DISTRIBUTION: Native to Venezuela, Colombia, South Mexico, Florida (USA), Cuba, Brazil and West Indies. Grows at an altitude of 1000 to 2000m (3280 to 6561′).
FLOWERING TIME: All year, ever-blooming.
DESCRIPTION: Pseudobulbs ovoid-ellipsoid, compressed, 5 to 20cm (2 to 8″) long. Leaves oblong-lanceolate up to 37cm (15″) long. Flowers up to 9cm (3½″) long. Labellum inverted.

Encyclia cordigera var. *alba* 'Henrique' syn. *Epidendrum atropurpurea*

Encyclia cordigera var. *alba* syn. *Epidendrum atropurpurea*

COMMON NAME: None.
COLOUR: Flowers light green. Labellum white.
SIZE: Growing up to 56cm (23″) high.
CLIMATE: Intermediate to warm.
DISTRIBUTION: Native to Mexico and Peru, growing from sea level to 900m (2952′) in dry forest.
FLOWERING TIME: Spring.
DESCRIPTION: Pseudobulbs clustered, erect, ovoid-conical, up to 10cm (4″). Leaves are strap-shaped, up to 45cm (18″). Inflorescence long, paniculate, with large flowers. The species *E. cordigera* has many colour variations. Many growers consider it to be one of the best Mexican *Encyclia* for cultivation.

Encyclia fragrans syn. *Epidendrum fragrans*

Encyclia fragrans syn. *Epidendrum fragrans*

COMMON NAME: None.
COLOUR: Labellum creamy white with purple streaks.
SIZE: Grows up to 30cm (12″) high.
CLIMATE: Intermediate.
DISTRIBUTION: Native to Mexico, Central America, northern South America, West Indies, Ecuador, Peru and Brazil. Grows at altitudes from sea level up to 1800m (3300′).
FLOWERING TIME: Winter to spring.
DESCRIPTION: A variable species. Pseudobulbs ellipsoid 5 to 11.5cm (2 to 4½″) long. Leaves are oblong-lanceolate to 20cm (8″) long. Flower inverted and grows to 5cm (2″) across.

Encyclia hanburii syn. *Epidendrum hanburii*

Encyclia hanburii syn. *Epidendrum hanburii*

COMMON NAME: None.
COLOUR: Flowers red-brown. Labellum white or pink with purple veins.
SIZE: Growing up to 30cm (12″) high.
CLIMATE: Intermediate.
DISTRIBUTION: Native to Mexico. Grows at altitudes of 1200 to 1800m (4000 to 6000′) in scrub oak forests.
FLOWERING TIME: Summer to autumn.
DESCRIPTION: Pseudobulbs are clustered, conical-ovoid, up to 8cm (3¼″) high. Leaves are elliptic-lanceolate to oblong, up to 23cm (9″) long. Inflorescence paniculate, with ten to thirty-five blooms, grows up to 90cm (3′) long. Flowers are up to 5cm (2″) across.

Encyclia linkiana syn. *Epidendrum linkianum*

Encyclia linkiana syn. *Epidendrum linkianum*

COMMON NAME: None.
COLOUR: Flowers olive-green, veined maroon. Labellum white, marked with green and maroon.
SIZE: Growing up to 30cm (12″) high.
CLIMATE: Intermediate.
DISTRIBUTION: Native to Mexico, Venezuela and Peru. Growing at elevations of 500 to 2300m (1650 to 6600′).
FLOWERING TIME: Spring to summer and probably most of the year.
DESCRIPTION: Pseudobulbs fusiform borne on creeping rhizome. Leaves are strap-like and flowers are sparse.

Encyclia livida syn. *E. tessellata*

COMMON NAME: None.
COLOUR: Flowers outside greenish-yellow, inside brown and streaked with a darker brown. Labellum pale yellow streaked with purple.
SIZE: Grows up to 30cm (12″) high.
CLIMATE: Intermediate to warm.
DISTRIBUTION: Native from Mexico to Panama, Venezuela and Colombia.
FLOWERING TIME: Generally summer.
DESCRIPTION: Pseudobulbs are compressed, fusiform, ellipsoid or ovoid, up to 7.5cm (3″). Leaves are ligulate-elliptic, growing up to 22.5cm (9″) long. Flowers grow up to 2cm (¾″) across.

Encyclia livida syn. *E. tessellata*

Encyclia microbulbon

COMMON NAME: None.
COLOUR: Flowers light green, may be veined brown. Labellum white spotted pink.
SIZE: A small plant, growing up to 15cm (6″) high.
CLIMATE: Intermediate.
DISTRIBUTION: Native to Mexico.
FLOWERING TIME: Late spring.
DESCRIPTION: Pseudobulbs are clustered, conical, up to 4cm (1½″) high. Leaves are strap-shaped, up to 12.5cm (5″) long. Flowers grow up to 4cm (1½″) across.

Encyclia tampensis syn. *Epidendrum tampense*

COMMON NAME: None.
COLOUR: Flowers light yellow-brown or yellow-green, suffused and veined brownish purple. Labellum white, blotched red-purple.
SIZE: Growing up to 45cm (18″) high.
CLIMATE: Intermediate to warm.
DISTRIBUTION: Native to Bahamas, Florida (USA) and with *Encyclia tampense* var. *amessianum* in Cuba.
FLOWERING TIME: Spring to winter.
DESCRIPTION: Pseudobulbs are clustered, ovoid, up to 7.5cm (3″) high and are mat-forming. Leaves are linear-lanceolate and grow up to 37.5cm (15″) long. Flowers are fragrant and may measure up to 5cm (2″) across, but are generally smaller; their colour is most variable.

Encyclia microbulbon

Encyclia tampensis syn. *Epidendrum tampense*

Encyclia odoratissima syn. *Epidendrum odoratissium*

COMMON NAME: None.
COLOUR: Flowers green. Labellum yellow-cream, veined red.
SIZE: Growing up to 30cm (12″) high.
CLIMATE: Intermediate.
DISTRIBUTION: Native to Brazil.
FLOWERING TIME: Summer.
DESCRIPTION: Pseudobulbs are erect, elongate-ovoid, up to 30cm (12″) high. Leaves are long and linear. Inflorescence branched. Flowers are fragrant, growing to about 2.5cm (1″) across.

Encyclia odoratissima syn. *Epidendrum odoratissium*

EPIDENDRUM
(eh-pi-den-drum)

Epidendrum from the Gk *epi* (upon) *dendrum* (tree) with reference to epiphytic habit of the plants. From their discovery in the early 1700s, all epiphytes were called *Epidendrum*. Since that time, researchers have revised the genus on several occasions, with the result that today we have *Amblostoma, Arachnis, Barkeria, Brassavola, Cymbidiums, Encyclia* together with many other genera all originally included in *Epidendrum*. Today *Epidendrum* is still an extremely large genus of over one thousand species spread throughout Central America, Florida, the West Indies, and northern South America. This is a genus of epiphytic or perhaps lithophytic or terrestrial plants; they are variable, either small or large, erect or on creeping rhizomes not always conspicuous, sympodial, and stems which rarely develop pseudobulbs. Leaves vary almost as much as the stems, being thick, fleshy, coriaceous, linear or terete, apical on pseudobulbs, alternate on reed-like stems, and few to many.

The inflorescence is terminal and can be one or many-flowered. Flowers are 2 to 7.5cm (1 to 3″) across. Sepals and petals are similar—uniform, equal, reflexed or spreading. The labellum is tri-lobed, with lateral lobes adnate to column, and the mid-lobe broad, lobed, fringed or with serrate margins.

Culture: Compost. The pseudobulb group do best in pots. The creeping rhizome group grow best in pans or mounted on tree-fern fibre. The reed-like group do well in pots or grown as terrestrials. Plants require shade, especially during the summer months, and regular watering while growing, less during the rest period.

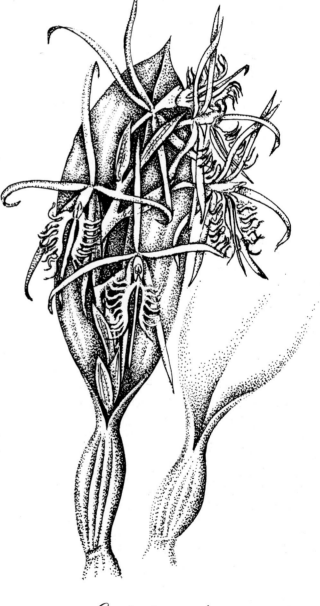

Epidendrum ciliare

SOUTH AMERICA

Epidendrum anceps

COMMON NAME: None.
COLOUR: Flowers yellow-brown to green-brown. Labellum pale green, flushed pink.
SIZE: Growing up to 70cm (28″) high.
CLIMATE: Intermediate.
DISTRIBUTION: Native to Mexico, southern Florida (USA), tropical America to Brazil, Peru and Ecuador.
FLOWERING TIME: Throughout the year, nearly always in bloom.
DESCRIPTION: An epiphytic, and at times, lithophytic plant. Stems are clustered and erect up to 70cm (28″) high. Leaves are oblong-elliptic, up to 15cm (6″) long. Inflorescence terminal. Flowers grow up to 1.5cm (½″) across.

Epidendrum anceps

Epidendrum ciliare

COMMON NAME: None.
COLOUR: Flowers yellow-green. Labellum white.
SIZE: Grows up to 30cm (12″) high.
CLIMATE: Intermediate.
DISTRIBUTION: Native to Mexico, West Indies, tropical America, Colombia, the Guyanas and Brazil.
FLOWERING TIME: Autumn to spring.
DESCRIPTION: A common epiphytic or lithophytic plant. Creeping rhizome, pseudobulbs fusiform, up to 20cm (8″). Leaves are oblong-lanceolate, growing to 12.5cm (5″) long. Flowers spreading to 7.5cm (3″) across.

Epidendrum ciliare

Epidendrum coriifolium

COMMON NAME: None.
COLOUR: Flowers pale green-brown, sepals and petals narrow. Labellum darker.
SIZE: Growing up to 35cm (14″) high.
CLIMATE: Intermediate.
DISTRIBUTION: Native to Mexico and Peru.
FLOWERING TIME: Autumn to winter.
DESCRIPTION: Epiphyte. Pseudobulb cane-like up to 30cm (12″). Leaves are fleshy, rigid, channelled, growing up to 25cm (10″) long. Inflorescence zig-zag, 25cm (10″) long. Flowers are narrow with a broad labellum.

Epidendrum difforme syn. *E. latilabre*

Epidendrum difforme syn. E. latilabre

COMMON NAME: None.
COLOUR: Flowers white, yellow or green.
SIZE: Growing up to 50cm (20″) high.
CLIMATE: Intermediate.
DISTRIBUTION: Native to Mexico, southern Salvador, West Indies, Central America to Brazil and Peru.
FLOWERING TIME: Almost throughout the year.
DESCRIPTION: This is a wide-ranging variable species. Stems are erect and numerous and grow up to 50cm (20″) high. Leaves are oblong-lanceolate, growing up to 10cm (4″) long. Inflorescence terminal and short.

Epidendrum coriifolium

Epidendrum nocturnum

Epidendrum nocturnum

COMMON NAME: None.
COLOUR: Flowers light green. Labellum white with yellow markings.
SIZE: Growing up to 1m (40″) high.
CLIMATE: Intermediate.
DISTRIBUTION: Native to Brazil, Peru, tropical America, Ecuador, Mexico and Florida (USA); introduced to tropical West Africa.
FLOWERING TIME: Summer to autumn.
DESCRIPTION: A variable epiphyte. Stem canes, clustered up to 1m (40″) high, with papery-sheaths bearing shiny distichous, oval to lanceolate leaves, 18cm (7″) long. Compact inflorescence with flowers variable in size and colour; white is rare.

Epidendrum parkinsonianum syn. *E. falcatum*

Epidendrum paniculatum syn. E. floribundum

COMMON NAME: None.
COLOUR: Flowers pale green. Labellum white to cream.
SIZE: Growing up to 2.5m (10′) tall.
CLIMATE: Intermediate to warm.
DISTRIBUTION: Native throughout tropical America.
FLOWERING TIME: Generally summer, and usually more than once annually.
DESCRIPTION: A common variable epiphytic or terrestrial plant. Stems are terete, clustered and covered in leaf sheaths. Leaves are lanceolate, up to 20cm (8″) long. Inflorescence paniculate with numerous flowers, sometimes up to 250 blooms. The flower is about 1cm (½″) across.

Epidendrum paniculatum syn. *E. floribundum*

Epidendrum parkinsonianum syn. E. falcatum

COMMON NAME: None.
COLOUR: Flowers white or creamy green and may be tinted with mauve. Labellum white with disc blotched yellow.
SIZE: A large pendulous epiphytic.
CLIMATE: Intermediate to warm.
DISTRIBUTION: Native to Mexico, Guatemala, Honduras, Panama and Costa Rica.
FLOWERING TIME: Summer to autumn, usually several times annually.
DESCRIPTION: Pseudobulbs are clustered, terete, curved-ascending, and up to 10cm (4″) long. Leaves are fleshy, linear, channelled, acuminate, up to 75cm (30″) long. Flowers, borne from new growth on short peduncles, are fragrant and grow up to 15cm (6″) across.

Epidendrum schlechterianum

Epidendrum schlechterianum

COMMON NAME: None.
COLOUR: Flowers yellow-green, brown-green to pink-purple.
SIZE: Small epiphyte, mat-forming.
CLIMATE: Intermediate.
DISTRIBUTION: Native to Peru, Central America, Mexico to Panama, West Indies and Brazil. Altitude 670 to 1700m (2000 to 3000′). Found in dense forest.
FLOWERING TIME: Summer.
DESCRIPTION: A variable dwarf species. Stem enclosed by leaf sheaths, up to 5cm (2″). Numerous elliptic-oblong leaves, growing up to 3.2cm (1¼″) long. Flowers are small, about 1.2cm (½″) across.

Epidendrum stamfordianum

Epidendrum stamfordianum

COMMON NAME: None.
COLOUR: Flowers green-yellow, spotted purple-red. Labellum yellow with mid-lobe margins red.
SIZE: Growing up to 40cm (16″) high.
CLIMATE: Intermediate to warm.
DISTRIBUTION: Native to Venezuela, Colombia and Mexico to Panama.
FLOWERING TIME: Winter to spring.
DESCRIPTION: Pseudobulbs are clustered, fusiform, up to 25cm (10″) high. Leaves apical, oblong-linear, obtuse, growing up to 15cm (6″) long. Inflorescence borne from base of pseudobulbs, occasionally one may be borne apical, and often branching. Flowers are numerous, showy, fragrant and are 4cm (1½″) long. Labellum tri-lobed.

EPIGENEIUM

(eh-pi-jee-nee-um)

Epigeneium from the Gk *epi* (upon) *geneion* (chin) meaning 'on the chin' with reference to the sepals and petals on the column foot. This is a genus of about thirty rare species scattered across South-east Asia, from China in the north to India in the west, as far as the Philippines in the east, and to Papua New Guinea in the south. It is a medium-sized erect epiphytic herb. Pseudobulbs are angular, occurring at intervals along elongated creeping rhizomes. Leaves are apical, coriaceous, oblong to obovate. Pseudo-terminal with one to few flowers. The flowers are attractively showy and are medium to large. The dorsal sepal encloses the column; lateral sepals form a mentum with column foot. Petals are deltoid, decurrent along the mentum. The labellum is tri-lobed and pandurate; lateral lobes are erect and the callus has a ridge or lobulate. Column is short with a long foot.

Culture: Mount the plant on a tree-fern slab or in a shallow basket. Allowance must be made for the creeping habit of the elongated rhizome. It requires warm, humid, shady conditions. Potted plants are easily set back by stale or sour conditions at the roots. Perfect drainage is essential. The fleshy foliage will burn from over exposure if left in a sunny spot. Plants from this genus are rare in collections.

Epigeneium coelogyne

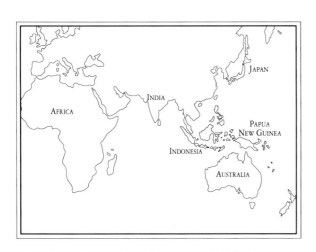

Epigeneium coelogyne

Epigeneium coelogyne

COMMON NAME: None.
COLOUR: Flowers brownish yellow with purple markings. The mid-lobe is almost purple-black.
SIZE: Growing up to 10cm (4″) high.
CLIMATE: Intermediate.
DISTRIBUTION: Native to Thailand and Burma.
FLOWERING TIME: Autumn.
DESCRIPTION: Pseudobulbs are borne on a stout creeping rhizome, ellipsoid, tetragonal, up to 6cm (2½″) high. Leaves grow in pairs, oblong-elliptic, emarginate to 7.5cm (3″) long. The fragrant flower grows to 10cm (4″) across.

ERIA
(ear-ee-a)

Eria from the Gk *erion* (wool) with reference to the woolly covering of the perianth. This is one of the larger aggregations of orchids into one genus in Orchidaceae. It has about five hundred species divided into thirteen groups, spread across tropical Asia from the Himalayas, China, the Philippines, Indonesia, Papua New Guinea, Pacific Islands to Fiji. Habitats range from hot humid coastal rainforests to the snow-line of the Himalayas. Primarily epiphytic, often lithophytic and rarely terrestrial, the genus has a variable habit. Stems are pseudobulbous, round, along creeping rhizomes, or often lengthy, cylindrical, fleshy, leafy stems, others short and heavily tomentose. The plant has two or many leaves often carpeted with hairs. Inflorescence is terminal or axillary, possessing either single flowers or dense racemes. Flowers have a distinctive shape and range from small to medium size. Sepals are free, hirsute or glabrous; lateral sepals adnate to elongate column foot; mentum saccate or spur-like; petals are similar, but smaller. The labellum is entire or tri-lobed, with the disc one to five keeled.

Culture: Depends on the species. Certain species do well in pans, while others grow best when mounted on tree-fern fibre slabs. Most plants require humid, shady conditions. Others may be grown outdoors even in cool climates. Make sure plants have good drainage and water with care. Consult your local orchid society about caring for these plants.

Eria vestita

Eria albido-tomentosa

COMMON NAME: None.
COLOUR: Flowers yellowish green. Labellum marked with red.
SIZE: Growing up to 30cm (12″) high.
CLIMATE: Intermediate.
DISTRIBUTION: Native to Thailand, Burma, Java, Sumatra, Laos and Cambodia.
FLOWERING TIME: Autumn.
DESCRIPTION: Pseudobulbs are borne on a creeping rhizome, ovoid, up to 12.5cm (5″) high. Leaves are apical from pseudobulb, are narrow-lanceolate and grow up to 20cm (8″) long. Inflorescence basal, 15cm (6″) or more long, stem very white and tomentose. Flowers grow up to 2.5 cm (1″) across.

Eria inornata

Eria aliciae

COMMON NAME: None.
COLOUR: Flowers whitish pink and marked with pink.
SIZE: Growing up to 1.5m (5′) high.
CLIMATE: Intermediate to warm.
DISTRIBUTION: Native to the Philippines, growing at an altitude of 1500m (4920′).
FLOWERING TIME: Autumn to winter.
DESCRIPTION: Long cane-like pseudobulbs, up to 1.5m (5′) long. Leaves are alternate, linear, acute, up to 25cm (10″) long. Inflorescence short, clustered and produced at the leaf axis. Flowers are small and numerous.

Eria albido-tomentosa

Eria inornata

COMMON NAME: None.
COLOUR: Flowers pale yellow.
SIZE: Growing up to 40cm (16″) high.
CLIMATE: Warm.
DISTRIBUTION: Native to far north-eastern Australia.
FLOWERING TIME: Late winter to spring.
DESCRIPTION: An epiphytic-lithophytic plant. Pseudobulbs are stout, ovate, conical, up to 20cm (8″) high. Leaves are 20cm (8″) long, or more. Raceme is vertical and grows up to 25cm (10″) long. Flowers are numerous.

Eria javanica

Eria javanica

COMMON NAME: None.
COLOUR: Flowers whitish cream. Labellum white with side lobes spotted red.
SIZE: Growing up to 37.5cm (15″) high.
CLIMATE: Intermediate to warm.
DISTRIBUTION: Native to Himalayas, Burma, Thailand, Indonesia and the Philippines.
FLOWERING TIME: Autumn.
DESCRIPTION: Pseudobulbs are ovoid, sheathed, up to 7.5cm (3″) high. Leaves are shiny, linear, growing up to 30cm (12″) long. Inflorescence pubescent, nodding, and longer than the leaves. Flowers are fragrant. The labellum is tri-lobed.

Eria aliciae

Eria undicaulius

COMMON NAME: None.
COLOUR: Flowers creamy white. Labellum marked with rosy pink.
SIZE: Growing up to 30cm (12″) high.
CLIMATE: Intermediate.
DISTRIBUTION: Native to Taiwan.
FLOWERING TIME: Spring to summer.
DESCRIPTION: Pseudobulbs are clustered, elongate, up to 25cm (10″) high. Leaves are broad-lanceolate, and grow up to 12.5cm (5″) long. Inflorescence arching to 15cm (6″) long, with dense numerous flowers, up to 2.5cm (1″) across.

Eria undicaulius

EUANTHE

(yew-an-thee)

*E*uanthe from the Gk *euanthes* (blooming) with reference to the showy inflorescence. A monotypic genus established in 1914 by Schlechter. This is an extremely popular monopodial epiphytic orchid from the Philippines. Originally, it was labelled *Vanda sanderiana*. The distinction from *Vanda* is based on the structure of the flattened flower, in particular the formation of the labellum which is bipartite not tri-lobed as in other *Vanda* species.

Culture: As for *Vanda*. Use compost in large, well-drained pots or baskets. In the wild, *Euanthe* grows on trees close to the ocean, often on branches overhanging waves, and in tropical sunshine.

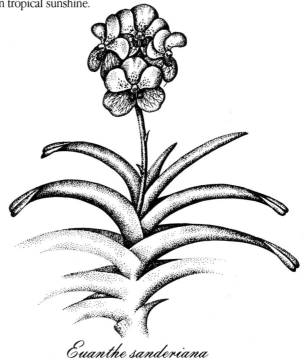

Euanthe sanderiana

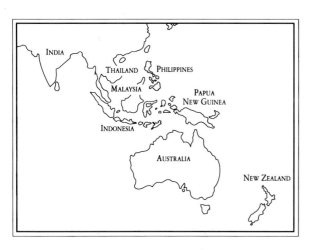

Euanthe sanderiana syn. Vanda sanderiana

COMMON NAME: None.
COLOUR: Flowers are a blend of white-pink, mauve to dull yellow, suffused with white.
SIZE: Growing up to 1m (3′) high.
CLIMATE: Warm.
DISTRIBUTION: Native to the Philippines, south-east Mindanao (Davao).
FLOWERING TIME: Autumn to spring.
DESCRIPTION: A large showy epiphytic species. Stems are elongated, generally solitary, branching from the base. Leaves are strap-shaped, unequally emarginate, growing up to 40cm (16″) long. Inflorescence generally shorter than leaves, with up to ten blooms. Flowers are variable in size and colour, but are generally large and fragrant. *Euanthe* is separate from *Vanda* by having no spur.

Euanthe sanderiana

GALEOLA
(gal-ee-oh-la)

*G*aleola from the Lat. *galeaola* (a small helmet) with reference to the helmet or hood-like dorsal appendage of the anther. This is a genus of about seventy species of leafless epiphytes or saprophytes whose distribution extends through India, Japan, Malaysia, Indonesia, Papua New Guinea, New Caledonia and Australia. This genus includes some of Orchidaceae's most spectacular and unusual species. *Galeola foliata* is the tallest-growing orchid in the world; with its sucker-like roots biting deep into the bark, its vine-like stem attains heights of 20 to 30m (60 to 100′), producing panicles of flowers often measuring as much as 180cm (6′) in length, with thousands of handsome blooms.

Culture: It is almost impossible to keep this gigantic saprophytic vine alive for more than several years. Several growers have had interesting but limited success by taking a very young plant together with a large quantity of *mycelium* and its host to a specially prepared and selected site, and by continuing to duplicate original growing conditions, and to feed the *mycelium*.

Galeola cassythoides

Galeola cassythoides

Galeola cassythoides
COMMON NAME: Climbing Orchid.
COLOUR: Flowers yellow-brown with green-brown markings.
SIZE: This saprophyte climbs as high as 6m (20′) with the aid of sucker-like roots.
CLIMATE: Cool.
DISTRIBUTION: Native to the Australian eastern coast.
FLOWERING TIME: Spring to summer.
DESCRIPTION: Flowers are numerous and measure about 3cm (1¼″) across. Stems are leafless and coloured chocolate brown.

GOMESA
(go-mee-sa)

Gomesa was named in honour of Dr Bernardino Antonio Gomes, a Portuguese naval physician and botanist. This is a genus of about twenty species of dwarf epiphytic plants from Brazil. The genus is closely allied to *Oncidium* and is often confusing for the novice. The unusual shape of the flower segments and the labellum is distinctive. *Gomesa* are commonly called the 'little men orchids'. Pseudobulbs are nearly elliptical and flattened, grow up to 10cm (4″) long, and are closely spaced along the rhizome. The plant has one or two leaves, which are apical, elongate, soft and arching. Inflorescence comes from the base of the pseudobulb, is short and arching with up to twenty or more flowers. Flowers are small, very fragrant, and are off-white, yellow or pale green in colour. Dorsal sepal and petals are free and spreading; the lateral sepals are adnate for half their length forming an inverted 'Y' beneath the labellum. Sepals and petals are similar in size and length. The labellum is tri-lobed, short, curved and u-shaped sectionally, with lateral lobes erect; the mid-lobe is fixed to the base of column foot, and is spurless; the disc has two prominent keels.

Culture: Compost. Plants grow well in pots, but be careful with watering. They require good drainage, shade and humidity.

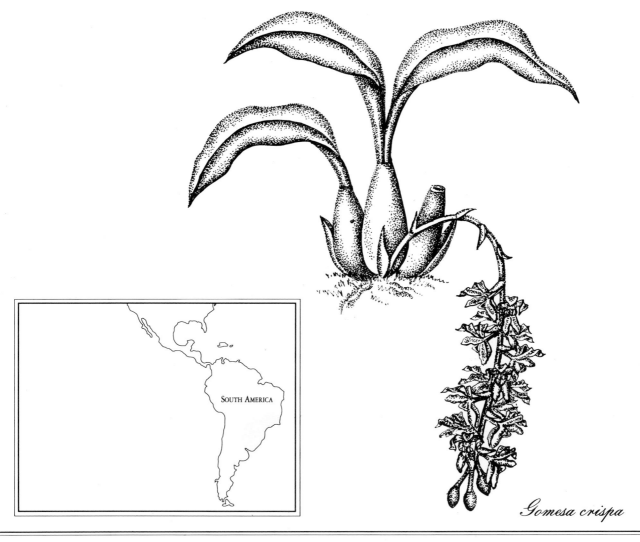

SOUTH AMERICA

Gomesa crispa

Gomesa barkerii

COMMON NAME: None.
COLOUR: Flowers are yellow.
SIZE: Growing up to 30cm (12″) high.
CLIMATE: Intermediate.
DISTRIBUTION: Native to Brazil.
FLOWERING TIME: Spring.
DESCRIPTION: Pseudobulbs are compressed,
smooth, ovoid-elongate, up to 10cm (4″) high.
Leaves grow up to 30cm (12″) long and are
oblong-lanceolate. Inflorescence is basal from
sheaths of new growth, is arching, and grows up
to 20cm (8″) long. Flowers are 2.5cm (1″) long.

Gomesa barkerii

Gomesa recurva syn. *Rodriguezia recurva*

Gomesa crispa

COMMON NAME: None.
COLOUR: Flowers are yellow-green.
SIZE: Growing up to 30cm (12″) high.
CLIMATE: Intermediate.
DISTRIBUTION: Native to Brazil.
FLOWERING TIME: Spring to early summer.
DESCRIPTION: Pseudobulbs are compressed,
oblong and 10cm (4″) high. Leaves are strap-
shaped, growing up to 20cm (8″) long.
Inflorescence is up to 22cm (8¾″) long.
Flowers are dense and numerous, are fragrant,
and grow to 2cm (¾″) long. Floral segment
margins are undulate.

Gomesa crispa

Gomesa recurva syn. Rodriguezia recurva

COMMON NAME: None.
COLOUR: Flowers are yellow-green. Labellum has
a yellow basal streak.
SIZE: Growing up to 30cm (12″) high.
CLIMATE: Intermediate.
DISTRIBUTION: Native to Brazil.
FLOWERING TIME: Spring to autumn.
DESCRIPTION: Pseudobulbs are compressed,
narrowly ovoid, up to 7.5cm (3″) high. Leaves
are linear-oblanceolate, acute, growing up to
30cm (12″) long. Inflorescence is up to 35cm
(14″) long. Flowers are densely numerous,
small and fragrant.

GONGORA

(gon-gor-uh)

Gongora is named in honour of Don Antonio Caballero Gongora, Viceroy of New Granada, and later Bishop of Cordova, Spain. This genus of about fifteen species of monopodial epiphytes, and their variants, is distributed through the tropical Americas, from Mexico to Peru and Brazil. The genus is divided into two groups by several workers: (a) *eugongora* (e.g. *G. quinquenervis*), and (b) *acropera* (e.g. *G. armeniaca* var. *biconuta*). Fundamentally, the difference is the floral shapes.

This is a most extraordinary small epiphyte. The short stems develop into strongly ridged pseudobulbs. The two leaves are apical, soft and plicate. Inflorescence rises from the base of the pseudobulbs and is pendulous and flexuous. The flowers are most unusual being intricate, 'grotesque' and 'fascinating'. The dorsal sepal is adnate to the column foot for one third of its length; lateral sepals are attached to the column foot. Petals emerge from the middle of the column and appear like wings. The extreme complexity of the fleshy labellum makes description difficult. The labellum is continuous with the column foot, is narrow and fleshy, complex and tri-lobed; the lateral lobes form a hypochile, erect, saccate and bear horns or bristle-like appendages; the mid-lobe (epichile) is complicate-saccate or laterally compressed, the apex is bi-lobed, elongate, lanceolate, acute or acuminate. The column is more or less clavate above.

Culture: Use moisture-retaining compost. Grow in a hanging basket as for *Stanhopea*. The plant requires high humidity, shade, plenty of water and good drainage. The winter temperature should be a minimum of 10°C (50°F).

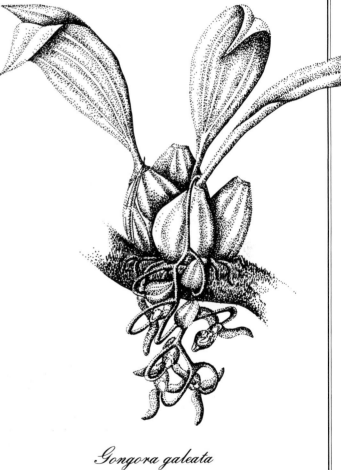

Gongora galeata

SOUTH AMERICA

Gongora galeata

COMMON NAME: None.
COLOUR: Flowers are brown-buff to greenish cream, mottled orange. Labellum yellow-brown with spotted purple column.
SIZE: Growing up to 30cm (12″) high.
CLIMATE: Intermediate.
DISTRIBUTION: Native to Mexico.
FLOWERING TIME: Summer to early autumn.
DESCRIPTION: An epiphytic species. Pseudobulbs are ovoid to pyriform with sheaths, up to 5cm (2″) long. Leaves are broad-lanceolate, growing up to 30cm (12″) long. Pendulous inflorescence grows up to 30cm (12″) long.

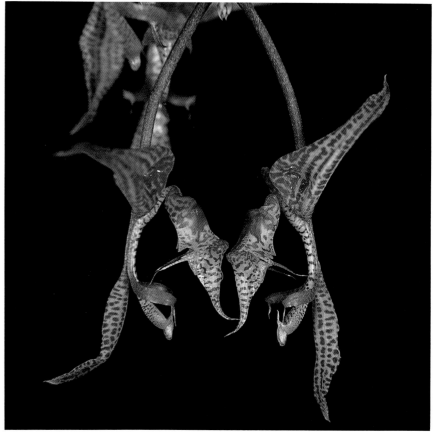

Gongora quinquenervis

Gongora galeata

Gongora quinquenervis

COMMON NAME: None.
COLOUR: Flowers are generally yellow, spotted maroon.
SIZE: Growing up to 40cm (16″) high.
CLIMATE: Intermediate.
DISTRIBUTION: Native to Peru, Ecuador, Trinidad, Mexico, Guyana, Venezuela and Colombia.
FLOWERING TIME: Autumn.
DESCRIPTION: Pseudobulbs are oblong-ovoid to conical, up to 8cm (3¼″). Leaves occur in apical pairs, strap-like, acute, plicate, margins undulate, and grow up to 40cm (16″) long. The inflorescence is long and pendulous. The numerous flowers are fragrant.

Gongora truncata

Gongora truncata

COMMON NAME: None.
COLOUR: Flowers are white with red marks. Labellum yellow.
SIZE: Growing up to 40cm (16″) high.
CLIMATE: Intermediate.
DISTRIBUTION: Native to Mexico.
FLOWERING TIME: Summer.
DESCRIPTION: Pseudobulbs are angular, up to 7.5cm (3″) high. Leaves are broad-lanceolate, growing up to 40cm (16″) long. Inflorescence pendulous, 60cm (2′) long. Flowers are numerous, fragrant, and are 5cm (2″) across.

GRAMMATOPHYLLUM
(gram-mat-o-fill-um)

Grammatophyllum from the Gk *gramma* (a letter) *phyllum* (leaf) with reference to the dark markings on the sepals and petals. This genus of about eight species has several varieties of sympodial epiphytic orchids. It is scattered throughout Burma, Thailand, Malaysia, the Philippines, Indonesia, Papua New Guinea and Polynesia. The genus has two distinct growth forms: (a) *Gabertia* has very elongated pseudobulbs which are really fleshy stems with many leaves, for example, *G. speciosum*, which has plants as large as 12.75m (42.5') high; and (b) *Pattonia* with short ovoid or ellipsoidal pseudobulbs with two to eight apical leaves, for example, *G. scriptum.*

Leaves are lanceolate with a pronounced mid-rib on the underside, are flexible and grow up to 60cm (2') long. Erect or arching inflorescence rises from the base of pseudobulbs, with spikes up to 2.4m (8') long, bearing up to a hundred flowers. Flowers are distinctive, being yellow-green or olive-green with purple markings, and growing 5 to 15cm (2 to 6") in diameter. Sepals and petals are sub-similar. The labellum is small, tri-lobed, with lateral lobes partially enclosing the column, and the mid-lobe small with three low brown-purple keels.

Culture: In native habitat, the plant grows in full sunlight as well as in partial shade. If potted, it requires a very large container. Compost as suggested for other large species. Humid, sticky heat is needed at all times. The genus produces gigantic inflorescences and requires a very large area. Fertilise monthly, and pay attention to drainage and fresh compost.

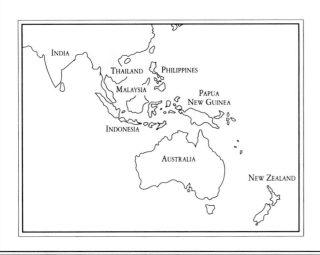

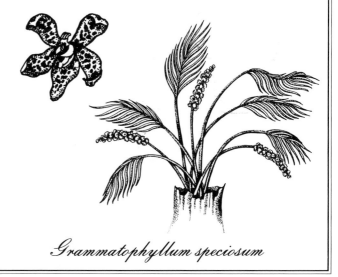

Grammatophyllum speciosum

Grammatophyllum scriptum

COMMON NAME: None.
COLOUR: Flowers are yellow-green, blotched with brown.
SIZE: Growing up to 75cm (30") high.
CLIMATE: Warm to hot.
DISTRIBUTION: Native to Papua New Guinea, Solomon Islands, the Philippines, Moluccas, Celebes and Borneo.
FLOWERING TIME: Usually summer.
DESCRIPTION: An extremely epiphytic plant in all parts. Pseudobulbs are clustered, ellipsoidal, up to 25cm (10") high. Leaves are usually apical, lanceolate, undulate, growing up to 50cm (20") long. Inflorescence long, up to 2m (6'); with numerous flowers and as many as a hundred fragrant blooms.

Grammatophyllum scriptum

ISABELIA
(is-a-<u>bell</u>-ee-a)

Isabelia is named in honour of Isabel, Countess d'Eu, patroness of science and floriculture in Brazil during the reign of Pedro II. *Isabelia* is now referred to as *Neolauchea* (q.v.). This single species genus comes from the damp humid forests of Brazil. It is a rare genus in orchid collections. It is a dwarf-growing, mat-forming epiphytic plant. Pseudobulbs are tightly clustered and are covered with a fine network of grey fibres; the rhizome forms a mat. Leaves are needle-like. Inflorescence is a single snow-white flower. Sepals form a sac with labellum.

Culture: Grow in a shallow pan or on a flat slab of tree-fern fibre. The plant has a creeping, mat-forming habit. Water carefully; plant needs to be kept just damp—not too wet or too dry.

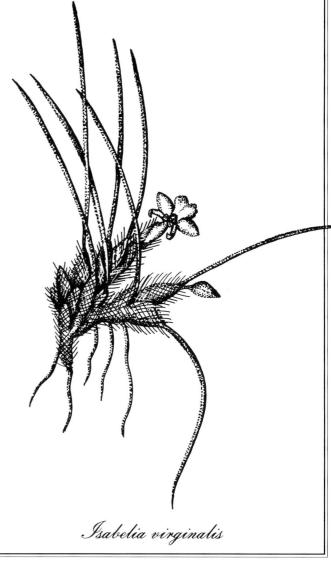

Isabelia virginalis

SOUTH AMERICA

Isabelia virginalis

COMMON NAME: None.
COLOUR: Flowers white and may have a flush of rose or lilac.
SIZE: Growing up to 7.5cm (3″) high.
CLIMATE: Intermediate.
DISTRIBUTION: Native to Brazil.
FLOWERING TIME: Winter.
DESCRIPTION: This small rare species grows in humid forests. Pseudobulbs clustered on a creeping rhizome are tiny and ovoid-conical. Pseudobulbs are densely covered in brown to grey networks of fibres. Leaves are solitary, needle-like and grow up to 7.5cm (3″) long.

Isabelia virginalis

ISOCHILUS
(eye-so-kye-lus)

Isochilus from the Gk *isos* (equal) *chilos* (a lip) with reference to the labellum which is more or less equal to the sepals in size. This genus of just two species and four varieties is found in West Indies, Central and northern South America, and from Mexico to Argentina and Jamaica. *Isochilus* is a sympodial, epiphytic, lithophytic or terrestrial creeping herb, which forms dense masses. Stems grow up to 60cm (2′) tall, are reed-like, with the upper two thirds clothed with small soft leaves. Leaves are flat, sub-coriaceous or soft, distichous, green, linear, base stem-clasping, and grow to about 6cm (2.5″) long. Inflorescence is terminal with one to several flowers. The flowers do not open fully, and are coloured pink to magenta. Sepals and petals are alike in shape, size and colour and are concave, forming a tube around the labellum. The labellum is tri-lobed, shortly clawed, sigmoid. It has a different shade of colour to the sepals and petals, and two pronounced dark dots close to the lateral lobes. The column is erect. The anther cap is partially enclosed by the lateral lobes at the apex.

Culture: Compost using mainly tree-fern fibre in pots or pans. *Isochilus* requires moderate humidity and shade and regular fertilisation. Water carefully as roots will rot with too much water and shrivel with too little water.

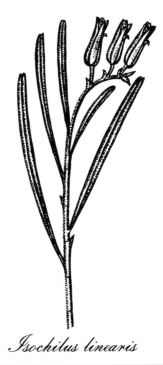

Isochilus linearis

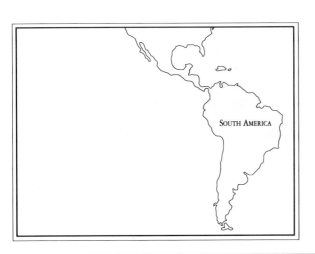

SOUTH AMERICA

Isochilus linearis

Isochilus linearis

COMMON NAME: None.
COLOUR: Flower colour variable from white to pink-purple, but is usually pink-purple.
SIZE: Variable in height, up to 60cm (2′) high.
CLIMATE: Intermediate.
DISTRIBUTION: Native to Cuba, Argentina and Mexico.
FLOWERING TIME: Throughout the year and usually more than once.
DESCRIPTION: A terrestrial, epiphytic or lithophytic plant. Stems form clumps, covered by verrucose leaf sheaths. Leaves are linear, obtuse, measuring up to 6.5cm (2½″) long.

KINGIDIUM

(king-ee-de-um)

*K*ingidium is named in honour of Sir George King, co-author with R. Pantling of *Orchids of the Sikkim-Himalaya*. This genus was previously known as *Kingiella*. In 1970, P. F. Hunt established the genus as *Kingidium* in the *Kew Bulletin*, explaining that under the International Code of Botanical Nomenclature the name *Kingiella* was invalid.

The genus is closely allied to *Phalaenopsis*, and is much confused with *Doritis*. *Kingidium* is a small genus of about six species of epiphytic monopodial orchids. They are distributed from India, east to the Philippines, and south to Indonesia. Stems are free rooting. The succulent leaves are 12 to 18cm (5 to 7″) long. Inflorescence is erect with numerous small flowers which do not open fully. The dorsal sepal and petals are free; lateral sepals unite with the base of the labellum to form a spur-like mentum. The labellum is tri-lobed, saccate at base without a claw, with side lobes erect, and mid-lobe widening from the base.

Culture: Compost as for *Phalaenopsis* and *Doritis*, that is with coarse 5cm (2″) chunks in baskets where roots can grow exposed to the air. Plants require humidity and shade, with plenty of water while growing and less on maturity.

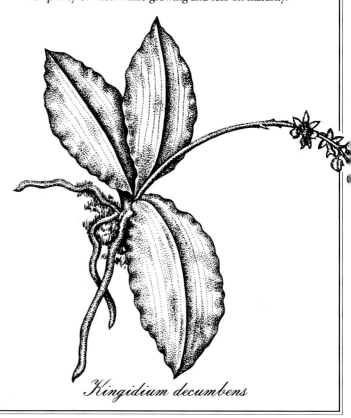

Kingidium decumbens

Map showing: INDIA, THAILAND, PHILIPPINES, MALAYSIA, PAPUA NEW GUINEA, INDONESIA, AUSTRALIA, NEW ZEALAND

Kingidium decumbens syn. *Kingiella decumbens, Phalaenopsis decumbens*

Kingidium decumbens syn. *Kingiella decumbens*

COMMON NAME: None.
COLOUR: Flowers white with the dorsal sepal spotted purple.
SIZE: Growing up to 25cm (10″) across.
CLIMATE: Warm.
DISTRIBUTION: Native to India, throughout eastern Asia, Malaysia, Indonesia and the Philippines.
FLOWERING TIME: Varies, usually flowering more than once annually.
DESCRIPTION: This is a variable epiphytic species. Short stems, up to 1cm (½″) high. Oblong-obovate leaves grow up to 15cm (6″) long. Inflorescence erect, may be branching, up to 20cm (8″) long with numerous, small flowers.

LAELIA
(lay-lee-a)

Laelia is thought to be dedicated to Laelia, one of the Vestal Virgins, or possibly the name derives from Laelius, the name given to the female members of Roman families. The genus of about sixty species is widespread from Mexico, West Indies and Panama, through Peru to Venezuela and Brazil. This genus is often divided into subdivisions, such as the following:

Cattleyoides—those resembling *Cattleyas*, e.g. *L. lobata*, *L. tenebrosa*;

Hadro-laelia—those with heteroblastic pseudobulbs and with a prominent labellum-keel, e.g. *L. jongheana*;

Eu-laelia—those with homoblastic pseudobulbs, e.g. *L. speciosa*;

Micro-laelia—similar to *Eu-laelia* but having sepals and petals of equal width, e.g. *L. lundii*;

Podo-laelia—those whose stems are articulate, e.g. *L. rubescens*.

Laelia is a genus of epiphytic, lithophytic or terrestrial herbs. Pseudobulbs develop along creeping rhizomes, varying considerably in shape and size; they may be fusiform, egg-shaped or ovoid, flat, cylindrical or almost reed-like. The one or several leaves per pseudobulb are apical, coriaceous, entire and varying in length. Inflorescence is terminal, and occurs either singly, close to apex of pseudobulb, or in a cluster of up to twenty flowers, or in a spike up to 1.5m (5′) in length. Flowers are large and showy, and display various colours, such as white, cream, yellow, orange, pink, red or purple. Sepals are narrow and spreading. Petals are generally broader, but are the same colour as sepals. The labellum is the longest and most showy segment of the flower; it is free or adnate to column base, tri-lobed, with lateral lobes forming a tube around the column. The mid-lobe is flat and spreading, and the apex is colourful. The column is toothed at the apex.

Culture: Compost. Most species grow well in pots, others do better in hanging baskets, while some grow well on tree-fern slabs. All require moderate shade, humid conditions and good drainage. Mexican species, however, need cooler conditions than Brazilian species. Fertilise monthly. With this genus it is a good idea to consult your local orchid club for more guidance.

Laelia anceps

SOUTH AMERICA

Laelia anceps

COMMON NAME: None.
COLOUR: Flower colour is variable with the typical form being pale rose-purple. Labellum dark purple.
SIZE: Growing up to 30cm (12") high.
CLIMATE: Intermediate.
DISTRIBUTION: Native to Mexico and Honduras.
FLOWERING TIME: Summer.
DESCRIPTION: Pseudobulbs are borne on a creeping rhizome, ovoid-oblong, compressed, up to 7.5cm (3") high. Leaves are oblong-lanceolate, leathery, generally solitary, growing up to 20cm (8") long. Inflorescence terminal long. Flowers measure up to 10cm (4") across.

Laelia anceps var. *chamberlainiana*

Laelia anceps var. chamberlainiana

COMMON NAME: None.
COLOUR: Flower pale pink-mauve. Labellum pink-purple. Throat yellow with maroon veining.
SIZE: Growing up to 30cm (12") high.
CLIMATE: Intermediate.
DISTRIBUTION: Native to Mexico and Honduras. Habitat same as its type.
FLOWERING TIME: Same as type.
DESCRIPTION: Same as type except for colour variation in the flower.

Laelia anceps

Laelia anceps var. *williamsiana*

COMMON NAME: None.
COLOUR: This variety is the white form. Labellum has a flush of yellow and maroon veining.
SIZE: Growing up to 30cm (12") high.
CLIMATE: Intermediate.
DISTRIBUTION: Native to Mexico. Habitat same as its type.
FLOWERING TIME: Same as type.
DESCRIPTION: Same as type except for the flower colour variation.

Laelia anceps var. *williamsiana*

Laelia crispa var. *candissima*

COMMON NAME: None.
COLOUR: Flowers are white. Labellum throat yellow veined red-purple.
SIZE: Growing up to 45cm (18") high.
CLIMATE: Intermediate.
DISTRIBUTION: Native to Brazil.
FLOWERING TIME: Autumn.
DESCRIPTION: Pseudobulbs are compressed, furrowed, clavate, up to 22cm (10") high. Solitary leaves are broad-oblong, up to 20cm (8") long. Inflorescence terminal, up to 15cm (6") long. Flowers are large and showy, measuring 12.5cm (5") across.

Laelia crispa var. *grandiflora*

COMMON NAME: None.
COLOUR: Flowers are lilac. Labellum veined dark purple with throat white.
SIZE: Growing up to 60cm (24") high.
CLIMATE: Intermediate.
DISTRIBUTION: Native to Brazil. Altitudes 800 to 1150m (2500 to 4000').
FLOWERING TIME: Summer.
DESCRIPTION: Pseudobulbs are compressed, clavate, up to 30cm (12") high. Leaf is solitary, erect, lanceolate-oblong, and grows up to 30cm (12") long. Flower margins are undulate crisped; the flowers are fragrant and grow up to 12.5cm (5") across.

Laelia crispa var. *grandiflora*

Laelia crispa var. *candissima*

Laelia esalqueana

COMMON NAME: None.
COLOUR: Flowers are yellow.
SIZE: A diminutive plant.
CLIMATE: Intermediate.
DISTRIBUTION: Native to Brazil.
FLOWERING TIME: Summer.
DESCRIPTION: Pseudobulbs are compressed, up to 3cm (1¼″) high. Leaf apical from the pseudobulbs, fleshy, up to 5cm (2″) long. Flower scape up to 4.5cm (1½″) long. There are usually four flowers, growing up to 3cm (1¼″) across.

Laelia esalqueana

Laelia gouldiana

Laelia gouldiana

COMMON NAME: None.
COLOUR: Flowers are rose-pink.
SIZE: Growing up to 30cm (12″) high.
CLIMATE: Intermediate.
DISTRIBUTION: Native to Mexico.
FLOWERING TIME: Summer.
DESCRIPTION: Pseudobulbs are oblong-elliptic, up to 15cm (6″) high. The two leaves are oblong or strap-shaped, growing up to 17.5cm (7″) long. The flower scape is up to 80cm (32″) long. Inflorescence has three to five flowers, each flower growing up to 10cm (4″) across.

Laelia harpophylla

COMMON NAME: None:
COLOUR: Flowers are orange-red.
SIZE: Growing up to 65cm (26″) high.
CLIMATE: Intermediate.
DISTRIBUTION: Native to Brazil.
FLOWERING TIME: Autumn.
DESCRIPTION: Pseudobulbs are long, erect, canes up to 45cm (18″) high; membranous sheaths. Leaf is solitary, ensiform up to 20cm (8″) long. Inflorescence has clustered flowers, each being 5 to 7.5cm (2 to 3″) across.

Laelia harpophylla

Laelia lindeyanum

Laelia lindeyanum

COMMON NAME: None.
COLOUR: Flowers are creamy white and may be tinted and spotted with lilac. Labellum tinted lilac, throat lemon and blotched.
SIZE: Growing up to 25cm (10″) high.
CLIMATE: Intermediate.
DISTRIBUTION: Native to Brazil.
FLOWERING TIME: Spring.
DESCRIPTION: Pseudobulbs are cylindrical, up to 20cm (8″) high. Leaves are linear-lanceolate, acute, slightly channelled, and grow up to 15cm (6″) long. Inflorescence short. Flowers are showy, measuring up to 10cm (4″) across.

Laelia purpurata var. *carnea*

COMMON NAME: Lady Godiva.
COLOUR: Flowers are white. Labellum crimson and throat yellow.
SIZE: Growing up to 50cm (20″) high.
CLIMATE: Intermediate.
DISTRIBUTION: Native to southern Brazil. It is an epiphyte growing in jungle conditions.
FLOWERING TIME: Spring.
DESCRIPTION: Pseudobulbs are up to 15cm (6″) high, fusiform, somewhat compressed and furrowed when matured. The solitary leaf is strap-shaped and grows up to 35cm (14″) long. Inflorescence short. Fragrant flowers measure up to 15cm (6″) across.

Laelia purpurata var. *carnea*

Laelia reginae

COMMON NAME: None.
COLOUR: Flowers are pink. Labellum white and yellow.
SIZE: Growing to 7.5cm (3″) or more high.
CLIMATE: Intermediate to hot.
DISTRIBUTION: Native to Brazil.
FLOWERING TIME: Spring.
DESCRIPTION: A small epiphytic plant. Pseudobulbs are ovoid, up to 3.5cm (1½″) high. Leaves are solitary, apical, ovate-lanceolate, acute, growing to 3.5cm (1½″) or more long. Inflorescence short, up to 6.5cm (2½″) long. Flowers measure 4cm (1½″) across.

Laelia tenebrosa

Laelia tenebrosa

COMMON NAME: None.
COLOUR: Flowers are a coppery bronze to yellow. Labellum pink-mauve, veined dark purple.
SIZE: An epiphytic plant up to 50cm (20″) high.
CLIMATE: Intermediate.
DISTRIBUTION: Native to Brazil.
FLOWERING TIME: Spring.
DESCRIPTION: Pseudobulbs are compressed, furrowed, fusiforme, up to 15cm (6″) high. Leaves are erect, up to two, apical from pseudobulb, narrow to broad and oblong, emarginate, growing up to 30cm (12″) long. Inflorescence short, with usually three blooms. Flowers measure up to 15cm (6″) across. Labellum trumpet-shaped. It has a beautiful flower and is a parent for many cultivated hybrids.

Laelia reginae

Laelia wendlandii

Laelia wendlandii

COMMON NAME: None.
COLOUR: Flowers are green-brown. Labellum green-white to pale yellow, marked with purple.
SIZE: Growing up to 40cm (16″) high.
CLIMATE: Intermediate to warm.
DISTRIBUTION: Native to Guatemala, Honduras and Nicaragua.
FLOWERING TIME: Summer.
DESCRIPTION: Pseudobulbs are fusiform, grooved, up to 17.5cm (7″) high. Leaves are apical oblong-elliptic, up to 22.5cm (9″) long. Inflorescence erect, up to 2.1m (7′) long. Flowers are fragrant and measure 5cm (2″) across. Petal margins are undulate.

LYCASTE

(lye-kass-tee)

Lycaste is named after Lycaste, the beautiful daughter of King Priam of Troy. The genus is distributed throughout the West Indies, Mexico and south to Peru and Bolivia. Many of the species have at one time or another been transferred into the *Maxillaria* genus then back to *Lycaste*. The distinguishing feature is the plicate leaves of *Lycaste*. This genus is divided into two groups: (a) those in which the mid-lobe of the labellum is fimbriate and the callus is bifid; and (b) those in which the mid-lobe of the labellum is not fimbriate and the callus is entire (finger-like). *Lycaste* plants are epiphytic, terrestrial or may be lithophytic herbs with short thick pseudobulbs. Leaves are plicate and apical. Inflorescence comes from the base of the pseudobulb and is erect. Flowers are showy, large, and usually fragrant. Sepals are spreading, forming saccate mentum with column foot. Petals are similar but smaller than the sepals, and are often of a different colour. Labellum is tri-lobed.

Culture: Compost in well-drained pots, or on a tree-fern slab. *Lycaste* requires shade and humidity. Provide plenty of water only while the plant is growing, that is, after new shoots appear and while new pseudobulbs are forming. During the rest period use less water.

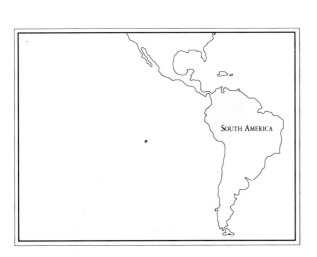

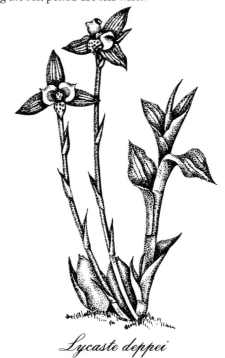

Lycaste deppei

Lycaste cruenta

COMMON NAME: None.
COLOUR: Sepals yellow-green with maroon flecks and a crimson blotch.
SIZE: Growing up to 50cm (20″) high.
CLIMATE: Cool to intermediate.
DISTRIBUTION: Native to Costa Rica, Mexico, Guatemala and El Salvador. Altitude up to 2200m (7250′).
FLOWERING TIME: Spring.
DESCRIPTION: Pseudobulbs are ovoid, compressed, and grow up to 10cm (4″) high. Leaves are deciduous, elliptic-lanceolate, plicate, growing up to 38cm (15″) long. Flowers are large, waxy and fragrant.

Lycaste cruenta

MALLEOLA
(mal-ee-oh-la)

M*alleola* The name's derivation is uncertain. It is a small genus of about thirty species found from India and Burma, through Malaysia and Indonesia to Papua New Guinea. Little is known of its genetic affinities, but it is thought to be closely allied to *Sarcanthus. Malleola* is an epiphytic herb. Stems are pendulous and branching. Leaves are fleshy, often with a waxy appearance. Inflorescence is pendulous with many flowers. The flowers are small, less than 1.2cm (½"); they look insignificant, but are exceedingly fragrant. The labellum is erect, fleshy and tri-lobed; lateral lobes are short with tips incurved, almost joining. The mid-lobe is short and fleshy, and almost closes the spur entrance. The spur is pendulous.

Culture: Compost in well-drained pots, as for *Vandas.* Water carefully, making sure not to over water. This genus is uncommon in collections.

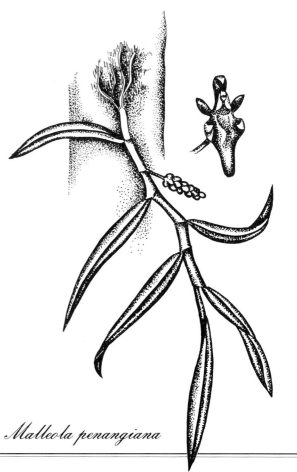

Malleola penangiana

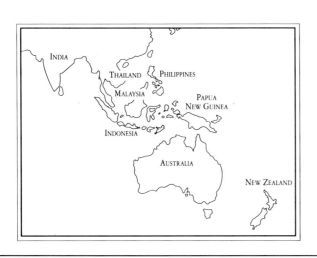

Malleola witteana

Malleola witteana

COMMON NAME: None.
COLOUR: Flowers greenish yellow, mottled and marked brown-red. Labellum white-cream.
SIZE: Pendulous, to 30cm (12") long.
CLIMATE: Warm.
DISTRIBUTION: Native to Sumatra, Java and Malaysia.
FLOWERING TIME: Spring to summer.
DESCRIPTION: Stems are pendulous, up to 30cm (12") long. Leaves are elliptic, may be purple-green, up to 8.5cm (3½") long. Inflorescence is pendulous and 20cm (8") long.

MASDEVALLIA
(maz-de-val-lee-a)

$Masdevallia$ is named after Dr Jose Masdevall, a Spanish physician and botanist. This is a large genus of almost three hundred species classified. It is distributed throughout Mexico, Panama and tropical South America to Peru and Venezuela with the greatest development in the cloud forests of the Andes of Colombia. Here, three-quarters of the known species occur. *Masdevallia* is a small to medium-sized epiphytic herb with creeping rhizomes. Stems are short, erect with an apical leaf, without pseudobulbs. Leaf is erect, fleshy, coriaceous, and is oblong to linear. Inflorescence is either erect, arching or pendulous, and is racemose with several flowers. These flowers are unusual; they are showy and have various vivid colours. Sepals are connate forming a tube at the base, with the upper part free, spreading with long or short filaments. Petals are small, as is the labellum which is parallel to the column. The petals and labellum are often hidden in the tube formed by the sepals. The short column is also hidden and is either winged or has a narrow margin. The sepals are the showy segments of the flower.
Culture: Compost in well-drained pots. Plants require moist, shady situations. Water carefully: neither too little nor too much water. This genus is very popular in collections.

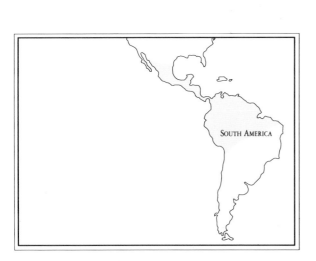

SOUTH AMERICA

Masdevallia pandurilabia

Masdevallia burfordensis

COMMON NAME: None.
COLOUR: Flowers yellowish orange, speckled and marked heavily with maroon.
SIZE: Growing up to 14cm (5½") high.
CLIMATE: Intermediate to cool.
DISTRIBUTION: Native to Peru.
FLOWERING TIME: Autumn.
DESCRIPTION: A tufted herb. Leaves are lanceolate-oblong, up to 14cm (5½") high. Inflorescence is shorter than the leaves. The solitary flower is triangular in shape and up to 8cm (3¼") across.

Masdevallia floribunda

Masdevallia burfordensis

Masdevallia floribunda

COMMON NAME: None.
COLOUR: Flowers pale yellow, spotted brown-purple. Labellum white with red-brown blotch.
SIZE: Small plant, growing up to 10cm (4") high.
CLIMATE: Cool to intermediate.
DISTRIBUTION: Native to Costa Rica, Mexico, Guatemala and Honduras. Altitude 900 to 1300m (3000 to 4500').
FLOWERING TIME: Spring.
DESCRIPTION: A tufted herb. Leaves are oblong-lanceolate and grow up to 10cm (4") long. Inflorescence is up to 7.5cm (3") high.

Masdevallia infracta

COMMON NAME: None.
COLOUR: Flower colour variable, pink-purple to red-brown and flushed yellow outside; purple-red inside with pale yellow tails.
SIZE: A small epiphytic plant, up to 20cm (8") high.
CLIMATE: Cool.
DISTRIBUTION: Native to Brazil and Peru. Altitude 200m (6561'), growing on mountain slopes, covered by grass steppe.
FLOWERING TIME: Winter.
DESCRIPTION: Leaves are lanceolate, shiny green, petiolate, and grow up to 10cm (4") long. Flowers are bell-shaped, up to 6cm (2½") long.

Masdevallia infracta

Masdevallia mezae

COMMON NAME: None.
COLOUR: Flower cream-yellow, spotted dark pink, tips ochre-yellow.
SIZE: Growing to 15cm (6") or more high.
CLIMATE: Intermediate to warm.
DISTRIBUTION: Native to Mexico.
FLOWERING TIME: Late winter to spring.
DESCRIPTION: A tufted epiphytic or lithophytic herb. Leaves are lanceolate, emarginate, growing to 15cm (6") or more high. Flower scape is shorter than the leaves. Flowers are solitary and about 9cm (3½") long.

Masdevallia mezae

Masdevallia torta

COMMON NAME: None.
COLOUR: Flower pale greenish yellow, spotted and striped red.
SIZE: Growing up to 22cm (8½") high.
CLIMATE: Cool.
DISTRIBUTION: Native to Mexico; growing on mossy trees in damp forests, at altitudes of 2000 to 2400m (7150 to 7800').
FLOWERING TIME: Winter to spring.
DESCRIPTION: Leaves are lanceolate, the mid rib is prominent and it grows up to 22cm (8½") long. Petiole is long. Inflorescence is erect and short, up to 7.5cm (3") long. Flower is solitary, bell shaped and about 15cm (6") long.

Masdevallia torta

Masdevallia tovarensis

COMMON NAME: None.
COLOUR: Flowers white.
SIZE: Growing up to 15cm (6") high.
CLIMATE: Cool.
DISTRIBUTION: Native to Venezuela.
FLOWERING TIME: Summer.
DESCRIPTION: Leaves clustered, shiny, green, elliptic-spathulate, growing up to 15cm (6") long. Scapes are long, carrying up to five waxy, white flowers, about 7.5cm (3") long. Sepals are tri-nerved with short tails.

Masdevallia tovarensis

Masdevallia veitchiana

COMMON NAME: None.
COLOUR: Flowers orange-red within, outer bluish sheen with numerous red-purple papillae.
SIZE: Growing up to 30cm (12") high.
CLIMATE: Cool.
DISTRIBUTION: Native to Peru, common at the Inca ruins of Macchu-Picchu; altitude 2200 to 4000m (11 000 to 13 000').
FLOWERING TIME: Winter.
DESCRIPTION: A large tufted, showy, lithophytic species. Leaves are linear-oblong, up to 30cm (12"). Flower scape is longer than leaves. Flowers grow up to 12.5cm (5") long.

Masdevallia ventricularia

COMMON NAME: None.
COLOUR: Flower maroon with darker markings, inside yellowish brown.
SIZE: Growing up to 15cm (6") high.
CLIMATE: Cool.
DISTRIBUTION: Native to Colombia and Ecuador, growing at altitudes of 1800 to 2200m (5095 to 7100') on trunks of forest trees.
FLOWERING TIME: Spring to summer.
DESCRIPTION: Leaves are oblong-lanceolate, clustered and up to 15cm (6") long. Flower scape is about the same length as the leaves. Flowers are terminal, solitary, tubular and up to 12.5cm (5") long.

Masdevallia ventricularia

Masdevallia veitchiana

MAXILLARIA
(max-il-lair-ee-a)

Maxillaria derives from the Lat. *maxillae* (jaw-bone) because the labellum and column of some species reminded Ruiz and Pavon of the jaws of insects. This genus of over three hundred species is found in tropical and subtropical America, from Mexico to Peru and Brazil. The plant is epiphytic or lithophytic, very rarely terrestrial, and has short, matted or creeping rhizomes. Pseudobulbs are tightly clustered, flattened, smooth or fluted. Leaves are coriaceous, with one or more per pseudobulb. Inflorescence rises from the base of the pseudobulb. The flower is solitary, but several scapes may rise from the base of one pseudobulb. Sepals are alike in size and colour with the dorsal sepal erect. Petals are smaller than sepals, but have the same colour. The labellum is tri-lobed and is attached to the column by a short claw. Lateral lobes are incurved and almost surround the column; the mid-lobe is decurved.

Culture: Compost in well-drained pots or mount on a tree-fern slab. Water freely and fertilise regularly.

Maxillaria picta syn. *M. fuscata*

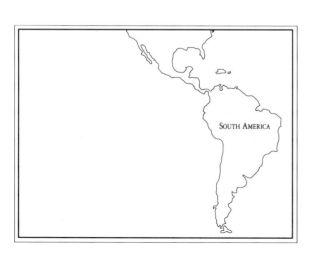

SOUTH AMERICA

Maxillaria densa syn. Ornithidium densum

COMMON NAME: None.

COLOUR: Flower colour variable, green-white, yellow-white, tinged purple to maroon.

SIZE: Growing up to 38cm (15″) high.

CLIMATE: Cool to warm.

DISTRIBUTION: Native to Mexico, Guatemala, and British Honduras. An epiphyte or terrestrial plant, growing at low elevations in damp woodlands of altitudes up to 2500m (8400′) in cloud forest; also occurs in pine forests where it has a terrestrial habit.

FLOWERING TIME: Usually late winter to spring.

DESCRIPTION: Pseudobulbs are oblong-elliptic on a creeping rhizome, compressed-ancipitous, up to 7.5cm (3″) high. Leaf is solitary, apical, linear to lanceolate, 30cm (12″) long. Flower grows 1cm (¼″) long.

Maxillaria densa syn. *Ornithidium densum*

Maxillaria luteo-alba

Maxillaria luteo-alba

COMMON NAME: None.

COLOUR: Flowers variable in colour and size, but generally white outside, yellow inside.

SIZE: Growing up to 50cm (20″) high.

CLIMATE: Intermediate to warm.

DISTRIBUTION: Native to Ecuador, Costa Rica, Panama, Colombia and Venezuela.

FLOWERING TIME: Spring to early summer.

DESCRIPTION: Pseudobulbs clustered, somewhat compressed, oblong-ovoid to elliptic-ovoid, up to 5cm (2″) high. Solitary leaf is shiny, linear-lanceolate, acute, growing up to 50cm (20″) long. Inflorescence is numerous, growing up to 15cm (6″) long. Flowers are variable in size, but about 10cm (4″) across.

Maxillaria picta syn. M. fuscata

COMMON NAME: None.

COLOUR: Flowers yellow with purple spots. Labellum yellow-white; column purple.

SIZE: Growing up to 45cm (18″) high.

CLIMATE: Intermediate.

DISTRIBUTION: Native to Brazil.

FLOWERING TIME: Autumn.

DESCRIPTION: Pseudobulbs mostly clustered on a creeping rhizome, compressed, ovoid, furrowing when old, growing up to 8cm (3″) high. Leaf is usually solitary, leathery, shiny, narrow, strap-shaped, acute, growing up to 38.5cm (15″) long. Flowers measure about 6.5cm (2½″) across.

Maxillaria picta syn. *M. fuscata*

Maxillaria porphyrostele

Maxillaria porphyrostele

COMMON NAME: None.

COLOUR: Flowers yellow with purple stripe near base of petals. Labellum column purple.

SIZE: Growing up to 25cm (10″) high.

CLIMATE: Intermediate.

DISTRIBUTION: Native to Brazil.

FLOWERING TIME: Late winter to spring.

DESCRIPTION: Pseudobulbs are clustered, compressed, orbicular-ovoid, up to 4.5cm (1¾″) high. Leaves are usually paired, linear, obtuse at the apex, growing up to 20cm (8″) long. Inflorescence is up to 7.5cm (3″) long. Flowers measure about 3.5cm (1¼″) across. Labellum is tri-lobed.

Maxillaria tenuifolia

COMMON NAME: None.
COLOUR: Flowers dark red, mottled yellow.
Labellum dark red; the apical yellow with
purplish spots.
SIZE: Growing up to 40cm (16″) high.
CLIMATE: Intermediate to warm.
DISTRIBUTION: Native to Mexico, Honduras,
British Honduras, Guatemala, Nicaragua and
Costa Rica.
FLOWERING TIME: Spring and summer.
DESCRIPTION: Pseudobulbs are about 2.5cm (1″)
apart on ascending rhizome, compressed, ovoid,
about 2.5cm (1″) long and are produced
further along the stem than preceding
pseudobulbs. Leaves are linear, acuminate, grass-
like, measuring up to 38.5cm (15″) long.
Inflorescence is usually numerous and about
5cm (2″) long. Flowers are up to 5cm (2″)
across. The tropical species has a creeping
rhizome, growing in a vertical position with
oval pseudobulbs; its scent is similar to the
coconut.

Maxillaria tenuifolia

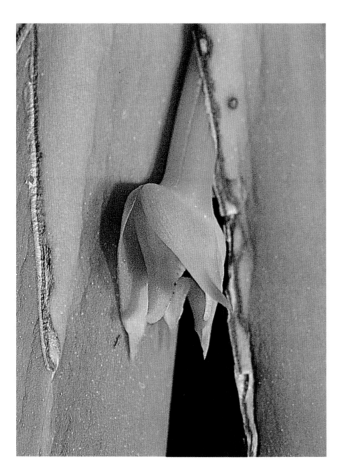

Maxillaria valenzuelana

Maxillaria valenzuelana

COMMON NAME: None.
COLOUR: Flowers light green or green-yellow.
Labellum light brown, spotted purple.
SIZE: Pendulous to 20cm (8″) long.
CLIMATE: Warm.
DISTRIBUTION: Native to central and southern
tropical America and West Indies.
FLOWERING TIME: Summer.
DESCRIPTION: An epiphytic species with short
stems. Leaves are compressed, falcate, acute
(fan-like), pendulous, measuring up to 20cm
(8″) long. Flowers are about 2cm (¾″) long.

MENADENIUM

(men-a-dee-nee-um)

Menadenium This is a genus of four exceptionally rare and beautiful epiphytes from Venezuela and northern Brazil. *Menadenium* are rare, even in the best collections, and are scarce even in their native land. The genus is thought to be rather closely allied to *Zygopetalum*. It is truly an epiphytic plant; rhizomes branch frequently forming a large mass. Pseudobulbs occur at regular intervals along rhizomes, usually with leaf-like bracts, and become shrivelled with age. The one or two leaves are apical, glossy, and five to seven nerves are prominent. Inflorescence from the base of the pseudobulb is erect. Flowers are large, showy, fragrant and variable in colour. Sepals and petals are free and spreading. The labellum is entire with a thickened basal part; the callus is semi-circular and fleshy. The column has two antenna-like projections.

Culture: For this truly epiphytic plant use compost in a hanging basket or shallow fern-pan. It does best mounted on a tree-fern slab. The plant requires warm, humid conditions at all times. Allow it to rest for several weeks after flowering.

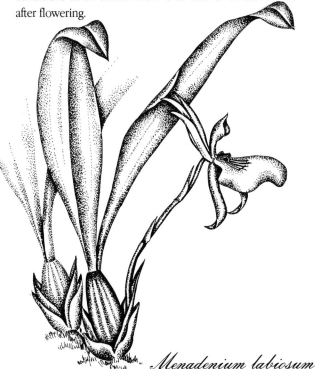

Menadenium labiosum

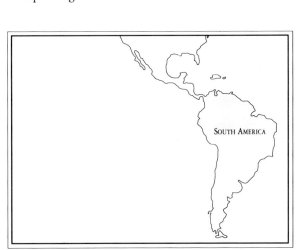

SOUTH AMERICA

Menadenium labiosum

COMMON NAME: None.

COLOUR: Colour variable, usually green-yellow, suffused with pink or grey. Labellum white with purple-red callus and veins.

SIZE: Growing up to 35cm (14″) high.

CLIMATE: Intermediate to warm.

DISTRIBUTION: Native to northern Brazil, Venezuela and Guyana.

FLOWERING TIME: Spring to early summer.

DESCRIPTION: Pseudobulbs borne at wide intervals, compressed, ovoid-oblong. One to two leaves are lanceolate, strap-shaped, acuminate and grow up to 30cm (12″) long. Flowers are fragrant, large and handsome.

Menadenium labiosum

MILTONIA
(mil-toh-nee-a)

*M*iltonia is named after Earl Fitzwilliam Viscount Milton. This small genus of about twenty species is found from the Andes to south-east Brazil, with one species from Panama and Costa Rica. *Miltonia* are characterised as having scandent rhizomes, compressed pseudobulbs with leaves, and an auriculate column. In 1977, *Miltonia* was divided into two groups: (a) those having terete peduncles, e.g. *M. clowesii*; and (b) those having compressed ancipitous peduncles, e.g. *M. spectabilis. Miltonia* is a genus of epiphytic plants, which have very small pseudobulbs at intervals along creeping, climbing rhizomes. The two leaves are apical and coriaceous. Inflorescence emerges from the base of the pseudobulb, and is short, erect or arching, with one or many flowered racemes. Flowers are medium to large and are showy. Sepals are free and spreading. Petals are similar to sepals, though often broader. The labellum is entire, broad and spreading. The column has ear-like appendages.

Culture: Compost. These plants have creeping, climbing rhizomes, so grow in shallow pans or baskets, or mount on tree-fern slabs. They require frequent watering and moderate shade. Provide warm but not hot conditions.

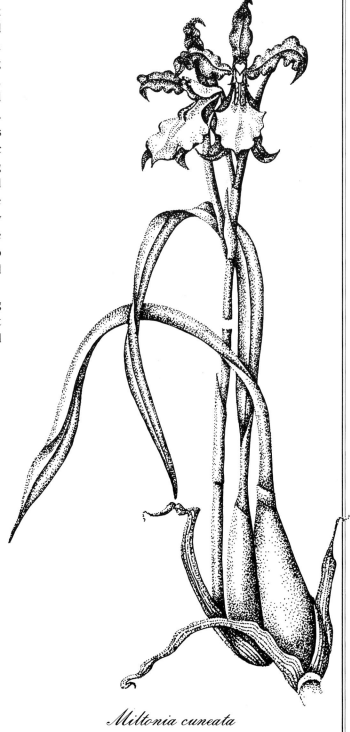

Miltonia cuneata

SOUTH AMERICA

Miltonia X *bluntii*

COMMON NAME: None.
COLOUR: Flowers red-purple. Labellum pink-purple.
SIZE: Growing up to 30cm (12″) high.
CLIMATE: Intermediate.
DISTRIBUTION: Native to Brazil.
FLOWERING TIME: Spring.
DESCRIPTION: A natural hybrid between *M. clowesii* and *M. spectabilis.* Two leaves. Inflorescence sheathing. Flowers are handsome, fragrant, usually produced one at a time and measure about 7.5cm (3″) across.

Miltonia X *bluntii*

Miltonia candida

Miltonia candida

COMMON NAME: None.
COLOUR: Flowers red-brown, tipped and spotted with yellow. Labellum white marked with purple.
SIZE: Growing up to 50cm (20″) high.
CLIMATE: Intermediate.
DISTRIBUTION: Native to Brazil.
FLOWERING TIME: Spring.
DESCRIPTION: Pseudobulbs are somewhat compressed, elongated, narrow-ovoid, up to 10cm (4″) high. Leaves grow in pairs, are linear-oblanceolate, acute and up to 38.5cm (15″) long. Flowers are fragrant, waxy and 7.5cm (3″) across.

Miltonia clowesii

COMMON NAME: None.
COLOUR: Flowers red-brown, barred and tipped yellow. Labellum purple and white.
SIZE: Growing up to 45cm (18″) high.
CLIMATE: Intermediate.
DISTRIBUTION: Native to Brazil.
FLOWERING TIME: Spring.
DESCRIPTION: An epiphytic plant. Pseudobulbs are compressed, narrowly ovate-oblong, up to 10cm (4″) high. Leaves are apical in pairs, strap-shaped, up to 46cm (18″) long. Inflorescence up to 45cm (18″) long with seven to ten blooms. Flowers measure up to 7.5cm (3″) across.

Miltonia clowesii

Miltonia cuneata

Miltonia cuneata

COMMON NAME: None.
COLOUR: Flowers red-brown, tipped with lemon, may have yellow streaks at the base.
SIZE: Growing up to 45cm (18″) high.
CLIMATE: Intermediate.
CLIMATE: Native to Brazil.
FLOWERING TIME: Summer to autumn
DESCRIPTION: Robust creeping rhizome. Pseudobulbs are compressed, oblong-ovoid and up to 10cm (4″) high. Two leaves are narrow-lanceolate, acute and grow up to 38.5cm (15″) long. Inflorescence is up to 60cm (2′) long. Flower measures 7.5cm (3″) across.

Miltonia flavescens

COMMON NAME: None.

COLOUR: Flowers ochre yellow. Labellum white with purple-red streaks on basal area.

SIZE: Growing up to 45cm (18″) high.

CLIMATE: Intermediate.

DISTRIBUTION: Native to Paraguay and Brazil.

FLOWERING TIME: Spring.

DESCRIPTION: Rhizome creeping. Pseudobulbs are compressed, oblong-oval, up to 12.5cm (5″) high. Two leaves are linear, strap-shaped and grow up to 30cm (12″) long. Flowers are fragrant. Petals and sepals are narrow, star-shaped and are about 10cm (4″) across.

Miltonia flavescens

Miltonia regnellii

Miltonia regnellii

COMMON NAME: None.

COLOUR: Flowers white with basal pink tint, streaked with pink, and purple-pink and white margins, and crest has yellow lines. Labellum pink and veined purple.

SIZE: Growing up to 45cm (18″) high.

CLIMATE: Intermediate.

DISTRIBUTION: Native to Brazil.

FLOWERING TIME: Spring.

DESCRIPTION: Pseudobulbs are compressed, oblong-ovoid and grow up to 10cm (4″) high. Two leaves are linear, strap-shaped, acute and 40cm (16″) long. Inflorescence is erect and grows up to 60cm (2′) long. Flowers measure about 7.5cm (3″) across. Labellum is tri-lobed.

Miltonia spectabilis

Miltonia spectabilis

COMMON NAME: None.

COLOUR: Flower colour variable, usually cream-white, may be tinted with pink near the base. Labellum red-purple, with deeper hue on longitudal veins.

SIZE: Growing up to 25cm (10″) high.

CLIMATE: Intermediate.

DISTRIBUTION: Native to Brazil.

FLOWERING TIME: Autumn.

DESCRIPTION: Creeping rhizome. Pseudobulbs are compressed, oblong-ovoid and measure up to 10cm (4″) high. Leaves are linear, strap-shaped, growing up to 25cm (10″) long. Inflorescence is erect and about 20cm (8″) high. Solitary flower is about 7.5cm (3″) long.

Miltonia spectabilis var. moreliana

COMMON NAME: Parsley Orchid.

COLOUR: This variant differs from its type in that it has a larger plum-purple flower. Labellum rose colour with darker veins.

SIZE: Growing up to 25cm (10″) high.

CLIMATE: Intermediate.

DISTRIBUTION: Native to Brazil.

FLOWERING TIME: Autumn.

DESCRIPTION: Pseudobulbs borne on a creeping rhizome, compressed, oblong-ovoid, up to 10cm (4″) high. Strap-shaped leaves grow in pairs up to 25cm (10″) long. Inflorescence is short. Flowers are solitary measuring up to 10cm (4″) long. It is more common in cultivation than is the type.

Miltonia spectabilis var. *moreliana*

MILTONIOPSIS

(mil-toh-nee-opsis)

Miltoniopsis from the Gk *opsis* (appearance) with reference to the flower's similarity to that of genus *Miltonia*. This is an epiphytic genus of six species and is found in the central Americas, Panama, Costa Rica, Venezuela, Colombia and Ecuador. The genus was first established in 1889, but failed to gain approval by many authors. In 1976 when describing a new species, Garay and Dunsterville revived the name for four other central American species previously in the *Miltonia* group of Brazil. *Miltoniopsis* is different from *Miltonia* in that the pseudobulbs are bilaterally flat in clusters, the single apical leaf and the exauriculate column is joined to the labellum by a raised ridge and is not excavate at the base.

Culture: Mount the plant on a tree-fern slab.

Miltoniopsis vexillaria

Miltoniopsis vexillaria syn. *Miltonia vexillaria*

COMMON NAME: None.

COLOUR: Flowers pink, white, or white striped and flushed pink. Labellum rose pink, white at base, marked with red and yellow.

SIZE: An epiphytic plant up to 30cm (12″) high.

CLIMATE: Cool to intermediate.

DISTRIBUTION: Northern Ecuador and Colombia, growing at an altitude of 1300 to 2150m (4265 to 7053′), in marginal areas of montane forests.

FLOWERING TIME: Spring.

DESCRIPTION: Pseudobulbs are conical-ovoid, compressed, up to 7.5cm (3″) high. Leaves are apical, strap-like, growing up to 25cm (10″) long. Inflorescence is borne from the base of the pseudobulbs, and is up to 30cm (12″) long. Flowers are showy and large, up to 10cm (4″) long.

Miltoniopsis vexillaria syn. *Miltonia vexillaria*

NEOBENTHAMIA
(nee-o-ben-tham-ee-a)

Neobenthamia is named after George Bentham, an English botanist. This single species genus is from tropical eastern Africa. It is a terrestrial orchid often cultivated in domestic gardens. The handsome robust plant often grows to 2.5m (8′) tall, with leaves to 20cm (8″) long. Inflorescence is a terminal cluster of white flowers, each 2.5cm (1″) across, in a hemisphere up to 30cm (12″) diameter on a tall leafy stem.

Culture: As for *Phaius*. Grows best in full sun. The plant requires water, a coarse moisture-retaining soil with very good drainage, and careful fertilising. *Neobenthamia* is a must for all orchidists.

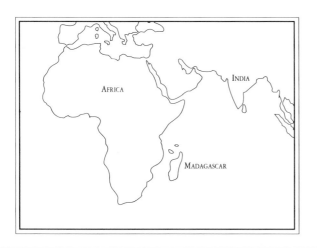

Neobenthamia gracilis

Neobenthamia gracilis

Neobenthamia gracilis

COMMON NAME: None.

COLOUR: Flowers white. Labellum white, with yellow stripe and red-purple markings either side.

SIZE: Growing up to 1.8m (6′) high.

CLIMATE: Intermediate.

DISTRIBUTION: Native to tropical eastern Africa.

FLOWERING TIME: Throughout the year.

DESCRIPTION: A robust species. Stems are slender, often branching and variable in size but usually up to 1.8m (6′) high. Leaves are shiny, linear-lanceolate, acute and grow up to 20cm (8″) long. Terminal inflorescence, up to 12.5cm (5″) high. Flowers are numerous and measure up to 2.5cm (1″) across.

NEOFINETIA
(nee-o-fi-net-ee-a)

*N*eofinetia is named after M. Achille Finet, a French botanist, who worked in China and Japan. This single species genus from China, Japan and Korea is a dwarf epiphytic monopodial plant. Leaves are distichous, fleshy and channelled above. Inflorescence is in the form of an axillary raceme with several white flowers. Sepals and petals are free and spreading. The labellum is tri-lobed, erect with arcuate spur at base. This species has some eight synonyms and several hybrids.

Culture: Compost. Grow in a small pot or basket. The plant requires humid conditions, light shade, frequent watering and good drainage. (Same treatment as for dwarf *Vandas.*)

Neofinetia falcata

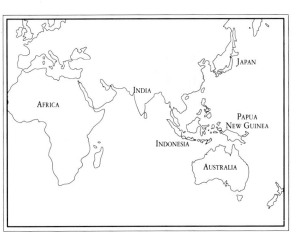

Neofinetia falcata

COMMON NAME: None.
COLOUR: Flowers white.
SIZE: Growing up to 15cm (6″) high.
CLIMATE: Intermediate.
DISTRIBUTION: Native to Korea and Japan.
FLOWERING TIME: Summer to autumn.
DESCRIPTION: A genus of one species, with many varieties. Small plant, stems branching from base, about 15cm (6″) high. Leaves are curving, linear, acute and grow up to 15cm (6″) long. Flowers are fragrant at night and measure about 3cm (1¼″) across. Sepals and petals are linear. Labellum is triangular with a long curved spur, up to 10cm (4″) long. Inflorescences short, bearing three to seven flowers.

Neofinetia falcata

NEOLAUCHEA
(nee-o-lau-chee-a)

*N*eolauchea may be named after Lauche, or after the Spanish *lauchea* (struggling) as the plant is difficult to establish. This single species genus comes from southern Brazil and is a most uncommon dwarf epiphytic orchid. The plant has small pseudobulbs at intervals along creeping rhizomes. Leaves are terete and coriaceous. Inflorescence is terminal with attractive rose-red flowers. This genus is found in only the most comprehensive collections. Nothing is known of its genetic affinities.

Culture: Use compost of finely chopped fibre, tightly packed, in a small basket. *Neolauchea* is difficult to handle because all vegetative parts of the plant are exceedingly fragile; however, once established it grows readily. The plant requires frequent watering, perfect drainage, a shady and perpetually moist situation, and warm but never hot conditions. Disturb as little as possible.

SOUTH AMERICA

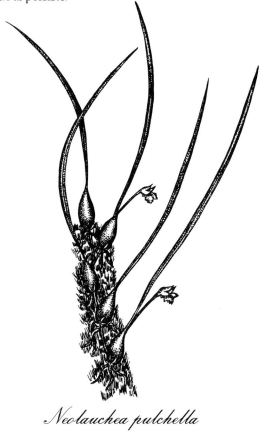

Neolauchea pulchella

Neolauchea pulchella

Neolauchea pulchella

COMMON NAME: None.
COLOUR: Flowers rose-red or mauve.
SIZE: Growing up to 7.5cm (3″) high.
CLIMATE: Intermediate.
DISTRIBUTION: Native to southern Brazil.
FLOWERING TIME: Summer.
DESCRIPTION: Pseudobulbs are narrow ovoid, 1cm (½″) high, borne at intervals on a creeping rhizome. Leaf is solitary, linear to almost terete, up to 6cm (2½″). Inflorescence is terminal and short. Flowers are about 1cm (¼″) long.

NEOMOOREA

(nee-o-moor-ee-a)

Neomoorea is named after F. W. Moore, curator at Glasnevin Botanic Gardens in Dublin. The genus has two epiphytic or terrestrial species and comes from Colombia and Panama. *Neomoorea* is closely allied to *Stanhopea*, but the labellum hypochile of *Neomoorea* is not saccate-concave like *Stanhopea*. Pseudobulbs are ovoid. The two leaves are apical and plicate. Inflorescence is erect from the base of the pseudobulb. Flowers are large and showy. Sepals and petals are free and spreading, with petals narrower at the base. The labellum is tri-lobed; lateral lobes are large and spreading, and the mid-lobe is concave with two lateral erect and spreading wings.

Culture: Use a compost of finely chopped tree-fern fibre, rich loam, gritty sand, and add sphagnum moss (ratio 5:1:1:1). If bark is used, sift out all the dust and use well-drained pots. Water frequently during growth periods and restrict watering during rest periods. New growth is very sensitive to over watering and stale compost. *M. irrorata*, a magnificent epiphytic orchid, is highly prized by orchidists. These majestic orchids deserve and require the best care and attention.

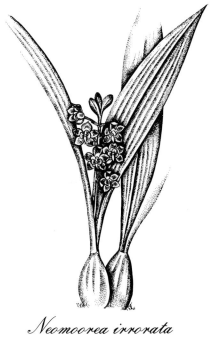

Neomoorea irrorata

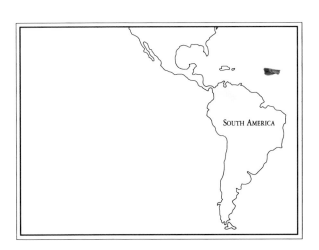

SOUTH AMERICA

Neomoorea irrorata

Neomoorea irrorata

COMMON NAME: None.
COLOUR: Flowers red-brown with white bases. Labellum lemon, marked and banded with brown-purple. Mid-lobe is lemon, spotted with red.
SIZE: Growing up to 1m (40″) high.
CLIMATE: Warm.
DISTRIBUTION: Native to Colombia and Panama.
FLOWERING TIME: Spring.
DESCRIPTION: Pseudobulbs are ovoid-ovate, compressed, furrowed and up to 12.5cm (5″) high. Two leaves are lanceolate-elliptic, folded and are about 1m (40″) long. Inflorescence is erect with many fragrant, waxy flowers about 6cm (2½″) across. Labellum is tri-lobed.

OCTOMERIA
(ok-toh-may-ree-a)

Octomeria from the Gk *octo* (eight) *meros* (part) with reference to the eight pollinia which are characteristic of the species in this genus. This is a relatively little known genus of about seventy species of epiphytic or lithophytic orchids. Mostly they originate from Brazil with widespread representation from the Honduras, Costa Rica, West Indies, Colombia and Guyana. The plant is small and insignificant in appearance. It has creeping rhizomes as the primary stem, with erect secondary stems, each with a single apical leaf. The leaf is coriaceous to fleshy, and flat to terete. Inflorescence arises from the base of the leaf. It has one to many flowers. The sepals and petals are connate at the base, or free and spreading. The labellum is very short and either tri-lobed or entire. The column also is very short with eight pollinia.

The *Octomeria* genus is a highly diverse plant, which is poorly known and exceptionally scarce in collections. Although quite small, many species are attractive with white, yellow or green flowers.

Culture: Use a fine compost in small pots. Depending on its place of origin, each species requires individual attention. Basically, treat as for *Pleurothallis*. Plants require shade and humidity during growth. Apply water regularly to roots and fertilise monthly. Always check with your local orchid club for advice when growing these species.

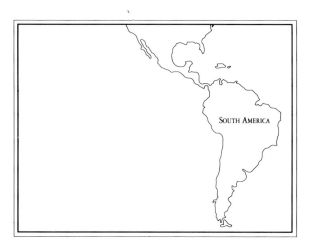

SOUTH AMERICA

Octomeria semiconnata

Octomeria gracilis

COMMON NAME: None.
COLOUR: Flowers lemon.
SIZE: A small plant, growing up to 18cm (7″) high.
CLIMATE: Intermediate.
DISTRIBUTION: Native to Brazil.
FLOWERING TIME: Throughout the year.
DESCRIPTION: Leaves are needle-like on a linear petiole. Flowers are clustered, small and up to 7mm (¼″) across.

Octomeria gracilis

ODONTOGLOSSUM

(o-don-toh-gloss-um)

Odontoglossum from the Gk *odonto* (tooth) *glossa* (tongue) with reference to the tooth-like crest of the labellum callus. This is a genus of over two hundred polymorphic species having several distinct forms. Its distribution extends from Mexico in the north down through the central Americas to Bolivia and Brazil. The larger number of species occur in the mountains of Ecuador, Peru and Venezuela. The genus is highly diverse in both appearance and vegetation; it is epiphytic or lithophytic, but rarely terrestrial. Rhizomes are short. Pseudobulbs are compressed, often with leaf-like distichous bracts, with one to three apical leaves. Leaves are fleshy or coriaceous and may be rigid or flexible. Inflorescence arises from the base of the pseudobulb, is erect or arching, and pendulous in several species. Flowers are large and either showy or small and inconspicuous. Sepals and petals are spreading. The labellum is often complex, tri-lobed or entire, erect or parallel to column, with lateral lobes erect or revolute; the mid-lobe is spreading.

The column is long with two pollinia. The genus is freely compatible genetically, hence the reports of thousands of hybrids. This genus is extremely popular with breeders.

Culture: Depends heavily on the place of origin of the specimen. Genus habitats range from sea level to 3000m (10 000′) elevation. Species from the coastal lowlands require moist humid conditions, while those from the Andes of Peru and Bolivia need 'cool-house' conditions. The roots must never be allowed to dry out. Fresh moving air is essential. Check with your local orchid society concerning growing conditions, such as use of fertiliser.

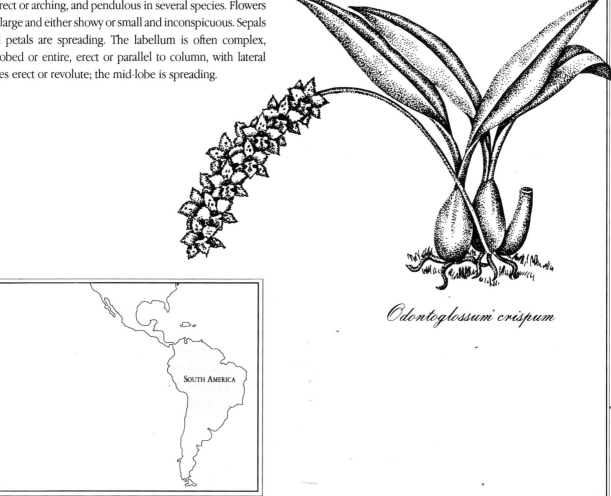

Odontoglossum crispum

SOUTH AMERICA

Odontoglossum bictoniense

COMMON NAME: None.
COLOUR: Flowers yellow-green, banded with red-brown. Labellum white, streaked purple.
SIZE: Growing up to 60cm (2') high.
CLIMATE: Warm.
DISTRIBUTION: Native to Mexico, El Salvador and Guatemala.
FLOWERING TIME: Winter to spring.
DESCRIPTION: Pseudobulbs are compressed, ovoid to ellipsoid, up to 17.5cm (7") high and are mostly concealed by leaf sheaths. Two to three leaves are oblong-elliptic to linear, acute and measure 45cm (18") long. Inflorescence is up to 90cm (3') high. Flowers are numerous, fragrant and 4cm (1½") across.

Odontoglossum bictoniense

Odontoglossum cariniferum

COMMON NAME: None.
COLOUR: Flowers red-brown with tips and margins yellow. Labellum white.
SIZE: Growing up to 50cm (20") high.
CLIMATE: Intermediate to warm.
DISTRIBUTION: Native to Colombia, Venezuela and Costa Rica, found growing in montane forest.
FLOWERING TIME: Autumn to spring.
DESCRIPTION: Pseudobulbs are compressed, oblong-elliptic and up to 10cm (4") high. Leaves are linear, strap-like, up to 45cm (18") long. Inflorescence is branching with many flowers, up to 1.2m (4'). Flowers measure up to 5cm (2") across.

Odontoglossum pulchellum

Odontoglossum pulchellum

COMMON NAME: None.
COLOUR: Flowers white. Labellum has yellow blotch.
SIZE: Growing up to 45cm (18") high.
CLIMATE: Warm.
DISTRIBUTION: Native to Mexico, Costa Rica, El Salvador and Guatemala.
FLOWERING TIME: Winter.
DESCRIPTION: Pseudobulbs are clustered, compressed, ovoid to ovoid-elliptic, up to 10cm (4") high. Leaves are strap-like, linear, acute and up to 40cm (16") long. Flowers are fragrant and 4cm (1½") long.

Odontoglossum cariniferum

Odontoglossum rossii

COMMON NAME: None.
COLOUR: Flowers lemon, white or pink; sepals barred red-brown. Labellum white with yellow callus.
SIZE: Growing up to 20cm (8") high.
CLIMATE: Warm.
DISTRIBUTION: Native to Mexico, Honduras, Guatemala and Nicaragua.
FLOWERING TIME: Spring.
DESCRIPTION: Pseudobulbs are compressed, wrinkling when old and measure up to 6cm (2½"). Leaves are lanceolate-elliptic and up to 20cm (8") long. Erect inflorescence is up to 20cm (8") high. Flowers are 7.5cm (3") across.

Odontoglossum rossii

Odontoglossum stellatum

COMMON NAME: None.
COLOUR: Flowers bronze or purple with yellow apex and petals may be yellow-white. Labellum pink or white, tinted with mauve.
SIZE: Growing up to 20cm (8") high.
CLIMATE: Warm.
DISTRIBUTION: Native to Mexico and Guatemala.
FLOWERING TIME: Spring.
DESCRIPTION: Pseudobulbs are clustered, almost cylindrical, up to 5cm (2") high. Solitary leaf is narrowing and folding at the base and measures up to 15cm (6") long. Flowers are about 5cm (2") across.

Odontoglossum stellatum

ONCIDIUM

(on-sid-ee-um)

Oncidium comes from the Gk *onkos* (pad or mass) with reference to the fleshy, warty callus of the labellum. This is one of the largest and most cultivated of genera. At the same time it is very controversial, for the taxonomists who try to delineate between *Miltonia, Odontoglossum* and *Oncidium*. The latter is a genus of over seven hundred species, widespread from Florida (U.S.A.) to Mexico, and throughout tropical and subtropical America to Argentina, Brazil and the Andes of Colombia, Ecuador and Peru.

Oncidium is not an easy genus to describe. All segments of the plants are extremely variable. Primarily *Oncidiums* are epiphytic, with several lithophytic species growing on rock outcrops; while another group exists as pure terrestrials. Often the pseudobulbs are compressed, while other plants appear to be without pseudobulbs. The leaves may be papery, rigid, fleshy, coriaceous, distichous, flat, terete or deltoid. Inflorescence is usually from the base of the pseudobulb with one, two or several flowers. Their colours may be yellow and brown, or of a different hue such as white, magenta or red. The flower size also is quite variable from small to large, up to 7.5cm (5″) across. Sepals and petals are free and of various shapes. The labellum is tri-lobed and usually pandurate, but with many variations.

Culture: Compost in well-drained pots. Plants require humid conditions. Water frequently. They are most intolerant to stale conditions. Care must be taken with fragile new growth; do not allow water to lie around newly growing tips as rotting may occur. *Oncidium* is popular in collections.

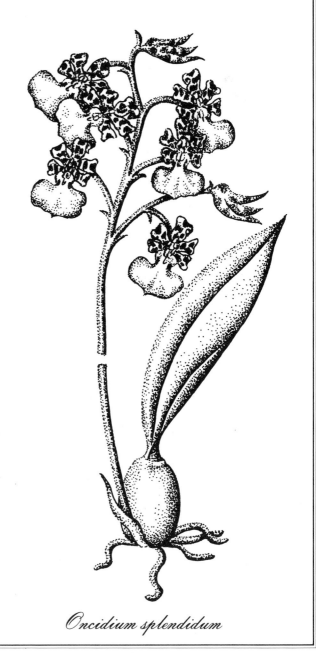

Oncidium splendidum

SOUTH AMERICA

Oncidium ampliatum

COMMON NAME: None.
COLOUR: Flowers yellow, spotted with red-brown. Labellum tri-lobed, white with red spots.
SIZE: Growing up to 50cm (20″) high.
CLIMATE: Intermediate to warm.
DISTRIBUTION: Native to Peru, Guatemala, Venezuela and Trinidad.
FLOWERING TIME: Spring.
DESCRIPTION: Pseudobulbs are clustered, compressed, ovoid, up to 12.5 cm (5″) high. Leaves are elliptic-oblanceolate, up to 38cm (15″) long. Inflorescence is erect, up to 1.2m (4′) long. Flower size is variable, about 2.5cm (1″) across. Labellum is tri-lobed.

Oncidium ampliatum

Oncidium barbatum

COMMON NAME: None.
COLOUR: Flowers yellow, marked red-brown. Labellum yellow, the crest spotted red.
SIZE: Growing up to 16.5cm (6½″) high.
CLIMATE: Intermediate.
DISTRIBUTION: Native to Brazil.
FLOWERING TIME: Spring.
DESCRIPTION: Pseudobulbs are compressed, clustered, oval-oblong, up to 6.5cm (2½″). Solitary leaf is linear to oval-oblong and up to 10cm (4″) long. Inflorescence is slightly panicled, up to 35cm (14″) long. Flowers are waxy and up to 4cm (1½″) long.

Oncidium barbatum

Oncidium carthagenense syn. *O. kymatoides*

COMMON NAME: None.
COLOUR: Flowers white or ochre yellow, blotched red-brown, lilac or red-purple.
SIZE: Growing up to 40cm (16″) high.
CLIMATE: Intermediate to warm.
DISTRIBUTION: Native to Mexico, Venezuela, Brazil, southern Florida (U.S.A.) and the West Indies. A common widespread epiphytic plant, growing from sea level to 1500m (4291′).
FLOWERING TIME: Spring to summer.
DESCRIPTION: Pseudobulbs are up to 2.5cm (1″) high and are covered by sheaths. Solitary leaf is apical lanceolate, oblong-elliptic, acute and up to 40cm (16″) long. Inflorescence is paniculate, erect with numerous flowers. Inflorescence is up to 2m (6′6″) long. Flowers are showy and 2.5cm (1″) across.

Oncidium carthagenense syn. *O. kymatoides*

Oncidium cavendishianum

COMMON NAME: None.
COLOUR: Flowers may be entirely yellow, but are generally yellow-green, spotted with red. Labellum yellow.
SIZE: Growing up to 60cm (2′) high.
CLIMATE: Warm.
DISTRIBUTION: Native to Mexico and Guatemala.
FLOWERING TIME: Winter to early spring.
DESCRIPTION: Pseudobulbs are small, borne from a robust rhizome. Leaves are oblong-lanceolate and up to 60cm (2′) high. Inflorescence is erect and up to 90cm (3′) long. Flowers are waxy, fragrant and about 4cm (1½″) across. Labellum is tri-lobed.

Oncidium cavendishianum

Oncidium crispum

COMMON NAME: None.
COLOUR: Flowers brown. Labellum brown-yellow, blotched red-brown.
SIZE: Growing up to 30cm (12″) high.
CLIMATE: Intermediate.
DISTRIBUTION: Native to Brazil.
FLOWERING TIME: Summer.
DESCRIPTION: Pseudobulbs are clustered, compressed, oblong, furrowed and ribbed on the flat side and are up to 10cm (4″) high. Leaves are lanceolate-oblong, acute, and grow up to 20cm (8″) long. Erect inflorescence are up to 90cm (3′) long, carrying as many as 80 blooms. Flowers are variable in size, but are about 7.5cm (3″) across.

Oncidium crispum

Oncidium enderianum syn. *O. crispum*
var. *grandiflorum*

Oncidium enderianum syn. O. crispum var. grandiflorum

COMMON NAME: None.
COLOUR: Flowers brown, margins slightly edged with yellow. Labellum brown, splashed yellow; orange callus.
SIZE: Growing up to 30cm (12″) high.
CLIMATE: Intermediate.
DISTRIBUTION: Native to the southern mountains of Brazil.
FLOWERING TIME: Autumn.
DESCRIPTION: Pseudobulbs are compressed, ovate, furrowed and up to 10cm (4″) high. Leaves are broad-lanceolate, up to 20cm (8″) long. Inflorescence is branching, 90cm (3′) long with numerous flowers. Flowers are up to 6cm (2½″) across.

Oncidium longipes

Oncidium flexuosum

COMMON NAME: None.
COLOUR: Flowers deep yellow, generally with a red blotch at the base of segments.
SIZE: Growing up to 30.5cm (12″) high.
CLIMATE: Intermediate.
DISTRIBUTION: Native to Brazil, Paraguay and Uruguay.
FLOWERING TIME: Autumn to winter.
DESCRIPTION: Pseudobulbs are compressed, oblong-oval, up to 7.5cm (3″) high. Predominantly two leaves, linear to linear-lanceolate, acute and up to 23cm (9″) long. Inflorescence is up to 90cm (3′) long. Flowers are numerous and up to 3cm (1¼″) long.

Oncidium gravesianum

Oncidium gravesianum

COMMON NAME: None.
COLOUR: Flowers brown. Labellum blotched yellow.
SIZE: Growing up to 15cm (6″) high.
CLIMATE: Intermediate.
DISTRIBUTION: Native to Mexico and Panama.
FLOWERING TIME: Autumn.
DESCRIPTION: Pseudobulbs are compressed, up to 5cm (2″) high. Leaves are narrow-lanceolate and up to 15cm (6″) long. Inflorescence is basal and 45cm (18″) long. Flowers are large, showy, with variable colour and are up to 7.5cm (3″) across.

Oncidium flexuosum

Oncidium leaneri

COMMON NAME: None.
COLOUR: Flowers yellow with brown markings.
SIZE: Growing up to 50cm (20″) high.
CLIMATE: Intermediate.
DISTRIBUTION: Native to Brazil.
FLOWERING TIME: Autumn.
DESCRIPTION: Pseudobulbs are compressed, furrowed, conical, up to 15cm (6″) long. Leaves are strap-shaped, acute and up to 50cm (20″) long. Branching inflorescence is up to 1.5m (5′) and densely flowered. Flowers are 4cm (1½″) long.

Oncidium leaneri

Oncidium longipes

COMMON NAME: None.
COLOUR: Flowers yellow, blotched with brown. Labellum yellow, marked with red-brown.
SIZE: Growing up to 15cm (6″) high.
CLIMATE: Intermediate.
DISTRIBUTION: Native to Brazil.
FLOWERING TIME: Summer to autumn.
DESCRIPTION: Closely allied to *O. uniflorum*. Pseudobulbs are ovoid and up to 2.5cm (1″) high. One to two leaves are linear-lanceolate and up to 15cm (6″) long. Inflorescence is short. Flower is up to 4cm (1½″) long.

Oncidium ornithorhynchum

COMMON NAME: Bird Beak Orchid.
COLOUR: Flowers pink-lilac.
SIZE: Growing up to 35cm (14") high.
CLIMATE: Intermediate.
DISTRIBUTION: Native to Mexico, Costa Rica, El Savador and Guatemala.
FLOWERING TIME: Winter.
DESCRIPTION: Pseudobulbs are clustered, somewhat compressed, oblong-oval, and 12.5cm (5") high. Leaves are linear-lanceolate, acute and up to 30cm (12") long. Inflorescence is up to 60cm (2') long. Flowers are numerous, fragrant and 2cm (¾") long.

Oncidium ornithorhynchum

Oncidium papilio syn. Psychopsis picta

Oncidium papilio syn. Psychopsis picta

COMMON NAME: None.
COLOUR: Flowers yellow with orange-brown markings.
SIZE: Growing up to 25cm (10") high.
CLIMATE: Warm.
DISTRIBUTION: Native to Trinidad, Venezuela, Colombia, Ecuador and Peru. A widespread epiphytic plant, growing in the lower montane forests.
FLOWERING TIME: Throughout the year.
DESCRIPTION: Pseudobulbs are compressed, wrinkled, clustered, orbicular and up to 5cm (2") high. Leaves are oblong-elliptic, mottled maroon, obtuse and up to 20cm (8") long. Inflorescence is up to 90cm (3') long. Flowers are up to 10cm (4") long.

Oncidium rio grandense

COMMON NAME: None.
COLOUR: Flowers yellow.
SIZE: Growing up to 20cm (8") high.
CLIMATE: Cool to intermediate.
DISTRIBUTION: Native to Brazil.
FLOWERING TIME: Summer.
DESCRIPTION: A medium sized epiphytic plant. Pseudobulbs are cylindrical, slightly compressed, furrowed and up to 10cm (4") high. Bracts are sheathing for three-quarters of the length of the pseudobulbs. Leaves are apical, lanceolate and up to 10cm (4") long. Inflorescence rises from basal sheathing bracts, up to 25cm (10") long; raceme has up to 15 blooms or more. Flowers are 2.5cm (1") across.

Oncidium rio grandense

Oncidium sphacelatum

Oncidium sphacelatum

COMMON NAME: None.
COLOUR: Flowers variable, yellow, barred red-brown.
SIZE: Growing up to 75cm (30") high.
CLIMATE: Intermediate.
DISTRIBUTION: Native to Mexico, British Honduras, Guatemala, El Salvador and Honduras.
FLOWERING TIME: Spring.
DESCRIPTION: Pseudobulbs are compressed, almost oblong and up to 20cm (8") high. Leaves are linear, strap-shaped and grow up to 60cm (2'). Inflorescence is branched, up to 1.5m (5'). Numerous flowers are up to 3cm (1¼") across.

Oncidium splendidum

COMMON NAME: None.
COLOUR: Flowers yellow, spotted and blotched, red-brown. Labellum deep yellow.
SIZE: Growing up to 35cm (14″) high.
CLIMATE: Warm.
DISTRIBUTION: Native to Honduras and Guatemala.
FLOWERING TIME: Spring to early summer.
DESCRIPTION: Pseudobulbs are clustered, ovoid, somewhat compressed and up to 5cm (2″) high. Solitary leaf is oblong to oblong-elliptic, acute, keeled behind and up to 30cm (12″) long. Inflorescence is up to 120cm (4′) long. Flowers are showy and 7.5cm (3″) long.

Oncidium splendidum

Oncidium stipitatum

Oncidium stipitatum

COMMON NAME: None.
COLOUR: Flowers yellow, marked with red-brown.
SIZE: Growing up to 60cm (2′) high.
CLIMATE: Warm.
DISTRIBUTION: Native to Panama, Honduras and Nicaragua.
FLOWERING TIME: Summer.
DESCRIPTION: Pseudobulbs are very small, almost obsolete. Solitary leaf is terete, acuminate and up to 65cm (26″) long. Flowers are clustered, numerous, variable in size, about 2.5cm (1″) long.

Oncidium teres

Oncidium teres

COMMON NAME: None.
COLOUR: Flowers yellow with red-brown spots.
SIZE: Growing up to 60cm (2′) high.
CLIMATE: Warm.
DISTRIBUTION: Native to Panama.
FLOWERING TIME: Winter to spring.
DESCRIPTION: Pseudobulbs are very small. Solitary leaf is terete, acuminate and up to 65cm (26″) long. Flowers are clustered, numerous, variable in size, but about 1cm (½″) long. Inflorescence is up to 45cm (18″) long.

Oncidium wentworthianum

COMMON NAME: None.
COLOUR: Flowers yellow, blotched red-brown.
SIZE: Growing up to 40cm (16″) high.
CLIMATE: Intermediate.
DISTRIBUTION: Native to Mexico, Guatemala; growing at an altitude of 1500m (5000′).
FLOWERING TIME: Summer to autumn.
DESCRIPTION: Pseudobulbs are compressed, ovoid-ellipsoid, up to 10cm (4″) high. Leaves are strap-shaped, acute, up to 35cm (14″) long. Inflorescence is paniculate and up to 2m (6′6″) long. Flowers are numerous and 3cm (1¼″) across.

Oncidium wentworthianum

ORTHOCERAS
(or-tho-ser-as)

*O*rthoceras from the Gk *orthos* (straight, upright) and *ceras* (horn) with reference to the lateral sepals which spread like the horns of a buffalo. This genus of a single terrestrial species is found in Australia, New Zealand and New Caledonia. The genus is similar to *Diuris*, but differs from that genus in technical detail—the almost sessile flowers, the minute sessile petals and the erect filiform lateral sepals. Although cultivated by several Australian species growers, the genus is not found in many collections.

Culture: As for *Caladenia*, which is not easy to grow. Plants require rich, well-drained, free moving compost. In pots, use broken crock, granulated or crushed brick, topped with equal parts of shredded tree-fern, leaf mould, crumbled loam, sharp, gritty sand and sphagnum moss. Use liquid fertiliser regularly.

Orthoceras strictum

Orthoceras strictum

Orthoceras strictum

COMMON NAME: Bird Beak Orchid or Horned Orchid.
COLOUR: Flowers green-purple-brown.
SIZE: Robust terrestrial, up to 75cm (29½″) high.
CLIMATE: Cool.
DISTRIBUTION: Native to eastern Australia (Tasmania), New Zealand and New Caledonia; grows close to damp, swampy areas.
FLOWERING TIME: Late spring to early summer.
DESCRIPTION: Robust terrestrial, up to 75cm (30″) high. Leaves are radical, linear and channelled. The one to nine flowers are 2cm (¾″) long. Dorsal sepal has the appearance of a bird's beak.

PAPHIOPEDILUM

(paf-ee-oh-ped-i-lum)

Paphiopedilum from the Gk *paphos* (the island with a temple dedicated to Venus) and *pedilon* (sandal) meaning Venus' sandal or ladies' slipper. This is a genus of about one hundred species of terrestrial or occasionally epiphytic orchids. It is widespread from India, Burma, South-east Asia, China, Malaysia, Java, Borneo, the Philippines, Papua New Guinea to the Solomon Islands. *Paphiopedilums* are unique and unmistakable. They are stemless, pseudobulbless, sympodial plants, with fans of conduplicate coriaceous leaves. Each fan comprises six or more leaves. Flowers can be single or a few in number. The dorsal sepal is showy; lateral sepals are fused to form a symsepalum almost hidden by the labellum. The lateral petals are long and narrow, often with wavy margins and tufts of hairs. Because of the fusion of the sepals, the petals may be mistaken for sepals. The labellum is saccate, pouch-forming, with side lobes incurved. *Paphiopedilum* is closely related to *Cypripedium, Phragmipedium* and *Selenipedium*. All four are often referred to as 'Cyps', having been treated in the past as one genus, *Cypripedium*.

In 1896, R. A. Rolfe established the following key to separate the genera: (a) Leaves plicate, alternate; rhizome prominent; ieafy shoots with conspicuous internodes: (i) *Selenipedium* (three species). Leafy shoots often branching; inflorescence of numerous small flowers having trilocular ovaries; up to 3m (10') tall; Central and South America. (ii) *Cypripedium* (about 28 species). Leafy shoots never branching; inflorescence of numerous small flowers with unilocular ovaries; up to 1m (40") tall; temperate and subtropical America. (b) Leaves conduplicate, distichous; rhizomes present but condensed; leafy shoots without conspicuous internodes; often with lengthy axillary inflorescence: (i) *Paphiopedilum* (about 60 species). Sepals imbricate in bud; unilocular ovaries; South-east Asia. (ii) *Phragmipedium* (about 12 species). Sepals valvate in bud; trilocular ovaries; Central and South America.

Culture: Compost. Species such as *P. insigne* require 'cool-house' conditions and species such as *P. concolor* require 'warm-house' conditions. All species require humid conditions, shade from direct sunlight and good air movement. Water frequently as plants are unable to store water. Never allow plants to become dry.

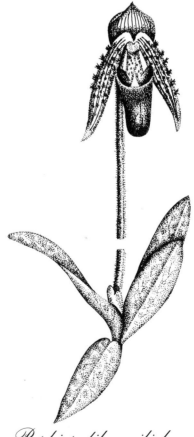

Paphiopedilum ciliolare

Paphiopedilum acmodontum

COMMON NAME: None.
COLOUR: Flower a blend of white, pink and green with red-brown spots and vertical veins.
SIZE: Growing up to 25cm (10″) high.
CLIMATE: Intermediate.
DISTRIBUTION: Native to the Philippines (Visayan areas).
FLOWERING TIME: Late spring.
DESCRIPTION: Leaves are broad-ovate, tessellated with dark green or light green and are up to 30cm (12″) long. Flower scape is up to 30cm (12″) high and usually solitary. Labellum is pouched.

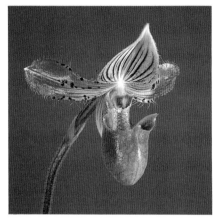

Paphiopedilum acmodontum

Paphiopedilum adductum

COMMON NAME: None.
COLOUR: Flowers white, with crimson vertical veins; petals white, blotched with crimson. Labellum white, veined, tinted with rose-pink.
SIZE: Growing up to 40cm (16″) high.
CLIMATE: Warm.
DISTRIBUTION: Native to Mindanao in the Philippines.
FLOWERING TIME: Summer.
DESCRIPTION: Leaves up to 45cm (18″) long. Flower scape bears up to five blooms. Pouched labellum.

Paphiopedilum adductum

Paphiopedilum appletonianum

COMMON NAME: None.
COLOUR: Flowers white with green and brown vertical veins. Petals marked with black-purple hairy warts. Labellum green-brown.
SIZE: Growing up to 15cm (6″) high.
CLIMATE: Cool to intermediate.
DISTRIBUTION: Native to Thailand, Himalayas, Assam and south-western Laos.
FLOWERING TIME: Late winter to early spring.
DESCRIPTION: Leaves are strap-shaped, up to 17.5cm (7″) long and faintly tessellated. Scape up to 45cm (18″) high. Solitary flower is about 10cm (4″) across.

Paphiopedilum appletonianum

Paphiopedilum argus

COMMON NAME: None.
COLOUR: Flower white with green vertical veins. Petals covered in black-purple hairy warts. Labellum brown-purple with green veins.
SIZE: Growing up to 25cm (10″) high.
CLIMATE: Cool to intermediate.
DISTRIBUTION: Native to the Philippines, Negros and Luzon. Growing at an altitude of 700 to 3000m (2300 to 10 000′).
FLOWERING TIME: Spring to early summer.
DESCRIPTION: Leaves are strap-shaped, dark green, tessellated with yellow-green and up to 30cm (12″) long. Flower scape is up to 60cm (2′) high. Flower is solitary and 10cm (4″) across.

Paphiopedilum argus

Paphiopedilum armeniacum

COMMON NAME: None.
COLOUR: Flower yellow.
SIZE: A small growing species.
CLIMATE: Intermediate.
DISTRIBUTION: Native to China—Bijiang, south Yunnan.
FLOWERING TIME: Spring.
DESCRIPTION: Leaves are oblong, up to 12.5cm (5″) long, with white tessellation and underside spotted with purple. Scape is up to 25cm (10″) high. Solitary flower has a pouched labellum.

Paphiopedilum armeniacum

Paphiopedilum barbatum

COMMON NAME: None.
COLOUR: Flower green-white, dark warts on petals, green and purple vertical stripes. Labellum brown-purple.
SIZE: Growing up to 25cm (10″) high.
CLIMATE: Intermediate.
DISTRIBUTION: Native to Peninsula Maylasia and coastal islands, Sumatra, Thailand and Mt Ophir, Singapore. Habitat is mountains at elevation of 200 to 1300m (1200 to 4000′). Preference for intermediate temperature and moist sheltered conditions.
FLOWERING TIME: Spring to autumn.
DESCRIPTION: Leaves are mottled, underside silver-green, and grow up to 30cm (12″) long. Scape is up to 35cm (14″) high. Flower is 10cm (4″) across.

Paphiopedilum barbatum

Paphiopedilum bellatulum syn. Cypripedium bellatulum

COMMON NAME: None.
COLOUR: Flower white, densely spotted with purple.
SIZE: Growing up to 30cm (12″) high.
CLIMATE: Cool to intermediate.
DISTRIBUTION: Native to Thailand, Burma (Moulmein); grows in limestone country at elevations of 1000 to 1600m (3300 to 5300′). Habitat varies from exposed cliff faces to moist mossy areas.
FLOWERING TIME: Spring to summer.
DESCRIPTION: Varied conditions affect leaf growth; they range from 20cm × 6cm (8″ × 2½″) wide in ideal conditions to 10cm × 3cm (4″ × 1¼″) in drier conditions. Leaves are narrow-elliptic, pale green mottled and under-surface is purple-maroon. Scape is short. Solitary flower is 8cm (3¼″) across.

Paphiopedilum bellatulum syn. *Cypripedium bellatulum*

Paphiopedilum birkii syn. P. sublaeve

COMMON NAME: None.
COLOUR: Flowers a blend of white, green and rose-pink. Labellum pouch rose-pink.
SIZE: Growing up to 25cm (10″) high.
CLIMATE: Intermediate to warm.
DISTRIBUTION: Native to western Malaysia, (Kedah Peak). It is a terrestrial liking warm conditions.
FLOWERING TIME: Summer.
DESCRIPTION: Leaves are up to 22.5cm (9″) long, are tessellated and lanceolate. Flower scape bears one to two blooms. Flowers are about 10cm (4″) across.

Paphiopedilum callosum

Paphiopedilum callosum

COMMON NAME: None.
COLOUR: Flower colour variable: white and green, purple-pink and green veins, black warts on petals. Labellum brown-purple.
SIZE: Growing up to 30cm (12″) high.
CLIMATE: Intermediate.
DISTRIBUTION: Native to Thailand and Cambodia. Grows at an altitude of 600 to 1200m (2000 to 4000′), lower slopes of mountains in moist areas.
FLOWERING TIME: Spring to summer.
DESCRIPTION: Leaves are tessellated and up to 22.5cm (9″) long. Scape is 40cm (16″) high. Flower is solitary and 9cm (3½″) across.

Paphiopedilum birkii syn. *P. sublaeve*

Paphiopedilum charlesworthii

COMMON NAME: None.
COLOUR: Dorsal sepal rose-pink, veins darker; rest of flower yellow-brown with darker veins.
SIZE: Growing up to 30cm (12″) high.
CLIMATE: Cool.
DISTRIBUTION: Native to Burma (Arakan Mountains), India (Bengal). Grows at an altitude of 1700m (5500′) on limestone mountains with westerly or north-westerly positions.
FLOWERING TIME: Autumn.
DESCRIPTION: Leaves are broad-linear, up to 20cm (8″) long and undersides are dotted with purple. Scape is up to 15cm (6″) high. Solitary flower is about 10cm (4″) across.

Paphiopedilum charlesworthii

Paphiopedilum ciliolare

Paphiopedilum ciliolare

COMMON NAME: None.
COLOUR: Flower blend of white and green with purple and green vertical veins, purple spots and warts. Labellum green-brown.
SIZE: Growing up to 25cm (10″) high.
CLIMATE: Intermediate.
DISTRIBUTION: Native to the Philippines (Luzon, Dinagat and Mindanao).
FLOWERING TIME: Spring to early summer.
DESCRIPTION: Broad, strap-shaped leaves with tessellation grow up to 17.5cm (7″) long. Scape is up to 30cm (12″) high. Solitary flower is about 10cm (4″) across.

Paphiopedilum concolor

Paphiopedilum concolor

COMMON NAME: None.
COLOUR: Flower colour variable, usually cream-yellow, spotted maroon-purple.
SIZE: Growing up to 30cm (12″) high.
CLIMATE: Intermediate.
DISTRIBUTION: Native to southern Thailand, southern Burma, Cambodia, Laos and Vietnam. Found growing at elevations of 300 to 1000m (1000 to 3300′) in limestone crevices near coastal areas, liking intermediate conditions.
FLOWERING TIME: Summer to autumn.
DESCRIPTION: Leaves are up to 15cm (6″) long, dark mottled green, underside spotted red-purple. Flower scape is up to 8cm (3″) long, bearing up to three blooms. Flower is up to 7.5cm (3″) across.

Paphiopedilum fairrieanum

Paphiopedilum delenatii

COMMON NAME: None.
COLOUR: Flower white tinted with pink. Labellum white and pink, tinted with lilac.
SIZE: Growing up to 15cm (6″) high.
CLIMATE: Warm.
DISTRIBUTION: Native to North and central Vietnam. Growing in crevices of limestone mountains, at low altitudes.
FLOWERING TIME: Spring to early summer.
DESCRIPTION: Leaves are rigid and thick with tessellation, underside green mottled with red-purple. Scape is up to 20cm (8″) high. Flower has a velvet texture. Labellum is almost rounded.

Paphiopedilum esquirolei

Paphiopedilum esquirolei

COMMON NAME: None.
COLOUR: Flower cream-green, with purple-brown suffusions and purple vertical veins and spots. Labellum cream-green, spotted with pink-purple.
SIZE: Growing up to 45cm (18″) across.
CLIMATE: Cool to intermediate.
DISTRIBUTION: Native to northern Thailand and southern China.
FLOWERING TIME: Spring.
DESCRIPTION: Leaves are notched apically, keeled, glossy green and 30cm (12″) long. Scape 20cm (8″) high. Flower is 14cm (5½″) across; labellum is helmet-shaped.

Paphiopedilum delenatii

Paphiopedilum fairrieanum

COMMON NAME: None.
COLOUR: Flower colour variable; blend of white and green with purple marks and veining. Labellum green with purple veins.
SIZE: Growing up to 30cm (12″) across.
CLIMATE: Cool.
DISTRIBUTION: Native to Himalayas, northern Burma, Bhutan and Assam in India. Grows on the edges of high river banks and forests at an altitude of 1200 to 3000m (4000 to 10 000′).
FLOWERING TIME: Late autumn.
DESCRIPTION: Leaves are channelled and up to 15cm (6″) long. Scape is up to 25cm (10″) high; usually has a solitary flower, 6cm (2½″) across.

Paphiopedilum fowliei

COMMON NAME: None.

COLOUR: Flower a blend of white, green, pink-purple with red-brown and green veining, dark warts. Labellum yellow-brown, veined dark brown.

SIZE: Growing up to 20cm (8″) across.

CLIMATE: Intermediate to warm.

DISTRIBUTION: Native to the Philippines and Palana Island. A lithophytic species, growing in leaf mould on limestone at an altitude of 700m (2300′).

FLOWERING TIME: Summer.

DESCRIPTION: Leaves are narrow elliptical, tessellated and up to 14 cm (5½″) long. Scape is up to 28cm (11″) high. Flower is about 10cm (4″) across.

Paphiopedilum fowliei

Paphiopedilum glaucophyllum

COMMON NAME: None.

COLOUR: Flowers pale green, stripes and marks brown. Labellum pouched, mauve-pink.

SIZE: Growing up to 40cm (16″) across..

CLIMATE: Warm.

DISTRIBUTION: Native to central Sumatra and Java. Habitat is rock pockets of humus on volcanic mountain slopes. Elevation 200 to 300m (660 to 1000′).

FLOWERING TIME: Spring to summer.

DESCRIPTION: Leaves are broad, strap-shaped, obtuse and 25cm (10″) long. Scape is up to 40cm (16″) high. Several flowers are 7cm (3″) across.

Paphiopedilum glaucophyllum

Paphiopedilum gratrixianum

COMMON NAME: None.

COLOUR: Flower blend of white, yellow-brown and green, spotted with brown-purple. Labellum cream-brown.

SIZE: Growing up to 22.5cm (9″) high.

CLIMATE: Cool to intermediate.

DISTRIBUTION: Native to central Vietnam.

FLOWERING TIME: Winter.

DESCRIPTION: Leaves are up to 22.5cm (9″) long. Solitary flower is similar in shape to *P. villosum*, but has a spotted dorsal sepal.

Paphiopedilum gratrixianum

Paphiopedilum haynaldianum

COMMON NAME: None.

COLOUR: Flower blend of yellow-green, pink with large brown apical spots, suffused with brown. Labellum helmet-shaped, yellow-green, suffused with brown-purple.

SIZE: Growing up to 30cm (12″) high.

CLIMATE: Warm.

DISTRIBUTION: Native to the Philippines (Luzon). Grows on mountain slopes at an altitude of over 1000m (3300′).

FLOWERING TIME: Spring to summer.

DESCRIPTION: Leaves are strap-shaped and up to 30cm (12″) long. Scape bears up to six blooms and is up to 50cm (20″) high. Flower is about 15cm (6″) across.

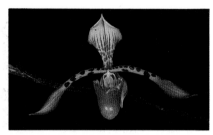

Paphiopedilum haynaldianum

Paphiopedilum hirsutissimum

COMMON NAME: None.

COLOUR: Flower blend of green and purple-pink, speckled with dark purple. Labellum helmet-shaped, green tinted and speckled with purple and tiny black warts.

SIZE: Growing up to 30cm (12″) high.

CLIMATE: Cool.

DISTRIBUTION: Native to Himalayas, Assam, Khasi Hills, Thailand and Burma. A terrestrial often found in epiphytic or lithophytic habitat. Grows at an altitude of 1000 to 1300m (3300 to 4300′).

FLOWERING TIME: Autumn to spring; early summer.

DESCRIPTION: Leaves are linear-oblong, keeled, acute and up to 30cm (12″) long. Flower scape is up to 30cm (12″) high. Solitary flower is up to 15cm (6″) across.

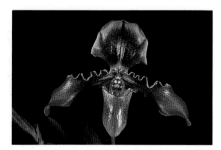

Paphiopedilum hirsutissimum

Paphiopedilum insigne

Paphiopedilum insigne

COMMON NAME: None.
COLOUR: Flower blend of white, light green with purple-brown spots and veining. Labellum helmet-shaped, yellow-green with brown marking.
SIZE: Growing up to 30cm (12″) high.
CLIMATE: Cool.
DISTRIBUTION: Native to Himalayas, Sylhet (Bangladesh), Nepal and Assam. Grows in exposed areas.
FLOWERING TIME: Autumn, winter, spring.
DESCRIPTION: Leaves are linear, acute and up to 30cm (12″) long. Scape is up to 27.5cm (11″) high. Solitary flower is about 10cm (4″) across. Labellum helmet-shaped. A common species of many varieties and prolific flowering.

Paphiopedilum insigne var. *Harefield Hall*

Paphiopedilum insigne var. Harefield Hall

COMMON NAME: None.
COLOUR: Flower purple-brown.
SIZE: Growing up to 30cm (12″) high.
CLIMATE: Cool.
DISTRIBUTION: Nepal, Assam.
FLOWERING TIME: Winter.
DESCRIPTION: Similar to *P. insigne*, but flower is much larger than the type form, 14cm (5½″) across. Flower is hairy and has shiny texture.

Paphiopedilum insigne var. *sanderae*

Paphiopedilum insigne var. sanderae

COMMON NAME: None.
COLOUR: Dorsal sepal light green with white margins, sparsely speckled with brown. Petals green. Labellum yellow-brown.
SIZE: Grows up to 30cm (12″) high.
CLIMATE: Cool.
DISTRIBUTION: Nepal, Assam.
FLOWERING TIME: Autumn, winter.
DESCRIPTION: Flower scape is up to 25cm (10″) high. Flower is about 12cm (5″) across. Labellum helmet-shaped.

Paphiopedilum javanicum var. *virens*

Paphiopedilum javanicum var. virens

COMMON NAME: None.
COLOUR: Flowers light green; petal base light green; lamina rose-pink with white margins. Labellum pale brown-green, lightly veined.
SIZE: Growing up to 30cm (12″) tall.
CLIMATE: Intermediate to warm.
DISTRIBUTION: Native to Mt Kinabalu, northern Borneo.
FLOWERING TIME: Autumn to winter.
DESCRIPTION: Closely allied to *P. virens*. Found growing in dense shade. Leaves 10 to 15cm (4 to 6″) long, pointed and coloured grey-green. Flower scape is up to 30cm (12″) high. Dorsal sepal is broad, pointed, light green with longitudinal dark striations and is horizontal. Petal bases are green, blade rose-pink with white margins. Petal margins are dotted with blackish warts and rose-purple ciliate. Labellum is pale brown-green and lightly veined. Staminode has green centre; upper margin white with three lobes; lower margin yellow-green with two lobes pointing downward.

Paphiopedilum malipoensis

COMMON NAME: None.
COLOUR: Flower green.
SIZE: Growing up to 15cm (6″) high.
CLIMATE: Intermediate.
DISTRIBUTION: Native to China.
FLOWERING TIME: Spring.
DESCRIPTION: Leaves are green, tessellated green, underside purple, margins wavy, broad-lanceolate and up to 15cm (6″) long. Inflorescence is up to 30cm (12″) high. Flower is solitary.

Paphiopedilum malipoensis

Paphiopedilum micranthum

Paphiopedilum micranthum

COMMON NAME: None.
COLOUR: Flower cream-white, tinted and veined with pink-purple.
SIZE: Growing up to 20cm (8″) across.
CLIMATE: Intermediate.
DISTRIBUTION: Native to China (south-east Yunnan).
FLOWERING TIME: Spring.
DESCRIPTION: A dwarf terrestrial. Leaves are oblong, obtuse with spotted underside. Erect scape is up to 22.5cm (9″) high. Solitary flower resembles *Cypripidium* and is about 6cm across. Labellum is elliptical-ovate.

Paphiopedilum moquetteanum

COMMON NAME: None.
COLOUR: Flower a blend of yellow-green, white, spotted and marked with red-purple. Labellum rose-pink.
SIZE: Growing up to 25cm (10″) high.
CLIMATE: Warm.
DISTRIBUTION: Native to West Java and Bogor.
FLOWERING TIME: Summer.
DESCRIPTION: Leaves are 25cm (10″) long and scape is up to 40cm (16″) high. Flower measures 11cm (4½″) across. Petal margins are undulate, twisted and cimiate.

Paphiopedilum moquetteanum

Paphiopedilum niveum

Paphiopedilum niveum

COMMON NAME: None.
COLOUR: Flowers white, marked with fine purple spots.
SIZE: Growing up to 15cm (6″) high.
CLIMATE: Warm to hot.
DISTRIBUTION: Native to Thailand Peninsular, Malaysia, Satun, Borneo, Langkawi Island, Longcavi Island, and Tambulan Island.
FLOWERING TIME: Spring and summer.
DESCRIPTION: This dwarf species grows in crevices of limestone rocks close to the sea. Leaves are oblong, mottled green, underside purple, and grow up to 15cm (6″) long. Scape is short, 12cm (5″) high. Flowers are about 7cm (3″) across. Edges of dorsal sepal are waved.

Paphiopedilum parishii

COMMON NAME: None.
COLOUR: Flowers pale green; petals green turning red-purple towards the apex; margins with hairy, purple warts.
SIZE: Growing up to 30cm (12″) high.
CLIMATE: Cool to intermediate.
DISTRIBUTION: Native to Burma, Thailand and China. Found growing at elevations of 1200m (4000′).
FLOWERING TIME: Spring to summer.
DESCRIPTION: Leaves are 30 to 50cm (12 to 20″), arching, coriaceous with rounded tip. Inflorescence is up to 50cm (20″) high, branched with four to six flowers. Dorsal sepal is bent forward; petals are 12.5cm (5″) long, pendulous, twisted, with hairy warts along margins. Labellum is deep green tinged with purple. Staminode is pale yellow marbled with green. Similar in habit to *P. philippinense.*

Paphiopedilum sukhakulii

Paphiopedilum parishii

Paphiopedilum philippinense
(very similar to *P. roebbelenii*)

COMMON NAME: None.
COLOUR: Flowers a blend of white, yellow-green, veined purple-red. Labellum pouch cream-green.
SIZE: Growing up to 30cm (12″) high.
CLIMATE: Warm to hot.
DISTRIBUTION: Native to the Philippines, Guimares, Mindanao, Palawan to northern Borneo. Coastal terrestrial growing in association on the roots of *Vanda batemanii* in brightly lit positions, liking warm conditions.
FLOWERING TIME: Summer to autumn.
DESCRIPTION: Leaves are strap-shaped and up to 30cm (12″) long. Flower scape is up to 40cm (16″) long. Flowers are large. Petals are linear, pendulous, twisted and up to 15cm (6″) long.

Paphiopedilum sukhakulii

COMMON NAME: None.
COLOUR: Flower blend of white-cream and green, spotted with red-purple. Labellum green with purple veining.
SIZE: Growing up to 30cm (12″) across.
CLIMATE: Intermediate.
DISTRIBUTION: Native to Vietnam and north-eastern Thailand. Grows at elevations up to 1000m (3250′), in leaf litter at the base of a tree, usually along creek banks and humid places. Grows in association with *P. callosum* at lower altitudes.
FLOWERING TIME: Autumn to winter.
DESCRIPTION: Leaves 20cm by 4cm wide (8″ by 1½″) tessellated, mottled green, absence of blotches at base of leaf helps to distinguish this plant from its close relative *P. wardii.* Solitary flower is about 16cm (6½″) across. Labellum is helmet-shaped.

Paphiopedilum philippinense

Paphiopedilum superbiens

Paphiopedilum superbiens

COMMON NAME: None.
COLOUR: Flower white, veined with purple and green. Petals white-pink veined with purple and black warts. Labellum purple.
SIZE: Growing up to 15cm (6″) high.
CLIMATE: Warm.
DISTRIBUTION: Native to Java, Sumatra and the islands of Malacca Straits. Grows at an altitude of 300m (1000′).
FLOWERING TIME: Spring to summer.
DESCRIPTION: Terrestrial herb. Leaves up to 15cm (6″) long, tessellated and elliptic to oblong. Flower scape is up to 30cm (12″) long. Flower is solitary; dorsal sepal is 4cm (1½″) across.

Paphiopedilum urbanianum

COMMON NAME: None.
COLOUR: Flowers blend of white, green and purple.
SIZE: Growing up to 20cm (8″) high.
CLIMATE: Warm.
DISTRIBUTION: Native to the Philippines (Mindoro). Semi-terrestrial growing at elevations of 500 to 800m (1600 to 2600′).
FLOWERING TIME: Autumn.
DESCRIPTION: Leaves are mottled, narrow-elliptic and up to 20cm (8″) long. Flower scape grows up to 25cm (10″) high. Flowers measure 12cm (5″) across.

Paphiopedilum urbanianum

Paphiopedilum venustum

Paphiopedilum venustum

COMMON NAME: None.
COLOUR: Flower blend of white with green, pink with dark warts.
SIZE: Growing up to 25cm (10″) across.
CLIMATE: Cool.
DISTRIBUTION: Native to Assam and Nepal. Growing at elevations of 1000 to 1500m (3300 to 5000′) in sheltered valleys.
FLOWERING TIME: Winter.
DESCRIPTION: Leaves are mottled, strap-shaped, elliptic and 15cm (6″) long. Flower scape grows up to 25cm (10″) high. Flower is 12cm (5″) across.

Paphiopedilum villosum

COMMON NAME: None.
COLOUR: Flower blend of white, green and maroon.
SIZE: Growing up to 35cm (14″) high.
CLIMATE: Cool.
DISTRIBUTION: Native to Thailand, Laos, Assam and Burma. Grows at elevations of 1200 to 1600m (4000 to 5200′). Found growing in decaying leaf mould and moss.
FLOWERING TIME: Autumn.
DESCRIPTION: Leaves are up to 35cm (14″) long and narrow-lanceolate. Flower scape is about 30cm (12″) high and flower about 12cm (5″) wide.

Paphiopedilum villosum

Paphiopedilum virens

Paphiopedilum virens

COMMON NAME: None.
COLOUR: Flower pale green with dark mottled marking.
SIZE: Growing up to 15cm (6″) high.
CLIMATE: Intermediate to warm.
DISTRIBUTION: Native to Mt Kinabalu and northern Borneo.
FLOWERING TIME: Spring, summer to autumn.
DESCRIPTION: Leaves are 10 to 12.5cm (4 to 5″) long. Flower grows to 10cm (4″) across. Closely allied to *P. javanicum*; the two main differences are the shape of the staminodes and the much lighter leaves. In *P. virens*, the staminode is wide, pink with a marble green centre. Upper incisure is v-shaped with lower margins having four incisions. In *P. javanicum*, the staminode is light green, darker markings in centre, white mark below upper margin, with two incisions on lower margin forming three lobes pointing downwards. Habitat is in semi-shade conditions.

PAPILIONANTHE
(pa-pil-ee-oh-nan-thee)

Papilionanthe from the Lat. *papilio* (butterfly) *anthos* (a flower) with reference to the resemblance of some flowers to a butterfly. This is an epiphytic, monopodial genus of some eleven species. It was first established in 1915 when Schlechter separated *Vanda teres* from other *Vanda* species creating a new genus *Papilionanthe*. The separation was based on the intermediate characteristics of *V. teres*, between *Vanda* and *Aerides*. This segregation was ignored by many and overlooked by others. On re-examining Schlechter's criteria of limitations, Leslie Garay agreed and added another ten species to the genus *Papilionanthe*. *Papilionanthe* differs from both *Vanda* and *Aerides* in the spur of the labellum and the structure of the column foot. *Papilionanthe* species are characterised by a short, stout, non-pyramidal column extending with a long prominant foot.

Culture: Compost. As for *Vanda*. Use large, well-drained pots or baskets. Pots and bench soon become overgrown because of strong aerial root growth.

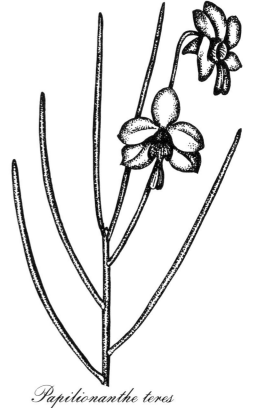

Papilionanthe teres

Papilionanthe teres syn. *Vanda teres*

Papilionanthe teres syn. *Vanda teres*

COMMON NAME: None.
COLOUR: Petals deep rose-pink, sepals white, tinged with rose-pink. Labellum yellow, outer lobe rose-pink, veined.
SIZE: Climbing.
CLIMATE: Warm.
DISTRIBUTION: Native to India and Burma.
FLOWERING TIME: Summer.
DESCRIPTION: Plant is large and showy. Leaves alternate terete and grow up to 20cm (8″) long. Labellum is large and tri-lobed. Flower measures up to 10cm (4″) across.

PESCATOREA
(pess-ka-tor-ee-ah)

Pescatorea is named after V. Pescatore of Chateau Cella St Cloud near Paris, who owned a very fine collection of orchids. *Pescatorea* is a small genus of about fifteen pseudobulbless epiphytic species, distributed from Costa Rica to Colombia. These spectacular orchids are closely allied to *Chondrorhyncha*, *Huntleya* and *Zygopetalum*. The distinguishing technical features are: (a) *Chondrorhyncha* lacks a conspicuous clawed labellum; (b) *Huntleya* has broad projecting apical column wings; (c) *Zygopetalum* has pseudobulbs. *Pescatorea* is an erect, tufted herb without pseudobulbs. Leaves are plicate, distichous and fan-shaped. Inflorescence is short and axillary. Flowers are large, showy and fragrant. Sepals and petals are fleshy and concave. The labellum is tri-lobed, fleshy with conspicuous linguate claw and the callus is deeply ribbed. These large, showy, wax-like, fragrant orchids are increasingly evident in collections and at orchid shows.

Culture: Compost as for *Zygopetalum*. Plants require shade and roots must be kept moist continually in perfectly drained pots.

SOUTH AMERICA

Pescatorea cerina

Pescatorea cerina

Pescatorea cerina

COMMON NAME: None.
COLOUR: Flower white. Labellum yellow.
SIZE: Growing up to 60cm (2') high.
CLIMATE: Warm.
DISTRIBUTION: Native to Panama and Costa Rica.
FLOWERING TIME: Autumn.
DESCRIPTION: Leaves are clustered in a loose fan arrangement, are linear-lanceolate and grow up to 60cm (2') long. Flower scape is 10cm (4") high. Flower is 7.5cm (3") across.

PHAIUS
(fay-us)

Phaius from the Gk *phaios* (dusky) with reference to the flowers which turn dark with age or if damaged. This is a genus of about thirty species. It is widespread throughout Africa, Madagascar, Asia, Indonesia, Papua New Guinea, Australia and the Pacific Islands. *Phaius* is a genus of robust sympodial terrestrial plants closely allied to *Calanthe*. Plants have pseudobulbs or stem-like pseudobulbs, each having up to eight large petiolate, plicate, grooved leaves. Inflorescence is from the base or is lateral on the pseudobulb, or emerges part way up the thickened stem. Flowers are often many, conspicuous, showy, moderately large, opening successively, remaining in bloom for a long period of time. Sepals and petals are fleshy and spreading. The labellum is tubular, extending into a basal spur, erect, convolute, spreading at the apex. Flower colours occur in a wide range of hues.

Culture: Coarse compost as for larger terrestrials, in perfectly drained pots. Roots need to be kept moist, not wet. Plants require shady cool conditions, with much less water once growth is complete. Excessive watering causes leaves to 'damp off'; so when watering avoid wetting leaves, otherwise they will go black.

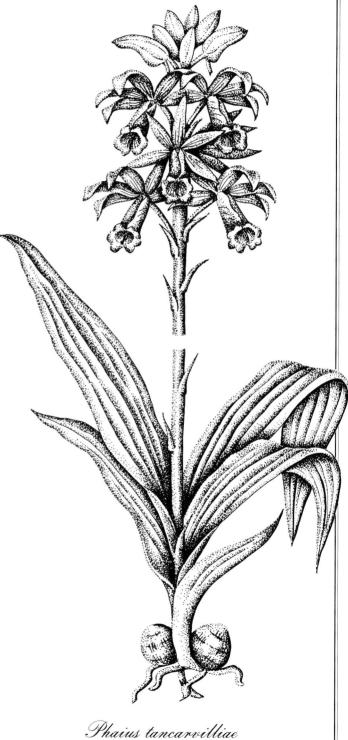

Phaius tancarvilliae

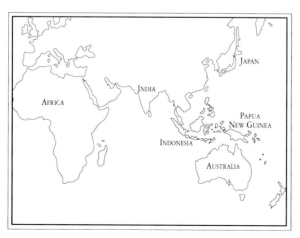

Phaius australis

COMMON NAME: Swamp Orchid.
COLOUR: A blend of red-brown and white.
SIZE: Growing up to 60cm (25″) high.
CLIMATE: Cool to intermediate.
DISTRIBUTION: Native to eastern Australia in moist areas.
FLOWERING TIME: Spring.
DESCRIPTION: Robust terrestrial species. Pseudobulbs are small and ovate. Leaves are large, ovate-lanceolate and fluted. Inflorescence is erect and up to 1.5m (5′) long. Flowers are fragrant, showy, large and numerous

Phaius australis

Phaius graffii

Phaius graffii

COMMON NAME: None.
COLOUR: Flowers yellow; petals and sepals reverse side white. Labellum throat white.
SIZE: Growing up to 75cm (30″) high.
CLIMATE: Warm.
DISTRIBUTION: Native to Fiji.
FLOWERING TIME: Late winter to spring.
DESCRIPTION: Pseudobulbs are conical and grow up to 5cm (2″) high. Leaves are sheathing at the base, plicate, broad lanceolate and 75cm (30″) high. Inflorescence is 1m (40″) high with numerous blooms. Flowers are up to 10cm (4″) across. Labellum is tubular and spreading at the apex.

Phaius tancarvilliae syn. *P. tankervilliae*

Phaius tancarvilliae syn. P. tankervilliae

COMMON NAME: Swamp Orchid.
COLOUR: A blend of red-brown and white.
SIZE: Growing up to 90cm (3′) high.
CLIMATE: Intermediate to warm to hot.
DISTRIBUTION: Native to Australia, the Pacific Islands, Malaysia, Indonesia, southern China and is naturalised in Panama, Hawaii, Cuba and Jamaica.
FLOWERING TIME: Spring to summer.
DESCRIPTION: A robust species closely allied to *P. australis*. *P. australis* differs from *P. tancarvilliae* in that the column is superior; at no time is it enclosed within the labellum tube. Only the base of the labellum embraces the foot of the column.

PHALAENOPSIS
(fal-en-op-siss)

P*halaenopsis* from the Gk *phalaina* (moth) *opsis* (appearance) with reference to the delicate, moth-like white flowers; this 'moth orchid' is considered by many authors as the most beautiful of all. Possibly the first discovery of *Phalaenopsis* was by Rumphius in 1750 on the island of Amboina when he mis-identified a plant as *Angraecum*. In 1825, Blume officially established the genus and since then *Phalaenopsis* has been revised several times. In about 1969, the genus was divided into nine sections. The sixty species of the genus extend from the Himalayas through Burma, Malaysia, Formosa, Borneo, the Philippines to Indonesia, Papua New Guinea and Australia.

Phalaenopsis species have very short stems. Leaves are stem clasping, distichous, coriaceous, up to 60cm (20″) long and either shiny or mottled green. Inflorescence is lateral, erect, arching or pendulous. Flowers are small to large, showy, white, pink, or violet in colour with red-brown or yellow markings. Sepals and petals are free and spreading. The labellum is tri-lobed and jointed; lateral lobes are erect and parallel to the column; the mid-lobe or lamina is of various shapes, entire or forked, or without appendages (antennae or tendrils). The type species is *Phalaenopsis amabilis.*

Culture: Compost should be 5cm (2″) coarse. Pot in baskets where roots can grow and be exposed to the air. If in pots, allow the roots to escape over the side of the pot. Plants require shade, warmth and humidity. Water frequently. Check with your local nursery for advice on a fertiliser program.

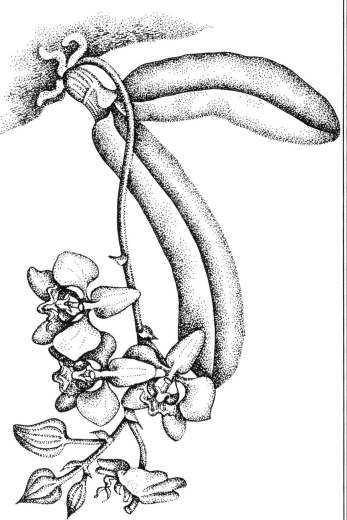

Phalaenopsis amabilis

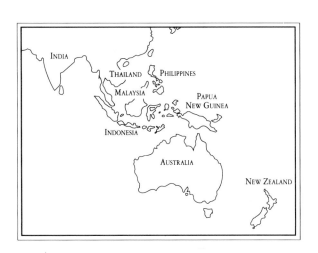

Phalaenopsis amabilis syn. *P. amabilis* var. *papuana* and syn. var. *rosenstromii*

COMMON NAME: White Moth Orchid.
COLOUR: Flowers white. Labellum marked with yellow.
SIZE: Growing up to 45cm (18″) across.
CLIMATE: Hot.
DISTRIBUTION: Native to northern Australia, Indonesia, Papua New Guinea and New Britain.
FLOWERING TIME: Spring to summer.
DESCRIPTION: A tropical epiphyte. Leaves are few, oblong-ovate and about 35cm (14″) long. Inflorescence is up to 90cm (3′) long. Flowers are showy and up to 10cm (4″) across.

Phalaenopsis amabilis syn. *P. amabilis* var. *papuana* and syn. var. *rosenstromii*

Phalaenopsis amboinensis

COMMON NAME: None.
COLOUR: Flowers pale yellow, blotched and barred with red-brown. Labellum white marked with yellow.
SIZE: Growing 25cm (10″) high.
CLIMATE: Hot.
DISTRIBUTION: Native to Ambon Island, Papua New Guinea and Indonesia.
FLOWERING TIME: Winter.
DESCRIPTION: An epiphytic plant. Leaves are elliptic-oblong and grow up to 20cm (8″) long. Flower measures up to 5cm (2″) across.

Phalaenopsis amboinensis

Phalaenopsis aphrodite

COMMON NAME: None.
COLOUR: White with lip-disc marked red.
SIZE: Growing up to 40cm (16″) across.
CLIMATE: Hot.
DISTRIBUTION: Native to the Philippines.
FLOWERING TIME: Winter to early spring.
DESCRIPTION: Closely allied to *P. amabilis*, the major differences being that the lip-disc is marked with red and the mid-lobe is nearly triangular in shape. Flowers are smaller, measuring about 7.5cm (3″) across.

Phalaenopsis aphrodite

Phalaenopsis cornu-cervi

COMMON NAME: None.
COLOUR: Flowers yellow-green, marked with brown. Labellum white.
SIZE: Growing up to 25cm (10″) high.
CLIMATE: Hot.
DISTRIBUTION: Native to Thailand, Sumatra, Malaysia, Borneo, Java and Burma.
FLOWERING TIME: Throughout the year (especially spring to autumn).
DESCRIPTION: Leaves are oblong, obtuse, coriaceous and up to 25cm (10″) long. Flower spike bears six to twelve blooms, each growing to 5cm (2″) across.

Phalaenopsis cornu-cervi

Phalaenopsis equestris var. *apparri* syn. *P. rosea* var. *apparri*

COMMON NAME: None.
COLOUR: Flowers rose-pink. Labellum deep rose.
SIZE: Growing up to 15cm (6″) high.
CLIMATE: Hot.
DISTRIBUTION: Native to the Philippines.
FLOWERING TIME: Autumn to winter.
DESCRIPTION: Leaves are oval and grow to 15cm (6″) long. Arching inflorescence grows up to 30cm (12″) long. Numerous flowers are up to 3cm (1¼″) across. Labellum is 2.5cm (1″) across.

Phalaenopsis equestris var. *apparri* syn. *P. rosea* var. *apparri*

Phalaenopsis fasciata

Phalaenopsis fasciata

COMMON NAME: None.
COLOUR: Flowers green-yellow, barred red-brown. Labellum marked yellow and pink.
SIZE: Growing up to 25cm (10″) across.
CLIMATE: Hot.
DISTRIBUTION: Native to the Philippines.
FLOWERING TIME: Summer to autumn.
DESCRIPTION: A rather robust epiphytic plant. Stems are short and enclosed by leaf sheaths. Leaves grow up to 20cm (8″) long and are distichous, elliptic-ovate. Inflorescence bears a few flowers which are usually waxy, fleshy and about 5cm (2″) across. Flowers open one to two at a time. Labellum is yellow and marked with red.

Phalaenopsis hieroglyphica

Phalaenopsis hieroglyphica

COMMON NAME: None.
COLOUR: Flowers cream-white spotted with brown. Labellum white flushed with pink-purple.
SIZE: Growing up to 30cm (12″) high.
CLIMATE: Hot.
DISTRIBUTION: Native to the Philippines (Polillo and Palawan only).
FLOWERING TIME: Spring.
DESCRIPTION: Leaves are oblong-lingulate and grow up to 30cm (12″) long. Inflorescence grows up to 32cm (12½″) long. Numerous flowers are long lasting. Labellum is tri-lobed, short clawed, truncate, with a central ridge. Mid-lobe is erose toward the apex, fleshy, centre hairy with a pair of long appendages in front.

Phalaenopsis X *intermedia*

Phalaenopsis X intermedia

COMMON NAME: None.
COLOUR: Petals and sepals white, speckled with deep pink at the base. Labellum violet, mid-lobes speckled with crimson, with middle lobe crimson.
SIZE: Growing up to 30cm (12″) across.
CLIMATE: Hot.
DISTRIBUTION: Native to the Philippines.
FLOWERING TIME: Winter to spring.
DESCRIPTION: A natural hybrid, *P. aphrodite* X *P. equestris*. Flower measures 5cm (2″) across. Leaves are green, oblong-elliptic with the underneath purple.

Phalaenopsis lindenii

Phalaenopsis lindenii

COMMON NAME: None.
COLOUR: Flowers white suffused with pink and dots at the base. Labellum pink and white, speckled with yellow and purple lines.
SIZE: Growing up to 25cm (10″) high.
CLIMATE: Hot.
DISTRIBUTION: Native to the Philippines.
FLOWERING TIME: Winter to autumn.
DESCRIPTION: Leaves are lanceolate to oblong, mottled and up to 25cm (10″) long. Flowers measure up to 3cm (1¼″) across.

Phalaenopsis lueddemanniana

Phalaenopsis lueddemanniana

COMMON NAME: None.
COLOUR: Flowers variable in colour, usually purple transverse bars on white-cream background.
SIZE: Growing up to 25cm (10″) high.
CLIMATE: Warm to hot.
DISTRIBUTION: Native to the Philippines.
FLOWERING TIME: Spring.
DESCRIPTION: Leaves are waxy and elliptic, but variable in shape and growing up to 25cm (10″) long. Flowers generally measure less than 5cm (2″) across. Five varieties of *P. lueddemanniana* are illustrated showing the colour variants: var. *bartonii*, var. *deltonii*, var. *luzon*, var. *purpurea* and var. *ochracia* syn. *P. ochracia*.

Phalaenopsis lueddemanniana var. *bartonii*

Phalaenopsis lueddemanniana var. *deltonii*

Phalaenopsis lueddemanniana var. *luzon*

Phalaenopsis lueddemanniana var. *ochracia* syn. *P. ochracia*

Phalaenopsis leuddemanniana var. *purpurea*

Phalaenopsis pallens

COMMON NAME: None.
COLOUR: Flowers white or lemon with brown lines. Labellum white and yellow.
SIZE: A dwarf epiphytic.
CLIMATE: Hot.
DISTRIBUTION: Native to the Philippines.
FLOWERING TIME: Winter to spring.
DESCRIPTION: Drooping leaves are distichous, elliptic to ovate and up to 18cm (7″) long. Inflorescence is sparsely flowered and about 18cm (7″) long. Flowers measure up to 5cm (2″) across.

Phalaenopsis pallens

Phalaenopsis pantherina

COMMON NAME: None.
COLOUR: Flowers lemon-green, barred and blotched red-brown.
SIZE: Growing up to 10cm (4″) high.
CLIMATE: Hot.
DISTRIBUTION: Native to Borneo.
FLOWERING TIME: Throughout the year.
DESCRIPTION: A robust epiphytic plant. Leaves are fleshy, oblong-oblanceolate and grow up to 25cm (10″) long. Inflorescence is compressed with angled, fleshy bracts, usually bearing solitary blooms. Flowers are waxy, fleshy and 4cm (1½″) long. *P. pantherina* is considered rare and is similar to *P. cornu-cervi*, differing in lateral sepal markings. With *P. pantherina*, lateral sepals are fully barred and all perianth segments are broader; also the plant tends to be more robust, while in *P. cornu-cervi* the lateral sepals carry only a marginal line of barring.

Phalaenopsis pantherina

Phalaenopsis parishii var. lobbii

COMMON NAME: None.
COLOUR: Flowers white. Labellum barred with yellow-orange to brown.
SIZE: Spreading to 15cm (6″) across.
CLIMATE: Warm.
DISTRIBUTION: Native to India and Burma, growing at elevations of 400 to 500m (1300 to 1660′).
FLOWERING TIME: Spring.
DESCRIPTION: Leaves are broad-elliptic and up to 7.5cm (3″) long. Raceme is shorter than the leaves. Flowers are up to 2.5cm (1″) across. Labellum is tri-lobed. The species is often deciduous in nature.

Phalaenopsis parishii var. *lobbii*

Phalaenopsis sanderiana

COMMON NAME: None.
COLOUR: Flowers white-pink to pink-purple.
SIZE: Growing up to 40cm (16″) across.
CLIMATE: Hot.
DISTRIBUTION: Native to the Philippines, growing at low altitudes.
FLOWERING TIME: Throughout the year.
DESCRIPTION: An epiphytic species with short stems. Leaves are elliptic-oblong, fleshy with the underneath purple-green. Inflorescence is long, bearing few to numerous flowers, each up to 7.5cm (3″) across.

Phalaenopsis sanderiana

Phalaenopsis sanderiana var. alba

COMMON NAME: None.
COLOUR: Flowers white. Labellum throat marked with yellow, spotted purple at the base.
SIZE: Growing up to 40cm (16″) across.
CLIMATE: Hot.
DISTRIBUTION: Native to the Philippines.
FLOWERING TIME: Throughout the year.
DESCRIPTION: An epiphytic species. Leaves are green, elliptic-oblong, fleshy, with the underneath purple-green. Inflorescence is long with few to numerous flowers, each growing to 7.5cm (3″) across.

Phalaenopsis sanderiana var. *alba*

Phalaenopsis schilleriana

COMMON NAME: Tiger (in the Philippines).
COLOUR: Flowers variable in colour, lilac to white. Labellum white with yellow and crimson markings.
SIZE: Growing up to 45cm (18″) high.
CLIMATE: Warm to hot.
DISTRIBUTION: Native to the Philippines. Grows at 750 to 900m (2500 to 3000′).
FLOWERING TIME: Spring.
DESCRIPTION: Leaves are dark green, oblong-elliptic and up to 45cm (18″) long. Inflorescence is up to 90cm (3′) long. The numerous flowers are variable in size and colour, but are generally about 6.5cm (2½″) across.

Phalaenopsis stuartiana

Phalaenopsis schilleriana

Phalaenopsis stuartiana

COMMON NAME: None.
COLOUR: Petals white lightly spotted, purple at the base. Sepals white, lateral sepals lemon on the inner half and spotted at the base with red. Labellum yellow, margins white, marked with purple.
SIZE: Growing up to 35cm (14″) high.
CLIMATE: Hot.
DISTRIBUTION: Native to the Philippines.
FLOWERING TIME: Autumn to spring.
DESCRIPTION: Small epiphyte. Leaves are grey-green, mottled when young, growing up to 35cm (13½″) long, with a purple underside at maturing. Inflorescence is up to 90cm (3′) long. Flowers are numerous and up to 5cm (2″) across. Labellum has double horns at the tip.

Phalaenopsis veitchiana syn. P. X gertrudes

COMMON NAME: None.
COLOUR: Flowers variable pink. Labellum white-purple, spotted purple at the base.
SIZE: Short and spreading.
CLIMATE: Hot.
DISTRIBUTION: Native to the Philippines.
FLOWERING TIME: Spring.
DESCRIPTION: This epiphytic species is a natural hybrid between *P. equestris* and *P. schillariana*. Leaves are silver-green and elliptic-oblong. Inflorescence is simple. Flowers are variable in size, but usually about 5cm (2″) across. Labellum is tri-lobed.

Phalaenopsis veitchiana syn. *P. X gertrudes*

Phalaenopsis violacea

Phalaenopsis violacea

COMMON NAME: None.
COLOUR: Flower colour variable green-white with violet markings. Labellum yellow and violet.
SIZE: Growing up to 25cm (10″) high.
CLIMATE: Hot.
DISTRIBUTION: Native to Peninsula Malaysia, Borneo and Sumatra. Growing at low altitudes in shady position along rivers.
FLOWERING TIME: Spring to summer.
DESCRIPTION: Leaves are variable, oblong-elliptic, obovate and up to 23cm (9″) long. Inflorescence is stout, flexuose and up to 12.5cm (5″) long. Flowers are up to 7.5cm (3″) across.

PHRAGMIPEDIUM
(frag-mi-pee-dee-um)

*P*hragmipedium from the Gk *phragma* (a fence, division or partition) *pedion* (slipper) with reference to the divisions of the trilocular ovary and the slipper-like shape of the labellum. This is a genus of about 12 to 20 either terrestrial or epiphytic species. They come from Panama, south to Brazil, Bolivia, Peru, Venezuela and Costa Rica. This genus forms part of the complex group often referred to as 'Cyps'. R. A. Rolfe separated the tropical American species from *Paphiopedilum* in about 1896. (See *Paphiopedilum*.) *Phragmipedium* species are sympodial herbs with short stems, fibrous roots, having tufted fans of six to eight coriaceous dark green leaves, growing up to 90cm (3') long. Inflorescence is erect, axillary, with a many-flowered raceme. Flowers are large and showy, with up to 15 blooms. The dorsal sepal is free; lateral sepals unite for the full length into a synsepalum. Petals are free spreading. The labellum is sac- or slipper-shaped. (The ovary is tri-celled.) The species *P. lindenii* is of notable interest in that the labellum is replaced by a third petal; initially, it was described as a new genus, but after much discussion it remains in *Phragmipedium*.

Culture: As for *Paphiopedilum*. Compost in pots. Fertilise monthly. Plants require humidity, shade from direct sunlight, good air movement, plenty of water and perfect drainage.

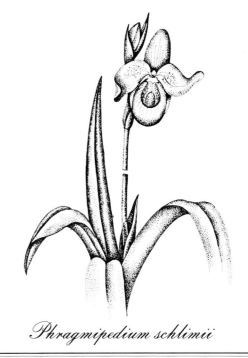

Phragmipedium schlimii

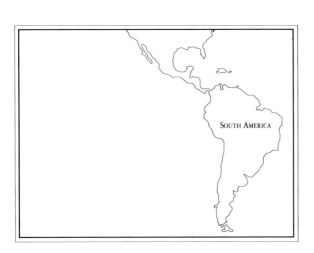

SOUTH AMERICA

Phragmipedium schlimii

COMMON NAME: None.
COLOUR: Flower colour variable, white mottled with pink. Labellum rose-pink.
SIZE: Growing to 30cm (12") high.
CLIMATE: Intermediate.
DISTRIBUTION: Native to Colombia, growing at an altitude of 1500 to 1800m (5000 to 6000') in moist areas.
FLOWERING TIME: Mostly spring.
DESCRIPTION: Leaves are strap-shaped, acute and up to 30cm (12") long. Inflorescence is up to 60cm (2') high with five to eight blooms. Flower is up to 5cm (2") across.

Phragmipedium schlimii

PLEIONE
(play-oh-nee)

Pleione is named after Pleione, mother of the pleiades (the seven daughters of Atlas) in Greek mythology, who were transformed into a cluster of stars by Zeus. *Pleione* comprises a small group of about twenty species of epiphytic, or on occasions lithophytic or terrestrial, plants closely allied to *Coelogyne*. They are found in the Himalayas through Burma, southern China to Formosa. This genus is well known in European collections. It is a dwarf plant often occurring in clusters. Stems are thickened to pseudobulbs. Leaves are plicate and deciduous. Flowers appear after leaf-fall, are attractive, large and delightfully showy. The labellum is tri-lobed, frilled or incised, trumpet-shaped, rather like the *Cattleyas*.

Culture: Compost. It is important to remember these plants grow from 1000 to 3000m (3000 to 11 000'), so require shade, 'cool-house' humid conditions, and repotting in small pots or shallow pans after flowering.

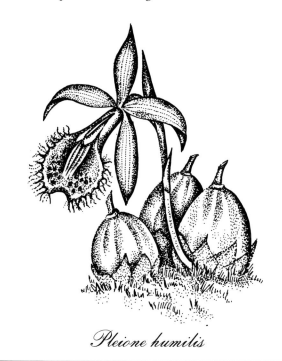

Pleione humilis

Pleione bulbocodiodies
syn. *P. pricei, P. formosana*

COMMON NAME: None.
COLOUR: Flowers pink to deep pink. Labellum white to pink, spotted and marked pink-purple to soft brown.
SIZE: Growing up to 50cm (20") high.
CLIMATE: Cool.
DISTRIBUTION: Native to China, Taiwan, Tibet, Thailand and Burma. Growing on mossy rocks and trees at 700 to 2900m (2300 to 9500') in altitude.
FLOWERING TIME: Spring.
DESCRIPTION: A variable epiphytic or lithophytic species. Pseudobulbs are small, pear-shaped, clustered and up to 2.5cm (1") high. Leaves are linear, elliptic-lanceolate and grow up to 50cm (20") long. Inflorescence is up to 20cm (8") long, appearing at the same time as immature leaves. Flowers are large, showy and up to 8cm (3¼") across. Labellum is tri-lobed, sub-ovate with side lobes erect and mid-lobe margins erose.

Pleione bulbocodiodies syn. *P. pricei, P. formosana*

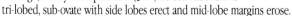

PORPHYROGLOTTIS
(por-feer-oh-glott-is)

Porphyroglottis from the Gk *porphyros* (purple) *glottis* (mouth of wind-pipe) with reference to the labellum's dark purple throat. This is a single species genus. This most unusual plant comes from Sarawak, Borneo. *Porphyroglottis* is almost unknown in collections.

Culture: As for *Dendrobiums*. Compost in a basket or on a tree-fern slab for this pendulous variety. Consult your local orchid society for the care of the plant.

Porphyroglottis maxwelliae

Porphyroglottis maxwelliae

COMMON NAME: None.

COLOUR: Sepals and petals white-pink (rose colour). Labellum dark purple-brown with yellow blotch towards tip.

SIZE: Growing up to 90cm (3′) high.

CLIMATE: Hot.

DISTRIBUTION: Native to Borneo (Sarawak) and Johor.

FLOWERING TIME: Spring.

DESCRIPTION: Stems are long. Leaves are linear, acute and up to 50cm (20″) long. Inflorescence grows up to 1.5m (5′) long, flowering in succession with two to three blooms at a time. Flowers are up to 4cm (1½″) long with sepals and petals reflexed. Vegetatively identical to a small *Grammatophyllum speciosum*.

Porphyroglottis maxwelliae

PRASOPHYLLUM

(praz-oh-fill-m)

*P*rasophyllum from the Gk *pason* (leek) *phyllum* (a leaf) with reference to the leek-like leaf which sometimes exceeds the flower spike in length. This genus of about 80 species is confined to Australia and New Zealand. At present, the genus is divided into two sections: (a) *Euprasophyllum* in which the labellum is either sessile at the base of the column, or connected to a short rigid claw but not moveable; and (b) *Micranthum* in which the labellum is articulate and moveable on a claw attached to the column foot.

This glabrous terrestrial has a root system of globular tubers. It has a single, leek-like leaf. There are several flowers in a terminal raceme or spike. Flower colour is inconspicuous, but is usually greenish white or purple. The flower is reversed, in that the labellum stands above the column. The dorsal sepal is erect or concave, curved about the column and is often recurved. Lateral sepals are as large as the dorsal sepal.

Petals are usually shorter. The labellum is oval, oblong or lanceolate, but divided; margins are crisped, ciliate, denticulate or entire.

Culture: As for *Caladenia*. Use rich, well-drained, free-moving compost. In pots, use broken crock, crushed brick, topped with equal parts of shredded tree-fern, leaf mould, crumbled loam, sharp gritty sand and sphagnum moss. Apply liquid fertiliser regularly.

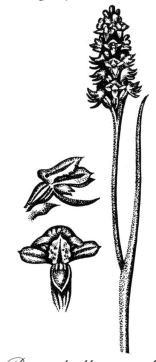

Prasophyllum cucullatum

Prasophyllum elatum

Prasophyllum elatum

COMMON NAME: Tall Leek Orchid.
COLOUR: Flowers yellow-brown, yellow-green or purple-black. Labellum white and green, but may be green to purple-black.
SIZE: A robust terrestrial, up to 1.3m (52″) high.
CLIMATE: Cool.
DISTRIBUTION: Native to Australia (coastal and nearby tablelands).
FLOWERING TIME: Spring.
DESCRIPTION: Solitary leaf is sheathing at the base. Inflorescence is up to 1.2m (4′) high. Flowers are inverted, large and numerous, forming a dense spike.

PTEROSTYLIS

(ter-o-stye-liss)

P*terostylis* from the Gk *pteron* (a wing) *stylos* (a column) with reference to the wing of the column. This genus of over 70 species is native to Australia, extending to Papua New Guinea, New Caledonia and New Zealand. 'Green Hoods,' as they are affectionately known, are not well represented in collections, although the number of collectors exhibiting Australian natives is increasing. The distinguishing feature of this genus is the manner in which the dorsal sepal and the petals appressed to it form a galea or hood surrounding the column. In several species the lateral sepals are reflexed, exposing the labellum. The column is elongated and curved within. The galea is winged on both sides.

Culture: As for *Caladenia*. Use rich, well-drained, free-moving compost. In pots, use broken crock, crushed brick, topped with equal parts of shredded tree-fern, leaf mould, crumbled loam, sharp gritty sand and sphagnum moss. Apply liquid fertiliser regularly.

Pterostylis nutans

Pterostylis grandiflora

Pterostylis grandiflora

COMMON NAME: Cobra Greenhood.
COLOUR: Flowers white with green and red markings.
SIZE: Small terrestrial up to 35cm (14″) high.
CLIMATE: Intermediate.
DISTRIBUTION: Native to Australia and New Zealand.
FLOWERING TIME: Autumn to winter, later in Tasmania.
DESCRIPTION: Plant has radical leaves. Leaves are basal. Large elegant blooms, galea 6cm (2½″) around the curve.

RENANTHERA

(ren-ann-ther-a)

Renanthera from the Gk *renes* (kidney) *anthera* (anther) with reference to the kidney-shaped anthers, a characteristic which helps in the separation of *Renanthera* from *Vanda* and *Aerides*. This genus of about 15 species of robust monopodial epiphytic orchids comes from Burma, Peninsula Malaysia, Indonesia and Papua New Guinea to the Pacific Islands. Stems grow up to 4.5m (15') and become almost woody with age. Leaves are coriaceous and unevenly lobed at apex. Inflorescence is axillary in the upper leaves, paniculate, many-flowered (up to 150 flowers). Individual flower spikes are up to 1.2m (4') long. Flowers are showy, predominantly red or yellow, and measure 6 to 9 cm (2.5 to 3.5") across. Dorsal sepal and petals are similar, free and spreading. The lateral sepals are the largest segment of the flower. The labellum is tri-lobed with a sack-like basal spur. Lateral lobes are erect and the mid-lobe is reflexed. The small callus is lamellate and directly below stigmatic surface.
Culture: Compost in pots. Plants require humid conditions and plenty of indirect sunlight. Fertilise each month.

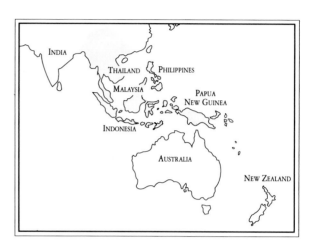

Renanthera imschootiana

Renanthera matutina

COMMON NAME: None.
COLOUR: Flowers dark red with dark spots, may be tinted with yellow. Labellum chrome yellow, white and spotted red.
SIZE: Scrambling plant, up to 2m (6'6") high.
CLIMATE: Hot.
DISTRIBUTION: Native to Sumatra, Java and Peninsula Malaysia.
FLOWERING TIME: Autumn.
DESCRIPTION: Leaves are oblong-linear and emarginate. Inflorescence is branched with numerous flowers and is up to 60cm (2') high. Flowers measure about 5cm (2") across.

Renanthera monachica

Renanthera matutina

Renanthera monachica

COMMON NAME: None.
COLOUR: Flowers yellow-orange, spotted red.
SIZE: An erect epiphytic plant 50cm (20") high.
CLIMATE: Warm.
DISTRIBUTION: Native to the Philippines.
FLOWERING TIME: Late winter to spring.
DESCRIPTION: Leaves are strap-shaped, unequally emarginate, up to 12.5cm (5") long. Inflorescence is densely flowered, up to 17.5cm (7") long. Flowers are 2.5cm (1") across.

Renanthera storiei

Renanthera storiei

COMMON NAME: None.
COLOUR: Flowers scarlet, mottled red. Base of labellum mid-lobe white.
SIZE: Growing up to 3m (10') high.
CLIMATE: Hot.
DISTRIBUTION: Native to the Philippines. A tropical lowland species.
FLOWERING TIME: Summer.
DESCRIPTION: Stems are up to 3m (10') long. Leaves are oblong, emarginate and up to 20cm (8") long. Inflorescence is paniculate. Numerous flowers measure up to 4.5cm (1¾") across. Closely related species *Renanthera coccinea*.

RHINERRHIZA
(rye-ner-rye-za)

*R*hinerrhiza from the Gk *rhis* (snout) *rhiza* (root) with reference to the raspy tuberculate roots which give rise to the common name 'Raspy Root'. This genus of a single epiphytic species is confined to eastern Australia. Originally it was included in *Sarcochilus*, but it differs in the thick raspy roots and the filiform segment of the perianth. The inflorescence has as many as six to eight racemes, up to 90cm (3′) long, each with up to 40 or more fugacious flowers. These flowers open simultaneously overnight, so by dawn, a somewhat unattractive plant has been transformed into a showy blaze of red and orange blooms which last but a few days. The flower wilts when picked and the colours fade quickly. This genus is rare in collections, although it responds well to cultivation. *Rhinerrhiza* is a must for growers of unusual botanical orchids.

Culture: As for the smaller *Vanda*. Plants respond well when mounted on a tree-fern slab. They require light shade (indirect sunlight), water, drainage and light dressings of fertiliser.

Rhinerrhiza divitiflora

Rhinerrhiza divitiflora

COMMON NAME: Raspy Root Orchid.
COLOUR: Flowers orange marked with red-brown.
SIZE: Epiphytic plant growing up to 17.5cm (7″) high, supported by flat raspy roots.
CLIMATE: Cool.
DISTRIBUTION: Native to north-eastern Australia (coastal and nearby ranges).
FLOWERING TIME: Autumn.
DESCRIPTION: Leaves are oblong, corrugated and grow up to 18cm (7″). Inflorescence is up to 90cm (3′) long. Flowers are numerous with as many as 80 blooms; they are spider-like in appearance. Petals are up to 3cm (1¼″) long.

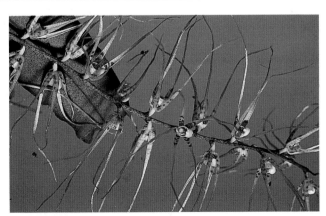

Rhinerrhiza divitiflora

RHYNCHOSTYLIS
(rink-oh-stye-liss)

Rhynchostylis from the Gk *rhynchos* (a beak) *stylos* (a pillar) with reference to the beaked column (although the beaked column is not exclusive to the genus). This genus of about four species was originally described as *Saccolobium*, a closely allied genus, but later was renamed *Rhynchostylis*. Its distribution ranges from India, Sri Lanka, Burma, South-east Asia, Malaysia, the Philippines, Borneo and Indonesia. These species are often called Fox-tail Orchids because of the erect or pendulous inflorescence of densely crowded, small, colourful flowers. The plant is a stout, short-stemmed monopodial epiphyte. Leaves are coriaceous, with a distinct keel and unequal apical lobes. The many flowers are showy, are 2 to 2.5cm (¾ to 1″) across and are coloured white with pink, blue or purple markings. Sepals and petals are spreading and waxy. The labellum is short, adnate to the base of the column foot, compressed, deeply saccate or with a sac-like spur at base. The genus is freely inter-fertile with numerous hybrids.

Culture: Compost. Pot in a hanging basket, allowing the numerous aerial roots to hang freely. Plants require high humidity, shade and lots of frequent watering while growing. Apply less water when roots show signs of inactivity.

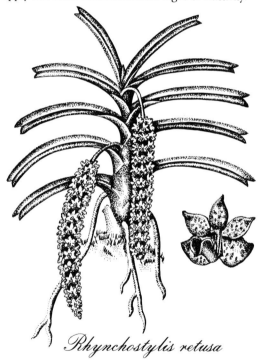

Rhynchostylis retusa

Rhynchostylis praemorsa

Rhynchostylis praemorsa

COMMON NAME: One of the Fox-tail Orchids.
COLOUR: Flower colour variable, usually white, spotted pink-lilac; may be pink or purple.
SIZE: Growing up to 60cm (2′) high.
CLIMATE: Warm.
DISTRIBUTION: Native to the Philippines.
FLOWERING TIME: Summer to autumn.
DESCRIPTION: A variable epiphytic plant. Robust stems are up to 60cm (2′) high. Leaves are lingulate, arching, coriaceous and up to 50cm (20″) long. Inflorescence is pendulous, up to 60cm (2′) long and many-flowered. Flowers are fragrant, waxy and about 2cm (¾″) across. This species is consistently confused with *Rhynchostylis retusa*.

ROBIQUETIA
(roe-bi-quet-ee-ah)

Robiquetia is named after Pierre Robiquet, a French chemist who discovered caffeine and morphine. This genus has about 25 species of pendulous, monopodial, epiphytic orchids. It is widespread in Indonesia, Malaysia, the Philippines, Papua New Guinea, Australia and the Pacific Islands to Fiji. Leaves are distichous. Inflorescence is racemose, pendulous and many-flowered. Flowers are small. Sepals and petals are free. The labellum is joined to the column, is tri-lobed and spurred, but the spur lacks appendages within; side lobes are small and fleshy. The spur is long and bent or flattened.

Culture: Mount on a tree-fern slab or may be grown in pans. Plants require humidity, reasonable shade and plenty of water while growing. *Robiquetia* are rare in collections; these plants are attractive and deserve more attention from growers.

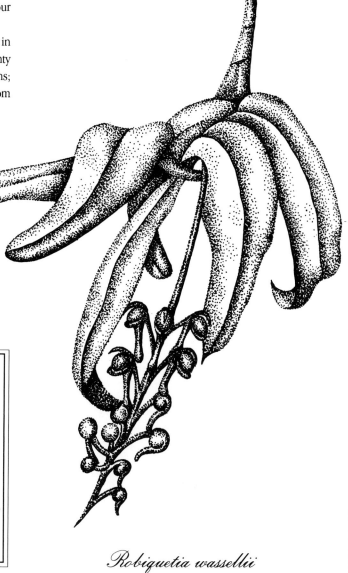

Robiquetia wassellii

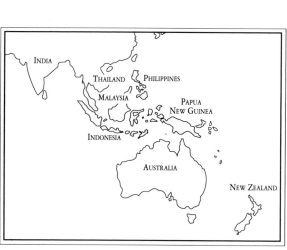

Robiquetia cerina syn. *R. merrillii*

Robiquetia cerina syn. R. merrillii

COMMON NAME: None.
COLOUR: Flowers purple and yellow.
SIZE: Growing up to 15cm (6″) high.
CLIMATE: Warm.
DISTRIBUTION: Native to the Philippines. Growing at 350 to 3200m (1200 to 10 500′) in altitude, on rocks of mountain slopes.
FLOWERING TIME: Throughout the year.
DESCRIPTION: An epiphytic or lithophytic plant. Leaves are oblong, strap-shaped, unequally emarginate, overlapping and up to 20cm (8″) long. Inflorescence grows up to 12.5cm (5″) long. Flowers are numerous, small and up to 1.5cm (1½″) across. Labellum is spurred.

Robiquetia tierneyana syn. Saccolabium tierneyanum

COMMON NAME: None.
COLOUR: Flowers pale green-yellow, mottled brown.
SIZE: A large robust epiphyte, growing up to 60cm (2′) high.
CLIMATE: Warm.
DISTRIBUTION: Native to Australia (north-eastern Queensland).
FLOWERING TIME: Autumn.
DESCRIPTION: Roots are thick, creeping or aerial. Leaves are oblong, emarginate and up to 14cm (5½″) long. Raceme is short. Numerous flowers are up to 2cm (¾″) across.

Robiquetia tierneyana syn. *Saccolabium tierneyanum*

Robiquetia wassellii

COMMON NAME: None.
COLOUR: Flowers green. Spur yellow.
SIZE: Pendulous epiphytic.
CLIMATE: Hot.
DISTRIBUTION: Native to Australia (northern Queensland rainforest).
FLOWERING TIME: Spring.
DESCRIPTION: Leaves are up to 14cm (5½″) long and narrow-oblong and unequally emarginate at apex. Raceme is pendulous. Numerous flowers are small.

Robiquetia wassellii

ROSSIOGLOSSUM

(ross-ee-o-gloss-um)

Rossioglossum is named after John Ross, an orchid collector in Mexico (1830–1840). This is a very small genus of six species which originates from Mexico to Panama. Originally these species were in the genus *Orchis*. In 1916, they were considered to be a section of the genus *Odontoglossum*. In 1976, Garay and Kennedy showed that these species do not conform to the taxonomic key of the genera *Odontoglossum*, thus giving rise to the genus *Rossioglossum*. The difference is that the labellum of *Rossioglossum* is free, at right angles to the column, the side lobes are auriculate, and the mid-lobe is large and pandurate. This medium to large epiphytic plant has short rhizomes. Pseudobulbs are ovoid. It has two leaves at apex which are large and petiolate. Flowers are large, showy and yellow with red markings. Sepals and petals are free and spreading. The labellum is free, pandurate, the mid-lobe is large and the callus fleshy.

Culture: As for *Odontoglossum* and *Oncidium*. Compost in well-drained pots. Provide humid conditions and frequent watering. Take care with fragile new growth; don't allow water to sit around newly growing tips as they may rot.

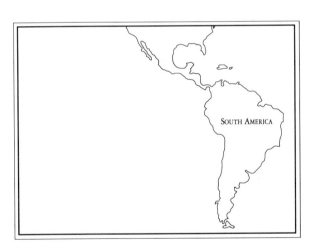

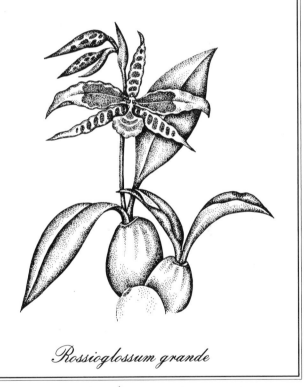

Rossioglossum grande

Rossioglossum grande syn. *Odontoglossum grande*

COMMON NAME: None.
COLOUR: Flowers yellow, barred and marked red-brown.
SIZE: Growing up to 50cm (20″) high.
CLIMATE: Intermediate to warm.
DISTRIBUTION: Native to Mexico and Guatemala.
FLOWERING TIME: Autumn.
DESCRIPTION: Pseudobulbs are clustered, compressed, ovoid and up to 10cm (4″) high. Leaves are lanceolate to elliptic, acute and up to 40cm (16″) long. Inflorescence is up to 30cm (12″) long. Flowers are large, showy and measure about 10cm (4″) across. Labellum is pandurate and tri-lobed; side lobes are auriculate; mid-lobe is shortly clawed and emarginate; disc is bi-lobed with callus between the lobes.

Rossioglossum grande syn. *Odontoglossum grande*

SARCOCHILUS
(sar-kok-i-lus)

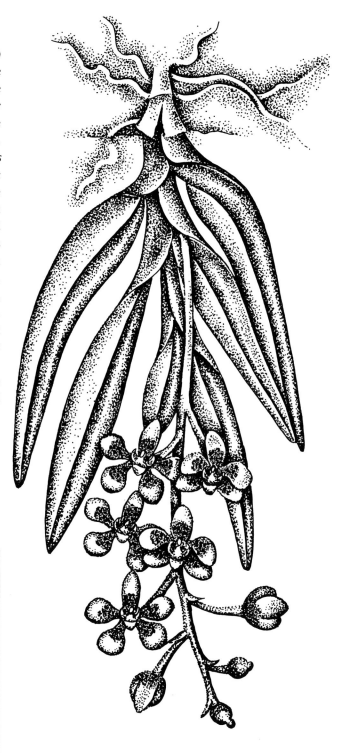

Sarcochilus from the Gk *sarx* (flesh) *chilos* (lip) with reference to the fleshy labellum. This was once a large genus, but over the last several decades many species have been reclassified and transferred to other genera, especially the Asian and Indonesian species which differ from the Australian species. There is now a small number of species. Most of the transferred species went to *Pteroceras*. *Sarcochilus* is now a genus of about a dozen epiphytic or lithophytic plants found in northern and eastern Australia. Roots are smooth and fleshy. The base of stems is covered with persistent scarious leafy-bases. The few leaves are channelled and the apex is unequally bi-lobed. The few to many flowers are showy and often fragrant. Sepals and petals are free, with the lateral sepals adnate to the column foot for a distance. The labellum is tri-lobed, articulate to apex of column foot, shallowly saccate. The large side lobes are erect and curved. The mid-lobe is small and fleshy and is attached to a short spur which is often poorly developed. The basal sac or disc is almost filled by callus thickenings.

Culture: Most species do best on tree-fern fibre slab or pans filled with gravel. All species require high humidity and moderate shade.

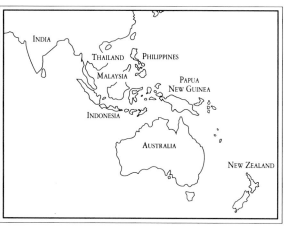

Sarcochilus ceciliae

COMMON NAME: Fairy Bells.
COLOUR: Flowers pink, mauve-pink or purple.
Labellum white.
SIZE: Growing up to 10cm (4″) high.
CLIMATE: Cool.
DISTRIBUTION: Native to Australia (eastern coast
and nearby mountains), growing in clumps on
rocks.
FLOWERING TIME: Late spring to summer to early
autumn.
DESCRIPTION: A variable species in growth and
flower form. Stems are erect. Leaves are linear to
lanceolate and grow up to 12.5cm (5″) long.
Inflorescence is in the form of a loose raceme.
Flowers measure about 1.5cm (½″) across.

Sarcochilus ceciliae

Sarcochilus falcatus

COMMON NAME: Orange Blossom Orchid.
COLOUR: Flowers white. Labellum marked with
orange, having a crimson-purple stripe.
SIZE: Growing up to 15cm (6″) high.
CLIMATE: Cool.
DISTRIBUTION: Native to Australia (eastern
rainforests).
FLOWERING TIME: Spring.
DESCRIPTION: Small, very fragrant epiphytic herb,
growing on trunks and limbs of softwood trees.
Leaves are flat, oblong-lanceolate and falcate,
measuring up to 15cm (6″) long. Flower scape
carries three to twelve blooms. Flower is about
2.5cm (1″) across with a showy display.

Sarcochilus fitzgeraldii

Sarcochilus fitzgeraldii

COMMON NAME: Ravine Orchid.
COLOUR: Flowers white, spotted pale purple-
pink. Labellum with yellow-orange markings.
SIZE: Growing up to 17.5cm (7″) high.
CLIMATE: Cool.
DISTRIBUTION: Native to eastern Australia
(rainforest areas). A prostrate epiphyte and
lithophyte growing chiefly on rocks in deep
shady ravines.
FLOWERING TIME: Spring.
DESCRIPTION: Leaves are falcate, channelled and
up to 17.5cm (7″) long. Inflorescence is
racemose with numerous flowers measuring up
to 3cm (1¼″) across.

Sarcochilus falcatus

Sarcochilus hartmannii

COMMON NAME: Hartmann's Orchid.
COLOUR: Flowers white with red blotches.
Labellum tri-lobe marked with yellow.
SIZE: Growing up to 10cm (4″) high.
CLIMATE: Cool.
DISTRIBUTION: Native to eastern Australian coast
and nearby mountains, growing on cliffs and
rocks.
FLOWERING TIME: Spring.
DESCRIPTION: Stems are erect, stout and up to
10cm (4″) high. The six to eight leaves are up to
17.5cm (7″) long, are oblong-lanceolate, falcate
and channelled. Inflorescence is erect to
arching and is 20cm (8″) long. Flowers measure
up to 2.5cm (1″) across.

Sarcochilus hartmannii

Sarcochilus moorei

COMMON NAME: None.
COLOUR: Flowers ochre-yellow, spotted and
blotched with brown.
SIZE: A pendulous epiphyte, up to 45cm (18″)
long.
CLIMATE: Hot.
DISTRIBUTION: Native to Australia (northern
Queensland) and Papua New Guinea.
FLOWERING TIME: Winter to spring.
DESCRIPTION: Leaves are up to 30cm (12″) long,
are narrow-oblong and unequally emarginate.
Raceme is pendulous and up to 45cm (18″)
long. Numerous flowers measure 2.5cm (1″)
across.

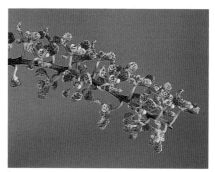

Sarcochilus moorei

SCHOMBURGKIA

(shom-berg-kee-a)

*S*chomburgkia is named after Dr Richard Schomburgk, a German botanist who explored and collected with his elder brother Sir Robert, in British Guiana (Guyana). In 1865, at the age of 54, he became director of Adelaide Botanic Gardens in Australia. Unfortunately, many taxonomists do not consider *Schomburgkia* a valid genus, so include it within *Laelia*. *Schomburgkia* has recently been divided into two sections: (a) *Schomburgkia*: pseudobulbs are fusiform, resembling those of *Cattleya*, but with a stalked base; leaves coriaceous, long and narrow. Inflorescence up to 15 flowers and up to 1.8m (6′) long, e.g. *S. undulata*. Found in South America, Venezuela and Guyana. (b) *Chaunoschomburgkia*: pseudobulbs are thick, cylindrical or conical, yellow-green, becoming hollow with age, and a favourite nesting place for a certain species of ant; leaves short and broad, e.g. *S. tibicinis*. Found in Central America and West Indies, Mexico to Costa Rica.

Schomburgkia is a genus of about twelve species from central and northern South America. Pseudobulbs are fusiform or conical and are often hollow. Leaves are coriaceous and spreading. Inflorescence is erect and very long. The flowers are large, showy and cream, red-brown, red-purple or wine-purple in colour. Sepals and petals are similar and free with undulating margins. Labellum is tri-lobed with side lobes erect on either side of the column; the mid-lobe is spreading with five longitudinal keels. *Schomburgkias* are distinguishable from *Laelia* by the beautiful undulate sepals and petals, and the labellum which does not enclose the column.

Culture: Compost in well-drained pots as for *Cattleya* and *Laelia*. Both the fusiform and hollow pseudobulb groups require plenty of water while growing, as well as shade with plenty of light. The hollow pseudobulb group require a longer dry period once growth and flowering is complete. Avoid frequent repotting.

SOUTH AMERICA

Schomburgkia undulata

Schomburgkia superbiens syn. *Laelia superbiens*

Schomburgkia superbiens syn. *Laelia superbiens*

COMMON NAME: None.
COLOUR: Flowers purple, variegated with yellow.
SIZE: A large epiphyte or terrestrial plant, growing up to 5m (16') high.
CLIMATE: Intermediate.
DISTRIBUTION: Native to Mexico, Guatemala and Honduras. Growing at altitudes up to 2000m (6600') in rainforests; uncommon in the open.
FLOWERING TIME: Autumn.
DESCRIPTION: Pseudobulbs are oblong-fusiform, furrowed and up to 3m (10') high. Leaves stem from the apex, are oblong-lanceolate and up to 30cm (1') long. Inflorescence measures up to 80cm (32") long. Flowers are numerous, large, showy, with sepals up to 7.5cm (3") long and petals up to 5cm (2") long. Labellum is tri-lobed and 5cm (2") long. Margins are convolute and enfold the column. Side lobes are short-oblong and the apex is crisp. Mid-lobe is obovate and the disc has five or six prominent, crisp, longitudinal lamellae.

SOBRALIA
(so-bral-ee-a)

Sobralia is named after Dr Francisco Sobral, a Spanish physician and botanist. This is a genus of about 35 terrestrial, lithophytic and epiphytic species. They are widespread from Mexico to Brazil in South America. This group of interesting, vegetative orchids has reed-like short to very long stems with few coriaceous or papery, plicate, distinctly nerved leaves. The flowers are large and spectacular. Their beauty often excels that of the *Cattleyas*. The single, successive flowers bloom over a period of many weeks; each bloom is short-lived, lasting not more than a day or two. The labellum is tri-lobed or entire, with the base adnate to the column, the basal half tubular then spreading and the disc with or without calli. The glorious beauty of these handsome orchids always makes them a centre of attraction.

Culture: Compost in well-drained pots. Plants require careful watering with moderate shade. As a note of warning, these plants are susceptible to toxic fumigants! Before importing any species of this genus discuss this problem with your customs and quarantine officers. Other than that concern, *Sobralias* are not difficult to grow if careful attention is given to their requirements.

Sobralia macrantha

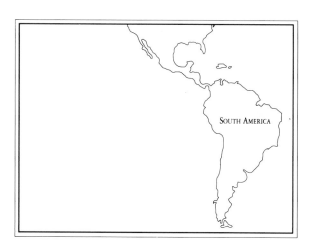

SOUTH AMERICA

Sobralia decora

COMMON NAME: None.

COLOUR: Flowers white. Labellum flushed with lilac.

SIZE: Growing up to 75cm (30″) high.

CLIMATE: Intermediate to warm.

DISTRIBUTION: Native to Mexico, British Honduras, Honduras, Costa Rica, Guatemala and Nicaragua.

FLOWERING TIME: Spring to summer.

DESCRIPTION: Stems are cane-liké, clustered and up to 75cm (30″) high. Leaves are linear-lanceolate, acute and up to 23cm (9″) long. Inflorescence is terminal with few blooms. Flowers are fragrant and grow up to 10cm (4″) across.

Sobralia xantholeuca

Sobralia xantholeuca

COMMON NAME: None.

COLOUR: Flowers yellow. Labellum marked orange.

SIZE: Growing up to 2m (6′6″) high.

CLIMATE: Warm.

DISTRIBUTION: Native to central America, liking warm conditions.

FLOWERING TIME: Late spring to summer.

DESCRIPTION: Leaves alternate on reed-like stem and are linear-lanceolate. Flowers bloom in succession for as long as the season lasts and measure up to 15cm (6″) across.

Sobralia decora

Sobralia macrantha

COMMON NAME: None.

COLOUR: Flower colour is variable, generally rose-purple. Labellum marked with white and yellow. A white form has been recorded.

SIZE: Growing up to 2.4m (8′) high.

CLIMATE: Intermediate.

DISTRIBUTION: Native to Mexico through to Costa Rica.

FLOWERING TIME: Spring to autumn.

DESCRIPTION: Stems are clustered and grow up to 2.4m (8′). Leaves are sheathing, lanceolate and up to 30cm (12″) long. Flowers open singly over a long period. Flowers are large, but size is variable.

Sobralia macrantha

SOPHRONITIS
(sof-roe-nye-tis)

Sophronitis from the Gk *sophronia* (modest) with reference particularly to *Sophronitis cernua*. This is a very small genus of less than ten species found in eastern Brazil and Paraguay. As recently as 1977, J. A. Fowlie set the taxonomic limits of this genus. *Sophronitis* is a genus of dwarf epiphytic or lithophytic sympodial plants. The pseudobulbs are small, ovoid, thickly clustered on a rhizome, each pseudobulb having a single, erect, apical, coriaceous, shiny or grey-green leaf. Inflorescence is terminal with one or many flowers. These flowers are showy and scarlet or orange-red in colour which is quite vivid at times. Sepals and petals are alike in shape, with petals slightly broader. The labellum is tri-lobed, with the lateral lobes partially encircling the column; the mid-lobe is smaller with a yellow disc; the spur is adnate to the ovary.

Culture: Mount on a tree-fern fibre slab. Plants require humidity; *never* allow them to become dry, but be careful with watering. Provide moderate shade.

SOUTH AMERICA

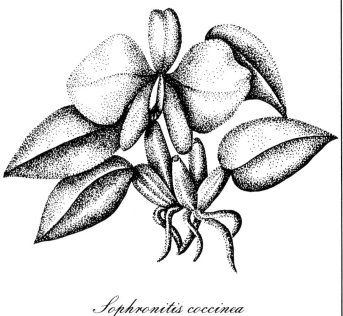

Sophronitis coccinea

Sophronitis coccinea

COMMON NAME: None.
COLOUR: Flower colour variable, generally scarlet. Labellum yellow-orange marked with scarlet.
SIZE: Growing up to 12.5cm (5″) high.
CLIMATE: Intermediate.
DISTRIBUTION: Native to Brazil.
FLOWERING TIME: Autumn to winter.
DESCRIPTION: Pseudobulbs are clustered, fusiform and grow up to 4cm (1½″) high. Solitary leaf is oblong-lanceolate and up to 7.5cm (3″) long. Flowers are usually solitary with variable size.

Sophronitis coccinea

SPATHOGLOTTIS
(spath-oh-glot-is)

Spathoglottis from the Gk *spathe* (a spath) *glotta* (a tongue) with reference to the broad lamina of the labellum. This genus of about 40 species is found from India across South-east Asia, China, Indonesia, Papua New Guinea, to the Pacific Islands, with two species in Australia. The largest number of species is found in Papua New Guinea. Covered with dry leaf sheaths, the pseudobulbs look more like *Gladiolus* corms. Closely allied to *Calanthe* and *Phaius*, *Spathoglottis* are quite handsome terrestrials, gaining popularity yearly. The pseudobulbs are green with up to four plicate, ribbed, lanceolate leaves, each up to 60cm (2′) long. Racemes are erect with up to 25 blooms in a tight cluster. Flower segments are free and showy. Sepals and the floral stem are covered with soft hairs. Petals are larger than sepals. Flowers vary in colour from yellow to red purple. The labellum is tri-lobed; lateral lobes are narrow and erect. The mid-lobe is interestingly narrow in the middle and flared at each end; the basal third is bi-lobed with two ear-like projections or appendages covered with fine, soft hairs. The lamina is apically bi-lobed.

Culture: Compost is three parts peat, one part sand and one part sphagnum moss. Plants can be grown in full sunlight, though moderate shade is desirable. Water and fertilise frequently.

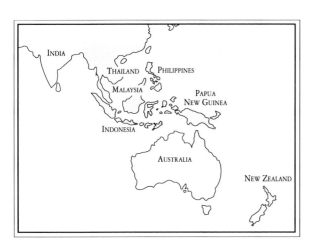

Spathoglottis paulinae

Spathoglottis pacifica

COMMON NAME: Known as 'Varavara' in Fiji.
COLOUR: Flowers pink, mauve or rarely white.
SIZE: Growing up to 1.5m (5') high.
CLIMATE: Warm to hot.
DISTRIBUTION: Native to Fiji.
FLOWERING TIME: Throughout the year.
DESCRIPTION: A common terrestrial orchid.
Pseudobulbs are conical and up to 10cm (4")
high. Leaves are ribbed, broad-lanceolate and
1.5m (5') long. Inflorescence is basal, up to 2m
(6'6") high, with a dense head of flowers
opening in succession. Flowers measure 3.5cm
(1½") across.

Spathoglottis pacifica

Spathoglottis paulinae

Spathoglottis paulinae

COMMON NAME: None.
COLOUR: Flowers light purple. Labellum deep
purple.
SIZE: Terrestrial herb growing up to 60cm (2')
high.
CLIMATE: Warm.
DISTRIBUTION: Native to Australia (far north-
east).
FLOWERING TIME: Winter to end of summer,
peaking in early summer.
DESCRIPTION: Leaves are plicate and strongly
ribbed. Flowers on slender scape, measure
2.5cm (1") across. Similar to *S. plicata,* but
S. plicata has larger, and more, flowers opening
at one time. The labellum side lobes are at right
angles in *S. plicata* and at 45 degrees in
S. paulinae.

Spathoglottis plicata

COMMON NAME: Solomon Islands Orchid.
COLOUR: Flowers pink, mauve, purple or white.
SIZE: A terrestrial species up to 90cm (3') high.
CLIMATE: Warm to hot.
DISTRIBUTION: Native to South-east Asia,
Indonesia, India, the Philippines to Papua New
Guinea, Solomon Islands, Fiji and Australia
(north-east).
FLOWERING TIME: Spring to autumn.
DESCRIPTION: Pseudobulbs are covered in old
leaf fibres, are ovoid and are up to 5cm (2")
high. Leaves are fine, plicate, linear-lanceolate,
acuminate and 30 to 120cm (1 to 4') long.
Inflorescence is lateral and up to 90cm (3')
long. Flowers measure 3cm (1¼") across.

Spathoglottis plicata

Spathoglottis vanoverberghii

Spathoglottis vanoverberghii

COMMON NAME: None.
COLOUR: Flowers yellow, usually sparsely
spotted crimson on the mid-lobe of the
labellum.
SIZE: Growing up to 45cm (18") high.
CLIMATE: Intermediate.
DISTRIBUTION: Native to the Philippines, Luzon,
growing at high elevations.
FLOWERING TIME: Late winter to spring.
DESCRIPTION: Pseudobulbs are ovoid-cylindrical
and grow up to 4cm (1½") high. Leaves are
plicate, lanceolate and up to 38.5cm (15").
Inflorescence is erect and is usually shorter than
the leaves.

STANHOPEA
(stan-hope-ee-a)

Stanhopea was named in honour of the Right Honorable Philip Henry, Fourth Earl of Stanhope, President of the London Medico-Botanical Society. This genus of about 50 species of interesting and fascinating orchids extends from Mexico (where it is affectionately known as 'el toro', the bull) to the tropics of northern South America, Peru and Brazil. At first, species were described by colour, but with further work, colour variation was no longer valid as an indicator of species differentiation. *Stanhopea* is allied to *Coryanthus*, differing in that the epichile of the labellum of the former does not have the saccate of the latter.

Pseudobulbs are deeply ribbed and in tight clusters, each with a single apical leaf. This leaf is plicate and deeply veined beneath. Inflorescence arises from the base of the pseudobulb and is pendulous, burrowing down through the leaf litter and debris in the crutch of the tree or rock crevice and into the open, forming a raceme of one to ten short-lived flowers. The flowers, which emerge from large, inflated buds which open with an audible click, are fleshy and exceedingly fragrant. Sepals and petals are alike in colour, are subsimilar, free, spreading and reflexed; petals often have wavy margins. The labellum is the extraordinary segment of the flower; it is fleshy, waxy and is divided into three distinct sections. The basal third, the hypochile, is usually hollow, calceiform or shoe-shaped where it joins the column. The middle third, the mesochile, is divided, having two prominent horn-like projections. The upper third, the epichile, is articulated to the mesochile and is very variable in shape, from cordate to oblong. The column is long, with the wings extending almost to the apex of the labellum; they are gracefully arched.

Culture: In a basket, use a compost of tree-fern fibre and sterilised bark. Use a 1:1:1 ratio fertiliser monthly. Plants require high humidity, regular water and moderate shade. The most commonly cultivated species is *S. nigroviolace* which is often wrongly named *S. tigrina*.

Stanhopea tigrina

Stanhopea eburnea

Stanhopea nigroviolacea

SOUTH AMERICA

Stanhopea anfracta

COMMON NAME: None.
COLOUR: Flowers orange to yellow, spotted purple-red. Column white; spotted. Hypochile eye spot is often in varying colours.
SIZE: Growing up to 40cm (16").
CLIMATE: Intermediate.
DISTRIBUTION: Native to Panama, Peru and Ecuador. A forest epiphytic growing at altitudes of 1100 to 1200m (3500 to 4000').
FLOWERING TIME: Spring to summer to early winter.
DESCRIPTION: Pseudobulbs are ovoid-conical and grow up to 6cm (2½") high. Leaves are petioled at base, are plicate and broad-elliptic. Inflorescence is pendulous, carrying five to twelve blooms. Flowers are fragrant and up to 7.5cm (3") across.

Stanhopea anfracta

Stanhopea candida

COMMON NAME: None.
COLOUR: Flowers white. Labellum interior spotted purple.
SIZE: Epiphytic plant growing up to 30cm (12") high.
CLIMATE: Intermediate.
DISTRIBUTION: Native to Mexico, Panama, Peru, Colombia and Brazil.
FLOWERING TIME: Summer.
DESCRIPTION: Pseudobulbs are ovoid-conical and up to 6cm (2½") high. Leaves are plicate, broad-elliptical and up to 45cm (18") long. Inflorescence is pendulous, bears three to seven blooms, each up to 7.5cm (3") across.

Stanhopea candida

Stanhopea embreei

COMMON NAME: None.
COLOUR: Flowers ivory-white to rich cream. Sepals and petals may be spotted maroon. Labellum orange-yellow; hypochile with a maroon eye spot on either side.
SIZE: Growing up to 55cm (22") high.
CLIMATE: Intermediate.
DISTRIBUTION: Native to Guatemala, Panama and Ecuador.
FLOWERING TIME: Spring.
DESCRIPTION: Pseudobulbs are ovoid-conical and up to 6cm (2½") high. Leaves are plicate, broad-elliptical and grow up to 45cm (18") long. Inflorescence is pendulous, usually a raceme of three to seven blooms. Flowers are large and showy, measuring 12.5cm (5") across. The orange-yellow hypochile of the labellum is squared, flat-based with a maroon eye spot on either side of the hypochile. Column and epichile are spotted maroon.

Stanhopea embreei

Stanhopea inodora

Stanhopea graveolens

COMMON NAME: None.
COLOUR: Flowers yellow-gold, spotted red-maroon.
SIZE: Growing up to 60cm (2') tall.
CLIMATE: Cool to intermediate.
DISTRIBUTION: Native to Mexico, Guatemala and Honduras in forests up to 2700m (9000') altitude.
FLOWERING TIME: Summer.
DESCRIPTION: An epiphytic or lithophytic plant. Pseudobulbs are ovoid-conical, somewhat depressed and are 5 to 7.5cm (2 to 3") long. Leaf is apical and elliptic-lanceolate. Inflorescence is pendulous with three to nine flowers. Flowers are showy, but have a foul smell. Sepals are concave and petals recurved. Labellum is 5cm (2") long; hypochile is short, saccate and toothed at base; mesochile horns are porrect; and epichile is ovate to revolute. Column is up to 5cm (2") long. Species is closely allied to, and often mistaken for, *Stanhopea wardii*.

Stanhopea graveolens

Stanhopea inodora

COMMON NAME: None.
COLOUR: Flowers ice green-white. The hypochile is partly tinted gold.
SIZE: This epiphytic plant is one of the largest and most vigorous of the *Stanhopeas*.
CLIMATE: Intermediate to warm.
DISTRIBUTION: Native to Mexico and Nicaragua.
FLOWERING TIME: Spring to summer.
DESCRIPTION: Pseudobulbs are ovoid-conical, furrowed, clothed with large sheaths, and grow up to 8cm (3¼") high. Leaves are very broad, elliptic, acute, cuneate near the base and are up to 50cm (20") long. Inflorescence is lateral, basal and pendulous. Raceme has six to ten blooms. Flowers are large, about 10cm (4") long.

Stanhopea insignis

COMMON NAME: None.
COLOUR: Flowers cream to orange-yellow,
covered with purple blotches. Labellum white,
spotted with dark and light purples.
SIZE: Growing up to 60cm (2') high.
CLIMATE: Intermediate.
DISTRIBUTION: Native to Peru and Brazil.
FLOWERING TIME: Autumn.
DESCRIPTION: Pseudobulbs are clustered, ovoid
and up to 7.5cm (3") high. Leaves are plicate,
oblong, acute and up to 45cm (18") long.
Inflorescence is pendulous and grows up to
25cm (10") long. Flower measures up to 12.5cm
(5") long.

Stanhopea insignis

Stanhopea nigroviolacea

Stanhopea nigroviolacea

COMMON NAME: None.
COLOUR: Flowers lemon-yellow with maroon
blotches and spots. Labellum white, spotted
purple. *S. tigrina* is spotted with two small
blotches, but is not blotched.
SIZE: Growing up to 60cm (2') high.
CLIMATE: Intermediate.
DISTRIBUTION: Native to Mexico. Grows up to
2000m (7000') in altitude.
FLOWERING TIME: Summer.
DESCRIPTION: This epiphytic species has been
mistakenly identified for many years as
S. tigrina. Pseudobulb is ovoid with corrugated
grooves and is up to 5cm (2") long. Leaves are
petiolate, broad, acute and up to 60cm (2')
long. Inflorescence is pendulous and fragrant
flowers are large and showy, each measuring up
to 15cm (6") long. In *S. nigroviolaceae* the
hypochile is deeper and the horns broader than
S. tigrina.

Stanhopea oculata

COMMON NAME: None.
COLOUR: Flower colour variable, generally
yellow with red-purple spots.
SIZE: Growing up to 50cm (20") high.
CLIMATE: Intermediate.
DISTRIBUTION: Native to Mexico, Honduras,
British Honduras, Guatemala, Costa Rica and
Panama.
FLOWERING TIME: Summer.
DESCRIPTION: *S. ocullata* is distinguished from its
close ally *S. Wardii* by the hypochile being
transversely cleft below, which forms a hump
below the mesochile. Pseudobulbs are
obliquely ovoid and are up to 6.5cm (2½")
high. Leaves are elliptic, petiolate, acute and
grow up to 45cm (18") long. Inflorescence is
pendulous with three to six blooms. Flowers
are fragrant, each up to 12.5cm (5") across.

Stanhopea oculata

Stanhopea wardii

Stanhopea wardii

COMMON NAME: None.
COLOUR: Flowers lemon to cream, spotted with
red-purple. Hypochile of the labellum maroon
or orange-yellow with purple spots on either
side.
SIZE: Growing up to 52.5cm (21") high.
CLIMATE: Intermediate to warm.
DISTRIBUTION: Native to Mexico and Panama.
FLOWERING TIME: Autumn.
DESCRIPTION: Closely allied to *S. oculata*, but
differing in the structure of the hypochile as
described in that species. Pseudobulbs are
ovoid-conical, angled, somewhat compressed
and grow up to 7.5cm (3") long. Leaves are
elliptic-lanceolate, plicate and are up to 45cm
(18") long. The one to six blooms are showy,
fragrant and 12.5cm (5") across.

STENOGLOTTIS
(sten-oh-glott-is)

Stenoglottis from the Gk *stenos* (narrow) *glotta* (a tongue) with reference to the narrow irregular lobes of the labellum. This genus of three species comes from eastern, central and southern Africa. Two of the three species are well known in choice collections, but *S. zambesiaca* from Nyasaland (Malawi) is exceedingly rare. These terrestrial herbs have fleshy, tuber-like roots, short stems, and the leaves form a basal rosette. Inflorescence is erect and many-flowered. The flowers are interesting and are coloured pink with dark spots. Sepals are adnate to the column and labellum for a short length, then are spreading. Petals are wider than sepals and are erect. The labellum is united to the column with or without the spur; it is wedge-shaped with three to seven lobes or tails.

Culture: Compost in small well-drained pots. Plants require moist, shady conditions. The leaves die back during and after flowering. Supply a little water until new growth appears.

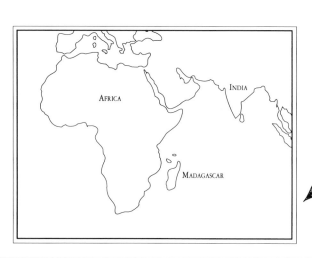

Stenoglottis longifolia

Stenoglottis longifolia

Stenoglottis longifolia

COMMON NAME: None.
COLOUR: Flowers mauve or rarely white. Labellum spotted purple.
SIZE: Growing up to 20cm (8″) high.
CLIMATE: Intermediate.
DISTRIBUTION: Native to South Africa, Zululand.
FLOWERING TIME: Autumn.
DESCRIPTION: A terrestrial or lithophytic or epiphytic species. Leaves are linear-oblong, acuminate, margins undulate, up to 18cm (7″) and form a dense basal rosette. Inflorescence is erect, up to 50cm (20″) long with a densely flowered raceme.

THELYMITRA
(thel-ee-mye-tra)

Thelymitra from the Gk *thelys* (female) *mitra* (head-dress or headband) with reference to the ornate wings that decorate the head of the column. This genus of over 80 species of terrestrial orchids is indigenous principally to Australia, with several species scattered through the Philippines, Indonesia, Papua New Guinea, the Pacific Islands and New Zealand. They are commonly known as Sun Orchids, because of their habit of opening only in bright sunlight. These species are true terrestrial herbs with a root system of two underground tubers. The solitary leaf is fluted and narrow. Inflorescence is a tall raceme of one or many wide open un-orchid-like blooms. Flowers are graceful; all segments of the perianth are similar and spreading. They open only in warm sunshine. The column is complex; it is erect with lateral wings united in front at the base and extending upwards at side of anther into plumed, brush-like appendages.

Culture: As for *Caladenia*. In Australia cultivated *Thelymitra* hybrids are freely available from nurseries specialising in Australian native species. These nurseries will also supply complete information on cultivating *Thelymitra*.

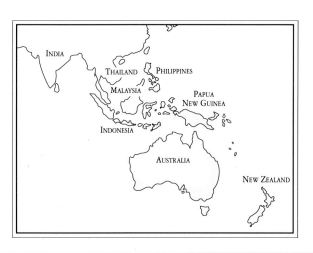

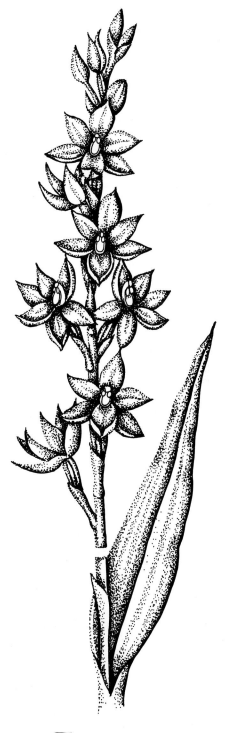

Thelymitra nuda

Thelymitra aristata

COMMON NAME: Scented Sun Orchid.
COLOUR: Flowers pink, blue or mauve.
SIZE: A variable terrestrial plant up to 90cm (3′)
high.
CLIMATE: Cool.
DISTRIBUTION: Native to Australia (moist areas)
in close association with *Dendrobium
kingianum.*
FLOWERING TIME: Spring.
DESCRIPTION: Leaves are sheathing, broad,
lanceolate and 15 to 25cm (6 to 10″) long.
Inflorescence 1 to 35 blooms, up to 90cm (3′)
high. Flowers are fragrant, each measuring to
3.5cm (1½″) across.

Thelymitra aristata

Thelymitra ixioides

Thelymitra ixioides

COMMON NAME: Spotted Sun Orchid.
COLOUR: Flowers blue-mauve with dark blue
spots, rarely pink.
SIZE: A robust terrestrial 20 to 60cm (8 to 24″)
high.
CLIMATE: Cool.
DISTRIBUTION: Native to Australia and New
Zealand (dry areas).
FLOWERING TIME: Spring.
DESCRIPTION: Leaves are channelled and 12.5 to
20cm (5 to 8″) long. Flowers are in a terminal
raceme, are numerous or solitary and about 3 to
6cm (1¼ to 2¼″) across.

Thelymitra venosa

COMMON NAME: Veined Sun Orchid.
COLOUR: Flowers blue with darker veins.
SIZE: A slender terrestrial. Grows to 75cm (30″) high.
CLIMATE: Cool.
DISTRIBUTION: Native to Australia (common in alpine moss beds and moist
swampy areas).
FLOWERING TIME: Summer.
DESCRIPTION: Leaves are narrow to broad-lanceolate and deeply channelled.
Terminal raceme with one to three flowers, each 2 to 5cm (¾ to 2″) across.

Thelymitra venosa

THUNIA
(too-nee-a)

Thunia is named in honour of Count von Thun Hohenstein of Tetschin, Bohemia. This is a small genus of less than ten very beautiful terrestrials from India, Burma, South-east Asia and China. In early times *Thunia* was included in *Phaius*; however, it lacks pseudobulbs. The leaves are deciduous. Inflorescence is terminal on thick, clustered, leafy stems or cane-like pseudobulbs, often 5cm (2″) thick, racemose and drooping. Flowers are large, attractive and white or purple-magenta in colour. Sepals and petals are free. The labellum is tubular or bell-shaped, entire. The front margin is fringed and has yellow markings with a short, obtuse spur at the base of the labellum.

Culture: Compost. As for *Phaius*. Once the flowers fade and die, the leaves turn yellow and drop. Any repotting may be carried out once all the leaves have fallen. This genus is very easily grown and grows best in pots. Plants require moderate shade.

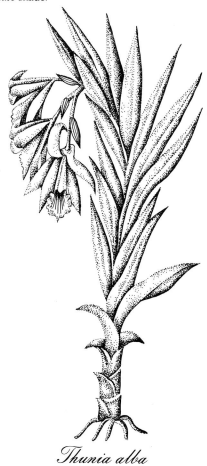

Thunia alba

Thunia marshalliana

COMMON NAME: Orchid of Burma.
COLOUR: Flower white. Labellum marked with yellow.
SIZE: Growing up to 90cm (3′) high.
CLIMATE: Intermediate.
DISTRIBUTION: Native to Burma.
FLOWERING TIME: Summer.
DESCRIPTION: Pseudobulbs are terete, stem-like, robust and up to 90cm (3′) high. Leaves are lanceolate. Inflorescence is arching and clustered. Flower measures 12½cm (5″) across.

Thunia marshalliana

TRICHOPILIA
(trik-o-pill-ee-a)

Trichopilia from the Gk *tricho* (hair) *pilos* (of felt, such as in a hat or cap) with reference to the fringed margin or hood of the column. This genus of about 30 species of large fragrant flowers is widespread throughout central and South America, from Mexico and the West Indies to Peru and Brazil. It is a small to medium epiphytic, sympodial orchid. The pseudobulbs are almost flattened and are clustered along a creeping rhizome. The single leaf is apical, oblong to lanceolate and coriaceous. Inflorescence is a spike from the base of the pseudobulb with one to many blooms. Flowers are exceptionally attractive; individual flowers measure up to 15cm (6″) across, are free flowering and have a wide range of colours. They somewhat resemble *Cattleya*. Sepals and petals are similar in shape, size and colour. The labellum is tri-lobed, fused at base to column, is trumpet-shaped or tubular-involute, is spreading above, with wavy margins and is sweetly fragrant. The column is usually hidden. The orchid's distinguishing feature is the ciliated hood of the anther cap.

Culture: Mount on a tree-fern fibre slab. Water well. Be careful how you use fertiliser as foliage is subject to burn. Plants require humidity and moderate shade.

SOUTH AMERICA

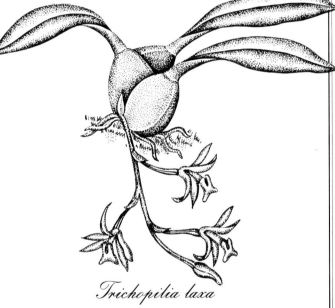

Trichopilia laxa

Trichopilia suavis

Trichopilia suavis

COMMON NAME: None.
COLOUR: Flower colour variable, usually white to cream, spotted with pink. Labellum marked with yellow.
SIZE: Growing up to 25cm (10″) high.
CLIMATE: Warm.
DISTRIBUTION: Native to Costa Rica, Peru and Colombia.
FLOWERING TIME: Spring.
DESCRIPTION: An epiphytic plant. Pseudobulbs are clustered, broad, oblong-ovoid and compressed. Leaves are solitary, apical, broad ovate, coriaceous and about 20cm (8″) or more long. Flower spike is short. Flowers are fragrant and grow up to 10cm (4″) across. Labellum margins are frilled.

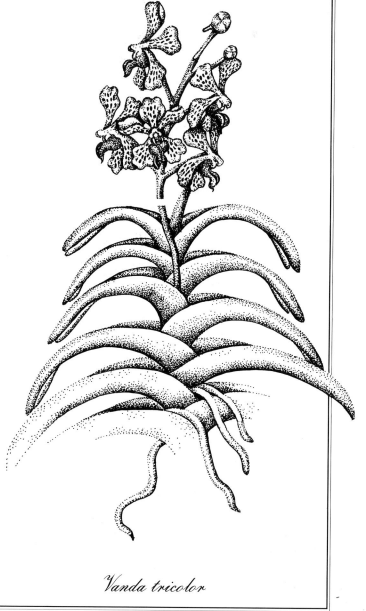

VANDA
(van-da)

*V*anda comes from the Sanskrit word describing the plant we today know as *Vanda tesselata* from Bengal, (India), Sri Lanka and Burma. It was discovered in 1795 by Sir W. Jones. This genus of over 70 species of monopodial epiphytic orchids extends from India to South-east Asia and Borneo, and south to Indonesia, Papua New Guinea and Australia. Vandas are as popular as *Cattleyas, Cymbidiums, Dendrobiums, Laelias, Oncidiums, Paphiopedilums* and *Phalaenopsis*, being found in most collections. *Vanda* is divided into two main groups: (a) *Vanda tricolour:* with strap-like, distichous, stem-clasping leaves, keeled, green above and light beneath, the apex erose; (b) *Vanda teres:* with terete leaves about as thick as a pencil. The base of these leaves encircle the stems.

The plant's inflorescence is axillary, erect, racemose, with few to many flowers. In group (b) the inflorescence is on the side of the stem opposite the leaf. Flowers are showy, with a wide range of colours. Sepals and petals are subsimilar, free and spreading. The labellum is tri-lobed, the base is spurred or saccate and is adnate to the column; lateral lobes may be small or long auricle appendages, almost encircling column. The spur is conical; the mid-lobe is porrect, varying in size with the fleshy disc.

Culture: Compost in large well-drained pots or baskets. Because of their habit of strong aerial root growth, pots and bench soon become overgrown. *Vandas* do exceptionally well on large tree-fern slabs, and on trees in the open garden.

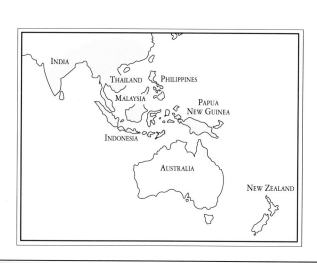

Vanda tricolor

Vanda coerulea

COMMON NAME: Blue Vanda.
COLOUR: Flowers blue. Labellum tri-lobed with front lobe deep blue.
SIZE: Monopodial, growing up to 90cm (3') high.
CLIMATE: Intermediate.
DISTRIBUTION: Native to Thailand, Burma and northern India at high elevations.
FLOWERING TIME: Autumn.
DESCRIPTION: Blue is considered a rare colour in orchids. Leaves are coriaceous, distichous, strap-like and 7.5 to 25cm (3 to 10") long. Inflorescence is erect or suberect, with 6 to 20 flowers, each up to 10cm (4") across. Sepals and petals equal. Labellum is small, tri-lobed, with small lateral lobes, and the mid-lobe has ridges terminating in bituberculate apex. Conical spur.

Vanda coerulea

Vanda cristata

Vanda cristata

COMMON NAME: None.
COLOUR: Flowers yellow to green-yellow. Labellum green underneath, tawny above, spotted with deep red stripes.
SIZE: Growing up to 30cm (12") high.
CLIMATE: Intermediate.
DISTRIBUTION: Native to Bhutan, Nepal and Sikkim. Growing at high elevations.
FLOWERING TIME: Spring to summer.
DESCRIPTION: Plant erect, with coriaceous leaves which are 15cm (6") long. Flowers are waxy and fragrant. Labellum is tri-lobed: lateral lobes erect and deltoid shaped; mid-lobe subpandurate; spur short and conical.

Vanda dearei

COMMON NAME: None.
COLOUR: Flowers cream, floral segment tips generally flushed with buff-brown. Labellum marked with lemon, streaked with crimson.
SIZE: A robust plant reaching height of up to 2.4m (8').
CLIMATE: Hot.
DISTRIBUTION: Native to Borneo, growing at low elevations.
FLOWERING TIME: Mainly summer, but throughout the year.
DESCRIPTION: Leaves are broad, and compact. Inflorescence is short with few blooms. Flower is fragrant and about 5cm (2") across. Labellum is tri-lobed.

Vanda dearei

Vanda denisoniana

Vanda denisoniana

COMMON NAME: None.
COLOUR: Flower colour variable from white-green to white. Labellum has a basal yellow blotch.
SIZE: Growing up to 45cm (18") high.
CLIMATE: Intermediate.
DISTRIBUTION: Native to Burma and Arakan Mountains, growing at elevations of 600 to 750m (2000 to 2500').
FLOWERING TIME: Spring.
DESCRIPTION: Stems are leafy throughout. Leaves are linear, emarginate and up to 30cm (12") long. Flower is fragrant, measuring about 5cm (2") long.

Vanda hindsii syn. V. whiteana

COMMON NAME: None.
COLOUR: Flower colour variable, usually red-brown with yellow margins, or may have yellow-brown flecks. A rare pure yellow form exists.
SIZE: Growing up to 90cm (3′) high.
CLIMATE: Hot.
DISTRIBUTION: Native to far north-eastern Australia and Papua New Guinea.
FLOWERING TIME: Late spring to summer.
DESCRIPTION: Stems are up to 90cm (3′) high. Leaves are strap-like, distichous, compact and grow up to 40cm (16″) long. Raceme is about 30cm (12″) long with up to seven blooms. Flowers measure up to 3.5cm (1½″) across.

Vanda hindsii syn. *V. whiteana*

Vanda lamellata

Vanda lamellata

COMMON NAME: None.
COLOUR: Flowers lemon with brown markings.
SIZE: A dwarf species.
CLIMATE: Warm.
DISTRIBUTION: Native to the Philippines and northern Borneo.
FLOWERING TIME: Winter.
DESCRIPTION: Leaves are slender, coriaceous, recurved and strap-like. Plant has a profusion of flowers. Flower measures about 5cm (2″) across.

Vanda pumila

COMMON NAME: None.
COLOUR: Flowers cream or yellow. Labellum streaked with purple.
SIZE: A small epiphytic species with short stout stem.
CLIMATE: Intermediate.
DISTRIBUTION: Native to Himalayas, India (Sikkim), Bhutan and Thailand, growing at altitudes of 600m (1000′).
FLOWERING TIME: Winter.
DESCRIPTION: Leaves are strap-shaped, curved, emarginate and grow up to 20cm (8″) long. Inflorescence is erect, as long as the leaves and is axillary. Flower is fragrant, showy and up to 6cm (2½″) across.

Vanda pumila

Vanda roeblingiana

Vanda roeblingiana

COMMON NAME: None.
COLOUR: Flowers yellow, striped irregularly with red-brown. Labellum yellow-cream streaked with red-brown.
SIZE: Growing up to 90cm (3′) high.
CLIMATE: Intermediate.
DISTRIBUTION: Native to the Philippines, Luzon, growing at elevations of 1200 to 1500m (4000 to 5000′).
FLOWERING TIME: Summer.
DESCRIPTION: Erect stems grow to about 90cm (3′) high. Leaves are linear, unequally emarginate, acuminate and up to 20cm (8″) long. Inflorescence grows up to 30cm (12″) long. Flowers measure 5cm (2″) across and are fragrant. Labellum is tri-lobed.

Vanda stangeana

COMMON NAME: None.

COLOUR: Flowers golden-green, tessellated with red-brown. Labellum white, marked and spotted red, tip gold-green.

SIZE: Growing up to 45cm (18″) high.

CLIMATE: Intermediate.

DISTRIBUTION: Native to India, Assam and Nepal, growing between 1200 to 1500m (4000 to 5000′) in altitude.

FLOWERING TIME: Spring.

DESCRIPTION: Stems are erect, robust and grow up to 45cm (18″) high. Leaves are distichous, strap-like, emarginate, recurved and up to 15cm (6″) long. Inflorescence is usually erect and about 12.5 cm (5″) long. Flowers are almost 6cm (2½″) long with undulate margins.

Vanda tricolor

Vanda stangeana

Vanda tricolor

COMMON NAME: None.

COLOUR: Flower colour variable, usually pale yellow, spotted and flecked red-brown. Labellum white, streaked red-brown and tinted purple and mauve.

SIZE: A large erect epiphytic, lithophytic or terrestrial, growing up to 1.2m (4′) high.

CLIMATE: Warm.

DISTRIBUTION: Native to Java, Bali and Laos.

FLOWERING TIME: Autumn to winter.

DESCRIPTION: Leaves are imbricate, strap-like, curved, unequally emarginate and grow up to 45cm (18″) long. Inflorescence is shorter than the leaves. Flower measures up to 7.5cm (3″) across, is fragrant, large and showy.

Vanda tricolor var. insignis

COMMON NAME: None.

COLOUR: Flowers yellow-green, blotched brown. Mid-lobe of labellum red-purple.

SIZE: Growing up to 1.2m (4′) high.

CLIMATE: Same as type.

DISTRIBUTION: Native to Mollucas, Timor and Alor Islands.

FLOWERING TIME: Usually autumn, but may flower three times annually.

DESCRIPTION: Same as type, except labellum is wider.

Vanda tricolor var. *insignis*

Vanda tricolor var. *suavis*

Vanda tricolor var. suavis

COMMON NAME: None.

COLOUR: Flowers white, spotted and flecked, red-purple.

SIZE: Same as type form.

CLIMATE: Warm.

DISTRIBUTION: Native to Java.

FLOWERING TIME: Autumn to winter.

DESCRIPTION: Differing from its type form by having a longer inflorescence with more numerous flowers. Labellum is slightly more linear with reflexed margins.

VANDOPSIS
(van-dop-sis)

Vandopsis from the Gk *opsis* (appearance; resembles) with reference to a resemblance to the genus *Vanda. Vandopsis* is a genus of less than ten species of very robust monopodial epiphytic orchids. They are widespread, occurring from Burma, through South-east Asia to Borneo, the Philippines, Indonesia and Papua New Guinea. *Vandopsis* was probably first recognised as a genus by Gaudichaud in about 1817; from then until about 1850 various species were continually being shifted from one genus to another and at about that time Pfitzer established *Vandopsis* as a recognised genus. The plants are erect. Leaves are distichous, coriaceous yet fleshy, strap-like and keeled. Inflorescence is axillary, up to 1.8m (6′) long and many-flowered with up to 22 blooms. Flowers are fleshy, thick-textured like a banana skin, or coriaceous, remaining open over a long period of time (*V. lissochiloides* for as long as four months). Sepals and petals are subsimilar. The labellum is tri-lobed; lateral lobes are joined across the base of the mid-lobe by a fleshy bridge. The mid-lobe is elongated, fleshy and keeled from the apex almost to the base. Flowers are yellow with purple or brown markings or blotches.

Culture: As for *Vanda*, use coarse compost in well-drained pots, or better still, mount on a large tree-fern slab.

Vandopsis parishii

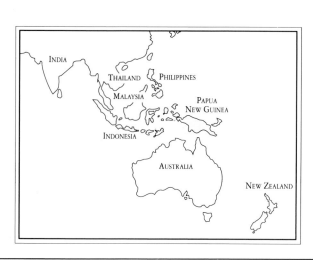

Vandopsis lissochiloides

COMMON NAME: None.
COLOUR: Flowers yellow marked with purple and red-purple underneath.
SIZE: Growing up to 1.8m (6′) high.
CLIMATE: Warm.
DISTRIBUTION: Native to the Philippines.
FLOWERING TIME: Spring to summer.
DESCRIPTION: Is often mistaken for *V. batemani*. Numerous flowers, each up to 7.5cm (3″) across.

Vandopsis lissochiloides

VANILLA
(va-nil-la)

Vanilla from the Spanish *vainilla*, a diminutive of the Spanish *vaina* (meaning a pod or sheath) with reference to the slender pod-like fruit. Several species of the genus are grown in various countries of the world as a commercial agricultural crop. This tall climbing monopodial herb is widely distributed throughout the tropics and subtropics of the world. It is closely related to *Pogonia*. *Vanilla* is a genus of over 100 species of terrestrial or epiphytic plants branching with leaves and roots at each nodes. Roots attach to bark or twigs for support. Species of the genera *Vanilla* and *Galoelia* are the only orchids to have developed the climbing habit so well. Leaves are alternately large or reduced to scale-like appendages, thus giving the plant an appearance of a leafless vine. Inflorescence is axillary, clustered with few or many flowers which do not open fully.

They are 7.5cm (3″) long, are fleshy and often showy. Sepals and petals are equal in shape, colour and size; segments are free. The labellum is tri-lobed or entire with the distinct claw adnate to the column, with lateral lobes encircling the column; the mid-lobe is flaring at the apex and the margins are wavy having appendages. The column is long, slender and often pubescent. The fruit is a long fleshy pod, not necessarily dehiscent.

Culture: Compost in a large pot with plenty of support or in a well-drained flower bed. The growing stems need to be supported with a tree-fern trunk or can be grown along a wall or with wires. Plants require humidity at all times with shade. Generally the flowers do not appear until the plant is well grown.

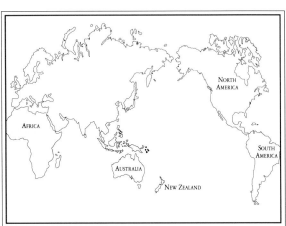

Vanilla planifolia

Vanilla pompona

Vanilla pompona

COMMON NAME: Vanilla Orchid.
COLOUR: Flowers green-yellow. Labellum white to yellow-orange.
SIZE: Climbs up to 6m (20′) high.
CLIMATE: Warm.
DISTRIBUTION: Native to Mexico, throughout Central America to Peru, Bolivia and Brazil.
FLOWERING TIME: Summer.
DESCRIPTION: A climbing, succulent, robust plant. Leaves are fleshy, ovate-oblong and grow up to 30cm (12″) long. Inflorescence is axillary with numerous, clustered flowers. Flowers are shy openers, are fragrant and measure up to 9cm (3¾″) long.

ZYGOPETALUM
(zye-go-pet-a-lum)

Zygopetalum from the Gk *zyon* (a yoke, occurring as a pair) *petalon* (a petal) with reference to the yoke-like callus on the base of the labellum, which appears to hold the petals together. This genus of almost twenty species is found in tropical South America from Paraguay, Peru, Bolivia, the Guyanas and south to Brazil. It is a genus of sympodial epiphytes.

Pseudobulbs are ovoid, short, stout, distinctly sheathed, wrinkling with age. It has two or more leaves which are apical, distichous, glossy, plicate, veined and becoming deciduous. Inflorescence from the base of the pseudobulb is a raceme of three to twelve flowers. Flowers are showy and interesting. Sepals and petals are usually alike in size and colour, are green with brown or purple blotches, with undulating margins. The labellum is tri-lobed, with a small spur attached to the base of the column. Lateral lobes are erect and small, encircling the column. The mid-lobe is broad with a wavy margin. Disc has an entire fleshy callus. The flower is often highly perfumed.

Culture: Compost. Best treated as a terrestrial, so plant in large well-drained pots. Plants require humid conditions and shade. Provide plenty of water while growing and far less once bulbs are fully grown.

Zygopetalum intermedium

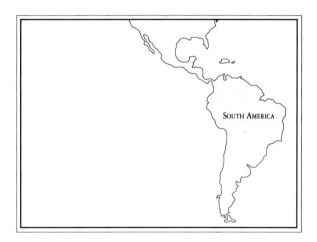

SOUTH AMERICA

Zygopetalum mackayi

COMMON NAME: None.
COLOUR: Petals and sepals green, blotched with green-brown. Labellum has violet stripes.
SIZE: Growing up to 55cm (22″) high.
CLIMATE: Intermediate.
DISTRIBUTION: Native to Brazil.
FLOWERING TIME: Autumn.
DESCRIPTION: Pseudobulbs are 10cm (4″) high. Leaves grow up to 45cm (18″) long. Flower scape bears five to ten flowers, each up to 7.5cm (3″) across and very fragrant.

Zygopetalum mackayi

Pests and Diseases

By far the most damaging of orchid diseases are caused by virus infection. Although much work has been done, no cure has been discovered. Most growers burn all affected plants, a safe precaution considering the ease with which viruses spread through plant collections. When an orchid is infected with a virus, the disease affects all parts of the plant, and cannot be eliminated by tissue culturing the *meristematic* tissue, as is done with some other types of plants. However the seed is not affected and can be used for propagation providing the pod is allowed to dry and split, ejecting the seed onto a sterile surface.

More than fifty different viruses have been identified in orchids but only two are easily detected by growers and are our concern here: Cymbidium Mosaic Virus (C.M.V.) and Tobacco Strain 'O' Virus (often called *Odontoglossum* Ring Spot Virus).

Plants may be infected with either of these viruses, or with any of the viruses, without showing any signs of the disease. It is only when some abnormality occurs that a virus is detected, unless tests are carried out in a laboratory on an indicator plant. Tests on healthy plants are usually undertaken when a plant is to be mericloned or used as a seed carrying parent.

HOW TO DETECT A VIRUS

Cymbidium Mosaic Virus can infect any genera of orchid, but as the name suggests, it is found mostly in *Cymbidiums*. It is usually detected by the leaves becoming streaked with broken lines of a paler colour. The flowers will often be deformed or have variations of colour, but the leaves are the main clue in detecting the disease.

Tobacco Strain 'O' Virus is detected in a wider range of genera, but particularly in *Odontoglossum, Cattleya* and *Dendrobium*. One symptom is a distinct ring spot, that is, an outer ring of necrotic black tissue, with some green tissue inside and then a necrotic black spot in the centre. Several such spots may occur on a single leaf. It is often called 'colour break virus' because the flowers are marked with irregular colour patterns. A third sign is the appearance of shallow dimples on the leaves. These signs and any other abnormality should be regarded as suspect and plants should be destroyed. If not destroyed, then plants should be isolated completely from the rest of the collection.

As viruses are seldom detected early, all plants must be regarded as possible carriers of the disease. As the disease is spread by innoculating one plant with the sap of another, we can reduce the spreading by simply using sterile tools and by using only sterilised pots. Likewise do not re-use potting material and thoroughly wash hands after working on each plant. Practising these simple procedures will not eliminate the spread of the disease, but it will certainly help keep your collection healthy.

FUNGAL AND BACTERIAL DISEASES

Other diseases affecting orchids are usually of fungal or bacterial origin, and they too can be reduced by good house-keeping practices—keep the growing area clean and free from unnecessary debris and allow for plenty of fresh air to circulate around the plants. However, sometimes problems occur in the cleanest houses. For practical purposes it is best to regard fungi problems in two categories: (a) Those that affect the plant above the potting mix; and (b) Those that affect the root area.

If the problem is in the pseudobulb or leaf area then it is best to use a contact fungicide. Some growers use these fungicides regularly as a preventative measure. Mancozeb is very good, but before using check to see if its use in your area is prohibited.

If the disease is in the root area, it will usually be found when the new leads appear; they will suddenly die, leaving a soft squashy mess, called damp-off. This can be controlled with a systemic fungicide. Benomyl or Furalaxy are good, but again check to see if its use is prohibited.

Bacterial diseases are usually not identified as such, but are thought to be of fungal origin until it is found that fungicides do not control the problem. There are relatively few bacteriacides on the market, but your local nursery may offer a product to help with your problem. Regulations vary from state to state and from country to country, so consult your local nursery or orchid society. However the writers use 'Physan 20' when necessary.

PESTS

Pests in orchids are numerous and destructive but all can be controlled to acceptable levels with proper treatment. Of the insect pests which cause ugly disfiguration of both plant and flower, the Red Spider Mite (*Tetranychus urticae*) is the most difficult to eradicate. Their favourite host plant is the *Cymbidium*, where they feed on the underside of the leaves. Regularly inspect your *Cymbidiums*. The mite is just visible to the naked eye and a build-up can be rapid. With a heavy infestation the leaves turn yellow, and a network of fine webs will be seen on the underside of the leaves. Control can be effected by the use of azobenzene fumigation, followed by an alternate treatment using a malathion aerosol spray. These chemicals do not kill eggs, so a follow up of three or four applications about ten days apart will be necessary. As a note of caution, remember that chemicals affect humans as well as insects. Read and follow instructions carefully.

False mite (*Brevipalpus russulus*) is red and attacks many plants, but seems to prefer *Phalaenopsis*. It causes pitting on the upper surface of the leaves. If treatment is neglected, a fungal infection will quickly develop, defoliating the plant. Here, again, a fumigation followed by a malathion aerosol spray should give complete control.

Brown or soft scales (*Diaspis boisluvalii* or *Coccus hesperidum*) are protected by a dome-shaped hard shell which resists chemical sprays. Likewise the Mealy Bug (*Pseudococcus longispinus*) is protected from sprays by a white waxy substance. Since both are sap-sucking pests, a systemic insecticide makes the plant toxic, thus the pests can be controlled with three applications, each about ten days apart. Should only several plants be affected, then paint the infection with methylated spirits using a small paint brush.

Aphids (*Cerataphis lantaniae*) attack young buds and tender new growth. There are several commercial sprays available for the treatment of Aphids. Check with your supplier or nursery. Liquid derris spray is usually most effective. Slugs and snails can be controlled by using common garden-snail baits. Most of the other insect pests, such as thrips, caterpillars, etc., can be controlled with the well-known and recommended garden insecticides.

As with fungal diseases, insect pests and other problems can be reduced considerably with good housekeeping. Close your houses as much as possible against insect entry. Keep overgrown grass and weeds away from the outside and, above all, check newly acquired plants carefully so you don't introduce new problems; treat new plants properly before introducing them to your collection.

Government regulations may prohibit dangerous chemicals, so always check with your local nursery or orchid society; they will recommend the best available legal sprays and chemicals if you are confronted with pests or diseases.

CLUBS AND ORGANISATIONS

For the novice and professional alike, orchid and general gardening societies can prove valuable sources of information. Most countries throughout the world have orchid societies which amateurs can join.

The American Orchid Society is a large organisation which publishes a monthly magazine *The Orchid Digest*. Botanical gardens throughout the world are also helpful, especially when trying to identify a plant.

For both interest and competition, orchid shows are held throughout the year in numerous countries. On a large scale, international orchid shows are conducted in Asia with entries from all over the world.

American Orchid Society Inc.
84 Sherman Street
Cambridge, Massachusetts 02140
United States of America

Orchid Society of South-East Asia
Phoon Yoon Seng
22 Tosca Street
Singapore 1545

Honolulu Orchid Society Inc.
1710 Pali Highway
Honolulu Hawaii 96813

Royal Horticultural Society
Vincent Square
London SW1P 2PE United Kingdom

Orchid Society of Great Britain
9 Harlands Close
Haywards Heath, West Sussex
RHY16 1PS, England

Sydney Orchid Society
75 Quigg Street
Lakemba NSW 2195
Australia

ORCHID HYBRIDS

There is a special procedure for registering hybrids. Application forms must be completed and submitted with The Royal Horticultural Society in England for the cross to be officially recognised. All new hybrid names are published in an English journal called *The Orchid Review*. Every three years an international list is published in the *Sanders List of Orchid Hybrids*.

GLOSSARY

Actinomorphic: radially symmetrical.

Acuminate: tapering to a point.

Acute: sharp point.

Adnate: attached along the whole length to a part of unlike kind (e.g. of a petal attached to a column).

Aerial: exposed to the atmosphere as adventurous from tree or stem.

Ancipital: two-edged, as stem of plant.

Anterior: on the side of an organ farthest from the axis or stem on which it grows.

Antero-lateral: anterior and at the side.

Anther: the part of the stamen that holds pollen.

Anticous: on the anterior side.

Apetalous: without petals.

Apex: (Plural apices): tip.

Apical: at or pertaining to the tip of any structure.

Apiculate: tipped with a short and abrupt point.

Apomixis: reproduction which replaces or serves as a substitute for sexual reproduction; reproduction from cells other than ovules.

Arcuate: arched.

Aromatic: fragrant.

Articulate: jointed.

Ascending: growing upward.

Asexual: sexless, without sex involvement.

Auricle: ear-like lobe at the base of lamina.

Awn: a stiff bristle-like appendage (eg. a beard of barley)

Axil: the angle formed by a leaf or bract with the branch or stem.

Axillary: arising from the axil of a leaf or bract.

Axis: the main stem or the central column from which organs originate.

Back bulb: old pseudobulb.

Bicalcarate: two-spurred.

Bidentate: having two teeth.

Bifarious: into two rows.

Bifid: divided by a deep cleft into two parts.

Bifurcate: branched into, or twice forked.

Bilobate: having two lobes.

Bipartite: divided into two parts.

Bisexual: of a flower containing both stamens and pistil.

Boss: swelling.

Botryoidal: resembling a bunch of grapes.

Bract: modified leaf or a flowering stem.

Bracteate: having bracts.

Bracteole: a small bract below an individual flower.

Calceiform: shoe-shaped or shoe-like.

Calceolate: slipper-shaped.

Callosities: alternative term for calli especially in *Microtis*.

Callosity: a hard lump.

Callus: (plural calli) thickened region, especially of labellum.

Campanulate: bell-shaped.

Canaliculate: with a longitudinal groove.

Capillary: hair-like.

Capitulum: inflorescence with sensile flowers compacted into a dense cluster, as in daisies; also known as a head.

Capsule: the fruit or seed case of most orchids.

Carinate: with a keel.

Cauda: a tail-like appendage; adjective caudate.

Caudicle: a star-like structure connected with the pollinia of orchids.

Cauline: attached to or pertaining to the stem (e.g. leaves on the stems).

Cavate: hollowed out.

Chelate: shaped like a lobster's claw.

Cilia: (singular cilium) fine hair-like structures usually around the margins of an organ.

Circinate: coiled into a tight spiral.

Clavate: club-shaped.

Claw: the stalk-like base of the petal, sepal or labellum.

Clinandrium: the depression on the top of the column on which the anthers rest.

Clone: a group of individuals (each a ramet) produced asexually from a single parent, normally of uniform genetic identity.

Column: the central organ of the orchid flower, formed by the fusion of the stamens and pistils.

Complicate: folded upon itself.

Confluent: running together.

Conical: cone-shaped.

Connate: of parts of like kind, closely united at their bases.

Connivent: converging but not fused.

Convolute: rolled together so margins overlap, furled like an umbrella

Cordate/Cordiform: heart-shaped.

Coriaceous: of leathery texture.

Corolla: the second lower-most whorl of sterile parts in a flower; each member is termed a petal.

Corymb: a racemose inflorescence in which the lower flowers are at more or less the same height.

Corymbiform: with the shape of a corymb.

Crassinode: nodes swollen in shape, thick and thin.

Crenulate: with tiny rounded teeth along the margins.

Cruciform: shaped like a cross.

Cucullate: arched into a hood.

Cuneate: wedge-shaped; broadest at apex.

Cuspidate: terminating in a sharp rigid point.

Cymbiform: boat-shaped.

Decurrent: extending downwards from the place of insertion; applied to leaves when their blades continue down the stem, forming raised lines.

Decurved: curved downwards.

Deflexed: bent downwards.

Deltoid: triangular with corners rounded.

Dentate: with outward facing acute teeth along the margins.

Denticulate: finely dentate.

Depressed: flattened down.

Dichotomous: forked in pairs; repeatedly dividing into branches.

Dilatation: a widening into a blade.

Disc: in orchids, the face or upper surface of the middle portion of the labellum.

Distal: towards the free end of an organ.

Distichous: arranged in two ranks, as leaves on opposite sides of stem.

Divaricate: widely diverging.

Dorsal: relating to the back of a structure; that is, the side facing away from the axis; but note that most orchid flowers twist around as they develop so that the dorsal side becomes the side *towards* the axis.

Dorsiventral: having distinct surfaces on both sides.

Dorsum: the back of an organ, that is, the side facing away from the axis.

Ellipsoid: compressed sphere; an elliptic solid.

Elliptic: shaped like an ellipse.

Emarginate: notched at the apex.

Endemic: confined to a particular region.

Ensiform: shaped like a sword blade.

Entire: without any division or irregularity (used especially of leaf margins or labellum).

Epichile: the terminal part of the jointed labellum of some orchids.

Epigeal: on or above the surface of the soil.

Epiphyte: a plant which grows upon trees, but which does not derive nourishment from their tissue.

Equitant: of leaves, arranged in such a way that each leaf is folded along its length and encloses the leaves younger than it.

Erect: upright.

Erose: jagged; as though bitten or gnawed off.

Evanescent: soon vanishing.

Exserted: protruding.

Eye: the incipient bud of a growth, particularly in sympodial orchids.

Falcate: sickle or scythe shaped.

Farinaceous: resembling flour; containing starch.

Flabelliform: fan-shaped.

Flagelliform: whip-like; long and slender like a lash.

Faucet gland: a tap-like gland that drips fluid.

Filiform: thread-like.

Fimbriate: fringed with long hairs or thread-like outgrowth; noun fimbria.

Flexuose: zig zag.

Foliaceous: leaf-like in appearance.

Foveolar: having pits or small depressions.

Fugacious: soon withering.

Furcate: forked into two.

Furfuraceous: scruffy; scaly or flaky.

Fused: amalgamated into one whole.

Fusiform: spindle-shaped.

Galea: a helmet-shaped structure, such as is formed in the flowers of *Pterostylis* in the fused dorsal sepal and lateral petals.

Gammate: shaped like the Greek capital letter *gamma* (i.e. upside down L).

Genus: the smallest natural group of species having certain essential characteristics in common. The first word in the botanical name of a plant is the genus to which it belongs.

Gibbous: with a swollen spur.

Glabrous: without hairs; having a smooth surface.

Globose: almost round.

Gynostemium: alternate name for column.

Hastate: spear shaped.

Herbaceous: without woody tissue.

Hirsute: covered with rough, fairly long hairs; pubescent.

Hydroponic: method of growing plants using nutrient solutions alone.

Hispid: with strong hairs or bristles.

Hypochile: lower or basal section of jointed labellum of some orchids.

Imbricate: overlapping, especially in bud.

Incumbent: lying upon a surface; distinct from erect.

Incurved: curved inwards; of the margins of the lamina of a leaf, curving towards the upperside or the side facing the axis.

Indent: notched.

Indigenous: native.

Inferior: describing the ovary when it is situated beneath the perianth, as in all orchids.

Inflexed: turned or bent sharply inwards.

Inflorescence: arrangement of the flowers on a plant; the flowers and shoot on which they are borne.

Inrolled: rolled inwards on the upper side.

Insectiform: insect-like in appearance

Inverted: turned upside down; reverse position.

Involute: rolled inwards on the upperside.

Irritable: sensitive to touch.

Keiki: a plantlet produced as an offshoot from a plant. (A Hawaiian term used by orchidists.)

Labellum: the lip-like petal of orchids, usually very distinct in appearance.

Lamellate: composed of thin plates.

Lamina: a flattened expansion of an organ, e.g. a leaf blade or the broad middle part of the labellum.

Laminate: blade-like.

Lanceolate: shaped like the head of a lance or a spear and broadest below the middle.

Lateral: at the side, as in the two lateral sepals of an orchid flower.

Leaf-fistula: the opening in a hollow leaf, through which the stem emerges.

Lenticular: lens-shaped.

Linear: long and narrow, having parallel sides.

Lingulate: strap-shaped.

Linear: long and narrow, having parallel sides.

Linguiform: tongue-shaped.

Lithophytic: growing on rocks; noun lithophyte.

Lobe: a division in the leaf or petal.

Lobule: a small lobe.

Lorate: strap-like.

Membranaceous: thin; more or less translucent.

Mentum: a chin; a pouch-like extension formed by the union of the column foot and bases of lateral sepals.

Mericlone: a plant produced by meristem propagation.

Meristem: the growing tissue made up of actively dividing cells, particularly at the tips of roots and at the apex of the vegetative or floral shoot.

Mesial: towards or on the middle line of a part.

Mesochile: middle section of jointed labellum of some orchids.

Monopodial: a form of growth in which there is a single vegetative shoot which continues to grow from year to year from its terminal bud.

Monotypic: of a genus having a single species.

Mucro: a sharp, abrupt terminal point.

Mucronate: having a mucro.

Mutation: a sudden departure from the parent type due to change in a gene or chromosome (a sport).

Nomenclature: a system of names and naming.

Obclavate: Club-shaped; widest at the base.

Obfalcate: Inversely sickle-shaped; that is, sickle-shaped but broadest above the middle.

Oblanceolate: lance-shaped in reverse, widest at the apex.

Oblong: moderately elongate but blunt at each end.

Obovate: tapering to both ends, about one-and-a-half times as long as broad, and widest above the middle.

Obtuse: bluntly pointed or rounded at the apex.

Operculate: like or furnished with a cap or lid.

Orbicular: circular or almost circular.

Orifice: the mouth of a cavity.

Ovary: the lowest part of the pistil containing the ovules; when fertilised becomes the fruit.

Ovate: shaped like a lengthwise section of an egg; more or less elliptical but broader below the middle.

Ovoid: of three-dimensional objects, shaped like an egg.

Ovule: an unfertilised seed in the ovary.

Panicle: an inflorescence in which the axis is divided into branches, both bearing a group of flowers.

Papilla: (plural papillae) minute wart-like glands or protuberances.

Papillose: having papillae.

Patelliform: shaped like a saucer.

Patent: spreading.

Pectinate: resembling the teeth of a comb.

Pedicel: the stalk of an individual flower of an inflorescence.

Peduncle: stalk of a flower cluster, or individual flower when flower is the sole member in an inflorescence.

Peltate: the stalk is attached at the back and in the centre of the leaf.

Pendulous: hanging.

Penicillate: ending in a tuft of hairs.

Perianth: single term for calyx and corolla.

Persistent: not withering or falling.

Petals: an individual member of the corolla; orchids have three petals.

Petaloid: resembling a petal, as a petal-like sepal.

Petiole: the leaf-stalk.

Pistil: in an orchid, the fertile part of the flower consisting of ovary, styles and stigma.

Placenta: parts of the ovary to which the ovule or ovules are attached.

Plicate: folded like a fan.

Plumose: feathery or feather-like.

Pollinium: (plural pollinia) A pollen mass formed by aggregation of individual pollen grains.

Porrect: directed forward and downwards.

Posterior: the parts of an organ closest to an axis or stem on which it grows.

Praemorse: bitten off at the apex.

Process: any projecting appendage or extension.

Procumbent: trailing over the ground without rooting.

Proliferation: producing offshoots; growing by multiple division.

Prostrate: lying on or trailing over the ground.

Protocrom: a tuber-like structure formed in an early stage of a plant's development, prior to the production of leaves and roots.

Proximal: part nearest the axis;

Pseudobulb: the swollen bulb-like part of the stems of many epiphytic orchids.

Pubescent: having soft short downy hairs.

Pulvinate: cushion- or pad-shaped.

Pyriform: pear-shaped, but broadest below the middle.

Quadrate: rectangular or square.

Raceme: an indefinite inflorescence with undivided axis and equally pedicellate flowers; adjective racemose.

Radical: springing from the root or near the junction of the stem and root.

Ramet: individual of a clonal line or group.

Reclinate: turned or bent downwards from the apex.

Recomplicate: folded back on itself, then folded again.

Recurved: curved backwards or downwards.

Reflexed: suddenly bent backwards.

Reniform: kidney-shaped.

Resupinate: having the flower reversed by a 180 degree twist of the pedical during development.

Reticuate: net-like.

Retinaculum: the attachment of stipitate pollinia to the rostellum.

Retracted: drawn back.

Retroflex: bent or turned backwards.

Retuse: a shallow notch in a rounded apex.

Reversed: of the flower, without a twisted pedicel; not resupinate.

Revolute: the margins of leaves rolled back towards the mid-rib.

Rhizome: a prostrate or subterranean stem.

Rhombic: of a lamina, nearly square, with petiole at one of the acute angles.

Rosette: a cluster of radiating leaves.

Rostellum: a structure on the column of the orchid; an extension of the upper edge of the stigma.

Rostrate: beaked.

Rostrum: a beak or beak-like extension.

Rugose: wrinkled.

Rugulose: somewhat wrinkled.

Runcinate: sharply incised with teeth pointing backwards.

Saccate: short and rounded like a little bag.

Sagittate: arrow-head shaped.

Saprophyte: a plant which lives upon dead organic matter.

Scape: a stalk from the base of the plant bearing flowers, not leaves.

Scarious: dry, thin, more or less transparent, and usually brownish as if scorched.

Sclerophyll forest: a forest dominated with sclerophyllous trees such as eucalypts.

Sclerophyllous: a plant with hard textured leaves.

Scutiform: shield-shaped.

Secund: with the flowers or other organs all directed to one side; often applied to an inflorescence.

Semilunar: shaped like a half moon.

Sepal: an individual calyx segment; orchid flowers have three sepals.

Septate: divided by partitions (septa).

Serrate: toothed like a saw.

Serrulate: minutely serrate.

Sessile: without stalk.

Seta: (plural setae) stiff hair or bristle.

Sigmoid: S-shaped.

Sinuate: wavy margins.

Sinus: a cavity or gap.

Solitary: occurring singly.

Spathulate: spoon-shaped.

Spicate: disposed in a spike or resembling a spike.

Spike: an unbranched inflorescence having the youngest flowers at the top and all sessile.

Spreading: diverging outwards.

Spur: a hollow, horn-like extension of a petal.

Stamen: male organ in a flower, consisting of a fertile, pollen bearing anther attached to a sterile filament.

Stem-clasping: leaf basal clasping around stem.

Stigma: the top of the pistil which is the receiving surface for the pollen.

Stipe: (plural stipitate) stalked, applied to the ovary.

Stoma: (plural stomata) a pore, usually on the underside of leaves, through which gaseous exchange takes place.

Striate: marked with parallel lines.

Subtend: to be positioned immediately below.

Subulate: narrow and tapering to a fine point; awl shaped.

Suffusion: an overspread of colour.

Sympodial: having an axis or stem which simulates a simple stem, but which is made up of the bases of a number of axes which rise as branches one from another.

Taxonomy: the science of classification.

Terete: almost rounded; cylindrical, not angular.

Terminal: situated at the tip.

Terrestrial: growing in the earth or on the ground.

Tessellate: divided or marked into small squares, like a mosaic.

Tetragonal: four sided.

Tomentose: covered in matted hairs.

Trapezoid: four-sided figure with two sides parallel.

Trapeziform: shaped like a four-sided figure with no pair of sides parallel.

Tridentate: three toothed.

Trifid: divided into three parts by clefts or notches.

Trilobate: having three lobes.

Trullate: trowel shaped.

Truncate: blunt-ended, as if cut off abruptly.

Tuber: a swollen, underground stem used for food storage.

Tuberculate: beset with little tubercles or knobby projections.

Tumid: swollen or inflated.

Turbinate: top shaped like an inverted cone.

Umbel: an inflorescence in which all flowers arise from the apex of the peduncle, similar to the spokes of an umbrella; adjective umbellate.

Uncinate: hooked or barbed at the apex.

Undulate: wavy sides.

Unguiculate: clawed.

Unilocular: having one cavity or chamber.

Urceolate: like a pitcher or urn.

Valvate: opening by valves; of members of a whorl of floral parts, arranged in the bud so that the margins of each are pressed against those of the next, without overlapping.

Venation: the way the veins of the leaves are arranged.

Verrucose: covered with wart-like projections.

Villous: covered with long soft hairs.

Viscid: sticky.

Whorl: a set of organs coming from the same node and arranged in a circle round the axis.

Wings: the membranous margin of the seed or fruit; also applied to the two lateral petals of pea flowers.

Zygomorphic: divisible into two halves in one plane only; bilaterally symmetrical.

BIBLIOGRAPHY

Bechtel, Helmut & Phillip Cribb & Edmund Launert *The Manual of Cultivated Orchid Species* London, Blandford Press, 1981.

Bennett, Keith S. *The Tropical Asiatic Slipper Orchids* Sydney, Angus & Robertson, 1984.

Hawkes, Alex D. *Encyclopaedia of Cultivated Orchids* London, Faber and Faber Limited, 1965.

Hodgson, Margaret & Roland Paine *Field Guide to Australian Orchids* Sydney, Angus & Robertson, 1988.

Lavarack, P. S. & B. Gray *Tropical Orchids of Australia,* Melbourne, Thomas Nelson, 1985.

Millar, Andree *Orchids of Papua New Guinea* Canberra, Australian National University Press, 1978.

Pottinger, Mollie *African Orchids* Berkshire, H. G. H. Publications 1983.

Schweinfurth, Charles *Orchids of Peru* Chicago, Natural History Museum, 1970.

Sheehan, Tom & Marion *Orchid Genera Illustrated* New York, Comstock Publishing Associated, a division of Cornell University Press, 1979.

Shuttleworth, Floyd S. & Herbert S. Zim and Gorden W. Dillon *A Golden Guide to Orchids* New York, Golden Press, 1970.

Williams, Mark L. Isaac *An Introduction to the Orchids of Asia* Sydney, Angus & Robertson, 1988

Valmayor, Helen *Orchidiana Philippiniana* USA, Eugenio Lopaz Foundation, 1984.

INDEX OF COMMON NAMES

Index of Botanical Names

Karen Brown's
ITALY B&B
2009

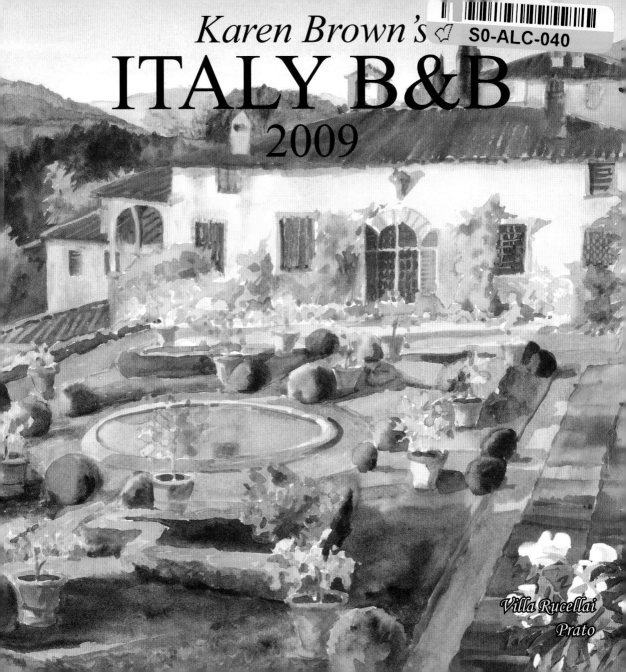

Villa Rucellai
Prato

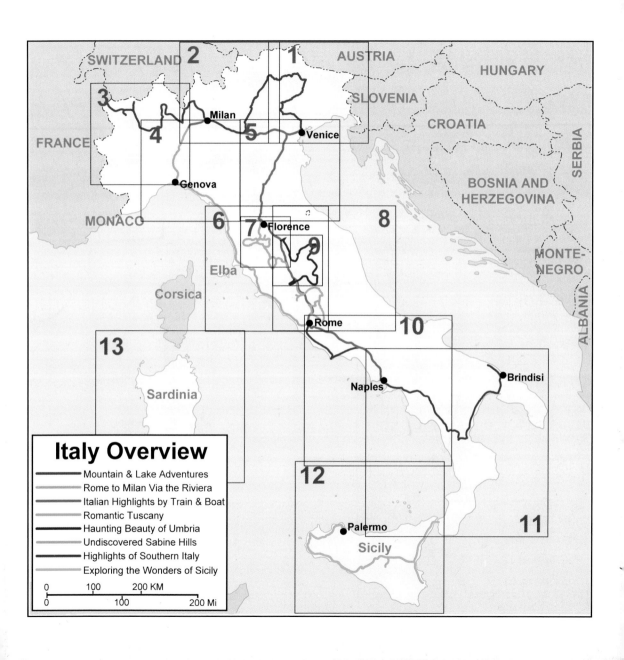

Italy Overview

- Mountain & Lake Adventures
- Rome to Milan Via the Riviera
- Italian Highlights by Train & Boat
- Romantic Tuscany
- Haunting Beauty of Umbria
- Undiscovered Sabine Hills
- Highlights of Southern Italy
- Exploring the Wonders of Sicily

| 0 | 100 | 200 KM |
| 0 | 100 | 200 Mi |

SWITZERLAND

AUSTRIA

HUNGARY

SLOVENIA

CROATIA

SERBIA

BOSNIA AND
HERZEGOVINA

FRANCE

MONACO

MONTE-
NEGRO

ALBANIA

Milan

Venice

Genova

Florence

Elba

Corsica

Rome

Naples

Brindisi

Sardinia

Palermo

Sicily

1
2
3
4
5
6
7
8
9
10
11
12
13

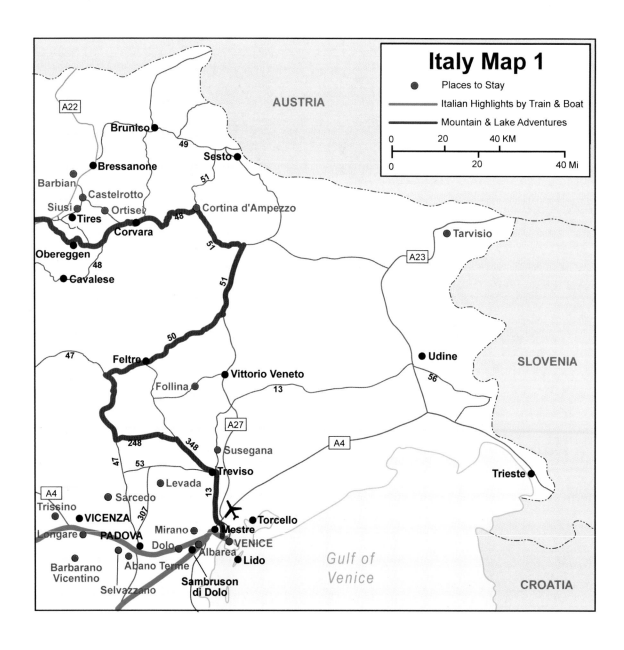

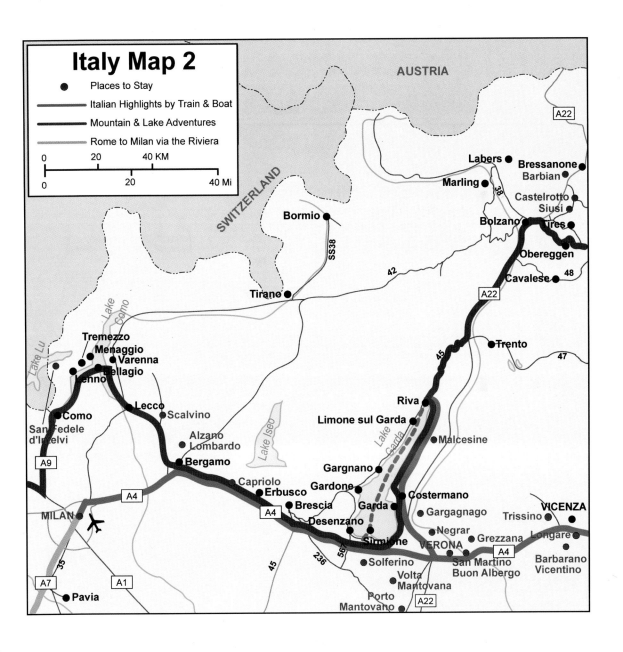

Italy Map 2

● Places to Stay
━━ Italian Highlights by Train & Boat
━━ Mountain & Lake Adventures
━━ Rome to Milan via the Riviera

0 — 20 — 40 KM
0 — 20 — 40 Mi

AUSTRIA

SWITZERLAND

A22

Labers ●   ● Bressanone
Marling ●   Barbian

Castelrotto ●
Siusi
Bolzano ● Fires

Obereggen ●

Cavalese ● 48

Bormio ●

SS38

42

A22

45

Tirano ●

Trento ●

47

Lake Como

Lake Lu

Tremezzo ●
Menaggio ●
● Varenna
Lenno ● Bellagio

Riva ●
Limone sul Garda ●

● Malcesine

Lecco ●
● Scalvino

Lake Iseo

Lake Garda

Gargnano ●

Como ●
San Fedele
d'Intelvi ●

Alzano
Lombardo ●

Gardone ●
● Costermano

A9

Bergamo ●

Capriolo ●
● Erbusco

Garda ●
● Gargagnago

VICENZA

A4

Brescia ●
Desenzano ●

Negrar ●

Trissino ●
● Longare

MILAN ●

A4

Sirmione ●
VERONA

Grezzana ●

A4

Solferino ●

San Martino
Buon Albergo

Barbarano
Vicentino

A7

A1

45

236

56

Volta
Mantovana

A22

Pavia ●

Porto
Mantovano ●

35

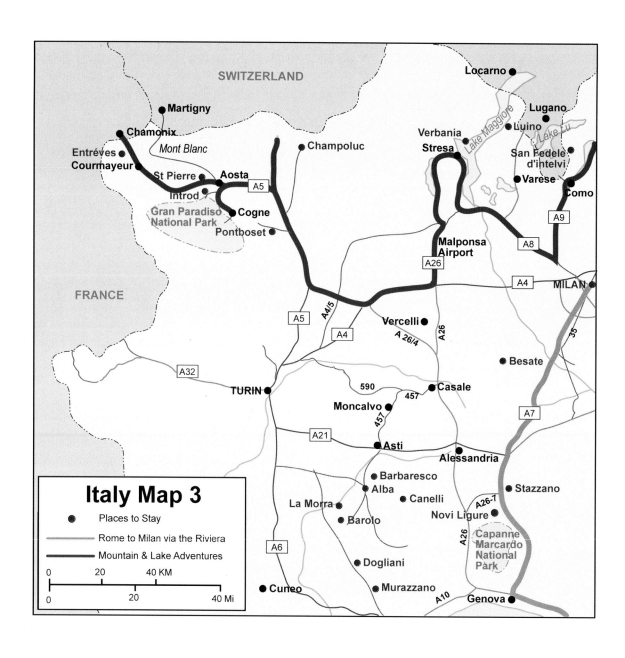

Italy Map 3

● Places to Stay

Rome to Milan via the Riviera

Mountain & Lake Adventures

0   20   40 KM

0   20   40 Mi

SWITZERLAND

● Martigny

● Chamonix

Entréves ●

Courmayeur ●

Mont Blanc

St Pierre ●

Introd ●

● Aosta

A5

Gran Paradiso National Park

● Cogne

Pontboset ●

● Champoluc

FRANCE

A5

A4/5

A4

A32

TURIN ●

Verbania

● Stresa

Locarno ●

● Lugano

● Luino

Lake Maggiore

Lake Lu

San Fedele d'intelvi ●

● Varese

● Como

A9

A8

Malponsa Airport

A26

A4

MILAN ●

Vercelli ●

A 26/4

A26

● Besate

590

● Casale

457

Moncalvo ●

457

A7

A21

● Asti

● Alessandria

35

● Barbaresco

● Alba

La Morra ●

● Canelli

● Barolo

Novi Ligure ●

A26-7

● Stazzano

A26

Capanne Marcardo National Park

A6

● Dogliani

● Cuneo

● Murazzano

A10

Genova ●

Italy Map 4

- ● Places to Stay
- ── Italian Highlights by Train & Boat
- ── Mountain & Lake Adventures
- ── Rome to Milan via the Riviera

0   20   40 KM

0   20   40 Mi

Candelo

A26

A8 A9

A4 Bergamo

Capriolo
Erbusco
Brescia
A4

MILAN

A5

A4/5

A4

A 26/4

590

457

457

Casale
Monferato

Besate

Pavia

A1

A21

236

567

Cremona

A7

A21

Piacenza

A21

Asti

Alessandria A21

Barbaresco
Alba
La Morra

Canelli

Barolo

A26-7

Novi Ligure

Stazzano

Salsomaggiore Terme

Fidenza

Tabiano

Parma

A1

Capanne
Marcardo
National
Park

A26

Dogliani

Murazzano

A6

A10 GENOVA

Savona

Gulf of
Genoa

Santa
Margherita
Portofino

Sestri Levante

Monéglia

Tavarone di
Maissana

A15

Bagnone

Finale
Ligure

A12

Levanto
Monterosso al Mare

Apuan Alps
National
Park

Vernazza
Corniglia
Manarola
Riomaggiore

La Spezia
Lerici
Tellaro
Porto
Venere

Imperia

Viareggio

A12

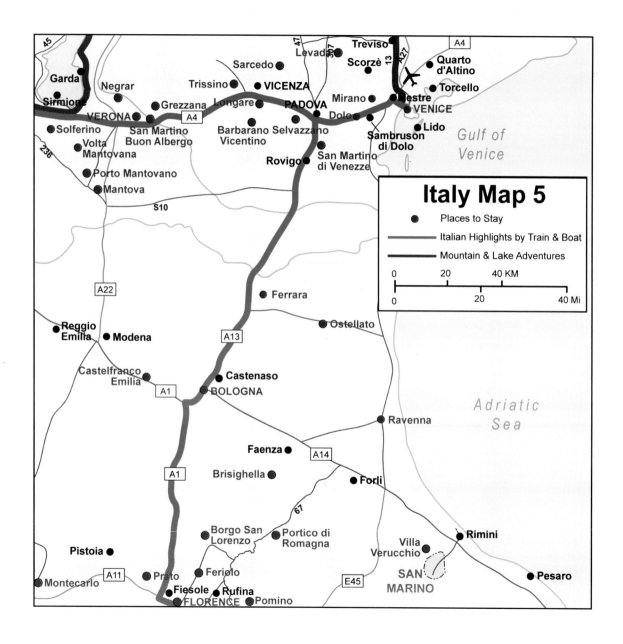

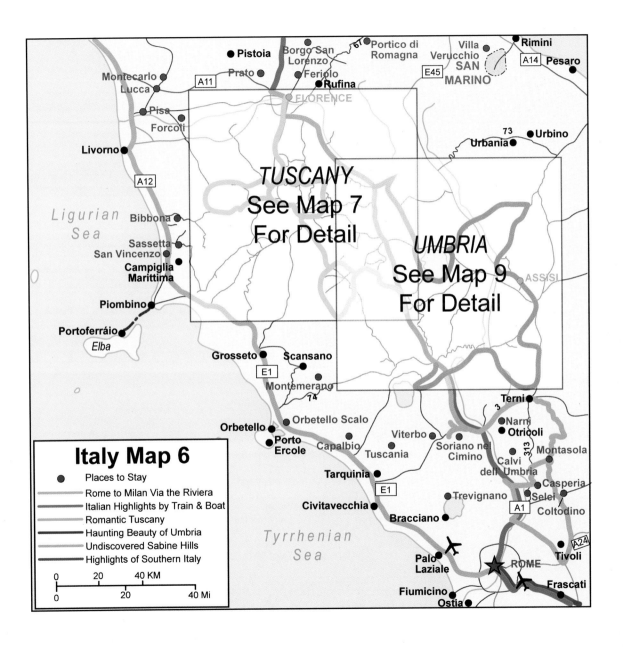

Italy Map 6

- ● Places to Stay
- Rome to Milan Via the Riviera
- Italian Highlights by Train & Boat
- Romantic Tuscany
- Haunting Beauty of Umbria
- Undiscovered Sabine Hills
- Highlights of Southern Italy

0   20   40 KM
0   20   40 Mi

Ligurian Sea

Tyrrhenian Sea

Pistoia
Borgo San Lorenzo
Prato
Feriolo
Rufina
Portico di Romagna
Villa Verucchio
Rimini
Pesaro
SAN MARINO
E45
A14
67
Montecarlo
Lucca
A11
FLORENCE
Pisa
Forcoli
Urbania
Urbino
73
Livorno
A12
TUSCANY
See Map 7
For Detail
UMBRIA
See Map 9
For Detail
ASSISI
Bibbona
Sassetta
San Vincenzo
Campiglia
Marittima
Piombino
Portoferráio
Elba
Grosseto
Scansano
Montemerano
74
Terni
3
Narni
Otricoli
Montasola
313
Calvi
dell'Umbria
Casperia
Selci
Coltodino
Orbetello
Orbetello Scalo
Capalbio
Viterbo
Tuscania
Soriano nel Cimino
A1
Porto Ercole
Tarquinia
E1
Trevignano
Civitavecchia
Bracciano
Palo Laziale
Fiumicino
Ostia
ROME
Tivoli
A24
Frascati
E1

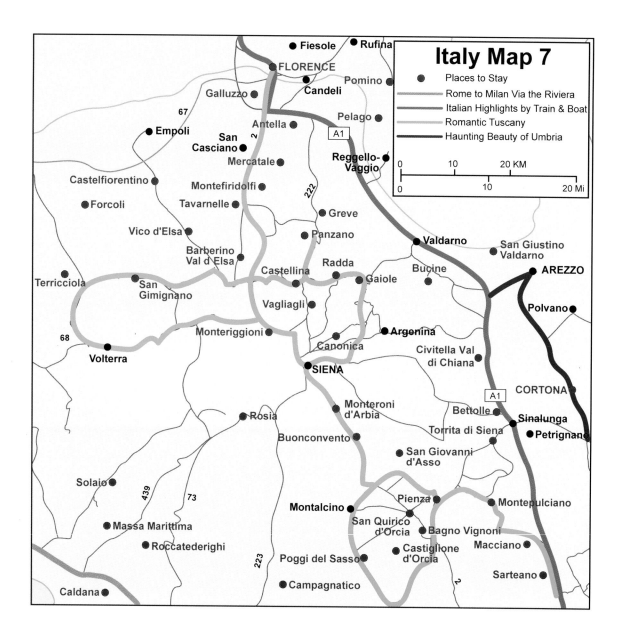

Italy Map 7

- ● Places to Stay
- Rome to Milan Via the Riviera
- Italian Highlights by Train & Boat
- Romantic Tuscany
- Haunting Beauty of Umbria

0   10   20 KM
0   10   20 Mi

Fiesole
Rufina
FLORENCE
Pomino
Candeli
Galluzzo
67
Pelago
Empoli
Antella
San Casciano
A1
2
Mercatale
Reggello-Vaggio
Castelfiorentino
Montefiridolfi
Forcoli
Tavarnelle
222
Greve
Vico d'Elsa
Panzano
Barberino Val d'Elsa
Radda
Bucine
Valdarno
San Giustino Valdarno
Terricciola
Castellina
Gaiole
AREZZO
San Gimignano
Vagliagli
Polvano
68
Monteriggioni
Canonica
Argenina
Volterra
Civitella Val di Chiana
SIENA
CORTONA
Monteroni d'Arbia
Bettolle
A1
Rosia
Torrita di Siena
Sinalunga
Buonconvento
Petrignan
San Giovanni d'Asso
Solaio
439
73
Pienza
Montepulciano
Montalcino
Massa Marittima
San Quirico d'Orcia
Bagno Vignoni
Macciano
Roccatederighi
223
Poggi del Sasso
Castiglione d'Orcia
Sarteano
Caldana
Campagnatico
2

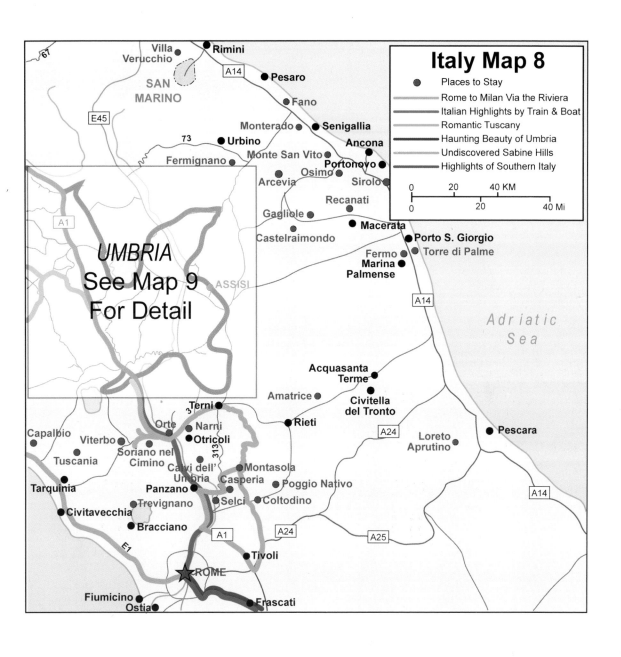

Italy Map 8

- Places to Stay
- Rome to Milan Via the Riviera
- Italian Highlights by Train & Boat
- Romantic Tuscany
- Haunting Beauty of Umbria
- Undiscovered Sabine Hills
- Highlights of Southern Italy

0 20 40 KM
0 20 40 Mi

67

Villa Verucchio
Rimini
A14
Pesaro
SAN MARINO
E45
Fano
73
Monterado
Senigallia
Urbino
Ancona
Monte San Vito
Fermignano
Osimo
Portonovo
Arcevia
Sirolo
Gagliole
Recanati
Castelraimondo
Macerata
Porto S. Giorgio
Torre di Palme
Fermo
Marina Palmense
A14

UMBRIA
See Map 9
For Detail

A1
ASSISI

Adriatic Sea

Acquasanta Terme
Amatrice
Civitella del Tronto
Terni
3
Rieti
A24
Orte
Narni
Otricoli
Loreto Aprutino
Pescara
Capalbio
Viterbo
Soriano nel Cimino
313
Montasola
Tuscania
Calvi dell' Umbria
Casperia
Poggio Nativo
Tarquinia
Panzano
Selci
Coltodino
Trevignano
Civitavecchia
A14
Bracciano
A1
A24
A25
E1
Tivoli
ROME
Fiumicino
Frascati
Ostia

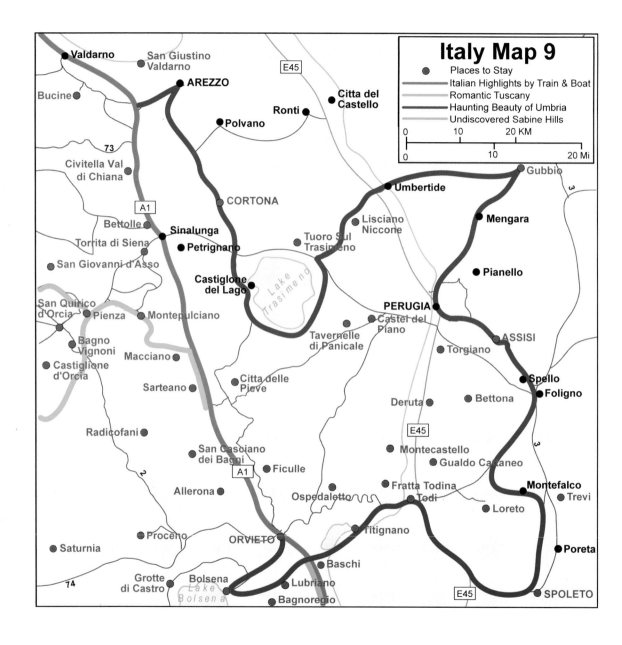

Italy Map 10

- ● Places to Stay
- ⋰ Archaeological Site
- ── Highlights of Southern Italy
- ── Italian Highlights by Train & Boat

0   25   50 KM

0   25   50 Mi

A1

A24

Tivoli

ROME

Frascati

Frosinone

148

A1

Latina

Anzio

Formia

Gaeta

Caserta

Rozzuoli

A30

Cuma

A3

NAPLES

Ponza

Ventotene

Ischia

Castellamare

Arola

Sorrento

Capri

Herculaneum

Pompeii

Ravello

Amalfi

Positano

Salerno

Paestum

Santa Maria di
Castellabate

Potenza

A3

Acquafredda

Maratea

Bay of
Naples

Bay of
Salerno

Tyrrhenian
Sea

A14

Vieste

Gargano
National Park

Monte
S. Angelo

Foggia

A16

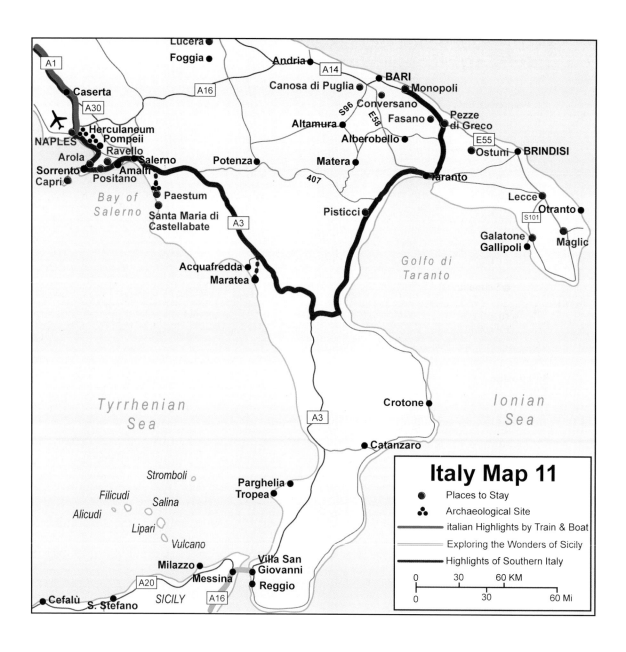

Italy Map 11

- ● Places to Stay
- ⋯ Archaeological Site
- ▬ italian Highlights by Train & Boat
- ▬ Exploring the Wonders of Sicily
- ▬ Highlights of Southern Italy

| 0 | 30 | 60 KM |
| 0 | 30 | 60 Mi |

Lucera
Foggia
Andria
Canosa di Puglia
BARI
Monopoli
Conversano
Pezze di Greco
Fasano
S96
E58
Altamura
Alberobello
E55
Ostuni
BRINDISI
Caserta
A14
A16
A30
Herculaneum
Pompeii
Ravello
Potenza
Matera
NAPLES
Arola
Salerno
Lecce
Sorrento
Amalfi
Otranto
Capri
Positano
407
Taranto
S101
Bay of Salerno
Paestum
Pisticci
Galatone
Santa Maria di Castellabate
A3
Gallipoli
Maglic
Golfo di Taranto
Acquafredda
Maratea
Tyrrhenian Sea
Ionian Sea
Crotone
A3
Catanzaro
Stromboli
Filicudi
Salina
Parghelia
Tropea
Alicudi
Lipari
Vulcano
Villa San Giovanni
Milazzo
Messina
Reggio
A20
Cefalù
S. Stefano
SICILY
A16

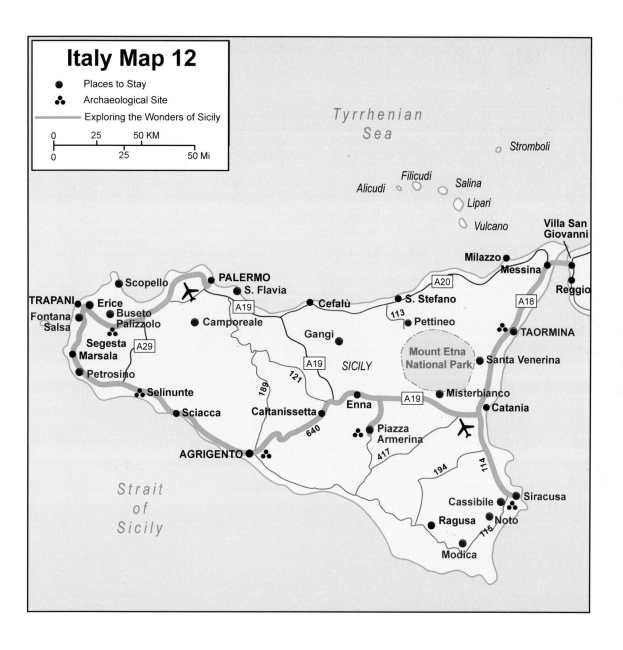

Italy Map 12

● Places to Stay

✦ Archaeological Site

▬▬ Exploring the Wonders of Sicily

0   25   50 KM

0   25   50 Mi

Tyrrhenian Sea

Stromboli

Filicudi

Alicudi

Salina

Lipari

Vulcano

Villa San Giovanni

Milazzo

Messina

Reggio

Scopello

PALERMO

S. Flavia

Cefalù

S. Stefano

A20

A18

TRAPANI

Erice

Buseto Palizzolo

Fontana Salsa

Camporeale

Gangi

Pettineo

113

TAORMINA

Segesta

A29

Marsala

A19

Mount Etna National Park

Santa Venerina

Petrosino

SICILY

A19

189

121

Selinunte

Misterbianco

Sciacca

Caltanissetta

Enna

A19

Catania

640

Piazza Armerina

AGRIGENTO

417

194

114

Strait of Sicily

Cassibile

Siracusa

Ragusa

Noto

115

Modica

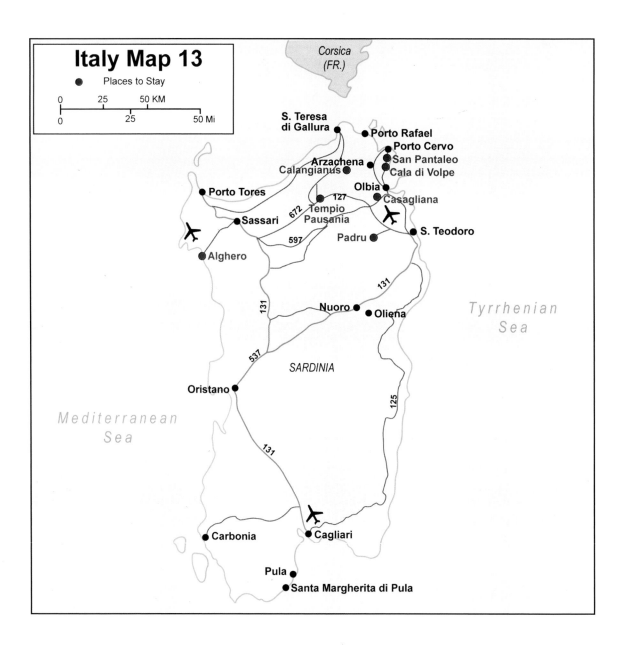

Italy Map 13

● Places to Stay

0   25   50 KM

0   25   50 Mi

Corsica (FR.)

S. Teresa di Gallura

Porto Rafael

Porto Cervo

San Pantaleo

Arzachena

Calangianus

Cala di Volpe

Olbia

Casagliana

Porto Tores

127

Sassari

672

Tempio Pausania

597

Padru

S. Teodoro

Alghero

131

131

Nuoro

Oliena

Tyrrhenian Sea

537

SARDINIA

Oristano

125

Mediterranean Sea

131

Carbonia

Cagliari

Pula

Santa Margherita di Pula

Contents

To Veronique and True Friendship

2009 Cover painting: Villa Rucellai di Canneto, Prato

Authors: Nicole Franchini and Clare Brown.

Editors: Clare Brown, Karen Brown, June Eveleigh Brown, Melissa Jaworski, Debbie Tokumoto.

Illustrations: Elisabetta Franchini.

Color photos: Ben Kong.

Cover painting: Jann Pollard.

Maps: Rachael Kircher-Randolph.

Technical support: Andrew Harris.

Distributed by National Book Network, 15200 NBN Way, Blue Ridge Summit, PA 17214, USA. Tel: 717-794-3800 or 1-800-462-6420, Fax: 1-800-338-4500, Email: custserv@nbnbooks.com

A catalog record for this book is available from the British Library.

ISSN 1532-8775

Introduction

BED AND BREAKFAST ITALIAN-STYLE—*Agriturismo*, as the bed and breakfast activity is called in Italy, has made great strides over the past decade or so. The bed and breakfast concept is relatively new to Italy, which followed suit after France and England originated the trend but has become a veritable boom in the past ten years. Accommodations vary from simple farmhouses to noble country villas, all promising unique and memorable stays. "*Agritourism*" travel offers visitors to Italy the unique opportunity to observe daily life "up close" as a guest in someone's home. It is a superb way to interact directly with Italians, experiencing their way of life as a participant rather than just an observer. It offers a more intimate contact with the country's traditional ways of life than can ever be experienced during hotel stays. It is the alternative vacation for curious visitors who wish to explore the back roads of this fascinating country and depart with a more in-depth understanding of Italians and their lifestyles than they could possibly get from city stays and sightseeing alone. The individual who will benefit most from agritourism will have an open, inquiring mind and a certain amount of flexibility. In return, agritourism rewards the traveler with a feeling of being "at home" while abroad. The warm welcome and the value you'll receive will tempt you back year after year.

HISTORY: *Agriturismo*, defined as agricultural tourism, was launched in 1965 as part of the Italian government's national agricultural department's plan to make it possible for farmers to supplement their declining income in two ways: through offering accommodation to tourists and through direct sales of their produce.

After World War II, during reconstruction and the subsequent industrial boom, Italians abandoned the countryside in droves in search of employment in urban centers, reducing the rural population from eight to three million people. Consequently, farmhouses, villas, and castles all across the country were neglected and went to ruin. This phenomenon also disrupted the centuries-old tradition of passing property from one generation to the next.

The agritourism concept—with its government funding, proclaimed tax breaks, and an increasing need to escape congested cities—has lured proprietors back to their land and ancestral homes, providing them with the incentive to restore and preserve these historical buildings (with many treasures among them) without spoiling the natural landscape. An additional consequence is an improved distribution of tourism between Italy's overcrowded cities and the countryside, which serves to raise awareness of the many marvelous historical and cultural attractions, from art and architecture to scenery and cuisine, that await tourists off the beaten track.

Each of Italy's 20 regions participates in agritourism, with over 12,000 properties offering accommodation and a full 60% of participants concentrated in Tuscany and Trentino-Alto Adige. This edition includes selections from 17 of Italy's regions. Unfortunately, this type of accommodation is still very scarce in Italy's southernmost regions such as Calabria, Basilicata, and Campania. We are happy to offer a new selection of bed and breakfasts in Sardinia and Sicily, where the activity is gradually taking hold, although mostly in more spartan accommodation.

In practical terms, agritourism was developed to stimulate the local economy in rural areas by encouraging the creation of accommodations (rooms, apartments, and campgrounds) in places where they had never before been available. In a more long-term and idealistic sense, it was hoped that the promotion and development of tourism in rural Italy would also bring about greater environmental awareness as well as rescue traditional folklore and customs, such as regional cuisine and handicrafts, from oblivion.

For Italians, agritourism facilitates an exchange of views between farmers and urbanites who come in search of a peaceful vacation surrounded by natural beauty. In fact, agritourism and the rich culture of the farmer represent for many an affirmation and validation of their heritage. Lamentably, some Italians still have a misconception of agritourism because it was originally organized as an exchange of very basic room and board for work in the fields. A wave of positive press in recent years and higher quality standards however, have helped enormously to change this outdated image.

Controversy also surrounds the fact that there are few established regulations governing this type of activity, and they differ greatly from one region to another. Consequently, few clearly defined quality standards exist and those participants with limited economic resources resent wealthier proprietors, whom they accuse of running accommodations resembling hotels more than farm stays. Moreover, it does not simplify matters that agritourism is organized in typical Italian fashion, with responsibility divided among three associations, each with its own regulations, politics, and guidelines. Each association produces a directory and may be contacted by writing to:

AGRITURIST, Corso Vittorio Emanuele 101, Rome 00168, Italy
www.agriturist.it, Email: *agritur@confagricoltura.it*

TERRANOSTRA, Via 14 Maggio 43, Rome 00187, Italy
www.terranostra.it, Email: *terranostra@coldiretti.it*

TURISMO VERDE, Via M. Fortuny 20, Rome 00196, Italy
www.turismoverde.it, Email: *info@turismoverde.it*

About Bed & Breakfasts

Our goal in this guide is to recommend outstanding places to stay. All of the bed and breakfasts featured have been visited and selected solely on their merits. Our judgments are made on charm, setting, cleanliness, and, above all, warmth of welcome. However (no matter how careful we are), sometimes we misjudge an establishment's merits, or the ownership changes, or unfortunately sometimes standards are not maintained. If you find a recommended place is not as we have indicated, please let us know, and accept our sincere apologies. The rates given are those quoted to us by the bed and breakfast: please use these figures as a guideline only and be certain to ask at the time of booking what the rates are and what they include.

ACCOMMODATION

The most important thing to remember as you consider an agritourism vacation is that you will be staying in the private homes of families who are obligated to run their bed and breakfasts without hiring additional personnel aside from family and farmhands. Do not forget that, in most cases, the primary responsibility of your hosts is the running of their farm, so, with a few exceptions, do not expect the service of a hotel. **Rooms may not necessarily always be cleaned daily** (sometimes linens are changed every three to seven days). Nevertheless, do anticipate a comfortable and enjoyable stay, because the proprietors will do everything possible to assure it. Cost will vary according to the level of service offered. (For the traveler's convenience, some city hotels have been included that are similar to a bed and breakfast in style, but go by the name *Albergo*, *Pensione*, or Hotel.)

ROOMS: Agritourism accommodations should not be thought of strictly in terms of the British or American definitions of bed and breakfasts, as in Italy they vary greatly according to each proprietor's interpretation of the concept. The bed and breakfasts in this guide have been described in terms of the criteria used in their selection—warmth of hospitality, historic character, charm of the home, scenery, proximity to sites of touristic interest, and quality of cuisine. Obviously, all of these attributes are not always found in each one. Most of them have an average of six rooms situated either within the family's home or in a separate guesthouse. Unless otherwise indicated in the bottom description details, all bedrooms have private bathrooms. Furthermore, we have tried to include only those with ensuite bathrooms. Having another bed or two added to a room at an extra charge for families with small children is usually not a problem. According to laws of the European Community, all new or renovated establishments must now offer facilities for the handicapped. It is best to enquire about the individual bed and breakfast's facilities when making reservations to see if they have accommodation that is suitable for you.

AFFILIATIONS

A number of properties recommended in our guide books also belong to other private membership organizations. These associations impose their own criteria for selection and membership standards and have established a reputation for the particular type of property they include. The Abitare La Storia is an affiliation of accommodations in historic residences, including castles, 3, 4, and 5-star hotels and country estates. They include some of the finest places to stay in Italy. The majority of their properties are featured either in this guide or our companion guide *Karen Brown's Italy Hotels: Exceptional Places to Stay & Itineraries*. Their search for quality, welcome and charm is a perfect match with our own selection criteria. Another affiliation is the History Traveller group. If a property that we recommend is a member of Abitare La Storia or History Traveller, we note their membership reference in the bottom details of the property description.

APARTMENTS: Since more and more travelers are learning that it is much more advantageous to stay for longer periods in one place (distances are so short between towns within a specific region), apartment-type accommodations with fully equipped kitchenettes are flourishing. Apartment accommodation is offered either within the farmhouse along with other units for two to six persons, or as a full house rental for six to ten persons. They are rented by the week from Saturday to Saturday throughout the country, the exception being during the low season. No meals are included unless the bed and breakfast also has a restaurant or makes special arrangements for breakfast. Rates include use of all facilities (unless otherwise indicated), linens, and utilities. There is usually an extra charge for heating and once-a-week cleaning. Average apartments for four persons run approximately $850 weekly, a rate hotels cannot beat.

CREDIT CARDS

Whether or not an establishment accepts credit cards is indicated in the list of icons at the bottom of each description by the symbol ▨. We have also specified in the accommodation description which cards are accepted as follows: AX–American Express, MC–MasterCard, VS–Visa, or simply, all major.

ENGLISH

English and other languages spoken at each bed and breakfast are indicated as follows: fluent, good, some, very little, and none. We would like to note, however, that this is just an indication, as the person who speaks English may or may not be there during your stay. In any case, it is helpful (not to mention rewarding) to have a few basic Italian phrases on hand. A phrase book or dictionary is indispensable. And when all else fails, the art of communicating with gestures is still very much alive in Italy!

FINDING YOUR BED AND BREAKFAST

At the front of the book is a key map of the whole of Italy plus maps showing each recommended bed and breakfast's location. The pertinent regional map number is given at the right on the *top line* of each bed and breakfast's description. Directions to help you find your destination are given after each bed and breakfast description. However, they are only guidelines, as it would be impossible to find the space to give more details, and to know from which direction the traveler is arriving. The beauty of many of these lodgings is that they are off the beaten track, but that characteristic may also make them very tricky to find. If you get lost, a common occurrence, first keep your sense of humor, then call the proprietors and/or ask locals at bars or gas stations for directions. It is important to know that addresses in the countryside often have no specific street name. *A common address consists of the farm name, sometimes a localita' (an unincorporated area, or vicinity, frequently not found on a map and outside the actual town named), and the town name followed by the province abbreviated in parentheses. (The bed and breakfast is not necessarily in that town, but it serves as a post office reference.)* The *localita'* can also be the name of the road where the bed and breakfast is located, to make things more confusing. We state the *localita'* in the third line of the bed and breakfast details and many times that name is the map reference name as well. Ask to be faxed a detailed map from the B&B upon confirmation.

Detailed maps for the area in which you will be traveling are essential and we recommend purchasing them in advance of your trip, both to aid in the planning of your journey and to avoid spending vacation time searching for the appropriate maps.

FOOD

A highlight of the agritourism experience is without a doubt the food. Most travelers would agree that a bad meal is hard to find in Italy, a country world-famous for its culinary skills. In the countryside you'll be sampling the traditional regional recipes from which Italian cuisine originates. Since, whenever possible, all of the ingredients come directly from the farms where you'll be staying and are for the most part organically grown (watch for the certificate), you'll discover the flavorful difference freshness can make. Even the olive oil has a special certificate of quality (DOP) similar to that of wines (DOC). A peek into the farm kitchen is likely to reveal pasta being rolled and cut the old-fashioned way—by hand. Many country cooks prefer to prepare food using traditional methods, and not rely on machines to speed up the process. Guests are usually welcomed into the kitchen for a look around and cooking lessons are becoming very popular.

MEALS OFFERED: Bed and breakfasts often serve only a continental breakfast of coffee, tea, fresh breads, and jams. However, many prepare a buffet breakfast plus other meals and offer (sometimes require) half- or full-board plans. Half board means that breakfast and dinner are both included in the daily per-person room rate. Full board includes the room and all three meals and is less common, since most guests are out and about during the day, or prefer one lighter meal. Dinner is a hearty three-course meal, often shared at a common table with the host family, and normally does not include wine and other beverages. Menus might be set daily, according to the availability of fresh produce, or a limited choice may be given. Some farms have a full-fledged restaurant serving non-guests as well. Travelers who are not guests at a particular bed and breakfast may take advantage of this opportunity to sample other fare (it is advisable to reserve in advance). When a listing offers dinner by arrangement we indicate this with the icon ▲. If a property has a restaurant, we use the icon ⍥ .

ICONS

Icons allow us to provide additional information about our recommended properties. We have introduced the following icons in this guide to supplement each property's description. For easy reference, an icon key can also be found on the inside back cover flap.

Services:

❄ Air conditioning

⊥ Beach nearby

🍽 Breakfast included

👟 Children welcome

♨ Cooking classes offered

▦ Credit cards accepted

🍲 Dinner upon request

☎ Direct-dial tel. in room

🐕 Dogs by special request

👪 Elevator

🏋 Exercise room

@ Internet for guests

⏉ Mini-refrigerator

🚭 Some non-smoking rooms

P Parking (free or paid)

🍴 Restaurant

💆 Spa (massage etc.)

🏊 Swimming pool

🎾 Tennis

📺 Television with English channels in guestrooms

💒 Wedding facilities

♿ Wheelchair friendly

W Wireless for guests

Activities:

🏌 Golf course nearby

🚶 Hiking trails nearby

🏇 Horseback riding nearby

⛷ Skiing nearby

🏄 Water sports nearby

🍷 Wineries nearby

LENGTH OF STAY

Agritourism is most advantageous for those who have more than the standard one week to travel. Bed and breakfast accommodations take longer to reach, for one thing, and *often they are neither set up nor staffed for one-night stays*, which increase costs and defeat the purpose of this type of travel. There are numerous exceptions, however, especially in bed and breakfasts near cities, where overnight guests are accepted. It is noted in the description where a minimum stay is required.

RATES

Room rates vary according to size, location, season, and level of service. Rates range from $110 to $300 for two people with breakfast (indicated as B&B in the following descriptions) and from $90 to $170 per person for room with half board (dinner also included). *Approximate prices for two persons in a room for 2009 are indicated in euros and are by no means fixed. Rates include tax and must be confirmed at the time of reservation.* If breakfast is included this is indicated with the ☕ icon. Because of its cost advantages, agritourism is an ideal choice for families. Children under eight are offered a discount and hosts will almost always add an extra bed for a small charge. There are some wonderful benefits to traveling in Italy in the low season (November to March with the exception of holidays). The considerable reduction in bed and breakfast rates combined with irresistibly low air fares makes for a super-economical vacation. And then, there's the ultimate advantage of not having to fight for space with crowds of other tourists. Italy is all yours!

RESERVATIONS

Whether you plan to stay in several bed and breakfasts or decide to remain for an extended period in just one, *advance reservations are preferred.* Not only do many of the bed and breakfasts have only a few bedrooms available, but also they are often in private homes that are not prepared to take walk-in traffic. It is important to understand that once reservations for accommodation are confirmed, whether verbally by phone or in writing, you are under contract. This means that the proprietor is obligated to provide the accommodation that was promised and that you are obligated to pay for it. If you cannot, you are liable for a portion of the accommodation charges plus your deposit. As a courtesy to your hosts, in the case of cancellation, please advise them as soon as possible. Although some proprietors do not strictly enforce a cancellation policy, many, particularly the smaller properties in our book, simply cannot afford not to do so. Similarly, many airline tickets cannot be changed or refunded without penalty. We recommend insurance to cover these types of additional expenses arising from cancellation due to unforeseen circumstances.

When making your reservations, be sure to identify yourself as a "Karen Brown traveler." The hosts appreciate your visit, value their inclusion in our guide, and frequently tell us they take special care of our readers. We hear over and over again that the people who use our guides are the most wonderful and appreciative guests!

THERE ARE SEVERAL WAYS TO MAKE A RESERVATION:

Email: This is our preferred way of making a reservation. All hotels/bed and breakfasts featured on the Karen Brown Website that also have email addresses have those addresses listed on their web pages (this information is constantly kept updated and correct). You can often link directly to a property from its page on our website. (Always spell out the month as the Italians reverse the American month/day numbering system.)

Fax: If you have access to a fax machine, this is a very quick way to reach a bed and breakfast. If the place to stay has a fax, we have included the number in the description. Following is a reservation request form in Italian with an English translation. (See comment above about spelling out the month.)

Reservation Service: If you want to pay for the convenience of having the reservations made for you, pre-payments made, vouchers issued, and cars rented, any of the bed and breakfasts in this guide can be booked through **Hidden Treasures of Italy**, a booking service run by an author of this guide, Nicole Franchini. Further information can be found at the back this book.

Telephone: You can call the bed and breakfast directly, which is very efficient since you get an immediate response. The level of English spoken is given in each bed and breakfast description. To telephone Italy from the United States, dial 011 (the international code), then 39 (Italy's code), then the city area code (including the "0" unless it is a cellular phone number), and then the telephone number. Italy is six hours ahead of New York.

WHEELCHAIR ACCESSIBILITY

If a property has *at least* one guestroom that is accessible by wheelchair, it is noted with the symbol ♿. This is not the same as saying it meets full disability standards. In reality, it can be anything from a basic ground-floor room to a fully equipped facility. Please discuss your requirements when you call your chosen place to stay to determine if they have accommodation that suits your needs and preference.

RESERVATION LETTER IN ITALIAN

BED & BREAKFAST or HOTEL NAME & ADDRESS—clearly printed or typed

Vi richiediamo la seguente prenotazione:
We would like to request the following reservation:

Numero delle camere o appartamenti _____ con bagno o doccia privata a _____ posti letto
Number of rooms or apartments with private bath or shower for how many persons

Numero di adulti _____   Numero di bambini _____ Età _____
Number of adults   Number of children and ages

Numero delle camere o appartamenti _____ senza bagno o doccia privata a _____ posti letto
Number of rooms or apartments without private bath or shower for how many persons

Numero di adulti _____   Numero di bambini _____ Età _____
Number of adults   Number of children and ages

Data di arrivo _____ Data di partenza _____ Totale notti_____
Date of arrival   Date of departure   Number of nights

Tipo di servizio richesto:
Type of meal plan requested:

_____ Pernottamento con prima colazione (*B&B*)

_____ Mezza Pensione (*Half Board—breakfast and dinner included*)

_____ Pensione Completa (*Full Board—all three meals included*)

Costo giornaliero: B&B (two persons) _____

Daily rate   MP (Half Board—per person) _____

        PC (Full Board—per person) _____

Sono previsti sconti per bambini e quanto? _____
Is there a discount for children and what is it?

E' necessaria una caparra e quanto? _____
Is a deposit necessary and for how much?

Ringraziando anticipatamente per la gentile conferma, porgo cordiali saluti,
Thanking you in advance for your confirmation, cordial greetings,

YOUR NAME, ADDRESS, TELEPHONE & FAX NUMBER—clearly printed or typed

REGIONAL FARM NAMES

The following names for farms, seen throughout this guide, vary from area to area.

azienda agricola—a general term meaning farm, not necessarily offering hospitality

borgo—a small stone-walled village, usually of medieval origins

casale, casolare—variations of farmhouse, deriving from "casa"

cascina and ca'—farmhouse in Piedmont, Lombardy, and Veneto

fattoria—typically a farm in Tuscany or Umbria

hof and maso—terms meaning house and farm in the northern mountain areas

locanda—historically a restaurant with rooms for travelers passing through on horseback

masseria—fortified farms in Apulia, Sicily

podere—land surrounding a farmhouse

poggio—literally describes the farm's position on a flat hilltop

stazzo—typical stone farmhouse in Sardinia

tenuta—estate

torre—tower

trattoria—a simple, family-run restaurant in cities and the countryside

villa and castello—usually former home of nobility and more elaborate in services

WHAT TO SEE AND DO

Bed and breakfast proprietors take pride in their farms and great pleasure in answering questions about their agricultural activity. They will often take time to explain and demonstrate procedures such as wine making, olive pressing, or cheese production. They are the best source for, and are happy to suggest, restaurants and local itineraries including historic sites, picturesque villages, and cultural activities. Your hosts feel responsible for entertaining their guests and many have added swimming pools or tennis courts if they are not already available in the vicinity. Other activities such as archery, fishing, hiking, and biking are sometimes offered. Horseback riding has made an enormous comeback and farms frequently have their own stables and organize lessons and/or excursions into the countryside. In most circumstances, a charge is made for these extra activities.

WHEN TO VISIT

Since agritourism accommodation is usually in permanent residences, many remain open all year, but most are open only from Easter through November. If you are traveling outside this time, however, it is worth a phone call to find out if the bed and breakfast will accommodate you anyway (at very affordable rates). The best time for agritourism is without a doubt during the spring and fall months, when nature is in its glory. You can enjoy the flowers blossoming in May, the *vendemmia*, or grape harvest, at the end of September, the fall foliage in late October, or olive-oil production and truffle hunts in November and December. Southern Italy can be mild and pleasant in the winter, which might be perfect for travelers who like to feel they are the only tourists around. The vast majority of Italians vacation at the same time, during the month of August, Easter weekend, and Christmas, so these time periods are best avoided, if possible.

About Itineraries

In the itinerary section of this guide you'll be able to find an itinerary, or portion of an itinerary, that can be easily tailored to fit your exact time frame and suit your own particular interests. If your time is limited, you can certainly follow just a segment of an itinerary. In the itineraries we have not specified the number of nights at each destination, since to do so seemed much too confining. Some travelers like to see as much as possible in a short period of time. For others, just the thought of packing and unpacking each night makes them shudder in horror and they would never stop for less than three or four nights at any destination. A third type of tourist doesn't like to travel at all—the destination is the focus and he uses this guide to find the perfect place from which he never wanders except for daytime excursions. So, use this guide as a reference to plan your personalized trip. Part of the joy of traveling is to settle in at a property that you like and use it as a hub from which to take side trips to explore the countryside.

SIGHTSEEING

Ideas on what to see and do are suggested throughout the itineraries. However, we just touch on the wealth of wonders to see. Make it a habit to always make your first stop the local tourist office to pick up maps, schedules of special events, and sightseeing information. Even more important, before you drive out of your way to see a particular museum or place of interest, check when it is open. As a general guideline, most museums are closed on Mondays except for the Vatican museums, which are closed on Sundays (except for the last Sunday of the month—free entrance). The most important museums now have continuous hours and either have a full- or half-day schedule but do not close for a few hours and then reopen. Smaller museums are usually open until 2 pm. Outdoor museums usually open at 9 am and close about an hour before sunset. Most monuments and museums close on national holidays. NOTE: To save waiting in line for hours to buy entrance tickets, buy tickets for most major museums well in advance on line, from travel agencies, or directly from the bed and breakfasts.

MAPS

Each itinerary is preceded by a map showing the route and each property listing is referenced on its top line to a map at the front of the book. All maps are an artist's renderings and are not intended to replace detailed commercial maps. We use the *Michelin Tourist and Motoring Atlas of Italy,* a book of maps with a scale of 1:300,000 (1 cm = 3 km). We also find the regional Michelin maps very useful and we state which Michelin 500-series map each property's town is found on in the property description. To outline your visit to Italy you might want to consider the one-page map of Italy, Michelin map 735. Italy Places to Stay maps in this book can be cross-referenced with those in our companion guide, *Karen Brown's Italy Hotels: Exceptional Places to Stay & Itineraries.* We sell Michelin country maps, city maps, and regional green guides (sightseeing guides) in our website store at *www.karenbrown.com.*

Another fine choice is The Touring Club Italiano map set, in an easy-to-read three-volume format divided into North, Central, and South. Even the smallest town or, better, *localita* is listed in the extensive index.

View of Assisi

About Italy

The following pointers are given in alphabetical order, not in order of importance.

AIRFARE

Karen Brown's Guides have long recommended Auto Europe for their excellent car rental services. Their air travel division, Destination Europe, an airline broker working with major American and European carriers, offers deeply discounted coach- and business-class fares to over 200 European gateway cities. It also gives Karen Brown travelers an additional 5% discount off its already highly competitive prices (cannot be combined with any other offers or promotions). We recommend making reservations by phone at (800) 835-1555. When phoning, be sure to use the Karen Brown ID number 99006187 to secure your discount.

BANKS–CURRENCY

Normal banking hours are Monday through Friday from 8:30 am to 1:30 pm and 3 to 4 pm, with some city banks now opening on Saturday mornings. Cash machines accepting U.S. bank cash cards and credit cards are now widely distributed throughout Italy. An increasingly popular and convenient way to obtain foreign currency is simply to use your bankcard at an ATM machine. You pay a fixed fee for this but, depending on the amount you withdraw, it is usually less than the percentage-based fee charged to exchange currency or travelers' checks. *Cambio* signs outside and inside a bank indicate that it will exchange traveler's checks or give you cash from certain credit cards. Also privately run exchange offices are available in cities with more convenient hours and comparable rates. The euro is the official currency of most European Union countries, including Italy, and has completely replaced European national currencies. Visit our website (*www.karenbrown.com*) for an easy-to-use online currency converter.

CAR RENTAL

An International Driver's Permit is not necessary for renting a car as a tourist: a foreign driver's license is valid for driving throughout Italy. Readers frequently ask our advice on car rental companies. We always use Auto Europe—a car rental broker that works with the major car rental companies to find the lowest possible price. They also offer motor homes and chauffeur services. Auto Europe's toll-free phone service, from every European country, connects you to their U.S.-based, 24-hour reservation center (ask for the Europe Phone Numbers Card to be mailed to you). Auto Europe offers our readers a 5% discount (cannot be combined with any other offers or promotions) and, occasionally, free upgrades. Be sure to use the Karen Brown ID number 99006187. You can make your own reservations online via our website, *www.karenbrown.com* (select *Auto Europe* from the home page), or by phone (800-223-5555).

DRIVING

A car is a must for this type of travel—most bed and breakfasts are inaccessible by any other means of transportation. A car gives the traveler a great deal of independence (public transportation is frequently on strike in Italy), while providing the ideal means to explore the countryside thoroughly. It is best to reserve a vehicle and pre-pay by credit card before your departure to ensure the best rates possible.

Italy is not quite the "vehicular-free-for-all" you may have heard about, at least not outside big cities (particularly Rome, Florence, and Milan). When visiting Rome, it's advisable to do so at the beginning or end of your trip, before you pick up or after you drop off your car, and, by all means, avoid driving within the city. Italians have a different relationship with the basic rules of the road: common maneuvers include running stop lights and stop signs, triple-parking, driving at 100 mph on the highways, passing on the right, and backing up at missed highway exits. But once out of the city, you will find it relatively easy to reach your destination. Road directions are quite good in Italy and people are very willing to help.

DISTANCES: Distances are indicated in kilometers (one kilometer equals 0.621 miles), calculated roughly into miles by cutting the kilometer distance in half. Distances between towns are also indicated in orange alongside the roads on the Touring Club Italiano maps. Italy is a compact country and distances are relatively short, yet you will be amazed at how dramatically the scenery can change in an hour's drive.

GASOLINE: Gas prices in Italy are the highest in Europe, and Americans often suspect a mistake when their first fill-up comes to between $120 and $150 (most of it in taxes). Most stations now accept Visa credit cards, and the ERG stations accept American Express. Besides the AGIP stations on the autostrade, which are almost always open, gas stations observe the same hours as merchants, closing in the afternoon from 12:30 to 4 and in the evening at 7:30. Be especially careful not to get caught running on empty in the afternoon! Fortunately now many stations have a self-service pump that operates on off-hours (€10 or €20 and €50 bills accepted as well as credit cards at times).

ROADS: Names Of Roads In Italy Are As Follows:

Autostrada: a large, fast (and most direct) two- or three-lane toll highway, marked by green signs bearing an "A" followed by the autostrada number. As you enter you receive a ticket from an automatic machine by pushing a red button. Payment is made at your exit point. If you lose your card, you will have to pay the equivalent amount of the distance from the beginning of the autostrada to your exit. Speed limit: 130 kph.

Superstrada: a one- or two-lane freeway between secondary cities marked by blue signs and given a number. Speed limit: 110 kph.

Strada Statale: a small one-lane road marked with S.S. followed by the road number. Speed limit: 90 kph.

Raccordo or *Tangenziale*: a ring road around main cities, connecting to an autostrada and city centers.

ROAD SIGNS: Yellow signs are for tourists and indicate sites of interest, hotels, and restaurants. Black-and-yellow signs indicate private companies and industries.

TOLLS: Tolls on Italian autostrade are quite steep, ranging from $15 to $28 for a three-hour stretch, but offering the fastest and most direct way to travel between cities. Fortunately for the agritourist, tollways are rarely necessary. However, if it suits your needs, a *Viacard*, or magnetic reusable card for tolls, is available in all tollway gas stations for €20–€50, or even more convenient, a MasterCard or Visa card can be used in specified blue lanes (the lines for these automatic machines are notably shorter).

HOLIDAYS

It is very important to know Italian holidays because most museums, shops, and offices are closed. National holidays are listed below:

New Year's Day (January 1)
Epiphany (January 6)
Easter (and the following Monday)
Liberation Day (April 25)
Labor Day (May 1)

Assumption Day (August 15)
All Saints' Day (November 1)
Christmas (December 25)
Santo Stefano (December 26)

In addition to the national holidays, each town also has its own special holiday to honor its patron saint. Some of the major ones are listed below:

Bologna—St. Petronio (October 4)   Palermo—Santa Rosalia (July 15)
Florence—St. John the Baptist (June 24)   Rome—St. Peter (June 29)
Milan—St. Ambrose (December 7)   Venice—St. Mark (April 25)

The Vatican Museums have their own schedule and are closed on Sundays (rather than on Mondays as in the case with all other National museums), with the exception of the last Sunday of each month when admission is free of charge.

INFORMATION SOURCES

Italian Government Travel Offices (ENIT) can offer general information on various regions and their cultural attractions. They cannot offer specific information on restaurants and accommodations. If you have access to the Internet, visit the Italian Tourist Board's websites: *www.italiantourism.com* or *www.enit.it*. Offices are located in:

Chicago: Italian Government Travel Office, 500 N. Michigan Ave., Suite 2240, Chicago, IL 60611 USA; email: *enitch@italiantourism.com*, tel: (312) 644-0996.

Los Angeles: Italian Government Travel Office, 12400 Wilshire Blvd., Suite 550, Los Angeles, CA 90025, USA; email: *enitla@italiantourism.com*, tel: (310) 820-1898.

New York: Italian Government Travel Office, 630 5th Ave., Suite 1565, New York, NY 10111, USA; email: *enitny@italiantourism.com*, tel: (212) 245-4822.

Toronto: Italian Government Travel Office, 175 Bloor Street East, Suite 907, Toronto, Ontario M4W 3R8, Canada; email: *enit.canada@on.aibn.com*, tel: (416) 925-4882.

London: Italian State Tourist Office, 1 Princes Street, London WIB 2AY, England; email: *italy@italiantourism.co.uk*, tel: (020) 7408-1254.

Sydney: Italian Government Travel Office, Level 4, 46 Market Street, Sydney NSW 2000, Australia; email: *italia@italiantourism.com.au*, tel: (61292) 621.666.

Rome: ENTE Nazionale Italiano per il Turismo (Italian Government Travel Office), Via Marghera, 2/6, Rome 00185, Italy; email: *sedecentrale@cert.enit.it*, tel: (06) 49711.

PROVINCES

Italy is divided into Provinces, which appear in abbreviated form in addresses. Some of the provinces you are likely to see and their abbreviated codes are as follows:

AG	*Agrigento*	CS	*Cosenza*	MN	*Mantova*	RM	*Rome*
AL	*Alessandria*	CT	*Catania*	MO	*Modena*	RN	*Rimini*
AN	*Ancona*	CZ	*Catanzaro*	MS	*Massa*	RO	*Ravigo*
AO	*Aosta*	EN	*Enna*	MT	*Matera*	SA	*Salerno*
AP	*Ascoli Picino*	FE	*Ferrara*	NA	*Naples*	SI	*Siena*
AR	*Arezzo*	FG	*Froggia*	NO	*Novara*	SO	*Sondrio*
AT	*Asti*	FI	*Florence*	NU	*Nuoro*	SP	*La Spezia*
AV	*Avellino*	FO	*Forli*	OR	*Oristano*	SR	*Siracusa*
BA	*Bari*	GE	*Genova*	PA	*Palermo*	SV	*Savona*
BG	*Bergamo*	GO	*Gorizia*	PC	*Piacunga*	TA	*Taranto*
BL	*Belluno*	GR	*Grosseto*	PD	*Padova*	TE	*Teramo*
BN	*Benevento*	IM	*Imperia*	PE	*Pescara*	TN	*Trento*
BO	*Bologna*	IS	*Isermia*	PG	*Perugia*	TO	*Torino*
BR	*Brindisi*	LA	*Latina*	PI	*Pisa*	TR	*Terni*
BS	*Brescia*	LC	*Lecco*	PR	*Parma*	TS	*Trieste*
BZ	*Bolzano*	LE	*Lecce*	PS	*Pesaro*	TV	*Treviso*
CA	*Cagliari*	LI	*Livorno*	PT	*Pistoia*	VB	*Verbano*
CB	*Campobasso*	LT	*Latino*	PV	*Pavia*	VC	*Vercelli*
CE	*Caserta*	LU	*Lucca*	PZ	*Potenza*	VE	*Venice*
CH	*Chieti*	MC	*Macerata*	RA	*Ravenna*	VI	*Vicenza*
CO	*Como*	ME	*Messina*	RE	*Reggio Emilia*	VR	*Verona*
CR	*Cremona*	MI	*Milan*	RI	*Rieti*	VT	*Viterbo*

REGIONS

Italy is divided into 20 regions. A map and description of each region is found in the next section of this book, beginning on page 31. Beginning on page XXX is a list of all the *Places to Stay* grouped alphabetically by region from Abruzzo to Veneto. For reference, the 20 regions of Italy from north to south, with their capital cities in parentheses, are as follows:

NORTH—Aosta Valley (Aosta), Liguria (Genova), Piedmont (Turin), Friuli Venezia Giulia (Trieste), Trentino-Alto Adige (Trento & Bolzano), Lombardy (Milan), Veneto (Venice), and Emilia-Romagna (Bologna).

CENTRAL—Tuscany (Florence), Umbria (Perugia), Marches (Ancona), Lazio (Rome), Abruzzo (L'Aquila), and Molise (Campobasso).

SOUTH—Campania (Naples), Apulia (Bari), Calabria (Cantazaro), Basilicata (Potenza), Sicily (Palermo), and Sardinia (Cagliari).

SAFETY

If certain precautions are taken, most unfortunate incidents can be avoided. It is extremely helpful to keep copies of passports, tickets, and contents of your wallet in your room in case you need them. Pickpocketing most commonly occurs in cities on buses, train stations, crowded streets, or from passing motorbikes. WARNING: At tollway gas stations and snack bars, **always** lock your car and beware of gypsies and vendors who try to sell you stolen merchandise. This practice is most prevalent south of Rome. In general, **never** leave valuables or even luggage in the car. Also, **never** set down luggage even for a minute in train stations.

SHOPPING

Italy is a shopper's paradise. Not only are the stores brimming with tempting merchandise, but the displays are works of art, from the tiniest fruit market to the most chic boutique. Each region seems to specialize in something: in Venice hand-blown glass and handmade lace are popular; Milan is famous for its clothing and silk; Florence is a center for leather goods and gold jewelry; Rome is a fashion hub, where you can stroll the pedestrian shopping streets and browse in some of the world's most elegant shops boasting the latest designer creations. Religious items are also plentiful in Rome, particularly near St. Peter's Cathedral. Naples and the surrounding area (Capri, Ravello, and Positano) offer delightful coral jewelry and also a wonderful selection of ceramics. You will be enticed by the variety of products sold at the farms such as wines, virgin olive oil, jams and honeys, cheese, and salami, along with local artisans' handicrafts. NOTE: For reasons of financial control and the tax evasion problems in Italy, the law states that clients **must** leave commercial establishments with an official receipt in hand, in order to avoid fines.

For purchases over €155 an immediate cash refund of the tax amount is offered by the Italian government to non-residents of the EU. Goods must be purchased at an affiliated retail outlet with the "tax-free for tourists" sign. Ask for the store receipt **plus** the tax-free shopping receipt. At the airport go first to the customs office where they will examine the items purchased and stamp both receipts, and then to the "tax-free cash refund" point after passport control.

U.S. customs allows U.S. residents to bring in $800-worth of foreign goods duty-free, after which a straight 10% of the amount above $800 is levied. Two bottles of liquor are allowed. The import of fresh cheese or meat is strictly restricted unless it is vacuum-packed.

TELEPHONES

The Italian phone company (TELECOM) has been an object of ridicule, a source of frustration, and a subject of heated conversation since its inception. More modern systems are gradually being installed, and most areas have touch-tone phones now. Telephone numbers can have from four to eight digits, so don't be afraid of missing numbers. Cellular phones have saved the day (Italians wouldn't be caught dead without at least one) and are recognized by three-digit area codes beginning with 3. We have added cellphone numbers many of properties in the guide. Cellphones offer the B&B owner great flexibility and give guests the advantage of always finding someone "home."

It is now very easy to rent cellular phones for your stay in Italy either through car rental companies or directly at airports.

All calls to Italy need to include the "0" in the area code, whether calling from abroad, within Italy, or even within the same city, *cellphone numbers drop the "0" in all cases.*

Dial 113 for emergencies of all kinds—24-hour service nationwide.

Dial 116 for Automobile Club for urgent breakdown assistance on the road.

Dial 118 for Ambulance service.

Remember that no warning is given when the time you've paid for in a public phone is about to expire (the line just goes dead), so put in plenty of change or a phone card. There are several types of phones (in various stages of modernization) in Italy:

Bright-orange pay phones, with attached apparatus permitting insertion of a *scheda telefonica,* reusable magnetic cards worth €5–€25, or now more rarely, coins.

To call the United States from Italy, matters have been eased by the ongoing installation of the Country Direct System, whereby you can reach an American operator by dialing 800-900-5825 for AT&T. Either a collect call or a credit-card call can then be placed. If you discover this system doesn't work from some smaller towns, dial 170 to place a collect call, or, in some cities, try dialing direct (from a *scatti* phone), using the international code 001 + area code + number.

TIPPING

HOTELS: Service charges are normally included in four- and five-star hotels only. It is customary to leave a token tip for staff.

RESTAURANTS: If a service charge is included, it will be indicated on the bill, otherwise 10–15% is standard tipping procedure.

TAXIS: 10%.

TRANSPORTATION

BOATS: Italy has gorgeous islands dotting her shorelines, a glorious string of lakes gracing her mountains to the north, and romantic canals in Venice.

Luckily for the tourist, the country's boat system is excellent. All of Italy's islands are linked to the mainland by a wonderful maritime network. The many outlying islands sometimes have overnight ferries that offer sleeping accommodations and facilities for cars. The closer islands usually offer a choice—the hydrofoil that zips quickly across the water or the regular ferry that is slower. Italy also offers you an enchanting selection of lakes. One of the true highlights of traveling in Italy is to explore these wondrous lakes by hopping on one of the nostalgic ferry boats that glide romantically between little villages clustered along the shorelines. Again, there is usually a choice of either the hydrofoil that darts between the hamlets, or the ferry that glides leisurely across the water and usually offers beverage and food service on board. The boat schedules are posted at each pier, or you can request a timetable from the Italian tourist office. NOTE: These little boats are punctual, to the minute. Be right at the pier with your ticket in hand so you can jump on board during the brief interlude that the boat stops at the shore. If at all possible, try to squeeze in at least one boat excursion—it is a treat you will long remember.

TRAIN TRAVEL

Although a car is an absolute necessity to reach most bed and breakfasts, it is often convenient and timesaving to leave the car and take a train for day trips into the city. NOTE: **Your ticket must be stamped with the time and date <u>before</u> you board the train;** otherwise, you will be issued a €20 fine. Tickets are stamped at small (and not very obvious) yellow machines near the exits to the tracks. Unstamped tickets may be reimbursed with a 30% penalty. In order to avoid long lines at the station it is strongly advised that you purchase your ticket (including seat reservation) in advance through a local travel agency when you arrive in Italy or online at *www.europerail.com* or *www.trenitalia.com*. The ES (Eurostar) trains to major cities are the fastest and most efficient. (Note that many special fares and passes are available only if purchased in the United States.) For information and the best possible fares, and to book tickets online, visit our website, *www.karenbrown.com*.

Introduction–About Italy

TRANSFERS INTO CITIES

Travelers from abroad normally arrive by plane in Florence, Milan, Rome, or Venice and pick up their rental car at the airport. However, if your first destination is the city and you plan on picking up your car after your stay, approximate transfer rates are as follows:

MILAN

From Malpensa to city by taxi (70 min)	€80
From Malpensa to Cadorna station by train (every 30 min)	€12
From Malpensa to several city stops by bus (every 20 min)	€5.50
From Linate to city by taxi (20 min)	€40
From Linate to city by bus (every 20 min)	€6

ROME

From Da Vinci to city by train (every 30 min)	€12
From Da Vinci to city by taxi (45 min)	€50

VENICE

From airport to city by waterbus (40 minutes)	€15
From airport to city by private waterbus	€110
From station to city by waterbus (15 min)	€6
From station to city by private waterbus	€80

FLORENCE

From airport to city by taxi (30 min)	€40

WEATHER

Italy is blessed with lovely weather. However, unless you are a ski enthusiast following the promise of what the majestic mountains have to offer in the winter, or must travel in summer due to school holidays, we highly recommend traveling in spring or fall. Travel at either of these times has two dramatic advantages: you miss the rush of the summer tourist season when all of Italy is packed and you are more likely to have beautiful weather. In spring the meadows are painted with wildflowers. In fall the forests are a riot of color and the vineyards are mellow in shades of red and gold. Although the mountains of Italy are delightfully cool in summer, the rest of the country can be very hot, especially in the cities. NOTE: Many properties are not air conditioned. Those that are sometimes charge extra for it.

WEBSITE

Please visit the Karen Brown website (*www.karenbrown.com*) in conjunction with this book. Our website provides trip planning assistance, new discoveries, post-press updates, feedback from you, our readers, the opportunity to purchase goods and services that we recommend (rail tickets, car rental, travel insurance, etc.), and one-stop shopping for our guides, associated maps and watercolor prints. Most of our favorite places to stay are featured with color photos and direct website and email links. Also, we invite you to participate in the Karen Brown's Readers' Choice Awards. Be sure to visit our website and vote so your favorite properties will be honored.

WHAT TO WEAR

During the day informal wear is most appropriate, including comfortable slacks for women. In the evening, if you are at a sidewalk café or a simple pizzeria, women do not need to dress up nor do men need to wear coats and ties. However, Italy does have some elegant restaurants where a dress and coat and tie are definitely the proper attire. A basic principle is to dress as you would in any city at home. There are perhaps a few special situations: the churches are still very conservative—shorts are definitely inappropriate, as are low-cut dresses. Some of the cathedrals still insist that women have their arms covered. It is rare that a scarf on the head is required, but to wear one is a respectful gesture. If you have an audience with the Pope, then the dress code is even more conservative. The layered effect is ideal. Italy's climate runs the gamut from usually cool in the mountains to frequently very hot in the south. The most efficient wardrobe is one where light blouses and shirts can be reinforced by layers of sweaters that can be added or peeled off as the day demands.

We wish you the best in your travels to Italy and always welcome your comments and suggestions. *Buon Viaggio!*

Regions of Italy

Aosta Valley

Milan

Piedmont

Lombardy

Trentino-Alto Adige

Friuli-Venezia Giulia

Veneto

Venice

Emilia-Romagna

Genova

Liguria

Florence

Tuscany

Marches

Umbria

CORSICA (France)

Abruzzo

ROME

Lazio

Molise

Bari

Campania

Naples

Basilicata

Apulia

Sardinia

Calabria

Cagliari

Palermo

Sicily

31

ABRUZZO: Although it is one of the smallest regions of Italy, rugged Abruzzo boasts the highest peaks of the Apennine range, the Gran Sasso. In fact, most of the territory is made up of majestic mountains spilling down to the coast of the Adriatic Sea. Unsuitable for agriculture, the region's economy depends on pastoral activity and specialty artisans (goldsmiths, wood and stone carvers, wrought-iron craftsmen) and  tourism. Abruzzo is the ancestral land of many Americans who return to Italy in search of their roots. The region's four major national parks and nature reserves are ideal for hiking, free climbing, and alpine, cross-country, and downhill skiing. Our favorite medieval villages to explore include Sulmona, Scanno, Penne Atri, Tagliacozzo, Saepinum and the historic capital town of L'Aquila with its Fontana delle 99 Cannelle, a fountain built in 1272 with 99 spouts. In Sulmona you find Ceramics of Castelli, a tradition since the Middle Ages. *Gastronomic specialties:* A large variety of pastas come from this region. Inland you find lamb dishes and a special variety of pecorino cheeses, while the coast offers seafood delights including stuffed squid. Highly prized wines come from Montepulciano d'Abruzzo.

AOSTA VALLEY: In the uppermost corner of northwest Italy is Valle d'Aosta, a region made up entirely of mountains, with its Alps bordering France and Switzerland. The capital city, Aosta, derives its name from Ottaviano Augusto who founded the city in 25 AD. It is one of two Italian regions that have been run as completely autonomous administrations since 1946, with its own constitution and laws. Besides  having preserved Patois, its original dialect, both French and Italian are also spoken fluently. This region has many ski resorts including: Cervinia, Courmayeur, and Mont Blanc on the French-Swiss border. You will also find 130 medieval castles in Aosta, with the Fenis and Issogne being the most famous. The Gran Paradiso National Park, with its Alpine refuges, is a haven for nature and wildlife lovers, hikers, and climbers. *Gastronomic specialties:* Fontina cheese (excellent in fondues) and many prestigious wines (including Pinot Gris) come from the Aosta Valley.

APULIA: Apulia is a delightful surprise with unique scenery barely resembling that which you see in the rest of Italy. Over the centuries it was invaded by Greeks, Arabs, Normans, Swedes, Aragonesi, Spaniards, and Saraceni, all of whom left their mark on the land. There are many castles in Apulia including: Castel del Monte, di Trani, d'Otranto, and di Copertino. Octagonal-shaped Castel del Monte is the most impressive of  the buildings commissioned by Frederick II. This region is also home to Gargano Peninsula National Park, which is heavily forested and has scenic beaches. Our favorite towns to explore are Vieste and Monte Sant'Angelo. You must also visit the whitewashed towns of Ostini, Alberobello, and Locorotondo, the touristic heart of the region and home to the trulli (whimsical-looking, cone-shaped houses). Located on the "heel" of the boot, and not to be forgotten, are the beautiful baroque cathedral cities of Lecce, San Matteo, Santa Chiara, and Santa Croce. *Gastronomic specialties:* Olive oil and wine (which are strong and full-flavored), various cheeses from sheep's milk; local ear-shaped pasta (called orecchiette), seafood dishes with mussels; fava beans and chicory are all found in the region.

BASILICATA: Basilicata, located at the "instep" of the boot, is another of Italy's smaller regions that is not often visited by tourists. It reaches the shores of the Gulf of Taranto as well as a small stretch of the Tyrrhenian Sea on the western coast. Matera is no doubt the most interesting city in this region. Its ancient neighorhood, Sassi, has been  preserved as an outdoor museum with cave-like dwellings built into the tufo rock where many citizens of this impoverished and forgotten region lived along with their livestock. While in Matera you must also visit its Romanesque cathedral and its several 9th-century churches with Byzantine frescoes. Another highlight of Basilicata is picturesque Maratea—a medieval village tucked in the hills above a beautiful coast that is enhanced by pretty beaches and hidden coves. The archaeological ruins of Eraclea and Metapontum are also part of this region.

CALABRIA: One of the most mountainous regions of Italy, Calabria, at the "toe" of the boot, is a peninsula flanked by two seas, the Ionian and the Tyrrhenian. Agriculture remains its mainstay even though the mountains are arid and the terrain subject to landslides. The rugged highlands of Aspromonte and the wooded Sila areas in the center are sparsely inhabited. Our favorite cities include: Catanzaro, Cosenza, Reggio di Calabria (ferryboats to Sicily) and Crotone. Damage from four major earthquakes and the effects of bombing in World War II have left these cities with few historic monuments. The National Museum of Magna Graecia in Reggio di Calabria (colonized by the Greeks in 750 B.C.) contains the most important art collection in southern Italy. When exploring this region, take the coastal road from Maratea going south towards Sicily which is far more scenic than the autostrada. There are gorgeous cliffs at Capo Vaticano, near Tropea, on the road from Vibo Valentia. One long beach with clear blue water runs along the Gulf coast from Reggio di Calabria all the way up to Taranto (500 km).

CAMPANIA: The Campania region, hugging the Tyrrhenian coast, is squeezed between its four neighbors: Lazio, Molise, Apulia, and Basilicata. With the country's third-major city, Naples, as its capital, Campania boasts one of the most famous coastlines in the world: the Amalfi Coast. The restored historic center of Naples (with its Piazza del Plebiscito, Palazzo Reale, Galleria Umberto, San Francesco di Paola, San Gennaro, Piazza Mercato, and Piazza Garibaldi) is definitely the highlight of this region. Nearby Naples, the archaeological sites of Pompeii, Paestum, Herculaneum, Capua, and Velia are also a must-see. Santa Maria di Castellabate and Acciaroli are two favorite towns on the Cilento coast south of the Amalfi Coast. This coastal area offers lovely, quiet, seaside resorts. Campania also boasts many gorgeous islands. After seeing the famed Capri, try lesser-known islands with more local flavor such as Ischia (specializing in thermal spas) and Procida. *Gastronomic specialties:* Campania is home of fresh Buffalo mozzarella from Paestum, pizza from Naples, and spaghetti with clams.

EMILIA-ROMAGNA: Emilia Romagna covers a large stretch of territory from the Adriatic Sea to almost the opposite side of the country. The bordering regions to the north are Veneto, Lombardy, Piedmont, and Liguria; and to the south, Tuscany and Marches. Italy's main autostrada runs right through Emilia-Romagna, dividing the flat plains to the north from the lush fertile hills to the south. There is a
wealth of precious works of art in this region from the magnificent Byzantine mosaics in Ravenna, wonderful Romanesque churches in Modena and Parma, to Renaissance art and architecture in Ferrara and Bologna. From the beaches of Rimini where international youth swarm in the summer months, dancing until dawn, to some of the most important opera and music festivals of international fame in Modena, Bologna, and Parma, this region has it all. *Gastronomic specialties:* Emilia–Romagna produces Italy's best and most famous food, starting with Parmesan cheese, Parma ham, balsamic vinegar, endless varieties of salami, tortellini and many other pastas.

FRIULI-VENEZIA GIULIA: In the far northeastern corner of Italy, is the Friuli-Venezia Giulia region. Half of its territory is made up of mountains, with the remaining area flatland bordering the Adriatic Sea. Its capital city, at the region's most easterly point, is Trieste, located on the Slovenian border and home to many shipyards. The highlighs of this region include the medieval villages of Portogruaro, Summaga, Sesto Al
Reghena, and Aquileia (the Roman colony founded in 181 B.C. whose artifacts are displayed in the Museo Archeologico). Also Cividale del Friuli, another city of ancient Roman origins (founded by none other than Caesar himself), boasts an interesting museum located in the Palladio-designed Palazzo Pretorio. If you like art, Giambattista Tiepolo, Venice's favorite 18th-century painter, is well represented in Udine, within the cathedral and Museo Diocesano. *Gastronomic specialtie*s: This region is home to some of the sweetest of prosciutto hams made in the town of San Daniele dei Friuli. Fine DOC regional wines including Pinot Bianco, Riesling, Riva Rossa, Carso Terreno, and Refosco come from this region (wine estates are concentrated around the hillsides of Gorizia).

LAZIO: It is only in the past decade or so that foreigners have begun to explore and appreciate the many historic, artistic, and natural wonders of the Lazio region, home to the nation's capital city Rome. Highlights of this region include the fascinating world of the Etruscans with more than 30 sites, a comprehensive archaeology museum in Tarquinia, and well-preserved tombs in the area of Tarquinia and Cerveteri. Lazio is  home to many famous gardens including the Tivoli and the extraordinary gardens and fountains of Villa d'Este. In addition, one of Italy's best-preserved Renaissance gardens, the Villa Lante, is also in Lazio. This region also boasts picturesque lakes. Lakes to the north of Rome include Bracciano, Bolsena, and Vico; and to the south are lakes Nemi and Albano. Rieti, backed by the Terminillo mountains and the scenic Sabine mountain area dotted with medieval villages is perfect for those seeking spots off the beaten path. Our favorite seaside attractions are the charming fishing villages on the islands of Ponza and Ventotene, plus the coast from Circeo to Gaeta. *Gastronomic specialties:* Top-rated olive oil, which rivals that of Tuscany and Puglia, is made in Riete.

LIGURIA: Liguria is best known for its Riviera tourism. The Ponente coast, including the flower capital of Italy, San Remo, is a highlight of this region. The gardens of Ventimiglia and the villages of Alassio, Albenga, Cervo, Dolceacqua, and Taggia are also worth visiting. Of course one must also visit the Levante coast which has stolen the spotlight with such gems as Portofino, Camogli, San Fruttuoso abbey,  Santa Margherita, and the very popular stretch of hill towns above the sea called Cinque Terre. We also love "Poet's Gulf," just south of the Cinque Terre where you find the charming fishing villages of Tellaro, San Terenzo, and Fiascherino. The hilly and mountainous inland areas, which give the region its verdant reputation, have yet-to-be-discovered villages (such as Uscio), and offer quiet havens from the more popular coastal destinations. A mountain excursion can be taken to Santo Stefano d'Aveto, an hour and a half's drive from the coast. *Gastronomic specialtie*s: Focaccia pizza using its famed olive oil, delectable pesto sauces, and many seafood specialties are common here.

LOMBARDY: The Lombardy region's capital, Milan, does not steal the  limelight from the rest of its territory, which encompasses the beloved lake regions. Still, a shopping expedition down the famed Via Monte Napoleone and a peek at Leonardo da Vinci's "Last Supper," plus the Duomo and La Scala are all a must. Regional highlights include the historic small city of Vigevano near Milan with its magnificent arcaded piazza and baroque cathedral. Our favorite Lombard cities include the beautifully austere Bergamo with its ancient stone center on the upper half of the city; Pavia with its monumental Certosa abbey and surrounding Pavese wine country; Cremona, the capital of violins and homeland of Monteverdi; and Mantova with its three interconnecting lakes. Tourists have always been highly attracted to the romantic northern lakes in Italy. Como sits at the top of the list, then Maggiore; Garda, the largest, with its fairy-tale medieval town; Sirmione; then minor lakes, Orta, Varese, Lugano, Iseo, all dotted with charming villages. The Franciacorta wine area, stretching between Brescia (Lombardy's second-biggest city), and Lake Iseo, is in this region and produces Italy's best sparkling wines.

MARCHES: The Marches, stretching along the Adriatic coast, runs  close behind Tuscany and Umbria in the way of scenic beauty, history, art, and cultural offerings. It is a prosperous region offering seaside resorts, the Sibillini mountain peaks, bucolic countryside, and Renaissance towns. Urbino, Ascoli Piceno, and Loreto are the most outstanding of the Renaissance towns in the region. Other highlights include the towns of Pesaro (on the sea and the birthplace of Rossini) and Macerata (a medieval city with summer music festivals). The scenically situated Renaissance town of Recanati is also wonderful. The Monte Conero coast south of Ancona is decidedly the most beautiful seaside area of the region, with intimate, rocky beaches and coves best reached by boat. This is a regional park with cliffs swooping down to the sea. Our favorite village here is the charming Sirolo, a walled town perched above the coast. Torre di Palma is another enchanting ancient village by the sea with delightful outdoor dining. The fascinating pink stalactite caves of Grotte di Frasassi are also worth seeing.

MOLISE: Molise, another of Italy's forgotten, mostly mountainous regions, is relatively isolated and sparsely populated. Until recently there were very few roads here, with just three main arteries cutting across the entire region. Isernia and Campobasso, the two main cities of Molise, are its highlights. Isernia has been severely damaged over the years by earthquakes and bombing and little remains of its history. It  does have, however, a museum with relics of the Paleolithic civilization recently discovered here, the most ancient finding in all of Europe to date. There are remote mountaintop villages in the area surrounding Isernia including Capracotta, Agnone, Pietrabbondante, and Scapoli, where the zampogna bagpipes, a local tradition among shepherds, are demonstrated in the yearly fair. The quaint villages of Larino, Ferrazzano, and Garanello surrounding Campobasso are lovely. The Tremiti islands of Molise and can be reached by ferryboat from Termoli or Vasto.

PIEDMONT: Piedmont is at the foothills of the Alps, which make up almost half of the region—the rest being divided between hillside and plains. Piedmont has a colorful past and today boasts one of Italy's strongest economies. Turin, the capital city of Italy until 1860 (now the  home of Fiat industries) maintains an impressive historic center (Piazza San Carlo), and has the world's most important collection of Egyptian art. The Langhe and Monferrato wine country is certainly the favorite area as far as tourism is concerned; this countryside south and east of Turin is characterized by medieval villages, ancient fortified castles, and hills lined with kilometer after kilometer of vineyards and fruit orchards. Other towns of interest include Alba, La Morra, Cherasco, Barolo, and Monforte. *Gastronomic specialties*: Risotto is common in Piedmont (the region along with Lombardy being Europe's rice capital). The region also boasts prized white truffles, and some of the country's finest wines: Barbaresco, Barbera, Barolo, and Dolcetto.

Regions of Italy

SARDINIA: Until recently, Sardinia was Italy's forgotten island, the farthest from the mainland with a rocky, arid interior covered with grazing sheep. Its Caribbean-blue waters, hidden coves, and isolated white beaches have attracted the sailing and yachting set who all converge in the summer months on the northern Emerald Coast. The rest of the year the island is a haven for explorers discovering it's fascinating ancient history,  dating back to 300 B.C. Over 7,000 ancient nuraghes (stone structures built for defense as far back as the 9th century B.C. up to the Roman period) are scattered about the entire island in various states of preservation. A vast variety of traditional festivals occur throughout the year where Sardinians, mostly dressed in traditional costumes, express their identity. These festivals are the best way to really come to understand their unique culture. The region also includes the picturesque islands of Sant'Antioco, San Pietro, La Maddalena, Caprera, and Asinara. *Gastronomic specialties:* A wide variety of good wines are made in Sardinia, especially sweet wines (Vernaccia). Recipes that are based either on lamb and wild boar or seafood specialties, including octopus, are popular.

SICILY: The culture, traditions, and history of Sicily are intensely rich. Its fertile terrain is just as varied with rugged mountains (including Europe's highest volcano, Mount Etna), flatland lined with endless citrus groves, spectacular coastlines, and 16 unique islands. The classic tour takes you to Palermo, Segesta's temple and amphitheatre, medieval Erice, the Greek ruins at seaside Selinunte, the Valley of the Temples in  Agrigento, the Roman villa and mosaics at Piazza Armerina, Siracusa, and the resort town of Taormina. Other areas worth visiting are the town of Cefalù on the northern coast, the ceramic center at Santo Stefano, Marsala and the Egadi Isles on the western coast, and the Madonie Mountains with their intact heritage. *Gastronomic specialties:* Fresh pastas made with a variety of Mediterranean vegetables; seafood combinations with sardines, tuna, and a range of local fish; rich desserts with ricotta and marzipan; and sweet wines including Moscato and Marsala, are all indicitive of this region.

TRENTINO-ALTO ADIGE: Trentino-Alto Adige combines two regions that have distinctly different flavors and traditions. Trentino is the southern tip of this far northern mountainous region, bordering Veneto's portion of the Dolomites on one side and Lombardy on the other. Whereas Trentino is Italian in tradition, the upper section of Alto Adige touching Austria is Tyrolian in flavor (more German is spoken than Italian).  The town of Trento is a highlight, featuring a 13th-century cathedral, Palazzo Pretorio, medieval tower, art museum Diocesano Tridentino, and Buonconsiglio Castle. The scenic Fassa and Fiemme valleys, a cross-country skiers' paradise where the ancient Ladin language is still in use, are also of interest. The Brenta Dolomites, where skiers gather at the Madonna di Campiglio resort, is in this region. Visit Alto Adige's capital city, Bolzano, with its Gothic cathedral and archaeological museum displaying the 5,300-year-old mummy, Otzi, discovered under the glaciers in 1991. We also love the beautiful Val Gardena valley extending to Cortina in neighboring Veneto, featuring the Siusi Alps with fairy-tale-like scenery and the centuries-old tradition of woodcarving.

TUSCANY: Tuscany has become synonymous with Italy. Travelers flock to its famous cities and well-preserved countryside not only to view the breathtaking art found here, but also to be swept away by the magic of its enchanting landscapes. Florence is a highlight with its rich display of Renaissance masterpieces all concentrated within the historical center of 3 square kilometers. One must also visit the Piazza  del Campo in Siena, one of Italy's most stunning squares, hosting the world-famous Palio horse races in July and August. The charming medieval hill towns of Montepulciano, Montalcino, and San Gimignano are home to some of the region's finest wines. The small historic cities of Lucca, Pisa, Arezzo, and Cortona, each with its own individual architectural characteristics, are also well worth visiting. Tuscany is also home to the famous Chianti area, with its endless vineyards and monumental castles. Maremma, in the southern, lesser-known reaches of the region touching the sea, is rich in Etruscan history and dotted with numerous stone villages to explore.

UMBRIA: Enchanting Umbria, bordering Tuscany, is located in the lush heart of Italy. A circular road in the center of the region touches the well-known cities of Perugia, Assisi, Spello, Spoleto, Todi, and Deruta. The two most spectacular towns outside of the loop are Gubbio and Orvieto. Highlights include the town of Perugia, a modern-day town with the stunning Palazzo Dei Priori where the majority of the finest Umbrian paintings are exhibited in the Galleria Nazionale dell'Umbria.

Assisi is another highlight with its many beautiful churches, including the mystic Basilica di San Francesco. The northern reaches of Umbria offer remote countryside and unspoiled landscapes. Umbria is home to world-famous ceramic centers, first and foremost, Deruta, and then Gubbio, producing hand-painted pieces for the past 600 years. Umbria also boasts the famous Orvieto Classico wine: varieties can be tasted at enotecas in Orvieto with its monumental cathedral and astounding façade.

VENETO: Wealthy Veneto boasts a handful of stunning artistic cities; the most beautiful slice of the Dolomites surrounding the popular resort, Cortina; the many villas of Andrea Palladio in and around Vicenza; and the eastern half of scenic Lake Garda. Venice with its 120 inlets, 100 canals, and 400 bridges is the highlight of this region. Venice's neighboring islands of Burano with its colorfully painted houses; Murano,

the glass center; and Torcello, are all of interest. Farther south you find Chioggia and its wondrous fish market; Cappella Scrovegni with Giotto's frescoed masterpiece and the 13th-century university (where Galileo taught). Verona, a magical well-preserved city, is also part of this region. Verona is famous for its still-standing 1st-century amphitheatre, its summer opera festival, the Piazza Erbe with its open market, the Renaissance square, and the Piazza dei Signori. The houses of both Romeo and Juliet in Verona are a pilgrimage point where lovers sign a book of confessions, enhancing the fairy-tale aura. Top wines from Valpolicella, Soave, and Barbarano, and grappa from Bassano del Grappa are produced in Veneto.

Florence

Regions of Italy

Italian Highlights
by Train & Boat–or Car

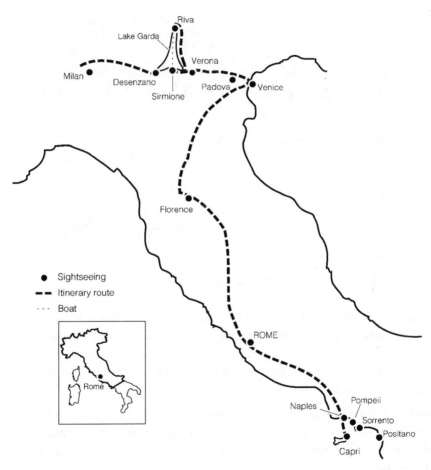

Italian Highlights by Train & Boat–or Car

Island of Burano, near Venice

This itinerary provides you with a glimpse of some of the highlights of Italy and will tempt you to return to delve more deeply into the wonders that Italy has to offer. This itinerary is woven around towns that are conveniently linked by public transportation. Although this itinerary shows how to travel by train and boat, if you prefer to drive, you can easily trace the same route in your car.

Approximate train and boat times have been included as a reference to show you how the pieces of this itinerary tie together. Schedules are constantly changing, so these must be verified. Also, many boats and some trains are seasonal, so check schedules before making your plans.

Remember to travel lightly—when burdened by heavy suitcases, the charm of public transportation quickly diminishes!

Recommended Pacing: To follow this itinerary in its entirety you need a minimum of three weeks—and this is really rushing it. We recommend two nights in Milan to see its major sights and enjoy shopping in its multitude of gorgeous boutiques, three nights in Sirmione to give you time to take boat trips on Lake Garda, two nights in Verona to wander its quaint streets and superb Roman amphitheater, three nights in Venice to enjoy its rich beauty, three nights in Florence to visit its many museums, three nights in Rome (an absolute minimum for its many sights to see and shopping), three nights in Naples to give time to visit its fabulous museums plus side trips to Pompeii and the Amalfi Drive, and three nights in Capri to just relax and play on this romantic island. If your time is limited, this itinerary lends itself well to segmentation, so if you can't include all of the suggested stops, choose just a portion of the itinerary and "finish up" on what you have missed on your next trip to Italy.

ORIGINATING CITY   MILAN

This highlight tour begins in **Milan**, a most convenient city since it is the hub of airline flights and trains. While it is a sprawling industrial city at its heart is a truly charming old section.

While in Milan you must not miss visiting the **Duomo**, the third-largest cathedral in the world. There is no denying the beauty of the interior but best of all is the exterior, so take an elevator or the stairs to the roof where you can admire the view and examine at close hand the statues that adorn this lacework fantasy.

Facing the Duomo is one of the world's most beautiful arcades, the forerunner of the modern shopping mall, but with far more style. Even if you are not a shopper, be sure to just browse and have a cup of tea in the **Galleria Vittorio Emanuele.** In this Victorian-era fantasy creation, there are two main intersecting wings, both completely domed with intricately patterned glass. Along the pedestrian-only arcades are boutiques and beautiful little restaurants with outside tables for people watching.

Duomo, Milan

After more than two decades of controversial restoration, Leonardo da Vinci's famous mural, **The Last Supper**, is once again on view in the church of **Santa Maria delle Grazie**. The mural, which covers an entire wall of the church, has been a problem for many years mainly because Leonardo experimented with painting onto drywall rather than employing the more usual fresco technique of applying paint to wet plaster. In an effort to prevent further damage, air filters, special lights, and dust-absorbing carpets have been installed, and the small groups of visitors are limited to a stay of 15 minutes. It is vital that you make an appointment in advance: from the USA 011-39 (Europe, 00-39) 0289-421146; from within Italy, (199) 19 91 00, *www.cenacolovinciano.org*. The unilingual Italian-speaking reservationists will make you an appointment and give you a confirmation number. Arrive at the church about 15 minutes before your appointment, confirmation number in hand, and pay cash for your ticket.

Milan's other great claim to fame is **La Scala**, one of the world's most renowned opera houses. In addition to wonderful opera, other types of performances are given here. If it is opera season, try your best to go to a performance; if not, try to get tickets for whatever is playing. It is such fun to watch the lights go down and the curtains go up in this magnificent theater with row upon row of balconies rising like layers on a wedding cake. Tickets are sold in the ticket office located around the left-hand side of the theater.

DESTINATION I   SIRMIONE

Sirmione is located on Lake Garda. The station where you need to disembark is in the town of Desenzano, which is on the main rail route between Milan and Venice. There are many trains each day between Milan and Venice, but not all stop in Desenzano. One we suggest runs as follows:

1:10 pm	depart Milan Central Station by train
2:21 pm	arrive Desenzano

When the train arrives in the ancient port of **Desenzano**, you can take a taxi to the pier where hydrofoils, steamers, and buses leave regularly for Sirmione. However, although it is more expensive, we suggest you splurge and take a taxi directly to Sirmione (about 10 kilometers away). This is definitely the most convenient means of transportation since you are taken directly to where you are staying.

Sirmione is a walled medieval village fabulously located on a tiny peninsula jutting out into **Lake Garda**. This peninsula seems more like an island because it is connected to the mainland by just a thread of land. To enter the ancient town, you first cross over a moat, and then enter through massive medieval gates. Unless you are one of the lucky ones with confirmed accommodations for the night, you cannot take your automobile inside the town walls, since only pedestrians are allowed through the entrance. But if you have reservations for the night, stop near the entrance at the information office where you are given a pass to enter in taxi.

It is an easy walk to the dock in the center of town where you can study the posted schedule to decide which boat you want to take for your day's excursion. You can glide around the lake all day and have a snack on board, or get off in some small jewel of a town and enjoy lunch at a lakefront café. There is a choice of transportation: either the romantic ferry boats or the faster hydrofoils.

There are some Roman ruins on the very tip of the Sirmione peninsula which can be reached either on foot, or, if you prefer, by a miniature motorized train that shuttles back and forth between the ruins and the village.

DESTINATION II   VERONA

There are trains almost every hour that cover the half-hour journey between Desenzano and Verona. But if it is a beautiful day, it is much more romantic to incorporate sightseeing into your transportation and take a boat and bus instead of the train. If this appeals to you, the following gives an idea of how this can be done.

  10:20 am depart Sirmione by ferry
  2:20 pm   arrive Riva

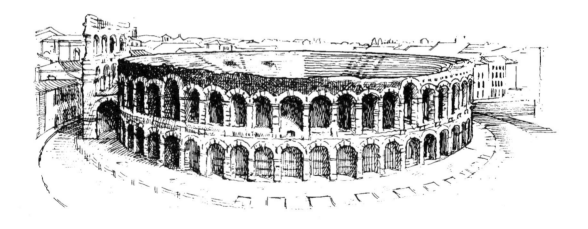

Amphitheater, Verona

You can have lunch on board the ferry or else you can wait until you reach the medieval town of **Riva**, located on the northern shore of Lake Garda. The interesting ancient core of Riva is small, so it doesn't take long to stroll through the old city.

After lunch and a walk through the old part of town, leave Riva by bus for Verona (buses run every 15 minutes in summer), tracing a scenic route along the eastern shore of the lake.

When you arrive in **Verona** you are in for a treat. This is a town that is all too frequently bypassed by the tourist, but what a prize it is. This medieval gem is the perfect city to explore on foot. Buy a detailed map and be on your way.

Definitely not to be missed is the **Roman amphitheater**, one of the largest in Italy. This dramatic arena, dating from the 1st century, has perfect acoustics and hosts operatic performances in summer. As you continue to wander through Verona's enchanting streets, you discover many delights, including the **Piazza delle Erbe** (Square of Herbs), which is the old Roman forum where chariot races used to take place. Follow your map to nearby 21 Via Cappello to find the 13th-century **Casa di Giulietta** and the balcony where Juliet rendezvoused with Romeo. Another colorful square, the **Piazza dei Signori**, features a statue of Dante in its center and 12th-and 13th-century buildings. The **Castelvecchio** (Old Castle) built by Congrande II of the Della Scala family in the 14th century, houses an art museum with paintings, sculptures, jewelry, and armaments. The 14th-century **Ponte Scaligero** (Scaliger Bridge) links the Castelvecchio with the opposite side of the river. The **Cathedral**, dating from the 12th century, is well worth a visit to see its fine red marble columns and richly adorned interior. Just across the river from the heart of the old city, visit the old **Roman theater** where performances are still held in summer.

St. Mark's Square, Venice

When you are ready to leave Verona, there is frequent train service to **Venice** so the following departure time is just a suggestion. NOTE: As you approach Venice, be sure not to get off the train at the Venice Mestre station, but instead wait for the next stop, the Santa Lucia station (about ten minutes further).

2:33 pm   depart Verona, Porto Nuova station by train
3:55 pm   arrive Venice, Santa Lucia station

As you come out of the front door of the train station, you find that the station is directly on the **Grand Canal**. It is a few short steps down to where you can board a boat to take you to where you are staying. The **vaporetti** are the most popular means of transportation and are a very inexpensive means of getting about the city. They are like boat buses that constantly shuttle back and forth from the train station to St. Mark's Square. If you have a lot of luggage you might want to consider a watertaxi. The **motoscafi** (watertaxis) cost about € 50 but deliver you right to the door of your accommodations, provided there is a motorboat dock (noted in the property's description). The third choice of transportation is the **gondola**, but these are much slower and very expensive, so save your gondola ride for a romantic interlude rather than a train connection.

Venice has many places to stay in every price range. In our description we give the closest boat stop to each so that you know where to disembark if you come by canal from the train station. For a few of our recommendations, you need to change boats at the San Marco boat stop.

Venice has so many sights—marvelous restaurants, beautiful boutiques, and fascinating little alleyways to explore—that you could happily stay for weeks.

Of course, you must savor the incomparable ambiance of **Piazza San Marco** (St. Mark's Square). Late afternoon is especially romantic as music wafts across the enormous square, courtesy of the tiny orchestras entertaining visitors as they enjoy an aperitif. A colonnaded walkway encloses the square on three sides, forming a protected path for window-shoppers at the beautiful boutiques and fancy cafés. The fourth side of the square is dominated by the **Basilica di San Marco** (St. Mark's Cathedral), richly endowed with gold and mosaics. The church dates back to the 12th century when it was built to house the remains of St. Mark. Next to the church rises the 99-meter-tall **campanile** (bell tower) where in the 15th-century priests were suspended in a cage to repent their sins. If you are in the plaza on the hour, watch the two Moors strike the hour with their huge bronze hammers as they have for 500 years. To the right of the basilica is the **Palazzo Ducale** (Doge's Palace), a sumptuous fantasy of pink and white marble— open now as a museum. The Palazzo Ducale faces on to the **Piazzetta**, a wide square opening onto the Grand Canal. The square's nickname used to be the *Piazzetta Il Broglio* (Intrigue) because in days of yore, only nobles were allowed in the square between 10 am and noon, at which time the area buzzed with plots of intrigue. Adorning the center of the square are two granite columns, one topped by the Lion of St. Mark and the other by a statue of St. Theodore.

Glass Blowing, Island of Murano

There is no better way to get into the mood of Venice than to join the crowd at St. Mark's pier as they climb aboard one of the ferries that ply the city's waterways. It is a real bargain to board the vaporetto and enjoy the many wonderful palaces bordering the Grand Canal. In addition to exploring the canals that lace Venice, you can take ferries to the outlying islands. Go either on your own or on a tour to the three islands: **Murano** (famous for its hand-blown glass), **Burano** (famous for its colorfully painted fishermen's cottages and lace making), and **Torcello** (once an important city but now just a small village with only its lovely large church to remind you of its past glories).

Another all-day outing by boat is to take the **Il Burchiello**, named for a famous 17th-century Venetian boat. From March to November, this boat departs Tuesdays, Thursdays, and Saturdays at 8:45 am from the Pontile Giardinetti pier near St. Mark's Square and travels the network of rivers and canals linking Venice and Padova. (The schedule might change, so verify dates and times.) This little boat, with an English-speaking guide on board, stops at several of the exquisite palaces en route. Lunch is served and there is time for sightseeing in **Padova** before returning to Venice by bus. Reservation office: Siamic Express, Via Trieste 42, 35121 Padova, Italy, tel: (049) 66 09 44, fax: (049) 66 28 30.

A favorite pastime in Venice is wandering—just anywhere—exploring the maze of twisting canals and crisscrossing back and forth over some of the 400 whimsical bridges. One of the most famous, the **Rialto Bridge**, arching high over the canal, is especially colorful because it is lined by shops. Also much photographed is the **Bridge of Sighs**, so named because this was the bridge prisoners passed over before their execution.

Although all of Venice is virtually an open-air museum, it also has many indoor museums. Two excellent ones are both easy to find near the Accademia boat stop. The **Galleria dell'Accademia** abounds with 14th- to 18th-century Venetian paintings. Within walking distance of the Galleria dell'Accademia is the **Peggy Guggenheim Museum**, featuring 20th-century art. The paintings and statues were the gift of the now-deceased wealthy American heiress, Peggy Guggenheim. The lovely museum was her canal-front home.

DESTINATION IV   FLORENCE

There are several direct trains each day from Venice to Florence: however, in summer, space is at a real premium, so be sure to reserve a seat in advance. Some of the express trains must have prior seat reservations and require a supplemental fee. NOTE: During the busy season, if you want to dine on the train, it is necessary to make advance reservations when you buy your ticket.

    11:45 am   depart Venice, Santa Lucia station (reservations obligatory)
    2:42 pm   arrive Florence

When you arrive in **Florence** take a taxi to where you are staying.

Be generous with your time and do not rush Florence—there is too much to see. You must, of course, pay a visit to Michelangelo's fabulous **David** in the **Galleria dell'Accademia** located just off the **Piazza San Marco**.

Ponte Vecchio, Florence

During your explorations of Florence, you will cross many times through the **Piazza della Signoria**, located in the heart of the old city. Facing this characteristic medieval square is the 13th-century **Palazzo Vecchio**, a stern stone structure topped by a crenellated gallery and dominated by a tall bell tower. It was here that the *signoria* (Florence's powerful aristocratic ruling administrators) met for two months each year while attending to government business. During this period they were forbidden to leave the palace (except for funerals) so that there could not be a hint of suspicion of intrigue or bribery. Of course, you cannot miss one of Florence's landmarks, the **Ponte Vecchio**. Spanning the Arno in the heart of Florence, this colorful bridge is lined with quaint shops just as it has been since the 14th century.

Don't miss the fantastic museums and cathedrals—the world will probably never again see a city that has produced such artistic genius. Florence's **Duomo** is one of the largest in the world. The cathedral's incredible dome (over 100 meters high) was designed by Brunelleschi. Climb the 464 steps to the top of the dome for a superb view of Florence. The **Baptistry** has beautiful mosaics and its bronze doors by Ghiberti were said by Michelangelo to be worthy of serving as the gates to paradise. The main door shows scenes from the life of John the Baptist, the north door shows the life of Jesus, and the east door shows stories from the prophets of the Old Testament. The **Uffizi Museum** (housed in a 16th-century palace) is undoubtedly one of the finest museums in the world. You can make advance reservations at the Uffizi Museum (tel: 055 23 88 651), *www.virtualuffizi.com,* or call Hidden Treasures (888) 419-6700 (U.S.). Also, do not miss the **Pitti Palace** with its fabulous art collection, including paintings by Titian and Raphael. NOTE: In addition to regular hours, museums stay open during June, July, August, and September until 11 pm. Be sure to buy a guidebook and city map at one of the many magazine stalls and study what you want to see. We just touch on the many highlights. Florence is best appreciated by wandering the historic ancient streets: poke into small boutiques; stop in churches that catch your eye—they all abound with masterpieces; sit and enjoy a cappuccino in one of the little sidewalk cafés and people watch; stroll through the

Palazzo Vecchio, Piazza della Signoria, Florence

piazzas and watch the artists at their craft—many of them incredibly clever—as they paint portraits and do sculptures for a small fee. End your day by finding the perfect small restaurant for delicious pasta made by mama in the back kitchen.

There is an excellent train service from Florence to Rome. EUROSTAR trains offer rapid, excellent service from Florence to Rome and vice versa. Trains take one hour and 38 minutes and depart several times an hour. It is probably best to take one of the midday trains—this allows you to enjoy lunch as you soak in the beauty of the Tuscany hills flowing by your window. Remember that you need both seat and dining reservations.

As the train pulls into Rome, you feel overwhelmed by its size and confusion of traffic, but once you get settled in, you realize that Rome is really not as cumbersome as it looks. The ancient part of the city is manageable on foot—a fabulous city for walking with its maze of streets and captivating boutiques just begging to be explored.

"She Wolf" with Romulus and Remus

According to legend, Rome was founded in 753 B.C. by **Romulus**, who, along with his twin brother, **Remus** (whom he later conveniently "did in"), were suckled by a "she wolf." Although a far less colorful story, historians concur that it was the Etruscans who first settled here and gave the city its name. By the time Christ was born, Rome controlled the entire Italian peninsula plus many areas around the Mediterranean.

Rome is bursting with a wealth of fantastic museums, ancient monuments, spectacular cathedrals, gourmet restaurants, beautiful boutiques, colorful piazzas, whimsical fountains, inspiring statues, theater, and opera—the city itself is virtually a museum. You cannot possibly savor it all. Either before you leave home or once you arrive in Italy, purchase a comprehensive guidebook and decide what is top priority for your special interests. There are many stalls along the streets as well as bookstores throughout Rome where guidebooks are available and most places to stay have brochures that tell about sightseeing tours. If there are several in your party, a private guide might be money well spent since he will custom-tailor your sightseeing—with a private guide you squeeze much more sightseeing into a short period of time.

To even begin to do justice to Rome's many wonders, this entire book would need to be devoted to its sightseeing possibilities. However, we cannot resist mentioning a few places you must see.

The first must-see is the **Vatican City** which includes in its complex **St. Peter's Basilica**, the largest church in the world. The original construction was begun in the 4th century by Emperor Constantine over the site of St. Peter's tomb. In 1447 Pope Nicolas V began plans for the new cathedral, which took over 100 years to build. It is no wonder the complex is so utterly breathtaking—all of Italy's greatest Renaissance artists were called upon to add their talents—Bramante, Michelangelo, Raphael, and Sangallo, to name just a few.

The Vatican is a miniature nation tucked within the city of Rome. It is ruled by the Pope, has its own flags, issues its own postage stamps, has its own anthem, mints its own coins, and even has its own police force—the Swiss Guard who still wear the uniform designed by Michelangelo.

Fronting the cathedral is the **Piazza San Pietro**, a breathtaking square designed by Bernini. It is so large that it can hold 400,000 people (making the square a favorite place for the Pope to address large audiences).

Vatican–Swiss Guard

St. Peter's Basilica, Rome

A double semicircle of columns encloses the square, so perfectly designed that the columns fade into each other, giving the illusion that there is a single row. In the center of the square is a towering ancient Egyptian obelisk—adorned, of course, by a Christian cross. As you stand at a distance, the **Piazza San Pietro** forms a visual frame for the cathedral.

To fully appreciate all the Vatican City has to offer, you could easily spend two days, one in St. Peter's Basilica and one day in the **Vatican museums**. The Basilica is like a museum. Not only is the structure magnificent, but the vast collection of works of art inside are almost unbelievable: imagine gazing at such masterpieces as the **Pietà** (the ethereal sculpture of Mary holding Jesus in her arms after the crucifixion, carved by Michelangelo when he was only 25) and the **Baldacchino**, the bronze canopy over the papal altar created by another master, Bernini. Also, be aware when you gaze up at the double-columned dome, that this too was designed by Michelangelo.

The **Sistine Chapel** alone is well worth a trip to Rome. Savor the breathtaking beauty of its ceiling painted by Michelangelo. In addition to St. Peter's Basilica and the Vatican museums, the gardens and the rest of the Vatican can be visited, but only on guided tours. If you are interested, inquire at the Ufficio Informazioni Pellegrini et Turisti in St. Peter's Square. NOTE: The Vatican museums are closed on Sundays, except for the last Sunday of the month when they are open free of charge.

Vatican City, as spectacular as it is, is just one small part of what Rome has to offer. You must see the gigantic **Colosseum**, the entertainment center for the citizens of ancient Rome. Here 50,000 people gathered to be entertained by flamboyant spectacles that included gladiatorial contests, races, games, and contests where Christian martyrs fought against wild beasts.

Another landmark is the **Forum**. It is difficult to make out much of this site because it is mostly in ruins, but at one time this was the heart of Rome. Once filled with elegant palaces, government buildings, and shops, it teemed with people from throughout the known world.

My favorite building in Rome is the **Pantheon**. It is difficult to imagine that this perfectly preserved jewel of a temple dates back to 27 B.C. Step beyond the heavy bronze doors which open into a relatively small, beautifully proportioned room lit only by light streaming in from an opening in the top of the dome.

No trip to Rome would be complete without a stroll down the **Via Veneto**, lined by fancy hotels and luxury boutiques. There are also many outdoor restaurants where a cup of coffee costs almost as much as a meal in a simple trattoria. However, along with your coffee, you are paying the price for the fun of people watching along one of Rome's most elite avenues.

While walking the back streets of Rome, you find many picturesque squares, usually enhanced by a fountain adorned with magnificent sculptures. Especially popular is the **Trevi Fountain** into which tourists go to throw a coin—assuring that they will return to Rome.

Rome has many festivals including the **Festa de Noantri** (Our Festival), which starts on the third Sunday in July. It takes place in **Trastevere**, which is transformed into the venue of a village fair with stalls, open-air taverns, band music, and theatrical shows throughout the entire neighborhood. The event is wrapped up with fireworks over the River Tiber.

The **Spanish Steps** is definitely a landmark of Rome. Topped by the twin spires of the Church of the Trinity of the Mountains, the wide avenue of steps leads down to the Piazza di Spagna (Spanish Square). This large square is highlighted by the Fountain of Baraccia (Fountain of the Boat), a masterpiece by Bernini. The steps are usually crowded both with tourists who come to capture the moment on film and vendors who lay out their wares to sell.

Spanish Steps, Rome

Italian Highlights by Train & Boat—or Car

Leading from the Piazza di Spagna, the Via Condotti is an avenue lined by shops and boutiques selling the finest of merchandise. Branching off the Via Condotti are the narrow lanes of Old Rome, again featuring exquisite small boutiques.

When you are ready to relax, walk to the **Villa Borghese**, a splendid large park in the center of Rome that originated in the 17th century as the private gardens of the Borghese family. Stroll through the park watching the children at play. If you are not saturated with sightseeing, there are many museums to see in the park. One of the loveliest is the **Museo di Villa Giulia**, a museum in a pretty villa that features artifacts from the Etruscan era.

DESTINATION VI   NAPLES

You could spend endless weeks discovering the museum that is Rome, but if you have time to add a few more highlights, venture farther south to visit Naples, using it as a hub from which to take side trips to Pompeii, Capri, Sorrento, and the Amalfi Drive. If you want a special treat, instead of visiting romantic Capri as a day excursion, end your holiday there.

There is frequent train service from Rome to Naples. A suggestion for your departure is given below:

    10:45 am   depart Rome, Termini station
    12:30 pm   arrive Naples, Main station

When you arrive in Naples, take a taxi from the train station to where you are staying. If you are arriving by car, be sure to buy a detailed city map in advance and mark with a highlight pen your route. In addition, ask for exact directions when making your reservations because Naples is a confusing city in which to find your way by car. However, once you get settled in your accommodations, you will discover Naples an excellent city to explore on foot.

Naples, a fascinating city whose history dates back 25 centuries, reflects its rich heritage in its architecture and culture. It seems everyone at one time claimed Naples as "theirs," including the Greeks, the Romans, the French, and the Spanish. Until the unification of Italy, Naples was an important European capital, and is still today a vibrant, exciting city with a stunning setting on the edge of the sea. For many years Naples had the reputation of being a dirty city that was plagued by petty crime. Most tourists came to see its fabulous Museo Archeologico Nazionale and then move quickly on. However, recently a great effort has been made to freshen up the entire city plus deal with the crime issue. Today a great transformation has taken place and Naples is indeed well worth a visit. It is a wonderful city filled with intriguing small squares, an unbelievable assortment of churches, a colorful waterfront, palaces, fortresses and world-class museums. Plus Naples makes an excellent base from which to take side trips.

Below are some suggestions on what to see and do in and around Naples:

SIGHTSEEING IN NAPLES

If you enjoy walking, you can visit almost all of the sights listed on foot. Or, at least walk one way and return to where you are staying by taxi.

Museo Archeologico Nazionale: The Museo Archeologico Nazionale is considered one of the finest museums in the world, and rightly so. It has an incredible collection of jewels of antiquity, including unbelievably well-preserved statues, intricate mosaics, and delicate frescoes. There are endless marvels to see. You are bound to be awestruck as you stroll through the corridors lined with the dazzling Farnese collection of ancient sculptures. You could spend endless hours gazing in wonder at the huge statues and deftly carved marble busts that line the well-lit hallways. If you include a visit to Pompeii (which you *must*) you will find that the originals of the most outstanding mosaics and sculptures have been transferred to the Museo Archeologico Nazionale for safekeeping. The mosaics alone are worth a trip to Naples.

Within the museum there is an "off limits" section that is called the *secret cabinet* which is a series of rooms that display a collection of quite risqué paintings, sculptures and mosaics discovered under the ash at Pompeii (only a limited number of people are allowed in at a time and you need a special ticket that can be bought when you arrive at the museum).

Arrive at the Museo Archeologico Nazionale when it opens in the morning in order to be among the first visitors. As the day progresses, busloads of tourists descend. After looking at your map, if you decide walking round trip is too strenuous, we suggest taking a taxi to the museum then strolling back to where you are staying since the return will be downhill. NOTE: Museum closed on Tuesdays.

Capodimonte Hill: Perched on Capodimonte Hill, which rises above the city, is a splendid park with over 4,000 varieties of centuries-old trees. Within these grounds is the Palazzo Capodimonte, built in 1738 as a hunting lodge for the King Charles III. Housed within the palace is the Museo e Gallerie Nazionale di Capodimonte featuring a breathtaking art collection of the wealthy Bourbon kings, including works by such masters as Bellini, Michelangelo, Titian, and Botticelli.

You can walk to Capodimonte from the Museo Archeologico, but it is a steep, uphill climb so you might well want to take a taxi, or save the excursion for a separate day. NOTE: Museum closed on Mondays.

Spaccanapoli District: For savoring the delights and charm of Naples, our favorite tour is in the Spaccanapoli District. Here, on the site of the old Greek-Roman city, you find tiny plazas, little boutiques, outdoor restaurants, coffee shops, markets, and a seemingly endless number of churches. Make your way to the pretty **Piazza Gesù Nuovo**, where you will find the tourist office facing the square. Pop in here and ask for their map that outlines a walk exploring the Spaccanapoli District. If for any reason, the office is closed, the route is easy to find on your own. Basically what you do is follow streets in a rectangular pattern, returning where you began in Piazza Gesù Nuovo. Leaving the square, head east on Via Benedetto Croce that soon changes its name to Via San Biagio dei Librai. Continue on until you come to Via Duomo where you turn left and go a couple of streets to until you see on your right the **Cathedral** (**Duomo di San Gennaro**). Next, retrace your steps on Via Duomo for a half a block and turn right, heading west on Via Tribunali. When the road dead-ends at Via San Sebastiano, turn left, go one block, turn right and you are back where you began. You will see many churches along your way, including two that are on the Piazza Gesù Nuovo (The **Church of Guesù Nuovo** and the **Cloister of Santa Chiara**). Most of the churches are open only during services, but the fun of this walk is not so much sightseeing as savoring the flavor of this colorful, ancient part of the city. Make this a leisurely stroll, looking into the little shops, sitting in the small square, maybe a cappuccino at a small café or a pizza, which originated in Naples.

The Piazza Plebiscito and Places to Visit Nearby: The Piazza Plebiscito is a large, bustling square located just at the lower part of one of Naples's principal boulevards, Via Toledo. This is a major square, so it is not surprising there are many monuments and museums nearby. Listed below are some of the recommended places to visit.

Palazzo Reale: Dominating the east side of the Piazza Plebiscito is the large, impressive Palazzo Reale, an outstanding palace that was built for the Spanish Viceroys in 1600, in honor of King Philip II's arrival in Naples. Accenting the façade are niches with statues of the kings of Naples. This is a massive complex, and it might take a while to find your way to the ticket office. Once you have your tickets, you climb an imposing double

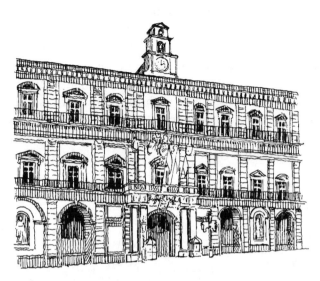

Palazzo Real, Naples

staircase that sweeps to the floor above where the royal quarters have been opened as a museum. You might want to rent a cassette which gives commentary on what you will be seeing. It is fun to wander through the endless rooms in this noble residence, including the queen's private chapel, the throne room, a quaint 18th-century theater, and an assortment of sumptuously adorned apartments. NOTE: Closed on Wednesdays.

Theatre San Carlo: Just around the corner from the Piazza Plebiscito, in a wing of the Palazzo Reale that faces the Piazza Trieste e Trento, you find the dazzling Theatre San Carlos. Commissioned by Charles of Bourbon in 1737, this jewel is reminiscent of La Scala Theatre in Milan. It looks like an ornate wedding cake with 186 private, gilt adorned boxes that rise in six tiers that face an imposing stage. Sometimes there are tours of the theater so you might want to drop by to check the schedule before visiting the museum in the Palazzo Reale.

The Umberto Gallery: Just to the north of Piazza Plebiscito, facing a second small square, the Piazza Trieste e Trento, is the belle-époque-style Umberto Gallery, a shopping arcade dating to 1887 which is made of four wings radiating like a cross from its core (if you have been to Milan, the Umberto Gallery is similar to the Galleria there). Wander in to admire the handsome mosaic floor and the ornate, glass-domed ceiling which soars over 50 meters.

Castel Nuovo: Just to the east of the Palazzo Reale, the Castel Nuovo rises on a bluff above the Porto Beverello, the dock from which the ferries leave for Capri and Sorrento. The Castel Nuovo (New Castle) certainly isn't very new—it dates back to the 13th century. The building is definitely dramatic, a rectangular stone building punctuated by huge round stone towers. In the 15th century a splendid white marble Triumphal Arch was added, a true masterpiece whose beauty contrasts pleasantly with the stern, fortress like castle. A deep moat, originally filled with sea water, embraces the fortress. Within the museum you can visit the Museo Civico that contains 14th-century frescoes. It is also possible to visit the Palatine Chapel and the Baron's Hall.

Castel Nuovo, Naples

Castel dell'Ovo: Leaving the Piazza Plebiscito, head down to the waterfront and turn right, following the Via Nazario Sauro as it traces the waterfront. As it rounds a bend, the name of the boulevard changes to Via Partenope, which is fronted by deluxe hotels that face onto Santa Lucia Harbor. Built on a rocky peninsula, that juts into the sea and forms one side of the harbor, is the Castel dell'Ovo built by the Norman King William I in the

12th century. The name means Castle of the Egg, which supposedly originated from a legend that a magic egg was buried in the castle, and if ever broken, bad luck would descend upon Naples.

SIDE EXCURSIONS FROM NAPLES

Naples makes a convenient hub from which to make side trips to some of Italy's jewels, including Sorrento, the Amalfi Drive, Capri and the archaeological sites of Herculaneum and Pompeii, all accessible by either organized tour or "do it yourself" by public transportation.

Pompeii & Herculaneum: Near Naples are two exciting archaeological wonders: Herculaneum and Pompeii. Both are fascinating, but if you don't have time to visit both, don't miss Pompeii. You can choose between joining a guided tour or taking a train to the site. A company called **Circumvesuviana** has narrow-gauge trains leaving Naples' Central Station about every half hour, arriving at the Pompeii Villa dei Misteri station (located across from the entrance to the site) about 40 minutes later. At the entrance to Pompeii, we suggest either buying a map explaining what to see or hiring a certified guide.

An aura of mystery lingers in the air as you wander the streets of Pompeii. All visitors are touched by this ancient city of an estimated 25,000 inhabitants, which in one day became frozen for all time. Probably there is nowhere else in the world where you can so vividly step back in time. Much of what you see today has been reproduced, but the reality is pure. Plaster was poured into molds formed by the lava that demolished the buildings and buried so many families that fateful day. Thus it became possible for latter-day archaeologists to reconstruct houses and make reproductions of people and pets. Walk through the town along the sunken streets crossed by high stepping stones, strategically placed so that pedestrians did not get their feet wet on rainy days. Be sure not to miss some of the reconstructed villas that allow you a glimpse into the daily life of long ago. The **Casa del Fauno**, a fine example of how the wealthy lived, has two inner courtyards and several dining rooms. The **Casa del Poeta Tragico**, a more modest home, has a sign in mosaic saying "Cave Canem" (beware of the dog). At the **Villa di Giulia Felice** you see the example of an entrepreneur—in addition to using it as a private villa, the owner rented out rooms, had shops on the ground floor, and operated an adjacent bathhouse. If traveling with children, you might want to go alone into the **Lupanare** (Pompeii's brothel) where there are erotic paintings on the walls. At the **Terme Stabiane** you see a sophisticated underground water-heating system.

There are many more places to visit than those listed above. As you explore Pompeii, there is no need to watch the time. There is a narrow-gauge train departing from the Pompeii Villa dei Misteri station about every 20 minutes for the half-hour scenic journey to Sorrento.

Sorrento: Sorrento is a charming city that sits on the top of a bluff overlooking the sea. Below is a colorful harbor with ferries constantly gliding in and out, en route to such picturesque destinations as Capri, Positano and Amalfi. The historic center is charming, richly reflecting its ancient Greek and Roman legacy. Pretty boutiques and outdoor cafes beckon as you stroll the narrow streets and explore intimate plazas. The same Circumvesuviana trains that depart Naples's Central Station for Pompeii, continue on to Sorrento. The total time is a little over an hour. Another option for visiting Sorrento, is to take one of the hydrofoils that ply between the two towns.

Amalfi Coast: The strip of coast that runs south from Sorrento to Salerno is world famous for its beauty. A two lane road hugs the steep, winding coastline, capturing breathtaking views as the bluffs fold around the brilliant blue Mediterranean. Enchanting villages dot the coast, further enhancing its idyllic beauty. One of the most accessible of these villages is **Positano**, a postcard-perfect fishing hamlet snuggled in a cove that is wrapped by an exceedingly steep hill. Colorfully painted houses, trendy boutiques, cute restaurants, and cascades of brilliant bougainvillea add to the appeal of this jewel. From Naples you can take a ferry to Sorrento and then on to Positano, or take the train to Sorrento and a bus from there (the buses leave from the train station).

Capri: Several shipping companies have ferries that leave frequently from Naples to the romantic island of Capri, leaving from Molo Beverello, the dock below Castel Nuovo. By choosing an early morning departure, it is easy to visit Capri and return in time for dinner in Naples. However, if time permits, we would suggest spending a few days in this beautiful small island. For sightseeing in Capri, see the following destination.

DESTINATION VII   CAPRI

There is frequent boat service between Naples and Capri. Boats leave from either the Mergellina Pier (Boat Companies: Alilauro and S.N.A.V.) or the Molo Beverello Pier (Boat Companies: Caremar and N.L.G.). You can take a ferry (traghetto), which takes one hour and fifteen minutes or a hydorfoil (aliscafo), which takes forty-five minutes.

Your boat arrives at the **Marina Grande**, a small harbor filled with colorful boats and edged by brightly painted shops. When the boat docks, you find porters on the pier along with carrier services that go to all of the places to stay. They relieve you of your luggage and take it directly to the accommodations of your choice, freeing you to take either a minibus or the funicular to the main town of Capri, which is located on a flat saddle of land high above the sea. There are many charming places to stay on Capri.

Capri has many wonders. The most famous is its submerged cave, the **Blue Grotto**, which can be accessed by boat when the seas are calm. Large boats begin leaving the harbor every day at 9 am for the short ride to the entrance to the grotto, where you are transferred into tiny rowboats. The earlier you go the better since the seas are calmer in the morning. The excursion is an adventure in itself. As you approach the tiny cave opening, it seems impossible that there is adequate room for a boat to enter, but suddenly the sea surges forward and in you squeeze. Like magic, you see it—the mysterious, stunning blue light reflecting from some hidden source that illuminates the grotto. The cost isn't great, but be aware of the system: You pay for a ticket for the motorboat that takes you to the cave, and then you pay again, on site, to the oarsman who skillfully maneuvers his little rowboat through the hole and into the grotto. It is appropriate to tip

Marina Grande, Capri

your boatman—he will do his best to make your short ride memorable and quite probably serenade you within the cave.

Capri is a superb island for walking. As you stroll the trails, all your senses are treated by the fragrant flowers, the gorgeous vistas of the brilliant blue waters, and the sound of birds luring you ever onward. There are many spectacular walks. Follow the trail winding down the cliffs to the small harbor **Marina Piccola**, located on the opposite side of the island from the ferry dock. At the Marina Piccola there are lovely views of the shimmering aqua waters as you make your way to the small beach where you can enjoy a swim before your return. Instead of walking back up the hill, take the little bus that delivers you quickly back to the main square.

Another absolutely spectacular walk—although a long one of at least 45 minutes each way—is to Emperor Tiberius's Palace, **Villa Jovis**, perched high among the trees on the cliffs on the western tip of the island. This is the grandest of the palaces left by Tiberius. Although it is mostly in ruins, you can easily appreciate its former magnificence as you climb about exploring the ruins of the terraced rooms. From the palace there are stunning panoramic vistas: you have an overview of the whole island and can watch the ferries shuttling back and forth to the mainland. A much shorter walk, but one equally beautiful, is to the **Cannone Belvedere**. This path guides you near delightful private villas hidden behind high walls (you get glimpses through the gates) and on to a promontory overlooking the sea.

Another excursion is to **Anacapri**, the only other town on the island, to visit the **Villa San Michel**, a lovely villa overlooking the sea that was the home of the Swedish scientist Axel Munthe. His residence is now open as a museum. Anacapri is a bit too far to walk easily but buses leave regularly from the main square in town.

During the day, Capri is swarming with tourists on package tours that descend like a swarm of locusts from the constant stream of hydrofoils and ferries. You might surmise that in the evening the activity subsides, but it isn't so. The tour groups leave at dusk but then a new group of people emerges from the secreted villas and fancy hotels. Guests in chic clothes and fancy jewelry stroll the streets—both to see and be seen.

When the real world calls and you must leave Capri, there is frequent ferry or hydrofoil service back to Naples. From Naples, you can take a train to Rome or a plane to your next destination.

Capri

Romantic Tuscany

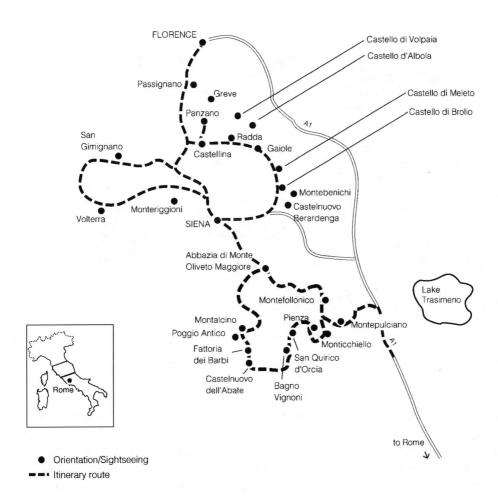

FLORENCE

Castello di Volpaia

Castello d'Albola

Passignano

Greve

Castello di Meleto

Panzano

Castello di Brolio

A1

San
Gimignano

Radda

Gaiole

Castellina

Montebenichi

Monteriggioni

Castelnuovo
Berardenga

Volterra

SIENA

Abbazia di Monte
Oliveto Maggiore

Montefollonico

Lake
Trasimeno

Montalcino

Pienza

Poggio Antico

Montepulciano

Fattoria
dei Barbi

Monticchiello

A1

San Quirico
d'Orcia

Castelnuovo
dell'Abate

Bagno
Vignoni

Rome

to Rome

● Orientation/Sightseeing

▬ ▬ ▪ Itinerary route

Romantic Tuscany

Monteriggioni

Nothing can surpass the exquisite beauty of the countryside of Tuscany—it is breathtaking. If you meander into the hill towns any time of the year, all your senses are rewarded with the splendors that this enchanting area of Italy has to offer. Almost every hillock is crowned with a picture-perfect walled town; fields are brilliant with vibrant red poppies; vineyards in all their glory and promise lace the fields; olive trees dress the hillsides in a frock of dusky gray-green; pine forests unexpectedly appear to highlight the landscape. As if these attributes were not enough, tucked into the colorful villages is a treasure-trove of some of the finest small hotels and bed and breakfasts in Italy. If this is still not sufficient to tempt you away from the normal tourist route, remember that the food and wines are unsurpassed.

If you are planning to include Florence on your trip to Italy, slip away into the countryside and treat yourself to Tuscany. You will be well rewarded with a wealth of memories that will linger long after you return home. The following itinerary suggests two stops—one in Chianti Classico wine region and the other in Southern Tuscany.

A convenient place to begin your journey is in **Florence**, Tuscany's jewel. Magnificent art is not confined to the city limits of Florence and you will see impressive cathedrals and museums hosting spellbinding works of art throughout Tuscany. See the *Italian Highlights by Train & Boat—or Car* itinerary for sightseeing suggestions for Florence.

Pacing: To explore the hill towns of Tuscany you need at least a week (in addition to the time you allocate to Florence). We recommend a minimum of four nights in the heart of Tuscany's Classico Wine Region, which stretches from Florence south to Siena. This will give the minimum time needed to enjoy the tranquil beauty of the hill towns and to sample the delicious Chianti wines. The second suggested stop is southern Tuscany where we suggest three nights to explore the stunning small towns that dot the hillsides, visit breathtaking monasteries, and taste more of Italy's superb wines: Vino Nobile, grown near Montepulciano, and Brunello, grown near Montacino.

Tuscany is laced with narrow roads that twist through the picturesque countryside. Take a detailed map so that if you get lost, you can find your way home, but part of the joy of Tuscany is to be unstructured. Enjoy the freedom to discover your own perfect village, your own charming restaurant, and your own favorite wine. Although in your wanderings you are sure to find some very special places that we have missed, we share below some of the towns we find irresistible and vineyards that are especially fun to visit.

CHIANTI CLASSICO WINE REGION

This idyllic area lives up to every dream of Tuscany—hills crowned by picture-perfect villages, medieval walled towns, straight rows of towering cypresses, romantic villas, ancient stone farmhouses, vast fields of brilliant poppies, forests of pine trees, vineyards stretching to the horizon. Instead of moving about, packing and unpacking, choose a place to stay anywhere within the area and use it us your hub for exploring this utterly beguiling region of Italy. Below we give suggestions for towns to visit and some of our favorite wineries.

SUGGESTED SIGHTSEEING: TOWNS TO VISIT

Monteriggioni: If you are looking for a town that is truly storybook-perfect, none can surpass the tiny, magical hamlet of Monteriggioni. It is such a gem that it is hard to believe it is real and not a creation by Disney! You can spot it from afar, nestled on the top of a small hill, with 14 towers punctuating the perfectly preserved enclosing walls.

Monteriggioni

No cars are allowed here, so you have to park in the designated area below the walls before walking up to the town, which is composed almost entirely of a main square with small streets radiating from it. On the square you find a Romanesque church, restaurants, boutiques, and shops selling olive oil, cheeses, and wine. It takes only a few minutes to stroll from one end of the town to the other but I assure you, you will be enchanted. As a bonus, Monteriggioni produces its own fine wine, Castello di Monteriggioni.

Passignano in Chianti: Passignano in Chianti is rarely on a tourist route, but we can't help mentioning this tiny hamlet that exudes such a tranquil beauty. For sightseeing, there really isn't much to see except the **Badia a Passignano Abbey**, founded by Benedictine monks in the 11th century. The abbey is set in a pocket of lush landscape and dominates the village, which is no more than a cluster of houses and a restaurant. However, as you drive into the valley, approaching from the west, the abbey with its towering ring of cypresses has such an idyllic setting that it is one of our favorites—a photographer's delight. The abbey can be visited on Sundays at 3 pm; tours leave from the church (please check to verify the abbey is open the Sunday you want to visit). Fine wines, produced by the abbey's vineyards, can be purchased at the Osteria, tel: (055) 80 71 278.

Radda: Located in the very heart of the Chianti wine region, Radda makes a good base of operations. However, not only is the town very conveniently located for sightseeing, it is also extremely quaint and some of its walls are still intact. It was in Radda in 1924 that 33 producers gathered to create a consortium to protect a very special blend of wine that was known as **Chianti Classico**. Only vintners who maintain the standards of the consortium are allowed to proudly display its symbol of the black rooster.

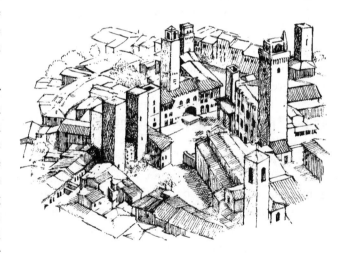

San Gimignano

San Gimignano: During your exploration of Tuscany, one town you must not miss is San Gimignano. What is so dramatic about San Gimignano is that at one time the walls of the town were punctuated by 72 towers. During the Middle Ages it was a status symbol for noble families to build their own personal towers for their protection—the higher the tower, the greater the image of wealth and importance. It is amazing that 14 of the original towers are still standing. They make a striking silhouette, soaring like skyscrapers, and on a clear day you can see them on the horizon from far away. San Gimignano is truly a jewel—plan to spend at least a day here. There are many shops and marvelous restaurants tucked along the maze of streets. On Fridays there are walking tours with English-speaking guides that leave from the Porta San Giovanni at 11 am (best check with the tourist office to be sure the time and day haven't changed). One of our favorite restaurants in San Gimignano is the delightful **Ristorante Dorando,** which has great food served in cozy rooms with coved ceilings that create the ambiance of an old wine cellar. Located on Vicolo del Oro 2, a small side street just off Piazza Duomo, tel: (0577) 94 18 62. Another favorite, **Ristorante Il Pino**, offers mouthwatering homemade pastas—some of the best we have ever eaten. Located on Via Collolese, 8–10, just down the street from L'Antico Pozzo, tel: (0577) 94 04 15.

Siena: This is an entrancing walled hill town that deserves many hours to savor its rich delights—you should allow yourself at least one full day here. The ramparts are perfectly preserved with a series of massive gates guarding a meticulously maintained medieval stronghold. Drive as close as you can to the main square, park your car, and set out to explore on foot. You cannot drive into the center of the city, but there are designated parking areas (marked by "P") near each of the gates. One of the most convenient is the parking at the Porta Romana. Once you leave your car, strike off for the giant **Piazza del Campo**. This central piazza is immense and, instead of being square, is fan-shaped and slopes downward like a bowl. Eleven streets surrounding the square converge into it like spokes of a massive wheel. Like the Spanish Steps in Rome, the Piazza del Campo is a favorite for tourists who linger here just enjoying the medieval ambiance. It is in this gigantic piazza that the colorful **Palio delle Contrade** (dating back to the 11th century) takes place twice a year, on July 2 and August 16. The horse race is only a part of a colorful spectacle of medieval costumes, impressive banners, and parades, and the festivities extend beyond the actual date of the races. Monopolizing one side of the Piazza del Campo is the 13th-century Gothic **Palazzo Pubblico** (Town Hall) whose graceful arches are embellished with Siena's coat of arms. The Palazzo Pubblico is open as a museum where you can stroll through the governor's living quarters.

Although Siena looks like a large city, it is easily negotiable on foot and most of the museums are in one small area. After visiting the Piazza del Campo, most of the other major places of interest are just a few minutes' walk away, clustered about the Piazza del Duomo. There are excellent tourist signs that will guide you along the maze of narrow streets to all the museums.

You absolutely must not miss Siena's 12th-century **Duomo**, facing the Piazza del Duomo. This is one of Italy's most astounding cathedrals. Not only is its exterior breathtaking, but once you enter, you will be overwhelmed by its dramatic black-and-white, zebra-striped marble columns. Don't miss the intricately carved, 13th-century panels depicting the life of Christ on the octagonal pulpit. Also, be sure to see the **Piccolomini Library**. You need to buy a ticket to enter, but it is well worth it. This relatively small room is totally frescoed with gorgeous murals in still-vibrant colors portraying the life of Pope Pius II. The cathedral also has 59 fabulous inlaid-marble mosaic panels on the floor depicting religious scenes. However, some of the most precious of these are covered to protect them and are on display only from the end of August to the first of October.

After visiting the Duomo, the following museums are just steps away. One of our favorites is the **Ospedale di Santa Maria della Scala**, located across from the entrance to the Duomo. At first glance, it is difficult to truly appreciate its wealth of things to see. The museum goes on and on—it is enormous. Just when you think you have finished, a discreet sign will lead you ever downwards to a lower level and a stunning array of artifacts. The building, dating back to the 800s, was originally constructed as a hospital. Be sure not to miss the former infirmary with its lushly colored frescoes by the master Domenico di Bartolo depicting scenes of patients being treated by their doctors. Another nearby museum is the **Baptistry**, a small museum that, as its name implies, houses the baptismal font for the Duomo. In addition to its beautifully frescoed walls and vaulted ceiling, of prime interest is the 15th-century baptismal font, which is adorned by religious scenes cast in bronze by some of Italy's most famous Renaissance masters, including one panel by Donatello. The **Museo dell'Opera Metropolitana** is worth a visit if for no other reason than to see the sublime *Maestá* by Duccio, painted in 1311. The central scene of the Virgin Mary is truly awesome. For art lovers, the **Museo Civico** must not be missed. Here you will see stunning masterpieces by Ambrogio Lorenzetti, Spinello

Aretino, and Simone Martini. It is overwhelming to ponder how Italy could have produced so many geniuses.

NOTE: There is a comprehensive ticket valid for three days that allows you entrance into many of Siena's prime sightseeing attractions—this is a bargain compared to buying individual tickets. When you buy your ticket for the first museum ask about it and which museums it includes.

Volterra: Just a short drive from San Gimignano, Volterra is a delightful, non-touristy town enclosed by still-intact, 12th-century walls. Like so many of the cities founded by the Etruscans, Volterra is built upon the flat top of a steep hill. As you drive toward the city, the landscape becomes increasingly barren, since the soil is not conducive to growing grapes or olive trees. Instead, alabaster is king here and objects made of alabaster are sold in all of the shops. Not to be missed is the alabaster museum called **Museo Etrusco Guaracci**, which has a fabulous collection of works of art, including sculptures and beautiful vases, displayed with great taste in a series of interlinking rooms that show the art to perfection. There is an adjacent shop selling many alabaster items. The whole town is a jewel whose charm is best experienced by strolling through the narrow cobbled streets. Its main square, **Piazza dei Priori**, the heart of the town, is surrounded by fine examples of beautifully preserved medieval buildings and with its towers, splendid town hall (the oldest in Tuscany), and Romanesque church, it is considered by some to be one of the finest squares in Tuscany. Stroll to visit one of the main gates, the **Porta all'Arco**, the origins of which date back to the 7th century B.C. During World War II, the loyal citizens of Volterra buried the stones of the gate to keep the Nazis from blowing it up.

SUGGESTED SIGHTSEEING WINERIES:

The production of wine plays an enormous role throughout Tuscany, and between Florence and Siena (where **Chianti Classico** is produced) you are constantly reminded of this as you pass through vast rolling hills splendidly adorned with neatly tended vineyards. The Chianti Classico area covers over 172,000 acres, with Siena and Florence being the two "capitals" of the region. Included in the area are the towns of Castellina, Gaiole, Greve, Radda, and some of Barberino Val d'Elsa, Castelnuovo Berardenga, Poggibonsi, San Casciano Val di Pesa, and Tavarnelle Val di Pesa. Even if you are not a wine connoisseur, it would be a pity not to make at least one winery stop both for the fun of observing the production process and for an understanding of the industry that is so central to the soul and character of Tuscany. Many of the wineries also have gift shops and sell marvelous olive oils and cheeses in addition to wine.

As you meander through the countryside you see signs with Chianti Classico's black rooster symbol and you can buy directly from the producer where you see *Vendita Diretta*. In some cases there are also tours of the winery (these are sometimes free, but sometimes there is a charge). A *Cantina* sign means that the winery has a shop where wine is sold and can usually be sampled. One of the delights of touring the back roads of Tuscany is just to stop on whim. When you spot a *Vendita Diretta*, drive in, introduce yourself, and sample some wines. You might well discover one that will become one of your favorites.

Some of our favorite wineries to visit are listed below:

Castello di Brolio: If you visit only one winery, Castello di Brolio should be it since this is not only one of the oldest wineries the world, but also where Chianti wine was "born." Although the production of wine in Tuscany dates back to Etruscan times, the enormously wealthy Ricasoli family, owners of the Castello di Brolio since 1167, are responsible for the special blending of grapes we now consider "Chianti Classico." At one time the extremely powerful Ricasoli family owned most of the land and castles lying between Florence and Siena. The remote family castle, Castello di Brolio, had largely been abandoned when Bettino Ricasoli decided to move into it (so the story goes) after becoming jealous at a winter ball in Florence when his young bride danced a bit too closely to one of her young admirers. Thinking it best to take his wife away from temptation, he rebuilt the huge, remote, crenellated castle, replanted the vineyards, and experimented with the blending of grapes, coming up with the original formula that forms the basis of what is known today as Chianti Classico. The fortified castle tops a high, forested hill. You leave your car in the designated parking area and climb for about 20 minutes up a path or on the road through a parklike forest to the castle gates. Open daily from 9 am to noon and 3 pm to sunset. The castle is located about 10 kilometers south of Gaiole. Tel: (0577) 73 02 20, *www.ricasoli.it.*

Castello d'Albola, winetasting

Castello d'Albola: The Castello d'Albola, a spectacular property just a short drive north of Radda on a gentle hill laced with grapes, is owned by the Zonin family, who have restored the entire medieval complex beautifully. This is an intimate, extremely pretty place to taste wines and take a tour. What we particularly like about the Castello d'Albola is that it is in such a beautiful setting and offers delightfully informal, friendly, free tours. Drive up the hill to the castle, leave your car in the parking area, and walk into an inner castle courtyard, off which you find the winetasting room and cantina. Before or after winetasting, your hostess leads you on a short, professional tour showing you how fine wines are produced. The owner has other enormous estates as well as the Castello d'Albola and is one of the largest producers of wine in the world. Tours start at noon, 2 pm, and 5 pm daily. The cantina is open for complimentary wine tasting daily, April to

October from 10 am to 6:30 pm (9 am to 5 pm November to March). Tel: (0577) 73 80 19, *www.albola.it.*

Castello di Volpaia: The 12th-century Castello di Volpaia, located on a narrow lane about 7 kilometers north of Radda, is one of our favorite places for winetasting. Plan to spend a day on this outing, with ample time to meander through the countryside en route, tour the winery, taste the superb wines, and enjoy a wonderful lunch at the winery's excellent restaurant, La Bottega. Although the winery is called *Castello* it really isn't located inside a castle at all, but rather in various medieval stone houses in a picture-perfect village wrapped by vineyards where you find a small church, a cluster of houses, La Bottega Ristorante, and the winetasting room. You need to preplan this wine tour and also make reservations for lunch since both are very popular and usually booked far in advance. There is a fee for the tour based on the number of people in the group. Tel: (0577) 73 80 66, *www.volpaia.com.*

Castello di Meleto: Another favorite destination for wine-tasting is the beautiful Castello di Meleto, which has an idyllic setting in the gentle hills near the town of Gaiole. Just across from the dramatic castle you find a pretty winetasting room and gift shop where fine wines and olive oils produced on the estate can be purchased. On request, tastings of olive oil and aromatic vinegars can be arranged. What makes this a very special experience is that there is an added bonus: not only can you sample wines, but you can

Castello di Meleto

also visit the beautiful interior of the castle. In addition to splendidly frescoed rooms, the castle has one exceptionally intriguing feature—a whimsical private theater complete with its original stage settings. Call ahead, tel: (0577) 73 80 66, to find out the time and cost of the guided tours of the cellars and castle. The Castello di Meleto also offers bed & breakfast accommodation.

SOUTHERN TUSCANY

The area of Tuscany that lies south/southeast of Siena is famous for its superb wines. A great bonus is that these vineyards are in one of Italy's most picturesque regions, filled with quaint villages and amazing abbeys, thus making your adventures even more enchanting. Whereas Chianti Classico wine is renowned in the area between Florence and Siena, the vineyards farther south also produce some of the mostly highly regarded wines in the world, the most famous of these being **Vino Nobile**, grown near Montepulciano, and **Brunello**, grown near Montacino. There are many wineries open to the public where wine can be tasted and purchased. Many winetastings are free, although some wineries charge a minimal fee. As you drive through the countryside look for signs reading *Cantina* (wine shop) or *Vendita Diretta* (direct sales).

LOOP VISITING WINERIES, ABBEYS, AND QUAINT VILLAGES

We suggest a loop that covers some of our favorite wineries, medieval towns, and picturesque abbeys. It would be impossible to squeeze everything in this itinerary into one day unless you rush madly from place to place. Therefore, if your time is limited, don't stop at each place suggested but just choose a few of the sightseeing suggestions below that most appeal to you. But better yet, take several days and follow the itinerary in its entirety, covering a small section each day at a leisurely pace.

This loop begins in **Montepulciano**, a rare jewel of a walled hill town that not only oozes charm in its narrow, cobbled streets but is also center stage for the delicious Vino Nobile di Montepulciano. This wealthy town was home to many aristocrats who built magnificent palaces here. The heart of the city is the **Piazza Grande** where you find the dramatic 13th-century **Palazzo Comunale** accented by a stone tower. Also facing the square is the picturesque **Palazzo Contucci**, fronted by a charming Renaissance well decorated with the Medici coat of arms and highlighted by two stone lions. Leading off the Pizza Grande are small streets that crisscross the town, connected by staircases.

A masterpiece you absolutely must not miss when visiting Montepulciano is the **Temple of San Biagio**, a stunning church located on the west edge of town. You can walk from town, but it is a long way down the hill and then back up again, so you might want to drive, especially in hot weather. Made of creamy travertine, the church's façade is extremely picturesque and its elegant interior is equally lovely—nothing cluttered or dark but rather light and airy, with fine marble pastel-colored walls.

Within Montepulciano there are many boutiques, restaurants, and cantinas selling wine. Our favorite wine shop here is an extremely special one, the very old **Cantina del Redi**, located just down the street from the Piazza Grande with its entrance next to the Palazzo Ricco. Once you enter, an ancient staircase leads ever deeper into the hillside, passing rooms filled with huge wooden casks of wine. When you finally reach the lowest level, you wind your way through more casks until you arrive at the cantina where you can sample and purchase wine. When finished, you discover that you have descended quite a way down the hillside and the main entrance to the winery faces onto a lower terrace.

Another of our favorite wineries, **Dei**, is just a few kilometers outside Montepulciano's city walls. What is especially fun about this winery is that it is family-owned and managed by the lovely daughter, Maria Caterina Dei, who still lives in the beautiful family villa on the property. Maria Caterina is passionate about wine and with great professionalism can explain about the production of the Dei wines, which have won many awards. Before taking over the family's vineyards, the multi-talented Maria Caterina trained in music and the theater, and sometimes she entertains the guests during wine tours. There is a fee for tours, depending upon what is requested. Lunches and winetasting can be prearranged. Call in advance for tours: Dei, Villa Martiena, Montepulciano, tel: (0578) 71 68 78, *www.cantinedei.com*.

Leaving Montepulciano, take the S146 west toward Pienza. After driving about 3 kilometers, take a small road on the left marked to **Monticchiello**. You soon arrive at a sweet, tiny, charming walled town whose allure is its unpretentious, non-touristy ambiance. Park your car in the designated area outside the main gate. As you enter through the gate, you will see on your left La Porta, a charming restaurant with an outside terrace sitting on the town walls—a great place to stop for lunch. As you stroll through Monticchiello (it won't take you long), take a look inside the 13th-century church where you will see a beautiful altarpiece by Pietro Lorenzetti.

Il Chostro di Pienza, Pienza

Romantic Tuscany

From Monticchiello, continue on the back road to **Pienza**. This is one of our favorite walled hill towns in Tuscany, a real gem that mustn't be missed. The town is perched on the top of a hill and is pedestrian-only so you need to park your car outside the walls. It is no wonder that the town is so perfect even though so tiny: it was here in the 15th century that Pope Pius II hired a famous architect, Bernardo Rossellino, to totally redesign the town where he was born, making it into a masterpiece. You will find many restaurants if you are inclined to dine.

Leaving Pienza, take S146 west to **San Quirico d'Orcia**, a very attractive small medieval town with a lovely Romanesque church. If you stop to see the town, you must not miss its lovely garden, called **Horti Leonini**. An entrance about a block from the main square leads into a tranquil Renaissance garden, originally designed as a beautiful resting place for the pilgrims who stopped here on the road to Rome. This cool oasis with clipped box hedges and shade trees makes an interesting stop. If you are hungry, the **Osteria del Leone** makes a good choice for lunch.

From San Quirico d'Orcia, head south on S2 for about 6 kilometers and watch for a small road to the right leading to **Bagno Vignoni**. This is a most unusual, very small town, known for the curative value of its hot sulphur springs. In the center of town, you find what would have been the town square made into a huge sulphur bath built by the Medicis. The pool is surrounded by picturesque medieval buildings that complete the interesting scene.

Leaving Bagno Vignoni, don't continue on the S2, but take S323 directly south for 12 kilometers and then turn right following signs to Montalcino. In a few minutes you come to **Castelnuovo dell'Abate** where, just a few minutes outside town, you will find the superb Romanesque **Abbey Sant'Antimo**, whose origins date back to the 9th century when it was founded as a Benedictine monastery. The abbey—a simple, pastel-pinkish stone church serenely set amongst fields of olive trees—makes a beautiful picture. Try to arrive at 11 am or 2:45 pm when the Benedictine monks, clad in long, pure-white robes, gather at the altar to chant their prayers in Latin. This is a haunting, beautiful experience.

The singing lasts only a short time, and the times might vary from the ones we mention above, so to confirm the schedule call, tel: (0577) 83 56 59.

Leaving Castelnuovo dell'Abate, drive north on the road for Montalcino. In a few minutes you will see a sign to the **Fattoria dei Barbi**. Turn right and follow a small road up the hill to the Barbi winery, an excellent winery to visit. It is extremely pretty with many gardens and a charming cantina where you can sample the vineyard's fine wines and purchase wine and other gift items. Its restaurant serves wonderful meals made with only the freshest products, accompanied, of course, by their own wines. Free tours of the winery are given hourly from 10 am to noon and 3 pm to 5 pm, tel: (0577) 84 82 77, *www.fattoriadeibarbi.it.*

After your visit to the Fattoria dei Barbi, continue north for 5 kilometers to **Montalcino**, which is world famous, along with Montepulciano, for its superb wine, Brunello di Montalcino. There are many places in town where wine can be tasted and purchased. In addition to wine, the town is famous for its fine honey, which can be purchased in many of the shops. Montalcino is fun for wandering—it is not large and you can in no time at all cover the area within the walls by foot. On the east edge of town is an imposing 14th century fortress.

From Montalcino, head south on the road to Grosetto for a little over 3 kilometers to another of our favorite wineries, **Poggio Antico**. Excellent tours are offered and, of course, you can also sample the superb wines. These tours are very popular so you should reserve in advance at tel: (0577) 84 80 44, *www.poggioantico.com*. For dining, the winery's **Ristorante Poggio Antico** serves outstanding Tuscany cuisine. Reservations for the restaurant are also highly recommended—tel: (0577) 84 92 00, email: rist.poggio.antico@libero.it.

After visiting Poggio Antico, retrace your way north to Montalcino and continue on for 9 kilometers to where the road intersects with the S2. Turn left here, going north toward Siena. In 10 kilometers, turn right on S451 and continue for another 10 kilometers to the **Abbazia di Monte Oliveto Maggiore**. Founded in the early 14th century by wealthy merchants from Siena as a Benedictine retreat, this fascinating abbey is well worth a detour. Be prepared to walk since you must park your car and follow a long path through the forest to the abbey's entrance, which is through a gatehouse crowned by a beautiful della Robbia terracotta. Once through the gate, you continue through the woodlands to the huge brick complex. After visiting the church, it seems you could wander forever through the various hallways. Before you get too distracted, however, ask directions to the cloister because you don't want to miss this marvel. Here you find 36 frescoes depicting scenes of the life of St. Benedict, some painted by Luca Signorelli, others by Antonio Bazzi.

In the region around the abbey you will come across an entirely different type of landscape, called the *crete*. Here, tucked among the green rolling hills, you unexpectedly come across bleak, canyon-like craters, caused by erosion. These are especially out of character as the surrounding scenery is so soft and gentle.

From Abbazia di Monte Oliveto Maggiore, weave your way through the small back roads to Montepulciano. Follow signs to San Giovanni d'Asso, then Montisi, then Madongino, then **Montefollonico**. Take time to stop in Montefollonico because this is another "sleeper"—a quaint, small, medieval walled town that is fun to explore. For the gourmet, there is a superb restaurant on the edge of town called **La Chiusa.**

From Montefollonico, go south on S327. When you come to the S146, turn left to complete your loop back to Montepulciano.

Duomo, Orvieto

The Haunting Beauty of Umbria

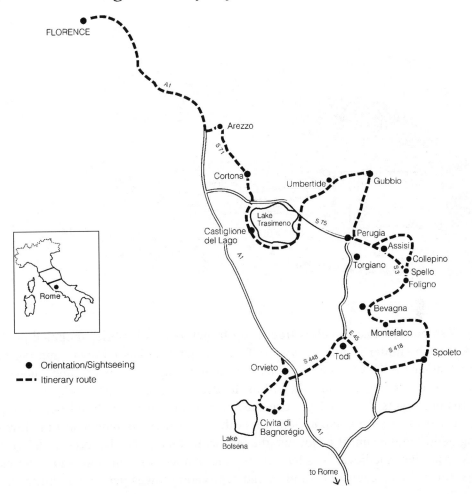

- ● Orientation/Sightseeing
- ▪ ▪ ▪ Itinerary route

The Haunting Beauty of Umbria

Assisi

Tuscany is so popular that travelers frequently forget to visit Umbria, snuggled just "next door." Although similar in many ways to Tuscany, Umbria has its own haunting beauty and the advantage of fewer tourists. This is a region seeped in history and imbued with romantic charm. Here you find a beguiling landscape—a blend of rolling hills, craggy forests, rushing rivers, lush valleys, chestnut groves, and hillsides laced with vineyards. Adding further to Umbria's magic is that its hills and valleys radiate a soft mellow light, gleaming gently in the sun. It is not just the landscape that makes Umbria so delightful. It also has stunning medieval castles, incredible cathedrals, ancient monasteries, art treasures, fine wines, beautiful ceramics, and captivating towns perched on hilltops.

Pacing: You can conveniently follow this itinerary either before or after a tour of Tuscany. If you already have visited Tuscany on a previous trip to Italy, this itinerary stands alone. After the finishing the itinerary, you can loop back to Florence by heading north on the A1, or head south on the A1 to Rome. Whichever way you choose, in order to capture its beauty and many sightseeing possibilities, you need at least five nights in the Umbria region: We suggest three nights in the eastern part of Umbria. Choose a place to stay and in use it as a hub from which to journey out each day to explore a different sightseeing target. Next, loop south and choose a place to stay for two nights in the western part of Umbria, somewhere near Orvieto.

EASTERN UMBRIA

NOTE: This itinerary of Eastern Umbria is much too long for one day. Use it only as a framework for how the most interesting towns can be looped together. Once you choose which town you are going to use as the hub for your explorations, tailor the itinerary to visit the places mentioned in the itinerary that most appeal to you.

As you depart from Florence you are bound to run into a lot of traffic, but there are many signs to the expressway. Follow signs that lead to the A1 and take it south toward Rome.

Arezzo: About 65 kilometers after leaving Florence you come to a turnoff to **Arezzo,** located about 10 kilometers east of the highway. Arezzo is still in Tuscany, but since it is so close to Umbria and "on the way," now is the time for a visit. Arezzo has a rich history dating back to the Etruscan era, but is not as quaint as some of its smaller neighbors. It is well known as one of the largest gold centers in Europe and has many shops selling gold jewelry. Arezzo is also famous for its **Antique Fair** that is held in the Piazza Grande on the first Saturday and Sunday of every month. Here you find many unusual items such as antique coins, jewelry, furniture, stained glass remnants, paintings, light fixtures, handmade linens, pottery, trunks, etc. The fair is considered one of the most important ones in Italy and so popular that people come from far and near to browse the rich collection of antiques. Arezzo was the birthplace of Guido Monaco who around the year 1000 A.D. devised musical notes and scales. One of Arrezo's famous inhabitants was the powerful 14th-century poet Pietro Aretino who took great glee in writing scandalous poetry about the rich and famous. Aretino's greatest skill was gentle blackmail, extorting great sums from princes and popes who paid him not to expose their indiscretions in poetry.

Cortona: From Arezzo follow S71 south to Cortona, a gem of a walled town terraced up a steep hillside covered with olive trees and vineyards. Like Arezzo, Cortona is still in Tuscany, but fits more conveniently into the itinerary for Umbria since it is on the route. Stop to enjoy the atmosphere of this medieval town: its narrow, twisting, cobbled streets, jumble of small squares, lovely boutiques, excellent restaurants, and colorful buildings are delightful. The heart of the town is the **Piazza della Repubblica**, the main square, which has many narrow streets feeding into it. If you are up for walking, climb the twisting streets to the old fortress standing guard over the town.

Lake Trasimeno: Leaving Cortona, continue driving south on S71 toward Lake Trasimeno. In about 11 kilometers you come to a four-lane expressway. Do not get on the highway, but instead continue south on S71, which traces the west shore of Lake Trasimeno, Italy's fourth largest lake, which is fed by underground channels linked to the Tiber river basin. Fascinatingly, the early Romans built these underground waterways many centuries ago. Follow the road south for 9 kilometers to **Castiglione del Lago**, the most interesting town on the lake. Built on a high rocky promontory that juts out into the water, the old walled city with its battlements and towers has lots of character. Artifacts and tombs nearby indicate it was originally an Etruscan settlement, but what you see today dates from the Middle Ages. In the 1500s it was the dukedom of the Corgna. In the church of Santa Maria Maddalena you can see a 16th-century panel with paintings of the Madonna and Child by Eusebio da San Giorgio. Also visit the Palazzo del Capitano del Popolo, the Palazzo della Cornna, and the Leone fortress.

Umbertide: Continue the loop around the lake then take the road toward Magione, which is just before the junction with the expressway heading to Perugia. In a few minutes, you see the four-lane expressway, but do not get on it. Instead, continue over the highway and follow the back roads through the countryside to Umbertide. Stop for a short visit to this small, 10th-century town that hugs the banks of the Tevere River. In addition to the castle, you might want to visit the Church of Santa Maria della Reggia, which is an intriguing octagonal, three-tired building topped by a cupola. Another church, the Holy Cross, is famous for its lovely painting by Signorelli, called *Deposition from the Cross*.

Gubbio: Leaving Umbertide, take the road that passes over the highway E45 and continue on to Gubbio. This splendidly preserved, medieval walled town is perched high on the slopes of Monte Ingino. The setting is superb and the view from the plaza that sits like a shelf overlooking the countryside is breathtaking. The narrow, cobbled streets and walkways lacing the hillside are delightful to explore. The town is filled with architectural masterpieces, one of these, the Basilica, dominates the town. There is much to see including the Cathedral, the Consuls Palace, the Piazza Pensile, the Pretorio Palace, and the Santa Maria Nuova church where you can see Ottaviano Nelli's *Madonna del Belvedere*. Outside the city walls, nestled below the town, there are the remains of a Roman theater—another reminder of how important the city was in its prime.

Perugia: From Gubbio head south on S298 in the direction of Perugia. There is a turnoff to Perugia, which is surrounded by many modern commercial buildings. If time is short, bypass Perugia (which is not as pristine as many of Umbria's other jewels) and continue on to the junction of S75 and continue east following signs to Assisi. However, if you want to "see it all," Perugia is rich in history and has many delights. Perugia is a large medieval city surrounded by ramparts. An important Umbrian city since Etruscan days, the old town has at its heart the **Piazza IV Novembre**, a beautiful square with an appealing fountain, the **Fontana Maggiore**, built in the late 13th century.

Assisi: Coming from either Perugia or Gubbio, take S75 east following signs for Assisi, one of our favorite targets in Umbria. Built up the steep slopes of Mount Subasio, this magical city is a tribute to St. Francis. Although he was born into a family of wealth, after several visions in which Christ appeared to him, St. Francis left his privileged life. He was obviously a person with a deeply poetic soul and his tender teachings of reverence for the beauties of nature and kindness to all animals and birds still appeal to

St. Francis of Assisi

us today. To remember your visit, you might want to buy a statue of St. Francis to bring home. You will find statues in all sizes and price ranges in the many shops.

Even if it were not for the lingering memory of the gentle St. Francis, Assisi would be a "must see" for it is one of the most spectacular hill towns in Umbria. Perhaps there are a few too many souvenir shops, but this is a small price to pay for the privilege of experiencing such a very special place. The town walls begin on the valley floor and completely enclose the city as it climbs the steep hillside to the enormous castle at its summit. Assisi with its maze of tiny streets is a marvelous town for walking (you must wear sturdy shoes) and it is great fun as you come across intriguing little lanes opening into small squares. When you stop to rest, there are breathtaking vistas of the lovely Umbrian fields stretching out below. Along with many other historic buildings, Assisi's most famous monument,

St. Francis' Basilica, was severely damaged by an earthquake in September 1997. However, all of the repairs have now been completed and the town looks remarkably "back to normal." The basilica, which also houses a monastery, faces onto a large square bound by columns forming vaulted covered walkways. In addition to the monastery, there are two basilicas—upper and lower. Both are adorned with excellent frescoes that were unfortunately damaged by the earthquake. Also while in Assisi, visit **Santa Chiara** (St. Clara's Church). Clara, a close friend of St. Francis, founded the Order of St. Clares. Go into the church to view the lovely frescoes of Santa Clara and her sisters. Part of the enjoyment of Assisi is just to stroll through its narrow, cobbled streets—the whole town is like a living museum. If you have time, hike up to the **Rocca Medioevale**, an enormous 14th-century fortress perched on the hillside overlooking the city. From here you have a magnificent bird's-eye view of Assisi and beyond to the enchanting Umbrian countryside sweeping out to the distant hills.

Collepino: From Assisi you can continue on the S75 in the direction of Foligno. However, if you feel adventuresome and enjoy getting off the beaten path, there is a narrow, twisting, very scenic back road that leads through the hills making a loop from Assisi that ends up back on the S75 in Spello, about 5 kilometers before Foligno. The driving is difficult, but you can enjoy the beauty of the rugged forested mountains, an area of Umbria seldom seen by tourists. The road begins at the upper part of Assisi. Follow signs in the direction of Gualdo Tadino, but before you get there, take the road marked to Armenzano where you continue on following signs to Spello. After going through Armenzano, the road passes the adorable secluded hamlet of Collepino, which oozes charm with its winding cobbled streets and stone houses. It is so tiny that you quickly see it all. After Collepino, it is 7 kilometers on to Spello, where the road joins the S75, which you take going south.

Bevagna: Five kilometers south of Spello you come to **Foligno** where we suggest leaving the S75 and taking instead the back roads that to enjoy the lovely villages and scenery. From Foligno S316 toward Bevagna, which you reach after about 8 kilometers. Bevagna is an enticing, intimate, charming walled village, founded by the Romans. In addition to just enjoying the allure of the town, there is much to see including a stunning 19th-century opera house, the beautiful San Michele church, well-preserved mosaics in the old Roman baths, and a paper press making paper just as it has been for centuries. If it is mealtime, there is a wonderful place for lunch, L'Orto degli Angeli.

Montefalco: From Bevagna, take the road marked to Montefalco (located 7 kilometers from Bevagna). Montefalco is a walled town that crowns a hill with sweeping views of the Umbrian countryside. The town is a maze of small, narrow streets. For sightseeing, the main attraction is **San Francisco**, a church now converted into a museum that displays some of the finest work of Benozzo Gozzoli, including the fresco *Life of St. Francis*. Also, a delicious wine, *Sagrantino*, is produced here.

Spoleto: From Montefalco, loop back to the main road, S75, and continue south following signs to Spoleto. Not only is medieval Spoleto dramatically perched atop a hill, but it also has an almost unbelievable bridge dating from Roman times. This **Ponte delle Torri**, spanning the deep ravine between Spoleto and the adjoining mountain, was built over an aqueduct existing in the 14th century. This incredible engineering wonder is 230 meters long and soars 81 meters high. It is supported by a series of ten Gothic arches and has a fort at the far end as well as a balcony in the center. The 12th-century **Cathedral** in Spoleto is also so lovely that it alone would make a stop in this charming town worth a detour. The exterior of this very old cathedral, with its beautiful rose window and intricate mosaics, is truly charming. Although a great sightseeing destination at any time of the year, Spoleto is very popular in late June and early July when it hosts the world-famous Spoleto Festival, featuring great music, dance, and theater. During the festival season rooms are usually more expensive and almost impossible to secure so should be booked far in advance.

Torgiano: Torgiano, in the center of a rich wine region, has a lovely small wine museum. You would never dream that such a tiny town could boast such a gem, but it is not a coincidence: the Lungarotti family owns the vineyards for many kilometers in every direction. Signor Lungarotti furnished the museum with artifacts pertaining to every aspect of wine production from the earliest days, creating an interesting and beautifully displayed collection worthy of a detour by anyone interested in wines. In the center of town, the Lungarotti family owns, **Le Tre Vaselle**, a charming choice for lunch.

WESTERN UMBRIA

From Spoleto, a scenic route connecting the eastern part of Umbria to the western part of Umbria is to take the S418, which twists west from Spoleto for 25 kilometers through beautiful hills to the E45. Turn north on E45 for about 21 kilometers and turn west on S448, following signs to the A1 and Orvieto.

Todi: The picture-perfect village of Todi makes a great midway stop between Spoleto and Orvieto. It is located near the junction of E45 and S448 and is well signposted. This adorable small town crowning a hilltop like icing on a cake is one of our favorites. No, there isn't much to see—it is the town itself that is so picturesque. It is just fun to wander the twisting cobblestone streets, enjoy the medieval ambiance, and stop to enjoy a cappuccino in one of the sidewalk cafés. As you stroll through the small village, watch for the Cathedral, the People's Square, the intimate San Ilario Church, and the Roman/Etruscan Museum.

When you come to the A1, don't get onto the freeway, but instead follow signs to Orvieto. NOTE: When deciding on a town in the area to use as a hub for sightseeing don't limit your choice to those in Umbria. You will also find a rich selection of places to stay very nearby in Tuscany and Lazio.

Orvieto: Originally founded by the Etruscans, Orvieto later became a prosperous Roman city, famous for its production of ceramics. Orvieto is spread across the top of a hill that drops down on every side in steep volcanic cliffs to the Umbrian plain 200 meters below—you wonder how the town could ever have been built! Drive as far as you can up to the town, park your car, and proceed on foot. Have a good map handy because you pass so many churches and squares that it is difficult to orient yourself—Orvieto is a maze of tiny piazzas and narrow twisting streets. Continue on to Orvieto's center where a glorious **Duomo** dominates the immense piazza. You may think you have seen sufficient stunning cathedrals to last a lifetime, but just wait—Orvieto's is truly special, one of the finest examples of Romanesque-Gothic architecture in Italy. It is brilliantly embellished with intricate mosaic designs and accented by lacy slender spires stretching gracefully into the sky. Within the Duomo, you absolutely must not miss the **Chapel of San Brizio;** here you find frescos by Fra Angelico and Luca Signorelli. Also of interest in Orvieto is **St. Patrick's Well**, hewn out of solid volcanic rock. Pope Clement VII took refuge in Orvieto in 1527 and to ensure the town's water supply in case of siege, he ordered the digging of this 62-meter-deep well. It is unique for the 70 windows that illuminate it and the two spiral staircases that wind up and down without meeting. Other sights to see include the Papal Palace, the Town Hall, and the archaeological museum.

Civita di Bagnorégio: Although **Civita di Bagnorégio** is not in Umbria, it's located just southwest of Orvieto, so it conveniently ties in with this itinerary. If you are a photographer and love picturesque walled villages, few can surpass the setting of this small town. Take the N71, which twists west from Orvieto toward **Lake Bolsena.** Stay on N71 for about 20 kilometers and then turn left heading to Bagnorégio. Go into town and follow signs to Civita, which crowns the top of a steep, circular-shaped, rocky outcrop. There is no road into the village—the only access is by walking over a long, narrow suspension bridge that joins the two sides of a deep ravine. Once you arrive, you will find a few shops, some Etruscan artifacts, a church, and a restaurant. However, the main focus is the town itself with its narrow arcaded alleyways and a dramatic 180-degree view of the desolate, rocky canyons that stretch out around the town with a haunting beauty.

The Haunting Beauty of Umbria

The Undiscovered Sabine Hills

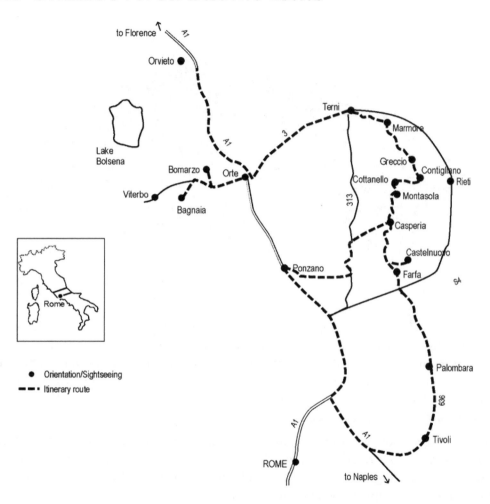

The Undiscovered Sabine Hills

Casperia

The Sabine Hills is an appealingly undiscovered niche of Italy, which—although blissfully lost in time—is an exceptionally convenient area to visit since the region is just north of Rome. We have suggested this itinerary as an "add on" to our Umbria itinerary (which precedes this one) since one flows gracefully into the other. However, you can just as easily reverse the route and start in Rome and include the Sabine Hills as you head north toward Umbria and Tuscany.

This adventure takes you over winding, tranquil mountain roads into the Sabine Hills (or Sabina as it is often referred to), an idyllic area in the region of Lazio offering splendid scenery with rolling, olive-clad hills and tiny, medieval hilltop villages. This part of central Italy—perhaps more than any other—has preserved its original rural character, and, not withstanding its proximity to Rome, is one of the least populated parts of the country. A wonderful time to visit is spring when the countryside explodes in color with yellow broom and fields of sunflowers, accented by the silver green of the olive trees which produce some of Italy's finest extra virgin olive oils.

Pacing: We suggest spending a minimum of two nights in this region of northern Lazio to savor the authentic charm of the long-forgotten villages in the Sabine Hills. Since the area is small, choose one town as your base of operation and go out from there each day for sightseeing.

As you study the map at the beginning of this itinerary, it is obvious that you could begin your drive to the Sabine Hills from numerous places in Umbria or Tuscany. However, since we ended the Umbria itinerary near Orvieto, we have chosen it as a suggested starting point. If your time is limited, the quickest way to get to Sabina from Orvieto is to take the A1 south and exit at Ponzano/Soratte, but we suggest in our itinerary a more leisurely approach through the less discovered corners of northern Lazio.

Parco dei Mostri and Villa Lante: Leaving Orvieto, drive south toward Rome on the A1. Because they are convenient to your route, we suggest stopping to visit two extraordinary gardens: the Parco dei Mostri and the Villa Lante. For these excursions, exit the A1 at Orte, and then take the superstrada 204 west toward Viterbo. About 27 kilometers after leaving the A1, take the exit marked to **Bomarzo** where the sacred garden of **Parco dei Mostri** is located. Dating back to 1552, the park was designed by Pirro Ligorio, who also created the incredible gardens of Villa d'Este in Tivoli. He is also responsible for the completion of Saint Peter's Cathedral, a commission he took over after the death of Michelangelo. A 30-minute walk through the wooded park with gigantic hidden statues of animals and mythological characters makes this a great destination for children. After visiting Parco dei Mostri, it is just a short drive on to the enchanting gardens of **Villa Lante.**

To reach Villa Lante from Parco dei Mostri, follow a small, ancient road flanked by olive and hazelnut groves in the direction of Viterbo. Before reaching Viterbo, follow signs for

Bagnaia, where you find the classic Italian renaissance gardens of **Villa Lante**, which date back to 1568. The lavish life style of those in the aristocracy of the Catholic Church is clearly evident; an opulent villa surrounded by sensational gardens seems to have been a perk of being a Cardinal. Villa Lante was built by Cardinal Gianfrancesco Gambara and later was occupied by a succession of Popes until the Lante family bought the property in 1657. The Duchess of Lante was born in France and when she moved to her new home in Italy, she brought with her a French agronomist who added a French flavor to the Villa Lante gardens. Open 9 am to 4:30 pm in winter, 9 am to 7:30 pm in summer.

Terni: After visiting both gardens, return east toward Orte. When you reach the A1, do not get on the freeway but continue east to Terni, which is on the border of Umbria and Lazio. Because it was rebuilt after extensive damage in World War II, Terni is a city of modern architecture. Although it does not have an old world ambiance, it is worth a stop for those who love fashionable couture—it seems every Italian designer is represented here. Our suggestion is to drive through Terni and get onto the smaller roads that lead to Marmore.

Marmore: From the center of Terni take route 79 to Marmore, a tiny village where **Cascata delle Marmore** is located. If you are a nature lover, you will not want to miss this side trip to the highest waterfall in Europe, which was created in 290 B.C. when the Romans changed the course of the River Velino. To admire the falls, leave your car and enter the parkland. The viewpoint is open year round for two hours a day: 1pm to 2pm and 4pm to 5pm. The times vary each month but you can check them on Google (Marmore waterfalls opening). The waterfall can be admired from below or above. You view the falls from above on the way to Greccio.

Greccio: As you leave Marmore the road divides. At this point, leave Route 79 that goes on to Rieti and take instead a very small road that parallels the river Velino. After 12 kilometers you will reach Greccio, a peaceful monastery in a spectacular position on the slopes of Mount Lacerone with views stretching across the green plain below to the peaks of Mount Terminillo. It was here in December, 1223, that Saint Francis of Assisi, along with the local noblemen, enacted the first live nativity scene. The tradition has continued ever since the 12th century and each year at Christmas people flock from all over Italy to see this traditional event in which a cast of a hundred people participate dressed in splendid costumes: the convent is open 9:30am to 1pm and 3pm to 6pm. After visiting the Greccio sanctuary, drive back down the steep winding road and continue south toward Sabina, following signposts for Contigliano. Before entering the town, make a sharp right. You find yourself on a mountain road with no traffic at all.

Cottanello: The first hilltop village you come to is Cottanello, a tiny, remote, picturesque hill town surrounded by mountains instead of olive groves. The inhabitants are mostly shepherds and you might need to stop along the way to let a shepherd with his flock of sheep cross the road. The typical regional products of the area are pecorino and ricotta cheese made with sheep's milk. Just outside this sleepy town is the tiny medieval cliff-side **Hermitage of Saint Cataldo**, carved out of rock hanging over the road. It is possible to have a guide open the hermitage for you if you have an appointment and arrive before lunchtime. Also of interest is the nearby archaeological remains of a Roman farmhouse, which belonged to Lucius Cotta, the brother in law of Julius Caesar, and features a lovely mosaic floor. The site is hard to find and rarely visited, so a reservation is essential. For both of these stops, call the Comune of Cottanello (0746) 66 122 or Sig. Stefano Petrucci, a guide, whose cell phone is (3287) 42 50 58. If you pass by in the afternoon and are planning to stay at one of the hotels or bed and breakfasts in the Sabine Hills, your hosts can call for you and make an appointment for the next morning.

Jewels of the Sabine Hills: Passing Cottanello, turn left at the bottom of the hill toward Poggio Mirteto and Casperia. As the road descends, the panorama widens to include the rolling plains of Lazio and the Tiber valley. You are now in the heart of Sabina which hasn't changed much in the last 1,000 years. Here you will discover authentic, off the beaten path, hilltop villages such as Casperia, Montasola, Roccantica, Poggio Catino, Farfa, and Stroncone and a romantic landscape of olive farms, abbeys and castles. To add to the enchantment, there is a total lack of souvenir shops and tour buses—a treat for those who enjoy experiencing the life of the local people. What fun it is to not rush about. Relax in one of hill towns where time seems to have stood still; enjoy a cappuccino or sip a glass of wine in the piazza and peer over the medieval walls at the inspiring landscape of the Tiber Valley. Happily, the area offers a rich selection of places to stay. Choose one of these as your hub for a few nights stay and venture out to explore the area, visiting the towns and sites featured in the following part of this itinerary. You will soon discover why the Roman emperor, Hadrian, chose Sabina as one of his favorite getaways from Rome. Some of the jewels of the Sabine hills are featured below.

Montasola

Montasola: This tiny, intact medieval hilltop village, typical of the region, has no more than 80 inhabitants. The entrance gate, dominated by a medieval tower, leads into the village. There are no famous monuments here, but stop to take some photos and enjoy the splendid panoramas (the town is at an altitude of 600 meters).

Casperia: Perched on a rocky outcrop and bound by the remains of its original stone walls and watchtowers, Casperia is one of the most picturesque medieval villages in the Sabine Hills. While enjoying the local food and wine, you can often listen to a live jazz pianist as you watch the sun set over Mount Soratte. In this completely pedestrian town every turning along the narrow cobble stoned alleyways offers a photo opportunity. A local craftsman, Gianni, has been making a wonderful model of the village for the last 10 years as a setting for the Christmas nativity crib. Every year he adds more. The model is located in the church of San Giovanni Battista, which is usually open in the afternoons around 5pm. A favorite place on a summer's evening is the panoramic café in the piazza of Casperia.

In 1852 the famous German historian, Gregorovius, described Casperia in his book *Wandering in Italy* "In all my travels I have never beheld a panorama of such heroic beauty as that offered to me from the top of the hill in the territory of Aspra (the old name for Casperia). It is truly a paradise on earth! A majestic solitude dominates both the nearby mountains where timeless castles stood, and the villages of the Sabines where ancient families still dwell, solidly preserving the customs and the ways of life of the past...the ideal place to dream." Little has changed since Gregorovius fell in love with Casperia and the Sabine Hills.

Abbey of Farfa

Farfa: Not to be missed is the **Abbey of Farfa**, one of the most famous European religious buildings of the Middle Ages, found in the town of the same name. Charlemagne was its protector, and at the height of his empire, a vast part of central Italy was owned by the abbey. A visit is not complete without including the magnificent, recently refurbished, library that contains more than 60,000 volumes and original manuscripts, including one of the first books ever printed. The staff in the herb store will arrange your visit. Do not miss a well preserved Roman sarcophagus that was found on the premises, attesting to the fact that the 6th-century abbey was built on the site of a Roman villa: tel: (0765) 27 73 15 (not much English spoken).

Castelnuovo di Farfa: A small winding road leads to the nearby village of Castelnuovo di Farfa where a contemporary museum of olive oil is located, the first of its kind in Italy. It has an unusual exhibit that interprets the history of the olive, which has always dominated the landscape of Sabina. International artists have participated in creating the exhibit, which also features a rare collection of oil presses. The museum is open weekends and on request for small groups, tel: (0765) 36 370.

Castel San Pietro: This small picturesque hilltop village built around a large 17th-century palace makes a fun place to stop for lunch after having visited Farfa. There is a great restaurant here, Re Burlone, located in the cellars of the palazzo.

Fara Sabina: The highest village in the Sabine hills is Fara Sabina. Once a Lombard stronghold the village offers the most spectacular view of the rolling plains of Lazio—the land of the Latins and birthplace of our western civilization. You can see across the Tiber valley as far as Rome, and, on a clear day, the dome of Saint Peter's is visible.

Tivoli, Villa d'Este, and Villa Adriana: While based in Sabina, enjoy a daytrip to one or more of Italy's famous renaissance gardens and the archeological site of Villa Adriana. To reach Tivoli, drive south from Fara Sabina, crossing the Via Salaria S4 and continuing on the small backroad 636 to Palombara Sabina. Then continue on to Tivoli. In Tivoli you find the Villa d'Este with its 16th-century fountains—a must see for Renaissance garden lovers. Nearby you find Villa Adriana, an incredible archaeological site with 300 acres of grounds.

After visiting Villa d'Este and Villa Adriana, take the link road to A1, direction Florence (the entrance is just a few kilometers from Tivoli). Exit at Ponzano/Soratte and head east, making your way back to your base in the Sabine hills. NOTE: Villa D'Este and Villa Adriana can also be visited en route to Rome, if this is your next destination.

Mountain & Lake Adventures

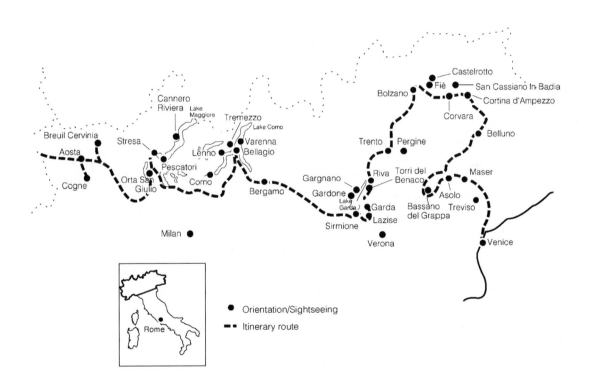

Castelrotto
Fiè
San Cassiano In Badia
Bolzano
Cortina d'Ampezzo
Corvara
Cannero Riviera
Lake Maggiore
Tremezzo
Lake Como
Belluno
Breuil Cervinia
Stresa
Varenna
Trento
Pergine
Aosta
Lenno
Bellagio
Pescatori
Maser
Cogne
Orta San Giulio
Como
Riva
Torri del Benaco
Asolo
Treviso
Bergamo
Gargnano
Gardone
Lake Garda
Garda
Bassano del Grappa
Sirmione
Lazise
Milan
Verona
Venice

● Orientation/Sightseeing
▪ ▪ ▪ Itinerary route

Rome

Mountain & Lake Adventures

Santa Maria Rezzónico, Lake Como

For the traveler who wants to combine the magic of seeing some of the world's most splendid mountains with the joy of visiting Italy's scenic northern lakes, this itinerary is ideal. Contrasts will heighten the impact of visual delights as you meander through dramatic mountains and then on to some of the most romantic lakes in the world. Along the way are giant mountains piercing the sky with their jagged granite peaks and lush meadows splashed with wildflowers. Continuing on you arrive at lazy blue lakes whose steep shorelines are decorated with villages wrapped in misty cloaks of siennas and ochres. This itinerary can stand alone. However, it is also perfect for the traveler arriving in or departing from neighboring countries. All too often the tourist thinks he has finished Italy when his tour ends in Venice, and he rushes north into Austria or Switzerland. What a waste—a very picturesque region still remains. Please linger to enjoy the mountains and lakes that truly are some of Italy's greatest natural treasures.

Recommended Pacing: To do this itinerary "well" you need three weeks. This may seem to be dawdling a bit, but less time than indicated would not allow you to enjoy your destinations. Remember that three nights really means only two full days with travel in between. Allow at least three nights in Venice—more would be preferable, especially if you want to explore some of the small islands such as Murano (famous for its hand-blown glass) and Burano (well-known for its colorful cottages and hand-made lace). Your next stop, Asolo, needs two nights. Not only is the town delightful, but also you will want to visit some of the Palladian mansions in the area. Your next suggested stop, the Dolomites, needs another three nights. The scenery is spectacular and you will want time to explore some of the exquisite mountain back roads and take hikes. From the Dolomites your next destination is spectacular Lake Garda. Again, you need three nights. You must have time to take advantage of the romantic boat trips around the lake and also a side trip to nearby Verona. Your next stop is another exquisite highlight, Lake Como. Here you need three nights to enjoy the boat excursions around the lake. From Lake Como, it is on to Lake Maggiore, another lovely destination. Here you need three nights to enjoy both boat trips around the lake and visits to the romantic islands in the lake. After Lake Maggiore it is on to Lake Orta, a much smaller lake with great personality. Because it is not so large, two nights should suffice here. From Lake Orta you leave the Lake District and are in the splendid Aosta Valley in the Alps, which trace the border with France and Switzerland. Here you need another two nights in order to have sufficient time to take walks and enjoy the awesome parks. You might not have the luxury of time to spend three weeks on this "*Mountain & Lake Adventures*." If not, tailor this itinerary for your own schedule. Perhaps visit just one of the lakes instead of all four, or save the lakes for another trip and leisurely enjoy just Venice and the Dolomites. Whatever your choice, you are in for a special treat in this incredibly beautiful region of Italy.

VENICE: This itinerary begins in **Venice**, one of the most romantic cities in the world. Venice's many narrow waterways are crisscrossed by storybook bridges and shadowed by majestic palaces whose soft hues reflect warmly in the shimmering water. Black gondolas quietly glide through the narrow canals as the gondolier in his red-and-white-striped shirt softly serenades his passengers with an operatic selection.

Venice is not a traditional city with streets and automobile traffic, but rather an archipelago of 117 islands glued together by 400 bridges.

There is a wealth of things to do and see in Venice. See our itinerary *Italian Highlights by Train & Boat–or Car* for sightseeing suggestions.

When it is time to leave Venice for Asolo, you need to take a boat to your car since all the "streets" in Venice are canals. If you are renting a car, take the boat to **Piazzale Roma** where most of the car rental companies are located. Also in the Piazzale Roma there are overnight car parks for storing your car if you drive into Venice. The choice of conveyance to the Piazzale Roma, Venice's hub of transportation, will depend upon your budget and your inclination. The **vaporetti** are the most reasonable: similar to river buses. They leave regularly from St. Mark's Square, stopping along the way to pick up passengers. It is approximately a half-hour ride to the Piazzale Roma. The **motoscafi** are motorboats that duck through the back canals and usually take about 15 minutes to the Piazzale Roma. The motoscafi are like private cabs and are much more expensive than the "bus," but can be very convenient, especially if where you are staying has a private dock. The most romantic mode of transportation is by private **gondola**: however, these are very expensive and usually take about an hour to reach the Piazzale Roma.

Once you have retrieved your car from the parking garage, head north from Venice toward **Treviso**, about an hour's drive. If time allows, stop here. Stroll through this picturesque city spider-webbed with canals and surrounded by 15th-h ramparts—perhaps have a cup of coffee or a bite of lunch. Treviso is famous for its arcaded streets, churches lavishly decorated with frescoes, and painted houses. You might want to climb the ramparts for a view of the Alps beckoning you on.

ASOLO: From Treviso it is approximately another hour north to Asolo. However, just a few kilometers before you reach Asolo you see signs for the town of **Maser** where the **Villa di Maser** (sometimes called by the name of **Villa Bararo**) is located. This is a splendid villa designed by **Andrea Palladio** and fabulously decorated with frescoes by Paolo Veronese. It also has a very interesting museum of old carriages and antique cars. This elegant villa has erratic days and hours when it is open to the public—usually in late afternoons on Tuesdays, Saturdays, and Sundays. However, it is only about 1½ kilometers out of your way, so it is well worth a detour to investigate.

Your prize tonight is **Asolo**, a gem of a medieval village snuggled on the side of a hill with exquisite views of the countryside. The town is so romantic that it is no wonder Robert Browning was captivated by it and chose Asolo as his home. As you drive toward Asolo, the terrain does not seem to hold much promise—just modern towns and industry. Then a side road winds up a lovely hillside and into the intimate little town. Although definitely a tourist destination, Asolo maintains the atmosphere of a *real* town with colorful fruit stands, candy shops, and the neighborhood grocer for those lucky few who live here. In addition, there are boutiques with exquisite merchandise for the tourist. Of course, a castle adorns the hill above the village—mostly in ruins but setting the proper stage. Naturally, there is a wonderful cathedral dominating the square, just as it should. You will find all this plus vineyards and olive trees on the hillsides and the scent of roses in the air.

There are a couple of towns that are worth seeing while you are in the Asolo area. If brandy holds a special interest for you, visit **Bassano del Grappa**, an old town famous for its production of grappa (or brandy). The town is also a pottery center. However, Bassano del Grappa is rather large and, in our estimation, much less interesting than **Marostica**, a tiny town just a few kilometers farther on. If you are in this area in September, check your calendar and consider a stop in Marostica. Here, during the first part of September (in alternate years) the central square is transformed into a giant chessboard and local citizens become the human chess pieces. Even if it isn't the year of the chess game, you will enjoy this picturesque little medieval town encircled by ramparts, its pretty central square enclosed by colorful buildings and castle walls. There is also a second castle guarding the town from the top of the hill.

THE DOLOMITES: From Asolo, you head north to one of the most stunning regions of Italy, the **Dolomites**—breathtaking mountains. It is important to have a very detailed map of the region because this is a confusing area for driving. Adding to the confusion of finding your way is the fact that most of the towns have two names: one Italian and one German. Before World War I this section of Italy belonged to the Austrian Empire, and most of the towns have retained their original names along with their new ones. The food is a mixture of Italian and German—strudel is the favorite dessert and ravioli stuffed with meat, vegetables, and cream cheese is called either ravioletti or schulpfkrapfeln.

There are various routes for driving north into the Dolomites. The major highway heads north through **Feltre** and **Belluno** and then goes on to Cortina d'Ampezzo. However, if the day is nice and your spirit of adventure high, there is really nothing more fun than taking the back roads through the mountains. Journey through tiny hamlets and gorgeous mountain valleys far from the normal tourist path—always keeping a map accessible so that you don't wind up hopelessly lost.

You might want to travel casually and stop in a village that captures your heart as you drive through the picturesque Dolomite valleys. A good base for exploring the region is **Corvara**, a small village ringed by breathtaking mountains. Another excellent choice is **Cortina d'Ampezzo**, a tourist center that is larger due to its excellent skiing facilities. Its location is truly breathtaking—the town spreads across a sunny meadow ringed by gigantic granite peaks. Although the true allure of Cortina is its beauty, there are a few other attractions—the lovely frescoes in the Romanesque **Church of SS Filippo e Giacomo**; the **stadium** where the 1956 Olympic ice-skating competition was held; and the **Museo Ciasa de Ra Regoles** with its geological display and contemporary art exhibition.

This is a mountain lover's area where the roads are slow and winding. The scenery is beautiful, with green valleys dominated by the stark mountain walls, but the driving is hard, with lots of hairpin bends. Many routes are spectacular. The 48 and 241 from Cortina to Bolzano form the stupendous **Great Dolomite Road** (*Grande Strada delle Dolomiti*). Another lovely route runs through the **Alpe di Siusi,** high Alpine meadowlands beneath towering mountains. (From the Verona-Brennero autostrada exit at Bolzano Nord and follow a route through Völs [Fiè allo Sciliar], Siusi, and Castelrotto.) It continues on into the **Val Gardena** (Grödner Tal) to **Ortisei** (Sankt Ulrich) and up to the **Sella Pass**. We enjoyed a sensational 50-kilometer drive over four mountain passes that ring the **Gruppo Sella** mountain group—from Corvara we took the Gardena Pass, the Sella Pass, the Podoi Pass, and the Campolongo Pass, which returned us to Corvara.

The only relaxing (albeit strenuous) way to truly appreciate the Dolomites is to get out of your car and walk the well-marked trails that feather out into the hills. Cable cars and ski lifts run in summer and are excellent ways to assist the walker to higher altitudes. At gift shops or tourist offices you can purchase detailed hiking maps that show every little path.

LAKE GARDA: Your next stop is Lake Garda. From the mountains, drive to Bolzano where you join the expressway (E7), heading south toward Trento (Trent). **Trent** is best known as the town where the Catholic Council met in the 16th century to establish important articles of faith that emphasized the authority of the Catholic Church.

Leave the freeway at Trent and head west on 45 toward the small, but lovely, green **Lake Toblino**, which is enhanced by a superb castle on its north shore where you can stop for lunch. From Toblino head south on the pretty country road, lined with fruit trees and vineyards, heading directly south toward Lake Garda, Italy's largest lake. When you come to Arco, the road splits. Take the road to the left and continue south to Lake Garda and then follow the 249 as it curves along the eastern shore of the lake.

Lake Garda abounds with romance. Don't rush. Take time to explore the lake by boat. Get off at colorful small hamlets that capture your fancy; it is hard to choose since each seems impossibly tempting. Have lunch, then hop back on a later boat to continue along your way. The boat schedules are posted at each dock, and if you ask the attendant, he can usually give you a printed timetable.

There are many alluring villages you should not miss, each a gem. One of the most charming towns is **Sirmione**, accessible by a picturesque drawbridge. This walled medieval village at the south end of Lake Garda is positioned on a miniature peninsula that juts into the lake. During the summer Sirmione is absolutely bursting with tourists, but you can easily understand why: this is another one of Italy's "stage-set" villages, almost too perfect to be real.

At the north end of the lake is the larger town of **Riva.** Although much of the town is of new construction, it has at its medieval core the **Piazza III Novembre** and 13th-century **Tower of Apponale**. A good place to eat lunch is on the terrace of the **Hotel Sole**, located directly across from the boat dock.

Along the western shore of the lake our favorite villages are **Gargnano** and its tiny adjacent neighbor, **Villa di Gargnano**. Both are medieval jewels hugging the waterfront with colorful fishing boats tucked into little harbors—truly adorable towns.

Also on the western shore of Lake Garda is **Gardone Riviera**. From here it is just a short drive to a **Vittoriale**, once the home of Gabriele d'Annunzio, the celebrated Italian poet. (For those who are fascinated by stories of romance, **Gabriele d'Annunzio** is also famous for his love affair with Eleanora Duse.)

The east side of Lake Garda also abounds with unbelievably quaint towns, each so perfect that you want to get out your camera or sketchbook to capture the beauty. Our favorites are the medieval walled towns of **Garda, Lazise**, and **Torri del Benaco**—each a gem. You mustn't miss them. Of the three, Torri del Benaco is our favorite.

It will be easier to leave the Lake Garda knowing that beautiful Lake Como awaits your arrival.

On your way from Lake Garda to Lake Como, stop at **Bergamo**, about an hour's drive west on the A4. As you approach Bergamo, the congested city doesn't appear to be worth a stop—but it is. The shell of the city is deceiving because it hides a lovely kernel, the **Cita Alta**, or high city. The lower part of Bergamo is modern and a bit dreary, but the old medieval city snuggled on the top of the hill holds such treasures as the **Piazza Vecchia**, the **Colleoni**

Chapel, and the **Church of St. Mary Major**. Should you want to time your stop in Bergamo with lunch, there are several excellent restaurants. One suggestion would be the **Agnello d'Oro**, a cozy, charming, 17th-century inn in the Cita Alta. From Bergamo it is a short drive on to **Lake Como**.

LAKE COMO: Lake Como is spectacular. The lower half of the lake is divided into two legs, the western branch called Lake Como and the eastern branch called **Lake Lecco**, enclosed by soaring cliffs that give a fjord-like beauty to the area. On the tip of land where the two lower sections of the lake join, is one of the lake's most delightful towns, **Bellagio**, a medieval jewel that exudes great charm. The town traces the shore of the lake and has a medieval walled entrance into the picture-perfect central square from which narrow lanes lined with colorful boutiques and restaurants lead up hill. Views of mountains, painted medieval buildings, flowers everywhere, promenades around the lake, and paths into the hills enhance your stay here. A particularly appealing walk follows a path that climbs up the wooded hill behind Bellagio and drops down into a tiny village, Pescallo, that nestles in a small cove on the other side of the peninsula.

Bellagio, Lake Como

In addition to Bellagio there is a rich selection of gems on the lake—picturesque, softly hued little hamlets, tucked into intimate coves around the shore. Most of these villages are accessible by boat. You can settle onto a steamer equipped with bar and restaurant and from your armchair lazily enjoy the constantly changing but always intriguing shoreline as the boat maneuvers in and out of the colorful little harbors, past elegant private villas, by enchanting villages. It is great fun to hop aboard one of the ferries and get off at one of the towns for lunch. There are also some swift hydrofoils that will whisk you about the lake and car ferries that transverse the lake, making it convenient to travel from one side to the other without going all around the lake.

Another bonus of Lake Como (besides the quaint towns to explore) is that it has exceptional villas to visit, many accessible by ferry. One of these on the western shore near **Tremezzo** is the **Villa Carlotta**, a fairy-tale-like 18th-century palace—worthy of the Prussian Princess Carlotta for whom it was named. Built by the Marquis Clerici, the villa with its surrounding formal gardens filled with rare plants and trees is outstanding. From the terrace you have an enchanting view over the lake to Bellagio. You reach the villa by a short drive from the ferry landing at Tremezzo along the beautiful tree-lined Via del Paradiso, *www.villacarlotta.it.* The interior of the villa with its prominent art collection and statues is open every day from 9 am to 6 pm from April to September. It is also open in March and October from 9 am to 11:30 am in the morning and in the afternoon from 2 pm to 4:30 pm.

Our favorite villa to visit because of its extraordinary beauty and romantic setting is **Villa del Balbianello** at **Lenno**, located on the west side of Lake Como. Built in 1700 by Cardinal Durini, this picture-postcard perfect villa is so beautiful it looks like a painting (and many artists have captured it on canvas). It is perched on the tip of a tiny peninsula with terraced gardens down to the lake. Have your camera ready and charged because as the ferry approaches the town of Lenno you will see the villa to your left and won't be able to stop taking photos. When your ferry arrives into Lenno, ask for directions to Sala Comacina, where you take a special motorboat to the landing where a flight of steps leads up to the gardens that are open to the public from the beginning of April until the end of

October on Tuesday, Thursday, Friday, Saturday, and Sunday from 10 am to 12:30 pm and again in the afternoon from 3:30 pm to 6 pm.

Como, located at the southern tip of Lake Como, is one of the larger towns on the lake. It is a pretty walled town with excellent shopping—including a colorful market every Saturday. Como is easily accessible from Milan and has many ferry departures from its dock.

Varenna is another small lakeside town accessible by ferry that is exceptionally attractive. Located about midway up the east side of the lake, it nestles on a promontory with great views. The heart of the town has a quaint, tiny square lined by medieval buildings. From Varenna about a half-an-hour hike takes you up to **Castello di Vezio,** a 13th-century castle with beautiful views of Lake Como. Varenna is a main hub for ferries, including car ferries that shuttle back and forth from Varenna to Bellagio and **Menaggio**, enabling you to quickly cross the lake without having to drive around it.

Cannero Riviera–Lake Maggiore

LAKE MAGGIORE: From Lake Como, the next stop is Lake Maggiore. Take advantage of the expressways to make your drive as easy as possible because there is usually heavy traffic in this part of Italy. It is best to head directly south in the direction of Milan to pick up the freeway.

Keep on the bypass that skirts the north side of Milan and take the freeway northwest to Lake Maggiore. Like Lake Garda and Lake Como, Maggiore offers ferries to many of its quaint towns and adds a special treat, the **Borromean Islands**, a small archipelago of three small islands, **Isola Bella**, **Isola Madre**, and **Isola dei Pescatori**. These enchanting islands can be reached by ferry from Stresa, Baveno, or Pallanza, but the most convenient of these departure points is **Stresa.** There are private taxi-boats available, but the most reasonable transportation is by public ferry.

Our two favorites of the Borromean Islands are Isola Bella and Isola dei Pescatori. You can easily visit them both in one day. If you enjoy gardens, be sure not to miss Isola Bella (Beautiful Island). Allow enough time to see its sumptuous palace, which is bound by formal gardens that terrace down to the lake. Fountains and sculptures make the gardens even more alluring. Afterwards, head to Isola dei Pescatori (Fisherman's Island) for lunch. Isola dei Pescatori is an enchanting island with twisting, narrow, alley-like streets and colorful fishermen's cottages. As the name implies, this is still an active fishing village. During the tourist season the island teems with people and the streets are lined with souvenir shops, but it is hard to dull the charm of this quaint town.

Another sightseeing excursion on Lake Maggiore is to the park at **Villa Taranto**. Its gardens, created in the 20th century by a Scottish captain, Neil McEacharn, are splendid with over 2000 species of plants, including huge water lilies, giant rhododendrons, and colorful azaleas. Adding to the botanical masterpiece, are fountains, waterfalls, beautiful trees and sculptures.

Isola Bella, Lake Maggiore

LAKE ORTA: Lake Orta, situated just west of Lake Maggiore, is one of our favorite lakes. Because it is so close to Lake Maggiore, it can be visited as a day trip from there. However, because it so appealing, we feel it deserves a stopover on its own. One doesn't hear much about Lake Orta, although it abounds with a charm and is filled with of Romanesque and Baroque treasures. It is probably less known because it is so small and doesn't have many quaint towns tucked along its shoreline. However, it does have one outstanding village, **Orta San Giulio**. It is picture perfect with a tiny square facing the water, narrow cobbled streets, noble mansions, a wonderful, very old, town hall, many boutiques, fragrant gardens, painted houses, and picturesque churches.

Adding to the perfection, just across from the town, you see **Isola San Giulio** shimmering in the water. You can take a boat out to this tiny island where you can walk the narrow street that circles the island and visit the Romanesque style church with 15th- and 16th-century frescoes.

THE ALPS: After visiting Lake Orta, drive south to the main freeway and head west on A4 toward Turin heading for the Italian Alps. Before Turin, when the freeway branches, take A5 heading northwest toward Aosta and beyond to the French border. As you head into the mountains, many small roads lead off to narrow valleys accented by gorgeous meadows, blanketed in summer with wildflowers. Most of these roads dead end when they are stopped by impregnable mountain ranges. In the winter, this is a paradise for downhill or cross-country skiing. One of the most famous ski areas is **Breuil-Cervinia**, almost at the Swiss border, just over the mountain from the Swiss resort, Zermatt. In summer the mountains beckon one to explore the beautiful paths that lead off in every direction.

Cogne-Valnontey

Our favorite place for walking or hiking is in the **Grand Paradis National Park**, just south of **Cogne**. To reach the park, from the A5, take the road south to Cogne. From here you can walk through a glorious meadow that stretches to the foot of the Grand Paradis, a majestic mountain that soars over 4,000 meters into the sky. If you drive a few kilometers beyond Cogne to where the road ends, you find Valnontey, a stunning hamlet of rustic, centuries-old, stone houses enhanced by pots of geraniums. As you stroll through the tiny village, it seems you have stepped back many centuries—it is so perfect, so untouched.

When it is time to continue your journey, the A5 continues on through the Mont Blanc tunnel and into France.

The Dolomites

Rome to Milan via the Italian Riviera

MILAN

Pavia Carthusian Monastery

SAVIGNONE

Genova

A12

Camogli

Sestri Levante

Portofino

Levanto

Monterosso al Mare

Colonnata

Cinque Terre

Carrara

La Spezia

Lucca

FLORENCE

Portovenere

Pisa

Livorno

Elba

Orbetello Peninsula

Orbetello

Porto San Stefano

Porto Ercole

Tarquinia

Civitavecchia

ROME

Rome

● Orientation/Sightseeing

▬ ▬ Itinerary route

125

Rome to Milan via the Italian Riviera

Vernazza, Cinque Terre

This itinerary traces the western coast of Italy as far as Genova before heading north for the final stretch to Milan. To break the journey, the first stop is Tarquinia for sightseeing, then Orbetello, a picturesque peninsula-like island joined to the coast by three spits of land. The next destination is Cinque Terre—a string of five tiny fishing villages along the coast that have not yet fallen prey to a great influx of tourists. As you follow the highway up the coast, it becomes a masterpiece of engineering—bridging deep ravines and tunneling in and out of the cliffs, which rise steeply from the sea. Along the way you pass picturesque small towns snuggled into small coves. Then it's on to Portofino—one of Italy's most treasured jewels—before the final destination of Milan.

Recommended Pacing: This itinerary can be run quickly if it is being used as simply as a means of transportation between Rome and Milan (or visa versa), but it is much more fun to savor the small towns along the way. You need a minimum of three nights in Rome—you could spend a week and still only touch on what this fabulous "living museum" has to offer. Once on your way between Rome and Milan, there are outstanding places to stay and things to see along the coast. However, if your time is strictly limited, choose just one of the three stopovers we recommend (Porto Ercole, Cinque Terre or Portofino) and plan to stay for three nights. Ideally, if you have the luxury to meander along the way, then plan to spend at least two nights in all three. Every suggested stopover is lovely in its own way and will give you a glimpse of the beauty of Italy's small, delightful, coastal towns.

This itinerary begins in **Rome**, a perfect introduction to Italy. The joy of Rome is that every place you walk you are immersed in history. The whole of the city is a virtual museum—buildings over 2,000 years old, ancient fountains designed by the world's greatest masters, the Vatican, Renaissance paintings that have never been surpassed in beauty. Buy a guidebook at one of the many bookstores or magazine stands to plan what you most want to see and do. Also buy a detailed city map and mark each day's excursion. Most places are within walking distance—if not, consider taking the subway, which stretches to most of the major points of interest.

For sightseeing suggestions in Rome, see the *Italian Highlights by Train & Boat—or Car* itinerary.

From Rome follow the well-marked signs for the expressway heading west toward the Leonardo da Vinci airport. About 5 kilometers before you arrive at the airport, head north on A12 in the direction of **Civitavecchia**.

About 13 kilometers beyond the Civitavecchia Nord exit, turn right (east) on S1 BIS in the direction of Viterbo. Continue a bit more than 3 kilometers and turn left toward **Tarquinia**, an Etruscan city that historians date back to the 12th century B.C. Even if it is not quite that old, archaeologists have established that people were living here as early as

600 years before Christ. Before you reach Tarquinia, you will see on your right an open-air museum—an open field dotted with **Etruscan tombs**. The site is not well-marked, but your clue will be tour buses lining the road. Park your car, buy a ticket at the gate, and explore the fascinating tombs. There are over a thousand tombs stretching over 5 kilometers, but only a small, select group is open to the public. You can wander at leisure. Each tomb has a sign describing what drawings are found within. You will find a rich treasure trove of paintings depicting the life of the ancient Etruscans, including scenes of hunting, dining, fishing, drinking, and frolicking. All of the burial sites are underground. To access a tomb, you have to climb down a narrow flight of steps and when you reach the bottom, everything is semidarkness. However, when you push a button, the tomb is magically illuminated behind a glass window. Each tomb is individually decorated with paintings that offer a poignant glimpse of life over a thousand years ago. There is no way you can visit all the burial chambers, but one of the most popular is the **Tomb of the Leopards** where there is a well-preserved banquet scene.

After viewing the tombs, ask the attendant at the gate for directions to the **Museo Nazionale Tarquiniese** which is located in the center of town in the 15th-century **Vitelleschi Palace**. Even if you do not have time to savor all of the beautiful Etruscan vases and handsome carved stone sarcophagi, you must make at least a brief stop to view the astonishing winged horses dramatically displayed in a large room on an upper floor. You will be spellbound by these superb horses on an ornate relief that adorned the altar of the Queen's temple.

After your brush with Etruscan civilization, continue north for approximately 50 kilometers to Scalo/Orbetello where you turn west. The road crosses 6 kilometers of lagoons on a narrow spit of land (going through the town of Orbetello) before reaching the large, bulbous peninsula dominated by Mount Argentario. Turn left when you reach the peninsula to reach the fishing village of **Porto Ercole** or right for the larger port town of **Porto Santo Stefano** where ferryboats depart for the islands of Giglio, Gianutri and Corsica. Beyond the town is a spectacular coastal cliff drive overlooking the sea.

Return to S1 and head north on the highway as it follows the coast. About 35 kilometers before you come to the large city of Livorno (which you want to avoid at all costs), the road divides. One split goes to Livorno and the other becomes the A12, which heads inland and bypasses the city. The next large town after Livorno is **Pisa.** Take the Pisa Nord exit which takes you directly to the city walls and the historic part of the old town. Your target is the **Piazza del Duomo**, a huge square studded by fabulous buildings, including Pisa's landmark, its **Leaning Tower.** However, it is not only the Leaning Tower that makes the Piazza del Duomo such a winner, it is studded with many other magnificent buildings, all of which are outstanding architectural jewels and happily are open to the public as museums. You can buy one ticket allowing entrance to all. Climb to the top of the Leaning Tower (which is once again open for visitors after being strengthened by massive cables). Also, don't miss the breathtaking **Duomo** or the **Baptistery**. Since we first visited Pisa many years ago, an awesome transformation has taken place. The buildings have been scrubbed cleaned and returned to their original splendor, making Pisa a joy to visit.

Leaning Tower of Pisa

About 25 kilometers northeast of Pisa is the extremely picturesque city of **Lucca.** Lucca too is an ancient, perfectly preserved city. Completely surrounding the town is an enormous wall—a wall so wide that it even supports pretty, small parks and a path that runs along the top that is a favorite for joggers. Lucca is truly a jewel. Take time to wander through her maze of narrow streets, admiring imposing mansions and colorful squares.

Leaving Lucca, return to the expressway A12 and head north to Genova. Along the way you see what appears to be a glacier shimmering white in the mountains that rise in the distance to the right of the highway. This is not snow at all, but rather your introduction to the renowned white Italian marble. Detour to visit some of the marble quarries. Exit the highway at Carrara and take the winding drive up into the hills to the ancient village of **Colonnata**—famous through the ages for its marvelous white marble. As you wander this tiny town you're following the footsteps of Michelangelo, who used to come to here to choose huge blocks of marble from which to carve his masterpieces.

Take the small road from Carrara west to join the A12 and continue north for an entirely different kind of experience—exploring the lovely, remote coast called **Cinque Terre**.

This area is quickly becoming linked with civilization, so do not tarry if you love the thrill of discovering old fishing villages hardly touched by time. En route you come to an exit to **La Spezia**, a large seaport and navy town. If you want to take a detour, go to La Spezia and from there take the short drive to the tip of the peninsula south of town to visit the old fishing village of **Portovenere** which clings to the steep rocks rising from the sea. This was one of Lord Byron's haunts when he lived across the bay at **San Terenzo**. After Portovenere, return to the A12 and continue north.

Along the Cinque Terre there used to be five completely isolated fishing villages dotted along the coast between La Spezia to the south and Levanto to the north. First, only a footpath connected these hamlets, then a train was installed, and now civilization is encroaching, with a road under construction, which will open them up to greater commercialism. Three of these little villages, (**Riomaggiore, Monterosso** and **Manarola)** are already accessible by road. Still completely cut off from car traffic are the colorful fishing hamlets of **Vernazza** and **Corniglia**.

If you want to spend the night in one of the villages along the Cinque Terre, **Monterosso al Mare** offers the best selection of accommodations. To reach the town of Monterosso al Mare, exit the A12 at Carrodano and follow signs to Levanto. From Levanto take the road up the hill at the south end of town, signposted Monterosso al Mare. A massive rock formation jutting into the sea divides Monterosso al Mare into two distinct sections that are connected by a train tunnel. You can walk between the two parts of town, but you cannot drive. So if you leave your car in the public parking area, which is located in the "north" village, you will need to take a taxi to places located in the "south" village.

You do not need a car to enjoy the Cinque Terre: this is a region that lures those who love to hike and be out of doors. You can explore the villages by train,

Cinque Terre

boat, or walking: the most fun is to combine all three. If you have the time, plan to spend several days here. If the weather is pleasant, hike the trail that traces the rocky coast and links the villages, stopping for lunch along the way (one of our favorite restaurants is the Pensione Cecio in Corniglia). After lunch, hop aboard one of the frequent trains (each of the towns has a train station and the schedules are clearly posted) or take one of the ferries (which only operate in the summer season) to return "home." Let your mood and the weather dictate your explorations. Although this is a remote coast, be prepared that you will not be alone: the path along the Cinque Terre is popular and always busy—filled with the vacationers who have come to enjoy the natural beauty.

If you have time to see only one of the scenic towns, **Vernazza**, which clings perilously to a rocky headland above a tiny harbor, is the most picturesque. This colorful jewel has brightly painted fishermen's houses, quaint restaurants, a harbor with small boats bobbing in the clear, turquoise water, and a maze of twisting narrow steps that lead up to the promontory overlooking the village.

Leaving Cinque Terre, continue north beside the coast. Stop in **Sestri Levante**, one of the most picturesque coastal villages en route. Continue along the small coastal road that goes through Chiàvari and on to San Margherita where you take the small road south for the short drive to the picture-book village of **Portofino**. This last section of the road, especially in summer, is jammed with traffic, but the prize at the end is worth the trials endured to reach it. Portofino is by no means undiscovered, but is well deserving of its accolades—it is one of the most picturesque tiny harbors in the world.

Portofino is a national treasure—it truly is a jewel. Its tiny harbor is filled with glamorous yachts, small ferries, and colorful fishing boats. Enveloping the harbor are narrow fishermen's cottages, poetically painted in warm tones of sienna, ochre, and pink and all sporting green shutters. Bright flower boxes accent the windows and the laundry flaps gaily in the breeze.

Vivid reflections of these quaint little houses shimmer in the emerald water. In the center of town is a small square, lined with restaurants, which faces the harbor. Forming a backdrop to the town are steep, heavily forested hills, which complete this idyllic scene.

Portofino

When it is time to leave Portofino, return to the A12 highway and continue west for about 30 kilometers to Genova. As you go through the city, watch for the A7 going north to Milan. An interesting detour on the last leg of your journey is the **Pavia Carthusian Monastery** (*Certosa di Pavia*). Probably the simplest way to find it is to watch for the turnoff to Pavia (96 kilometers north of Genova): take the road east to Pavia and from there go north about 10 kilometers to the monastery. Lavishly built in the 15th century, this splendid monastery is claimed by some to be one of the finest buildings in Italy. (Check carefully the days and hours open—the monastery is usually closed on Mondays and for several hours midday.) The outside of the building is lavishly designed with colorful marble and intricate designs. Inside, the small cloisters are especially charming with 122 arches framed by beautiful terracotta moldings. It also has a baroque fountain and several small gardens. Next to the monastery you find the **Palace of the Dukes of Milan**, which is now a museum. After your tour of the monastery it is approximately 26 kilometers farther north to **Milan**.

The outskirts of Milan are not very inviting—you find frustrating traffic and modern commercial buildings. However, the heart of Milan has much to offer. Take time to see Leonardo da Vinci's famous mural, **The Last Supper**, in the church of **Santa Maria delle Grazie**. It is vital that you make an appointment in advance: from the USA call 011-39 (Europe, 00-39) 0289-421146; from within Italy, (199) 19 91 00. The unilingual Italian-speaking reservationists will make you an appointment and give you a confirmation number. Arrive at the church about 15 minutes before your appointment, confirmation number in hand, and pay cash for your ticket.

If you enjoy shopping (and Milan has some of the finest shops in Italy), pay a visit to the splendid **Galleria Vittorio Emanuele**, one of the prettiest shopping arcades in the world. Even if you are not a shopper, you should take time to browse. Located between Milan's other two sightseeing stars, the Duomo and La Scala, the Galleria Vittorio Emanuele is the forerunner of the modern shopping mall, but with much more pizzazz. In this Victorian-era fantasy there are two main, intersecting wings, both completely domed with intricately patterned glass. Along the pedestrian-only arcades you find many boutiques and colorful restaurants with outside tables.

After a stroll through the arcade, you emerge into an imposing square dominated by the truly spectacular **Duomo**, the third-largest cathedral in the world. Not only is the size impressive, but this sensational cathedral has a multicolored marble façade enhanced by over 100 slender spires piercing the sky. This spectacular cathedral faces onto an enormous square lined with cafés, office buildings, and shops. Stop to have a snack at one of the outdoor restaurants—you could sit for hours just watching the people go by.

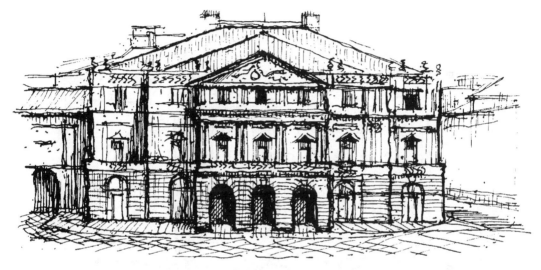

La Scala, Milan

Another site not to be missed is Milan's opera house. Every opera buff knows about **La Scala**. Even if you have not been an opera enthusiast in the past, if you are going to be in Milan during the opera season (which usually runs from December to May), write ahead and try to get tickets. The theater is stunning and an experience not to be missed. When it is not opera season, there is usually some other performance or concert featured. If you haven't purchased seats in advance, you can try to buy them on the day of the performance (the ticket office is located down a flight of stairs to the left of the opera house).

Highlights of Southern Italy

ROME

Abbey of
Monte Cassino

Trani
Polignano
a Mare

Anzio
Nettuno

Castel del Monte
Monopoli

to Corfu-Greece

Naples
Pompeii
Salerno
Matera
Alberobello

Sorrento
Brindisi

Capri
Taranto

Positano
Paestum

Amalfi
Ravello

Maratea
Sibari

●   Orientation/Sightseeing

▬ ▬ ▬   Itinerary route

......   Suggested sidetrips

Messina

Erice
PALERMO
Villa San Giovanni

Trapani

Marsala
Taormina

Selinunte
Enna
Catania

Agrigento
Piazza
Armerina
Siracusa

Rome

Highlights of Southern Italy

Amalfi Coast

Memories of childhood history lessons vaguely call forth such names as Pompeii, Herculaneum, and Paestum, yet, all too frequently, the urge to visit these jewels is lost in the misconception that southern Italy is a rather lackluster destination. What a mistake! Southern Italy has fascinating archaeological sites, appealing medieval towns, white sand beaches and the dazzling Amalfi Coast with its picture-perfect villages. Travelers who venture south from Rome are thrilled when they wander through the fabulous Greek site of Paestum with its splendidly preserved temples rivaling those found in Greece or discover the mysterious town of Alberobello with its twisting streets lined by cute, whitewashed, beehive-like Trulli houses.

Recommended Pacing: Spend a minimum of three nights in Rome. Then, choose one town along the Amalfi Coast and stay for a minimum of five nights so that you will have time to make an excursion to Capri. Your next stop, Maratea, does not have much sightseeing but is a perfect place to relax for a couple of nights. The final destination is near the "heel" of Italy. Choose one place to use as your home base in Apulia and plan to spend at least three nights so that you will have time to explore this remote, beautiful part of Italy.

This itinerary makes a circle of the south in order to suit the travel needs of a wide selection of tourists. Follow the entire route or select the portion best for you since this itinerary is particularly suitable for the traveler who wants to take only a segment. For instance, the journey from Rome to Brindisi is a favorite one for the lucky tourists on their way to Greece, while the west coast is a popular drive for the tourist who wants to visit Sicily and then return to Rome by air or ferry. Most popular of all is the segment from Rome to the Amalfi Drive. This itinerary allows you to custom tailor your journey and gives you tantalizing sightseeing along the way.

Rome is a most convenient starting point to begin a tour of southern Italy, since its airport is the destination of planes from all over the world. In Rome you can immerse yourself in a wealth of history, art, architecture, museums, and monuments—and build a foundation for the sights that will be encountered on your journey southward. For sightseeing suggestions in Rome, refer to the chapter *Italian Highlights by Train & Boat—or Car.*

If you arrive into Rome by plane, do not reserve your rental car until the day of your departure. Just take a taxi to your accommodations or board the train from the airport that whisks you to the center of the city. When it is time to leave Rome, bear in mind that the city has a monumental traffic problem. To guide you, look for strategically placed signs indicating that there is an expressway ahead. It might be quite a distance, but be patient as these signs lead you to the outskirts of Rome to the highway that makes a ring around the city with various spokes going off to different destinations. Follow the ring and take the exit for the A2, the expressway heading south toward Naples. Continue south for approximately 128 kilometers to the exit for **Cassino** where you leave the expressway. Actually, you can spot your destination from several kilometers away—the **Abbey of Monte Cassino** crowns the top of a large mountain to the left of the highway as you drive south. The road that winds up to the summit of the mountain to the Abbey is clearly marked about midway through Cassino. This abbey, founded by St. Benedict in 529 A.D., is extremely interesting both religiously and historically. For war historians it brings back many battle memories—this is where the Germans staunchly held out against the Allied forces for almost a year in World War II. When the mountain was finally conquered in May 1944, it opened the way for the Allies to move into Rome. As you read your history books, it seems strange that one fort could hold out for so long, but when you see the abbey you understand: it is an enormous building on the crest of a precipitous mountain. In the siege the abbey was almost destroyed, but it has been rebuilt according to the original plans.

NOTE: For those of you who for sentimental or for historical reasons are especially interested in World War II, there is another destination you might well want to visit in this day's journey. **Anzio** is a town on the coast about 56 kilometers south of Rome and could easily be included as a stop before Cassino. It was at Anzio that the British and Americans forces landed in January 1944. The emotional reminder of this terrible battle is a few kilometers south at **Nettuno** where 8,000 white crosses and stars of David range—row after row across the green lawn. There is a circular drive around the beautifully manicured, parklike grounds where you also find a memorial chapel and small war museum. For those who lost family or friends during the invasion, there is an information office to the right as you drive in, where you can stop to find out exactly where your loved ones are buried—you will need help because the park is huge.

From Cassino return to the expressway and continue south for about 60 kilometers until you see the sign for **Pompeii**. Unless you have absolutely NO interest in archaeology, you must see the city of your childhood history books. This is where time was frozen in 79 A.D. for the 25,000 people who were smothered by lava from the eruption of **Mount Vesuvius**. If you are a dedicated student of archaeology, you must also visit the **Museo**

Archeologico Nazionale (National Archaeological Museum) in Naples, which houses many of the artifacts from Pompeii.

Time slips back 2,000 years and you feel the pulse of how people lived in ancient times as you wander the streets of Pompeii and visit the temples, lovely homes, wine shops, bakeries, and public baths. Many of the private homes have been reconstructed so you can marvel at the pretty inner courtyards, sumptuous dining rooms in Pompeii-red with intricate paintings on the walls, fountains, servants' quarters, bathrooms, and gardens. At the entrance to Pompeii there are souvenir stands where you can purchase a guidebook to the city, or, if you prefer, you can hire a private guide at the entrance. There is a nice terrace restaurant by the entrance and also a café inside.

Much of what you see today has been reproduced, but the reality is pure. Plaster was poured into molds formed by the lava that demolished the buildings and buried so many families that fateful day. Thus it became possible for latter-day archaeologists to reconstruct houses and make reproductions of people and pets. Walk through the town along the sunken streets crossed by high stepping stones, strategically placed so that pedestrians did not get their feet wet on rainy days. Be sure not to miss some of the reconstructed villas that allow you a glimpse into the daily life of long ago. The **Casa del Fauno**, a fine example of how the wealthy lived, has two inner courtyards and several dining rooms. The **Casa del Poeta Tragico**, a more modest home, has a sign in mosaic saying *Cave Canem* (beware of the dog). At the **Villa di Giulia Felice** you see the example of an entrepreneur—in addition to using it as a private villa, the owner rented out rooms, had shops on the ground floor, and operated an adjacent bathhouse. If traveling with children, you might want to go alone into the **Lupanare** (Pompeii's brothel) where there are erotic paintings on the walls. At the **Terme Stabiane** you see a sophisticated underground water-heating system.

If you have time, visit the nearby ruins of **Herculaneum** which was also buried in the lava of Vesuvius.

Leaving Pompeii, head to the coast in the direction of Sorrento where the **Amalfi Drive** begins, tracing one of the most beautiful stretches of shoreline in the world. Be sure to make the journey in daylight because you want to savor every magnificent vista as well as safely negotiate this extremely twisty and precipitous road.

It is hard to recommend our favorite town along the Amalfi Drive since each has its own personality: **Sorrento**, is an old fishing town perched on a rocky bluff overlooking the sea. It makes an especially convenient place to stay if you want to make a side trip to Capri by ferry or hydrofoil. **Ravello** is a tiny village tucked high in the hills above the coast with absolutely dazzling views down to the sea. **Positano** is an especially romantic coastal town with a picturesque medley of whitewashed houses terracing down an ever-so-steep embankment to a pebble beach dotted with brightly painted fishing boats. **Amalfi** is a small harbor town nestled in a narrow ravine.

From whatever hub you choose as your base, venture out to do some exploring. The traffic during the tourist season is staggering, with buses, trucks, and cars all jockeying for position on the narrow twisting roads. Prepare for much shouting, waving of hands, honking, and general bedlam as long buses inch around the hairpin curves. The best advice is to relax and consider the colorful scene part of the sightseeing. Also, begin your excursions as early in the day as possible to try to avoid the major traffic.

If you are not overnighting in **Ravello**, you must plan to take the narrow winding road up to this romantic clifftop town. When you arrive, leave your car in one of the designated parking areas, pick up a map at the tourist office, then walk along the well-marked path to the **Villa Rufolo** and the **Villa Cimbrone**—both have beautiful gardens that are open to the public and enchanting views of the Bay of Salerno.

If you are not overnighting in **Positano**, by all means make this a day's excursion. The town is a photographer's dream—houses painted a dazzling white step down the impossibly steep hillside to a pebble beach lapped by brilliant blue water. To reach the small plaza dominated by a church topped by a colorful mosaic-tiled dome you have to climb one of the town's many staircases. Today Positano attracts artists and tourists from

Positano

around the world, but in the 16th and 17th centuries it was an important seaport with tall-masted ships bringing in wares from around the world. When steamships came into vogue in the 19th century, Positano's prosperity declined and three-quarters of its population immigrated to the United States.

If you have not been able to include an interlude on **Capri** during your Italian holiday, it is easy to arrange an excursion to this enchanted island as a side trip from the Amalfi Coast. Steamers and hydrofoils depart regularly from Sorrento, Amalfi, and Positano. Ask at the tourist bureau or where you are staying for the schedule.

We also highly recommend spending a day in **Naples**, which, although not on the Amalfi Coast, is conveniently close. Since it is quite difficult to drive into Naples without getting lost, we suggest the following options: Train from Sorrento, boat from Sorrento, or boat from Positano. Naples, the third largest city in Italy, is well worth a side trip; it has many places of interest plus one of the world's finest archaeological museums, the **Museo Archeologico Nazionale,** where most of the original artifacts from Pompeii are displayed. For more in depth suggestions for what to see and do in Naples, read the itinerary *Italian Highlights by Train & Boat—or Car.*

While exploring the Amalfi Coast, be sure to include the **Emerald Grotto**, located between the towns of Amalfi and Positano. After parking, buy a ticket and descend by elevator down the steep cliff to a small rocky terrace. Upon entering the water-filled cave, you're rowed about the grotto in a small boat. Your guide explains how the effect of shimmering green water is created by a secret tunnel allowing sunlight to filter from deep below the surface. The cave is filled with colorful stalactites and stalagmites which further enhance the mysterious mood. There is also a nativity scene below the water which mysteriously appears and then drifts again from view.

When it is time to leave the Amalfi area, take the coastal road south as it twists and turns along the dramatic cliffs toward Salerno. At Salerno, join the expressway A3 for about 19 kilometers until the turnoff for **Paestum** which is located on a side road about a half-hour drive from the freeway. Magically, when you enter the gates of the ancient city, you enter a peaceful environment of a lovely country meadow dotted with some of the world's best-preserved Greek temples. As you walk along the remains of streets crisscrossing the city, your senses are thrilled by the sound of birds singing and the scent of roses.

From Paestum return to the A3 and continue south until you come to the Lagonegro Nord-Maratea exit. Do not be tempted by some of the short cuts you see on the map that lead to the coast, but stay on the main road 585. In about 25 kilometers the road comes to the sea where you turn north at Castrocucco, following signs to **Maratea**. Plan on spending several days in the Maratea area.

Not well known to foreigners, this lovely section of coast, known as the **Gulf of Policastro**, is a popular resort area for Italians. The loveliest section of the road is between Maratea and Sapri where the road traces the sea along a high corniche, providing lovely vistas of small coves and rocky promontories. This is not an area for intensive sightseeing, but provides a quiet interlude for several days of relaxation.

Maratea, Gulf of Policastro

From the Gulf of Policastro, take road 585 back to the A3 and continue south for about 75 kilometers, turning east at Frascineto-Castrovillari toward the instep of Italy's boot. After about 25 kilometers you near the coast. Here you turn left on 106 to **Taranto**. Stop to see this ancient port, which is connected by a bridge to the modern city. Even if you are not interested in ancient history, it is fun to see the Italian naval ships—giant gray monsters—sitting in the protected harbor.

From Taranto take 172 north and continue on for about 45 kilometers following signs to **Alberobello**. You are now in the province of **Apulia**, not a well-known destination, but all the more fun to visit because it is off the beaten path. Choose a place to stay in the area as your hub, venture out to explore the fascinating sights that follow:

Trulli District: Trulli houses (whose origins date back to at least the 13th century) are some of the strangest structures in Italy—circular stone buildings, usually in small clusters, standing crisply white with conical slate roofs and whimsical, twisted chimneys. Outside ladders frequently lead to upper stories. Often several of these houses are joined together to form a larger complex. What a strange and fascinating sight—these beehive-like little houses intertwined with cobbled streets form a jumble of a small village that looks as though it should be inhabited by elves instead of *real* people. The heart of the Trulli region is **Alberobello** where there are so many Trulli houses (more than 1,000 along the narrow streets) that the Trulli district of town has been declared a national monument.

Trulli Houses, Alberobello

Highlights of Southern Italy

Trulli houses are not confined just to the town of Alberobello though this is where you find them composing an entire village. In fact, the Trulli houses you see outside Alberobello are sometimes more interesting than those in the town itself. As you drive along the small roads, you spot gorgeous villas cleverly converted from Trulli houses, now obviously the homes of wealthy Italians. Others are now farmhouses with goats munching their lunch in the front yard. Occasionally you spot a charming old Trulli home nestled cozily in the center of a vineyard. But most fun of all are the Trulli homes of the free spirits: their homes, instead of displaying the typical white exteriors, have been painted a brilliant yellow, pink, or bright green with contrasting shutters.

Grotte di Castellana: As you are exploring the countryside near Alberobello, take the short drive north to see the Castellana Caves—the largest in Italy. In a two-hour tour you see many rooms of richly colored stalagmites and stalactites.

Coastal Villages: Be sure to include in your sightseeing some of the characterful towns along the coast. They look entirely different from the colorful fishing villages in the north of Italy. These are Moorish-looking, with stark-white houses lining narrow, alley-like streets. The Adriatic looks an even deeper blue as it laps against the white buildings, many of which rise from the sea with small windows perched over the water. Besides **Monopoli** other coastal towns to see are **Polignano a Mare** and **Trani**.

Castel del Monte: On the same day that you explore the coastal villages, include a visit to the 13th-century Castel del Monte. Built by Emperor Frederick II of Swab, it is somewhat of a mystery, having none of the fortifications usually associated with a medieval castle. Nevertheless, it is dramatic—a huge stone structure crowning the top of a hill with eight circular towers, which stretch 24 meters into the sky. There are stunning views in every direction.

Matera: Plan one full day to visit Matera, an intriguing town of stark beauty (so extraordinary UNESCO has listed it as a World Heritage site). As you approach Matera, you can't help but wonder what is so special—it looks like quite an ordinary, modern city. But, continue on, following signs for "Sassi." Upon arrival, park your car and go to the central plaza in the heart of the old city. From the plaza, steps lead down to a secreted town beneath, hugging the walls of a steep canyon laced by narrow alley-like lanes and ancient houses. These dwellings, called **Sassi**, have facades fronting cave-like homes. The scene is haunting with a jumble of monotone houses and churches clinging to, and blending with, the hillside. There is not a hint of color to liven the scene. Some scholars think that this site, which began thousands of years ago as cave homes, might well be the oldest inhabited place in Italy. The city had been almost totally abandoned by the mid-1900s, but it is being rediscovered and, as a result, art galleries, restaurants, shops, and a few places to spend the night are reappearing. Mel Gibson is responsible for some of the most recent interest in the town, since he filmed here for his movie, *The Passion of the Christ*. The only way to explore this ancient part of Matera is on foot (the tourist office provides maps with various suggested routes).

When it is time to leave Apulia, you can breeze back to Rome by an expressway. Or, if your next destination is Greece, it is just a short drive to **Brindisi** where you can board the ferry for Corfu, Igoumenitsa, or Patras. Best of all, if you can extend your holiday in Sicily (see *Exploring the Wonders of Sicily* itinerary).

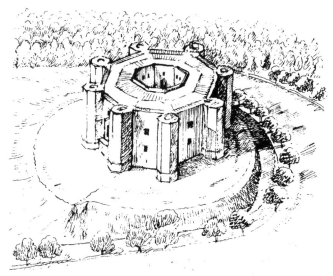

Castel del Monte

Exploring the Wonders of Sicily

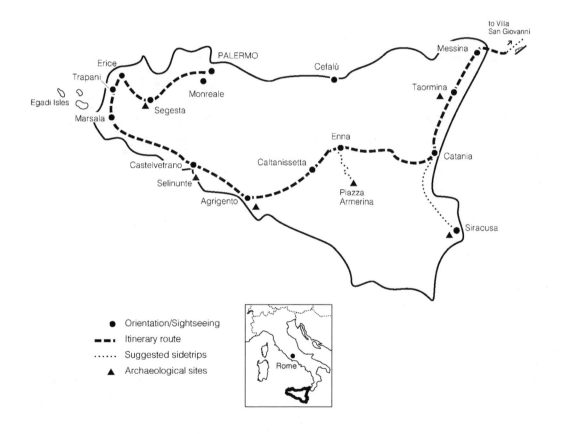

- ● Orientation/Sightseeing
- ■ ■ ■ ■ Itinerary route
- ..... Suggested sidetrips
- ▲ Archaeological sites

Exploring the Wonders of Sicily

Greek Theater, Taormina

Sicily, the largest island in the Mediterranean, is a wondrous destination. This triangular hunk of land jutting out from the tip of Italy's toe became the crossroads of the ancient world. Nowhere in your travels can you discover a more diverse archaeological treasure-trove. Stone-Age tools and figures carved in the Grotta di Addaura at Monte Pellegrino indicate people were living in Sicily during the Paleolithic Age. About 1270 B.C. the island was invaded by a Mediterranean tribe called Siculians, but they were not the only settlers: excavations show the arrival of tribes from Asia. Beginning in the 10th century B.C., pioneering Phoenicians took a fancy to this fertile land, followed later by their descendants, the Carthaginians. However, the true dawn of Sicily's reign of glory began with the colonization by the Greeks whose enormous influence permeates Sicily today. However, the rich fabric of Sicily's heritage does not end with the Greek influence: later the Romans invaded, then the Normans, then the Spanish, and on and on. This resulting melting pot of cultures makes Sicily an absolute MUST for those who delight in the romance of archaeology. The true magic of Sicily is that most of the ruins are so natural in their setting. Frequently you discover you are alone—the only tourist walking through a field of wildflowers to gaze in awe at an exquisite temple.

Recommended Pacing: We recommend a minimum of a week to follow this itinerary. If you are passionate about archaeology, you could stay in Sicily for a month or more to delve in depth with its many glorious sites. Plan to spend two nights in Taormina (one of Sicily's most attractive cities) two nights in Agrigento to see the incredible temples in the *Valle dei Templi*, and then three nights in northwest Sicily (Palermo or another hub) to visit Palermo, Segesta, Monreale, and Erice.

The greatest age of glory for Sicily began when the Greeks founded their first colony here about 770 B.C. Apparently these early Greeks left their native country for economic and political reasons, but many were also undoubtedly motivated by pure curiosity—the desire to discover what awaited across the sea. Like the immigrants who came to America, the early settlers wanted a fresh start in a new land and an opportunity to establish a better life for themselves. And they did. Prospering enormously from the richness of the fertile soil, the early Greeks became extremely wealthy. As the *nouveaux riches* tend to do, they flaunted their success, building great cities, elaborate houses, theaters, spas, and stadiums—all bigger and better than those they left at home. Siracusa, the mightiest city in Sicily, eventually became more powerful than Athens. The temples they built surpassed in size and splendor those left in their native land. Not losing their passion for sports, every four years the new colonialists sent their finest athletes back to Greece where they dominated the Olympic games.

Twice an hour ferries cross the narrow channel from **Villa San Giovanni** to **Messina**, Sicily. After buying your ticket, go to the indicated lane and wait with all the trucks, campers, and other cars for the signal to drive onto the boat. When on board, you may leave your car and go upstairs to the lounge area where you can buy snacks while traversing the short channel. In 35 minutes the large ferry draws up to the pier in Messina and you drive off to begin your adventures.

If you prefer to fly to Sicily, just reverse this itinerary. Start in Palermo and finish in Taormina. Alternatively, you can take a ferry from Naples to Palermo (a ten-hour journey).

Picture-perfect **Taormina** with the dramatic peak of **Mont Etna** as a backdrop, hugs the crest of a small peninsula that juts out to the sea. Steep cliffs drop to the unbelievably blue sea. Quaint streets wind through the colorful town where you can browse in the many smart boutiques, sip a cappuccino at a small café, or simply enjoy the incredible view. The scent of oranges is in the air and brilliantly colored bougainvilleas lace the medieval buildings.

However, it is not just the natural beauty of its spectacular setting that makes Taormina so popular. As in all of Sicily, your leisure pleasure is enhanced with fabulous sights to see. The prime archaeological target for your sightseeing is the **Greek Theater**. From the center of town an easy walk up Via Teatro Greco takes you to a magnificent theater dug into the sloping hillside above the town. Built by the Greeks in the 3rd century B.C., the open-air amphitheater has only a token few of its original columns remaining, making the effect even more romantic. As you gaze beyond the rows of seats to the stage below and out to the vivid blue sea beyond, you will think there is no prettier picture in all of Italy.

After visiting the Greek Theater, most of the remainder of your sightseeing can be done informally while strolling through town. First pick up a map and general information at the tourist office in the **Palazzo Corvaia**, a 15th-century palace located on the Piazza Vittorio Emanuele. From the Palazzo Corvaia, continue through town and stop at the 17th-century **St. Giuseppe Church** in Piazza Nove Aprile. As you walk on, be sure to

Exploring the Wonders of Sicily

step inside the 13th-century **Cathedral** in the Piazza del Duomo to enjoy the paintings. Farther on you come to the 12th-century **Torre dell'Orologio**, the portal that leads into the oldest and most colorful part of Taormina, **Borgo Medieval**.

Leaving Taormina, follow the A18 south toward Catania. When you reach Catania, take the A19 west in the direction of Palermo, then when the highway splits (not long after passing Enna), instead of continuing north to Palermo, head southwest in the direction of Caltanissetta and Agrigento. After Caltanissetta, the expressway ends and you are on a two-lane road for the final leg of your journey to Agrigento.

Along the route from Taormina to Agrigento, we recommend two excursions. It would make your day too long to include them both, but if you get an early start, you will have enough time to squeeze in one of them.

Suggested Excursion I: If you are a Greek history buff, take this 128-kilometer detour to see one of the wealthiest, most powerful cities of the ancient Greek Empire (rivaling only Athens in importance). When you reach Catania, don't turn west toward Palermo, but continue south, following signs to **Siracusa**, founded in 734 B.C. by the Corinthians. In the **Archaeological Park** at the edge of town are two theaters—a 6th-century B.C. **Greek Theater** (one of the most magnificly preserved in the world) and the ruins of a 2nd-century A.D. **Roman Amphitheater** (one of the largest arenas the Romans ever built). From the Archaeological Park, skip the sprawling modern city and cross the Ponte Nuovo that spans Siracusa's harbor to **Ortygia**, the island where the Greeks first founded Siracusa. Visit the two main squares, the beautiful **Piazza del Duomo** where the cathedral (built upon the ancient temple of Minerva) is located and the **Piazza Archimede** enhanced by a baroque fountain. After sightseeing in Siracusa, return to Catania and take A19 west in the direction of Palermo.

Suggested Excursion II: If you are a Roman history buff, take this 74-kilometer round-trip excursion to visit the Villa of Casale. En route from Taormina to Agrigento on the A19, turn south at Enna to **Piazza Armerina**. Continue southwest beyond Piazza Armerina for 5 kilometers to your sightseeing target, the **Villa of Casale**, rivaling in splendor the home built by Tiberius on the island of Capri. The foundations of this sumptuous Roman villa were hidden under a blanket of mud for 700 years—not discovered by archaeologists until 1950. The fact that this ostentatious villa was built when the Roman Empire was on the verge of financial ruin is all the more fascinating. You cannot help wondering if the obviously vast expense of its construction was indicative of the flamboyant spending style that led to the collapse of the Roman Empire.

Built in the 3rd century A.D., this mansion surely must have belonged to someone of enormous importance—perhaps Emperor Maximilian. The ruins are beautifully displayed in a covered museum with walkways guiding you from one opulent room to the next, each overlooking courtyards. But don't start until you have studied a mockup as you

enter showing an artist's rendering of what the huge villa looked like in its prime—a look at this will increase your appreciation of the incredible grandeur of what you will be seeing. In all, the home covers an area almost three times the size of a football field. The outstanding feature is the 3,500 square meters of mosaics that decorated the floors of this splendid villa. Following the home's foundations are 40 amazing mosaic floors of extraordinary quality. These beautifully preserved ancient Roman mosaics are considered the finest in the world. Slip back almost 1,700 years and imagine what life must have been like: the scenes show hunting expeditions, wild animals, mythical sea creatures, chariot races, cupids fishing, slaves working, girls cavorting. Once you have visited this Roman showplace, return north to Enna, then turn west following the route to Agrigento.

Agrigento is a congested, not very pretty city. We recommend you stay instead outside the heart of the city near the archeological zone. Follow the signs for the **Valle dei Templi**. The name is misleading: the archeological site is actually on a plateau to the west of town—not in a valley at all.

Plan to spend two nights in Agrigento so that you can spend one entire day leisurely seeing the ruins. A wide pedestrian road connects the temples—start at one end and savor the haunting beauty of each. Most of these Doric temples are in ruins, with only enough columns remaining to give you an idea of what they used to be in their glory. The best preserved is the **Temple of Concord** which dates back to 440 B.C. See them all: the **Temple of Juno**, the **Temple of Hercules**, the **Temple of Dioscuri**, the **Temple of Jupiter**, and the **Temple of Castor and Pollux**. The setting is beautiful with the sea in the distance and colorful wildflowers in the surrounding fields. It is a thrill to stroll from one temple to the other, marveling at their grandeur and trying to envision what these incredible structures dedicated to Greek gods looked like 2,000 years ago.

To complement your sightseeing at the temples, take a walk to the **Archaeological Museum**. The museum has a mock-up of the Temple of Jupiter, plus many vases and artifacts from the site.

From Agrigento, continue west on 115 toward Castelvetrano. About 10 kilometers before you arrive in Castelvetrano, turn left onto the 115 dir toward the coast, signposted to Selinunte. For such major ruins, there is little commercialism. You might well miss the main east entrance on the 115 dir—as you drive toward the coast, look for a parking area to the right of the road (if you go under the railroad tracks, you have gone too far).

Park your car in the designated area, buy your ticket, and walk through the tunnel into the enormous field where the remains of the temples of Selinunte lie scattered amongst the wildflowers. In its prime, **Selinunte** was one of the finest cities in Sicily. It met disaster in 407 B.C. when the Carthaginians (it is thought under the command of Hannibal) razed the city, slaughtered 16,000 people, and took thousands into slavery. The giant temples, however, were probably destroyed by earthquake, not by the sword. Here, spread along a huge plateau overlooking the ocean, are the impressive remains of some of the most gigantic temples built by the Greeks. It is staggering to imagine how more than 2,500 years ago they had the skill and technology to lift and piece together these huge blocks of stone weighing over 100 tons each (slaves undoubtedly helped). Of the original seven temples, only one has been reconstructed, but the massive columns lying on the ground indicate the scope and grandeur of what used to be.

From Selinunte, return to the 115, taking the coastal route to Erice. En route, stop for lunch at one of the restaurants along the seafront promenade in **Mazara del Vallo**, an ancient city that was at one time a colony of Selinunte. Browse through the historic center of town to see the beautiful **Piazza della Repubblica** and the **Cathedral**.

The next large town after Mazara del Vallo is **Marsala**, a city well known throughout the world for its excellent wine. Ironically, it was not an Italian, but an Englishman, named John Woodhouse, who experimented by lacing the native wine with an extra bit of alcohol. Based on Woodhouse's formula, Marsala quickly became one of the staples of the British Navy and a special favorite of Lord Nelson. Along the road between Selinunte and Marsala are various wineries that are open to the public. One of the most popular is the **Florio Winery**—one of the three original companies to produce Marsala.

From Marsala, the road heads north to Trapani. Bypass Trapani and head northeast to **Erice**. Positioned over 750 meters above the coast (about 10 kilometers from Trapani), Erice is a delightful medieval walled town, cooled by breezes from the sea. Park your car and walk through the **Porta Trapani** and up the cobbled street. Erice is best discovered by exploring on foot. Narrow cobblestone streets and steep stairways form a maze throughout the town, which is so small that you cannot get lost for long. Just wander, discovering tiny old churches, picturesque squares, characterful stone houses, arcaded passageways, and shops selling the locally produced handmade carpets with colorful geometric designs. Walk to the Castello Normanno, built

Erice, Sicily

upon the ruins of the Temple of Venus. From the tower you have a splendid view looking over the town of Trapani and out to the sea.

If you like to get off the beaten path, from Erice drive down to Trapani and take a hydrofoil to the **Egadi Isles**, all less than an hour away. Just a short distance off shore, **Favignana**, the largest of the three islands, was once a great center for tuna. The major cannery was owned by Ignazio Florio (the same Florio who founded the Florio Winery). **Levanzo**, the smallest of the islands, has a very small population due to its lack of fresh water. The island farthest from Trapani, **Maréttimo**, is basically a fishermen's island.

Wind down the hill from Erice and turn left on the A29 going east in the direction of Palermo. Thirty kilometers after getting on the freeway, take the Segesta exit and follow signs for the **Segesta** archaeological site, located close the highway. Although you have seen many ruins by this stage of your holiday in Sicily, don't miss this one—it is special. First drive to the designated parking area and walk up the hillside to visit what most experts believe to be the world's finest example of a **Doric temple**. The temple with 36 columns looks much as it must have in 400 B.C. There is no roof—there never was because this isolated temple to some unknown god was never completed. One of the most superb aspects of this temple is its setting—there is nothing to jar the senses. The temple stands alone in a field of wildflowers with great natural beauty all around. Enjoy the romance of this gem at your leisure, then drive down the hill and park your car by the information center where there is a nice restaurant. Eat lunch here and then walk the marked path to see the Greek Theater. It is about a kilometer away, but a lovely walk through untouched fields. There are so few signs, you'll wonder if you are going the right way and be tempted to verify your destination with a fellow tourist you pass en route. Again, the location is what makes this theater so special. What an eye the Greeks had for beauty: the stage is set in such a way that the spectators look out across the mountains to the sea. The theater is mostly in ruins, but sit on one of the ancient benches, enjoy the beautiful surroundings, and imagine dramas that took place over 2,000 years ago.

Continue to **Palermo**. Palermo is a commercial, traffic-congested city, but there are some very interesting places to see both within the city and on its outskirts.

The most dramatic sightseeing excursion (just 8 kilometers south of Palermo) is to visit **Monreale**, an awesome cathedral built by William II in 1174. It seems that William II was visited in a dream by an angel who told him of a secret treasure, and with his new-found wealth he built Monreale, one of the world's greatest medieval monuments. From the outside, the cathedral doesn't look special, but just wait: the interior is stunning. When you step inside you find 130 panels of shimmering mosaic, illustrating stories from both the Old and the New Testaments. The bronze doors of the cathedral are spectacular, designed by Bonanno Pisano in the 12th century. This is a cathedral not to be missed.

Another sight near Palermo is **Monte Pellegrino**, a 600-meter mountain rising on the west edge of the city. There are several caves in the mountain. The **Grotta di Addaura** is a three-chamber cave with carvings dating to the Paleolithic Age. Another cave has been transformed into a chapel, the **Sanctuary of Santa Rosalia**, commemorating Santa Rosalia, the niece of King William II, who became a hermit—living and dying in this cave. You need to obtain permission from the National Archaeological Museum in Palermo if you want to visit these caves.

Another recommended side trip from Palermo is to visit the ancient fishing village of **Cefalù** built on a rocky peninsula about an hour's drive east from Palermo. Not only is this a very colorful fishing village, complete with brightly-hued boats and twisting narrow streets, but there is also a splendid Norman **Cathedral** built by King Roger II in the 12th century in fulfillment of a promise he made to God for sparing his life during a storm at sea.

From Palermo you can take one of the many flights to Rome, board a ferry to Naples, or complete your circle of Sicily by driving to Messina for the short ferry ride back to the mainland.

Taormina, Greek Theater

Exploring the Wonders of Sicily

Places to Stay

A pleasant, budget choice for touring the Veneto region is found just outside Padua at Casa Ciriani, where Silvana and her mother, Mariantonia, thoroughly enjoy the international cultural exchange that their bed and breakfast business brings. Within the large family home, where Silvana grew up, are four simply decorated, homey bedrooms. All the bedrooms have a private, en suite bathroom (except one whose bath is located just outside the guestroom door). A bedroom with king bed, plus a twin bedroom combination and a bathroom, serves families well. The decor is much as it was before being converted to a bed and breakfast, complete with family photos, drawings, and other personal artifacts. Guests enjoy the large yard, and outside terrace overlooking the garden and grounds, where a breakfast of breads, cereals, fruit, cakes, and yogurt is served during the summer. Guests are also welcome to bring their own food and picnic. For those who love to explore, walks are organized on the nearby hills or tours of local wineries and artisans. Silvana be happy to teach guests over breakfast a few essential phrases that will make you feel comfortable shopping and ordering in restaurants. *Directions:* From Milan, exit the A4 at Padova Ovest and follow signs for Abano (10 km); from the south on A13, exit at Terme Euganee. Silvana can send a map.

CASA CIRIANI
Host: Silvana Ciriani
Via Guazzi 1
Abano Terme, (PD) 35031, Italy
Tel & Fax: (049) 715272
Cellphone: (368) 3779226
4 Rooms, Double: €65–€80
Family room: €112–€132
Minimum Stay Required: 2 nights
Open: all year, Credit cards: none
Other Languages: good English, German, French
Region: Veneto, Michelin Map: 562

In the heart of the wine valley of Piedmont, just above the town of Alba, lies the stately, cream-colored villa belonging to Giuliana, her doctor husband Giuseppe, and sons Andrea and Fabrizio—Cascina Reine's warm and gracious hosts. Accommodation is offered within the ivy-covered main house, each room finely decorated with antiques, paintings, and the family's personal collectibles. A suite consisting of a bedroom, sitting room with two extra beds, bath, kitchenette, and large terrace is ideal for a family of four. Other equally charming rooms and apartments (one with facilities for the handicapped) are on the ground and first floors of the adjoining wing, one with its own private terrace. A full breakfast is served either outside under big umbrellas overlooking the vineyards and woods or inside in the pristine dining room with vaulted ceilings. A swimming pool is set in the best possible position taking in views over the city, soft hillsides, river valley, and distant Alps. Alba boasts some of the finest restaurants in Italy and is also famous for its regional wines and prized truffle festival. The Giacosas have a piece of land dedicated to experimentation (with Torino University) of the cultivation of truffles. *Directions:* From Alba's center follow signs for Barbaresco and Mango. Halfway up the hill on a large curve, watch for a small white sign indicating a gravel road on the left and then the wrought-iron gates of the property at the end of the road.

CASCINA REINE (VILLA LA MERIDIANA)
Host: Giacosa family
Localita: Altavilla 9, Alba, (CN) 12051, Italy
Tel & Fax: (0173) 440112
Cellphone: (338) 4606527
5 Rooms, Double: €85–€95, 1 Suite: €95–€100
4 Apartments: €95 daily
Minimum Stay Required: 2 nights
Open: all year, Credit cards: MC, VS
Other Languages: good English
Region: Piedmont, Michelin Map: 561

This historic ex-convent dating back a thousand years is the oldest of the aristocratic Venetian Villas in the area of the Brenta canal, impeccably restored by descendants of the original aristocratic family. Guests have an extraordinary opportunity for a brief moment, to live the life of the Villa-Museum along with hosts who passionately recount the history of the property, its artifacts, original architecture details from various periods (medieval floors, renaissance frescoes, antiques and paintings). The elongated u-shaped home with front rose garden and romantic park (including a big, beautiful pool and lake with swans) incorporates the private residence, servants quarters, chapel, cloisters and barns. Rooms on the main floor, each more fascinating than the next, include the salon with its grand piano, libraries, and veranda where breakfast is served by the butler. Your host is a surgeon with a passion for vintage cars and car racing. Three of the seven junior suites adjoin an elegant salon—ideal for a group of friends. Bedrooms are appointed in style with canopy beds and antique furnishings. Another hall is dedicated to the extra features such as sauna, gym, solarium and massage treatments. *Directions:* Halfway between Venice and Padova, take the at Dolo exit from the autostrada and go for 2.5 km (passing two roundabouts). Before Dolo turn right for Albarea and follow the historical brown signs to the villa.

VILLA RIZZI ALBAREA
Hosts: Aida & Pierluigi Rizzi
Via Albarea, 53, Pianiga di Venezia
Albarea di Venezia, (VE) 30030, Italy
Tel: (041) 5100933, Fax: (041) 5132562
Cellphone: (348) 2681216
7 Rooms, Double: €195–€285, 3 Suites: €225–€295
1 Apartment: €295 daily, €1950 weekly
Minimum Stay Required: 2 nights
Open: all year, Credit cards: all major
Other Languages: English, French, German
Region: Veneto, Michelin Map: 562

On the island's west coast you find the ancient port town of Alghero, Sardinia's lobster and coral capital. With origins dating back as far as 1100, the walled seaside village still preserves evidence of a strong Spanish influence. The road bordering the coast takes you past the archaeological site of Palmavera with its typical Nuraghi construction from the Bronze Age; the bay of Porto Conte with its nature park; and the Capo Caccia scenic point with the fascinating Nettuno cave. In the near vicinity is the Porticciolo agritourism farm, named after the ancient watchtower on the coast. The flat property made up of cultivated fields surrounds the simple white rectangular house and restaurant. Like most farms in Sardinia, buildings are of recent construction as the agritourism is in its early stages. Just behind the building that houses the restaurant are six separate guesthouses for four persons each with a bedroom, bathroom, loft bed, and living area with kitchenette, nicely appointed with wood furnishings and wrought-iron beds. There is also a play area for children. The enormous glassed-in dining room with fireplace where fish and meats are grilled is where Maria and her entire family work together presenting delectable Sardinian specialties topped off with the island's myrtle-berry cordial. Local products from the farm are sold here. *Directions:* From Alghero (16 km) take the S.S.127 to Fertilla; go past Porto Conte Bay; turn right for S.M. La Palma. Turn left at the first road to Porticciolo.

PORTICCIOLO
Host: Maria Angius Floris family
Localita: Porticciolo, Alghero, (SS) 07041, Italy
Tel & Fax: (079) 918000
Cellphone: (347) 5231024
6 Rooms, Double: €40–€45
6 Apartments: €700–€1000 weekly
Open: May to Oct, Credit cards: all major
Other Languages: very little English
Region: Sardinia, Michelin Map: 566

Having made the decision to return to her native Italy after years in Venezuela, Liria elected to do it in style. She bought a 200-acre estate in the virgin hills north of Orvieto and set about restoring the four abandoned stone houses which once made up a farmer's village. Her natural flare for integrating soft muted color tones, gorgeous French fabrics and selected antiques has resulted in a refined and romantic country ambiance throughout. The five spacious bedrooms with canopy beds in the main house are tastefully appointed and harmonize well with handmade terracotta brick floors and original stone walls so typical of an Umbrian home. Two 2-bedroom apartments are found in an adjacent house complete with kitchenette and living room for longer stays. Alternatively you could rent an entire two-story house with three bedrooms. Sweeping valley views over soft green hills are enjoyed from any position whether it be out in the lavender garden surrounding the curved swimming pool or on the main terrace where most meals are served. The farm produces organic olive oil, wine, grain, honey and fruits. *Directions:* From the A1 autostrada exit at Fabro and turn right for Allerona. Pass through the town center of Fabro and continue for 5 km and fork left for Allerona Scalo. After 3.2 km turn right and stay to the right for the next two forks until you come to Monticchio.

I CASALI DI MONTICCHIO
Host: Liria Costantino family
Vocabolo Monticchio 34, Allerona, (TR) 05011, Italy
Tel: (0763) 628365, Fax: (0763) 629569
10 Rooms, Double: €200–€520
2 Apartments, €1500–€2500 weekly
Minimum Stay Required: 2 nights
Open: all year, Credit cards: MC, VS
Other Languages: good English, Spanish
Region: Umbria, Michelin Map: 563

Seven kilometers from historic Bergamo and within easy reach of beautiful Lakes Como, Iseo, and Garda is the home of the region's agritourist former president, Gianantonio Ardizzone. On the property, next to the recently constructed residence where he and his family live, is a sprawling 15th-century farmhouse and barn quad complex of the type known in Lombardy as a cascina. Installed within the cascina are five guest apartments, each including one or two bedrooms, bathroom, and kitchen (though breakfast is served). The apartments are furnished modestly but comfortably, with a decidedly rustic ambiance. The cascina is nestled in pretty surroundings, looking onto the small town of Nese and backing onto the green hills where well-tended riding horses are kept. Gianantonio delights in showing guests his hobbies—a collection of antique farm tools, fruit orchard, and ostrich breeding—and wife Lalla takes care of guests' daily requests including dinner with prior confirmation. The Grumello offers self-catering, conveniently located accommodation and outstanding value. Your hosts are exceptionally helpful and sincerely warm. *Directions:* Exit from the A4 autostrada at Bergamo and follow signs for Alzano Lombardo, Valle Seriana. Exit at Alzano after 6 km and follow hospital signs; go straight on for Nese and turn left on Via Grumello after 300 meters.

CASCINA GRUMELLO
Host: Gianantonio Ardizzone family
Localita: Fraz. Nese
Alzano Lombardo, (BG) 24022, Italy
Tel: (035) 510060, Fax: (035) 513210
Cellphone: (340) 2487185
5 Apartments: Double: €63–€68
Open: all year, Credit cards: VS
Other Languages: some English
Region: Lombardy, Michelin Map: 561

In the area referred to as the very center of Italy, facing the Laga and Sibillini mountains, is the historic home of Signor Sanguigni and his wife, who retired to Amatrice after a lifetime in Rome. At the very edge of the small village, the tall stone country home with surrounding garden, has been carefully restored respecting and conserving its unique features, white stone exposed walls, brick floors and beamed ceilings. The same care and attention has been given to the interiors, tastefully and simply decorated with just the right antiques and soft color choices as to not disturb the serene ambiance. Breakfast is served either in the garden or at one long table in the stone-walled dining room with an enormous gray-stone fireplace. On the two upper floors are the two sitting rooms and five country style guest bedrooms with wrought iron beds and fine embroidered linens. The large corner room has breathtaking views out towards the mountains. This is a great area for nature lovers with many hiking possibilities in the nearby National Park, horseback riding, and even hang-gliding. This far reach of the Lazio region borders Umbria, the Marches, and Abruzzo regions with the Adriatic sea at a distance of 50 km. *Directions:* From Rome take the S.S. 4, a historic Roman road that goes through Amatrice and down to the Adriatic sea. Five km before Amatrice turn off for Bagnolo. The house's gate is on the right hand side before town.

VILLA SANGUIGNI
Host: Domenico Sanguigni
Bagnolo Di Amatrice
Amatrice, (RI) 02012, Italy
Tel & Fax: (0746) 821075
5 Rooms, Double: €90–€100
Closed: Nov & Feb, Credit cards: none
Other Languages: English spoken well
Region: Lazio, Michelin Map: 563

One of the most attractive features of Florence is that its surrounding countryside hugs the city limits, giving the possibility of staying in the tranquil foothills of Chianti. In the nearby village of Antella warm hosts Azelio and Luisa have completely restored their part of an enormous estate divided into three 14th-century villas. The downstairs area includes a large living/dining room, main kitchen, and separate kitchenette for guests' use during the day. The vaulted antique cantina below displays an enviable collection of reserve wines. Up a steep flight of stairs are the well-appointed guestrooms, all with superb views over countryside all the way to Brunelleschi's cupola. The bedrooms are double-bedded, individually decorated with country antiques and one has a hydro-jet bathtub. The real treat is the large junior suite with its high wood-beamed mansard ceilings, sitting area, and canopy bed. Originally the outdoor loggia, it retains its columns and seven windows looking out to both sides of the property. A country breakfast is served either in the small breakfast room or in the garden. Do not miss a chance to sample one of Luisa's delectable Tuscan meals or, better yet, cooking lessons. *Directions:* Leave the A1 at Firenze Sud. After the toll, turn first right for Siena and after about 1.5 km turn left for Antella. In Antella the Via Montisoni starts from the square with the church on your left.

VILLA IL COLLE
Hosts: Azelio & Luisa Pierattoni
Via Montisoni 45
Antella–Florence, (FI) 50011, Italy
Tel & Fax: (055) 621822
Cellphone: (347) 8778178
4 Rooms, Double: €90–€120
1 Suite: €120–€160
Minimum Stay Required: 2 nights
Open: all year, Credit cards: MC, VS
Other Languages: good English
Region: Lazio, Michelin Map: 563

The Marches, bordering the Adriatic and continuing inland with rolling green hills reaching to the Apennine mountains, is a region full of historic, cultural and gastronomic discoveries. Taking the road inland from the sea at Senigallia for 30 km you arrive at the village of Palazzo. Just beyond is the 1400-acre wooded property of the Bartoletti family. Dynamic hostess, artist and sculptor, Francesca Romana transformed the family property, originally hunting grounds, into a nature lover's resort. Activities range from guided Jeep or quad bike tours to hiking, horseback riding, biking, swimming and tennis. A full spa features body and face treatments. Guestrooms and apartments are scattered about the estate in charming natural stone houses decorated in country style with modern bathrooms. Some apartments have a fireplace while others feature exposed stone walls and brick floors. Highlights include country furnishings accented with crisp and colorful fabrics and top-quality linens. Guests gather at the reception/panoramic restaurant for well-prepared meals based on local recipes, using ingredients produced in-house, including fresh pastas. A friendly and energetic staff is always available to arrange activities. *Directions:* Exit the A14 at Senigallia, turn left and then go right for Corinaldo an Castellone di Suasa. Proceed through Castelleone di Suasa towards Arcevia. After 10 km enter Palazzo di Arcevia and follow signs up to the Tenuta.

TENUTA SAN SETTIMIO
Host: Francesca Romana Bartoletti
Palazzo di Arcevia, Arcevia, (AN) 60011, Italy
Tel: (0731) 9905, Fax: (0731) 9912
12 Rooms, Double: €146–€178
8 Apartments: €800–€2200 weekly
Minimum Stay Required: 7 in apartments
Open: Mar to 7 Jan, Credit cards: all major
Region: Marches, Michelin Map: 563

On the crest between the Amalfi coast and Sorrento, Villa Giusso, once a 16th-century monastery for cloistered monks is a unique bed and breakfast. A long, very narrow road takes you up to the isolated, stone-walled property whose entrance is marked by an arched gateway with watchtower leading into a park. From there you have an enthralling view over Sorrento, the gulf, and Naples. The monastery itself is surrounded by a high stone wall within which is found a grass courtyard and ancient well still in use. The Giusso family has owned this beloved property for the past 200 years and siblings Onorina, Giovanna, Micaela, and Tullio continue the restoration process while preserving its monastic features. Several cells have been converted into two apartments suitable for four people. A long corridor leads to a suite and three double bedrooms, appointed with worn period furniture and huge paintings. Breakfast with local fresh ricotta, figs in season, and homemade cakes is served in the original kitchen tiled with 17th-century handcrafted Vietri ceramic. On display is an interesting collection of ancient objects. Though not for everyone, Villa Giusso is fascinating and offers the visitor a unique slice of Italian history. *Directions:* Exit the A3 at Castellammare (signed Sorrento). Drive to Seiano and just after Moon Valley Hotel take a left at the sign for Monte Faito. Drive to the Arola sign (4.6 km) and go first right up the narrow dirt road to the monastery.

VILLA GIUSSO
Host: Giusso Rispoli family
Localita: Arola, Via Camaldoli 51
Arola, (NA) 80069, Italy
Tel: (081) 8024392, Fax: (081) 403797
Cellphone: (329) 1150475
5 Rooms, Double: €90–€110, 1 Suite: €170–€190
2 Apartments: €650–€800 weekly
Open: Apr to Oct 30, Credit cards: none
Other Languages: good English
Region: Campania, Michelin Map: 564

The delightful Malvarina farm with its charming, country-style accommodations, excellent local cuisine, warm and congenial host family, and ideal location has been a long-time favorite of our readers. Just outside town, yet immersed in lush green vegetation at the foot of the Subasio Mountains, the property is comprised of the 15th-century stone farmhouse where the family lives and four independent cottages (converted barn and stalls) divided into bedrooms and suites with en suite bathrooms, plus three apartments with kitchenettes for two to four persons. Casa Angelo has several bedrooms plus a sweet breakfast room with a corner fireplace and cupboards filled with colorful Deruta ceramics. Great care has obviously been taken in the decor of rooms, using Mamma's family heirloom furniture. The old wine cellar has been cleverly converted into a cool and spacious taverna dining room with long wooden tables for dining "en famille" if not out on the veranda terrace. Cooking classes are very popular here. A collection of antique farm tools and brass pots cover walls near the enormous fireplace. Horses are available for three- to seven-day trekking trips into the scenic national park just beyond the house, led by gregarious hosts, Claudio and Filippe. A welcome feature is a swimming pool. *Directions:* Exit at Rivotorto from the Perugia-Spello route 75. Turn right then left on Via Massera (Radio Subasio sign) and follow the road up to Malvarina.

MALVARINA
Host: Claudio Fabrizi family
Localita: Malvarina 32, Assisi, (PG) 06080, Italy
Tel & Fax: (075) 8064280
9 Rooms, Double: €93
3 Suites: €105–€140
3 Apartments: €98 daily, €670 weekly
Minimum Stay Required: 3 nights
Open: all year, Credit cards: MC, VS
Other Languages: some English
Region: Umbria, Michelin Map: 563

Fabrizio and Bianca, the Milanese hosts originally from this part of Umbria, restored their farmhouse, situated in the very desirable location just 2 km from Assisi, with their guests' comfort foremost in mind. With careful attention to detail, six comfortable apartments and two guestrooms were fashioned within the three stone houses. Each apartment has one or two bedrooms, bathroom, fully equipped kitchenette, and eating area. Interesting decorating touches such as parts of antique iron gates hung over beds, terracotta and white ceramic tiles in the immaculate bathrooms, and antique armoires give the accommodations a polished country flavor. Le Pannocchie includes a corner fireplace, while Papaveri looks out over the flat cornfields up to magnificent Assisi and the Subasio Mountains beyond. Ambra looks after guests when the owners are away. A small dining room has been created on the ground floor, next to the 18th-century wood oven, for morning breakfast. At guests' request cooking classes and guided tours are arranged to Umbria's top sights. A lovely swimming pool, barbecue area, small gym, bikes, ping pong, and games for children are available for guests. *Directions:* From Perugia-Spoleto highway 75, exit at Ospedalicchio on route 147, turn left for Tordibetto after the bridge, then right for Assisi and follow signs for La Fornace.

PODERE LA FORNACE
Hosts: Bianca & Fabrizio Feliciani
Via Ombrosa 3, Tordibetto
Assisi, (PG) 06081, Italy
Tel: (075) 8019537, Fax: (075) 8019630
Cellphone: (338) 9902903
2 Rooms, Double: €65–€95*
6 Apartments: €70–€195 daily, €430–€1200 weekly*
*Breakfast not included: €6, Minimum Stay Required
Closed: Jan & Feb, Credit cards: all major
Other Languages: good English
Region: Umbria, Michelin Map: 563

Bagno Vignoni is a charming little village whose unique piazza is actually an ancient stone pool with thermal water. In medieval times the large bath was divided for men and women who came to soak in the rejuvenating waters, hoping to cure such ailments as arthritis and rheumatism. Today, tourists come to view this remarkable place and take advantage of these same curative properties in the nearby falls or modern pool facilities. With the success of their wine bar ("enoteca") here, it was only natural that the young Marinis should open a bed and breakfast for travelers. The stone building dates to the 1300's and was thoughtfully restored after having been abandoned for more than 30 years. The eight double bedrooms and large living room with loft and grand piano are very cozy and purposely old-fashioned in feeling. The beamed guestrooms and nice new bathrooms each have their own theme and corresponding soft pastel color schemes and are romantically appointed with lace curtains and pillows, antique beds and armoires, and painted stencil borders. Breakfast is served across the way in the historic enoteca, which was once part of the Capuchin friars' monastery. With its informal and warm hospitality, it is no wonder that the bar is a favorite place for artists and writers. *Directions:* Bagno Vignoni is 5 km south of San Quirico. Park in the town lot and walk the short distance to the locanda.

LA LOCANDA DEL LOGGIATO
Hosts: Sabrina & Barbara Marini
Piazza del Moretto 30, Bagno Vignoni, (SI) 53023, Italy
Tel: (0577) 888925, Fax: (0577) 888370
Cellphone: (335) 430427
8 Rooms, Double: €130–€150
Minimum Stay Required: 2 nights
Open: all year, Credit cards: MC, VS
Other Languages: some English, French
Region: Tuscany, Michelin Map: 563

After many years of traveling to Italy at any opportunity, Jennie and Alan left England to move to Tuscany and fell in love immediately with Villa Mimosa, a rustic, 18th-century home with a shady front courtyard facing the village street and the church. They have created three sweet bedrooms and one attic mansard suite for four persons, each with a different theme and lovely mountain views. A cozy sitting room and a library with grand piano are reserved upstairs for guests and decorated with the Pratts' own antiques imported from England. Jennie and Alan delight in sharing their passion for this part of the country known as Lunigiana (very near the Cinque Terre coastal area and one hour from both Parma and Lucca) and give their guests lots of personal attention, while making them feel right at home. Guests are treated to breakfast on the terrace overlooking the pretty garden and swimming pool with the Apennine Mountains as a backdrop and delight in Jennie's creative cuisine straight off the Aga, based on fresh garden vegetables and local recipes. Tea and homemade cakes are served in the shady garden. *Directions:* Leave the A15 autostrada (Parma-La Spezia) at Pontremoli from the north or Aulla from the south and take the autostrada S.S.62 to Villafranca, then Bagnone. Enter town through the yellow gateway, then over the bridge. Turn left following signs for Corlaga, and the villa is on the right 50 meters before the church.

VILLA MIMOSA
Hosts: Jennie & Alan Pratt
Localita: Corlaga, Bagnone, (MS) 54021, Italy
Tel & Fax: (0187) 427022
Cellphone: (335) 6264657
4 Rooms, Double: €80–€120
Open: all year, Credit cards: none
Other Languages: fluent English
Region: Tuscany, Michelin Map: 563

One of many wonders of Italy is that within a few kilometers, the landscape, wines, food, traditions and dialect change dramatically. Such is the case with the area of Lazio, between Orvieto and Viterbo, where rolling green hills transform into a gray crater-like landscape caused by soil erosion. Bagnoregio is a sleepy town often mentioned because of its smaller neighboring village Civita Bagnoregio, a recently re-inhabited protected village of Etruscan origins (population had dwindled down to 12 at one point). The village is accessed only by a foot bridge, and is surrounded by a dramatic valley of volcanic tufo rock used to build the local houses. You can explore Civita Bagnoregio from the Romantica Pucci. Hosts Pucci and Lamberto are retired and warmly welcome guests into their 200-year-old home. Five bright, comfortable and romantic bedrooms are named after flowers and have an old-fashioned feel with canopy antique beds, lace doilies and curtains, floral bedspreads and soft colors. The showers are particularly spacious. Family items give a homey feel to the place and the rustic style restaurant serves typical home-style meals, which are well worth a side trip. *Directions:* From the north exit Autostrada A1 at Orvieto and follow signs to Lago di Bolsena, then Montefiascone on SS71, turning off for Bagnoregio after 1 km. Follow signposts for the town center.

HOTEL ROMANTICA PUCCI
Hosts: Pucci & Lamberto Perno
Piazza Cavour 1
Bagnoregio, (VT) 01022, Italy
Tel & Fax: (0761) 792121
5 Rooms, Double: €80–€85
Open: all year, Credit cards: MC, VS
Region: Lazio, Michelin Map: 563

In the heart of the Veneto region, south of Vicenza, you find the Castello winery and estate, a handsome 15th-century villa watching proudly over the sweet town of Barbarano Vicentino and the home of the Marinoni family for the past century. Signora Elda, along with her two young children, Lorenzo and Maddalena, carries on the tradition. The large walled courtyard with manicured Renaissance garden is bordered by the family's home, the guesthouse (originally the farmer's quarters), and converted barn, where concerts and banquets are organized. A lovely courtyard overlooks the family's expansive vineyards from which top-quality (D.O.C.G.) red wines are produced. The independent two-story guesthouse overlooking the garden can be rented out as one house or divided into three apartments. Each apartment has one or two bedrooms, bathroom, and kitchenette with sitting area, and is decorated simply but pleasantly with the family's furnishings. This is an excellent, economical base from which to visit the beautiful Veneto region. It's an easy drive to Padua and Venice where you may opt to leave your car and take the train. *Directions:* Exit from the A4 at Vicenza Est towards Riviera Berica, then Barbarano Vicentino. From the center of town, follow signs to Il Castello (20 km total).

IL CASTELLO
Host: Elda Marinoni family
Via Castello 6, Barbarano Vicentino, (VI) 36021, Italy
Tel: (0444) 886055, Fax: (0444) 777140
3 Apartments: €26–€29 daily, per person*
*Apartment rental, no breakfast offered
Minimum Stay Required: 3 nights
Open: all year, Credit cards: none
Other Languages: good English
Region: Veneto, Michelin Map: 562

The area around the city of Alba is true wine country, where vineyards cover every possible inch of land. Giovanna, an independent vintner, admirably manages her grandparents' farm and bed and breakfast single-handedly and has taken on the ultimate challenge of producing Barbaresco, Barbera, and Dolcetto wines right on the premises. Giovanna loves welcoming travelers who are looking for a home away from home, wholesome foods, and the simple pleasures of country life. The mustard-colored house backed by striped hillsides has a separate guest entrance. A large informal living room filled with books and local wine itineraries includes a corner kitchen where guests sit at a table for a self-service breakfast. Upstairs are the three country-style bedrooms. The pink room has twin beds and a vineyard view while the green and blue rooms have queen beds. They each have new, immaculate bathrooms, and are decorated with grandmother's lace curtains, old photographs, brass beds, and patchwork quilts. Four similarly appointed apartments are situated on two floors in a wing off the main house. Also organized are truffle hunts and participation in the wine harvest activities. *Directions:* From Alba (6 km) drive towards Barbaresco. Before town, at the sign for Tre Stelle, look for the B&B on the left. From Asti follow signs for Alba-Barbaresco–Treiso. After Barbaresco, on the road for Alba, watch for Tre Stelle and the B&B on the right.

CASCINA DELLE ROSE
Host: Giovanna Rizzolio
Localita: Tre Stelle, Barbaresco, (CN) 12050, Italy
Tel: (0173) 638292, Fax: (0173) 638322
Cellphone: (339) 6075790
3 Rooms, Double: €90–€110
4 Apartments: €100–€180 daily, €600–€1100 weekly
Open: all year, Credit cards: all major
Other Languages: good English, French, German
Region: Piedmont, Michelin Map: 561

Casa Sola is just that—an ancient villa standing alone atop a hill on a gorgeous 400-acre vineyard estate in the heart of Chianti. The gracious Gambaro family produces prestigious Chianti Classico Riserva, Supertuscan-Montarsiccio, and extra-virgin olive oil of the highest quality. There are six large guest apartments on two floors of a rose-covered stone farmhouse down the road from the main villa. All the apartments consist of living room, kitchen, bedrooms, and baths, with private entrances and garden (flowers match the color scheme of each apartment!). The apartments are furnished stylishly with selected country antiques, and details such as botanical prints hung with bows, eyelet curtains, fresh flowers, and a bottle of wine are welcome touches. Number 5, for up to eight people, is the most spacious with four bedrooms, fireplace, and magnificent views over the Barberino Valley and cypress woods. Il Capanno, in the converted barn, is a delightful "nest" for honeymooners. An inviting pool overlooks the valley surrounding the main villa. Wine-cellar visits with wine tasting are organized once a week and marked hiking trails lead guests through picture-perfect landscapes. *Directions:* From the Autostrada del Sole, direction Florence, exit at Firenze Certosa joining the Firenze-Siena Superstrada. Exit S. Donato in Poggio and go beyond San Donato. Go 1 km past San Donato, look for the sign for Casa Sola on the right and follow the road for 2 km.

FATTORIA CASA SOLA
Host: Count Gambaro family
Localita: Cortine, Barberino Val d'Elsa, (FI) 50021, Italy
Tel: (055) 8075028, Fax: (055) 8059194
11 Apartments: €700–€2430 weekly* (Jul & Aug)
Off season rates for Apt: €90–€350 daily*
*Apartment rental, no breakfast offered
Open: all year, Credit cards: all major
Other Languages: good English, French, Spanish
Region: Tuscany, Michelin Map: 563

Strategically positioned midway between Siena and Florence sits the square stone farmhouse with cupola (actually one of the bedrooms!) dating from 1700 owned by Gianni and Cristina, a couple who have dedicated their lives to the equestrian arts. The Paretaio appeals particularly to visitors with a passion for horseback riding, for the Marchis offer everything from basic riding lessons to dressage training, and day outings through the gorgeous surrounding countryside. In fact, the Paretaio is recognized as one of the top riding "schools" in Italy, with more than 30 horses. On the ground floor is a rustic living room with country antiques, comfy sofas, and piano enhanced by a vaulted brick ceiling and worn terracotta floors, off which are two bedrooms. Upstairs, the main gathering area is the dining room, which features a massive fireplace and a seemingly endless wooden table. This room gives access to more bedrooms, each decorated with touches such as dried flowers, white lace curtains, and, of course, equestrian prints. A vast collection of over 300 pieces with an equestrian theme is displayed about the home. Il Paretaio also organizes courses in Italian and is an excellent base for touring the heart of Tuscany. The swimming pool gives splendid views over olive groves and vineyards. *Directions:* Head south from Barberino on route 2 and after 2 km take the second right-hand turnoff for San Filippo. Continue on 1.5 km of dirt road to the house.

IL PARETAIO
Hosts: Cristina & Giovanni de Marchi
Localita: San Filippo
Barberino Val d'Elsa, (FI) 50021, Italy
Tel: (055) 8059218, Fax: (055) 8059231
Cellphone: (338) 7379626
8 Rooms, Double: €65–€105
2 Apartments: €80 daily, €490 weekly
Open: all year, Credit cards: none
Other Languages: good English, French
Region: Tuscany, Michelin Map: 563

The Bad Dreikirchen is situated up in the Dolomite foothills with an enchanting view over a lush green valley and distant snowcapped mountain peaks. The young and energetic Wodenegg family works diligently at making guests feel at home in their lovely residence and running the busy restaurant, which serves typical local meals to non-resident patrons as well as guests. The restaurant shares the site of a unique historical monument—Le Tre Chiese, three curious, attached, miniature medieval churches. This unique inn is accessible only by taxi or Jeep, or on foot. An exhilarating half-hour hike takes you up to the typical mountain-style chalet with long wood balconies in front. The most charming rooms are those in the older section, entirely wood-paneled, with fluffy comforters and old-fashioned washbasins. The rambling house has several common areas for guests as well as a swimming pool. This is truly an incredible spot, near the Siusi Alps and Val Gardena where some of the best climbing in Europe can be found. *Directions:* Exit from the Bolzano-Brennero autostrada A22 at Chiusa, cross the river, and take S.S.12 south to Ponte Gardena. Take the road on the right up to Barbian and call the hotel from the village for a pickup by Jeep (€12).

BAD DREIKIRCHEN
Hosts: Annette & Matthias Wodenegg family
San Giacomo 6, Barbian, (BZ) 39040, Italy
Tel: (0471) 650055, Fax: (0471) 650044
Cellphone: (335) 5226585
27 Rooms, Double: €100–€130
1 Suite: €120–€150
Open: May 4 to Oct 26, Credit cards: MC, VS
Other Languages: good English
Region: Trentino-Alto Adige, Michelin Map: 562

Just 2 kilometers outside Barolo in the area where the famous wine is produced sits the long, rectangular, antique-pink-colored farmhouse of Raffaella Pittatore, passed down to her from her grandparents. After years of working for a major tour-operator company and living in many parts of the world, she came back home with her young son to impart her hospitality experience to her own guests. She is a natural hostess, friendly and accommodating, with a "joie de vivre" that is truly refreshing. One year after opening, four bedrooms in the attached former barn were added to those already existing on the first floor. These are simply furnished with the family's country furniture and each has its own bathroom. One also has a kitchenette. Downstairs you find an informal living room and breakfast room with original brick ceilings and floors. Guests can use the kitchen or barbecue, if desired, and breakfast is served out on the front patio in fine weather. Although there are no particular views, the crossroads location is convenient for touring this beautiful Piedmont wine country, the price is economical, and the hospitality exceptional. Raffaella has put together many interesting local itineraries including quaint villages, castles, wine museums, and vineyards. *Directions:* From Alba (10 km) follow signs for Barolo and at the turnoff stay to the left. The entrance to the bed and breakfast is on the right-hand side of the road just at this fork.

IL GIOCO DELL'OCA
Host: Raffaella Pittatore
Via Crosia 46, Barolo, (CN) 12060, Italy
Tel: (0173) 56206, Cellphone: (338) 5999426
6 Rooms, Double: €65–€75
Open: Feb to Dec, Credit cards: MC, VS
Other Languages: good English
Region: Piedmont, Michelin Map: 561

The expansive Pomurlo farm covers 370 acres of hills, woods, and open fields and is an excellent base for touring Umbria. A winding dirt road leads to the typical stone house, which contains a restaurant featuring organically grown, farm-fresh specialties. An antique cupboard and old farm implements on the walls enhance the rustic setting. A nearby converted stall houses two adorable independent rooms looking out over the lake. Other guestrooms and apartments with kitchens are found in two large hilltop homes commanding a breathtaking view of the entire valley with its grazing herds of longhorn cattle. The main house, a 12th-century tower fortress where the inn's personable hostess Daniela resides, accommodates guests in three additional suites of rooms. Breakfast fixings are provided in apartments. The acquisition of the neighboring property has resulted in a center (Le Casette) offering more service—two stone farmhouses containing 16 additional rooms and a restaurant around a large swimming pool (there's a second pool). Comfortable and cheerful, all rooms are decorated with wrought-iron beds, colorful bedspreads, and typical regional country antiques. Enjoy the pool and activities such as tennis, soccer, and mountain biking. Very affordable. *Directions:* The farm is located near the Rome-Florence autostrada. Take the Orvieto exit from the A1 and follow signs for Todi, not for Baschi. On route S.S.448 turn right at the sign for Pomurlo.

POMURLO VECCHIO
Hosts: Lazzaro Minghelli & family
Localita: Lago di Corbara, Baschi, (TR) 05023, Italy
Tel: (0744) 950190 or (0744) 957645
Fax: (0744) 950500, Cellphone: (336) 607708
18 Rooms, Double: €65–€85
13 Apartments: €65–€85 daily
Open: all year, Credit cards: MC, VS
Other Languages: some English, French
Region: Umbria, Michelin Map: 563

Only 30 kilometers from Milan, the Cascina Caremma is the essence of agritourism: a 100-acre working farm using strictly organic methods; offering accommodation and meals using produce from the farm, and organizing lessons in organic production and the agri-ecosystem. It is also part of the Ticino River Park Reserve, which can be explored by bike, horse, or foot only. This typical northern Italian cascina is a quad formation with large inner courtyard lined with multi-colored houses, stalls, and barns. Over the years the very involved hosts have vastly improved the comfort level and charming decor of the accommodations, which are situated in two colorful side-by-side houses. Cheerful, air-conditioned rooms have country furnishings and beamed ceilings and are accented with matching floral curtains and bedspreads. The delightful downstairs dining rooms maintain their true country flavor with antiques, fireplace, and ancient wood-burning oven. On weekends people from the city come to enjoy the excellent, wholesome meals. A new well-being center offers an indoor pool, steam bath, sauna, and yoga classes. Within reach are Malpensa airport and the lake region. *Directions:* Exit the A7 (Genova-Milano) at Binasco and head towards Casorate Primo, Besate. In the small town of Besate look for a sign for the cascina and follow this country road for 2 km to the farm.

CASCINA CAREMMA
Host: Gabriele Corti family
Strada per il Ticino, Besate, (MI) 20080, Italy
Tel & Fax: (02) 9050020
Cellphone: (348) 3049848
14 Rooms, Double: €80–€120
Closed: Aug, Credit cards: all major
Other Languages: good English
Region: Lombardy, Michelin Map: 561

The Locanda, a pale-yellow and brick house dating from 1830, sits on the border between Tuscany and Umbria and is an excellent base from which to explore this rich countryside. The villa's dining room features a vaulted ceiling in toast-colored brick, an enormous fireplace, French windows opening out to the flower garden, and antiques including a cupboard adorned with the family's blue-and-white china. The upstairs quarters are reserved primarily for guests, and contain five comfortable rooms all off one hallway and an inviting sitting room and library. The cozy bedrooms have mansard ceilings, armoires, lovely linens, and private bathrooms with showers. Additional guestrooms are located on the ground floor of the converted barn between the house and a small garden, where a swimming pool has been added. These are more spacious, private, and modern in decor. Cordial hostess Palmira assists with local itineraries. Excellent regional fare including divine vegetarian dishes with local produce is prepared by the chef who is happy to give cooking classes. Siena is only 45 kilometers away, and the quaint medieval and Renaissance villages of Pienza, Montepulciano, and Montalcino are close by. *Directions:* Exit from the Rome-Florence autostrada at Val di Chiana. Head toward Bettolle, then bear right toward Siena. Follow signs for La Bandita.

LOCANDA LA BANDITA
Host: Palmira Fiorini
Via Bandita 72, Bettolle, (SI) 53040, Italy
Tel & Fax: (0577) 624649
Cellphone: (335) 6945920
9 Rooms, Double: €90–€100
Open: Mar to Dec, Credit cards: all major
Other Languages: good English
Region: Tuscany, Michelin Map: 563

The vast Torre Burchio property is immersed in 1,500 acres of wooded wildlife preserve where wild boar, deer, hare, and pheasant abound. Seemingly far away from civilization, this Italian version of a ranch offers a relaxing holiday in close touch with nature, while still being in reach of Umbria's top sights. The reception, restaurant, and six guest bedrooms are within the main 18th-century farmhouse, which maintains the ambiance of the original hunting lodge with hunting trophies on the walls, large open fireplace, cozy living room, and library. The upstairs breakfast room, from which the bedrooms lead, is lined with colorful Deruta ceramics. An additional ten bedrooms are found in a single-story house just across from the lodge, while the very comfortable apartments with kitchenettes are in a beautifully restored 230-year-old stone house with inner courtyard 4 kilometers down the road. The rooms and apartments are very nicely appointed with antiques, pretty fabrics, paintings, and large bathrooms, and have telephones and televisions. Guests gather in the busy restaurant in the evening for a hearty meal based on organic products from the farm. Many activities such as cooking classes, horseback-riding weeks, and sports are available. *Directions:* 20 km from either Perugia or Assisi. From the center of Bettona, follow signs for 5 Cerri-Torre Burchio and follow the dirt road through the woods for 5 km to the main house/reception.

TORRE BURCHIO
Host: Alvaro Sfascia
Bettona, (PG) 06084, Italy
Tel: (075) 9885017, Fax: (075) 987150
Cellphone: (347) 8460995
16 Rooms, Double: €77–€104
13 Apartments: €672–€878 weekly*
Apartment rental, no breakfast offered
Closed: Jan, Credit cards: all major
Other Languages: good English
Region: Umbria, Michelin Map: 563

Luisa left her fashion business in Parma and settled in this peaceful spot 3 kilometers from the coast. The stylish, impeccable home clearly reflects the personality of the warm and yet reserved hostess who tastefully designed both the exterior and interior of this lovely accommodation. Each of the four corner bedrooms upstairs has its own large private terrace and beautiful floral-tiled bathroom. All offer beds with linen sheets and splendid views over fruit orchards and olive groves to the sea. While the hostess occupies the cupola, guests have a independent entrance to the upstairs rooms, giving utmost privacy to all. Common areas include the living room and open kitchen with large arched window and doors looking out to the surrounding garden. An ample fresh country breakfast with cakes all prepared by Luisa is served here at one long table. A separate cottage next to the main house offers a double room and beamed living room with stone fireplace and kitchen, and a second apartment is available within another cottage next door. Day trips include Elba Island, Volterra and San Gimignano, Lucca, Siena, private beaches, Etruscan itineraries, visits to the wine estates of Bolgheri, and biking in the nearby nature park. Sweet and simple. *Directions:* Exit from Aurelia on route 1 at Bibbona and turn left. Pass through La California and turn left for Bibbona. Podere Le Mezzelune is before town, well marked to the left. Pisa airport is 40 km away.

PODERE LE MEZZELUNE
Host: Luisa Chiesa family
Via Mezzelune 126, Bibbona, (LI) 57020, Italy
Tel: (0586) 670266, Fax: (0586) 671814
Cellphone: (329) 3712287
4 Rooms, Double: €160–€190, 2 Apts: €180–€195*
Minimum Stay Required: 2 nights
*Breakfast not included with apartments: €13
Open: all year, Credit cards: MC, VS,
Other Languages: French
Region: Tuscany, Michelin Map: 563

For some reason, the city of Bologna is often bypassed by visitors, despite its rich past, beautiful historic center, arcaded streets, and elegant shops. Cristina, Serena, and Mauro Orsi, the owners of the splendid, four-star Hotel Corona d'Oro, mentioned in our hotel guide, own three other centrally located hotels: the Orologio, the Commercianti and the sleek new Novecento. Just steps away from Bologna's main piazza and Basilica, the true heart of the city, you find the nicely renovated Orologio, so-called because it looks onto city hall with its clock tower. The reception desk on the ground floor leads upstairs to a large sitting and dining room where a buffet breakfast is served. From this level there is an elevator up to the guestrooms displaying unique antique clocks at each level. Rooms include occasional antiques, fabric walls, and white and gray marble bathrooms. The classically decorated rooms with carpeting have all amenities (including wireless internet) and most have great views of the square. Bicycles are available free of charge to our readers to visit the city's historical center and main monuments just like a native. The owners also organize personalized cooking classes, tickets for special events, and private tours of Bologna and surrounding cities. *Directions:* Located in the heart of the old city. Private garage facilities are available upon reservation (restricted traffic in historical center).

ART HOTEL OROLOGIO
Manager: Cristina Orsi
Via IV Novembre 10, Bologna, (BO) 40123, Italy
Tel: (051) 74 57 411, Fax: (051) 74 57 422
Cellphone: (335) 61 49 933
34 Rooms, Double: €189–€357
5 Suites: €285–€510
1 Apartment: €290–€492 daily
Open: all year, Credit cards: all major
Other Languages: good English
Region: Emilia-Romagna, Michelin Map: 562

Bolsena is a quaint, ancient village 18 kilometers from Orvieto right on picturesque Lake Bolsena with its small ports and two islands. Marco Zammarano, with his long hotelier experience in Rome, took over the family's 60-acre hillside farm property just above town and opened lovely bed and breakfast accommodation offering utter tranquility. The main stone farmhouse holds eleven beamed bedrooms each with en suite bathroom, satellite TV, and fridge, simply but comfortably appointed with a mix of wicker furniture and country antiques. All but two have gorgeous views over the manicured garden and swimming pool out to the lake. Five bedrooms are found farther up the wooded road in another house with its own swimming pool and there is a third residence with an additional eleven rooms and a third swimming pool. Two apartments are available within yet another separate building. A restaurant for guests only has an ample outside terrace enjoying sunsets over the lake and takes advantage of ingredients fresh from the farm. Here you have the convenience of being near town and many interesting Etruscan sights, while the lake itself offers many activities including a fascinating boat ride to the small, historic island of Bisentina. *Directions:* Exit the A1 autostrada at Orvieto and follow signs for Bolsena. Just before town at the Trattoria Castagneta, turn right up to La Riserva. Shuttle service is available from the Rome airport or Orvieto train station.

LA RISERVA MONTEBELLO
Host: Marco Zammarano
Strada Orvietana km 3
Bolsena, (VT) 01023, Italy
Tel & Fax: (0761) 798965
Cellphone: (339) 8947664
27 Rooms, Double: €120–€140
Per person half board: €85–€105
Closed: Jan, Credit cards: all major
Other Languages: good English
Region: Lazio, Michelin Map: 563

The prestigious Monsignor della Casa property extending over 600 acres is a true country resort with all the trimmings in the beautiful area north of Florence called Mugello. This is the land from which such masters as Giotto, Cimabue, and Fra Angelico came and was the actual home of 16th-century writer and Vatican secretary, Giovanni della Casa, whose portrait hangs in Washington's National Gallery. The Marzi family meticulously restored a cluster of six stone farmhouses on the vast estate next to their own stately villa. The refined bi-level apartments exude pure Tuscan charm and can accommodate from two to six guests. Two individual villas, each with private swimming pool, can take a group of twelve to sixteen. The finest linens and fabrics were chosen to accent exposed stone walls, brick floors, and wood-beamed ceilings. Spend your days touring or in any of a variety of activities for every age and interest: biking, hiking, or horseback riding in the nearby woods, golf, swimming in one of two pools, tennis, volleyball, and children's playground. An elegantly rustic restaurant and wine bar serves guests in the evening with cordial host Alessio making sure nothing is overlooked. The "wellness center" offers sauna, steam bath, Jacuzzi, and other services. Indulge! *Directions:* From Borgo San Lorenzo follow signs for Faenza. Just after the turnoff for Scarperia turn right for Mucciano and the resort (3 km total). 27 km from Florence.

MONSIGNOR DELLA CASA
Host: Marzi family
Via di Mucciano 16
Borgo San Lorenzo, (FI) 50032, Italy
Tel: (055) 840821, Fax: (055) 8408240
21 Rooms, Double: €160–€460
21 Apartments: €460–€3350 weekly
Minimum Stay Required: 2 nights, 7 in high season
Open: all year, Credit cards: all major
Other Languages: good English
Region: Tuscany, Michelin Map: 563

The town of Brisighella is a gem and comes to life during the first weekend of July with its annual Medieval Festival when games of the period are re-enacted, and medieval music, literature, and dance are produced. Locals attire themselves in appropriate costume and torches illuminate the village's narrow streets nightly for the occasion. Just out of town sits the sweet farmhouse of Ettore (a former architect) and Adriana, with its 25 acres of organically cultivated vineyards and orchards. Guests can learn about the production of the hosts' excellent Sangiovese and Chardonnay wines. The renovated barn next to their small brick house holds two guestrooms and a rustic dining area with exposed beams and a large fireplace where guests gather for typical Romagna-style meals. A third bedroom is within their own home and the ex-barn provides two cozy apartments for two to five people. Breakfast is served out on the covered terrace overlooking a quiet valley lined with vineyards. Rooms are decorated with simple country furnishings. The atmosphere is casual and the value excellent. "Must sees" are the mosaics in Ravenna, Bologna's historical center, and the international ceramic museum in Faenza. La Torre golf club is 8 kilometers away. *Directions:* Take the Faenza exit from the A14 between Bologna and Rimini, follow signs for Brisighella or Florence. At town turn left for Terme/Modigliana. Il Palazzo is on the left after the Hotel Terme.

IL PALAZZO
Host: Ettore Matarese family
Via Baccagnano 11, Brisighella, (RA) 48013, Italy
Tel & Fax: (0546) 80338
Cellphone: (328) 1462585
3 Rooms, Double: €62–€68
2 Apartments: €100–€130 daily
Minimum Stay Required: 3 nights
Open: Mar to Oct, Credit cards: all major
Other Languages: good English
Region: Emilia-Romagna, Michelin Map: 562

Tall cypress trees protect the cluster of ancient stone farmhouses making up the idyllic Iesolana property, situated atop 300 acres of cascading vineyards, olive groves, and sunflowers, with 360 degrees of breathtaking Tuscan views. After years of meticulous restoration of the three ochre-stained houses, eleven high-level apartments are offered, with private terraces. Apartments have from one to four bedrooms and are elegantly appointed with rustic furnishings, country fabrics, and modern kitchens and baths that harmonize beautifully with the cool stone floors and original wood-beamed ceilings. Among the many services available are individual telephones, satellite TV, barbecue facilities, and a swimming pool. The impeccable landscape is studded with terracotta pots overflowing with brightly colored geraniums. The fabulously restored barn now hosts a stylish wine bar for tastings of Iesolana's own wines, oils, and honey. Breakfast and dinners of regional cuisine are also served in the comfortable restaurant with outdoor seating as an option. A state-of-the-art meeting room is available for groups. Centrally located for day trips to Siena, Florence, and Rome, this is the perfect spot for relaxing and exploring. *Directions:* Leave the A1 at Valdarno for Montevarchi, Bucine (8 km). From town follow signs up to Iesolana, passing over a stone bridge (2 km) to the end of the road.

BORGO IESOLANA
Host: Giovanni Toscano
Localita: Iesolana, Bucine, (AR) 52021, Italy
Tel: (055) 992988, Fax: (055) 992879
11 Apartments: €140 daily, €850 weekly*
*Apartment rental, no breakfast offered
Minimum Stay Required: 2 nights, 7 in high season
Open: all year, Credit cards: all major
Other Languages: good English
Region: Tuscany, Michelin Map: 563

La Ripolina farm is a vast 500-acre farm comprised of several different brick farmhouses. Self-catering apartments (two for up to ten people) and individual guest bedrooms are divided among five farmhouses dotting the soft hills of the property. Two very charmingly authentic apartments are found within the Pieve di Piana, a cluster of houses grouped around an ancient church with bell tower dating to the 9th century. The richly historic Pieve sits on a hill and enjoys panoramic views of vineyards and fields of grain and sunflowers extending as far as the eye can see. Hostess and owner Laura Cresti resides in the house called S. Ferdinando where there are two apartments with two bedrooms with a separate entrance. Five rooms are next door in the Ripoli house, each being individually appointed with appropriate country local antiques. Walls are painted in warm earth colors and the upstairs loggia, a typical open porch with four large arched windows, has been enclosed and transformed into the breakfast room. A full country breakfast buffet includes fresh coffee cakes, fruit, cereals, yogurt, and cheeses. This is strikingly beautiful countryside, chock-full of hilltowns to explore. A beautiful swimming pool and bicycles are available for guests. *Directions:* From Siena (25 km) take the S.S.2 to Buonconvento and turn right in town following signs for Bibbiano. After crossing the river, turn right at La Ripolina and drive up to the main house.

LA RIPOLINA
Host: Laura Cresti
Pieve di Piana, Buonconvento, (SI) 53022, Italy
Tel & Fax: (0577) 282280
Cellphone: (335) 5739284
7 Rooms, Double: €75–€95
7 Apartments: €45–€70 daily, price per person
Minimum Stay Required: 3 nights
Open: all year, Credit cards: MC, VS
Other Languages: good English, French
Region: Tuscany, Michelin Map: 563

There are only a handful of hotels in Sicily meeting the charming, historic ambiance category of agriturismo. On the northwest corner of the island around Trapani, an ideal touring base for the island, a group of owners have transformed their ancient, ancestral baglio farm properties into accommodation for guests. Typically, the stone-walled structure with large, inner courtyard housed everything from the family residence, farmer's quarters, oil and wine press, to barns and stalls. The Baglio Fontana farm dates from the late 1700s and has been restored with care by the original Fontana family. On the outskirts of a small town, the huge, front doors of this fortress farm open to a stone courtyard. The courtyard leads to a large, rustic, beamed dining room with fireplace, and an ancient oil stone press, where dishes from typical, local recipes using all local farm products are served to guests. The austere, main villa has 6 guestrooms. Additional loft bedrooms and ground floor apartments are located in another section. The farm still produces wine, honey, and olive oil. Comfortable rooms, all with air conditioning, have new wood furnishings, bathrooms, and smart plaid fabrics. A cozy living room in the main villa, decorated with family antiques and paintings, is where guests gather after dinner to chat. An inviting pool is found in the large garden. *Directions:* From Palermo follow route 187 towards Trapani; exit at Buseto Palizzolo. After 3km, before town, turn left at sign.

※ ■ ⚡ ▣ ☎ 🐕 @ P ‖ ≋ 木 🏌 ⊥ 👫 🛶

BAGLIO FONTANA
Host: Di Vita family
Via Palermo, Buseto Palizzolo, (TP) 91012, Italy
Tel & Fax: (0923) 855000
Cellphone: (355) 5274874
11 Rooms, Double: €95–€120
Minimum Stay Required: 2 nights
Open: all year, Credit cards: all major
Other Languages: good English
Region: Sicily, Michelin Map: 565

We recommend the Piccolo Golf hotel in order to offer the less-adventurous traveler a more classic accommodation than the rather spartan agritourism choices of the region. It is also a more reasonable alternative to the expensive hotels for which the Emerald Coast is so famous. Beautifully positioned, the peach-colored stone hotel immersed in Mediterranean vegetation overlooks the Pevero Golf Club to one side and the bay of Cala di Volpe to the other. This is a more secluded and peaceful area of the Emerald Coast, with small, hidden coves and rocky beaches, between the more famous towns of Porto Cervo and Porto Rotondo. The large reception and bar area have wicker furnishings and lead out to the surrounding garden and swimming pool. To the right of the entrance is a simple veranda dining room where regional meals are served. Bedrooms are practical and basic, with light-blue bedspreads and trimmings accenting cream-colored walls. Rooms have either garden or sea views (slightly higher rate), with the top-floor rooms catching glimpses of the turquoise-blue sea, which is very reminiscent of the Caribbean. This is a perfect location for viewing the coast or exploring the more rugged interior landscapes of the island—the "real" Sardinia. *Directions:* 30 km from Olbia airport. Drive towards Palau and turn off right for Porto Cervo then right again for Capricciolo. Cala di Volpe is 4 km before town and the hotel is opposite the luxurious Hotel Cala di Volpe.

IL PICCOLO GOLF
Host: Mario Azzena
Localita: Cala di Volpe
Cala di Volpe, Porto Cervo, (SS) 07020, Italy
Tel: (0789) 96520, Fax: (0789) 96565
17 Rooms, Double: €73–€207
Minimum Stay Required: 14 nights in Aug
Open: all year, Credit cards: AX, VS
Other Languages: some English
Region: Sardinia, Michelin Map: 566

British expatriate Jane Ridd settled in Gallura, one of the most beautiful corners of Sardinia many years ago and, with her husband, took over his 150 acre family farm consisting mainly of cork woods, vineyards and pastures where horses now roam. Over the years, Jane has gained fame, and Michelin mention, for her completely homemade, and to a great extent home grown local Gallura cuisine. Three different dining rooms accommodate the many culinary enthusiasts who gather here. One, used during the winter, has an enormous fireplace, beamed ceiling and walls decorated with old farm implements and photos of the early 1900s. The lovely timbered veranda is opened on three sides during the summer months and looks over the stone terraces where diners eat under the trees and stars in midsummer. Completely immersed in the trees four guestrooms are found off a small piazzetta at the side of the restaurant, almost carved out of the enormous granite rock that backs the property. Decor is simple, white walls, beamed ceilings and typical hand-woven Sardinian bedcovers and curtains. Each has its own shower room. Beautiful sandy beaches are only 20 minutes away. Nearby are many prehistoric archaeological sites, hikes countryside drives. *Directions:* From Olbia (20 km away) head for Tempio-Calangianus via Via Barcellona and Monte Pino e Tempio. Turn left 2 km after Priatu. and follow the signs.

LI LICCI
Host: Jane Elizabeth Ridd Abeltino
Localita: Valentino-Priatu
Calangianus, (SS) 07023, Italy
Tel: (079) 665114, Fax: (079) 665029
Cellphone: (348) 0693700
4 Rooms, Double: €100–€120
Minimum Stay Required: 2 nights
Open: all year, Credit cards: none
Other Languages: fluent English, French
Region: Sardinia, Michelin Map: 566

The beautiful Montebelli resort property, situated in Maremma, with its wild Tuscan landscapes, covers 300 acres of mountain, hills laden with vineyards and olive groves, and sunflower fields, all close to the sea. The Filotico-Tosi family divides their time and energy between their guests and production of wines and olive oil. The main guesthouse, originally a centuries-old mill, holds most of the comfortable guestrooms, while the remaining accommodation is spread out in two, one-story wings, each with individual entrance. Rooms are decorated tastefully with typical Tuscan antiques. The latest addition to Montebelli is a magnificent 4-star, 24 room country hotel perfectly integrated with the existing structure. The new hotel rooms are modern in their furnishing and amenities. The hotel also integrates into the complex spa facilities, a billiard room and spacious common areas. As a result of the new addition, the Montebelli now can offer guests a choice between a bed and breakfast and a hotel stay. The half-board requirement allows guests to sample marvelous local cuisine by candlelight within the intimate dining rooms or out on the terrace. Scenic walks or biking on marked trails, a swimming pool, tennis courts, horse riding, and courses in cooking, yoga and wine-tasting are all available. *Directions:* From the north, exit at Gavorrano Scalo from Aurelia S.S.1, following signs for Caldana. Just before Caldana, turn at the Montebelli sign and take the dirt road to the end.

MONTEBELLI
Host: Carla Filotico Tosi family
Localita: Molinetto, Caldana, (GR) 58023, Italy
Tel: (0566) 887100, Fax: (0566) 81439
35 Rooms, Double: €210–€290*
10 Suites: €252–€320*
*Includes breakfast & dinner
Closed: Jan to Mar, Credit cards: all major
Other Languages: good English
Region: Tuscany, Michelin Map: 563

The quaint medieval village of Calvi is just on the border between Lazio and Umbria and conveniently located at 15 kilometers from the autostrada and 80 kilometers from Rome. Louise, from Sweden, divides her time between Rome and the countryside where the farm's activities include production of wine and olive oil on the 150-acre property. The fascinating family residence in town is a historic 15th-century palazzo filled with period furniture, paintings, and frescoed ceilings. Hospitality is offered in the ochre-colored farmhouse within four comfortable apartments, each with private garden area. Accommodations on the first and second floors are a combination of one or two bedrooms, living room with fireplace, fully equipped kitchen, bathroom, and outdoor barbecue. The house has been restored with new bathrooms and tiled floors, while maintaining original beamed ceilings and a country flavor in antique furnishings. Also to be enjoyed on the property is a lovely garden with swimming pool and a children's playground. From here, in addition to exploring the many surrounding villages, you can visit Rome, Viterbo, and Orvieto, within one hour by car. *Directions:* Leave the Rome-Florence autostrada A1 at Magliano Sabina. After Magliano turn left for Calvi, after 1km turn right. Just before Calvi you see signs for San Martino on the right.

CASALE SAN MARTINO
Host: Louise Calza Bini
Colle San Martino, Calvi dell'Umbria, (TR) 05032, Italy
Tel & Fax: (0744) 710644
Cellphone: (328) 1659514
4 Apartments: €60–€150 daily, €420–€1050 weekly*
*Apartment rental, no breakfast offered
Minimum Stay Required: 2 nights
Open: all year, Credit cards: none
Other Languages: English, French, German, Spanish
Region: Umbria, Michelin Map: 563

The Villa Bellaria is situated right in the picturesque village of Campagnatico with its stone streets and houses and magnificent views over the Ombrone Valley and up to Mount Amiata, it retains the authentic flavor of a noble country home from centuries past. Credit goes to gracious hostess Luisa who oversees the 900-plus-acre property, once belonging to such powerful families as the Aldobrandeschi and Medici. It was partially destroyed during World War II and completely restored by the Querci della Rovere family. Talented Luisa runs not only the hospitality activity but the entire farm as well, while her husband produces Morellino wine from another property. With its large surrounding balustraded park with cypress-lined trails and swimming pool, one forgets that it is all part of the actual town (with its many conveniences). The spacious bedrooms with family antiques and two of the apartments are situated within the main villa while the other newer but characteristic ones are spread out on three floors in the transformed olive-press building. They have either one or two bedrooms, bathroom, and sitting room with kitchenette and are appointed with the family's country furniture. This is a lovely base for exploring the area. *Directions:* From Siena (55 km) or Grosseto (20 km) exit from highway 223 at Campagnatico and continue for 4 km to the town. The villa is the second right in town—drive up to a brown gate.

VILLA BELLARIA
Host: Luisa Querci della Rovere
Campagnatico, (GR) 58042, Italy
Tel & Fax: (0564) 996626
Cellphone: (335) 6097438
2 Rooms, Double: €70–€80
1 Suite: €130–€150
10 Apartments: €550–€1000 weekly
Open: all year, Credit cards: all major
Other Languages: good English
Region: Tuscany, Michelin Map: 563

The vast Masseria Pernice property sits on the hills south of Palermo, in the Alcamo wine area of Sicily. The vast 300-acre estate has always been in the noble Sallier de la Tour family from Palermo. Gracious host, Prince Filiberto—combining his passion for the countryside, wine and olive oil making, horses, and entertaining—opened the farm home to guests just recently. Although, from the road, the rust-colored, 300-year-old house and surrounding working farm seem rather basic, the well-appointed interiors have obviously been given prime attention. One bedroom and three comfortable apartments have been reserved for guests, each with independent access from the cobblestone main courtyard, covered with magenta-colored bougainvillea vines. The spacious "Papare", with exposed beams, has a bedroom and sofabed and a living area, while the largest apartment comes complete with a kitchen. "Fiori" sleeps five persons in two bedrooms, one being a loft with three beds. "Piume" is a double bedroom, and "Caccia" has a kitchenette and sitting room. Perfect for a full house rental, as well. Accessible day trips include Palermo, Monreale, Segesta, Selinunte, Erice, Cefalu, and the cantinas of the wine roads in the area with visits arranged by your host. *Directions:* From Palermo take the highway straight south towards Sciacca. Exit Camporeale and follow signs to "Case Pernice."

MASSERIA PERNICE
Host: Prince Filiberto Sallier De La Tour family
Contrada Pernice Monreale
Camporeale, Sicily, (PA) 90043, Italy
Tel & Fax: (0924) 36797, Cellphone: (336) 892533
1 Room, Double: €215–€250
3 Apartments €215–€315 daily
Minimum Stay Required: 3 nights
Open: all year, Credit cards: all major
Other Languages: fluent English, French
Region: Sicily, Michelin Map: 565

For those who have a passion for horseback riding, or with an urge to learn, Tenuta La Mandria provides the opportunity to do either while on holiday. Host and horseman Davide Felice Aondio's horse farm has been in existence for over 35 years and has been a model for riding resorts. Situated near the foothills of the Alps and between the cities of Turin and Milan, the vast, flat property borders a 15,000-acre national park, offering spectacular scenery and endless possibilities for horseback excursions. The complex is made up of horse stables, indoor/outdoor ring, haylofts, guestrooms, dining room, and the private homes of the proprietor and his son Marco's family. The whole forms a square with riding rings in the center. As a national equestrian training center, it offers lessons of every kind for all ages. Six very basic bedrooms with bath are reserved for guests and good local fare is served in the rustic dining room. Golf, swimming, and tennis facilities are available nearby. Two side trips that must not be missed are first, to lovely Lake Maggiore, and then to the intriguing medieval town of Ricetto where the houses and streets are made of smooth stones. *Directions:* Take the Carisio exit from the Milan-Turin autostrada. Head toward Biella, but at the town of Candelo turn right for Mottalciata. La Mandria is on the right.

TENUTA LA MANDRIA
Host: Marco Aondio family
Candelo, (BI) 13062, Italy
Tel: (015) 2536078
Fax: (015) 2530743
Cellphone: (335) 710444
6 Rooms, Double: €90–€96
Open: all year, Credit cards: none
Other Languages: good English
Region: Piedmont, Michelin Map: 561

Poetically named after a classic Italian tale by Cesare Pavese, a native of this area, the Luna e i Falo' (meaning "the moon and the fire") farmhouse was lovingly restored by congenial hosts Ester and Franco Carnero. The ritual described in the story is still performed in August every year when local farmers burn old grapevines under the full moon in hopes of a good crop. On that night, the bonfires dotting hills surrounding the farm create quite a spectacle. The Carneros' brick home has arched windows and arcaded front and side terraces, with three double or triple rooms and one apartment for four persons within the villa, which they have made available to visitors. For a country home, the spacious living/dining area is elaborately furnished with Renaissance period pieces. The bedrooms enjoy a combination of old and new decor and sweeping views of the countryside, known for its wineries. The emphasis at the Luna e i Falo' is on the cuisine: the proprietors previously owned a top-rated restaurant in Turin and continue to practice their culinary skills, producing delicacies from ancient recipes to guests' delight. Regardless of the language barrier, they have a way of making guests feel right at home. *Directions:* From Asti follow the signs for Canelli and, before town, take a right up the hill to Castello Gancia. The farmhouse is on the right after Aie.

LA LUNA E I FALO'
Hosts: Ester & Franco Carnero
Localita: Aie 37, Canelli, (AT) 14053, Italy
Tel & Fax: (0141) 831643
Cellphone: (328) 7191567
3 Rooms, Double: €100–€110*
1 Apartment: €140–€160 daily*
*Includes breakfast & dinner
Open: Mar to Nov, Credit cards: none
Other Languages: French
Region: Piedmont, Michelin Map: 561

The Canonica a Cerreto property is truly a marvel to behold, with an extraordinary combination of features. Perfectly located in lower Chianti and equidistant from most of Tuscany's highlights, it offers not only very comfortable accommodation in a fascinating historic dwelling but also seemingly endless vistas of gorgeous countryside, and welcoming and gracious hosts. Iron gates open up to an entrance lined with gorgeous terracotta pots in the form of lions, overflowing with geraniums and oleander plants giving accents of color to the facade of the ancient stone church and attached canonica, the summer residence of the Vescovo of the Duomo of Siena. Within the walls is a complex including the family's residence, three guest apartments in the monks' former rooms, quarters for the farmhands, and a cantina. Signora Lorenzi proudly shows guests her museum-caliber art collection and magnificent home where large period paintings adorn frescoed walls and elegant antique pieces are displayed. The apartments, in an elegant country style, are tastefully appointed with antiques and include a bedroom, bathroom, and living area with kitchenette. The largest apartment has two bedrooms, each with its own bathroom. A lovely, secluded swimming pool has superb countryside views. *Directions:* From Siena follow the S.S.408 towards Gaiole and just after Pianella, take the first left (Canonica a Cerreto is marked on most maps).

CANONICA A CERRETO
Host: Egidio Lorenzi family
Canonica a Cerreto
Castelnuovo Berardenga, (SI) 53019, Italy
Tel & Fax: (0577) 363261
3 Apartments: €735–€1250*
*Apartment rental, no breakfast offered
Minimum Stay Required: 3 nights, 7 in high season
Open: Apr to Oct, Credit cards: all major
Other Languages: good English
Region: Tuscany, Michelin Map: 563

The Country House Cefalicchio, property of the locally prominent Rossi family, promises a memorable stay. The 200-year-old, monumental pale yellow residence complete with grand double staircase in front, sits on more than 200 acres of land. The plateau territory is covered with the region's primary crop; olive groves, plus vineyards, orchards and vegetable gardens, all cultivated using strictly bio-dynamic principles. These earthly foods are brought directly into the kitchen of chef Maurizio Gusman who creates magic before your eyes. A small dining room is in a separate house behind the residence with a patio for outdoor seating adjacent to the pool area. A second restaurant is currently being built. Within the historic home are two suites, seven bedrooms, and three apartments, one suitable for up to four guests. The two suites occupy the entire first floor and are the most characteristic with antique furnishings, high ceilings and French windows leading out to a terrace which winds around three sides of the palazzo. Living areas are more spacious than the bedrooms and the added bathrooms are quite small. Mansard bedrooms on the top floor, reached by a narrow staircase and all down one hall, have a common living room, which leads out to the loggia tower for extended views. Bikes are available and wine tastings and tours can be arranged. *Directions:* Exit at Canosa di Puglia from A16; drive through town; travel 3 km, following signs for Cefalicchio.

COUNTRY HOUSE CEFALICCHIO   **New**
Manager: Nicola Franco
Contrada Cefalicchio
Canosa di Puglia, (BA) 70053, Italy
Tel: (0883) 642123, Fax: (0883) 662736
7 Rooms, Double: €100–€200
2 Suites: €240–€390
3 Apartments: €240–€330 daily
Open: all year, Credit cards: all major
Other Languages: English, French, German
Region: Apulia, Michelin Map: 564

The turreted medieval village of Capalbio, perched on a hilltop, has the double advantage of being close to one of the prettiest seaside spots—Argentario—plus having the beautiful countryside and villages of Maremma to explore. Monica and husband Filippo run an efficient little bed and breakfast operation, having left a long career in the restaurant business. Breakfast, composed of fresh homemade cakes, breads, and jams, is served in the stone-walled dining room or out on the patio. Ten rooms in a row, each with independent entrance from the garden, are situated next door to the main house; while five new bedrooms have been added in the adjacent converted barn. Rooms are nicely decorated in a classic style, and have such amenities as television, telephone, hairdryer, and air conditioning. This comes in handy on hot summer evenings, although there is always a cool breeze passing through and the swimming pool surrounded by a manicured lawn is wonderfully refreshing. The farm property extends over 30 acres of olive groves and fields of grain and oats. Monica and Filippo run a little restaurant in town Trattoria Al Pozzo. Guests often eat here and at Tullio's well known for its excellent food. The sculpture park of Niki de St. Phalle is 4 km away. *Directions:* From Rome on the coastal highway 1, exit before Capalbio at Pescia Fiorentina. At Pescia stay left for 3 km. Ghiaccio is 1 km after the fork for Manciano.

GHIACCIO BOSCO
Hosts: Monica Olivi & Filippo Rinaldi
Strada della Sgrilla 4
Capalbio, (GR) 58011, Italy
Tel: (0564) 896539
Cellphone: (339) 5662578
15 Rooms, Double: €80–€120
Open: all year, Credit cards: none
Other Languages: some English
Region: Tuscany, Michelin Map: 563

La Minerva, a full-fledged hotel with many amenities, is located in a quiet section of Capri, slightly off the beaten track, yet still quite central, permitting easy access to the more bustling areas of town—a walkers' paradise with no motorized transportation allowed. Glass entrance doors look straight through the capacious reception/sitting area across glossy blue-and-white tiled floors out to a view of the sea through another set of glass doors at the opposite end of the room. The captivating sea views through umbrella pine trees will strike you every time you come and go, as well as from most bedrooms. Rooms, all below this level, are reached by elevator, as is a small breakfast area, although most guests prefer breakfast served in rooms on their private balconies. The hotel's royal-blue-and-white tile theme follows through in the luminous guestrooms (standard or larger superior doubles), which are accented by an occasional antique piece. Deluxe doubles have Jacuzzi bathtubs and larger terraces with sea view. A rooftop solarium is an unusual bonus and is a special location and treat for a summer breakfast buffet. *Directions:* Stop at the tourist office as you get off the hydrofoil for a detailed map indicating Via Occhio Marino. The cable car or a taxi takes you from the port to the piazza at the center of town. From there it's a ten-minute walk to the hotel. Prearrange to have your luggage picked up at the port, otherwise, pack light!

LA MINERVA
Host: Luigi Esposito
Via Occhio Marino 8, Capri, (NA) 80073, Italy
Tel: (081) 8377067, Fax: (081) 8375221
18 Rooms, Double: €150–€390
Closed: Jan & Feb, Credit cards: all major
Other Languages: good English
Region: Campania, Michelin Map: 564

The Villa Krupp, built in 1900, is a delightful, small, family-run hotel, whose claim to local fame can be found in its guest book, boasting such illustrious names as Lenin and Gorky. The warm Coppola family, who turned the property into a hotel in the '60s, offer charming accommodation in 12 bedrooms within a somewhat modern and boxy white building alongside their own residence. The Krupp is dramatically situated in one of the most beautiful corners of Capri's Augusto Park, atop a steep, sheer cliff dropping to the sparkling turquoise sea beneath. The site overlooks the Faraglioni rock formation and Marina Piccola, one of Capri's two ports. A set of stairs leads up to the best vantage point from which to admire this spectacular and privileged panorama away from crowds of tourists. The renovated light-filled guestrooms, featuring individual balconies, are decorated with scattered antiques and pastel-colored ceramic tiles and all have air conditioning. Breakfast is served either out on the front terrace overflowing with potted flowers or in the veranda bar/dining room. Mother-daughter team Valentina and Donatella do an excellent job of caring for their guests, many of whom are regulars. Reserve well in advance for a long stay. *Directions:* Take the cable car up to Capri center (la piazzetta). Walk to Via Emanuele, past the Quisisana hotel, down to Viale Matteotti. The hotel is signposted to the right up a ramp, a 10 minute walk from the main square.

VILLA KRUPP
Hosts: Valentina & Donatella Coppola
Viale Matteotti 12, Capri, (NA) 80073, Italy
Tel: (081) 8370362 or (081) 8377473
Fax: (081) 8376489, Cellphone: (338) 1954155
12 Rooms, Double: €130–€170
Minimum Stay Required: 2-3 nights
Open: Apr to Oct 31, Credit cards: MC, VS
Other Languages: some English, French, German
Region: Campania, Michelin Map: 564

Capri has long had a reputation as an exclusive island, with prices only the elite were able to afford. However, the cost of tourism across Italy has soared, bringing other destinations more in line with Capri in terms of expense and making it relatively more affordable than it once was. Besides the many hotels, there are just a few true bed and breakfasts and Villa Vuotto is one of the best. Antonino Vuotto and his wife, a local couple both with hotel experience, opened up their centrally located, prim, white home in the town of Capri, making four bedrooms down one hall available to guests. The very pleasant and airy rooms are extremely clean and neat, with typical tiled floors, and private baths and balconies in each. All have a full or partial view of the sea. Breakfast is not served because there are no common rooms for guests but the Villa Vuotto's convenient location makes it easy to get to any of Capri's fine restaurants for breakfast, lunch, and dinner. It would be impossible to find another accommodation with such an absolutely incredible price/quality rapport. A marvelous value! *Directions:* Take the cable car up to Capri. Go through the main town square to Via Emanuele, past the Quisisana Hotel, and continue to the end of the street. Turn left onto Via Certosa, then left again on Cerio. The Villa is on the corner of Campo di Teste and is marked with its original name, Villa Margherita.

VILLA VUOTTO
Host: Antonino Vuotto family
Via Campo di Teste 2
Capri, (NA) 80073, Italy
Tel & Fax: (081) 8370230
4 Rooms, Double: €85–€110
Open: all year, Credit cards: none
Other Languages: very little English
Region: Campania, Michelin Map: 564

Between the cities of Bergamo and Brescia is a vast commercial area that incorporates the wine region known as Franciacorta—or "land of bubbles." The Ricci Curbastro vineyards, made up of almost 80 acres, are located in the heart of the area based at the foot of Lake Iseo. The family is one of the most renowned producers of top-quality (D.O.C.G.) Franciacorta Brut sparkling wine, among 12 other varieties of wine. The large and busy family estate just on the main road is made up of a complex of houses, which include the family's villa, wine cellars, a wine-tasting showroom, an antiques store, and an interesting agricultural museum and library filled with ancient farm tools and wine presses. Across the street is the farmhouse, transformed into guest apartments of various sizes (studio, one and two bedrooms), each with living area and kitchenette facilities. Rooms are simply decorated with country antiques and stenciled borders around windows and doorways. Here you have the advantage of being close to town while having views of the flat vineyards from bedroom windows. Sports facilities in the area include golf, horseback riding, and biking. This is a conveniently located accommodation for independent travelers. *Directions:* Exit at Palazzolo from the A4 autostrada and follow signs to Capriolo (2 km). Turn right in town at the sign for Adro. After half a kilometer the farm is on the left-hand side of the road.

AZIENDA AGRICOLA RICCI CURBASTRO
Host: Ricci Curbastro family
Via Adro 37, Capriolo, (BS) 25031, Italy
Tel: (030) 736094, Fax: (030) 7460558
8 Apartments: €70 daily*
*Apartment rental, no breakfast offered
Minimum Stay Required: 2 nights
Open: all year, Credit cards: all major
Other Languages: good English
Region: Lombardy, Michelin Map: 561

Although many think of Sardinia as purely a sailors' paradise (which it is), the development and widespread publicity of the chic Emerald Coast has robbed the island of its true identity. The beauty of ancient Sardinia (dating back to the Neolithic and Bronze Age periods) lies in its stark and rugged windswept landscapes and its relatively simple lifestyle. With the strategic location of Monti Tundu, the traveler can take advantage of both coast and mountain excursions, exploring this corner of the island. Making your way up the steep dirt road, you are rewarded with mountaintop views over the rocky Mediterranean terrain stretching out to the Cugnana Gulf. Meals incorporating local delicacies such as the island's famed Percorino cheeses are served in the simple circular dining room with windows looking out over the striking vistas. A separate one-story L-shaped stone house contains the guestrooms, each with independent entrance from the exterior and more sweeping views. Newly refurbished double rooms (all of which can become triples) and bathrooms have soft pastel color schemes, beige tiled floors, and simple and practical furnishings. Hosts Gianni and Giuseppina offer warm Sardinian hospitality. *Directions:* 10 km from Olbia (airport and ferry port). From Olbia take the S.S.125 regional road towards Arzachena/Palau. Monti Tundu is marked on the right side of the road. Follow the very rough, steep road up to the very end.

MONTI TUNDU
Hosts: Gianni Spolittu & Giuseppina Serra
Localita: Casagliana, Via Francoforte 4
Casagliana, Olbia, (SS) 07026, Italy
Tel & Fax: (0789) 613072 or 58001
Cellphone: (348) 8504860
10 Rooms, Double: €90–€110
Open: all year, Credit cards: none
Other Languages: French, Spanish
Region: Sardinia, Michelin Map: 566

After 20 years of managing guided tours throughout Italy, Welsh-born Maureen, along with husband, Roberto, brought her expertise "home" to La Torretta. Restoration work on the three-story 15th-century building, tucked away in this yet-undiscovered medieval hilltop village, took three years to complete. The entrance stairway leads to a large open and elegant lounge room with a collection of the family's paintings, stone fireplace, and 16th-century frescoes discovered during the restoration process. All seven bedrooms are individually and tastefully decorated in soft beige tones, which harmonize with travertine bathrooms, and have stunning views over the town's rooftops. Meals are served upstairs in a dining area with panoramic terrace overlooking olive groves and the wooded Sabine hills. This virgin territory is filled with hilltop villages to explore, besides being on the border of Umbria, and is just a 45-minute train ride from Rome. Maureen and her daughters customize itineraries for guests and organize cooking courses, while Roberto specializes in ancient Roman architecture and archeology. A separate self-catering apartment across the street is available. *Directions:* From Rome or Florence exit the A1 at Ponzano-Soratte. Go straight then turn right at the T-junction. Turn left at second T-junction and follow signs to Casperia (20 mins). Cars are easily parked on the street below and luggage is delivered by special vehicle.

LA TORRETTA
Hosts: Maureen & Roberto Scheda
Via Mazzini 7, Casperia, (RI) 02041, Italy
Tel & Fax: (0765) 63202
Cellphone: (338) 1451859
7 Rooms, Double: €80–€90
1 Apartment: €100 daily
Open: all year, Credit cards: MC, VS
Other Languages: fluent English, French
Region: Lazio, Michelin Map: 563

Raised in the United States, Lusya came "home" to Sicily to restore her grandfather's 17th-century villa and farmhouse complex and open it to guests. The large peach-colored villa, surrounded by citrus groves, originally housed both the family residence and cantinas where the grapes were made into wine. The cantinas serve as a dining area with stone arches that divide the room and a wine cellar that offers many Sicilian labels. The nineteen bedrooms are found in the main villa and a one-story wing around the swimming pool. Comfortably appointed in various color schemes, all the rooms have large wooden or wrought iron beds, striped bedspreads, and wooden furnishings. Lusya is an enthusiastic and energetic hostess and suggests many different day trips in this fascinating area of southern Sicily. Guests can also take advantage of nearby activities such as scooter or bike rentals, horseback riding, scuba diving, guided tours, Jeep excursions, and sailing. Excursions to the most important tourist and cultural sites are available. The hotel is very close to beautiful sandy beaches, in the countryside where peace and quiet are guaranteed even in the center of high season. Shuttle service is arranged for the beaches, Siracusa or the Catania airport. *Directions:* From Catania E45 exit at Cassibile, turn right for Floridia and after 2 km turn at hotel sign, next to the horse racing tracks.

HOTEL LADY LUSYA
Host: Lusya Giardina family
Strada Spinagallo, 16
Cassibile, (SR) 96100, Italy
Tel: (0931) 710277, Fax: (0931) 710274
Cellphone: (348) 5354190
24 Rooms, Double: €112–€212
Open: all year, Credit cards: all major
Region: Sicily, Michelin Map: 565

A stay at the Villa Aureli with Count di Serego Alighieri (descendant of Dante) can only be memorable. With its back to the town and looking out over the Italian Renaissance garden and surrounding countryside, the imposing brick villa has been standing for the past 300 years. When it was bought by the di Serego family in the 18th century, it was meticulously restored and embellished with plasterwork, decorative painted ceilings, richly painted fabrics on walls, ornately framed paintings and prints, colorful tiles from Naples, and Umbrian antiques. Left intentionally intact by the Count, who disdains overly restored historical homes, the elegant apartments for guests maintain their original ambiance. They can accommodate from four to six persons and are spacious, having numerous sitting rooms with fireplaces; although don't expect updated bathrooms or kitchens. A small swimming pool set against the villa's stone walls is a refreshing spot for dreaming. The villa serves as an ideal base from which to explore Umbria and parts of Tuscany, as well as special local itineraries prepared for guests by the Count. *Directions:* Exit from the Perugia highway at Madonna Alta and follow route 220 for Citta della Pieve. After 6 km, turn left for Castel del Piano Umbro.

VILLA AURELI
Host: Sperello di Serego Alighieri family
Via Cirenei 70, Castel del Piano, (PG) 06071, Italy
Tel: (340) 6459061, Fax: (075) 5149408
2 Apartments: €900–€1250 weekly*
*Apartment rental, no breakfast offered
Open: all year, Credit cards: MC, VS
Other Languages: good English, French, German
Region: Umbria, Michelin Map: 563

Castelfiorentino is 40 kilometers from Florence, Siena and Pisa, and although its outskirts are very commercial, it is a strategic touring base and the surrounding countryside is lovely. Continuing a long tradition of making guests feel at home—their hotel in Florence has been in the family for four generations—Massimo and Susanna opened this bed and breakfast ten years ago after major restoration of two hilltop farmhouses. The completely refurbished rooms, with many modern amenities, new bathrooms, fresh landscaping, and recently installed swimming pool and tennis court, have a very new feeling. Spacious bedrooms are appointed with authentic and reproduction antiques and have colorful Sicilian ceramic tiles above beds, with matching ones in bathrooms. The former barn was converted into a small restaurant decorated with contemporary art, a kitchen with viewing window, and a common living room/library upstairs. The preparation of delectable Tuscan fare using ancestral recipes is another strong tradition and cooking lessons are happily arranged. A buffet breakfast is served. The side terrace, overlooking soft hills, is where guests can both enjoy breakfast and watch the sunset in the evening. Olive oil and wine tasting can be arranged. *Directions:* From Castelfiorentino turn off at signs for Renai (this can be tricky to locate) and follow signs for Locanda Country Inn Le Boscarecce (5 km).

LE BOSCARECCE
Hosts: Susanna Ballerini & Massimo Ravalli
Via Renai 19, Castelfiorentino, (FI) 50051, Italy
Tel: (0571) 61280 or (347) 901092
Fax: (0571) 634008, Cellphone: (347) 9010922
14 Rooms, Double: €80–€150
Open: all year, Credit cards: all major
Other Languages: good English
Region: Tuscany, Michelin Map: 563

The Villa Gaidello farm has received acclaim in many culinary publications. There is nothing extravagant about hostess Paola Bini's recipes—she has simply revived traditional dishes using the freshest possible ingredients. Pasta is made daily (a great treat to watch) and features all the local variations on tagliatelle, pappardelle, and stricchettoni. Reservations for dinner must be made several days in advance. Paola is one of the pioneers in agritourism, transforming her grandmother's nearly-200-year-old farmhouse into a guesthouse and restaurant more than 30 years ago. One to five guests are accommodated in each of the eight apartments, which include kitchen, sitting room and are cozy and rustic with exposed-brick walls, country antiques, and lace curtains. Two double bedrooms are found in a fourth house on the property, San Giacomo, each decorated in the style of Paola's two favorite countries, France and the U.S. The dining room, set with doilies and ceramics, is situated in the converted hayloft and overlooks the vast garden and a small pond. Handling all guest requests is niece, Marta. This is a convenient stopover just off the Bologna-Milan autostrada. *Directions:* Exit the A1 autostrada at Modena Nord (or Bologna Nord from the south). Follow Via Emilia/route 9 towards Castelfranco. Turn left at the stop light (or right) on Via Costa (hospital) and follow signs to Gaidello.

VILLA GAIDELLO
Host: Paola Bini
Via Gaidello 18
Castelfranco Emilia, (MO) 41013, Italy
Tel: (059) 926806, Fax: (059) 926620
2 Rooms, Double: €98
8 Apartments: €130 daily
Closed: Aug, Credit cards: MC, VS
Other Languages: little English
Region: Emilia-Romagna, Michelin Map: 562

There is no doubt that the spectacular Amalfi coast must be seen, but in high season when the traffic is unbearable and Positano's streets are packed, a welcome retreat is the coast farther south at Castellabate. This is a very quiet and modest resort area where the majority of summer tourists are Italians. The winding road climbs up to the medieval village of Castellabate and La Mola, the summer home of the Favilla family, is right on the road entering town. Rather nondescript from the roadside entrance, the four-story former olive-press building, perched on the cliffside, faces out to the bay. Each room takes in some angle of this amazing panorama, two having balconies and the two-bedroom suite having a terrace. With an occasional antique, the bedrooms and living room with spiral staircase are pleasantly uncluttered so as not to detract from the inspiring sea views. On a clear day the Amalfi coastline and even Capri are visible. Hostess Loredana takes care of guests, preparing cakes and bread for breakfast, which is served on a table made from the old stone press on the main terrace. It is difficult to tear oneself away to try one of the interesting itineraries with an emphasis on either nature or ancient history (temples of Paestum, Certosa, or Padula). *Directions:* 60 km from Salerno. Take the road up to the town center and La Mola is marked on the side of the gray building on the right, the first house as you enter town on Via Cilento.

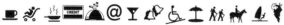

LA MOLA
Host: Francesco Favilla
Via A. Cilento 2, Castellabate, (SA) 84048, Italy
Tel: (0974) 967053, Fax: (0974) 967714
Cellphone: (335) 1292800
5 Rooms, Double: €114–€135
Minimum Stay Required: 2 nights
Open: Apr to Oct, Credit cards: all major
Other Languages: some English
Region: Campania, Michelin Map: 564

This idyllic location in the heart of Chianti, the Fattoria Tregole, five kilometers outside the charming village of Castellina, is reached by a gravel road. The ivy-covered stone farmhouse with hexagonal 18th century oratory (one of only two in Tuscany) is on the small road and opens out to the back to unspoiled hillsides covered with woods and vineyards. While husband Catello tends to the production of Chianti wine (visit the cantina with wood barrels for the reserve wines), gracious hostess Edith pays careful attention to her guests. There are five comfortable bedrooms and also two apartments complete with kitchen corner and living room, perfect for two to four guests. Particular care has been given to the décor, with peach-colored hand-stenciled walls and trim, soft colored quilts, antique pieces, painted wrought-iron beds, and dried flower arrangements all complimenting the terracotta brick floors. The breakfast room is set with white porcelain to match the white chairs and tables where Edith serves fresh cakes and breads each morning. With adequate notice an occasional dinner can also arranged. Outdoors the terrace and swimming enjoy inspiring views across the surrounding countryside. A great base for exploring Tuscany. *Directions:* From Castellina, follow south towards Siena and after 5 km turn left for Tregole and it's 1 km to Fattoria.

FATTORIA TREGOLE
Hosts: Edith Kirchlechner & Catello Conte
Località: Tregole 86
Castellina in Chianti, (SI) 53011, Italy
Tel: (0577) 740991, Fax: (0577) 741928
Cellphone: (333) 4329968
5 Rooms, Double: €130–€180, 2 Apts: €200–€360
Minimum Stay Required: 3 nights
Closed: Jan 15 to Mar 15, Credit cards: all major
Other Languages: good English
Region: Tuscany, Michelin Map: 563

While wandering in Marches through picture-perfect landscapes, we came upon the Giardino degli Ulivi bed and breakfast and were immediately intrigued. The absolutely charming accommodation is actually part of a 12th-century stone village and faces out to the rolling hills splashed with bright patches of yellow sunflowers. The scenery is enough to leave one in awe, let alone Maria Pia's marvelous cuisine with its Michelin rating. The carefully restored building, left ingeniously intact, thanks to her architect husband, Sante, includes the stone-walled restaurant with its many intimate nooks, centered around the ancient wine-making press. The five bedrooms upstairs off two sitting rooms with fireplace have wrought-iron beds, antique bedside tables, and beamed ceilings. The favorite corner bedroom (at a higher rate) has a large arched window taking in the breathtaking view. While their son, Francesco, tends to the breeding of horses, daughter Raffaela assists guests with the many interesting itineraries in the area (Camerino, San Severino, Matelica, and Fariano—famous for its paper industry). A real sense of discovery is experienced in this region, which keeps its traditions and folklore intact. *Directions:* From Castelraimondo follow route 256 towards Matelica, turning first left for Castel S. Maria then Castel S. Angelo.

IL GIARDINO DEGLI ULIVI
Host: Sante Cioccoloni family
Localita: Castel S. Angelo
Castelraimondo, (MC) 62022, Italy
Tel: (0737) 642121, Fax: (0737) 642600
Cellphone: (338) 3056098
5 Rooms, Double: €90–€140
Closed: Jan 8 to Mar 7, Credit cards: AX, VS
Other Languages: good English
Region: Marches, Michelin Map: 563

Tucked away off a winding mountain road in the enchanting Siusi Alps is a typical Tyrolean farmhouse where the Jaider family has resided ever since the 15th century, traditionally running a dairy farm. Their inviting home, with its authentic ambiance of the past, is colorfully accented with green shutters and flower-laden windowboxes. Two wooden barns are connected to the residence via a stone terrace. Paula Jaider runs her home with the hotel efficiency expected by visitors to this predominantly German-speaking area. Meals are served either out on the vine-covered terrace or in the original dining room, whose charm is enhanced by the low, wood-paneled ceiling and little carved wooden chairs. Be sure to reserve dinner: the food is excellent and it is just too far to go out for a meal. Cuisine in this region has an Austrian flavor, featuring speck ham, meat and potatoes, and apple strudel, and regulars come from afar to this well-known restaurant. Lovely country antiques are dispersed throughout the house and the eight very nice bedrooms, which are wood-paneled from floor to ceiling and have balconies with pretty valley views. A real charmer and a bargain. Book well in advance. *Directions:* Exit from the Bolzano-Brennero autostrada at Klausen and drive south to Ponte Gardena where you turn left across the river and first right towards Castelrotto. After 3.5 km make a sharp right for San Osvaldo and follow the narrow road for 2.5 km.

TSCHOTSCHERHOF
Host: Jaider family
San Osvaldo 19, Castelrotto, (BZ) 39040, Italy
Tel: (0471) 706013, Fax: (0471) 704801
8 Rooms, Double: €56–€80
Open: Mar to Nov, Credit cards: all major
Other Languages: very little English, German
Region: Trentino-Alto Adige, Michelin Map: 562

The lesser-known area of Tuscany south of Siena makes a delightful discovery and the variety of landscapes within an 8-kilometer drive provides one of the most fascinating excursions in the region. Besides the charming hilltowns of Montepulciano, Pienza, and Montalcino, there are the abbeys of Monte Oliveto and Sant'Antimo, plus the thermal baths of Bagno Vignoni. A perfect base in this richly historical and natural area is the fairytale castle of the Aluffi Pentini family, theirs for the past 400 years or so and practically a village in itself. The family resides in the upper reaches of the castle while guests are accommodated in several separate farmers' houses divided into a combination of apartments with one or two bedrooms, living room, and kitchenette, plus six simply and characteristically appointed bedrooms with country furniture. Rooms facing out have absolutely breathtaking views over the virgin valley (the same view that all guests enjoy from the lovely pool). Downstairs is the dining room with wood tables covered with cheery checked cloths, where breakfast and dinner are served using homegrown products. A common space for guests is the old granary, converted into a large cozy reading room with fireplace. *Directions:* The castle is well marked at 5 km from San Quirico d'Orcia. Ripa d'Orcia is marked on most maps.

CASTELLO DI RIPA D'ORCIA
Host: Aluffi Pentini family
Localita: Ripa d'Orcia
Castiglione d'Orcia, (SI) 53023, Italy
Tel: (0577) 897376 or (0577) 897317
Fax: (0577) 898038, Cellphone: (333) 5825181
6 Rooms, Double: €115–€170
8 Apartments: €110–€198 daily, €690–€950 weekly
Minimum Stay Required: 2 for rooms, 3 for apartments
Open: Mar to Nov, Credit cards: MC, VS
History Traveller
Region: Tuscany, Michelin Map: 563

This bed and breakfast has been added to the new group of agritourism accommodation in the Aosta Valley region. It offers a pleasant place to stay right in the center of charming Champoluc and is associated with the agritourism cheese farm, La Tchavana, up on the mountainside overlooking town. In the summer months the two establishments offer a very worthwhile four-day itinerary featuring a country lunch and tour of the Bagnod family's fontina cheese farm, a visit to an ancient mountain village with sabotier artisans, and two other mountain hikes. The scenic ride up through the valley leading to Champoluc takes you by many picturesque villages, ending at the ski/summer resort. Raul and Lorena took over the family's early-19th-century home in the center of town and recently had it refurbished into a small bed and breakfast. The prim white house with wood-trim balconies, conveniently located right next to the cable-car lift entrance, contains nine (non-smoking) bedrooms divided among the top two floors, decorated plainly and practically with new tiled flooring and wood-beamed mansard ceilings. The main entrance to the home opens directly into a welcoming living room with dark-wood furniture, burgundy armchairs, and combination wood and slate floors. A loft balcony overlooks the room. Breakfast is served downstairs in the dining room. *Directions:* On the main road in Champoluc.

LO MIETE VIEI
Hosts: Raul Chasseur & Lorena Blondin
Rue Prabochon 6, Champoluc, (AO) 11020, Italy
Tel: (0125) 308713, Fax: (0125) 308449
9 Rooms, Double: €90–€130
Open: all year, Credit cards: MC, VS
Other Languages: some English, French
Region: Aosta Valley, Michelin Map: 561

In the hills between Tuscany and Umbria, overlooking the Tiber and Chiana valleys, you find the Nannotti family's typical farm property. Renato and Maria Teresa used to run a restaurant nearby before deciding to open a bed and breakfast and serve delicious Tuscan-Umbrian recipes at home. The three adjacent red-stone houses include six guestrooms, two apartments, and the family's private quarters. Rooms, many with terrace or garden space, are all decorated in a simple, pleasant country style with a mix of reproduction armoires, wrought-iron beds, and some modern pieces. Ernesto and Renato specialize in organic produce and make their own honey, jams, grappa, D.O.C. red wine (Colli del Trasimeno), and extra-virgin olive oil, which are brought directly to their restaurant next door with large panoramic terrace, Le Due Valli, for Maria Teresa to use in her authentic homemade cooking. She creates an easy, informal ambiance and young daughter Aureliana helps out. Being close to the charming, historical village and having easy access to the autostrada make this a super touring location. There are also bikes, a swimming pool, hiking trails, a special spa package at nearby thermal waters, a park for children, many farm animals, a fitness track, and horses to ride. *Directions:* Exit at Chiusi from the north or Fabro from the south and follow signs for Citta della Pieve. In town follow signs for San Casciano Dei B., the B&B is signposted.

MADONNA DELLE GRAZIE
Host: Renato Nannotti family
Via Madonna delle Grazie 6
Citta della Pieve, (PG) 06062, Italy
Tel: (0578) 299822, Fax: (0578) 297749
Cellphone: (340) 8210564
6 Rooms, Double: €100–€140
2 Apartments: €600–€1100 weekly
Open: all year, Credit cards: MC, VS
Other Languages: some English, French, German
Region: Umbria, Michelin Map: 563

Il Caggio is a delightful agriturismo farm, distinguishing itself from the many others by the sincere and warm hospitality of its owners, Gabriella and Paolo, and the superb quality of the meals. Conveniently located close to the main autostrada, guests have this corner of Chianti at their fingertips, from Siena, Cortona, Chianti, to Arezzo. Two bedrooms and two apartments are in part of the main stone house and an adjacent house. All are carefully appointed in a creative, country-style with great attention to details and the comfort of guests. All accommodations have private entrances from the exterior. In the rustic main house, the ambiance really warms up around Gabriella's dinner table where a non-stop series of aperitifs, pasta specialties, and a dessert buffet are served, accompanied by good local wine. An abundant breakfast with more of Gabriella's homemade, baked cakes awaits guests in the morning. A swimming pool behind the house bordering the woods is available, as well as a six-person hot hydro-jet pool. Convinced that their guests will enjoy their stay, their brochure warns: An extended stay here generates a sense of well-being with a tendency to forget about problems, tempting one to postpone going back home! *Directions:* From the A1 autostrada exit at Monte Savino and turn left continuing for 6.7 km to Ciggiano. Turn right and then left at abandoned farmhouse and follow up to the house.

CASALE IL CAGGIO
Hosts: Gabriella & Paolo Magini
Località: Ciggiano
Civitella in Val di Chiana, (AR) 52040, Italy
Tel & Fax: (0575) 440022, Cellphone: (335) 5844811
2 Rooms, Double: €100–€135
2 Apartments: €600–€1200 weekly
Open: all year, Credit cards: all major
Other Languages: good English
Region: Tuscany, Michelin Map: 563

Venture north from Rome to explore the scenic countryside and medieval villages of Sabina and consider staying a few days in the area to experience the small-town life of an area famous for its production of top-quality virgin olive oil (there is even an oil museum). Definitely include the magnificent 6th-century Farfa Abbey which was one of the most important monasteries in Europe at the time of Charlemagne. Ten minutes further in Santo Pietro a cluster of stone houses actually served as a defense line for the Abbey. The Corradini family welcomes guests to a portion of this hamlet where they offer guest accommodations in six bedrooms (two with private bathrooms outside the room) above the popular country restaurant where fresh pasta and savory local recipes are served. As you would expect in this setting, bedrooms are appointed with family antiques, armoires, chests and wrought-iron beds. Each has a particular feature, such as the mansard or the corner room with spectacular views. A living room with kitchen is also for guest use. The whole Corradini family with three grown children gets involved, especially on weekends when residents of the area and Romans come for a meal. *Directions:* Exit the A1 autostrada at Fiano Romano; follow signs for Passo Corese. Turn left at intersection; then right at the first turnoff for Farfa. Continue for Farfa until Coltodino. After town turn left at sign for Santo Pietro. Located 25 km north of Rome.

SANTO PIETRO   **New**
Host: Carlo Corradini family
Loc. Santo Pietro di Coltodino
Coltodino, Fara in Sabina, (RI) 02030, Italy
Tel: (0765) 386748
Fax: (0765) 386818
6 Rooms, Double: €60–€76
Open: all year, Credit cards: VS
Other Languages: some English
Region: Lazio, Michelin Map: 563

Drive past thousands of gnarled secular olive trees divided by low-rising, dry-stone walls to the 17th-century stone Masseria Sacerdote, immersed amid groves of olive, cherry and almond trees and wildflowers. Once a simple shelter for livestock, the home has been restored by the Piccone family who took great care not to disturb the original character of the simple dwelling. The completely intact farmhouse is surrounded by seven trulli, those distinctive cone-shaped roofs found only in Puglia. Each of two of the trulli cottages has a double bedroom and bathroom appointed with extreme simplicity (it was once the home of a priest), incorporating design pieces which blend well with the bio-architecture concept. A third room is located on the first floor of the main house and has a small stone terrace with enchanting views over the lush countryside. A fourth choice of accommodation is an apartment with en suite double bedroom, a lounge/double bedroom with a fireplace and a single sofa-bed plus kitchenette. An organic breakfast with fresh fruits from the orchard is served in the kitchen or on the patio. The Masseria is a short a drive to the coast and 15 minutes from the historic town with its cathedral, churches and castle. Daughter Marta is on hand to suggest day trips to Alberobello, Ostuni, Locorotondo and the caves of Castellana Grotte and Grotta Bianca. *Directions:* From Conversano take the road towards Putignano. After 4 km turn left for Castellana. The house is on the right after 1 km.

MASSERIA SACERDOTE   New
Host: Marta Piccone family
Contrada Madonna dei Tetti
Conversano, (BA) 70014, Italy
Tel: (080) 4959725
Fax: (080) 5211286
Cellphone: (335) 7507985
4 Rooms, Double: €90
Open: Apr to Nov
Credit cards: VS, Other Languages: English
Region: Apulia, Michelin Map: 564

Cortina has enjoyed a long-standing reputation as one of the most "in" resorts of the Dolomites, helped also by its center-stage location. Prominent politicians, stars of television and cinema, socialites and nobility have vacation homes here and congregate three times a year at Christmas, Easter, and during the month of August. In town, there is a large range of accommodation available, but if you want to be part of the scene yet desire a quiet place to sleep, the Menardi family's Baita Fraina is the perfect choice. A baita is a typical chalet farmhouse where home and barn are incorporated into one building. Overlooking mountains to the back and a large park for children to the front, the Fraina is primarily a well-established and esteemed restaurant cited in top restaurant guides and specializing in pastas with fresh mushrooms as well as the exquisite local fartaies dessert with wild-berry sauce. Three paneled and intimate dining rooms have ceramic-tiled stove heaters, lace curtains, antique kitchen tools, and dried flower arrangements. Adolfo will show you his cellar which stocks over 500 Italian wines. The six simply decorated bedrooms done in pinewood were added later on the top two floors. A sauna, Jacuzzi, and sun terrace are extra features of this characteristic bed and breakfast. *Directions:* Entering Cortina on route 48, turn left before town for Fraina and take the road for 1.2 km.

☕ 🏊 💳 ☎ @ P 🍴 🚶 🚶‍♂️ 🐎 ⛷

BAITA FRAINA
Host: Adolfo Menardi family
Localita: Fraina
Cortina d'Ampezzo, (BL) 32043, Italy
Tel: (0436) 3634, Fax: (0436) 876235
Cellphone: (335) 265204
6 Rooms, Double: €100–€150
Closed: Apr 1 to Jun 26 & Sep 22 to Dec 1
Credit cards: all major
Other Languages: good English, German
Region: Veneto, Michelin Map: 562

Cortina is one of the most frequented spots for travelers passing through the Dolomites on their way up to Austria, or those who just want to get a taste of a mountain resort Italian-style. The multitude of ski lifts and variety of slopes along with the absolutely gorgeous scenery make it an easy winner. The Meublè Oasi is a pleasant, recently updated bed and breakfast on the outskirts of town (easily reached by foot) at the beginning of a pretty residential street. This former private residence dating to 1925 has ten rooms located on the ground and first floors, while the Luchetta family, the original owners, reside on the top floor. New bedrooms are comfortably appointed with pinewood beds topped with fluffy comforters and soft-pea-green curtains and matching chairs. Amenities include satellite TV and phones in the rooms. A good buffet breakfast is served in the downstairs breakfast room with bay window. A small garden to the side of the house offers a restful spot. This is an efficient little hotel maintaining the warmth of a home and the Seppis are true hosts. *Directions:* The Meublè Oasi is in town on the road leaving Cortina towards Dobbiaco and well marked.

MEUBLÈ OASI
Hosts: Lorenza Seppi & Tranquillo Luchetta
Via Cantore 2
Cortina d'Ampezzo, (BL) 32043, Italy
Tel: (0436) 862019, Fax: (0436) 879476
Cellphone: (340) 7383 822
10 Rooms, Double: €75–€170
3 Suites: €90–€190
Open: all year, Credit cards: MC, VS
Other Languages: good English, German
Region: Veneto, Michelin Map: 562

Borgo Elena, located in the hills outside one of our favorite Tuscan towns, Cortona, belongs to Mario Baracchi, whose brother owns the gorgeous inn, Il Falconiere (listed in our Inns guide). In fact, you can reach Borgo Elena by passing through the Falconiere property (stop in for an exquisite meal) on a narrow, steep gravel road that ends at the cluster of stone houses bordered by dense chestnut woods. Here you are totally immersed in nature and complete silence, with hilltop Cortona to one side and the immense Chiana Valley spread out before you. Seven quaint apartments, each with independent entrance, are dispersed among the various stone houses, which were the quarters for the farmhands of the Falconiere estate a century ago. Their original rustic ambiance remains while convenient modern utilities and amenities have been incorporated. The apartments, all charmingly appointed with Tuscan country pieces, accommodate from two to six persons and are all different in layout, most being on two levels. A lovely swimming pool sits higher up and takes in even more of the expansive view. The Borgo Elena is an ideal base for independent travelers who want to settle in one place for easily touring Tuscany's highlights. *Directions:* Instead of going into the center of Cortona, follow signs for Arezzo and drive past Camucia on the outskirts of town to Tavarnelle. Turn right at San Pietro a Cegliolo and drive 2 km up to Borgo Elena.

BORGO ELENA
Host: Mario Baracchi
Localita: San Pietro a Cegliolo
Cortona, (AR) 52042, Italy
Tel & Fax: (0575) 604773
Cellphone: (333) 9319320
7 Apts: €40 per person per night, €560–€750 weekly
Minimum Stay Required: 3 nights
Open: all year, Credit cards: all major
Other Languages: very little English
Region: Tuscany, Michelin Map: 563

The charming medieval Etruscan town of Cortona that gained international fame through Frances Mayes' bestseller, "Under the Tuscan Sun", has subsequently responded to the increased demand for tourist accommodation. The Mancini family decided to completely refurbish their lovely old farm (a village in itself on the site of an Etruscan settlement) to accommodate a variety of needs for the more demanding traveler. The 17th-century private home sits in the middle of its meticulously landscaped gardens boasting 2,500 rose plants and surrounded by ten other stone houses which are now home to the comfortable hotel, Locanda. Featuring a voluminous breakfast room, eight spacious one, two and three-bedroom apartments on two floors of the former olive oil mill and farmer's quarters, there are also two excellent restaurants, a wine bar, a stunning swimming pool with hydro-massage, and a chapel. The décor of all the rooms is in keeping with an air of elegant country ambiance. A complete country resort. *Directions:* Exit from autostrada A1 at Valdichiana, proceed towards Perugia. Exit from this highway at second exit for Cortona. Strategically located, Il Melone is well-marked on the main street leading to Arezzo, below Cortona center.

BORGO IL MELONE
Host: Carlo Livraga Mancini family
Il Sodo, Case Sparse 38, Cortona, (AR) 52042, Italy
Tel: (0575) 603330, Fax: (0575) 630001
12 Rooms, Double: €165–€240
8 Apartments: €1500–€2500 weekly
Minimum Stay Required: 7 nights in apartments
Closed: Jan 10 to Feb 10, Credit cards: all major
Other Languages: good English
Region: Tuscany, Michelin Map: 563

The Antica Fattoria came highly recommended by several readers who stayed there in the first year it opened. It is indeed a delightful combination of pretty countryside, strategic touring position, comfortable rooms, excellent meals, and warm hospitality. Following the increasingly popular lifestyle trend of abandoning the city for a rural pace, Roman couple Alessandro and Anna left their offices to become, essentially, farmers. They bought and restored two connected stone farmhouses and incorporated a combination of five rooms and two apartments, decorated pleasantly with a characteristic country flavor, for guests. While Alessandro tends to the crops and farm animals, Anna lives out her passion for cooking, much to guests' delight. Meals are served either outside at one long table or in the transformed cow stalls below with cozy sitting area and fireplace. At times the allegria and good food keep guests at the table until the wee hours. A lovely swimming pool looks over the wooded hills to the valley. The busy hosts take time to assist guests with the many local itineraries and organize a wide variety of games. Perfect for families and a great base for exploring Umbria. The town of Deruta is world famous for its painted ceramic pottery and filled with workshops and stores. *Directions:* From Perugia (18 km), exit from E45 at Casalina. Take the first right and follow signs to the Santuario Madonna dei Bagni and then to the Fattoria.

ANTICA FATTORIA DEL COLLE
Hosts: Anna & Alessandro Coluccelli
Strada Colle delle Forche 6, Deruta, (PG) 06053, Italy
Tel & Fax: (075) 972201, Cellphone: (329) 9897272
5 Rooms, Double: €90–€110
2 Apartments: €850–€1100 weekly
Minimum Stay Required: 2 nights, 7 in August
Per person half board: €75–€80
Open: Easter to Jan 11, Credit cards: none
Other Languages: good English
Region: Umbria, Michelin Map: 563

The prestigious Luigi Einaudi wine estate (he was the first president of the Italian republic), established in 1897, is the oldest in the area and extends over 300 acres of land of which some 160 acres are covered entirely with vineyards. Today, Luigi's granddaughter Paola and husband Giorgio Ruffo continue this strong family tradition as leading producers of top Barolo, Barbera, and Dolcetto wines. They have transformed one of the family residences dating to the 18th century into a refined bed and breakfast that preserves an authentic essence of the past. The very attractive and spacious bedrooms, all on the first floor and appointed with fine antiques and gorgeous fabrics, are joined by an elegant common living room where plenty of material on what the region offers is readily available. There is also a large terrace for guests on this same floor and a full country breakfast is served in the sunny dining room off the kitchen. Corner rooms and the one suite have terraces and all rooms have splendid views of the undulating hillsides with a backdrop of the Alps in the distance. Six additional bedrooms are found opposite the main house with an arched glassed-in living room and swimming pool. Elvira, who takes care of guests, lives with her family in the apartment downstairs next to the cantina. *Directions:* The Foresteria dei Poderi is 2 km outside of Dogliani on the road towards Belvedere.

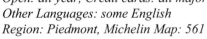

FORESTERIA DEI PODERI
Host: Elvira Raimondi family
Localita: Borgata Gombe 31
Dogliani, (CN) 12063, Italy
Tel: (0173) 70414, Fax: (0173) 742017
12 Rooms, Double: €120–€150
Open: all year, Credit cards: all major
Other Languages: some English
Region: Piedmont, Michelin Map: 561

The Villa Goetzen is an excellent choice as a base for visiting the villas of Palladio and the stunning historical centers of Verona and Padua (plus being 20 minutes from Venice). With a long tradition in hospitality, the local Minchio family bought the peach-colored home (dating from 1739) sitting on the Brenta Canal in town and transformed it into an elegant bed-and-breakfast accommodation. Although the house borders the main road, silence reigns within. You enter the iron gates into a courtyard, where on the right is a miniature coach house with two of the twelve rooms. These are the favorites and most romantic, with beamed mansard ceilings, parquet floors, and canal view. All rooms are decorated with classic good taste in the selection of antique pieces, wrought-iron beds, and coordination of fabrics and individual color schemes. Immaculate bathrooms have black-and-white checked tiles. Fortunate guests can sample delectable Venetian meals prepared by Paola and her son, Massimiliano, in one of the three intimate dining rooms of their well-known restaurant. Tables are also available outside bordering the canal. Son Christian is ready to receive and assist guests at the front desk. It would be virtually impossible to find a hotel with similar standards in Venice at this rate. *Directions:* Exit at Dolo from the A4 autostrada and go straight into town until you come to the canal. Turn left and follow signs for Venezia, the villa is on the right.

VILLA GOETZEN
Host: Minchio family
Via Matteotti 6, Dolo, (VE) 30031, Italy
Tel: (041) 5102300, Fax: (041) 412600
12 Rooms, Double: €110–€140
Open: all year, Credit cards: all major
Other Languages: good English
Region: Veneto, Michelin Map: 562

Picturesque Courmayeur, on the Italian side of the tunnel cutting through Mont Blanc into France, is a popular ski and summer resort. In the summer months comfortable temperatures and spectacular mountain scenery along with activities such as hiking, golf, horseback riding, and kayaking attract many visitors. The warm Berthod family have been offering hospitality to guests for some time, greeting them by name as they return "home" year after year. The old stone chalet and barn, squeezed between other houses in the center of the centuries-old village of Entreves, outside Courmayeur, has been restored using old and new materials. The cozy reception area maintains its original rustic flavor with flagstone floors and beams, hanging brass pots, typical locally made pine furniture, and homey touches like dried-flower arrangements and lace curtains. The 23 simply appointed rooms, divided between two buildings, offer the amenities of a standard hotel. A hearty breakfast is the only meal served; however, half-board arrangements can be made with local restaurants for longer stays. La Grange is an efficiently run bed and breakfast right at the foot of the snow-capped Alps. *Directions:* From Aosta where the A5 autostrada ends, continue on route 26 to Courmayeur. Entreves is 5 km beyond.

LA GRANGE
Host: Berthod family
Frazione Entrèves
Entrèves-Courmayeur, (AO) 11013, Italy
Tel: (0165) 869733, Fax: (0165) 869744
23 Rooms, Double: €100–€230
Minimum Stay Required: 3 nights
Closed: May, Jun, Oct, Nov, Credit cards: all major
Other Languages: good English, French
Region: Aosta Valley, Michelin Map: 561

The ancestral summer home of the aristocratic Passi family from Venice is a true charmer, overflowing with historic ambiance in every corner. It is special in every aspect having maintained its original character while being updated for modern comforts, yet what leaves guests so enamored is its best-of-both-worlds position. You are perched on a hill, immersed in a romantic garden with terraces and trails leading past ancient trees while having open views out to the Adriatic sea. As if all this were not enough, the property is part of an actual farm of olive groves. Your passionate hostess and world traveler, Anna Passi, can recount tales of her family's illustrious Franco-Italian roots (her great aunt Baroness Giulia de Rolland was the first woman to have climbed Mont Blanc) and original owners, Prince Eugène de Beauharnais, stepson of Napoleon. The refined ancient home full of family heirloom antiques from various epochs has been given a fresh look with marvelous French fabrics on sofas, curtains and bedspreads. Several sitting rooms plus many of the guest bedrooms and suites are in the main house, while the remaining rooms and apartments with kitchen facilities are located within two houses in the garden. There is also a swimming pool. Pure magic. *Directions:* Exit at Fano from the A14 autostrada, pass through the city following signs for Pesaro. After 3 km turn left for Via di Villa San Biagio and then right following signs to the villa.

RELAIS VILLA GIULIA
Host: Anna Passi
Localita: San Biagio, Via di Villa Giulia 40
Fano, (PU) 61032, Italy
Tel & Fax: (0721) 823159
10 Rooms, Double: €150–€280
5 Apartments, 1 Cottage: €170–€240 daily
Open: Mar to Dec, Credit cards: MC, VS
Other Languages: English spoken well
2 km from center Fano
Region: Marches, Michelin Map: 563

Although the Apulia region is decidedly one of the most intriguing and unusual areas of the less-traveled Italy, it is short of accommodation with that combination of comfort, charm, and history we search high and low for. The 350-year-old Masseria Marzalossa, however, is a true exception, being a romantic inn strategically placed between the highlights of the region with its unique trulli cone-shaped houses. The stunning 100-acre property, which produces top-quality olive oil, has belonged to the Guarini family since its origins and they take pride in sharing their piece of paradise with world travelers. A wall surrounding the ancient masseria conceals several inner courtyards leading to the massive stone main house and connecting houses where the elegant, ground-level bedrooms enjoy their own private courtyard entrances. The tastefully decorated rooms are appointed with period antiques in harmony with the stone floors and vaulted or beamed ceilings. Also available is a magnificent suite with high, vaulted ceilings, frescoes, and a marble bathroom. A passageway from the front garden leads to a divine enclosed swimming pool surrounded by columns, lemon trees, bougainvillea vines, potted geraniums, and utter silence. Full country breakfasts and occasional dinners are served in the intimate dining room. This property is impeccable. *Directions:* Two km from Fasano on the S.S.16 going towards Ostuni, turn right at their sign.

MASSERIA MARZALOSSA
Hosts: Mario & Maria Teresa Guarini
Contrada da Pezze Vicine 65
Fasano, (BR) 72015, Italy
Tel & Fax: (080) 4413780
8 Rooms, Double: €160–€270
4 Suites: €300–€500
Closed: Nov 15 to Dec 22, Credit cards: VS
Other Languages: some English
Region: Apulia, Michelin Map: 564

Casa Palmira, directly north of Florence, was originally a group of rural buildings attached to an 11th-century tower guarding the road to the Mugello area of Tuscany. Stefano and Assunta, the amiable hosts, named their bed and breakfast after the old lady who lived in the house her entire life. She represents perhaps the spirit of the place, reminding everyone of the basic values of simple country living. The seven bedrooms on the top floor are decorated in a fresh, simple, country style, with hardwood floors, dried and fresh flowers, patchwork quilts, botanical prints, and local country antiques. Rooms are accessed by a large open sitting area with skylights and green plants. The hosts' naturally informal style of hospitality has guests feeling so at home that they can't resist assisting as Assunta works wonders in the open kitchen. This is part of a multi-functional space incorporating kitchen, dining room, and cozy living area with wicker chairs and large fireplace. Meals based on fresh vegetables are served either here or out in the garden under the portico. Daily cooking lessons for individuals or weekly cooking courses for small groups are arranged. Transfers from train station or airport are also offered. *Directions:* Halfway between Borgo S. Lorenzo and Florence on route 302 (Via Faentina), 2 km after Olmo coming from Florence (16 km). Casa Palmira is on the right at the sign for Ristorante Feriolo. From the north leave the A1 at Barberino del Mugello.

CASA PALMIRA
Hosts: Assunta & Stefano Mattioli
Via Faentina–Polcanto, Feriolo, (FI) 50030, Italy
Tel & Fax: (055) 8409749
Cellphone: (339) 3331190
7 Rooms, Double: €85–€110
1 Apartment: €130 daily, €800–€900 weekly
Minimum Stay Required: 3 nights
Open: Mar to Dec, Credit cards: none
Other Languages: good English, French
Region: Tuscany, Michelin Map: 563

The Savini family transplanted from Milan to Urbino, open up their 185-acre organic cattle farm to guests in the summer months from June to October. Set in spectacularly scenic countryside, characterized by soft green hills, intermittent patches of woods and a mountain backdrop, the simple farmer's house built in the 1920s has been converted into a guesthouse with six double bedrooms all down one hall (tend to be on the small side). Each room has been given a specific color theme and the simple and practical furnishings and fabrics fit into the scheme, designed by Giulia's architect father, utilizing the principles of bio-architecture (solar heating, water purifying system). Both Giulia and her mother are directly involved with the hospitality duties and the general cooking—over 70% of the food served is organically sourced on the farm. This is an area famous for its white truffles, a true delicacy. A swimming pool facing the virgin landscapes is near the house as well as the stables and arenas where lessons can be taken or country walks organized. Bordering Umbria and Marches, there are many historic villages to explore including stunning Urbino and Gubbio. *Directions:* Exit the Fano-Roma highway at the Acqualagna/Piobbico exit, proceed for Piobbico until you reach Pole. After 750 m turn right towards Castellaro and follow the Valle Nuova roadsigns for 3.3 km.

LOCANDA DELLA VALLE NUOVA
Host: Giulia Savini
La Cappella 14, Fermignano, (PU) 61033, Italy
Tel: (0722) 330303, Fax: (0722)330303
Cellphone: (329) 8975940
6 Rooms, Double: €108
2 Apartments: €680 weekly
Minimum Stay Required: 3 nights, 7 in apartments
Open: Jun to Oct, Credit cards: MC, VS
Other Languages: English, Spanish, some French
Region: Marches, Michelin Map: 563

The noble Romani Adami family has resided for many generations in this fascinating 18th-century palace complex at the heart of the well-preserved walled medieval town of Fermo. Comprising the family residence, farmers' quarters, cantina, barns, kitchens and stables this was a flourishing agricultural area where grain, grapes and olives were transported to the village and processed literally in-house. After an ingenious restoration, fortunate guests have a choice of seven tastefully appointed apartments and rooms of varying sizes within the palazzo. All the rooms have independent entrances and some special features such as views, inner courtyard or large interior garden. A creative combination of family antiques, contemporary pieces, beautiful fabrics and modern bathrooms enhance the apartments. Gracious hostess Cecilia Romani Adami and her family live in another section of the vast palazzo and are always on hand to suggest interesting sightseeing. The apartments are ideal for groups of friends. Dinners can be arranged for larger groups while breakfast fixings are found in each of the apartments with kitchen facilities. Fermo is south of Ancona and just 5 km from the Adriatic sea. *Directions:* Exit the Autostrada A14 at Fermo/Porto San Giorgio and follow to Fermo center. Proceed to the main piazza with the stunning cathedral. Corso Cavour street descends from the other side of the piazza.

PALAZZO ROMANI ADAMI
Host: Cecilia Romani Adami
Corso Cavour 94, Fermo, (AP) 63023, Italy
Tel: (338) 8811300
6 Suites: €150–€200
2 Apartments: €360 daily, €2200 weekly
Open: all year, Credit cards: none
Region: Marches, Michelin Map: 563

The stunning ancient cities of Ferrara, Ravenna, and Mantova have recently become part of the more curious traveler's itinerary and Il Bagattino could not be a more perfect base for exploring this triangle of Emilia-Romagna as well as making day trips to Bologna or Venice. Congenial hostess Alessandra left a ten-year restaurant business and opened her six-room bed and breakfast in the apartment next door to her own. Just off the main square of the historic center with its impressive fortress Castello Estense, Il Bagattino is on the second floor (with elevator) of a completely refurbished brick building dating to the 1400s. You are warmly greeted in the cheery yellow front room where a breakfast of fresh croissants and homemade cakes is served at one table. The six bedrooms are divided on both sides of the main room, with a small sitting room for extra privacy. Each comfortable, identically-sized bedroom, with air conditioning, television, mini-bar, and hairdryer, has its own color scheme reflected in matching bedspreads and curtains, and a new checked-tiled bathroom. The entire historic center of this fascinating ancient city is closed off to traffic and is a cyclist's haven (bikes can be rented through Alessandra). Ferrara is a city not to be missed! *Directions:* Although this is a restricted traffic area, you can unload luggage in front of the bed and breakfast. Follow signs for the city center and Duomo—Corso Porta Reno begins from the piazza at the clock tower.

IL BAGATTINO
Host: Alessandra Maurillo
Corso Porta Reno 24, Ferrara, (FE) 44100, Italy
Tel: (0532) 241887, Fax: (0532) 217546
Cellphone: (349) 8696683
6 Rooms, Double: €100–€120
Open: all year, Credit cards: all major
Other Languages: good English
Region: Emilia-Romagna, Michelin Map: 562

Best friends Luciano and Tommaso, refugees from city life, have transformed the 1,000-acre property, La Casella, made up of woods, rivers, and valleys, into a veritable countryside haven for vacationers. Foremost attention has been given to the 32 rooms, which are divided between four separate stone houses. The Noci house contains seven doubles upstairs appointed with country antiques, and a large vaulted room downstairs used for small meetings or dining. La Terrazza, originally a hunting lodge, has nine rooms, one with namesake terrace looking over the oak woods. On the highest point sits San Gregorio, with a small pool, where guests revel in the utter silence and a spectacular 360-degree view over the entire property. The lively dining room offers delectable cuisine, with ingredients direct from the farm. The many sports facilities include a beautiful big swimming pool, tennis, and an equestrian center where numerous special outings and events are organized. There is also a spa program with natural treatments. Well-marked trails lead the rider, biker, or hiker to such marvels as Todi, Orvieto, or even Perugia. *Directions:* Exit at Fabro from the Rome-Florence A1 autostrada. Follow signs for Parrano (7 km), turning right at the Casella sign, and continue for another 7 km on a rough gravel road.

LA CASELLA
Hosts: Luciano Nenna & Tommaso Campolmi
Localita: La Casella
Ficulle, (TR) 05016, Italy
Tel & Fax: (0763) 86588
32 Rooms, Price per person: €70–€90
Minimum Stay Required: 7 nights in Aug
Open: all year, Credit cards: all major
Other Languages: English, Spanish, German, French, Swedish
Region: Umbria, Michelin Map: 563

The latest arrival in the group of independent city bed & breakfast properties, managed by Lea, is the very charming Antica Dimora Firenze. Located in part of an ancient palazzo owned by the Pandolfini family, just 5 blocks north of the Duomo Cathedral, it has similar characteristics to the other bed & breakfasts found in the same area (Johanna I & II, Johlea) owned by the same cordial owner, but offers a great deal more. Six smartly decorated rooms are located on the second floor of the ancient, residential building. Each room is individually and tastefully appointed as in a true home, with great attention to detail and guest comfort. A cozy living/reception room with inviting sofas plus breakfast room awaits guests. Breakfast is served in this same reception room or privately in the bedrooms. It is difficult to choose a preference among the six romantic rooms, each completely different in soft pastel color schemes and a unique, additional feature. There are two lovely corner rooms and two quiet ones with small back terraces. All have antique pieces, silk or hand-woven Busatti fabrics and linens, and canopy beds. The color-coordinated bathrooms have marble or brick floors. All are delightful giving the feeling of having your own private apartment in Florence, including the key to the front door! Guests have free wireless connection, television and DVD, plus other amenities. *Directions:* 3 blocks north of San Marco church and square.

ANTICA DIMORA FIRENZE
Host: Lea Gulmanelli
Via San Gallo 72, Florence, (FI) 50129, Italy
Tel: (055) 4627296, Fax: (055) 4634450
6 Rooms, Double: €125–€150
Open: all year, Credit cards: none
Other Languages: good English
Region: Tuscany, Michelin Map: 563

In the past few years, a new breed of bed and breakfasts has developed in Italy's favorite cities, especially in Florence and Rome. A small staff is on hand which makes this an appropriate choice for the independent traveler who enjoys good value for money. It is like having your own home in Florence with keys to the front door. Hostess Lea Gulmanelli had such success with her first three bed and breakfasts (Johanna I and II, Johlea) that she opened one additional place at a superior level, Antica Dimora Johlea, in the same neighborhood. The six bedrooms with four-poster-beds are very cozily appointed in muted soft colors, with beautiful fabrics, Oriental carpets, paintings by the owner, and original tiled or parquet floors. Lea has a real flair for decorating and, as in someone's home, each well-proportioned bedroom retains its own character. There is someone on duty all day (8:30am-8pm) to assist guests with their needs. A rich breakfast is set up in the tastefully decorated breakfast room. During the summer season guests may have breakfast on the delightful flower-potted terrace which offers dreamy views over Florence's rooftops and the Cupola of the Duomo. The guests have free internet service, television, DVD plus other amenities. This property offers very tasteful accommodation and excellent quality and value. *Directions:* The B&B is located between San Marco Square and Piazza della Libertà, north of the Duomo, reached in 12 minutes on foot.

ANTICA DIMORA JOHLEA
Host: Lea Gulmanelli
Via San Gallo 80, Florence, (FI) 50129, Italy
Tel: (055) 4633292, Fax: (055) 4634552
6 Rooms, Double: €100–€160
Open: all year, Credit cards: none
Other Languages: good English, German
Region: Tuscany, Michelin Map: 563

Another nice discovery in the category of small, renovated hotels in Florence is the Botticelli, hidden away on a narrow back street behind the Central Market. Many original features of this 16th-century building, once a private home, have been preserved including evidence of a tiny alley that divided the two now-united buildings. Guests enter into a painted, vaulted reception area appointed with large blue and gold armchairs and side sitting room. Other architectural features so typical of the Renaissance period in Florence are the austere gray stone doorways, beamed ceilings in bedrooms, and the delightful open loggia terrace on the second floor lined with terracotta vases of cascading red geraniums. The bedrooms are situated on the three upper floors, with two being up in the mansard and enjoying the best views, and are comfortably and practically decorated with clean wooden furniture and an occasional antique piece blending well with the pea-green fabrics. A full buffet breakfast is offered in the breakfast room with bar just behind the reception area. All the necessary modern amenities such as air conditioning, elevator, modern telephone system, and satellite TV were incorporated during the recent renovation. Fabrizio and his American wife, Janet, run two other hotels in Florence, one being the Villa Carlotta near Piazzale Michelangelo. Very helpful staff. *Directions:* The hotel is one block north of Piazza San Lorenzo and the Medici Chapels.

HOTEL BOTTICELLI
Hosts: Fabrizio & Janet Gheri
Via Taddea 8, Florence, (FI) 50123, Italy
Tel: (055) 290905, Fax: (055) 294322
34 Rooms, Double: €100–€240
Minimum Stay Required: 3 nights during fairs & New Year
Open: all year, Credit cards: all major
Other Languages: good English, French
Region: Tuscany, Michelin Map: 563

Another choice in the now wide selection of city bed and breakfasts is the well-located Dream Domus, a six-bedroom accommodation created from a former apartment in an historic palazzo. The building is conveniently located behind the San Lorenzo marketplace and two blocks from Florence's cathedral. While congenial hostess Perla resides next door, her B&B is on the second floor. The front door opens directly into the main living room where tables are set up side for a hearty buffet breakfast, a prerequisite before setting off to explore Florence with its myriad art museums and attractions. This room looks onto the main street while the six bedrooms off a hall to the back guarantee a peaceful sleep (hence Perla's logo, Parva Domus Magna Quies—small house, big silence. Polished black and white tiled floors lead you to the individually decorated rooms with antique armoires and fancy regal canopy beds. Golden brocade fabrics are mixed with either red, green or blue for the curtains and bedspreads. Comfortable rooms with many hotel style amenities are named after members of Florence's powerful De'Medici family from Lorenzo the great to Cosimo, Giovanni, Caterina, Lucrezia and Maria. An international traveler, Perla thoroughly enjoys taking care of her guests from all over the world and pointing out her favorite spots in Florence. *Directions:* The Via de Ginori is two blocks north of the Duomo cathedral. Garage parking is available.

FLORENCE DREAM DOMUS
Host: Perla Collini
Via de' Ginori, 26, Florence, (FI) 50123, Italy
Tel: (055) 295346, Fax: (055) 2675643
Cellphone: (335) 5820093
6 Rooms, Double: €160–€200
Minimum Stay Required: 2 nights
Open: all year, Credit cards: all major
Other Languages: good English
Region: Tuscany, Michelin Map: 563

The Hotel Hermitage is a small, characteristic hotel housed in a 13th-century palazzo with breathtaking views over the city's most famous monuments. The location could not be more central—on a small street between the Uffizzi Gallery and the River Arno. The fifth-floor reception area looking out to the Ponte Vecchio bridge has a cozy living-room feeling with selected antique pieces, Oriental rugs, and corner fireplace. Across the hall is the veranda-like breakfast room dotted with crisp yellow tablecloths and topped with fresh flowers where privileged guests view the tower of Palazzo Signoria. Color-coordinated, air-conditioned rooms, some quite small, others with hydro-jet baths, have scattered antiques, framed etchings of the city, and more views. However, the highlight of a stay at the Hermitage is spending time dreaming on the intimate rooftop terrace. The view embraces not only the previously mentioned marvels of Florence, but also the famous dome of the Duomo cathedral and Giotto's tower. Guests are served a basic continental breakfast under the ivy-covered pergola and among the many flower-laden vases lining its borders. Reserve well in advance. *Directions:* Consult a detailed city map. There is a parking garage in the vicinity. Call for instructions as car traffic in this part of the city is strictly limited.

HOTEL HERMITAGE
Host: Vincenzo Scarcelli
Piazza del Pesce, Florence, (FI) 50122, Italy
Tel: (055) 287216, Fax: (055) 212208
Cellphone: (335) 208042
28 Rooms, Double: €120–€220
Open: all year, Credit cards: all major
Other Languages: good English, German, Dutch
Region: Tuscany, Michelin Map: 563

The Residenza D'Epoca in Piazza della Signoria is a top-quality B&B hidden away on the corner of Florence's most famous square hosting the imposing city hall, Palazzo della Signoria. Delightful hosts Sonia and Alessandro initially bought the four-story ancient building as an investment but were touched by the magic spell of this very special historic spot just up the street from the house of Dante and decided to restore it and share it with friends. The fascinating restoration project became something of an archaeological adventure, with documents discovered dating back to 1427 along with a pair of woman's shoes from that same period, and 18th-century frescoes uncovered. Up one flight from street level, Sonia, Alessandro, and occasionally their three sons, greet guests in a small reception area. The ten bedrooms, named after Renaissance masters, are spread about the two floors, with the top floor being crowned with three apartments for those able to enjoy this marvelous city for a full week. To-die-for views from this level include the piazza, Giotto's tower, and Brunelleschi's cupola. The new breakfast room with one long table has the same advantage. Impeccably styled rooms with unique personalities display lovely antique furnishings, parquet floors, and rich colors of teal, peach, and rust. None of the innovative designer bathrooms are identical. A real treat. *Directions:* On the northeast corner of the square at the beginning of Via dei Magazzini.

IN PIAZZA DELLA SIGNORIA
Hosts: Sonia & Alessandro Pini
Via dei Magazzini 2, Florence, (FI) 50122, Italy
Tel: (055) 2399546, Fax: (055) 2676616
Cellphone: (393) 483210565
8 Rooms, Double: €220–€290
3 Apartments: €1200–€1400 weekly
Minimum Stay Required: 7 nights in apartments
Open: all year, Credit cards: all major
Other Languages: good English
Region: Tuscany, Michelin Map: 563

Orto de'Medici was named for the Medici family's extensive gardens and orchards that once existed on the site of this hotel. Capable father-and-son team Emilio and Giacomo Bufalini recently took over the reins and took on the challenge of completely refurbishing the family's prim, centuries-old palazzo. Public areas maintain the ambiance of an elegant private home—the frescoed foyer and sitting rooms are graced with portraits, chandeliers, overstuffed armchairs, and Oriental carpets—while services and facilities in bedrooms conform to European Community standards. The spacious upper-floor guestrooms are reached by an elevator and are decorated with classic style. They have matching armoires and beds and all but ten have smart new gray-and-white-marble bathrooms. Several rooms on the top floor have a terrace or balcony with dreamy views over red Florentine rooftops. Perhaps the architectural highlight is the gracious breakfast room (breakfast is a buffet), with high ceilings, original parquet floors, and frescoed panels depicting garden scenes all around. French doors lead from this area to an outdoor terraced flower garden with wrought iron chairs and tables and a lovely view of San Marco church. Wine and cheese tastings are held here in the late afternoon. Dynamic young host Giacomo and his efficient and friendly staff ensure a perfect city sojourn. *Directions:* Four blocks north of the Duomo.

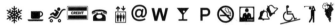

HOTEL ORTO DE'MEDICI
Host: Giacomo Bufalini family
Via San Gallo 30, Florence, (FI) 50129, Italy
Tel: (055) 483427, Fax: (055) 461276
31 Rooms, Double: €97–€280
Open: all year, Credit cards: all major
Other Languages: good English
Region: Tuscany, Michelin Map: 563

The Palazzo dal Borgo–Hotel Aprile, owned by the Cantini Zucconi family for almost four decades, is located in a 15th-century Medici palace behind the Piazza Santa Maria Novella, near the train station and many fine restaurants and shops. The historical building was restored under the strict ordinance of Florence's Commission of Fine Arts. Guests are invited to three complimentary evening lectures a week on Florence's art and history by a professor of the University of Florence. The small and charming hotel is full of delightful surprises: from 16th-century paintings and a bust of the Duke of Tuscany to the frescoed breakfast room and quiet courtyard garden. The old-fashioned reception and sitting areas are invitingly furnished with Florentine Renaissance antiques, comfy, overstuffed red armchairs, and Oriental carpets worn with time. There are 34 bedrooms that vary widely in their size and decor, all with private bathrooms, telephones, mini-bars, carpeted or tile floors, and high vaulted ceilings. A recent extensive renovation has made improvements in facilities while maintaining the original overall charm. Request one of the quieter rooms at the back of the hotel, overlooking the garden. At the desk you find Roberto Gazzini and Sandra Costantini looking after guests' needs. *Directions:* Use a detailed city map to locate the hotel, three blocks north of the Duomo. There is a parking garage.

460 - 780 -   *Good breakfast*

PALAZZO DAL BORGO–HOTEL APRILE
Host: Riccardo Zucconi
Via della Scala 6, Florence, (FI) 50123, Italy
Tel: (055) 216237, Fax: (055) 280947
34 Rooms, Double: €130–€300
Open: all year, Credit cards: all major
Other Languages: good English
Region: Tuscany, Michelin Map: 563

Palazzo Galletti, housed in an historic Florentine palazzo dating to the 1500s, comes under the category of Historic Residences—a glorified bed and breakfast. Young and enthusiastic partners, Francesca and Samuele acquired the entire upper first floor (historically referred to as the Noble floor and characterized by high ceilings and frescoed walls) with the idea of offering high quality accommodation in a more home-like ambiance. Enter from the street through ancient iron gates. Up a flight of stairs is the small reception area, from which a hallway with bedrooms extends and wraps around the center atrium. Softly styled guestrooms, each different from the next and named after the planets, are nicely appointed in beige tones contrasting with colorful abstract paintings. Many have original features such as the magnificent old frescoes in the two corner junior suites (well worth the extra euros!). A fresh buffet breakfast is served in the original kitchen with its vaulted brick ceilings, sink and oven dating to 1550. A day spa, Soul Space, offers massages and treatments. Palazzo Galletti offers all the amenities of a hotel and the hospitality and ambiance of a home. There are plans for two beautiful new suites for this coming year and for those who seek a quiet escape, inquire about their charming farmhouse, Fattoria Bacio! *Directions:* Take the Via dell'Oriuolo from behind the Duomo to the end and turn sharp left on Via Sant'Egidio.

PALAZZO GALLETTI
Hosts: Samuele Minucci & Francesca Cascino
Via Sant'Egidio 12, Florence, (FI) 50122, Italy
Tel: (055) 3905750, Fax: (055) 3905752
Cellphone: (348) 2547941 or (339) 1573276
7 Rooms, Double: €120–€160
4 Suites: €180–€260
Open: all year, Credit cards: all major
Other Languages: fluent English, French
Region: Tuscany, Michelin Map: 563

The refurbished Hotel Silla is located on the left bank of the River Arno opposite Santa Croce, the famous 13th-century square and church where Michelangelo and Galileo are buried. This position offers views from some of the rooms of several of Florence's most notable architectural attractions—the Duomo, the Ponte Vecchio, and the tower of the Palazzo Vecchio. Housed on the second and third floors of a lovely 15th-century palazzo with courtyard entrance, 36 new and spotless double rooms (non-smoking upon request) with private baths are pleasantly decorated with simple dark-wood furniture and matching bedspreads and curtains. Air conditioning and an elevator were recently added necessities. The fancy, cream-colored reception area is appointed in 17th-century Venetian style, with period furniture, a chandelier, and large paintings. Breakfast is served on the splendid and spacious second-floor outdoor terrace or in the dining room overlooking the Arno. The Silla is a friendly, convenient, and quiet hotel, near the Pitti Palace, leather artisan shops, and many restaurants. It offers tourists a good value in pricey Florence. A parking garage is available. *Directions:* Refer to a detailed city map to locate the hotel.

HOTEL SILLA
Host: Gabriele Belotti
Via dei Renai 5, Florence, (FI) 50125, Italy
Tel: (055) 2342888, Fax: (055) 2341437
35 Rooms, Double: €90–€220
Open: all year, Credit cards: all major
Other Languages: good English, French, German
Region: Tuscany, Michelin Map: 563

La Torricella, just on the outskirts of Florence, offers travelers the advantage of staying in a Tuscan home in a quiet residential area, yet with the city easily accessible by public transportation. Marialisa completely restored her great-grandfather's home and converted it into a comfortable and efficient lodging. She decided to offer all the trimmings of a hotel, with amenities such as satellite TVs, mini-bars, and telephones in rooms, plus daily cleaning service. The terraced front of the pale-yellow villa is lined with terracotta vases of flowers and intoxicating wisteria vines. Upon entering the home, you pass through a small reception area with brick arches and equestrian prints into the luminous breakfast room where a buffet is served in the morning. Accommodations are scattered about the large, pristine home on various levels and are each similarly appointed in soft-green and mustard hues with sparkling new white bathrooms. Reproduction armoires and desks and wrought-iron beds harmonize well with the brick floors and high, beamed ceilings. Marialisa offers cooking classes, teaching secrets of genuine Tuscan dishes, and is a rich source of information on the area. There is a small pool at the back of the house. *Directions:* From the Certosa exit of the A1, head for the center of the city, turning right at the stoplight in Galluzzo at Piazza Acciaiuoli. Take Via Silvani for several blocks, turning right on Via Vecchia di Pozzolatico just before the fork in the road.

LA TORRICELLA
Host: Marialisa Manetti family
Via Vecchia di Pozzolatico 25
Florence, (FI) 50125, Italy
Tel: (055) 2321818, Fax: (055) 2047402
Cellphone: (340) 2798856
7 Rooms, Double: €100–€130
1 Apartment: €800 weekly
Open: Mar 1 to Nov 20, Credit cards: VS
Other Languages: good English
Region: Tuscany, Michelin Map: 563

Country residences of wealthy Florentine families dating back to Renaissance times were all concentrated on the hills above the city. Villa Poggio San Felice is one of these, reached by way of a labyrinth of narrow (unbelievably two-way) winding roads past stone-walled gardens concealing magnificent villas. Livia inherited not only the actual property of her great-grandfather but also a long standing tradition in the hospitality field—he was the founder of two of Florence's most prominent hotels. This bed and breakfast is special as guests are given full run of the main part of the two-story villa with its library, gracious portrait-lined sitting rooms, and high-ceilinged dining room where a full buffet breakfast and dinner are served overlooking the garden through French doors. Hosts Livia and her husband Lorenzo's desire was that their guests experience the true flavor of a noble villa and consequently minimum possible modifications were made. This authentic ambiance prevails throughout the simple bedrooms, which are spread out on the upper floor and contain the family's original furniture. The romantic I Sposi honeymoon bedroom has fireplace, parquet floors, and hunter-green color scheme, while the spacious room Nonni features a large terrace looking out over hills to the famous dome of Florence's cathedral. *Directions:* Ten minutes from the center of Florence. Ask for the detailed map.

VILLA POGGIO SAN FELICE
Hosts: Livia Puccinelli & Lorenzo Magnelli
Via San Matteo in Arcetri 24
Florence, (FI) 50125, Italy
Tel: (055) 220016, Fax: (055) 2335388
Cellphone: (392) 9780816
5 Rooms, Double: €200–€250
Open: Mar to Dec, Credit cards: all major
Other Languages: good English
Region: Tuscany, Michelin Map: 563

Although considered a hotel, we include this property to give readers delightful accommodation in an area not well known to tourists. The Zanon family, whose other hotel, Villa Abbazia, features in our hotel guide, drew on their expertise when creating this property. With a true flair for details and decorating they have combined contemporary styles with classic, mixing fabrics, colors and materials with stunning results. The new building has been constructed on half of the Cisterian Abbey of Santa Maria, a convent complex of which the other half is still occupied. Architectural enhancements echo the ancient abbey with columns and vaulted ceilings. Each of the comfortable rooms, all down one long hall on each of two floors, maintains its own personality softly done in beige tones and highlighted by one special focal piece. Superb designer bathrooms matching room colors have all the latest fittings, including no-mist mirrors and rain shower heads. Breakfast is served downstairs with windows looking out to the ancient palazzo Rusca with loggia, as do many of the guest bedrooms. The quaint town of Follina with its mountain backdrop is a perfect spot from which to explore the upper portion of the Veneto region from Treviso, to Asolo, down the Prosecco wine roads. *Directions:* Exit at Conegliano from autostrada A27 and follow through town to Pieve di Soligo and on to Follina.

HOTEL DEI CHIOSTRI
Host: Zanon Family
Piazza IV Novembre 20, Follina, (TV) 31051, Italy
Tel: (0438) 971805, Fax: (0438) 974217
8 Rooms, Double: €130–€160
8 Suites: €190–€225
Open: all year, Credit cards: all major
Other Languages: English spoken well
Region: Veneto, Michelin Map: 562

The Fontanasalsa is a restored farm within a historic baglio farm complex in the countryside outside Trapani, where ferry boats depart for the beautiful Egadi islands. The vast property of the Burgarella family headed by Signora Maria Caterina, a retired pediatrician, is made up mostly of citrus and olive groves (10,000 trees!), the source of their award-winning olive oil. Cordial hospitality is offered within inviting bedrooms in a section of the quad-shaped structure which includes the wine cellars, olive oil press, a small agricultural tool museum, and the lofty beamed dining room with fireplace. Outside the courtyard, beyond a citrus grove, is the swimming pool and outdoor dining area. Individually decorated rooms appointed with family heirloom furniture and olive print curtains and bedspreads contribute to the feeling of being a truly doted upon house guest of Signora, exactly what she had in mind. The farm continues with its daily business. Guests get a first hand look (and taste!) at Sicilian country life. This is also an excellent location for exploring the Mozia salt islands, the majestic temple of Segesta, hilltop medieval Erice, and Trapani. *Directions:* From Palermo on autostrada A29 to Trapani, follow for Marsala-Birgi airport and exit at Fontanasalsa. At first stop light turn right and continue for a half km to the farm entrance.

BAGLIO FONTANASALSA
Host: Maria Caterina Burgarella
Via Cusenza, 78, Fontanasalsa
Sicily, (PA) 91020, Italy
Tel & Fax: (0923) 591001
Cellphone: (348) 5114998
10 Rooms, Double: €110–€140
2 Suites: €120–€160
Per person half board: €67–€75
Open: all year, Credit cards: all major
Other Languages: good English
Region: Sicily, Michelin Map: 565

The bed and breakfast boom of the last decade in Italy has brought about a vast variety of accommodation from classic, in-home hospitality to places with many amenities that more resemble small hotels. Il Torrino brings us back to the more traditional example, with four bedrooms offered within the hostess home. The large, old-fashioned family home of Signora Cesarina's grandparents is located in the Montechiari hills between Florence and Pisa east-west and between Volterra and Lucca north-south—a prime touring location. Here you will not find standardized rooms all decorated alike, but rather individual rooms filled with the family's personal belongings, heirloom furniture, and the authentic feeling of a Tuscan home. With her children grown and residing in various parts of the world, the very sweet hostess, Cesarina Campinotti, opened her home to travelers and welcomes guests into the downstairs living room and upstairs breakfast room where an abundant meal is served. A separate garden apartment for two persons has glass doors overlooking the small pool and countryside beyond. The four bedrooms with living room and kitchen can also be rented separately. Here you are in the center of Tuscany and there is a golf course 12 kilometers away. *Directions:* From Forcoli follow signs for Montechiari and Montacchita, continuing past Montacchita up to the group of houses called Montechiari (2 km). Il Torrino has the black iron gate and no sign.

VILLA IL TORRINO
Host: Cesarina Campinotti
Montechiari, Forcoli, (PI) 56030, Italy
Tel & Fax: (0587) 629181
Cellphone: (347) 3643411
4 Rooms, Double: €85–€90
1 Apartment: €420 weekly
Minimum Stay Required: 3 nights
Open: all year, Credit cards: all major
Other Languages: very little English, French, Spanish
Region: Tuscany, Michelin Map: 563

After many years working as managers of multinational corporations in separate cities, gracious hosts Stefano and Paola Zocchi changed lifestyles and location. They decided on Umbria—midway between Milan and Rome—and bought the Palazzetta property sitting on a hill near Todi. Complete with 360-degree countryside views, their beautifully restored 17th-century stone home is a gem where guests enjoy spacious bedrooms with all the amenities. While enhancing the original features, and capitalizing on the views, each romantic room has been styled with a muted color scheme enhanced by delightful hand-loomed local fabrics for curtains and bedspreads. The bathrooms are accented with lovely mosaic tiles. Guests enjoy breakfast in the lovely dining room or out on the terrace facing an infinity pool that seems to look out on all of Umbria. The sitting rooms on each floor, with similar inviting country chic décor, offer relaxing spots for reading or chatting. Besides sightseeing in the area, arrangements can be made for massages, personal trainers, helicopter transfers from the airport, vineyard visits and cooking lessons with Paola. *Directions:* Exit the E45 (Todi-Perugia) at Fratta Todina/Montecastello di Vibio for the 7 km drive to Fratta Todina. Pass the walls of the town and turn left to Spineta. Go through Spineta past the convent and after the vineyard turn right at the gate.

LA PALAZZETTA DEL VESCOVO
Hosts: Stefano & Paola Zocchi
Via Clausura, 17, Fratta Todina, (PG) 06054, Italy
Tel: (075) 8745183, Fax: (075) 8745042
7 Rooms, Double: €170–€220
2 Suites: €217–€250
Open: Mar to Jan 6, Credit cards: all major
Region: Umbria, Michelin Map: 563

The Locanda San Rocco is located in the heart of the Marches region, in spectacularly unspoilt countryside virtually unknown to international tourists. Here you have a chance to experience at first hand the beauty and simplicity of Italian country life. Nearby you can explore the historic hilltop towns of Camerino, Jesi, Osimo, Macerata, Loreto, and Recanati. The Pirri family from Rome return to their native Marches in the summer months and gracious hostess Signora Gisla opened her summer bed and breakfast business in order to share her love for this beautiful piece of the country. She offers very charming accommodation within an 18th-century stone farmhouse, part of a small village near their 132-acre property. Guests have full run of the house, which includes a large living area in a cozy exposed-stone and wood-beamed room, billiard room, and dining room looking out to a patio and garden at the back. The home is very tastefully appointed with fine country antiques, crisp striped fabrics on overstuffed armchairs, and sofas in sea-green and burgundy tones. The six bedrooms, divided between two floors and reached by an elevator, have wrought-iron beds, fine linens, and original brick floors. *Directions:* From Castelraimondo head towards San Severino and after 2 km turn left for Gagliole. The Locanda San Rocco is located in a small group of houses in Collaiello, before Gagliole.

LOCANDA SAN ROCCO
Host: Gisla Pirri Conforti
Frazione Collaiello 2, Gagliole, (MC) 62020, Italy
Tel: (0737) 642324, Fax: (0737) 636252
Cellphone: (338) 8461123
6 Rooms, Double: €80–€150
1 Apartment: €550 weekly
Minimum Stay Required: 2 nights
Closed: Oct to May, Credit cards: MC, VS
Other Languages: English, French, Spanish
Region: Marches, Michelin Map: 563

Borgo Argenina has all the elements of a "bestseller" bed and breakfast: the perfect location in the heart of Chianti surrounded by vineyards, very comfortable accommodation in an ancient stone farmhouse, glorious countryside views, and, above all, Elena, the Borgo Argenina's gregarious hostess. She left behind a successful fashion business in Milan and bought an entire abandoned village, restoring two of the stone houses for herself and the bed and breakfast. She chose the best artisans in the area and literally worked with them to create the house of her dreams. Everything from painting stenciled borders in rooms through restoring furniture to sewing quilted bedspreads was executed exclusively by Elena herself. The downstairs living rooms and breakfast room are beautifully done in rich cream and soft yellows that complement perfectly the brick-vaulted ceilings and terracotta floors. Elena is up at dawn baking cakes for breakfast and makes occasional dinners for the guests accompanied by classical music. Every little detail has been attended to in the pink-and-blue bedrooms adorned with white eyelet curtains, patchwork quilts, and dried flower arrangements. Across the way is a very comfortable three-bedroom, independent house. *Directions:* Follow S.S.408 from Siena for Montevarchi and after 15 km turn off to the right at Monti. Just before Monti and S. Marcellina there is a sign on the right for Borgo Argenina.

BORGO ARGENINA
Host: Elena Nappa
Localita: Argenina-Monti, Argenina
Gaiole in Chianti, (SI) 53013, Italy
Tel: (0577) 747117, Fax: (0577) 747228
5 Rooms, Double: €150–€170
2 Suites: €180–€200, 3 Houses: €240 daily
Minimum Stay Required: 3 nights
Open: Mar to Oct, Credit cards: all major
Other Languages: good English, French
Region: Tuscany, Michelin Map: 563

In the heart of the beautiful Chianti wine region, a cypress-lined lane leads up to the handsome, 13th-century Castello di Meleto, set upon a gentle hill just outside Gaiole. The fairytale-perfect castle with its imposing round watchtowers and arched stone doorway embraced by fragrant roses makes an enchanting stop while exploring the back roads of Tuscany. There is a double treat in store because you can not only sample delicious wines in the attractive tasting room, but also visit the interior of this splendid castle with its walls and ceilings lavishly enhanced by superb frescoes, lovely antique furnishings, and even an adorable baroque theater dating back to the mid-1700s (call ahead for tour times). The castle also offers nine attractively decorated guestrooms with antique furnishings, five within the castle and four in the chapel house. Breakfast is served each morning in the cozy kitchen with huge open fireplace. The castle gardens stretch out to a line of lacy trees that frame a superb vista of the idyllic Tuscan countryside. There is also a stunning view from the swimming pool, which is bordered on three sides by a flagstone terrace and on the fourth flows seamlessly into the horizon. If you are traveling with friends or family and want a place for a longer stay, the castle offers 11 beautifully furnished stone cottages with well-equipped kitchens and from one to three bedrooms. Advance reservations a must. *Directions:* From Gaiole in Chianti, follow signs to the castle.

CASTELLO DI MELETO
Hosts: Lucia Pasquini & Roberto Stucchi Prinetti
Gaiole in Chianti, (SI) 53013, Italy
Tel & Fax: (0577) 749129
9 Rooms, Double: €125–€148
11 Cottages: €630–€1953 weekly
Minimum Stay Required: 2 nights, 7 in cottages
Open: all year, Credit cards: all major
Other Languages: fluent English, German
Region: Tuscany, Michelin Map: 563

The Castello di Tornano, a strategically situated hilltop tower dating back almost 1,000 years, has a 360-degree vista of the surrounding valley and has been of great historical significance in the seemingly endless territorial battles between Siena and Florence. The owners are the Selvolini family and it is Patrizia who welcomes guests to the expansive wine estate. Nine charming rooms are situated in the actual castle and its monumental tower. Patrizia has personally taken care of the décor of the house using many of the family's own antiques. The "piece de resistance" is the superior suite on the top floor of the tower, offering a unique architectural style and a magnificent view from eight large windows. The tower-top terrace has a 6-person hydro-jet pool, a view not easily forgotten. In the stone farmhouse, in front of the tower, 7 one- and two-bedroom apartments are offered guests, each appointed in the typical rustic style of Tuscany. The kitchen serves authentic, traditional meals as well as cooking classes. The spectacular pool was built inside the ancient moat of the castle. Trails cut across the vineyards and the surrounding woods, enjoyable for walks. It is also possible to ride the owners' horses through the scenic countryside. *Directions:* From the A1 exit at Valdarno, follow the sign to Gaiole. Take the S.S.408 towards Gaiole and pass through the village, following signs for Siena. After 6 km you see the sign for Tornano on the left.

CASTELLO DI TORNANO
Hosts: Patrizia Selvolini & Francesco Gioffreda
Gaiole in Chianti, (SI) 53013, Italy
Tel: (0577) 746067, Fax: (0577) 746094
Cellphone: (335) 7606699
9 Rooms, Double: €140–€270
2 Suites: €300–€600
7 Apartments: €110–€280 daily
Open: Mar to Dec, Credit cards: VS
Other Languages: good English
Region: Tuscany, Michelin Map: 563

The heel of Italy offers a wealth of natural beauty but, because of its remoteness, few really charming places to stay. The Masseria Lo Prieno is run by the delightful Castriota family, whose crops are representative of the staples of the Apulia region, and include olives, almonds, fruits, and grains. Spartan accommodations are offered in bungalows scattered among the pine woods and palms on the family property. Each mini guesthouse includes one bedroom, kitchenette, bathroom, and an eating area containing basic necessities. Nine simply decorated rooms with bathrooms are now available within a newly constructed house on the property. Former animal stalls have been converted into a large dining space rustically decorated with antique farm tools and brass pots. Along with warm hospitality, the family makes meals a top priority and it is the food that makes the stay here special. For an exquisite and authentic traditional meal, the restaurant here is incomparable. Both Maria Grazia, the energetic daughter who runs the show, and her charming mother take pride in demonstrating how local specialties are prepared. This is a budget choice for touring this area. *Directions:* From Taranto take N174 to Galatone, then follow signs for Secli. From Bari take the Gallipoli-Galatone road. After the first traffic light, continue to the sign on the right for Masseria and follow signs to the farm.

MASSERIA LO PRIENO
Host: Francesco Castriota family
Localita: Contrada Orelle
Galatone, (LE) 73044, Italy
Tel: (0833) 865898, Fax: (0833) 861879
Cellphone: (335) 8432610
9 Rooms, Double: €58–€72
5 Bungalows: €64–€74 daily
Minimum Stay Required: 2 nights
Open: Apr to Sep, Credit cards: all major
Other Languages: some English, some Spanish
Region: Apulia, Michelin Map: 564

On the extreme outskirts of Florence, the Fattoressa offers a location for dual exploration of both the city and the Tuscan countryside. One of the many marvelous attractions of Florence is how the countryside comes right up to the doors of the city and just behind the magnificent Certosa monastery you find the 15th-century stone farmhouse of the delightfully congenial Fusi-Borgioli family. They have transformed the farmer's quarters into guest accommodations: four sweetly simple bedrooms plus two triples, each with its own spotless bathroom. Angiolina and Amelio, who have tended to this piece of land for many years, treat their guests like family and, as a result, enjoy receiving some of them year after year. Daughters-in-law Laura and Katia, who speak English, have been a great help in assisting guests with local itineraries. Visitors take meals "en famille" at long tables in the cozy, rustic dining room with a large stone fireplace (€25-€28 for dinner). Here Angiolina proudly serves authentic Florentine specialties using ingredients from her own fruit orchard and vegetable garden. *Directions:* Entering Florence from the Certosa exit off the Siena superstrada, turn left one street after the Certosa monastery stoplight onto Volterrana. After the bridge, turn right behind the building. The house is just on the left.

LA FATTORESSA
Hosts: Angiolina Fusi & Amelio Borgioli
Via Volterrana 58, Galluzzo, (FI) 50124, Italy
Tel & Fax: (055) 2048418
Cellphone: (339) 8027715
6 Rooms, Double: €80
Open: all year, Credit cards: none
Other Languages: good English, French, German
Region: Tuscany, Michelin Map: 563

Wandering off the main tourist trail in Sicily is recommended for the traveler who truly enjoys contact with local people and their culture (best to have some command of Italian) and is curious and open to new experiences, without being tied to rigid schedules. If you leave yourselves in the hands of the Contes, you will certainly be rewarded with a once-in-a-lifetime stay. Reaching Gangi is an adventure in itself, taking you far away from the main route through the scenic Madonie Mountains, which cut across the mid-northern part of Sicily. Villa Raino is just outside Gangi, with its tightly packed houses covering the tip of a mountaintop. Host, Aldo, left the family hotel business in town and restored this 100-year-old brick house once owned by a noble family, offering an excellent countryside restaurant for local families and city people coming from as far away as Palermo. On the first and second floors there are ten unique guestrooms with mansard ceilings, some having a small balcony. A mix of family antiques is scattered about the rooms, which have Tiffany bedside lamps and walls stenciled using an ancient technique that gives the effect of floral wallpaper. Bathrooms have brightly colored tiles. All in all Villa Raino provides a delightful opportunity to explore this off-track area. *Directions:* From A19 exit at Tre Monzelli; follow S.S.120 38 km to Gangi. A sign before town directs you down a rough, unpaved road to the property.

VILLA RAINO
Hosts: Nina & Aldo Conte
Contrada Raino, Gangi, Sicily, (PA) 90024, Italy
Tel: (0921) 644680, Fax: (0921) 644424
Cellphone: (3387) 798444
10 Rooms, Double: €80
Per person half board: €25
Open: all year, Credit cards: all major
Other Languages: some English
Region: Sicily, Michelin Map: 565

Situated in the heart of the Valpolicella wine country, equidistant from Verona and Lake Garda, Gargagnagno is a medieval village made up mostly of grape growers and wine producers. Signora Lucia, born in Colombia, and her late husband, a famous American neurosurgeon, settled here with the dream of producing fine wines. They bought the 300-year-old Villa Monteleone and began producing Valpolicella wines including Amarone and Recioto. Today, Lucia continues to produce wine and also offers hospitality in three very large bedrooms of her home. The San Vito Suite has direct access to the front courtyard, a mix of family furnishings and a bathroom with sauna. Upstairs the Santa Lena room has bright blue sponged walls and a terrace while the San Paolo has antique furniture. Both have their private bathrooms across the hall. An adjoining living room can be transformed into an additional bedroom for a family. Breakfast is served out in the wooded garden which for its variety of ancient trees and vegetation has been listed as a national monument, or within the dining room with its fireplace. The wine production and cellars are situated directly below the house, and wine tastings are offered. The informal ambiance is that of a home. *Directions:* Exit at Verona Nord. Take the highway, north towards S. Ambrogio di Valpolicella and exit at Gargagnago. Follow the signs to Villa Monteleone and turn right. The villa is the first gate on the left.

VILLA MONTELEONE
Host: Lucia Raimondi
Via Monteleone, 12, Gargagnago, (VR) 37015, Italy
Tel: (045) 7704974, Fax: (045) 6800160
Cellphone: (348) 5638811
3 Rooms, Double: €70–€85
Minimum Stay Required: 2 nights
Open: Mar to Oct, Credit cards: MC, VS
Other Languages: English, Spanish
Region: Veneto, Michelin Map: 562

Casa Mezzuola is part of a small group of farmhouses atop a hill 3 kilometers outside Greve where the land was divided into separate smaller properties. Friendly hosts, Riccardo, an antiques and jewelry dealer, Nicoletta, and their two girls live in the main house while hospitality is offered within three apartments for two to four persons in the adjacent stables and fienile where the hay was once stored. The stone walls, beams, and original brick openings to allow air into the barn were all preserved in the tower-like construction housing two of the apartments. A two-story apartment has a tiled kitchen/living area on one floor and bedroom and bathroom upstairs, while the snug studio apartment crowns the top of the tower. They are all nicely furnished with colorful rugs, local country furniture, satellite TV, and fully equipped kitchens. Breakfast is served within the apartments or outside under one of the pergola terraces. Just below the apartments is a swimming pool, which enjoys the expansive vistas, and there are bikes for guests' use. This is a convenient base for travelers in the heart of Chianti. Greve has a full program of festivals, concerts, and events, especially during the summer. *Directions:* Entering Greve from the north (Florence), turn right at the Esso Petrol Station. Follow signs for Mezzuola, Cologne, not Montefioralle. After 3 km of unpaved, bumpy road, you will come across the marked property.

CASA MEZZUOLA
Host: Riccardo Franconeri family
Via S. Cresci 30, Greve in Chianti, (FI) 50022, Italy
Tel & Fax: (055) 8544885
Cellphone: (347) 6135920
1 Room, Double: €80–€130
3 Apartments: €90–€150 daily, €400–€850 weekly
Minimum Stay Required: 3 nights
Open: all year, Credit cards: MC, VS
Other Languages: good English and good French
Region: Tuscany, Michelin Map: 563

North of Verona, bordering the Valpolicella wine region, is the magnificent palace of the Arvedi family. The enormous 13th century estate has been in the family since 1874. Featuring well-preserved Renaissance gardens and a 12-meter high frescoed hall, the house can be visited by appointment. Accommodation in twelve suites is reserved for guests in the family's former residence, a turn-of-the-century hilltop villa in the nearby village. Each spacious room located in the upper two floors of the large private residence has a living room area and an eclectic mix of family furnishings with modern amenities such as air conditioning, TV and minibar. The two bedrooms suites are ideal for families. Amiable daughter Anna resides in the main palace but is always present to take care of guests needs and assists in arranging wine tours and other itineraries in the area of Lake Garda and nearby Verona. An informal country breakfast is served in the downstairs kitchen, off the main sitting room with its French windows looking over the surrounding garden. *Directions:* From the autostrada exit Verona est, take the highway north for Valpanteiva-Lessinia exiting at Grezzana. Turn right and follow up to walled town to gate (the pink villa perched on top corner is easily visible).

BORGO 27
Host: Anna Carolina Arvedi
Via Borgo 27, Grezzana, (VR) 37023, Italy
Tel: (045) 8658311, Fax: (045) 8658399
12 Rooms, Double: €100–€250
Open: all year, Credit cards: all major
Other Languages: English spoken well
Region: Veneto, Michelin Map: 562

In the northern reaches of Lazio, bordering Umbria and Tuscany, is the stately, 17th-century castle of the noble Mancini Caterini family. Sociable hosts Antonello and Cristina decided to transfer their young family from Rome and reside permanently on the vast wooded property, overseeing the agricultural activity as Antonello's ancestors once did. They have done an admirable job of restoring the large, ivy-covered farmhouse just below the family's residence and creating four charming apartments plus twelve bedrooms for guests. The bi-level apartments maintain their original rustic flavor and are cheerfully decorated with antique armoires and dressers, country fabrics for curtains and bedspreads, and wrought-iron beds. Accommodation in low season and for shorter stays is offered in the Granaio 1 and 2, with four bedrooms on each floor and individual living rooms, which can also be used as separate apartments. On the ground floor you find outdoor and indoor eating areas, billiard room, and game room overlooking a lovely swimming pool. Activities include tennis, horseback riding, wine itineraries, and boat rides and sailing on nearby Lake Bolsena, besides exploration of the many ancient Etruscan towns in this very beautiful countryside. *Directions:* From the A1 autostrada exit at Orvieto and follow signs first for Bolsena then Castel S. Giorgio-S. Lorenzo Nuovo-Grotte di Castro. Just past town turn right at the Castello sign.

CASTELLO DI S. CRISTINA
Hosts: Cristina & Antonello Mancini Caterini
Grotte di Castro, (VT) 01025, Italy
Tel & Fax: (0763) 78011
Cellphone: (339) 8605166
12 Rooms, Double: €80–€135
6 Apartments: €450–€1620 weekly
Minimum Stay Required: 7 nights in apartments
Open: all year, Credit cards: all major
Region: Lazio, Michelin Map: 563

La Ghirlanda is an enchanting country home, glowing with warmth and color, charm and romance. The sprawling country estate home of Riccardo and Amalija and her brother, Riccardo who encourage you to make their house your home. From the hill top position, the rust-red stately home, originally the family hunting lodge, takes in sweeping views of the alternating wooded and cultivated landscapes, thankfully all theirs and therefore left unspoiled. The secluded pool area is an agreeable spot from which to literally breath in this inspiring scene. Each individually decorated bedroom has been thoughtfully appointed with antique pieces, fine linens and color coordinated fabrics. A cozy wine bar, dining room, library and sitting room with fireplaces are all open to guests and meals are enjoyed either within the golden hued dining room or out in the garden under the stars. Guests are offered freshly made totally Umbrian recipes accompanied by their own top-rated Sagrantino di Montefalco wine. Most ingredients come right from the farm, including meats, vegetables, fruits and of course, the extra virgin olive oil. *Directions:* From the S.S.3 Todi-Perugia, exit at the second Todi exit from the south, or Ripabianca from the north and follow signs for San Terenziano, then Saragano. Located 15 km from Todi.

LA GHIRLANDA
Hosts: Riccardo Pongelli & Amalija Tomassini Barbarossa
Localita: Saragano
Gualdo Cattaneo, (PG) 06035, Italy
Tel: (0742) 98731, Fax: (06) 233231544
Cellphone: (333) 4338231
8 Rooms, Double: €100–€132
4 Suites: €130–€162
Open: all year, Credit cards: all major
Other Languages: English spoken well
Region: Umbria, Michelin Map: 563

Emanuela and Paolo left behind advertising careers and a period of time living in Mexico and returned to their native Italy with the idea of changing lifestyles and opening a B&B. They purchased and carefully restored Casa Branca, a hilltop stone house surrounded by woods and a soothing babbling brook. Just above the house is a peaceful spot poolside which enjoys spectacular countryside views. The main house is divided between the couple's own residence and the guest quarters which are made up of six double rooms with nice new bathrooms. Down on the main floor is a large stone-walled room with tables to one side and a sitting area to the other. A separate cottage in back has two bedrooms with adjoining bathroom. Their Latin American stay has had a definite influence on décor decisions with yellow, orange, and red prominent in sofas and wall colors, an effective contrast to traditional brick, stone and wood materials. It is well worth staying for dinner as Emanuela is an exceptional cook, preparing a four-course meal with ingredients from the vegetable garden at an impeccable table either out on the terrace or in the dining room. Besides Gubbio there is lots to explore in this area bordering the Marches. *Directions:* From Spoleto follow signs for Foligno, then Nocera Umbra, then Branca. From Branca, turn right at the sign for Casa Branca up past new houses to the top. Gubbio is 12 km away.

CASA BRANCA
Hosts: Emanuela Notari & Paolo Coppola
Voc. San Simeone, 8\A, Gubbio, (PG) 06020, Italy
Tel: (075) 9270016, Fax: (075) 9270037
Cellphone: (334) 3561051
5 Rooms, Double: €90
2 Suites: €120–€160
Open: all year, Credit cards: all major
Other Languages: English spoken well, Spanish
Region: Umbria, Michelin Map: 563

The address says Gubbio but actually the Locanda, of ancient origins, is immersed in the wooded hills halfway between Gubbio and Perugia (each 20km away) where it once played a strategic role protecting the territory. Take the scenic road up to the group of stone houses (once an entire village with chapel) overlooking this peaceful landscape, a haven for those wanting to just take it easy. You can dine on healthy organic foods and recharge your batteries, literally immersed in noiseless nature. Furnished comfortably in Asian style, pleasantly blending in with the original stone, brick and wood architecture, gracious hosts Paola and Eric have faithfully and lovingly restored the residence, creating ten double pastel-colored bedrooms. Meals are served in the dining room or on the terrace at tables set with crisp yellow linen cloths and picture-perfect foods prepared by amiable Chef Jimmy. If guests are not out viewing the highlights of Umbria, they have given in and chosen just to relax; walking in the surroundings or lounging poolside, taking in the magical, undisturbed scenery and waiting for another spectacular sunset. Everyone seems content at this very special place and it is the owners and the setting that make it that way. *Directions:* From Perugia, follow for Cesena and after 15 km exit at Ponte Pattoli and follow for "Casa del Diavolo", then Santa Cristina. Continue for another 7 km and turn left into the Locanda after the restaurant, "La Dolce Vita". Located 30 km NE of Perugia.

LOCANDA DEL GALLO   New
Hosts: Paola & Erich Breuer
Loc. S. Cristina
Gubbio, (PG) 06020, Italy
Tel & Fax: (075) 9229912
10 Rooms, Double: €130–€140
Open: all year, Credit cards: MC, VS
Other Languages: English, French, German
Region: Umbria, Michelin Map: 563

We are pleased to include the first B&B property along the top half of the "Ponente" Riviera, running along the coast from Genoa to the French border. Congenial hosts Roberto and Pamela made a lifestyle decision to move to the soft hills above the seaside city of Imperia and create an agriturismo farm literally from scratch. Starting some years ago with just a patch of olive groves, they acquired more land and built their home along with the large guest complex holding nine suites, many on two levels with living room, fireplace and kitchenette. Each has an outdoor space, garden or terrace nicely decorated in country style and using a combination of local materials including terracotta, slate, marble, and wood. Guests become part of the home and are treated to a royal breakfast spread prepared daily by Pamela. The separate veranda breakfast room directly overlooks a borderless pool which literally spills into the sweeping valley below dotted with olive groves and stretching down to the sea and distant Imperia. Here is a chance to explore a lesser-known Liguria with its interesting villages or hop over the border to Nice or Monte Carlo. *Directions:* Exit from autostrada A10 at Imperia Ovest and proceed left towards Imperia. Turn left again at the next intersection until you come to a roundabout and stay left for Dolcedo. After another roundabout left, stay on the road leading right up to Vasia. The gate for San Damian is on the left and marked with a large stone oil press.

RELAIS SAN DAMIAN
Hosts: Roberto Gardini & Pamela Kranz
Strada Vasia 47, Imperia, (IM) 18100, Italy
Tel: (0183) 280309, Fax: (0183) 280571
Cellphone: (339) 4417632
10 Suites: €120–€150
1 Apartment: €500–€980 weekly
Open: all year, Credit cards: all major
Other Languages: English spoken well, German, French
Region: Liguria, Michelin Map: 561

The Aosta mountain area is known primarily as a ski resort, sharing the majestic Alps with France and Switzerland. Tourism during the rest of the year is in the developing stages and offers a myriad of attractions in a beautifully unspoilt environment, including mountain hikes on well-marked trails (the famous Walser trail stretches straight across the region starting on the Swiss border and ending on the French border), medieval castles, quaint villages, Roman archaeological sites, local artisans, artisan cheese production, and wine tours. Lo Triolet offers a strategic point from which to visit these treasures within two comfortable apartments in the restored 16th-century house with cantina next door. The group of stone houses near the road includes the family's own house, the guesthouse, and surrounding neighbors all backed by the hillside and woods. Everything in the one- and two-bedroom apartments—tiles on floors, kitchenettes, bathrooms, and furniture—is brand new. The immediate area lends itself well to the production of various grapes and Marco took advantage of this climate for the production of various Pinot Gris, which he enthusiastically explains to guests. His wife's family owns another winery in the next valley. *Directions:* Exit from A5 at Aosta Ovest, driving towards Courmayeur. After 5 km, just after the village of Villeneuve, follow signs for Introd. After another 2 km, Lo Triolet is marked on the right.

LO TRIOLET
Hosts: Marco Martin & Paola Bionaz
Fraz. Junod 7, Introd, (AO) 11010, Italy
Tel & Fax: (0165) 95437
Cellphone: (339) 1387092
2 Apartments: €50–€75 daily*
*Apartment rental, no breakfast offered
Minimum Stay Required: 3 nights, 7 Jul & Aug
Open: all year, Credit cards: none
Other Languages: French
Region: Aosta Valley, Michelin Map: 561

A highlight of your visit to the intriguing Apulia region is without a doubt the city of Lecce, known as the "Florence of the Baroque period" for its many well preserved examples of Leccese Baroque. Besides the splendid churches with ornately sculpted facades, Lecce's pedestrian-only center has a magnificent open piazza with cathedral, Roman amphitheater and ancient university giving it a youthful air. Placed in the square of the stunning Basilica Santa Croce is the Palazzo Personé, a refreshingly stylish accommodation within a historic building. Dynamic and creative owner Stefano Ramponi's intentions are clear: kind hospitality and personalized service within a historic home that has a contemporary touch of interior design. From the street you enter the large double doors to an inviting inner courtyard with tables adjacent the lounge bar, open all day and serving breakfast, light lunch and appetizers. Each of the four suites vary in shape and size and have been given a clean and attractive look with the combination of white against the sand-colored stone walls. The effect has enhanced the original architectural features, including stone arches, fireplace, columns (of the ex-synagogue), stone wheel (olive oil mill), wood rafters and ancient wood doors. At just 11 km from the sea, and in center Apulia, easy day trips to the southern Salento area are possible. *Directions:* The Palazzo Personé is located next to the Basilica Santa Croce in Piazzeta Riccardi.

PALAZZO PERSONÉ   **New**
Host: Stefano Ramponi
Via Umberto I, 5, Lecce, (LE) 73100, Italy
Tel: (333) 3745510, Fax: (0832) 792470
Cellphone: (335) 408384
4 Rooms, Double: €135–€180
Open: all year, Credit cards: none
Other Languages: English, French
Region: Apulia, Michelin Map: 564

An pleasant alternative to the city hotels of Venice is the quiet and charming Gargan bed and breakfast situated in the countryside just 30 kilometers away. The Calzavara family renovated the family's expansive 17th-century country house and opened the bed and breakfast activity, offering four sweetly and simply decorated bedrooms each with its own bathroom on the top floor plus two suites consisting of bedroom, sitting room, and bathroom. Signora Antonia, son Alessandro who looks after the farm activity, horses (his passion) and tree nursery, and his wife Nicoletta enjoy making their guests feel as "at home" as possible by having fresh flowers in the cozy, heirloom antique-filled bedrooms. The downstairs sitting and dining rooms display the family's country antiques as well as a large fireplace and nice touches such as lace curtains and family paintings. Guests are treated to a full breakfast of home-baked cakes and exceptional four-course dinners prepared especially for guests by Signora Antonia herself, using all ingredients from the farm. The Gargan is an ideal choice in this area, being a short drive from such marvels as Padova, Venice, Treviso, Vicenza, Verona, and Palladian villas plus many smaller medieval villages. *Directions:* From Venice take route 245 to Scorze, turning right for Montebelluna at the stoplight 1 km after town. After the town of S. Ambrogio turn left at the stoplight. Turn right at the church in Levada up to the house.

GARGAN
Host: Calzavara family
Via Marco Polo 2
Levada di Piombino Dese, (PD) 35017, Italy
Tel: (049) 9350308, Fax: (049) 9350016
6 Rooms, Double: €65–€85
Closed: Jan & Aug, Credit cards: none
Other Languages: some English
Region: Veneto, Michelin Map: 562

When Lois Martin, a retired teacher, spotted the lovely restored farmhouse at San Martino, she knew it literally had her name on it and purchased it immediately. The house is completely open to guests, from the upstairs cozy living room with large stone fireplace to the downstairs country kitchen and large family room. Ingredients for a full country breakfast await you in the kitchen with its impressive display of Deruta ceramics. One bedroom with king bed is joined by a bathroom to a small room with twin beds, ideal for a family. Each of the other two doubles has a bathroom, with one being en suite. Besides a swimming pool overlooking the wooded hills and valley, other extras are satellite TV, a travel library, American washer and dryer, bikes, guest bathrobes, and dinner upon request. Casa San Martino also offers onsite cooking and painting with a visiting professional teacher in off-season. Being right on the border of Umbria and Tuscany, Lake Trasimeno and towns such as Gubbio, Perugia, Cortona, Assisi, and Deruta are all easily accessible. The entire house can also be rented weekly for a group of up to eight persons. *Directions:* From Lisciano square, pass the bar and turn left for San Martino. Continue for 2 km and take a right up the hill at the sign for San Martino for just over 1.5 km to the house.

CASA SAN MARTINO
Host: Lois Martin
Localita: San Martino 19
Lisciano Niccone, (PG) 06060, Italy
Tel: (075) 844288, Fax: (075) 844422
4 Rooms, Double: €140–€150
1 House: €2000–€3000 weekly
Minimum Stay Required: 3 nights
Open: all year, Credit cards: none
Other Languages: fluent English, German, Spanish
Region: Umbria, Michelin Map: 563

This attractive bed and breakfast in the wooded Berici hills just outside Vicenza's city limits is a lovely base for enjoying Veneto. The three-story stone hunting lodge dating back to the 15th century has eight very comfortable and tastefully decorated guestrooms. All have views and many amenities, and all are enhanced by the original stone, wood, and brick building materials. The Savoia family antiques are found in the cozy living room with large fireplace and in the breakfast room. Well-known by locals for its high-quality country cuisine using products from the farm, the attractive restaurant is found in the original barn with loft ceilings and enormous windows. Guests can choose to relax in the lush garden poolside or take various hiking trails, visiting prehistoric caves in the back woods. Besides vegetables, fruits, and cereals, the farm produces its own olive oil and D.O.C.-level Cabernet, Chardonnay, Barbarano, and Sauvignon wines. Aside from the famous Palladian villas, you can explore many interesting itineraries in Verona, Venice (by boat), Vicenza and its surrounding areas: the Barbarano wine area, Asolo, Basssano, and Marostica (with its annual human chess game). *Directions:* Exit the A4 autostrada at Vicenza Est, heading for Rivera Berica. From Longare (on the southern edge of Vicenza) follow signs for Le Vescovane-Villa Balzana, turning right at the church onto the Via S. Rocco. Follow the road up to the left for 3 km.

LE VESCOVANE
Hosts: Luigi & Rita Maria Savoia
Via S. Rocco 19, Longare, (VI) 36023, Italy
Tel: (0444) 273570, Fax: (0444) 273265
Cellphone: (348) 4101191
7 Rooms, Double: €80–€110
1 Suite: €98–€135
Apartment: €140–€230 daily
Open: all year, Credit cards: all major
Other Languages: good English
Region: Veneto, Michelin Map: 562

Mario and Gabriella Tortella left an intense corporate life and returned to their peaceful Abruzzo region with the intention of concentrating on organic farming and hospitality. They have succeeded and today the 90-acre property overlooking the Apennines is made up of olive groves, woods, a kiwi plantation, orchards, pastures for farm animals, and fields of grain and cereals. Guests are welcomed like old friends and are accommodated within the six country-style bedrooms upstairs in the main 300-year-old house or in one of the more independent apartments next door. Very much in keeping with the simple rustic features of the farmhouse, they have wrought-iron beds, antique armoires, new tiled bathrooms, and a common living room. The largest has a fireplace and kitchenette. Guests convene in the evening for conversation and an excellent regional meal prepared with ingredients straight from the farm by Gabriella's mother, Olga, either out on the covered porch or in one of the vaulted brick dining rooms. This is a very pleasant base for exploring Loreto, Penne, Pescara, Atri, and three national parks, among other attractions. Alternatively, you can relax poolside and just enjoy the views, the tranquility, and superb meals. *Directions:* Exit the A25 at Pescara-Villanova and drive towards Penne on S.S.81. Six km before Penne, just before S. Pellegrino, turn right after a bar (or call from there) onto a gravel road up to Le Magnolie. (18 km total from exit.)

LE MAGNOLIE
Hosts: Mario & Gabriella Tortella
Contrada Fiorano 83
Loreto Aprutino, (PE) 65014, Italy
Tel: (085) 8289534, Fax: (085) 7992838
Cell: (335) 7787622
2 Rooms, Double: €65–€75
11 Apartments: €100–€125 daily
Closed: Feb, Credit cards: MC, VS
Other Languages: good English, Spanish, French
Region: Abruzzo, Michelin Map: 563

Still another undiscovered area is the peaceful countryside northeast of Todi, where you find the Castello di Loreto. After having meticulously restored part of this medieval fortress castle as a country home, Nino Segurini now coordinates restoration work on ancient buildings, besides continuing his own business as a consultant to antiques dealers. Nino is very knowledgeable on many subjects, and delights in introducing guests to the undiscovered treasures he has found in the immediate area. Nino and Francesca's home is a veritable museum, with collections of ancient artifacts naturally inhabiting the historical building. Within the base of the thick-walled fortress you find the main living room, two small bedrooms (one twin, one double) connected by a sitting area, and three bathrooms. The kitchen leads outside to the spacious patio with grape pergola overlooking the landscaped garden and swimming pool. The preferred and largest bedroom, arranged as a suite with its own sitting room, is reached by two flights of stairs past another living room with fireplace, appointed with antique armor and weaponry and an enclosed loggia. A fourth guestroom features a 16th-century carved, gilded bed of a noble Venetian family who once had Napoleon as a house guest. *Directions:* Leave highway E45 at Todi/Orvieto, heading for Pian di Porto, then San Terenziano. After 2 km, fork right towards Loreto for another 4 km. The entrance gate is opposite the church.

CASTELLO DI LORETO
Hosts: Nino & Francesca Segurini
Loreto–Todi, (PG) 06059, Italy
Tel & Fax: (075) 8852501
Cellphone: (335) 6249734
4 Rooms, Double: €110–€130
Minimum Stay Required: 2 nights
Open: all year, Credit cards: none
Other Languages: good English, Spanish, French
Region: Umbria, Michelin Map: 563

This 200-year-old farmhouse made of tuff stone, a sand-colored porous rock of volcanic origin, is one of many concentrated in this scenic area south of Orvieto. Gracious hostess Francesca bought and gradually put back the pieces of the home using all local materials to create a natural ambiance in harmony with the country setting. Warm earth tones as well as stronger provincial hues have been chosen for the interiors which include ten spacious, beamed bedrooms on the two upper floors, each with a different color theme. The furnishings in the bedrooms (from wrought-iron or wood beds and natural linen bedspreads to curtains and woven rugs) and common areas compliment the ambiance of the home. The two luminous guest rooms open to both sides of the house, each with an enormous stone fireplace and sofas or tables for sitting and enjoying a country breakfast. In fine weather this pleasant moment of the day is passed on the front portico overlooking hills, fruit orchards and woods. A small pool surrounded by a deck is steps away. Easily reached are interesting naturalistic or cultural excursions to neighboring towns, such as Orvieto, Civita Bagnoreggio (accessed by a pedestrian bridge), the thermal spa at Viterbo, Lake Bolsena and others of Etruscan origins. *Directions:* Exit at Orvieto from autostrada A1; travel 11 km following signs to Lubriano. Before town, turn left at sign for Locanda Settimo Cielo. Located 18 km S of Orvieto, 130 km N of Rome.

SETTIMO CIELO   New
Host: Francesca Anghileri
Locatlità Santa Caterina 28
Lubriano, (VT) 01020, Italy
Tel: (0761) 780451, Cell: (349) 3597732
9 Rooms, Double: €120
2 Cottages: €900-€1200 weekly
Open: all year, Credit cards: MC, VS
Other Languages: English
Region: Lazio, Michelin Map: 563

Lucca is decidedly one of the loveliest cities of Italy with its historical churches and circular piazzas interspersed among beautiful shops featuring original storefronts and signage. Besides the well-known summer Puccini Festival (this is his birthplace), there are antiques markets, artisan fairs, and some of the most beautiful formal gardens and villas in Italy surrounding the city. In March the villas and gardens open for a special tour when the area's famed flower, the camellia (tree size), is in bloom. Over the years we have patiently awaited the arrival of a charming place to stay within the city walls and we were eventually rewarded with the Alla Corte degli Angeli. The Bonino family, already very familiar with the hospitality business, took over a private residence in the very heart of Lucca and created ten spacious bedrooms with guests' comfort in mind. The ground-floor reception area includes a lovely dining room with fireplace where an abundant buffet breakfast is served, if not in your own room. Bedrooms on the upper two floors are reached by an elevator, and all follow a specific flower theme, with pastel-colored walls giving an overall fresh feeling. Complementing the well-put-together decor are antique dressers, parquet floors, and amenities such as air conditioning, Jacuzzi tubs, mini-bars, satellite TV, and WiFi. *Directions:* In the pedestrian-only center of Lucca near the famous Piazza Anfiteatro. Private garage parking can be arranged.

ALLA CORTE DEGLI ANGELI
Host: Pietro Bonino
Via degli Angeli 23, Lucca, (FI) 55100, Italy
Tel: (0583) 469204, Fax: (0583) 991989
12 Rooms, Double: €130–€175*
10 Suites: €190–€220*
*Breakfast not included: €10
Open: all year, Credit cards: all major
Other Languages: some English
Region: Tuscany, Michelin Map: 563

La Romea is a charming and informal B&B situated in a 14th century palazzo right in the very heart of Lucca's enchanting ancient city center. Walk up to the first floor and enter the spacious apartment with its reception desk, sitting area with black leather sofas, and three breakfast tables all under one beamed ceiling. Warm and friendly hosts, Gaia and Giulio heartily welcome guests. Off the main room are the five guest rooms each decorated and named by color (yellow, red, green, ivory and blue). Individually appointed rooms, each with new bathrooms and amenities such as direct telephone line, television, mini-bar, air conditioning and internet wireless connection, are spacious and well lit with large windows and antique furnishings. Their individual color themes are carried through the wall color, bedspreads and curtains. Features include stencil painted borders, beams and parquet floors. The celestial blue room is actually a junior suite, suitable for a family of four. A number of interesting itineraries are suggested and arranged by your knowledgeable hosts, including highlights of the city, wine and villa tours in the outlying countryside. *Directions:* On the corner of the Square Sant'Andrea (12th century church) and Via Ventaglie. A two-minute walk from Lucca's most important sights, the Torre Guingi and Piazza dell'Anfiteatro, plus the lovely Via Fillungo with its many shops and original storefronts.

❄ ☕ 🛵 ☎ 🏠 @ W Ŷ P ⛷ 🧍 👫 🐎 ⛷ ⛴ 💃

LA ROMEA
Hosts: Giulio & Gaia Calissi
Vicolo delle Ventaglie, 2, Lucca, (FI) 55100, Italy
Tel: (0583) 464175
5 Rooms, Double: €120–€170
1 Suite: €140–€170
Open: all year, Credit cards: all major
Other Languages: good English, French
Region: Tuscany, Michelin Map: 563

As you descend south towards fascinating Puglia, one of the first provinces is Foggia, which includes the "spur" and scenic nature reserve of Gargano. Head off the main road and just outside of Foggia is the interesting town of Lucera, whose ancient historical center includes a centuries-old cathedral, moschea, Roman amphitheater, and a massive fortress on a cliff dominating the valley below. The Elena degli Angeli bed and breakfast is within one of the city's most ancient edifices, the Palazzo d'Auria Secondo, built upon Roman ruins. One enters the main doors from the street into the courtyard of the family's restaurant, with tables set outside. Dining rooms feature exposed brick walls, domed or vaulted brick ceilings, fireplace and shelves lined with bottles of regional prized wines (200 labels, plus 400 labels from other regions of Italy). Guests are treated to an authentic meal based on fresh local ingredients and influences from neighboring Abruzzo. Upstairs are the six spacious, comfortable bedrooms with new bathrooms. Rooms are appointed with turn-of-the-century antiques and enhanced by painted ceilings and patterned marble floors. You are definitely on the discovery trail and should make time to explore this area and others farther south. It's well worth the drive. *Directions:* Enter Lucera and follow signs to center city and the cathedral. Piazza Oberdan is just around the corner.

ELENA DEGLI ANGELI   **New**
Host: Alberto Trincucci
Piazza Oberdan 3, Lucera, (FG) 71036, Italy
Tel & Fax: (0881) 530446
6 Rooms, Double: €75–€80
Open: all year, Credit cards: all major
Other Languages: some English
Region: Apulia, Michelin Map: 564

Ten years ago the Luz family of Luino refurbished another home, creating a second, more economical accommodation just 2 kilometers up the road from their hotel on Lake Maggiore (in our other guide). The Colmegna is run by their young and energetic daughter Lara and caters well to families—in fact, there is no charge for children under four. The two pale-yellow buildings run right along the waterfront bordered by an old stone port. There are several terraces for dining outdoors and another with a lawn for sunning or relaxing and enjoying the view. Beyond there is a gorgeous shaded park with romantic trails, tall trees, and wildflowers at one of the prettiest points of the lake. Simply appointed bedrooms are all situated lakeside on the two floors and accommodate from two to four persons. Swimming, sailing, and windsurfing sports can be arranged. Luino is famous for its open market on Wednesdays, a long-standing tradition since 1541. Within touring distance are the lakes of Lugano and Como, the ferry from Laveno across Lake Maggiore, and the Swiss border. *Directions:* Luino is halfway up the lake on the eastern side near the Swiss border. Heading north, Colmegna is on the left-hand side of the main road just past the town of Luino.

CAMIN HOTEL COLMEGNA
Host: Lara Luz
Localita: Colmegna, Luino, (VA) 21016, Italy
Tel: (0332) 510855, Fax: (0332) 501687
25 Rooms, Double: €150–€175
2 Apartments: €60–€140 daily
Minimum Stay Required: 3 nights in apartments
Open: Mar to Nov, Credit cards: all major
Other Languages: good English
Region: Lombardy, Michelin Map: 561

The noble Albertario family have four large countryside properties in Umbria and Tuscany that they have opened up to accommodate travelers. Macciangrosso, bordered by ancient cypress trees, is the most beautiful, with its hilltop position overlooking the sweeping valley. The large stone villa, which has been added on to at various times throughout its long history (15th-century origins), belonged to the noble Piccolomini ancestors. You enter through the side gate, walk over a large patio looking onto the delightful rose garden, and climb an external stairway up to the six bedrooms. These are all accessed by a main living room, more like a museum with its rare antique pieces and gilded frame paintings. Bedrooms, each with a small bathroom, are simpler, appointed with wrought-iron beds and coordinated bedspreads and curtains. Other common living areas are the transformed cantina and dining and game rooms. The swimming pool is bordered by a stone wall from the Etruscan period and a tennis court is nearby. Ten apartments of various sizes are found in the rest of the home and in a nearby house next to the chapel. Close to the thermal spas, Macciangrosso is on the edge of Umbria and Tuscany, offering easy access to the highlights of both regions. *Directions:* From Chiusi drive 3 km towards Chianciano. Turn right at the grocery store at the corner with "Via Pignattaia Alta" and go 1.5 km to the house.

MACCIANGROSSO
Hosts: Sonia & Luigi Albertario
Macciano, (SI) 53044, Italy
Tel & Fax: (0578) 21459
6 Rooms, Double: €130
10 Apartments: €440–€950 weekly
Minimum Stay Required: 2 nights, 4 in apartments
Closed: Nov, Credit cards: MC, VS
Other Languages: good English, French
Region: Tuscany, Michelin Map: 563

Deep in the heart of the Apulia region, in the south part of Italy's heel, is the Salento area and the inviting and informal Tenuta Le Pezzate, of typical masseria design. At a short distance from the main town of Maglie (where recent archaeological diggings revealed artifacts from the Bronze Age and fossils verifying the presence of primitive man) the farm property of the Parma family includes olive groves and a watermelon plantation. Enter the main doors to the large enclosed courtyard, with a single tree in the center, from which the four guest suites, private home and main dining room are accessed. Formerly these spaces were used as farmer's quarters, stalls and barn. A simple and appropriately country look decorates rooms with new bathrooms, wrought-iron beds, brick floors and painted wood furnishings. Two have a sitting room area with lofts for the bedroom. Cross the courtyard, past the Indian fig plants, and you find the door exiting the masseria to the ample-size pool surrounded by more of the cactus family plants. Breakfast is served either on the covered patio or in the long domed dining room with one long wood table and fireplace. Your congenial hosts, world travelers themselves, know just what guests require and can suggest a myriad of day trips. *Directions:* From Lecce, take exit after Maglie, "Scorrano Ospedale". Enter center of town to archway, Porta S. Domenica; continue for 2 km until you see the sign for the entrance. Located 15 W of Oltranto.

TENUTA LE PEZZATE   **New**
Hosts: Benedetta & Mario Parma
Località:, Maglie, (LE) 73024, Italy
Tel: (368) 3739551
Cellphone: (348) 3643697
6 Rooms, Double: €90–€110
Open: all year, Credit cards: all major
Other Languages: English, French, German
Region: Apulia, Michelin Map: 564

With its rocky cliffs edging the water and its many charming lakeside villages, Lake Garda has always been a classic vacation haven for northern Europeans. Most accommodations are very standard, so it was a delight to come across the charming Park Hotel positioned high up on the mountainside and offering spectacular views over the entire lake. These majestic vistas are visible from many of the twenty-two comfortable bedrooms (some of which feature terraces), the outdoor restaurant, the surrounding park and the cliff top swimming pool. The entire hotel has been renovated and given a mountain chalet décor with wood-lined walls, wooden floors and trim, giving the place a warm, cozy ambiance. A buffet breakfast and four-course dinner are offered in the dining room. Many guests often choose to eat on the terrace. Additional amenities include a tavern/cantina for wine tasting, sauna, Swedish shower and whirlpool tub. Members of the Biasi family are always on hand to make their guests feel at home and to suggest sightseeing forays to the many places of interest in the area. The hotel is a few steps from the intermediate aerial cableway to the top of Monte Baldo. *Directions:* Exit Autostrada A22 at Rovereto Sud from the north, or Affi from the south. Go to the lake and follow signs for Malcesine. Then follow signs for Funivia Monte Baldo (cable car). Continue up the Via Panoramica for 5 km to the hotel at the top.

PARK HOTEL QUERCETO
Host: Giorgia Biasi family
Via Panoramica 113
Malcesine, (VR) 37018, Italy
Tel: (045) 7400344, Fax: (045) 7400848
22 Rooms, Double: €124–€166
Open: May to Sep, Credit cards: all major
Region: Veneto, Michelin Map: 562

Mantova is a delightful discovery on the trail of lesser-known art cities of Italy, exceptional for its position on four miniature lakes, which are found right in the historic center. On the outskirts of the city is the San Girolamo property of the Mantovani family where guestrooms are also situated in a part of the former convent and watermill dating to the 17th century, complete with the sound of waterfalls. Four very simply appointed bedrooms are found above the breakfast room (two with en suite bathrooms and two sharing a bathroom) where Kim your host greets you in the morning with fresh cakes and coffee and makes suggestions on the many itineraries in the area. After years of world travel, he has come back to assist in the management of the family agricultural and hospitality business. Ten new guestrooms have been added on one level with individual entrances in the converted barn just across from the family's home. The almost 200 acres of cultivated land are divided up in various surrounding areas. An interesting bike or boat excursion starts from San Girolamo and follows the Mincio Park Preserve and river all the way to Lake Garda (20 kilometers). Bikes can also be used to ride into Mantova as the locals do, an excellent way to view the ancient monuments and squares. *Directions:* From Mantova center take the 62 north towards Villafranca-Verona, turn left at Cittadella, then left again at the sign for San Girolamo. (3 km from the city.)

CORTE SAN GIROLAMO
Host: Kim Mantovani family
Strada S. Girolamo 1, Mantova, (MN) 46100, Italy
Tel: (0376) 391018, Fax: (0376) 1999806
Cellphone: (347) 8008505
14 Rooms, Double: €70–€80
Open: all year, Credit cards: none
Other Languages: good English
Region: Lombardy, Michelin Map: 561

It would be difficult for anyone with a passion for the outdoors to resist the challenge offered Federico when he inherited this 1,000-plus-acre estate in the wilderness of Maremma. He and his energetic wife, Elisabetta, plunged in and in two years made this dream come true. The results are notable and very ambitious, with the complete restoration of six stone farmhouses scattered about the vast property comprised of wooded hills, olive groves, and cultivated fields of grain and sunflowers. Guests first arrive at the imposing 1850s main villa, which houses the private family quarters. Comfortable apartments and guestrooms (divided among the various farmhouses) are harmoniously furnished with country pieces old and new and can accommodate from two to ten persons. Guests have the use of five swimming pools (indoor and out), mountain bikes, sauna, exercise and game rooms, Jacuzzi, and massage therapy. They convene at Podernovo where Tuscan meals are served in the exposed-stone dining room with fireplace, or on the patio looking out over the valley and up to Massa Marittima. The Etruscan towns of Massa Marittima, Volterra, Vetulonia, and Populonia are waiting to be explored. The summer months offer a rich musical program of operas and classical concerts in the main piazza and villas. *Directions:* Drive for 2 km on the gravel road from Massa Marittima where signs indicate Il Cicalino.

TENUTA IL CICALINO
Hosts: Elisabetta & Federico Vecchioni
Localita: Cicalino, Massa Marittima, (GR) 58024, Italy
Tel: (0566) 902031, Fax: (0566) 904896
7 Rooms, Double: €74–€100*
Apartments & Houses: €518–€2070 weekly*
*Breakfast not included: €7
Minimum Stay Required: 2 nights
Open: Mar to Nov, Credit cards: MC, VS
Other Languages: English, French & German
Region: Tuscany, Michelin Map: 563

Florentine sisters Francesca and Beatrice Baccetti eagerly accepted the challenge of converting the family's country home and vineyards into an efficient bed and breakfast. Restoration work began immediately on the two adjacent stone buildings dating back to 1300. All original architectural features were preserved, leaving the five guestrooms and eleven apartments (for two to four people) with terracotta brick floors, wood-beamed ceilings, and mansard roofs, and many with generous views over the tranquil Tuscan countryside. The very comfortable and tidy rooms are furnished with good reproductions in country style and feel almost hotel-like with their telephones and modern bathrooms. A beautiful swimming pool with hydro-massage, tennis court, fitness room, and nearby horse stables are at guests' disposal, although finding enough to do is hardly a problem with Florence only 18 kilometers away and practically all of Tuscany at one's fingertips. Breakfast is served at wooden tables in the stone-walled dining room or out on the terrace. Readers give Salvadonica a high rating for service and warm hospitality. *Directions:* From Florence take the superstrada toward Siena for 6 km, exiting at San Casciano Nord. Follow signs for town, turning left at the sign for Mercatale. Salvadonica is on this road and well marked.

SALVADONICA
Hosts: Francesca & Beatrice Baccetti
Via Grevigiana 82
Mercatale Val di Pesa, (FI) 50024, Italy
Tel: (055) 8218039, Fax: (055) 8218043
5 Rooms, Double: €113–€125
11 Apartments: €135–€160 daily
Open: Mar to Nov, Credit cards: all major
Other Languages: good English
Region: Tuscany, Michelin Map: 563

In an industrial city where the word "charm" is practically nonexistent, the Hotel Regina, although not inexpensive, came as a pleasant surprise among the rather nondescript modern hotels in Milan. For those flying in and out of Milan, with a desire to catch a glimpse of the city center (and newly restored Last Supper of Da Vinci), this is an ideal selection. The attractive, typically 18th-century facade and entrance invite guests into a luminous reception area, converted from the original courtyard, with stone columns, arches, marble floors, large plants, and a small corner bar with sitting area and tables. Completely refurbished rooms include all modern amenities and are very quiet, being set off the street. Decorated comfortably and uniformly with identical furniture, rooms are warmed with soft-pastel-colored walls, parquet floors, and scattered Oriental rugs. A full buffet breakfast is served below and is included in the room rate. Manager Michela is helpful in satisfying guests' requests and bicycles are available for visiting the city's historical center. Linate airport is easily reached by cab in 20 minutes, while the Malpensa airport can be reached by bus from the train station. Rate discounts are given for weekend stays. *Directions:* Via Correnti is just off the Via Torino, which leads to Milan's famous cathedral and shopping area, and is between the basilicas of San Lorenzo and San Ambrogio.

HOTEL REGINA
Host: Michela Barberi
Via Cesare Correnti 13, Milan, (MI) 20123, Italy
Tel: (02) 58106913, Fax: (02) 58107033
43 Rooms, Double: €189–€310
Open: all year, Credit cards: all major
Other Languages: good English
Region: Lombardy, Michelin Map: 561

A recent and long-overdue updating of the regional agritourism laws of Veneto has paved the way for many farm property owners to offer accommodation. Villa Mocenigo is one such place and along with being an economical and pleasant choice, first and foremost it has the advantage of an ideal location right outside of Mirano. At just 20 kilometers from Venice (a bus for the 20-minute ride leaves in front of the farm every 20 minutes), guests have the marvels of Veneto at their fingertips: Padua, Vicenza, Treviso, Brenta and Palladian villas, Chioggia, Asolo. The Ribon family resides in the historic 16th-century villa, while the thirteen guestrooms are located within two other adjacent buildings, originally the farmer's quarters and converted stalls, one being all on ground level and each having an independent entrance from the garden. Damask fabrics and the family's antique beds and armoires adorn the rooms in contrast with the simplicity of the building. Cultivated fields and vineyards line the flat fields in the back and come right up to the house. Locals convene at the authentic country restaurant with checked green tablecloths to be treated to one of Luigina's famed meals with fresh pastas, breads, and their own choice of meats. We like the authentic family hospitality and the rate. *Directions:* Exit the A4 autostrada at Dolo-Mirano and drive 5 km to Mirano. Turn left at the roundabout on Via Cavin di Sala and after 1 km, left again on Via Viasana to the house.

💻 🛒 P ⑪ ♿

VILLA MOCENIGO
Hosts: Giorgio & Luigina Ribon
Via Viasana 59, Mirano, (VE) 30035, Italy
Tel & Fax: (041) 433246
Cellphone: (335) 5474728
13 Rooms, Double: €60–€80
Open: all year, Credit cards: none
Other Languages: English
Region: Veneto, Michelin Map: 562

The Alcala farm, made up of citrus and olive groves extends over 75 acres of fertile plain backdropped by the Etna volcano—a picture-perfect setting. Cordial hostess Anna Sappupo La Rosa and her family have taken over the family's agricultural business and have added hospitality activity as well. The main house is a hundred-year-old masseria, built in several sections. Guests are situated nearby in four different apartment setups (one has handicapped facilities) for two to six persons. Two of them are separate houses and all have terraces of varying dimensions. They include living room areas and kitchenettes simply decorated with floral sofas and a mix of modern and old family furniture. Although breakfast is not served, guests can help themselves in season to plenty of oranges, tangerines, and grapefruit. An occasional Sicilian dinner is served by request in your apartment. Anna, a native Sicilian, gladly assists her guests with touring suggestions, which include Catania city (important where not to go), Siracusa, Etna National Park, and the temples of Agrigento. She is also happy to arrange for a guided tour of the farm. *Directions:* Take the Palermo-Catania autostrada A19 and leave at the exit Motta S. Anastasia. Access is on S.S.192 at km 78. Turn left, backtracking towards Catania on route 192, pass the U.S. army base, then turn left again at the Alcala sign (milestone 78). Go to the end of the private road.

ALCALA
Host: Anna Sappupo family
Casella Postale 100-S.S.192 at km 78
Misterbianco, Sicily, (CT) 95045, Italy
Tel: (095) 7130029, Fax: (095) 7130342
Cellphone: (368) 3469206
4 Apartments: €56–€112 daily, no breakfast offered
Minimum Stay Required: 3 nights, 7 in high season
Open: all year, Credit cards: MC, VS
Other Languages: good English, French
Region: Sicily, Michelin Map: 565

Casa Talìa, a special property full of character and charm, reflects the careful restoration work of Marco and Viviana. Located on a hillside within a maze of ancient houses, the property was once a group of shepherd's cottages that have been transformed into enchanting guesthouses. With an environmentally sensitive philosophy, local building techniques and materials including stone, painted ceramic tiles, brick and wood were used to create an intimate and appealing ambiance. Full bathrooms with a designer's touch compliment each of the four simple rooms, reflecting the intense colors of Sicily. The rooms open onto small Mediterranean gardens, dotted with cactus, palm, olive and fig trees. Guests take in spectacular views of Modica, an intriguing city, including the imposing church of St. Giorgio. A full breakfast of homemade cakes and jams is served in another house. The house's living room has a wall of windows that opens up to the same fabulous view enjoyed from the cottages. As Casa Talìa's brochure states, "slow living" is a lifestyle choice and this is certainly the right place to just live in the moment. *Directions:* Casa Talìa is located within the group of houses on the hill above the main street of Modica, Corso Umberto. Via Exaudinos is a narrow one-way street and it is best to contact the owners for specific instructions. It's not easy to find but well worth the effort.

CASA TALÌA
Hosts: Marco Giunta & Viviana Haddad
Via Exaudinos 1/9
Modica, (RG) 97015, Italy
Tel: (0932) 752075
Cellphone: (335) 5486656
4 Rooms, Double: €130–€160
Minimum Stay Required: 3 nights
Open: all year, Credit cards: all major
Region: Sicily, Michelin Map: 565

If you wish to experience the true flavor of southern Sicily, a stay in the baroque town of Modica is essential. In the heart of town where the houses nestle between two facing hillsides, you find L'Orangerie, a 19th-century palazzo owned by the Cartia family. Walk up the steps from the main street to a small street which ends at the front doors of this charming and impeccable bed and breakfast. The guestrooms and bi-level mini apartments are spread over the two floors of the palace. The fresh décor combines the features of a historic home with antiques, fresco ceilings, contemporary furniture, parquet floors and modern bathrooms. Graphic art accents walls that are painted cream, forest green, coral and rust red. Some rooms have a terrace overlooking the lemon trees. Giovanni Cartia, whose family has owned the palazzo for several generations, offers warm hospitality and advice on where to go and what to see. Breakfast is served in the delightful kitchen with its hand-painted tiles. Guests often dine at the restaurant, Torre D'Oriente, savoring traditional cuisine and local sweet specialties including dark chocolate, cannoli, gelati and granitas. *Directions:* Before you reach Modica's piazza, park by the pharmacy on the right-hand side of the Corso Umberto (the main street that runs the center of town). Vico de Naro is reached by steps from behind the pharmacy.

L' ORANGERIE
Host: Giovanni Cartia
Vico de Naro 5, Modica, (RG) 97015, Italy
Tel: (0932) 754703, Fax: (0932) 754840
Cellphone: (347) 0674698
4 Rooms, Double: €96
3 Suites: €126
Open: all year, Credit cards: all major
Other Languages: fluent English, German
Region: Sicily, Michelin Map: 565

To one side of the Church of San Giorgio in the seaside village of Monéglia is the former convent and cloister where this intimate bed and breakfast is housed. Dating back to the 1300's the convent was dedicated to St. Francis, depicted in the painted frescoes on the walls of the cloister. The complex once included full guest quarters, infirmary and a precious library.It has been recently restored by partners Angelo and Giorgio, natives of Monéglia, who have set high standards of comfort in the eight rooms overlooking the courtyard, while maintaining the same calm and contemplative ambiance. Using the expertise of local artisans and selecting antique pieces and rich fabrics which harmonize splendidly, the romantic and luxurious results contrast with the convent's austere past. No two of the modern bathrooms, with marble sinks and a few with hydro-jet baths, are alike. Breakfast with freshly made jams and breads is served in the small refectory. Extra services are available as your hosts also own another hotel. This property has a swimming pool and sauna which can be used, a private beach facility and a boat for excursions along the coast of the famous Cinque Terre. The scenic drive over the mountain down to the secluded village is well worth all the curves to get there. *Directions:* Exit at Sestri Levante from the autostrada A12 and after turning left at the stop light, follow for Monéglia center (approx 15 minutes). Located 30 km south of Portofino.

❄ ☕ ✂ ☕ 💳 ☎ @ W Ⲩ P 🚭 🖼 🐾 🏃 🏇 ⛵ 🍇

ABBADIA SAN GIORGIO   New
Hosts: Angelo Sella & Giorgio Botto
Piazzale San Giorgio
Monéglia, (GE) 16030, Italy
Tel: (0185) 491119, Fax: (0185) 490270
Cellphone: (335) 6278356
6 Rooms, Double: €180–€250
2 Suites: €260–€315
Open: all year, Credit cards: all major
Abitare La Storia, History Traveller
Region: Liguria, Michelin Map: 561

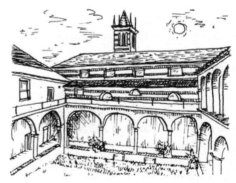

While many agritourism farms are run by transplanted urbanites, many are still owned and operated by farmers whose families have worked the land for generations. Such is the case with Onofrio Contento and his family, proprietors of Masseria Curatori, not far from the city of Monopoli and the Adriatic Sea, where, for five generations, the family has produced olives, almonds, and cattle. Inside the main coral-color house are very modest and immaculate quarters for guests, consisting presently of a large three-bedroom apartment with kitchen and living room, plus two doubles with private bathrooms. Old and new family furniture has been combined to decorate the rooms. The view is pleasingly pastoral, overlooking olive-tree-studded hills. Two apartments for two to four persons are found in a nearby one-story building overlooking a lovely stone-walled garden and fruit orchard. Breakfast and extra meals are taken together with the hospitable family in their dining room where Lucrezia delights guests with local dishes. Horseback riding can be arranged for guests. Curatori is an excellent base from which to visit the highlights of this unique region of Italy. *Directions:* 40 km from Bari. Take coastal route S.S.16 south, leaving at the sixth exit for Monopoli called Monopoli-San Francesco da Paola. Turn right for 300 meters and then left on S.C. Conchia Road, to a pink house on your right.

MASSERIA CURATORI
Hosts: Onofrio & Lucrezia Contento family
Contrada Cristo delle Zolle 227 (S.C. Conchia)
Monopoli, (BA) 70043, Italy
Tel & Fax: (080) 777472, Cellphone: (338) 6242833
2 Rooms, Double: €70–€80, 9 Suites: €120–€160
2 Apartments: €180 daily, €910 weekly
Minimum Stay Required: 2 nights
Open: all year, Credit cards: none
Other Languages: very little English
Region: Apulia, Michelin Map: 564

A well-kept secret among off-the-main-road travelers is the countryside north of Rome known as "Sabina" after the mountain range. It is unusual that agritourism has not developed close to Rome compared to what has occurred around Florence, but locals are beginning to wake up. Ancestors of the Gabbuti family came from this area and the principal palazzos in both medieval towns of Casperia and Montasola, plus a large farm with olive groves, have been in the family for generations. One of the daughters, Letizia, decided to leave a law career in Rome to work on restoration of these properties and offer hospitality in the form of apartments and one bedroom within her home. Spacious apartments include one to three bedrooms, living room, kitchen, and bathrooms, all warmly decorated with the family's own antiques. Characteristic architectural features have been preserved, and three apartments have terraces with a breathtaking panoramic view (our favorite is the one in the medieval tower). There is something very special about being a "resident" of a medieval village with its narrow stone alleyways. Lounge under the shady trees of a stone-walled garden, dine at the characteristic osteria in the village, or take 2-3 day cooking lessons. Other charming villages dot the area, Umbria is nearby, and Rome is just a 45-minute train ride away. Suitable for independent explorers. *Directions:* Arrangements to be met should be made at the time of reservation.

MONTEPIANO
Host: Maria Letizia Gabbuti
Via dei Casalini 8, Montasola, (RI) 02040, Italy
Tel: (0746) 675035, Fax: (0765) 63252
Cellphone: (328) 3813145 or (330) 749221
1 Room, Double: €150
4 Apartments: €100 daily, €980 weekly
Minimum Stay Required: 3 nights
Open: all year, Credit cards: none
Other Languages: some English
Region: Lazio, Michelin Map: 563

While Monte San Vito's official documents date back to 1177, recent evidence shows Neolithic origins. The Viadelcampo bed and breakfast is right on the road outside the town of Monte San Vito, a hilltop village which has brought traditional festivals back to life. Indeed 14 festivals are scheduled during the year. The deep salmon color of the house amid gardens and olive groves makes it unmistakable from the road. Silvia, a natural hostess and decorative painter, had the family farmhouse restored and all the walls became canvases for her trompe d'oeil and naive artwork. To give the simple house some personality, she designated a different bright color for each room and painted scenes in color schemes of green, yellow, pink and beige. Dècor is a mix of ethnic and country with patchwork bedspreads. The informal ambiance is ideal for one or two families traveling together as each pair of bedrooms share one bathroom. A country breakfast is served out under the pergola or at a long wood table in the living room. Silvia also has a passion for cooking and she organizes impromptu pasta or pizza lessons in the restored barn. Guests are surrounded by wine country, where fine Lacrima di Morro d'Alba red and Verdicchio whites are produced. *Directions:* Easily reached from Autostrada A14, exit at Ancona Nord. Follow for Jesi–Monsano–Chiaravalle–Monte S. Vito. The bed and breakfast is on the left at crossroads before town.

VIADELCAMPO
Host: Silvia Serrani
Via Martiri della Resistenza 66
Monte San Vito, (AN) 60037, Italy
Tel: (339) 3560989
4 Rooms, Double: €70
Open: all year, Credit cards: none
Other Languages: very little English
Region: Marches, Michelin Map: 563

Lucca, one of our favorite Italian cities, is well situated near Pisa, with the beautiful Valdera countryside to the south, the Apuane mountain range to the north, the seaside 20 kilometers away, and many splendid villas and famous gardens scattered in the vicinity. The city, however, is directly surrounded by a heavily commercial area until you get to the olive oil and wine country around the charming hilltop town of Montecarlo, 15 kilometers east of town. This medieval stone village with fortress walls has several good restaurants and cafés, its own theater where Puccini was known to put on operas, and many olive-oil-producing farms and wineries close by. A team of three women friends, Antonella, Marta and Miriam, take turns caring for their guests on a rotation basis, alternating with their own family duties. All bedrooms on two upper floors but two have en suite bathrooms and are simply appointed with wrought-iron beds, eyelet curtains and floral bedspreads. A rich and tasty breakfast, made with local and homemade products, is served either out on the front patio where you can observe the daily life of the locals, or in the miniature breakfast room to the right of the reception and mini sitting area (with internet point) where a wine and coffee bar is open all day. You are left a front door key when returning in the evening. *Directions:* From the A11 autostrada, take the Altopascio exit. Head towards Pescia (3 km) and turn left for Montecarlo for another 2 km.

ANTICA CASA DEI RASSICURATI
Hosts: Antonella Romanini, Marta Giusti & Miriam Keller
Via della Collegiata 2, Montecarlo, (LU) 55015, Italy
Tel: (0583) 228901, Fax: (0583) 22498
8 Rooms, Double: €50–€80
Minimum Stay Required: 2 nights
Open: all year, Credit cards: MC, VS
Other Languages: good English, German, French
Region: Tuscany, Michelin Map: 563

The scenic approach to the Fattoria di Vibio passes through lush green hills, by picturesque farms, and is highlighted by a romantic view of the quaint town of Todi, 20 kilometers away. Two handsome brothers from Rome run this top-drawer bed and breakfast consisting of several recently restored stone houses. The houses sit side by side and share between them 14 double rooms with private baths. Common areas for guests include a cozy, country-style living room with fireplace, games room, and country kitchen. The accommodations are enhanced by preserved architectural features such as terracotta floors and exposed-beam ceilings, and typical Umbrian handicrafts such as wrought-iron beds, renovated antiques, and Deruta ceramics. On the assumption that guests may find it difficult to leave this haven, the hosts offer half board plus lunch and snacks, along with spa facilities (massages and Turkish bath) indoor and outdoor heated swimming pools, tennis, hiking, horseback riding, fishing, and biking. Signora Gabriella, with a passion for cooking, gets all the richly deserved credit for the marvelous meals served either poolside or on the panoramic terrace. Four houses are also available for rent. *Directions:* From either Todi or Orvieto follow route S448 until the turnoff for Vibio at the sign for Prodo-Quadro and follow the well-marked dirt road for 10 km up to the farmhouse.

FATTORIA DI VIBIO
Hosts: Giuseppe & Filippo Saladini
Localita: Buchella-Doglio
Montecastello di Vibio, (PG) 06057, Italy
Tel: (075) 8749607, Fax: (075) 8780014
Cellphone: (335) 6686977
14 Rooms, Double: €140–€160, 3 Suites: €180–€200
4 Villas: €980–€2100 weekly
Open: Mar to Jan 8, Credit cards: all major
Other Languages: good English
Region: Umbria, Michelin Map: 563

La Loggia, built in 1427, was one of the Medici estates during the centuries of their rule. Owner Giulio Baruffaldi, weary of urban life in Milan, transplanted himself and his wife here and succeeded in reviving the wine estate's splendor while respecting its past, enhancing its architectural beauty while giving utmost attention to the preservation of the historic property. Their informal yet refined hospitality is reflected in the care given to retaining the rustic ambiance of the former farmers' homes, each containing one to three bedrooms, living room, and kitchen, some with fireplace, and adorned with country antiques and original paintings from the Baruffaldis' own art collection. In fact, many important bronze and ceramic sculptures by international artists are displayed throughout the gardens of the villa. Four double rooms have been added, some having a fireplace or hydro-massage bath and steam room. Apart from just basking in the pure romance and tranquility of this place, you can enjoy a heated seawater swimming pool, horseback riding, and nearby tennis and golf facilities. Other activities include the occasional cooking or wine-tasting lesson, and impromptu dinners in the cellar. The charming hostess Ivana personally takes care of guests' needs. *Directions:* Leave the Florence-Siena autostrada after San Casciano at Bargino. Turn right at the end of the ramp, then left for Montefiridolfi (3.5 km). La Loggia is just before town.

FATTORIA LA LOGGIA
Hosts: Giulio Baruffaldi & Cuca Roaldi
Via Collina, Montefiridolfi
San Casciano Val di Pesa, (FI) 50026, Italy
Tel: (055) 8244288, Fax: (055) 8244283
4 Rooms, Double: €100–€260
11 Apartments: €140–€570 daily
Open: all year, Credit cards: MC, VS
Other Languages: good English, French, Spanish
Region: Tuscany, Michelin Map: 563

It is only logical that the Antinori family, one of the most famous wine producers in Italy, has joined the ranks of landowners offering top-quality, agriturismo accommodation. They have done it in grand style, restoring and creating twenty apartments and seven guestrooms within the eight stone houses scattered about the vast property in the center. Chianti is composed of hills, woods, and, of course, infinite vineyards. In keeping with the general countryside ambiance, the high-level accommodation is appointed with wood furniture, smart striped or checked fabrics that harmonize well with the brick floors and beamed ceilings. While three of the ancient farmhouses are located up a road across the vineyards, the others are grouped together at the main entrance near the reception room, swimming pool, tennis courts, small gym, and restaurant serving typical Tuscan fare. The Fonte de Medici is heads above the rest with an offering of a wide range of amenities including air conditioning, kitchenette, fireplaces, dishwasher, barbecue, satellite TV, and internet access. Enjoy the classic, Tuscan landscapes coupled with classic Chianti wine and the marvels of this region surrounding you. *Directions:* Exit from A1 at Certosa-Firenze and follow the highway for Siena. Exit at San Casciano and follow for Montefiridolfi, then Badia di Passignano. Follow signs for Fonte de Medici-Antinori to the front gate.

FONTE DE MEDICI
Host: Gilberto Nori
Localita S. Maria a Macerata
Montefiridolfi, (FI) 50020, Italy
Tel: (055) 8244700, Fax: (055) 8244701
Cellphone: (348) 3979600
7 Rooms, Double: €150–€180
22 Apartments: €150–€390 daily
Open: all year, Credit cards: all major
Other Languages: good English
Region: Tuscany, Michelin Map: 563

Just opposite the lovely Fattoria La Loggia is a bed and breakfast that was actually one of the farmhouses belonging to the vast vineyard property. Gracious Signora Nadia fell in love with the ancient house and decided to retire here after having the entire place restored, leaving the ground floor for herself and the guests' breakfast room while the upstairs provides apartments of flexible configurations for travelers. The two adjoining apartments to the right (yellow and blue color schemes) can become a three-bedroom apartment with three colorful bathrooms, living room, kitchen, and large fireplace. The two one-bedroom apartments in green hues can be rented separately or adjoined as well. Rooms have a clean, country feeling to them with antique armoires, simple wrought-iron beds blending in nicely with stone walls, wood-beamed mansard ceilings and brick floors so typical in Tuscany. A lovely swimming pool sits close to the house overlooking the soft valley. This is a very easy base from which to visit most of the region's highlights besides being only 20 minutes from Florence and 30 from Siena. *Directions:* Exit at Bargino from the Florence-Siena highway and turn right and then immediately left at the sign for Montefiridolfi. After 3 km look for a stone house with large arched windows on the left side of the road before town.

MACINELLO
Host: Nadia Ciuffetti
Via Collina 9, Montefiridolfi
San Casciano Val di Pesa, (FI), 50020, Italy
Tel & Fax: (055) 8244459
4 Rooms, Double: €80–€110
4 Apartments: €210–€225 daily
Minimum Stay Required: 3 nights, 7 nights Jun to Aug
Open: all year, Credit cards: none
Region: Tuscany, Michelin Map: 563

The Villa Sant'Andrea is a prestigious wine estate on a hilltop dominating the Pesa valley in the Chianti region of Tuscany. An impressive villa and church are its focal points. So spectacular and strategic is the location that it has been occupied since Roman times. The vast property (over 1,300 acres!) spills down the vineyard-covered terrain to the horizon and includes three typical Tuscan farmhouses, (Zobi, Perticato and Montelodoli) that can be rented weekly or daily, each with its own private swimming pool. Luckily, for those desiring accommodation with breakfast, six quaint country style rooms are also available. Situated within the hamlet and across from the proprietors' gated historic villa, they are hidden by centuries-old cypresses and a lush garden. Wrought iron beds adorned with checked bedspreads and country antiques are authentically Tuscan. Superb views are to be enjoyed from each window. Two common rooms with large open fireplaces are reserved for guests for breakfast or simply lounging. For the more active, mountain bikes are available as well as hiking trails into the scenic countryside, through olive groves, vineyards and oak trees. The office is open for check in from 3pm to 6pm. The marvels of Tuscany are at your doorstep (Siena, San Gimignano, Volterra, and everything in between). *Directions:* From the Siena-Florence highway exit at Tavarnelle and follow road for 2 km to Fabbrica and the villa entrance.

VILLA SANT'ANDREA
Host: Vicini family
Via di Fabbrica, 63, Montefiridolfi, (FI) 50020, Italy
Tel: (055) 8544254, Fax: (055) 82442030
Cellphone: (393) 9912572 or (393) 9879116
6 Rooms, Double: €105–€125
3 Houses: €130–€216 daily
Open: all year, Credit cards: all major
Other Languages: English, French, German, Spanish
Region: Tuscany, Michelin Map: 563

Le Fontanelle country house sits in the heart of the Maremma area of Tuscany where, besides being pleasant and well run, it fills a need for the growing interest in this off-the-beaten-track destination. Signor Perna and his two lovely daughters, originally from Rome, searched and found this peaceful haven from the stress of city life, promptly transferring themselves and undertaking major restoration work. Looking over a soft green valley up to the nearby village of Montemerano, the stone farmhouse with its rusty-red shutters offers four comfortable rooms with spotless private bathrooms. The converted barn houses five rooms while the last room is in a separate cottage set in the woods. Sunlight pours into the front veranda-like breakfast room where coffee and cakes are taken together with other guests at one large table. The Pernas assist guests in planning local itineraries including visits to artisan workshops. With due notice, guests can find a wonderfully prepared dinner awaiting them under the ivy-covered pergola in the rose garden. The property is part of a reserve with deer, wild boar, and various types of wildlife, where Porcini mushrooms, wild asparagus, and berries are found in season. *Directions:* From Rome, take the A12 autostrada. Continue north on Aurelia route 1, turning off at Vulci after Montalto. Follow signs for Manciano then Montemerano. Turn left at the bed-and-breakfast sign before town and follow the dirt road for 1 km.

LE FONTANELLE
Hosts: Daniela & Cristina Perna
Localita: Poderi di Montemerano
Montemerano, (GR) 58050, Italy
Tel & Fax: (0564) 602762
10 Rooms, Double: €85
Open: Mar to Nov, Credit cards: MC, VS
Other Languages: some English
Region: Tuscany, Michelin Map: 563

One result of increasing interest in the singular attractions of the Maremma, or southern Tuscany, is the opening or expansion of several noteworthy places to stay. The Villa Acquaviva, once owned by nobility and a small family hotel for some years, was extensively remodeled to include seven guestrooms named for and painted in the colors of local wildflowers. The bedrooms all have private baths and are decorated with country antiques and wrought-iron beds. Breakfast of homemade cakes, breads, and jams can be eaten in the breakfast room near the enoteca. There are ten newer rooms in a stone farmhouse on the property plus eight in another, joined together by a glassed-in reception area. These are our favorites, with beautiful local antiques and colorful matching fabrics adorning beds and windows. Tennis courts and a swimming pool are attractive features of the complex. In the center of the park, in a scenic position by the swimming pool, the restaurant presents typical Maremman dishes made with fresh products from the farm. *Directions:* From Rome, take the Aurelia coastal road, exiting at Vulci. Follow signs for Manciano, then Montemerano. Acquaviva is well marked just outside the village.

VILLA ACQUAVIVA
Hosts: Valentina di Virginio & Serafino d'Ascenzi
Localita: Acquaviva
Montemerano, (GR) 58050, Italy
Tel: (0564) 602890, Fax: (0564) 602895
Cellphone: (335) 7509100
25 Rooms, Double: €102–€240
3 Suites: €220–€240
Open: all year, Credit cards: all major
Other Languages: good English, French, German
Region: Tuscany, Michelin Map: 563

A pleasant alternative to a countryside bed and breakfast is one right in the historical center of the marvelously preserved medieval town of Montepulciano. Most famous for its prized Rosso di Montepulciano wines, its striking charm of the past rivals that of its hilltop neighbors, Pienza and Montalcino. Here Cinzia Caroti offers bed and breakfast on the first floor of a 16th-century palazzo on the main street of town, which is lined with shops and restaurants and is off limits to cars, which adds much to its medieval aura. One flight of wide stairs takes you up to L'Agnolo's reception area. There are three bedrooms off this area and another two off the frescoed dining room with wrought-iron chandelier. The spacious, high-ceilinged rooms have a subdued ambiance, with wrought-iron beds, family antiques, and new white-tiled bathrooms. Better lighting could be used to show off lovely original frescoed ceilings and painted borders. A classic breakfast of cappuccino and fresh croissants is served in the coffee shop below the home, making one feel like a true local resident. Cinzia lives two doors down and is present throughout the day to assist guests and make suggestions from the many sightseeing possibilities in this rich area of Tuscany, bordering Umbria. *Directions:* Park your car nearby (north or east lot) outside the village walls and follow Via di Gracciano running north-south to the middle. There is a small gold name plaque at the door.

L'AGNOLO
Host: Cinzia Caroti
Via di Gracciano nel Corso 63
Montepulciano, (SI) 53045, Italy
Tel: (0578) 717070, Fax: (0578) 757095
Cellphone: (339) 2254813
5 Rooms, Double: €90
Open: Mar 20 to Jan 10, Credit cards: MC, VS
Other Languages: very little English
Region: Tuscany, Michelin Map: 563

Montepulciano, ancient hilltop town and home of the prized "Rosso di Montepulciano" wine, is one of Tuscany's best-preserved marvels. The scenic countryside leads to other enchanting towns, such as Pienza, Montalcino, Sarteano, and San Quirico. Set below the town, behind the Basilica, taking in upwardly sweeping views of Montepucliano, is the lovely San Bruno property. The owners from Milan restored a typical stone farmhouse, drenched in pink cascading geraniums, and found themselves (naturally) with so many house guests that they created two additional, one-story guesthouses across the informal garden dotted with lavender plants and roses. With guest comfort foremost in mind, large doubles have spacious, travertine bathrooms with hydro-jet tub and separate shower. They are impeccably appointed in a refined country décor, using the finest materials and reflecting the innate beauty of these famed landscapes. The "Royal" suite in the main house is a real splurge. A borderless, swimming pool awaits guests with a small, side gym and massage room. Home-baked goods are served in the morning until 11:00 in the dining room—located in a separate house incorporating the reception office and a soft-peach/yellow-colored living room with fireplace, inviting white sofas, and enormous glass doors with views. *Directions:* From Montepulciano, follow for Basilica San Biagio. Behind church, turn a sharp left on Via Pescaia, then into second gate on left.

RELAIS SAN BRUNO
Host: Alberto Pavoncelli
Via di Pescaia, 5/7, Montepulciano, (SI) 53045, Italy
Tel: (0578) 716222, Fax: (0578) 715084
Cellphone: (338) 2557450
8 Rooms, Double: €200–€340
Apartments: €200–€300 daily
Open: Mar to Nov, Credit cards: all major
Other Languages: good English, Spanish
Region: Tuscany, Michelin Map: 563

Starting out as an ancient monastery, the Castello di Monterado passed on to the Duchy of Urbino and later to the powerful Della Rovere family. Today the monumental fortress belongs to the Rodano family who have painstakingly brought it back to its original splendor. Orlando and Kira are young and attentive hosts. Four magnificently spacious suites (Atena, Afrodite, Amorini and the Bridal suite) are available with original antiques, chandeliers, period paintings, and restored whimsical frescoes on high ceilings. The Bridal Suite is the largest and the most special. It was commissioned by Napoleon's nephew for his wedding night with the daughter of Russia's Czar Alexander. Its private terrace overlooks soft hillsides and it has a refurbished but original (early 1900s) bathroom. Other suites have contrasting new designer bathrooms. A series of common rooms wraps around the courtyard; formal sitting rooms, library with century-old books, music room and terrace, and frescoed dining room where breakfast is served. The simply-appointed apartments, within a building across the street, can accommodate from four to six people. *Directions:* Exit autostrada A14 at Marotta (two exits north of Ancona) and follow signs for Pergola then Monterado (8km). Go straight into town up to the top where the castle awaits you. 10 km from the Adriatic coast.

CASTELLO DI MONTERADO
Host: Orlando Rodano family
Piazza Roma 19, Monterado, (AN) 60010, Italy
Tel: (071) 7958395, Fax: (071) 7959923
Cellphone: (392) 3179412
5 Suites: €190–€230
6 Apartments: €560 weekly
Open: all year, Credit cards: all major
Other Languages: good English
Region: Marches, Michelin Map: 563

Monteriggioni is a circular medieval town with turreted fortress walls, mentioned in Dante's Inferno. To the east is an extension of unspoiled land, preserved over the centuries because it was all owned by one proprietor. Within this mix of olive groves and dense woods, in the center of a peaceful forest reserve is the Poggiarello property. The three stone farmhouses dating back to the 1700s are reached by a 2 kilometer dirt road. The Giove family (brother and sister team) bought and restored the property creating apartments for 2-8 people, two doubles, a restaurant and swimming pool plus living quarters for both of their own families. They enjoy entertaining guests and attending to their comfort and ease, offering tasty regional meals, such as fresh pastas and country soups all made with local products and fresh produce. A casual ambiance prevails in room dècor which is basic and simple like the stone and beam houses, each with outdoor garden space or a nice wide open view. Another special feature is the Roman hot bath within its own stone house, perfect for a soak after a long day of Tuscan touring. Sights in the immediate area include Siena, San Gimignano, Volterra and Chianti. *Directions:* From the Florence-Siena highway, exit at Monteriggioni, turn right at the stop sign and after 1.4 km left for Abbadia. After 6 km turn left for Scogiano. After 4 km turn left signed Antico Borgo Poggiarello. Go 300m, turn left and follow the dirt road for 2 km.

ANTICO BORGO POGGIARELLO
Hosts: Roberto Giove & Paolo Ruggiero
Localita Poggiarello-Strada San Monti
12, Monteriggioni, (SI) , Italy
Tel & Fax: (0577) 301003
2 Rooms, Double: €140–€190
14 Apartments: €115–€280 daily
Open: all year, Credit cards: all major
Other Languages: some English
Region: Tuscany, Michelin Map: 563

After years of working in a hotel in Siena, then owning a wine bar, Marcello and his wife Maria Pia decided to put their hospitality experience into practice and opened the charming Bolsinina bed and breakfast. This is a perfect location for travelers, being so close to Siena (18 km) and having easy access to the main road, which passes through the magical Crete Senesi landscapes with their low, rolling clay hills punctuated by an occasional cypress tree against the horizon, to the hilltowns of Montalcino, Pienza, and Montepulciano. The 18th-century brick house has a courtyard where meals are served in season. To one side are the apartments of varying sizes, and to the other is the large house where the beamed guestrooms are located upstairs, along with a large common living room and loggia terrace with splendid views. Downstairs is an open multi-use space rotating around the center staircase with billiard table, cozy living room with fireplace and two large brick arches, and dining room. Guests reserve in the morning for dinner accompanied by excellent local wines. The house and rooms are filled with local antique country furniture and armoires and there is an immediate at-home informal air about the place. An inviting swimming pool is an added bonus. *Directions:* From Siena on the S.R.2, follow signs to Buonconvento. Before Buonconvento turn left at Casale-Gaggiolo (km 209). Take the gravel road up to the house.

❄ ☕ ⚗ 🃏 🔔 @ ☰ P 🚭 🏊 🖼 🚶

CASA BOLSININA
Hosts: Marcello & Maria Pia Mazzotta
Localita: Casale, Monteroni d'Arbia, (SI) 53014, Italy
Tel & Fax: (0577) 718477, Cellphone: (338) 2705153
6 Rooms, Double: €120–€140, 1 Suite: €145–€165 daily
4 Apartments: €700–€1000 weekly
Minimum Stay Required: 7 in apartments
Cleaning & heating extra for apartments
Closed: Jan 15 to Mar 15, Credit cards: all major
Other Languages: good English
Region: Tuscany, Michelin Map: 563

La Morra is a quaint village dominating the Langhe wine valley with spectacular views over undulating layers of striped hillsides. The village, dating back to the 12th century, has six historic churches and a bell tower from the 1600s. There is a comprehensive enoteca in town where most regional wines are presented and sold, plus five other wine bars and six restaurants. The Vibertis have returned to their farm property after living in Alba for some years and now the retired couple enjoys hosting guests from around the world in their pristine white brick farmhouse dating to 1885. Signora Teresa has done a wonderful job of maintaining an authentic ambiance of the farmer's home. Rooms with worn brick floors retain all the original country antiques, are decorated with embroidered curtains and bedspreads, and have immaculate new bathrooms. All four bedrooms face the road and are off a hallway up on the first floor of one half of the house, while the hosts' quarters remain separate on the opposite side. A country breakfast with fresh-baked cakes is served downstairs in the guests' common room. Son Franco speaks English well and is present mostly in the afternoons and weekends, while brother Bruno has just opened his own 14-room hotel in La Morra. Genuine hospitality and ambiance. *Directions:* Leaving Alba, follow signs for Barolo. At the town of Gallo d'Alba, turn right for La Morra-Santa Maria. Casa Bambin is right on the road 2 km before La Morra.

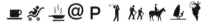

CASA BAMBIN
Host: Teresa Viberti family
Frazione Santa Maria 68, La Morra, (CN) 12064, Italy
Tel & Fax: (0173) 50785
Cellphone: (347) 4659272
4 Rooms, Double: €60–€65
Minimum Stay Required: 2 nights
Closed: Dec to Mar, Credit cards: none
Other Languages: good English
Region: Piedmont, Michelin Map: 561

Hostess Silvana's claim to fame is her innate ability to please guests at the dining table and she did this for years in her own restaurant in Alba, which was written up in many culinary guides. Now she concentrates on her privileged guests who can sample her regional specialties right at home. Gracious Silvana and her journalist husband, Gianni, have transformed the grandparents' farmhouse, a group of three attached wings forming a U, into an intimate bed and breakfast with just two rooms. Their idea was to offer couples maximum space and privacy in junior suites (Rosa and Azzurra). Each room has its own entrance from the garden, sitting area, bedroom, and bathroom and Azzurra also has a small loft with two extra beds. The most extraordinary feature here is the soul-soothing panoramic views encompassing layers and layers of unspoilt landscapes dotted with villages and farmhouses all the way to the distant Alps on the horizon. All this accompanied by silence or the occasional chirping of birds. At sunset the only thing that can possibly tear guests away from the patio with its huge pots of hydrangeas overlooking the deep-green countryside is the call to dinner for another one of Silvana's fabulous meals served on the veranda. *Directions:* From Murazzano follow signs for Dogliani. After 1 km turn left at a small chapel on the road marked Cichetti and follow it to the end. 35 km from Alba, 70 km from Turin.

CASCINA CICHETTI
Hosts: Silvana Faggio & Gianni Galli
Frazione Mellea 69, Murazzano, (CN) 12060, Italy
Tel: (0173) 798501, Fax: (0173) 798921
2 Rooms, Double: €100
Minimum Stay Required: 2 nights
Open: all year, Credit cards: VS
Other Languages: fluent English
Region: Piedmont, Michelin Map: 561

We have been informed that the Albergo Sansevero Degas has been closed. The Albergo Sansevero Degas belongs to the Sansevero properties, a group of small hotels in Naples that are within prestigious palaces dating to the 1700s. Our favorite, of the three more basic hotels in the affiliation, is the Albergo Sansevero Degas. As the name implies, the palace at one time belonged to the family of the painter Edgar Degas, who also stayed here. The location couldn't be more ideal; the hotel is located just off of the Piazza Gesù Nuovo, a gem of a small square in the historic heart of Naples. The charm of the Albergo Sansevero Degas is not immediately apparent. You enter through a handsome portal into a dreary courtyard, then up an elevator to the hotel, where you step out into a pleasant reception area. The Sanservero affiliation has done an excellent job in staffing personnel, since every property we visited had exceptionally friendly, knowledgeable hosts at the front desk. The Albergo Sansevero Degas is a simple hotel, but offers great value. The décor is not pretentiously antique, but instead offers fresh and pretty rooms decorated with bamboo furniture. Our favorite, room 305, looks out to the colorful piazza. Note: Not all of the rooms are with a private bathroom and the reservation telephone represents all the hotels in the group, so ask for the Albergo Sanservero Degas by name. *Directions:* Located just off of the Piazza Gesù Nuovo.

ALBERGO SANSEVERO DEGAS
Manager: Armida Auriemma
Calata Trinit à Maggiore 53
Piazza Gesù Nuovo
Naples, (NA), 80138, Italy
Tel & Fax: (081) 7901000
8 Rooms, Double: €95–€80
Open: all year, Credit cards: none
Region: Campania, Michelin Map: 564

The Hotel Il Convento, next to the shrine of Santa Maria Francesca in the historic heart of Naples, is tucked in the maze of narrow, alley-like streets that make up the interesting old Spanish quarter of the city. The location is excellent, with many of the most interesting places to visit very close to the hotel. Just two blocks away is the Via Toledo that leads down to one of Italy's most colorful squares, the Piazza del Plebiscito, where you can visit the Royal Palace and San Carlo Theater. The Hotel Il Convento, originally a 17th century palace, has been skillfully renovated to maintain its original architectural features while introducing modern comforts. You enter through a stone, arched doorway into a small lobby, where instead of a formal check-in counter, you are warmly greeted at an antique wood desk. Throughout the hotel wrought-iron accents, terracotta floors, and rustic antiques set an inviting, casual ambiance. Just off the reception area there is a cozy, wood-paneled bar; a welcome place to have a quiet drink. Upstairs, a buffet breakfast is set out each morning on a handsome wooden-trestle table. The spacious, immaculate guestrooms are attractively furnished. Our favorite guestroom, 44, has its own secluded, walled terrace complete with wrought-iron furniture and pretty potted plants. *Directions:* Located in the heart of the historic center on Via Speranzella, which is two blocks west of and parallel to Via Toledo a main street in Naples.

HOTEL IL CONVENTO
Manager: Liliana Boccalatte
Via Speranzella, 137
Naples, (NA) 80132, Italy
Tel: (081) 403977 or (333) 4591170
Fax: (081) 400332
6 Rooms, Double: €70–€160
4 Suites: €100–€200
Open: all year, Credit cards: all major
Region: Campania, Michelin Map: 564

In a small pocket of land in the southernmost point of Umbria is the Podere Costa Romana property, immersed in the green hillsides south of ancient Narni. Dynamic hostess Anna Maria left her native Naples for the peace and quiet of the Umbrian hills and meticulously restored the stone 18th-century farmhouse where she now hosts guests within six well-appointed apartments. Rooms have been thoughtfully decorated with antique country furnishings, which harmonize perfectly with the rustic quality of the original farmhouse. Each individual apartment (named for women) can accommodate from two (Giovanna is an adorable love nest) to five guests (Paola has two bedrooms) and is equipped with a kitchenette. Soft-peach and pale-yellow walls highlight exposed stones, beamed ceilings, and brick floors. The large main living room with fireplace and double arches opens out to the surrounding garden and swimming pool overlooking the hills. Travelers can easily reach many lesser-known Umbrian villages as well as the cities and from Orte frequent trains depart for either Rome or Florence. *Directions:* Exit the A1 autostrada at Magliano Sabina and turn right for Otricoli. 8 km after Otricoli turn right at the Narni-Testaccio-Itieli sign and then right again for the Podere Costa Romana.

PODERE COSTA ROMANA
Host: Anna Maria Giordano
S.S. Flaminia
Strada per Itieli, Narni, (TR) 05035, Italy
Tel: (0744) 722495, Fax: (0823) 797118
6 Apartments: €110 daily, €400–€600 weekly
Minimum Stay Required: 2 nights
Open: all year, Credit cards: none
Other Languages: some English
Region: Umbria, Michelin Map: 563

La Magioca is a wonderful discovery in the wine country of Valpolicella, close to Lake Garda and historic Verona. The elegant 17th-century country home of the Merighi family was transformed into a luxurious bed and breakfast under the direction of the family's youngest son, Matteo, who runs the operation with flair and efficiency. No detail has been overlooked in this ivy-covered home where many decorating ideas were inspired by innumerable trips to the French countryside. A golden-yellow hue prevails, giving common areas luminosity and warmth. A large living room with enormous arched windows gives access to the surrounding garden and extended lawns, which lead to a private 13th-century chapel and a hidden hydro-jet pool for six people. Three double bedrooms, and three junior suites, all very individually appointed with fine antiques and each more delightful than the other, are divided among the top floors. Rich fabrics, carpets, and paintings harmonize perfectly with wood-beamed mansard ceilings and parquet floors. Matteo's mother, Signora Marisa, is on hand as well and oversees the buffet breakfast. Romantic and peaceful and a great splurge. *Directions:* From Milan exit the A4 autostrada at Verona and follow signs for the city center (centro) for 3.5 km. After passing under a highway, turn left at the sign for the Valpolicella area and Negrar just after Pedemonte. From Negrar, follow signs for La Magioca just 1 km away.

LA MAGIOCA
Host: Matteo Merighi
Via Moron 3, Negrar, (VR) 37024, Italy
Tel: (045) 6000167, Fax: (045) 6000840
6 Rooms, Double: €220–€290
Open: all year, Credit cards: all major
Other Languages: good English
Region: Veneto, Michelin Map: 562

Situated in the Vendicari Nature Reserve, just 2 km from the sea at the Gulf of Noto, Monteluce makes an ideal base for those who want to explore the tip of Sicily. Imelda, who hails from Milan, offers four suites with kitchen facilities and one large double room for guests. Two suites are found in a nearby farmhouse, while the main house holds Imelda's private quarters, two additional suites, one bedroom (named Pilot after its aviator theme) and the dining room. Breakfast of freshly baked cakes and cappuccino is served here or under the pergola. Imelda's background in design and architecture is reflected in the décor of her home. An attractive contemporary look with modern lighting, top-of-the-line bathrooms, artwork and splashes of color accents harmonize well with the original features of the house. The enchanting surrounding countryside and utter peace and quiet is enhanced by the fact that only cell phone service reaches this area. The low rolling hills are covered with a combination of citrus and olive groves and paint a pretty picture against a clear blue sky. Besides land attractions, ferryboats depart daily to the island of Malta. *Directions:* From Catania and Syracusa, before the city (Noto) boundary, follow signs to Nature Reserve Vendicari/Pachino S.P.19 (county road n.19). Just past km sign 8 turn right on the S.P.11 (direction Codalupo). After 1km turn right at the sign for Vaddeddi and Monteluce. Monteluce is on the left-hand side.

 P ⚊ 👫

MONTELUCE
Host: Imelda Rubian
c.da Vaddeddi, Noto, (SR) 96017, Italy
Tel: (335) 6901871, Cell: (335) 6901871
1 Room, Double: €130–€150
4 Suites: €150–€190
Closed: Feb, Credit cards: all major
Region: Sicily, Michelin Map: 565

The La Federica estate is part of a nature reserve in the flat countryside on the border of Piedmont and Liguria. The Gambarotta family from Genova came back to live on the ancestral farm dating back some 400 years. In this typical quad structure called a cascina you will find the main home, chapel, farmer's quarters, stalls and barns. One upper floor wing, dedicated to guests, has rooms that each access a large terrace. Views are out to the courtyard and to the back cultivated fields of wheat, barley, corn, sunflowers, alfalfa, hay and straw. The family also breeds purebred horses which are a natural part of the scenery. Bedrooms are appropriately appointed with country antiques, wrought-iron beds, floral bedspreads and new bathrooms. A country breakfast is served downstairs in the informal dining room where a collection of horse bits hang over the fireplace, as well as equestrian prints. Gracious hostess Carla is a great resource for the area's attractions, from visits to the Gavi wine region, gastronomic tours, biking, choice of two golf courses, to a stop for shopping at one of the country's largest outlets. At an hour's distance is Genova and the Riviera in one direction and Milan and Turin in the other. *Directions:* At a crossroads of autostradas, coming from Genova, exit from A7 at Serravalle-Scrivia or at Tortona from the north, or at Novi Ligure from A26, and follow for approx. 12 km to Merella, and signs for La Federica.

LA FEDERICA   New
Host: Carla Ghisalberti Gambarotta
Via Villalvernia, 80, Frazione Merella
Novi Ligure, (AL) 15067, Italy
Tel & Fax: (0143) 329533
Cellphone: (388) 8483841
6 Rooms, Double: €90–€100
Open: all year, Credit cards: all major
Other Languages: English, French
Region: Piedmont, Michelin Map: 561

The Casalone farm estate, located between seaside resort Ansedonia and Orbetello Scalo, is a 700-acre property producing olive oil, wines, honey and the typical local breed of Maremman cows. It is in close proximity to the sea with a splendid view of Mount Argentario in the distance. Gracious Signora Marcella and husband, Giuseppe, live in the ivy-covered ancient stone tower and attached villa, while guests reside within seven comfortable self-catering apartments in a converted barn down the road. Spacious apartments have two bedrooms and two bathrooms, living/dining area, and kitchenette. Some apartments have the bedrooms on a second floor, while others have them split between the main floor and an open loft space. They are nicely appointed in a simple, cozy style, with fresh white walls, smart plaid cushions on built-in sofas, framed prints, wicker furniture, and wrought-iron beds. An alternative to sea bathing is a dip in the swimming pool, guarded by olive trees. For nature lovers, the area is full of marvelous expeditions on foot or bike, including the National Park of Uccellina, various forts on Mount Argentario, and the islands of Giglio and Giannutri, not to mention the Saturnia thermal spa. *Directions:* From Rome take the Aurelia Highway 1 and turn right at the sign "Piante-Vivaio" (140.5 km after the turnoff for Ansedonia). From the north you must exit at Ansedonia and return to the highway heading towards Grosseto.

IL CASALONE
Hosts: Marcella & Giuseppe Lignana
S.S. Aurelia sud km 140.5
Orbetello Scalo, (GR) 58016, Italy
Tel: (0564) 862160, Fax: (0564) 866308, Cell: (329) 2167397
7 Apartments: €600–€1390*
*Apartment rental, no breakfast offered
Minimum Stay Required: 2 nights, 7 in Jul & Aug
Open: all year, Credit cards: none
Other Languages: good English, French, Spanish
Region: Tuscany, Michelin Map: 563

The expansive Grazia farm is uniquely located at 3 kilometers from the sea. Gracious and warm hostess Signora Maria Grazia divides her time between Rome and the 300-acre property she inherited from her grandfather. The long cypress-lined driveway takes you away from the busy Aurelia road past grazing horses up to the spacious, rust-hued edifice with its arched loggia. The hosts' home, office, guest apartments, farmhands' quarters, and horse stables are all housed within the complex, which is surrounded by superb country and has peeks of the sea in all directions. From here one can enjoy touring Etruscan territory: Tuscania, Tarquinia, Sovana, Sorano, and the fascinating Roman ruins of Cosa, or stay by the coast on the beaches of Feniglia on the promontory of Argentario. Comfortably modest accommodations, including living area, kitchen, and breakfast basket, pleasantly decorated with homey touches, are offered within five apartments for two to four persons. Maria Grazia can suggest a myriad of local restaurants specializing in seafood or local country fare. Tennis and horseback riding lessons are available. Altogether a delightful combination. *Directions:* Take the coastal Aurelia road from Rome and after the Ansedonia exit turn right into an unmarked driveway immediately after the Pitorsino restaurant.

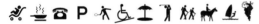

GRAZIA
Host: Maria Grazia Cantore family
Localita: Provincaccia, 110, S.S. Aurelia sud km 140.1
Orbetello Scalo, (GR) 58016, Italy
Tel & Fax: (0564) 881182, Cellphone: (347) 6471779
5 Apartments: €95–€140 daily*
*Apartment rental, no breakfast offered
Minimum Stay Required: 3 nights, weekly in Aug
Open: all year, Credit cards: none
Other Languages: good English, French
Region: Tuscany, Michelin Map: 563

The location of La Chicciola bed and breakfast, minutes from the main tollway from Rome to Florence and on the border of the Lazio and Umbria regions, is ideal. Added bonuses are the warm hospitality, deliciously prepared regional meals (set rate of €30), and lovely country-style bedrooms. Roberto and Maria Cristina from Rome bought the stone farmhouse dating back to 1400 several years ago and began restoration work while living in the newer house next door. The results of their efforts are six perfectly neat and spotless bedrooms and two separate private suites divided between the two houses, and a large stone-walled dining room with outdoor veranda. Obvious care and attention has been put into the decorating of the air-conditioned bedrooms with wrought-iron canopy beds, crisp, white linen curtains, and botanical prints. The scenic 50-acre property with fruit orchards and olive trees is part of the Tiber river valley and woods. A swimming pool and spa facilities are there for guests to enjoy. Innumerable day trips and itineraries of special interest are offered in the area of Umbria and Lazio and it's a 40-minute train ride to Rome. *Directions:* From Rome or Florence on the A1 autostrada, exit at Orte and turn immediately left for Orte, passing under the tollway. Then follow the signs for Penna in Tevenna. La Chicciola is 5 km along this road.

LA CHIOCCIOLA
Hosts: Roberto & Maria Cristina de Fonseca Pimentel
Localita: Seripola, Orte, (VT) 01028, Italy
Tel: (0761) 402734, Fax: (0761) 490254
Cellphone: (348) 5108309
8 Rooms, Double: €120–€160
Open: all year, Credit cards: MC, VS
Other Languages: good English, French
Region: Lazio, Michelin Map: 563

Whether you want to take advantage of some of the best skiing in the country or prefer invigorating hikes up lush green mountain trails in summertime, the Dolomites mountain range will leave you spellbound. Ortisei is one of the main towns in Val Gardena and a busy place, especially during Christmas and August. This is a region with a distinct Tyrolean flavor where more German is spoken than Italian and more wurstel served than pasta. The Stuflesser family, naturals in the hospitality business, have put an impressive addition onto their house near the old barn of the farm as a result of their success as a hotel. In fact, everything about the place is crisp and new, from the white exterior to the pinewood-paneled entrance, bar, and dining room, modeled after the typical stuben style, with a wood-burning ceramic heater where Signora Stuflesser creates traditional meals made with cheeses, yoghurt, marmalades and bread. There is also a large international selection of over 400 wines. Comfortable bedrooms with balconies to the back overlooking green-wooded hills, the town below, and distant mountains are slightly higher in rate. Typical of this area, they have built-in wooden furniture and white down covers on the beds. The Hotel Digon offers all the amenities of a hotel with the warmth of a family home. *Directions:* From Ortisei, take the road towards Castelrotto. The Hotel Digon is on the right-hand side of the road after 2 km.

HOTEL DIGON
Host: Stuflesser family
Via Digon, Ortisei, (BZ) 39046, Italy
Tel: (0471) 797266, Fax: (0471) 798620
Cellphone: (335) 1012052
12 Rooms, Double: €80–€180
2 Suites: €100–€200
Closed: Apr 15 to May 15 & Oct 15 to Dec 1
Credit cards: all major
Other Languages: English, German, French, Spanish
Region: Trentino-Alto Adige, Michelin Map: 562

After following directions up to the village of Bulla where the winding mountain road ends (1,400 meters up), 5 kilometers from Ortisei below, we thought this accommodation was in just a little too remote a location. Our opinion quickly changed, however, when we entered the Uhrerhof, a very special haven indeed. The Zemmer family have done a remarkable job of combining old and new in their recently renovated hotel, which just exudes warmth and welcome. Spacious antique-filled common rooms with fireplaces or stuben burners are strewn about the first floor, many opening out to terraces taking in the glorious mountaintop views. Walter treats guests to one of his divine five-course meals, which include fresh vegetables and salads from the garden and wonderful homemade pasta. The typical stuben dining rooms are thoughtfully divided between families and couples in consideration of noise level. Spacious bedrooms and suites, many with balconies for the uplifting views, are divided between the original house and the new addition and are traditionally appointed in light pinewood with white comforters. A beautiful mosaic-tiled wellness center below includes everything: bio-sauna, whirlpool, Turkish bath, and other special treatments. This place is all about serenity, slowing down, and pampering of the body and soul. *Directions:* From Ortisei, take the road for Castelrotto and after 1 km, turn left up to the road's end at Bulla.

❄ ☕ 🎿 💳 ☎ 🛗 🏋 @ W ⚐ P 🍴 🚭 ❀ 🖼 ♿ 🕴 👫 🏇 🎿

HOTEL UHRERHOF
Host: Walter Zemmer family
Localita: Bulla, Ortisei, (BZ) 39046, Italy
Tel: (0471) 797335, Fax: (0471) 797457
10 Rooms, Double: €166–€220, 3 Suites: €186–€244*
2 Apartments: €250 daily*
Minimum Stay Required: 3 nights
*Includes breakfast & dinner
Closed: Nov, Credit cards: VS
Other Languages: English, German
Region: Trentino-Alto Adige, Michelin Map: 562

The Locanda Palazzone distinguishes itself from the more standard agriturismo or bed and breakfast choices by its contemporary interiors wrapped up in a 14th-century building. Once a cardinal's home and a stopover on a pilgrimage to Rome, the hillside residence takes in wide open views over the valley. The Dubini family, originally from Milan, returned from abroad and settled in on their grandfather's property, surrounded by the vineyards which produce a pleasant Orvieto Superiore wine. The unusual limestone brick structure resembling a church was completely restored to its original dimensions by having a part of the roof raised. Interiors were carefully studied by a group of architects and were given a clean minimalist décor. Guests walk into an enormous open space, cross-sectioned by large arches with a central staircase and glass elevator. Spacious rooms and suites upstairs have designer bathrooms, hardwood floors and some have loft space for beds. The enoteca below is where breakfast is served or wine-tastings are arranged. Hosts Lodovico and Patrizia reside in the adjacent house and are on hand to assist guests. While dining by candlelight on the front terrace, guests delight at the magical view of illuminated Orvieto and its dominating Cathedral. *Directions:* From the A1 Autostrada, exit at Orvieto and follow for Orvieto then Allerona and just after stay left at the gas station. Continue for 2.5 km turning left at the Locanda sign.

LOCANDA PALAZZONE
Hosts: Lodovico & Giovanni Dubini
Rocca Ripesena 67
Orvieto, (TR) 05019, Italy
Tel: (0763) 393614
Fax: (0763) 394833
7 Suites: €173–€290
Open: Mar to Jan, Credit cards: all major
Region: Umbria, Michelin Map: 563

A very high rating goes to the Locanda Rosati on the border of Umbria and Lazio, and just steps away from Tuscany. Giampiero and sister, Alba, with their respective spouses, Luisa and Paolo, sold their cheese production business in Lucca and returned to Orvieto to transform the family farmhouse into a bed and breakfast. The results are splendid and guests, taking priority over the agricultural activity in this instance, are treated with extra-special care. The downstairs common areas include two cozy living rooms with fireplace and a large stone-walled dining room divided by a brick archway leading down to the "tufo" stone cellar. Seven bedrooms upstairs (one with access and bathroom for the handicapped) have been decorated with an animal theme evident in the carvings on bed boards and lamps. Three more bedrooms were added for guests on the top floor with mansard ceilings, leaving the entire home to the bed and breakfast business. Although the house is right on the road, most rooms face the countryside to the back where a large open lawn space leads to the inviting swimming pool. Paolo produces appetizing pastas, soups, and other specialties all written up in a recipe book for guests. *Directions:* Exit from the A1 autostrada at Orvieto and follow signs for Viterbo-Bolsena. Skirt town and continue towards Bolsena for about 8 km on route 71. After a series of sharp curves, the locanda comes up on the right.

LOCANDA ROSATI
Host: Rosati family
Localita: Buonviaggio 22
Orvieto, (TR) 05018, Italy
Tel & Fax: (0763) 217314
Cellphone: (348) 7466451
10 Rooms, Double: €100–€140
Closed: Jan & Feb, Credit cards: MC, VS
Other Languages: good English
Region: Umbria, Michelin Map: 563

In the countryside between the historic towns of Jesi and Osimo, La Commenda is a refined and upscale "Country House," a newly established accommodation category in the Marches and Umbria regions. It is distinguished from the bed and breakfast category by the number of rooms and the fact that proprietors do not necessarily reside on the premises. Signora Ezia, with a background in architecture, has carefully restored the ancient brick 15th-century residence, giving its interiors a contrasting and appealing contemporary style. The good-sized guestrooms, with designer bathrooms, on the upper two floors each have their own décor, clean and uncluttered. Attention has been given to choice of furniture and lighting. Mosaic tiles mix in with hardwood floors, sand-colored brick walls, and beamed mansard ceilings. Top quality crisp linens are provided as well as plasma televisions and Internet connection. Ezia, who lives in the house next door, leaves keys for guests giving them independence. Common areas include a large living area, breakfast room, swimming pool and open pergola with comfortable sofas and lovely valley views. This is a wonderful base from which to visit the many ancient towns of the area and the nearby coastline. *Directions:* Exit the A14 at Ancona Nord and follow to Osimo. After Polverigi follow the road to Casenuove, a group of houses on the main road. Just after this crossroad, turn right on Via Commenda to the first house.

■🍲▦☎@ P ≈ ⚓

LA COMMENDA
Host: Ezia Pugnetti
Via della Commenda
1, Osimo, (AN) 60027, Italy
Tel & Fax: (071) 7103360
Cellphone: (339) 6259866
8 Rooms, Double: €100–€140
Open: all year, Credit cards: all major
Region: Marches, Michelin Map: 563

Owner Claudia Spatola does an admirable job of single-handedly running a bed and breakfast in the complex of stone houses known as Borgo Spante, which dates back to the 15th century and has been in her family since 1752. Consisting of a main villa, connecting farmers' houses, chapel, barns, swimming pool, and garden, it is isolated in 500 acres of woods and hills, the true heart of Umbria, yet is located only 16 kilometers from Orvieto and not far from Assisi, Todi, and Perugia. Guests stay in a combination of rooms or apartments in the former farmers' quarters with their irregular-sized rooms, sloping worn-brick floors, and rustic country furnishings—very charming in its way. Authentic Umbrian meals (half-board required), prepared by local women, are served in the dining room with long wooden tables and fireplace. A larger dining area has been added in the former barn, along with four additional mini-apartments, simply and characteristically decorated. Memorable evenings are spent in the garden or poolside conversing with other guests or listening to an impromptu concert or lecture. *Directions:* From the A1 autostrada exit at Orvieto and follow signs for Arezzo on route 71. After 4 km, turn right at Morrano, Route 101, and proceed for 12 km to the sign for Spante. Turn left and continue for 2 km.

BORGO SPANTE
Host: Claudia Spatola
Loc. Spante, Ospedaletto, (TR) 05010, Italy
Tel: (075) 8709134, Fax: (075) 8709201
Cellphone: (347) 0023581
4 Rooms, Double: €120
5 Apts: €60 per person daily*
Minimum Stay Required: 3 nights
*Includes breakfast & dinner
Open: all year, Credit cards: none
Other Languages: some English, French
Region: Umbria, Michelin Map: 563

The Belfiore farm property certainly stands out among a very bland choice of bed and breakfasts in the area between the well-preserved Renaissance city of Ferrara and Ravenna with its extraordinary mosaics. The flat countryside is characterized by marshland and the National Delta del Po Park, a paradise for birdwatchers and bikers, where many excursions are organized. The Bertelli sisters, Fiorenza and Daniela, from Ferrara, transformed their farm into a country restaurant with 18 bedrooms on the upper two floors. They are identically appointed with rustic wooden beds painted with a floral motif and matching armoires. Guests can feel right at home in the spacious living room with antiques and enormous open fireplace. The restaurant, where locals come for excellent local fare based on organically produced fruits and vegetables, is divided among several beamed dining rooms and guests are invited into the kitchen for a demonstration of making various types of pastas and breads. Italian lessons are also offered free of charge. A neat garden surrounds the simple rectangular-shaped house with burgundy shutters and a swimming pool sits invitingly in one corner. A mini-spa center includes facial and body treatments, sauna, and massage. *Directions:* Exit from the Ferrara-Comacchio highway at Ostellato and pass through the rather nondescript town to the tall bell tower at the corner of Via Pioppa, following signs to Belfiore.

❄ ☕ ✎ ♨ 🆑 ☎ 🍴 @ P ⑪ ❀ ≈ ⛳ ⚕ 🏊 🚣 ⛷ 🏃 👫 🏇 ⛵

VILLA BELFIORE
Host: Tullio Bertelli family
Via Pioppa 27, Ostellato, (FE) 44020, Italy
Tel: (0533) 681164 or (0533) 681172
Fax: (0533) 681172, Cellphone: (335) 275702
18 Rooms, Double: €110–€120
Open: all year, Credit cards: all major
Other Languages: some English, some German
Region: Emilia-Romagna, Michelin Map: 562

The Balestrazzi family left behind a corporate life in order to bring this 72-acre property back to its original state as a self-sufficient farm where they could offer very special hospitality. Numerous articles written about this magical spot and a guest book overflowing with happy travelers' praise testify to the success of their labor of love. Eight lovely bedrooms, a large dining room, living room, game room, library, bird sanctuary, lemon grove, chapel, and agricultural museum are all part of the ancient whitewashed masseria complex. Outside the walls are horse stables, farm animals, fruit orchards, and a vegetable garden, then acres and acres of olive trees divided by rows of low stone walls, so typical of Apulia. No detail has been overlooked in the decor of the bedrooms, which are appointed with selected antiques, wrought-iron beds, fine linens and lace, and paintings. Many have an adjoining room for families and two of them have a kitchen for self catering. Dinner, either out in the candlelit courtyard or by the fire, is a very special time and requires full sensory attention. Course after course of unique culinary combinations are served and explained with anecdotes, poetry, or stories by Armando while Rosalba guides her team of local women in the kitchen. *Directions:* Seven km from the sea and close to Alberobello, Castellana Locorotondo, and Martina Franca. Il Frantoio is well marked at km 874 on S.S.16 between Fasano and Ostuni.

MASSERIA IL FRANTOIO
Host: Balestrazzi family
S.S.16, km 874, Ostuni, (BR) 72017, Italy
Tel & Fax: (0831) 330276
8 Rooms, Double: €184–€224
1 Apartment: €319-€350 daily
Minimum Stay Required: 2 nights
Open: all year, Credit cards: MC, VS
Other Languages: good English, French
Region: Apulia, Michelin Map: 564

For those who wish to become better acquainted with the real Sardinia, head inland where the natives live, the scenery is striking, and the food authentic. Sardinia presents travelers with its own unique scenery, layers of history, artisans' craftwork and folklore, traditional cuisine, and delightfully warm hospitality (not one single place we stopped at neglected to offer us refreshment). The 150-acre property of the Corda Altana family is isolated and completely immersed in the typical Sardinian landscape where huge time-worn granite rocks emerge on the horizon surrounded by cork trees and Mediterranean brush vegetation. Roads are bordered by low stone walls and the base of the family's prim white house was built on the granite foundation. The six bedrooms (two are adjoining for families), all on the first floor and separate from the family's quarters, are new and immaculate like the rest of Maria's house. Breakfast and dinner are served either out on a large granite table or within the spacious dining room, which caters to non-guests as well (Maria is well known for her homemade gnocchetti and soups). Innumerable hiking or horseback-riding excursions are organized from the property. *Directions:* From Olbia head south for San Teodoro and after 10 km turn right for Padru. After Padru drive another 8 km towards Buddusò, turning left for Pedra Bianca-Sas Concas. The house is marked on the right after 3 km.

■✍ P ¶ ⏬ ⋔ 🐎

TONINO CORDA
Host: Maria Sabina Altana family
Localita: Sas Concas-Pedra Bianca
Padru, (SS) 07020, Italy
Tel & Fax: (0789) 49125
6 Rooms, Double: €95–€110*
Minimum Stay Required: 2 nights
*Includes breakfast & dinner
Open: all year, Credit cards: none
Other Languages: none
Region: Sardinia, Michelin Map: 566

45 kilometers south of the Amalfi coast is the archaeological site of Paestum with its three well-preserved Greek temples. The area is surrounded by unattractive commercial strips and much new construction, although farther south are the lovely Cilento National Park and the coast. Here the Seliano farm provides an oasis of peace and tranquility very near the sea. Baroness Cecilia, her two sons, Ettore and Massimino, and manager, Nicola, are wonderful hosts and make the managing of this busy farm, the horseback riding center, restaurant, and bed and breakfast look like a delightful game. The emphasis here is on the preparation of meals using local recipes and their own produce, including fresh mozzarella, most famous in this area. In fact, the Baroness conducts week-long cooking classes including excursions to local cultural and gastronomic highlights. Pleasantly decorated rooms with tiled floors and family antiques are situated in the farmhouse or adjacent yellow house, with two comfortable living rooms for guests. Truly delectable meals are served out on the covered terrace or in the long dining/living room with fireplace and historic paintings. There is an inviting swimming pool for guests. *Directions:* Leave the A3 at Eboli (less traffic than Battipaglia) and head for Paestum. Turn right off the main road (S.S.18) at Paestum and after 1 km turn into the driveway marked Seliano. Pass the main villa (uninhabited) to the main gate.

SELIANO
Host: Baroness Cecilia Bellelli Baratta
Localita: Seliano, Paestum, (SA) 84063, Italy
Tel: (0828) 723634 or (0828) 726544
Fax: (0828) 724544, Cellphone: (335) 6674200
14 Rooms, Double: €75–€125
Closed: Jan & Feb, Credit cards: MC, VS
Other Languages: good English
Region: Campania, Michelin Map: 564

We look all over for bed and breakfasts that radiate a natural charm like that of Fagiolari, just outside Panzano. Cordial hostess Giulietta has seemingly unintentionally created a haven for travelers just by letting her home be a home. The unique stone farmhouse on three levels is brimming with character and has been restored with total respect for its innate simplicity using stone, terracotta brick, and chestnut-wood beams. Entering the front door into the cozy living room with large fireplace, I was impressed by the refreshingly authentic ambiance of this Tuscan home. Two bedrooms are just off this room, the larger having an en suite bathroom of stone and travertine. The main house and former barn, where you find two other good-sized bedrooms, are united by a connecting roof, left open in the middle to allow for an enormous fig tree. Bedrooms hold lovely antiques, book-lined shelves, collections of framed drawings and artwork, embroidered linens, and views of the delightful garden and cypress-lined paths. Overlooking the swimming pool, an adorable one-bedroom house on the property with a bookcase dividing the kitchen and living area is rented out weekly. Giulietta also teaches cooking classes lasting from one to four days. *Directions:* From the piazza in Panzano follow signs to centro and take the left fork for Mercatale. At a half km from the piazza turn left after a pale-green building and follow the gravel road downhill to the end.

FAGIOLARI
Host: Giulietta Giovannoni
Case Sparse 25, Panzano in Chianti, (FI) 50020, Italy
Tel & Fax: (055) 852351
Cellphone: (335) 6124988
5 Rooms, Double: €100–€120
1 Cottage: €120 daily, €840–€910 weekly
Minimum Stay Required: 3 nights in cottage
Open: all year, Credit cards: all major
Other Languages: English
Region: Tuscany, Michelin Map: 563

As you wind your way up a steep road through thick woods, you will no doubt wonder as we did how British patriot Edward ever found the secluded 70-acre property set above the Sieve river valley to the east of Florence. Upon arrival you will be greeted and rewarded with a glass of fresh spring water from the fountain "shower" (la doccia). It is understandable that long ago the farmhouse was originally a farm for the monks of the local abbey—the views are inspirational and the positions of both the house and the swimming pool take full advantage of the expansive panorama encompassing the Rufina wine valley nature reserve. Original features remain intact after a complete restoration of the house that created a variety of high-level accommodation in the form of four bedrooms, three suites with individual kitchenettes, and two independent houses with one bedroom each for weekly stays. The perfectly charming home is filled with lovely antiques (local and imported from England), queen- or king-sized beds, and beautiful linens and tiled bathrooms. Guests can wander about the many common rooms and have a glass of wine in front of a spectacular sunset while Edward works Mediterranean wonders in the kitchen. Prepare to be pampered. *Directions:* 40 minutes from Florence, 5 km from Pelago. Detailed directions are supplied at the time of reservation.

LA DOCCIA
Host: Edward Mayhew
Localita: Paterno, Ristonchi 19/20
Pelago, (FI) 50060, Italy
Tel: (333) 5966426, Cellphone: (9) 2430972
3 Rooms, Double: €75–€125
4 Apartments: €450–€700 weekly
2 Cottages: €130 daily, €800 weekly
Minimum Stay Required: 3 nights
Open: all year, Credit cards: all major
Other Languages: fluent English
Region: Tuscany, Michelin Map: 563

Located in southwest Sicily, 14 km from Marsala, is the historic Baglio farm estate, owned forever by the Montalto Spanò family. The 18th-century, fortified construction with two inner courtyards includes the main house, farmer's quarters, wine cellars, and barns and stalls; all in the center of over a thousand acres of vineyards where the famous Marsala wines derive. A long, dirt road through the vineyards and citrus groves leads to the front gate through the seemingly abandoned work area to the second courtyard, where the restored home is situated. On the ground floor of the owner's villa is a rustic dining room, where guests can enjoy a typical home-cooked, Sicilian country meal. A rooftop terrace offers views to the not so distant sea. Five guestrooms on two floors are each individually decorated with original, patterned-tile floors and family heirlooms, giving turn-of-the-last-century ambience. New bathrooms have been added to each bedroom. There are the Mozia salt and wine islands, the seaside archaeological site of Selinunte with temples still-standing and vast areas of fallen columns (best seen at sunset), and many wineries to visit in the area. *Directions:* Take the A29 past Mazara del Vallo onto the state road for 10 km. Pass Caffè Movida (on right) and after 300 meters turn left signed Baglio Spano. Go 4.5 km, of which 1.5 km are dirt surfaced.

BAGLIO SPANO
Host: Federico Montalto
Contrada Triglia Scaletta
Petrosino, (TP) 91020, Italy
Tel: (348) 8822095, Fax: (0923) 989840
Cellphone: (329) 4358442
5 Rooms, Double: €75–€130
Open: all year, Credit cards: none
Other Languages: good English
Region: Sicily, Michelin Map: 565

The coastal stretch from Messina to Cefalu has special appeal to the off-the-beaten-track traveler who will find the perfect place to stay at Casa Migliaca, a 200-year-old farmhouse nestling in the wooded hills 7 kilometers off the main road. This stone house just outside town, owned by Maria Teresa and Sebastiano, who left the city several years ago in favor of a rural lifestyle, offers a lovely sweeping view over olive and citrus groves down to the sea. The very congenial hosts love to converse with guests around the kitchen table or down in the cool dining room (originally the oil-press room) around the press wheel. A special effort was made to keep everything possible intact, giving the house its own very distinct character, maintaining all original floors, ceilings, beams, kitchen tiles, and furniture, although new bathrooms have been incorporated in most of the rooms. There are even extra showers out in the lovely informal garden! Guests are offered a choice of three double bedrooms upstairs or five downstairs appointed with family antiques. For those who desire direct contact with Sicilian culture, Casa Migliaca is a truly memorable experience. *Directions:* From coastal route 113, just 25 km after Cefalu, turn right at the sign for Pettineo and follow it right past town. Just after a gas station, on the right you will find a gate about 300 meters from Pettineo. Please ring the bell.

CASA MIGLIACA
Host: Maria Teresa Allegra
Contrada Migliaca
Pettineo, Sicily, (ME) 98070, Italy
Tel: (0921) 336722, Fax: (0921) 391107
Cellphone: (335) 8430645
8 Rooms, Double: €150*
*Includes breakfast & dinner
Open: all year, Credit cards: all major
Other Languages: good English
Region: Sicily, Michelin Map: 565

The southernmost, "heel-side" of Italy's boot-shaped peninsula, known as Puglia, presents another facet of the country's many-sided culture. It is a land with spectacular coastlines, villages with distinct Greek and Turkish influence, endless lines of olive groves, fields of wildflowers, and a rich history of art including baroque (Bari's Santa Nicola church is exquisite). All of this plus delectable cuisine and a warm and open people await in Puglia (Apulia), as does the Masseria Salamina, a 16th-century fortified farmhouse between Bari and Brindisi covering 100 acres of land and producing primarily olive oil. The long driveway leads to the sand-colored castle with turreted tower with expansive vistas over olive groves to the sea. The seven rooms, each with a separate courtyard entrance, are decorated with basic reproductions and wicker furniture, and are a notch up in level but not as luminous as the upstairs apartments. These eight one-bedroom apartments are available for longer stays, with simple and practical furnishings. Host Gianvincenzo and family live in the main wing and run their masseria like a small hotel. A lofty, vaulted restaurant with terracotta floors provides all meals for guests. In the low season a week-long stay including Mediterranean cooking lessons and local excursions for small groups is arranged. *Directions:* From the S.S.16 exit at Pezze di Greco. Just before town take the first right for 1 km to the masseria.

MASSERIA SALAMINA
Host: Gianvincenzo de Miccolis Angelini
Pezze di Greco, (BR) 72010, Italy
Tel: (080) 4897307, Fax: (080) 4898582
15 Rooms, Double: €115–€155
5 Suites: €205–€305
Minimum Stay Required: 3 nights, 7 in Jul & Aug
Open: all year, Credit cards: all major
Other Languages: some English
Region: Apulia, Michelin Map: 564

Originally a 12th-century monastery, and after 200 years in the possession of the aristocratic Bonnano family, the Gigliotto estate was purchased by the current owners, the Savoca family. They took on the challenge of transforming the 1,000-acre farm property into a tourism center for travelers. The impressive stone baglio formation with courtyard holds an elongated rustic restaurant to one side, the main house in the center and guestrooms on the other. From any angle or window of the large complex, and as far as the eye can see, are glorious sweeping views of the rolling hills, and vineyards from which originate their organic wines. In fact practically everything served in the restaurant is from the organic farm, including the wine, olive oil, honey, home-made liqueurs, patés, fresh and dried fruits, local cheeses, salami, game and meats. Meals here are an authentic Sicilian experience. New bedrooms have wrought -iron beds, tiled floors, wood furnishings and immaculate bathrooms. A large swimming pool offers respite on lazier days. The Gigliotto is a busy place, appropriate for families, offering a central base from which to explore a wide range of attractions. The mosaics of Piazza Armenina are very close, and within a circumference Agrigento, Ragusa, Modica, Siracusa and Taormina. *Directions:* Go beyond the city of Piazza Armerina following signs for Gela on the SS117bis. After10 km. at 60 km. marker, turn right at the gate of Agriturismo Gigliotto.

GIGLIOTTO   ***New***
Hosts: Elio & Laura Savoca family
SS 117bis, Km 60
Piazza Armerina, (EN) 94015, Italy
Tel: (0933) 970898, Fax: (0933) 979234
Cellphone: (335) 8380324
26 Rooms, Double: €80–€100
Open: all year, Credit cards: all major
Other Languages: English, French, German
Region: Sicily, Michelin Map: 565

The most striking images of southern Tuscany are in the Orcia Valley—enchanting landscapes with soft, rolling hills topped with rows of cypress trees silhouetted against the sky. This alternating with the area called Le Crete Senesi—barren hills made of clay and resembling moon craters—makes for fascinating scenery. Le Traverse, at 3 kilometers from Pienza, is submersed in this peaceful countryside to which your gracious hosts, Pinuccia and Enrico, retired from Milan. Their charming home has been very tastefully restored and all the right touches (such as terry bathrobes and the finest-quality bed linens) added to make guests feel right at home. The stone farmhouse with front courtyard is divided between the couple's own quarters, rooms for their visiting children, and two apartments for guests with independent entrance. The other two bedrooms are situated in the one-level converted barn nearby and are enhanced with the family's country antiques and prints. Huge terracotta vases overflowing with geraniums, trailing roses, and azalea plants dot the 50-acre property, which includes a swimming pool. Olive oil is produced as well as jams using homegrown fruit. The intimacy of the place with its four rooms makes you feel like a true house guest and the area is full of delightful day trips. *Directions:* Follow signs for Monticchiello from Pienza (circular piazza). After 3 km turn left on an unpaved road up to a group of cypress trees and the house.

LE TRAVERSE
Host: Pinuccia Barbier Meroni
Localita: Le Traverse, Pienza, (SI) 53026, Italy
Tel: (0578) 748198, Fax: (0578) 748949
Cellphone: (333) 4708789
4 Rooms, Double: €170–€210
Minimum Stay Required: 2 nights
Closed: Jan 22 to 30, Credit cards: all major
Other Languages: good English, French
Region: Tuscany, Michelin Map: 563

It has not been easy to find a charming, true bed and breakfasts in Pisa, a city famous for its leaning tower and basilica, and its quaint city center and excellent restaurants. Thankfully, the Relais dell'Orologio has opened a smaller accommodation down the street. The Relais dei Fiori, a 19th-century palazzo on the main pedestrian-only street has an attractive sidewalk café lining its front with gazebo, plants and bamboo tables and chairs. Breakfast is served here or in the small bar area in front, as well as other meals throughout the day. A small reception area to the side leads up to the bedrooms by stairs or elevator on the next two floors. Twelve rooms, four to a floor, have a white base between walls and armoires, and are given each a different color theme with bedspreads and carried through in the floral-painted motifs along ceiling borders. Four different size categories have been designated doubles, with the smallest being quite tight. Hallways display collections of French porcelain and lace items. Plenty of amenities and services are arranged by the helpful staff. Pisa is strategically based near the coastline and a lesser known side of Tuscany. An international airport makes it easy coming in or leaving the country. *Directions:* Via Carducci is the main street in town, hotel is well marked in city center.

RELAIS DEI FIORI   **New**
Host: Maria Luisa Bignardi
Via Carducci, 35/37
Pisa, (PI) 56127, Italy
Tel: 050 556054, Fax: 050 8311733
12 Rooms, Double: €220–€340
Open: all year, Credit cards: all major
Other Languages: English, French, German
Region: Tuscany, Michelin Map: 563

The San Teodoro Nuovo property offers the "way-off-the-beaten-track" traveler a delightful base for exploring the southernmost reaches of Italy. In the Basilicata region, just 5 kilometers from the beaches of the Gulf of Taranto, this 400-acre farm specializing in citrus fruits and olive oil has been in the noble Xenia Doria family for generations and the family resides here all year, offering guest accommodation in a variety of renovated buildings. Two apartments appointed with the house's original furniture are found in a wing of the large main brick villa covered with bougainvillea vines, while another five, simpler in decor, are just below on the ground floor facing out to the back orchards. These can accommodate from two to four persons and have a kitchen. The remaining four very pleasant apartments, for two to four people, are in the same building as the restaurant on the property and are appointed with the family's own furniture, with accents of color from the fresh country fabrics used. Meals at the restaurant are based on local traditional recipes and the farm's own products. In the vicinity are the highlights of Apulia and many Greek archaeological ruins, as well as two 18-hole golf courses and horse riding. *Directions:* From Taranto take the S.S.106 coastal highway and pass the S.S.407 for Potenza. Turn right at the sign for San Teodoro Nuovo at the km 442 sign of the S.S. 106.

SAN TEODORO NUOVO
Host: Maria Xenia Doria family
Localita: Marconia, Pisticci, (MT) 75020, Italy
Tel & Fax: (0835) 470042
Cellphone: (338) 5698116
11 Rooms, Double: €130–€150
11 Apartments: €80–€160 daily
Minimum Stay Required: 2 nights
Open: all year, Credit cards: all major
Other Languages: good English, French, German
Region: Basilicata, Michelin Map: 564

Castello di Vicarello, an historic country residence whose origins date to the 1100's, is an enchanting resort, a peaceful spot renowned for its quality wine & oil production. After traveling and living all over the globe the Baccheschi Berti family decided to restore this lovely old home and offer top of the line guest accommodation. The castle features three suites and two adjacent stunning stone guesthouses. The smaller guesthouse, I Sassi, has one bedroom, a large bathroom, a kitchenette and a glassed-in living room taking in the sumptuous view. The other guesthouse, La Chiesina, has two spacious bedrooms, two bathrooms, a kitchen and a living room with intarsia parquet. They are sophisticatedly appointed with family antiques and colonial pieces bought around the world, as are the luxurious suites, each with bedroom, bathroom, kitchenette and large living room. The property features two swimming pools; a travertine infinity pool which hangs on the edge of the manicured garden, and a pool secluded among the olive groves. Your gracious hosts serve lunch and dinner based on organic local products and are even willing to reveal traditional family recipes and organize cookery classes for curious gourmets. *Directions:* From the Grosseto-Siena highway 223, exit at Paganico. After 3 km turn right for Sasso d'Ombrone, and right for Poggi del Sasso. In town watch for Via di Vicarello on the right and follow the road, keeping left at the fork, for 3.5 km.

CASTELLO DI VICARELLO
Hosts: Aurora & Carlo Baccheschi Berti
Via di Vicarello 1, Poggi del Sasso, (GR) 58043, Italy
Tel & Fax: (0564) 990718, Cellphone: (339) 2546646
2 Rooms, Double: €400–€450
5 Suites: €580–€1100
2 Houses: €780–€1400 daily
Minimum Stay Required: 2 nights
Open: all year, Credit cards: all major
Abitare La Storia, History Traveller
Region: Tuscany, Michelin Map: 563

The picturesque countryside dotted with medieval hilltowns north of Rome called Sabina is finally getting some recognition after centuries of being just a sleepy rural area. Bed and breakfasts are springing up right and left and at long last the tourist, inexplicably foreign to this lovely area so close to the capital city, has the opportunity to explore this virgin territory with its ancient traditions still in practice. Maria Vittoria, the warm and enthusiastic hostess of Wonderland, as her bed and breakfast translates, is another newcomer to Sabina. She offers a very comfortable level of accommodation in her own home set down below the main road outside of town and facing out to an impressive panorama of hills covered with olive groves and distant mountains. Four bedrooms are found in the main house, elegantly appointed with precious antiques, paintings, and various collections from Maria's travels. Some have terraces from which you can watch sunsets over the magnificent valley. Two suites have been built into the hillside in front of the home. One has a loft bedroom with sitting area and kitchenette below. There's a swimming pool for guests to enjoy. A homemade breakfast is served on the front patio. *Directions:* From the Rome-Rieti Via Salaria (route S.S.4), turn right and left at km 52. Two hundred meters later turn left on the road called SP42 and continue for 5 km and you see the Paese delle Meraviglie sign and an iron gate on the right.

PAESE DELLE MERAVIGLIE
Host: Maria Vittoria Toniolo
Via Mirtense km 5, Poggio Nativo, (RI) 02030, Italy
Tel & Fax: (0765) 872599
Cellphone: (328) 6642954
4 Rooms, Double: €78–€90
1 Apartment: €400–€500 weekly
Minimum Stay Required: 2 nights
Open: all year, Credit cards: none
Other Languages: good English, French
Region: Lazio, Michelin Map: 563

Thirty-five kilometers northeast of Florence, in a beautiful, hilly area of Tuscany, lies the Rufina Valley, famous for its robust red wine. Crowning a wooded slope is one of the many residences of the noble Galeotti-Ottieri family. The interior of the 15th-century main villa reveals spacious high-ceilinged halls with frescoes depicting family history. The family has also restored several stone farmhouses on the vast property, one of which is the Locanda Praticino whose upper floor contains lovely, simple double rooms with countryside views down one long hall, each named after its color scheme. Downstairs is a large rustic dining and living room with vaulted ceiling, enormous stone fireplace, worn brick floors, and casual country furniture. Full country-fresh Tuscan meals are only €18. A swimming pool and tennis courts, plus the enchanting landscape, make it difficult to tear oneself away for touring. In order to retain the characteristic flavor of farmers' quarters, the properties have an intentionally unrestored, natural air to them. Available for longer stays are three very tastefully decorated apartments. The Petrognano is a tranquil spot where guests may enjoy the gracious hospitality of this historically important Florentine family. *Directions:* From Florence head toward Pontassieve. Pass the town of Rufina and after 1.5 km turn right for Pomino. Continue for 5km on this winding road and the Locanda is signpost on the right hand side.

FATTORIA DI PETROGNANO
Host: Cecilia Galeotti-Ottieri family
Localita: Pomino, Pomino, Rufina, (FI) 50060, Italy
Tel: (055) 8318867, Fax: (055) 8318812
8 Rooms, Double: €80–€90
3 Apartments: €400–€1000 weekly
Minimum Stay Required: 2 nights
Open: Apr to Oct, Credit cards: all major
Other Languages: good English, French
Region: Tuscany, Michelin Map: 563

In the undiscovered valley of Champorcher, Mauro and his wife Piera took over the ancient town grain mill and have reopened its doors as a bed and breakfast. The plain exterior on the road gives no clue to the fascinating interior where enormous dining-room windows look right out over the rushing torrents of Ayasse, which cut directly through this lush valley. In the middle of this spacious room is an antique carpenter's sawing machine, once part of the mill. Restoration work on the stone mill, just off the dining room, is being completed with the hopes of continuing the grain production activity using original methods. A loft living room with fireplace and burgundy sofas looks over the main room. Piera prepares the nightly meal for guests using traditional recipes from this mountain area. The Gontiers' agriculture activity produces various vegetables, berries, and chestnuts. The four sweetly decorated new bedrooms are located on the same floor and all have water views (and sounds!), brand-new bathrooms, lace curtains, and carved pinewood beds. Hiking trails in the valley take you up to the many waterfalls. There is complimentary rock climbing. This is a perfect spot for nature lovers wanting to explore. *Directions:* Exit at Verres from the A5 from the north, heading for Verres, then Bard. At Bard turn right for Hone, Champorcher. After 7 km, just after Pontboset, Le Moulin is located just before the stone bridge on the left-hand side of the road.

LE MOULIN DES ARAVIS
Hosts: Mauro Gontier & Piera Chanoux
Fraz. Savin 55, Pontboset, (AO) 11020, Italy
Tel: (0125) 809831 or (329) 8013184
4 Rooms, Double: €70–€80
Open: all year, Credit cards: none
Other Languages: very little English, French
Region: Aosta Valley, Michelin Map: 561

Leave the car and any desires of grandeur on the mainland, and take the ferry or hydro-jet to the pure beauty and simplicity of Ponza island. To really get a sense of this special place you need that most precious of commodities: time. And if you have at least three days to spare, head for Casa Giulia at the opposite bay overlooking the port. Manager Carlo will meet your ship with his typical wooden gozzo boat and take you across the bay in 10 minutes time. After a slight walk up a combination of stairs and soft inclines, you reach the white-washed house with 10 simply appointed bedrooms, tiled with colorful ceramic. No frills or special amenities except for a no-nonsense continental breakfast, swimming pool alternative to the beach below, and shuttle service at established times to and from town. The natural amenities should suffice for those seeking a peaceful retreat, breathtaking views, and a feeling of truly being far from it all. Carlo is omnipresent to suggest hiking itineraries right from the house, scuba diving excursions, reserve a table at one of the local seafood restaurants (don't miss an al fresco lunch under the bamboo shading at Gerardo's), or rent a boat or scooter to explore the secret bays and the rest of the rugged coastlines. It's a totally authentic experience. *Directions:* Take the ferry or hydro-jet from Anzio or Formia ports.

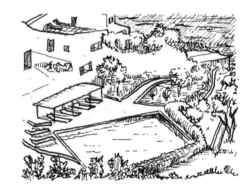

CASA GIULIA PONZA   ***New***
Manager: Carlo D'Ambrosio
Località: Frontone, Ponza, (LT) 04027, Italy
Tel: (0771) 80407, Fax: (0771) 80776
10 Rooms, Double: €120–€220
Open: May 1 to Sep 30, Credit cards: MC, VS
Other Languages: some English
Region: Lazio, Michelin Map: 563

As you approach the volcanic rock mountain emerging from the crystal waters, you begin to make out the amphitheater-shaped harbor and cluster of colorful box-shaped houses clinging to the hillside. Ponza, the largest of the four Pontine islands, is a favorite getaway because of its stunning marine landscapes. The charm of the island is immediate as you descend and mix among fishermen, locals and vacationing modern Romans. It is also the preferred retreat of the Fendi family who have opened up a delightful bed and breakfast just up the hill from the main port. The historic building dates to the Barbonic period and is squeezed among other residences in a maze of footpaths and narrow streets. Six small bedrooms each have a definite personality and the name of a particular spice, with an eclectic mélange of original pieces, and views out toward the sea. On the ground floor, carved out of the stone foundation, is an amazing kitchen and living room covered with antique tiles in earth tones, recalling the Arabian influences of the island's past. Breakfast is served in the shaded garden with an ancient stone wheel. Ponza is for those with strong legs, a love of sea life, and a sense of adventure. Explore the wild side of the island by scooter, or do as the Romans do, rent a gozzo boat and head for the nearest secluded bay. And don't miss a day trip to neighboring Ventotene island. *Directions:* Take the ferry or hydro-jet from Anzio or Formia ports; arrange to be picked up upon arrival.

VILLA LAETITIA   **New**
Host: Anna Fendi Venturini Family
Salita Scotti, Ponza, (LT) 04027, Italy
Tel: (06) 3226776
6 Rooms, Double: €150–€230
Open: all year, Credit cards: MC, VS
Other Languages: English
Region: Lazio, Michelin Map: 563

The Vecchio Convento is a real gem, offering quality accommodation for a moderate price. Its several dining rooms are brimming with rustic country charm and serve delicious meals prepared from local produce. There are 15 guestrooms tastefully decorated with antiques. The town of Portico di Romagna is like the inn, inviting yet unpretentious—an old village surrounded by wooded hills and clear mountain streams. A stroll through medieval pathways, which twist down between the weathered stone houses, leads you to an ancient stone bridge gracefully arching over a rushing stream. The inn, too, is old, but was not (as you might expect from its name) originally a convent. According to its gracious owner, Marisa Raggi, it was named for a restaurant located in a convent that she and her husband Giovanni (the chef) used to operate—when they moved here they kept the original name. The restaurant is still their primary focus, as its fine, fresh cuisine reflects. Italian lessons are also organized. *Directions:* Because of the winding, two-lane mountain highway that leads to the village, it takes about two hours to drive the 75 km from Florence. The inn is located 34 km southwest of the town of Forli.

ALBERGO AL VECCHIO CONVENTO
Hosts: Marisa Raggi & Giovanni Cameli
Via Roma, 7, Portico di Romagna, (FC) 47010, Italy
Tel: (0543) 967053, Fax: (0543) 967157
Cellphone: (347) 3719260
12 Rooms, Double: €100
1 Apartment: €300 weekly
Closed: Jan 12 to Feb 12, Credit cards: all major
Other Languages: some English
Region: Emilia-Romagna, Michelin Map: 562

On the outskirts of historical Mantova sits the Villa Schiarino Lena, one of the magnificent estates formerly belonging to the Gonzaga family, once among the most powerful nobility in Lombardy. The very cordial Lena Eliseo family, the present owners, have taken on the enormous task of restoring the 15th-century palace room by room. With high vaulted ceilings, completely frescoed rooms, wrought-iron chandeliers, and original terracotta floors, the seemingly endless parade of rooms reveals one delight after another. Besides being a museum, the villa is used for large parties, weddings, and business meetings, and guestrooms are also available. Surrounding the villa are small houses, once inhabited by farmhands, which are now offered to travelers on a daily or weekly basis. The three modest but spacious and comfortable apartments are appointed with a mixture of antique and contemporary furniture and can accommodate up to four persons. Each apartment has its own living area and one includes a kitchenette. A golf practice range is available on the property. This location is the ideal spot to base yourself while exploring less-touristy Ferrara, Cremona, Verona, and Mantua, which are filled with medieval and Renaissance buildings (Palazzo del Te and Palazzo Ducale are "must sees"). *Directions:* From Mantova take route N62 north past the church and turn left on Via Gramsci. Follow it for 1 km to the villa.

VILLA SCHIARINO LENA
Host: Giuseppe Lena Eliseo family
Via Santa Maddalena 7, Porto Mantovano, (MN) 46047, Italy
Tel: (0376) 398238, Fax: (0376) 393238
Cellphone: (347) 6097784
2 Rooms, Double: €150*
3 Apartments: €80 daily, €500 weekly*
*Breakfast not included: €5
Open: all year, Credit cards: MC, VS
Other Languages: good English
Region: Lombardy, Michelin Map: 561

All types of accommodation are available in Positano: from five-star luxury to simple bed and breakfasts like Casa Cosenza, with its sunny yellow facade. Sitting snug against the cliff side, halfway down to the beach, it is reached by descending one of the variety of stairways found in this unique seaside town. The front arched entranceway leads to an enormous tiled terrace overlooking the pastel-color houses of Positano and the dramatic coastline. Seven guestrooms on the second floor, each with a balcony and air conditioning, enjoy the same breathtaking panorama. The residence dates back 200 years, as evidenced by the typical cupola ceilings, originally designed to keep rooms cool and airy. Guestrooms have bright, tiled floors and are simply and sweetly decorated with old-fashioned armoires, desks, and beds. Room 7 (at a slightly higher rate), although smaller and with an older bathroom, has a lovely large terrace, as do two suites behind the main house that can accommodate three to four persons. Two apartments located in the back and above the B&B also have lovely views. A continental breakfast is served on the terrace. The Cosenza family is happy to arrange tours of the Amalfi coast, to Pompei and Naples and to arrange transfers to and from Rome. *Directions:* Park your car in Fratelli Milano parking garage in center of Positano and ask for directions to Cafe Positano, which is next to the stairway that takes you to Casa Cosenza. Pack light!

CASA COSENZA
Host: Salvatore Cosenza family
Via Trara Genoino 18, Positano, (SA) 84017, Italy
Tel & Fax: (089) 875063
6 Rooms, Double: €130–€150, 3 Suites: €150–€180*
2 Apartments: €320 daily, €2300 weekly*
*Breakfast not included: €10
Minimum Stay Required: 3 nights in high season
Open: all year, Credit cards: all major
Other Languages: some English
Region: Campania, Michelin Map: 564

The spectacular Amalfi coast offers a wide variety of accommodation, yet few as special as La Fenice—as fantastic as the mythological bird for which it is named. Guests leave their cars on the main road and climb the arbored steps to discover the white villa hidden amid lush Mediterranean vegetation. Costantino and Angela heartily welcome new arrivals on the shady front terrace, where a basic continental breakfast is served each clement morning. Seven luminous bedrooms, three with terrace and marvelous sea views, the others with lateral sea or no sea view, are simply and sparsely furnished with an occasional antique armoire or bureau in a wing off the family's home. Eight more rooms of varying dimensions, most with terraces, reached by many steps down from the road, are built separately into the side of the cliff and have colorful, tiled floors and similar furnishings. Descending yet more steps, you'll come to the curved seawater pool and Jacuzzi carved against the rock (open June to October), where an occasional salad or sandwich is served during summer months (at an extra cost). A coastal boat tour (pick-up at La Fenice's beach) including a stop for lunch can be arranged. This property has few or no amenities in the rooms, but is a natural wonder, cascading down to the sea and a small private beach. *Directions:* Located on the coastal highway south of Positano towards Amalfi. Two curves after town, watch for gates on both sides of the road.

LA FENICE
Hosts: Angela & Costantino Mandara
Via Marconi 4, Positano, (SA) 84017, Italy
Tel: (089) 875513, Fax: (089) 811309
15 Rooms, Double: €140
Open: all year, Credit cards: none
Other Languages: some English
Region: Campania, Michelin Map: 564

The Villa La Tartana, owned by the same delightful owners of the Villa Rosa, deserves more than a full page write-up. Very different than the Villa Rosa, which is located high above on the hillside above the main road of town, the Tartana is down at the seaside where one has easier access to restaurants, ferries to Capri, stores, and lounging on the popular beach. A three-story white house snuggled in between others, the bed & breakfast offers comfortable rooms each with its own terrace, many amenities, and the warm hospitality of the Caldiero family. In keeping with the seaside ambiance, local hand-painted tiles from Vietri are used in cool blue tones throughout. A main living room with bright, yellow sofas and colorful paintings of nautical themes is where guests are greeted and daily itineraries are arranged to Amalfi, Sorrento, or Ravello. The best way to get a real taste of Positano is to rent a gozzo boat (with or without a skipper) and view the dramatic coastline from the sea, stopping to swim at various beaches and coves or lunching at one of the delectable, waterside trattorias serving pasta with seafood and other local specialties. *Directions:* Arriving in Positano, take the main road down into town and continue until you reach a small fork. You can park the car here in the garage and call the hotel for assistance with baggage. The hotel is down at the beach reached by a pedestrian path.

VILLA LA TARTANA
Hosts: Franco & Virginia Caldiero family
Via Vicolo Vito Savino, 6/8, Positano, (SA) 84017, Italy
Tel: (089) 812193, Fax: (089) 8122012
12 Rooms, Double: €160–€200
Minimum Stay Required: 3 nights
Open: Apr to Oct, Credit cards: all major
Other Languages: some English
Region: Campania, Michelin Map: 564

Villa Rosa opened its doors six years ago after restoration work by local couple, Virginia and Franco, who own a clothing store, ceramic store and Cafe Positano which has a breathtaking view of Positano. The 150-year-old villa, built into the cliffside and hidden behind bougainvillea vines high above the road right in town, is on three levels. Taking the stairs up to the first level, you find the reception area where guests are greeted. The twelve bedrooms vary in size from small to a spacious king-bedded room with a terrace and a suite with a separate living room. All the rooms have access to the large front terraces which are divided by plants and grapevine-covered pergolas for privacy. Picturesque views of Positano's colorful houses and the spectacular coastline are enjoyed from any point. Breakfast is served either in rooms or out on individual terraces adorned with large terracotta vases laden with cascading pink and red geraniums, in sharp contrast to pure white walls. Bedrooms maintain original tiles and vaulted ceilings and are furnished with simple antiques, while bathrooms display typical yellow and blue hand-painted tiles from Vietri. Air conditioning is available. Easy day trips include Amalfi, Ravello, and the ruins of Pompeii, Paestum, or Herculum. *Directions:* Following the main road through town, you find Villa Rosa almost at the end just before the famous Sirenuse Hotel. Parking is possible only in a nearby public garage.

❄ 🍵 ⚙ 💳 ☎ 🍷 🖼 ⊥ 🚶 🏄

VILLA ROSA
Hosts: Virginia & Franco Caldiero
Via C. Colombo 127, Positano, (SA) 84017, Italy
Tel: (089) 811955, Fax: (089) 8122761
12 Rooms, Double: €165–€175
1 Suite: €290–€300
2 Apartments: €280–€290 daily
Minimum Stay Required: 3 nights
Open: Mar to Oct, Credit cards: all major
Other Languages: some English
Region: Campania, Michelin Map: 564

West of Naples from Pozzuoli to the tip of the gulf, where ferryboats depart for the islands of Ischia and Procida, is an area full of archaeological sites with noteworthy Roman and Greek ruins. After spending 30 some years living in London Signora Giulia returned to her birthplace with the desire to live in the country near the city. She bought and skillfully renovated an ancient farmhouse creating an oasis of gardens, orchards and vineyards in the midst of a maze of rather unsightly new construction. Do not let the approach deter you. The bedrooms are divided among five apartments each with its own living room and either kitchenette or full kitchen facilities (divine antique hand-painted tiles). Italian and British influences harmonize perfectly in rooms appointed with a variety of antiques, lovely linens, white sofas and crisp fabrics. Each refined apartment has a garden or patio space. Breakfast and an occasional dinner upon request is served out near the barbecue and wood-burning oven, cooking classes can be arranged. Guests enjoy lounging around the poolside. Just 5 km away is Pozzuoli where ferries depart for Capri, Ischia, Procida, Ponza, Ventotene Islands and Sardinia. *Directions:* From Naples take the "tangenziale" highway towards Pozzuolo and exit at Cuma. Pass Lake Averno and turn left then right at next crossing. Pass under the Roman arch and at the end turn right on Via Cuma Licola. Take the second dirt road after the supermarket MGM.

VILLA GIULIA
Host: Giulia Carunchio
Via Cuma Licola 178, Pozzuoli, (NA) , Italy
Tel: (081) 8540163, Fax: (081) 8044356
Cellphone: (335) 6759429
5 Rooms, Double: €90–€130
5 Apartments: €90–€130 daily
Open: all year, Credit cards: none
Other Languages: English spoken well
Region: Campania, Michelin Map: 564

From the moment you enter the grand foyer looking out over the classical Italian garden of this 16th-century country villa, all sense of time and place is lost. The Rucellai-Piqués' devotion to their estate (in the family since 1759) is apparent, as is their warm hospitality. Guests are given the run of the rambling old home, from the cozy bedrooms, varying in size and decor; antique-filled library; and spacious living room with fireplace, old comfortable sofas, and family portraits to a gracious buffet breakfast room where guests are seated at long tables. At the entrance is a duck pond, a large shady area with tables and a 15th-century swimming pool. Villa Rucellai serves as an excellent base for visiting Florence, Siena, Lucca, and Pisa. The nearby town with its many restaurant choices is conveniently just a 15–20 minute walk away. *Directions:* From Exit the A11 autostrada at Prato Est. Follow signs for centro and the railway station. Turn right at the first roundabout onto Viale della Republica. Go straight for 2km towards the hills. After crossing the river and railway circle left onto Viale Borgo Valsugana and go 2 km keeping the river on your left. After the road bends to the right, turn right at the small roundabout (do not cross the river). After 150 meters turn left at a small piazza onto Via del Palco. Follow signs for Villa Rucellai Loc. Canneto or Trattoria La Fontana. Continue for 1.5 km after Trattoria La Fontanta on the very narrow Via di Canneto to the entry gate.

@ W P

VILLA RUCELLAI DI CANNETO ***Cover painting***
Host: Rucellai Piqué family
Via di Canneto 16, Prato, (PO) 59100, Italy
Tel: (0574) 460392, Fax: (0574) 467748
Cellphone: (347) 9073826
8 Rooms, Double: €100
Open: all year, Credit cards: MC, VS
Other Languages: fluent English
Region: Tuscany, Michelin Map: 563

The fascinating Castello di Proceno is in the Lazio region bordering Tuscany and Umbria. This unique accommodation combines historical context, authentic ambiance, unspoiled landscapes, regional foods and wines, and congenial hosts. The Cecchini Bisoni family, owners of this 12th-century hilltop fortress for many generations, have done an outstanding job of restoring some of the farmers' quarters that make up part of the village grouped around the tower. They modernized plumbing, electricity, and heating systems without disturbing the innate quaintness of these stone dwellings. In addition, Signora Cecilia is a passionate decorator and has artistically displayed the family's antique collections and restored furniture. The restaurant, complete with cantina and fireplace, leads to a labyrinth of tunnels and stairways connecting to four of the apartments, while the remaining four are located in the fortress attached to the ancient pentagonal walls of the tower and castle, in a wooded area leading down to the pool. All apartments have one or two bedrooms and a kitchenette and all feature both a fireplace and garden area or terrace. For shorter stays, the bed and breakfast formula is available within a choice of four suites. Summer concerts accompanied by a buffet dinner in the castle's park are a highlight. *Directions:* The castello is in Proceno, 16 km north of Lake Bolsena. Follow S.S.2 from the lake to Acquapendente; after 3 km turn left for Proceno.

CASTELLO DI PROCENO
Host: Cecilia Cecchini Bisoni family
Corso Regina Margherita 155, Proceno, (VT) 01020, Italy
Tel & Fax: (0763) 710072, Cellphone: (335) 373394
4 Rooms, Double: €100*
8 Apartments: €110–€165 daily, €350–€1250 weekly*
*Breakfast not included, Minimum Stay Required: 2 nights
Restaurant closed Mon & Tue
Open: all year, Credit cards: MC, VS
Other Languages: good English
Region: Lazio, Michelin Map: 563

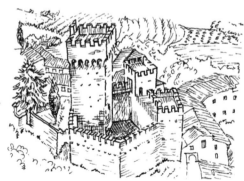

Weary of life in the intense financial world of Milan, Guido and Martina packed up and headed for the hills of Chianti and the "good life" that attracts so many there. After a long search they chose the scenic property where La Locanda now stands, primarily for its magnificent position facing out to medieval Volpaia and an endless panorama filled with layers of virgin hills. The results of their meticulous restoration of three simple stone farmhouses are formidable and today fortunate guests can share in their dream. Its remote location among woods and olive groves guarantees total silence and tranquility and the comfortable, decorator-perfect common rooms and luminous colors harmonize divinely with this idyllic setting. An understated elegance permeates the six bedrooms and the suite. They are tastefully appointed with antiques and smart plaid curtains, and four have the advantage of the views. Breakfast and dinner (except Sundays and Thursdays) are served out on the terrace above the swimming pool whose borderless edge disappears into the landscape. Guido and Martina, natural and gregarious hosts, exude a contagious enthusiasm for their new surroundings. *Directions:* From Radda follow signs for Florence and turn right for Volpaia. Continue on the unpaved road for another 3.8 km after Volpaia village, following signs to La Locanda/Montanino.

LA LOCANDA
Hosts: Guido & Martina Bevilacqua
Localita: Montanino
Radda in Chianti, (SI) 53017, Italy
Tel: (0577) 738833, Fax: (0577) 739263
Cellphone: (348) 4003835
6 Rooms, Double: €200–€280, 1 Suite: €300
Rent the entire house (min 3 nights): €1500 daily
Minimum Stay Required: 2 nights
Open: Apr to Oct, Credit cards: MC, VS
Other Languages: good English, French
Region: Tuscany, Michelin Map: 563

Podere Terreno combines idyllic location and authentic, charming ambiance with delightful hosts Sylvie and Roberto, a Franco-Italian couple, and son, Francesco. The 400-year-old rustic stone farmhouse is surrounded by terracotta flower vases, a grapevine-covered pergola, a small lake, and sweeping panoramas of the Chianti countryside. Inside are six sweet double bedrooms with small bathrooms, each decorated differently with country antiques and the family's personal possessions, which make the feeling very informal and homelike. Guests convene in the main room of the house around the massive stone fireplace on floral sofas for a glass of house wine before sitting down to a sumptuous candlelit dinner prepared by your hosts. This is a cozy, stone-walled room, filled with country antiques, brass pots, dried-flower bouquets hanging from the exposed beams, and shelves lined with bottles of the proprietors' own Chianti Classico wine. Wine tastings take place within the new cantina. The hosts are experts at suggesting local itineraries and directing guests to the many quaint villages waiting to be explored. *Directions:* From Greve follow signs to Panzano, then, on the way to Radda, pass Lucarelli. After 6 km turn left towards Volpaia and after 3 km turn right at the sign for Podere Terreno.

PODERE TERRENO
Hosts: Marie Sylvie Haniez,
  Roberto Melosi & Pier Francesco Rapisarda-Haniez
Via della Volpaia, Radda in Chianti, (SI) 53017, Italy
Tel: (0577) 738312, Fax: (0577) 738400
6 Rooms, Double: €200*
*Includes breakfast, dinner & wine
Open: all year, Credit cards: all major
Other Languages: good English, French, German
Region: Tuscany, Michelin Map: 563

Both Radda and Greve are excellent bases from which to explore the scenic Chianti wine country with its regal castles and stone villages, in addition to Siena, Florence, and San Gimignano. Radda in particular offers a myriad of possibilities for accommodation, including many private homes with rooms or apartments. The Val delle Corti is the home and vineyard property of gracious hostess Eli Bianchi and her son Roberto where they produce a high-quality Chianti Classico wine. The cozy pale-stone house with white shutters tops a hill overlooking the quaint town. The hosts, who moved here in 1974 from Milan, are extremely active in community affairs and are a superb source for area information. The guest accommodation is a lovely separate little house called il Fienile (hay barn), simply appointed with family antiques and newer pieces, which has a large open kitchen and living space looking out to the vineyards, and two bedrooms and one bathroom on the first floor. Meals can be taken at one of the excellent restaurants right in nearby Radda. *Directions:* Equidistant from Florence and Siena off the N222 Chianti road. Before entering Radda, turn right toward Lecchi-San Sano, then take the first left at Val delle Corti.

PODERE VAL DELLE CORTI
Host: Bianchi family
Localita: La Croce
Radda in Chianti, (SI) 53017, Italy
Tel: (0577) 738215
1 Apartment: €90–€110 daily; €690 weekly*
*Apartment rental, no breakfast offered
Minimum Stay Required: 3 nights
Open: all year, Credit cards: MC, VS
Other Languages: good English
Region: Tuscany, Michelin Map: 563

In the very heart of Chianti between Radda, Castellina, and Vagliagli sits the Pornanino farm surrounded by 90 acres of wooded hills and olive groves. Hosts Franco and Lia have carefully restored the main house for themselves plus two stone barns for guests, appointed with the same warm country style as their own home, with antique furniture enhancing beamed ceilings and terracotta floors. Il Capannino is completely refurbished and offers a large central room with open kitchen at an upper level, dining room/living room with open fireplace, and two bedrooms with two bathrooms. A large arched glass door opens onto the pergola-covered terrace for outside meals. Il Leccino is similar but has just one bedroom. Guests can also take advantage of the lovely swimming pool overlooking the olive groves. Franco and Lia are part of the increasing breed of "neo-farmers" migrating from major cities in search of a slower-paced lifestyle where the basic values of life are emphasized in everyday living. Franco has become a passionate producer of top-quality olive oil and even conducts small seminars and tastings on the subject. *Directions:* The farm is located 9 km south of Radda, 5 km from Castellina, and 4 km north of Vagliagli on route 102 but the turnoff is not marked, so it is best to call ahead. 18 km from Siena and 54 km from Florence.

PORNANINO
Hosts: Lia & Franco Lombardi
Localita: Pornanino 72
Radda in Chianti, (SI) 53017, Italy
Tel: (0577) 738658, Fax: (0577) 738794
Cellphone: (347) 7980012
2 Houses: €800–€1400 weekly*
*House rental, no breakfast offered
Minimum Stay Required: 4 nights
Open: all year, Credit cards: MC, VS
Other Languages: good English, French
Region: Tuscany, Michelin Map: 563

The new owners of La Palazzina, Eliana and Silvano Mamprin, were both international hoteliers before falling head over heels in love with this beautiful property. The stately 18th-century hilltop villa surrounded by a lush garden is located in the enchanting Orcia valley with views over wheat fields and soft green hills fringed by cypress trees. This region is part of a Unesco World Heritage preservation area. Eleven guestrooms are appointed with country antiques, botanic prints, lace curtains and wrought iron beds set on check tiled floors. The elegant dining room has been renovated in Tuscan style and looks out to a formal garden and expansive lawns. During the summer months the outdoor terrace is a special spot for enjoying Eliana's delectable Tuscan cuisine. A swimming pool hugs the side of the hill overlooking the surrounding countryside. Cooking courses and wine and olive oil tastings are offered as well as trips to the nearby hot springs and spa at San Casciano. This southeast corner of Tuscany offers a rich variety of sites to explore, including the Amiata Mountains, the Abbey of Sant'Antimo and the hilltowns of Montepulciano, Pienza, and Montalcino. *Directions:* From Florence on the A1 autostrada, exit at Chiusi and drive towards Sarteano on route 478, turning left for Radicofani. After 14 km turn left for Celle Sul Rigo then right at the sign for Fattoria La Palazzina.

FATTORIA LA PALAZZINA
Hosts: Eliana & Silvano Mamprin
Localita: Le Vigne, Radicofani, (SI) 53040, Italy
Tel: (0578) 55771, Fax: (0578) 283114
Cellphone: (338) 3267595
11 Rooms, Double: €80–€120
Open: all year, Credit cards: MC, VS
Other Languages: good English
Region: Tuscany, Michelin Map: 563

The Villa Maria is perhaps best known for its absolutely delightful terrace restaurant, which has a bird's-eye view of the magnificent coast. Whereas most of Ravello's hotels capture the southern view, the Villa Maria features the equally lovely vista to the north. The hotel is easy to locate, being on the same walking path that winds its way from the main square to the Villa Cimbrone gardens. After parking a level below the main square (or at the owner's other hotel, Giordano, where porters can handle your luggage and a heated pool can be used), look for signs for the Villa Maria, perched on the cliffs to your right (5 min. walk). The building is a romantic old villa with a garden stretching to the side where tables and chairs are set, a favorite place to dine while enjoying the superb view. Inside, there is a cozy dining room overlooking the garden. The bedrooms are air conditioned and furnished with antique pieces including brass beds. The bathrooms have been freshly remodeled and some have Jacuzzi tubs. Ingredients for excellent Mediterranean dishes come directly from the property's organic vegetable garden and for those wishing to know more about this regions fine cuisine, weekly cooking courses have become very popular here. A private garden down the road is another relaxing spot for guests who fill the comments book with appreciation of the warm hospitality. *Directions:* Ravello is about 6 km north of Amalfi on a small road heading north from the highway.

VILLA MARIA
Host: Vincenzo Palumbo
Via San Chiara 2, Ravello, (SA) 84010, Italy
Tel: (089) 857255, Fax: (089) 857071
22 Rooms, Double: €195–€475
Open: all year, Credit cards: all major
Other Languages: good English
Region: Campania, Michelin Map: 564

Ravenna is a splendid small city boasting one of the world's most prized collections of Byzantine mosaics housed within eight of its churches, basilicas, and mausoleums. The city comes alive in the summer months with a full program of theater, opera, and outdoor concerts, and also evening opening hours of churches to view the mosaics by night. There are lovely shops and the historical center of Ravenna is quiet since most residents get around by bicycle. Since we found bed and breakfast possibilities in the surrounding area to be much too spartan, the Hotel Diana with its yellow facade, in the center of Ravenna, is the best accommodation choice. A very friendly staff welcomes you into the luminous reception area with various sofas and armchairs arranged around a faux-marble fireplace, and a small patio outside. A buffet breakfast is served downstairs and an elevator takes you up to the second and third floors where the renovated bedrooms are located. These are rather standard but pleasant, with cream-colored walls and bedspreads, carpeting, and reproduction furniture. All have satellite television, air conditioning, and nice new bathrooms. The recommended superior doubles afford more space. Within a drive of an hour or less are Venice, Padua, Ferrara, Bologna, and the ancient ceramic center of Faenza. *Directions:* Follow signs for city center (centro) then follow yellow hotel signs. Near the San Vitale Basilica.

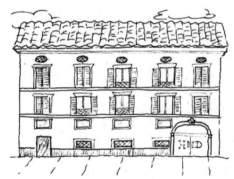

HOTEL DIANA
Manager: Filippo Donati
Via G. Rossi 47, Ravenna, (RA) 48100, Italy
Tel: (0544) 39164, Fax: (0544) 30001
33 Rooms, Double: €100–€135
Open: all year, Credit cards: all major
Other Languages: good English
Region: Emilia-Romagna, Michelin Map: 562

Recanati is a remarkably well preserved town characterized by its brick palazzo. It was one of the most important papal centers and the birthplace of the 17th-century poet, Giacomo Leopardi. The native home of the poet, still inhabited by his descendants, is open to the public, and its antique library is worth a visit. The Palazzo della Casapiccola, of the same period, once hosted bishops visiting the sacred Sanctuary of neighboring Loreto. The coat-of-arms emblems still visible on walls commemorate these visits. The Dalla Casapiccola family has resided here for the past five generations, and recently restored the fascinating historic home to provide guestrooms in four very charming apartments. The rooms and suites can be combined to accommodate from 2 to 6 persons. Accommodations are tastefully appointed with original antiques, fine fabrics, updated bathrooms and kitchenettes. Three of the apartments are within the more rustic original staff quarters, while the largest is within the actual patrician palazzo with frescoed ceilings. The complex includes an ancient barrel-domed cantina where wine and olive oil were once produced. It has access to either of the main streets of town or to the formal gardens in back with views of distant hillsides. *Directions:* Exit A14 autostrada at Loreto/Porto Recanati; follow signs for Porto Recanati. After 500 meters turn right towards Recanati for 8 km. The Palazzo is within the historic center. Located 25 km south of Ancona.

PALAZZO DALLA CASAPICCOLA   New
Host: Anna Maria dalla Casapiccola
Piazzola Vincenzo Gioberti 2
Recanati, (MC) 62019, Italy
Tel: (071) 7574818, Fax: (071) 7574352
Cellphone: (338) 1380055
7 Rooms, Double: €110–€130
3 Suites: €150–€170
Open: all year, Credit cards: all major
Other Languages: English, French
Region: Marches, Michelin Map: 563

Daniela and her architect husband, Piero, brought the family's ancient property back to life. Dating back to the 9th century the property contains a Romanesque church, now the site for concerts. The complex of stone houses is surrounded by vineyards, woods, olive groves (source of the family's prestigious olive oil), and a garden including a collection of English roses. Five suites and two apartments are attached to the main house. Each accommodate two to five persons. Simply furnished with the family's country antiques, wrought-iron beds, and original paintings by Daniela's father, a renowned fresco painter. They feature living rooms with fireplace and balconies with view to either the sweeping countryside, down to the sea, or out to the woods, All the units are rented on a self-catering basis but breakfast can be provided for a fee by request. Besides a pool with spectacular views and massage treatments, painting classes are organized in May and October. Along with Siena and Montalcino, there are plenty of off-the-beaten-track sights to see organized by son, Emiliano. Bikes can be rented. *Directions:* From Grosseto take Aurelia route 1 north and exit at Braccagni. Continue towards Montemassi and before town turn right for Caminino and Roccatederighi. After 1 km turn right at the gate for Caminino.

PIEVE DI CAMININO
Hosts: Daniela Locatelli & Piero Marrucchi
Via Provinciale di Peruzzo
Roccatederighi, (GR) 58028, Italy
Tel: (0564) 569736, Fax: (0564) 568756
Cellphone: (393) 3356605
5 Suites: €130–€170, 2 Apartments: €180–€230 daily
Minimum Stay Required: 2 nights in suites, 7 in apartments
Open: all year, Credit cards: all major
Other Languages: good English, French
History Traveller
Region: Tuscany, Michelin Map: 563

A delightful discovery on the city B&B scene in Rome is the Arco de' Tolomei, a sprawling ancient home on various levels situated in the Trastevere neighborhood, full of character with its narrow cobblestone streets, ancient buildings and excellent restaurants. Opening their cleverly restored home to guests was a natural choice for owners Signori Marco and Gianna Paola. The home is made up of two distinct sections divided by a terrace complete with pergola, vines and gravel pavement. An independent street entrance opens to a split level with stairs going up to five charmingly appointed bedrooms, three with their own small terrace, floral wallpaper, family antiques and nice new bathrooms. The remaining two rooms are down a level off the cozy living room and formal dining room where a buffet breakfast is served around one large table. Rooms are named after the ancient roads that lead to the capital city and are still in use today: Salaria, Appia, Latina, Cassia, and Tiburtina Valeria. A gracious hostess and movie actress, Signora Gianna Paola enjoys suggesting interesting itineraries in ancient Rome, all within easy reach from the home. The famous Trastevere restaurants, with their outdoor seating, are within walking distance. Special discount for stays over 4 nights. *Directions:* Four blocks south of Viale Trastevere, the main street dividing the two sections of the neighborhood.

ARCO DE' TOLOMEI
Hosts: Marco & Gianna Fe' d'Ostiani
Via dell'Arco de' Tolomei 27
Rome, (RM) 00153, Italy
Tel: (06) 58320819, Fax: (06) 5899703
Cellphone: (335) 8112952
5 Rooms, Double: €150–€220
Open: all year, Credit cards: all major
Other Languages: English, good French, German
Region: Lazio, Michelin Map: 563

A delightful alternative to our other accommodations in Rome is Casa Stefazio, the only true in-home bed and breakfast. The location and setting are as perfect as the dedication and warm hospitality offered by Stefania and Orazio in their large, ivy-covered suburban home, just 16 kilometers from the very center of the city, surrounded by several acres of manicured garden and utter silence. On the lower level, with a separate entrance, are one bedroom and two spacious suites (with sauna) accommodating a family of four, each with its own immaculate bathroom, satellite TV, air conditioning, and mini-bar. The main areas include living room, large American-style kitchen, where the Azzolas work wonders, and eating area overlooking the expansive lawn and distant woods. Dinner is served on request under the pergola. Their style, in both decorating and easy entertaining, has obviously been influenced by their yearly winter sojourn in the States, which they adore. Sports activities such as horseback riding, tennis, golf, and swimming are easily arranged. The hosts also organize excursions for groups of friends throughout Italy. Highly recommended by readers. *Directions:* Located north of Rome just outside the circular highway around the city (GRA), close to the tollway north to Florence and south to Naples. Call one day ahead for detailed directions.

CASA STEFAZIO
Hosts: Stefania & Orazio Azzola
Via della Marcigliana 553
Rome, (RM) 00138, Italy
Tel: (06) 87120042, Fax: (06) 87120012
Cellphone: (338) 2180612
3 Rooms, Double: €220–€275
Open: Apr to Nov, Credit cards: none
Other Languages: good English
Region: Lazio, Michelin Map: 563

The Due Torri, a small and charming city hotel, dates to the early 1800s and is tucked away on a tiny, narrow cobblestone street in the historical heart of Rome very near the Navona Square with its Bernini fountains. The 26 rather petite bedrooms, decorated with period antiques and matching burgundy drapes and bedspreads, are accompanied by newly tiled bathrooms. Amenities include an elevator and air conditioning, which provides welcome relief on hot Roman summer days. The contained reception and sitting area have Oriental carpets, pieced marble floors, brocaded draperies, gilt-framed mirrors and paintings, and red-velvet chairs accenting the cream-colored walls. The fifth-floor mansard rooms (even smaller size) have small terraces and fourth-floor rooms have balconies with enchanting views over typical tiled rooftops and terraces. A buffet breakfast is served in a windowless room made cheery with painted borders and paintings. Super hostess Cinzia (owner as well of the newer Fontanella Borghese, also featured in this book) and her courteous staff are very helpful at arranging everything from advance ticketing for museums to transfers and restaurant and itinerary suggestions. *Directions:* Use a detailed city map to locate the hotel, north of Navona Square in a maze of winding streets.

HOTEL DUE TORRI
Host: Cinzia Pighini Giordani
Vicolo del Leonetto 23, Rome, (RM) 00186, Italy
Tel: (06) 6875765, Fax: (06) 6865442
26 Rooms, Double: €180–€235
Open: all year, Credit cards: all major
Other Languages: good English
Region: Lazio, Michelin Map: 563

Many hotels in Rome can boast panoramic views over the city, but few have such a close-up view of a world-famous monument as the Hotel Fontana. Located directly on the square containing the magnificent Trevi Fountain, the Fontana's windows look out on to its gushing waters—you can practically toss a coin from your room. The sleek black-and-white breakfast room with wrought-iron chairs and tables is situated on the top floor of the 14th-century building, giving a bird's-eye view over the square from an enormous picture window. The small irregularly-sized bedrooms (14th century building with many building restrictions) are all individually decorated with understated furnishings some with canopy beds. Bathrooms were incorporated into each room later, and are quite small. Narrow, vaulted-ceilinged halls leading to the guestrooms are adorned with antique prints of Rome. Signora Elena and her welcoming staff at the desk attend to guests' every need. The noise commonly associated with a city hotel is not a problem here as the square is closed to traffic, although loud voices of tourists lingering into the early hours might be a problem in the summer. Preference goes to the side bedrooms with high beamed ceilings. *Directions:* Use a detailed city map to locate the hotel right in the Piazza di Trevi (at the fountain) off the Via Tritone.

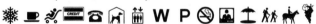

HOTEL FONTANA
Host: Elena Daneo
Piazza di Trevi 96, Rome, (RM) 00187, Italy
Tel: (06) 6791056, Fax: (06) 6790024
24 Rooms, Double: €215–€280
Minimum Stay Required: 2 nights
Open: all year, Credit cards: all major
Other Languages: good English
Region: Lazio, Michelin Map: 563

The many travelers who have enjoyed staying at the Due Torri can also experience the same charismatic hospitality offered by Cinzia in her other hotel very close by. The hotel has the same name as the triangular-shaped piazza where it is located, directly in front of the imposing Palazzo Borghese leading to the Spanish Steps. The enormous doors of the 17th-century building open up to a courtyard where you take the elevator up to the second floor. The lobby has a charming drawing room and a sitting corner and a sweeping spiral staircase up to additional rooms on the next floor. Guestrooms have sparkling new bathrooms and modern amenities and are appointed with either an antique desk or armoire, green or blue matching bedspreads and draperies, and prints of Rome. An effort was made to preserve the original gray-marble floors in some rooms, while parquet flooring was put in the others. Most have a view on a narrow and very characteristic cobblestone street, or on the inner courtyard, offering rare silence. Elegant describes the breakfast room with its green and burgundy marble floors and matching faux-marble doorways. Cinzia oversees every detail in both hotels and the secret to her success is that she obviously has guests' comfort foremost in mind. *Directions:* Largo Fontanella Borghese is at the end of the Via Condotti leading from the Spanish Steps.

HOTEL FONTANELLA BORGHESE
Host: Cinzia Pighini Giordani
Largo Fontanella Borghese 84
Rome, (RM) 00186, Italy
Tel: (06) 68809504, Fax: (06) 6861295
31 Rooms, Double: €180–€250
Open: all year, Credit cards: all major
Other Languages: good English
Region: Lazio, Michelin Map: 563

The Hotel Locarno is centrally located on the corner of a rather busy street, only two blocks from bustling Popolo Square. Its downtown location makes noise unavoidable, so it is advisable to request a room away from the street, even though the installation of thermal windows has helped. Even with the extensive renovations it has undergone, the hotel, dating from 1925, retains the distinct art-deco flavor it originally had. The reception area leads to a cozy bar and long, mirrored sitting room lined with cushioned banquettes and café tables. There is also a side patio with shady canvas umbrellas where guests can have breakfast in warm weather, if not in the breakfast room downstairs. A very special feature of the hotel is the rooftop garden accessed by the antique elevator, where you can gaze over Rome's tiled roofs and terraces to St. Peter's dome and the Villa Borghese Park while enjoying drinks and meals. The comfortable rooms are individually decorated with antiques, and gold-framed mirrors. The Locarno offers such extras as a parking garage and free use of bicycles—a perfect way with which to tour the Villa Borghese Park long a favorite among artists and writers. Reserve well in advance. *Directions:* Use a detailed city map to locate the hotel one block east of the River Tiber at the Flaminia Square sign.

HOTEL LOCARNO
Host: Caterina Valente
Via della Penna 22
Rome, (RM) 00186, Italy
Tel: (06) 3610841 or 3610842
Fax: (06) 3215249
66 Rooms, Double: €260–€450
Open: all year, Credit cards: all major
Region: Lazio, Michelin Map: 563

Marco and Giulia Di Tillo are enterprising hosts who continue the family tradition of being hoteliers. Leaving their careers as musician and writer (Marco just wrote a guide on seven romantic itineraries in Rome), they totally renovated a centuries-old building with the goal of offering comfortable and practical accommodation with many amenities (air conditioning, satellite TV, mini-bar, laundry service, motorbike and car rental, city tour excursions, nearby garage), topped off with an efficient but friendly staff. With its unbeatable central location close to Via Veneto and the Spanish Steps, they have all the elements for success. The front desk, sitting area, and spacious reception hall with comfortable sofas have a clean, contemporary look accented with Modigliani prints. A personalized touch has been given to the breakfast room with framed black-and-white photos of the couple's children and friends artwork. Bedrooms on the six upper floors, reached by an elevator, are decorated along the same clean lines with wood floors and olive-green-striped spreads and drapes. Most desirable are the top-floor rooms with balconies and views over rooftops to St. Peter's cupola while others face the inner courtyard (where breakfast can be enjoyed on warm mornings). The hotel is next door to a convent, quiet is guaranteed! *Directions:* Via della Purificazione is a side street just north of the Piazza Barberini, near the Spanish Steps.

HOTEL MODIGLIANI
Hosts: Marco & Giulia Di Tillo
Via della Purificazione 42, Rome, (RM) 00187, Italy
Tel: (06) 42815226, Fax: (06) 42814791
Cell: (06) 42027931
23 Rooms, Double: €135–€220
2 Suites: €200–€350
1 Apartment: €250 daily
Open: all year, Credit cards: all major
Other Languages: good English
Region: Lazio, Michelin Map: 563

With the success of his first venture in accommodations at the well established Hotel Santa Maria, Paolo Vetere opened a second establishment just across the square. Using his architectural know-how, he has converted the ground floor of one of colorful Trastevere's characteristic buildings into a pleasant hotel with the same look and feel of the first. Following the natural shape and features of the 18th century edifice, the six quiet rooms are positioned around an inner courtyard, reached by passing through the main reception/lounge area. A simple country style has been given to guest rooms with wood furniture, floral print bedspreads, stenciled motifs, beamed ceilings and brick archways. Bathrooms have a choice of showers or bathtubs. Both hotels are extremely family friendly, being on one level and offering a choice of triples or family suites, plus baby-sitting service. A hearty buffet breakfast is served a level below in what was once a Roman cistern, where relics of ancient Rome found during the renovation are cleverly installed within niches in walls. The amiable staff is always on hand to suggest tourist attractions, many at walking distance from the hotel, or to reserve private guides who take you right to the entrances, avoiding long lines. There is no problem for meals as this area has a high concentration of Rome's most popular trattorias. *Directions:* One block south of the Santa Maria in Trastevere square.

❄ ☕ 🛒 💳 ☎ 🐕 @ W 🚭 👥 🔔

RESIDENZA SANTA MARIA   **New**
Host: Paolo Vetere
Via Dell'Arco Di San Calisto 20
Rome, (RM) 00153, Italy
Tel: (06) 58335103, Fax: (06) 58157270
2 Rooms, Double: €175–€230
4 Suites: €200–€310
1 Apartment: €200 daily, €1000 weekly
Open: all year, Credit cards: all major
Other Languages: English, French, Spanish
Region: Lazio, Michelin Map: 563

We chose the Royal Court as a small hotel alternative in the vicinity of the main train station primarily because of its friendly staff, high quality accommodation and service level with the bonus of affordable rates in an otherwise expensive city. Originally a private town house, the 100-year-old home was recently revamped and under the capable hands of hoteliers the Di Rienzo brothers (Inn and View at the Spanish Steps in our hotel guide) is another winner. The 24 comfortable rooms in gold and burgundy combinations are tastefully and individually appointed in classic style with antique furnishings, parquet floors and nice new marble bathrooms, a few with hydro-jet baths. A full range of amenities including modem connection for personal computers, increase with the range of room type – from standard, deluxe to executive. A full buffet breakfast is offered in the elegant breakfast room downstairs. Outdoor spaces are also found in the inner courtyard or on the rooftop terrace, a section reserved for one of the guestrooms. The impressive extra services and facilities list (40 in all!) include tea-room, meeting room for up to 30 participants, pick up service from airport on request, travel desk, complimentary newspaper, laundry and dry cleaning and room service and rivals that of a four or five star hotel at a third of the cost. *Directions:* Three blocks to the left of the Termini train station.

HOTEL ROYAL COURT
Hosts: Mauro & Roberto Di Rienzo
Via Marghera 51, Rome, (RM) 00185, Italy
Tel: (06) 44340364, Fax: (06) 4469121
24 Rooms, Double: €120–€490
Open: all year, Credit cards: all major
Other Languages: English, French
Region: Lazio, Michelin Map: 563

Trastevere, literally translated as "across the Tiber", is the most authentically Roman neighborhood of the city's historic center. Tourists flock here to stroll down the narrow cobblestone streets, visit artisans' shops, dine in one of the many excellent sidewalk trattorias, or just watch the daily life of locals. What pleasure to have discovered the new Hotel Santa Maria, the first accommodation to speak of in the area, which has proved to be a true winner. Native Romans Paolo and Valentina had the ingenious idea of transforming a plot of open land between the jumble of ancient apartment buildings into a unique one-story hotel with rooms looking out to two courtyards with orange trees. The couple welcomes travelers as private house guests, serving a buffet breakfast with freshly baked cakes either out in the courtyard or in the inviting breakfast room/wine bar. Before going out for dinner in one of many nearby favorite restaurants, guests enjoy a glass of wine with nibbles from a local bakery. Bedrooms, each with its own entrance to the outside, are hand painted, with a splash of color on matching bedspreads and curtains, and enjoy amenities such as air conditioning, mini-bar, TV and internet. Bikes are available for guests to use. Identify yourself as a Karen Brown reader and receive a 10% discount. *Directions:* In the heart of Trastevere just behind the famous Piazza Santa Maria, on the tiny Vicolo del Piede. Garage parking is available.

HOTEL SANTA MARIA
Hosts: Paolo & Valentina Vetere
Vicolo del Piede 2, Rome, (RM) 00153, Italy
Tel: (06) 5894626, Fax: (06) 5894815
18 Rooms, Double: €175–€230
5 Suites: €340–€460
Open: all year, Credit cards: all major
Other Languages: good English
Region: Lazio, Michelin Map: 563

Beyond the city gates of Porta Pia, whose ancient walls lead from the Via Veneto, is tranquil, tree-lined Via Nomentana, once a luxurious residential street. Many elegant pastel-colored villas remain (including the last residence of Mussolini), but most have been converted into embassy-owned apartments over the years, while in 1956 the Villa del Parco was transformed into a lovely, quiet hotel with a bed-and-breakfast feel to it. A flower-edged driveway leads to the villa, passing by tables set up for breakfast in the small front garden. When you enter the pleasant lobby scattered with antiques and comfy sofas, you feel that you've arrived home. An inviting bar and breakfast room invite guests to relax and plan the days activities with the assistance of the friendly staff. All of the 30 comfortable guestrooms including bathrooms, have been renovated and vary greatly in size and decor, appointed in a classic style. The Bernardini family are on hand and are happy to make restaurant and itinerary arrangements. Special features are an elevator, central air, and five nice new bedrooms on the top floor with beamed mansard ceilings. Drinks and snacks are available round the clock. *Directions:* Rely on a detailed city map to locate the hotel in a residential district, a 15-minute walk from the city center.

HOTEL VILLA DEL PARCO
Host: Alessandro Bernardini
Via Nomentana 110, Rome, (RM) 00161, Italy
Tel: (06) 44237773, Fax: (06) 44237572
29 Rooms, Double: €145–€195
Open: all year, Credit cards: all major
Other Languages: good English, French
Region: Lazio, Michelin Map: 563

Offering hospitality to foreigners is nothing new to Rosemarie Diletti and family who run the Hotel Columbia right in the city. With the children grown and busy with their own careers, and because she misses the daily contact with international guests, Rosemarie decided to offer accommodation in the family home on the outskirts of the city. The sprawling, very modern home built in the sixties is located on a small road with other large estates and the property extends to the back overlooking lush green countryside. Two spacious air-conditioned apartments on the upper floor each have a double bedroom, bathroom, corner kitchenette, sitting room, and large terrace. A third suite is located at garden level. Rosemarie, being a collector of antiques, fills the house with pieces from the baroque period, both in the common rooms downstairs and in guestrooms. Breakfast is served out on the terrace looking out to the garden and a swimming pool. Transportation to the local train station is provided and the center of Rome is just 15 minutes away. The rate indicated is already reduced for our readers only. *Directions:* North of Rome 4 km from the GRA ring highway, Via Livigno is just off the Via Flaminia. Call in advance to arrange pickup at a nearby meeting point.

VILLA DELROS
Host: Rosemarie Truninger Diletti
Via Livigno 166, Rome, (RM) 00188, Italy
Tel: (06) 33679837, Fax: (06) 4740209
Cellphone: (340) 9295488
3 Suites: €170–€190
Minimum Stay Required: 2 nights
Open: Mar to Oct, Credit cards: none
Other Languages: good English, German
Region: Lazio, Michelin Map: 563

The intimate Villa Mangili, a fresh and updated accommodation has all the ingredients for which we search high and low. In the heart of Rome's most desirable residential section, Parioli, right on the Don Minzoni square, the villa's entrance is that of a true home, through a gate and front garden. Brother and sister team, Gualtiero and Claudia Bacci's intentions were to offer guests comfortable accommodation in an informal but super efficient ambiance, with all the details they look for when traveling. The contemporary décor, choice of colors and layout of this home harmonize to create a soothing haven from the busy city streets of Rome. The airy and luminous main hall doubles as the lounge and breakfast room while the 12 bedrooms are dispersed between two floors. Parquet floors, subdued tones chosen for walls are accented with colorful striped sofas, and abstract artwork. Rooms have individual personalities and unique features such as an outdoor patio, a marble tub right in the room, designer bathrooms in travertine stone. Amenities and services abound from laundry service, room service and airport transfers, plus lots of insider information on what is currently going on in the city. The Villa Borghese park is a two-minute walk away. *Directions:* In the heart of the Parioli neighborhood, north of city center. Consult a detailed city map.

VILLA MANGILI
Hosts: Claudia & Gualtiero Bacci
Via G. Mangili 31, Rome, (RM) 00197, Italy
Tel: (06) 3217130, Fax: (06) 3224313
12 Rooms, Double: €240–€250
Open: all year, Credit cards: all major
Other Languages: English, French, Spanish
Region: Lazio, Michelin Map: 563

The spectacular 2,500-acre hilltop farm property of Montestigliano is a rich combination of woods, cultivated fields, olive groves, and open meadows all surrounding the hamlet dating from 1730. British-born hostess Susan makes sure guests are comfortable in one of the ten independent apartments within the various houses scattered about the property. All retain their original Tuscan character in furnishings and have a combination of two or three bedrooms, kitchen, living room (some with fireplace), and essential modern amenities like washing machines and telephones. The granary has been restored and converted into a farm shop, recreation room, and dining room where meals are served upon request from Monday to Friday. Groups of up to 12 persons have the opportunity to reside in the main villa. Two swimming pools are at guests' disposal, plus many paths and trails. Montestigliano is a marvelous base for getting to know in depth a part of Tuscany whose traditions and lifestyles have remained intact, while still having Siena, San Gimignano, Pienza, Montalcino, and the Chianti area at one's fingertips. Plenty of places to dine are available in Rosia and Sovicille. Susan also arranges weddings. *Directions:* From Siena (12 km) take S.S.223 (towards Grosseto). After 12 km, just after a gas station, turn right and after 2 km turn left for Brenna, taking the unpaved road to the right up to the top of hill.

MONTESTIGLIANO
Host: Susan Pennington
Rosia, (SI) 53010, Italy
Tel: (0577) 342189, Fax: (0577) 342100
Cellphone: (347) 7778761
10 Apartments: €545–€1780 weekly*
1 Villa: €1538–€3880 weekly*
*Apartment/Villa rental, no breakfast offered
Open: all year, Credit cards: none
Other Languages: fluent English
Region: Tuscany, Michelin Map: 563

The climb up to L'Abri is worth the trip just for the spectacular view over the valley and for the warm welcome given by amiable hostess Antonella, a young, enterprising woman who opened her sweet and simple bed and breakfast within her grandmother's home in order to be able to live in her native area. The typical stone house with slate roof is part of a miniature village with just a few other houses, restaurant, church, and school. A collection of grandmother's lace and domestic work adorns the entrance to the left of a small breakfast room. Six small bedrooms are dispersed about this compact home's upper three floors, including the attic. Three have small balconies decorated with cascading geraniums and all are identically appointed using local pine for beds and wall paneling, accented with colorful Provençal curtains. A nice extra is the possibility of sampling local fare at the family's trattoria next door. For two generations traditional dishes such as polenta with meat, rice (no pasta served in this region!), soups, crêpes, and scrumptious desserts made with apples from their own orchards have been served in the cozy dining room covered with black-and-white photos of decades past. Enthusiastic Antonella is an expert on local tourism and can suggest many interesting itineraries for the area. *Directions:* Exit the A5 at Aosta-Ovest and follow signs for Saint Pierre (1 km) and then up to Vetan where L'Abri is located (15 km).

L' ABRI
Host: Antonella Montrosset
Fraz. Vetan Dessous 83
Saint Pierre, (AO) 11010, Italy
Tel: (0165) 908830, Fax: (0165) 908228
Cell: (333) 2095679
4 Rooms, Double: €60–€70, 1 Suite: €70–€80
Minimum Stay Required: 2 nights
Open: all year, Credit cards: VS
Other Languages: some English, French
Region: Aosta Valley, Michelin Map: 561

The Aosta mountain valley has just recently joined the agritourism trend in Italy, with 40 farms in the region currently offering hospitality. Les Ecureuils was one of the first to open, well ahead of the trend, and is the most established of the group. The Gontiers' large property—a cheese farm—overlooks the valley surrounding the capital city of the region, Aosta. The main chalet, which dates to the mid-1800s, houses five double bedrooms and a characteristic dining room adorned with ceramic plates, brass pots, and locally fashioned sabots. A modern barn for the goats and three typical stone houses make up the farm complex. The three front bedrooms have small balconies and valley views, while the remaining two look into the pine woods. The individually decorated, homelike rooms have floral wallpaper and carpeted or wood floors. Each room is equipped with a shower and sink and has a private toilet just outside. Plans to renovate and add full bathrooms are projected for the next season. Half board is required here and meals are based for the most part on fresh products from the farm including various salamis, vegetables, poultry, and their primary production of high-quality goat cheeses. *Directions:* After the A5 autostrada ends at Aosta, continue 8km up to Villa Sur Sarre, turn to the left and after 4km you arrive to Les Ecureuils.

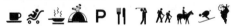

LES ECUREUILS
Hosts: Pepe & Glori Gontier Ballauri
Fraz. Homené Dessus 8
Saint Pierre, (AO) 11010, Italy
Tel: (0165) 903831, Fax: (0165) 909849
Cellphone: (368) 7185685
5 Rooms, Double: €44–€60
Per person half board: €37–€45
Closed: Jan & Dec, Credit cards: none
Other Languages: some English, French
Region: Aosta Valley, Michelin Map: 561

Parma is without doubt the city internationally most known for its Parmesan cheese and prosciutto ham. Thirty kilometers from Parma are found the curative thermal waters of Salsomaggiore and just beyond town is the Antica Torre, the ancient 13th-century tower that majestically crowns a hilltop overlooking the gorgeous soft green countryside. The tower was built to protect the cellar where Cistertian monks used to make salt, a valuable commodity, from the sodium rich waters of the river. The hard-working Pavesi family, proprietors of the ancient property and surrounding organic farm, have welcomed guests to their property for over 20 years. The family offers warm hospitality to their guests within the tower where one bedroom with bath is located on each of the four floors. In addition, there are five characteristic suites on two floors in the main stone residence, including a large two-bedroom suite with fireplace, which is ideal for a family. Rooms are simply decorated and have lovely views over the valley. The original barn has been converted into a dining room where guests sit down together to a hearty, homemade, Emiliana-style meal, including fresh pastas, vegetables, meat, and poultry direct from the farm (drinks not included in half-board rate). Amenities include a swimming pool, bicycles, and tasting local produce in the cellar. *Directions:* From Salsomaggiore, go through town, following signs for Cangelasio and then Antica Torre (3.5 km).

ANTICA TORRE
Host: Francesco Pavesi family
Localita: Cangelasio-Case Bussandri 197
Salsomaggiore Terme, (PR) 43039, Italy
Tel & Fax: (0524) 575425
9 Rooms, Double: €90–€110
Per person half board: €75
Open: Mar to Nov, Credit cards: none
Other Languages: good English, French, Spanish
Region: Emilia-Romagna, Michelin Map: 562

In the southeastern corner of Tuscany is a delightful, yet undiscovered pocket of absolutely stunning countryside. It was only natural that Andrea, with his expert culinary skills, and his lovely wife, Cristina, a born hostess, should open a bed and breakfast close to their vast 1,000-acre countryside property producing olive oil, wine, cereals and vegetables. La Crocetta sits at the crossroads leading up to the charming town of San Casciano, offering eight guestrooms. The small guestrooms with varying color schemes, each with a new bathroom, are pleasantly appointed with canopy beds and fresh country fabrics used for bedspreads and curtains. A pool has been added in the front garden. Inquire about the possibility of cooking and flower arranging courses. San Casciano dei Bagni is the home of several ancient thermal hot springs and is a real plus for those wanted to take a day off from touring to enjoy a swim in one of the thermal pools or take advantage of the many specialized treatments at the nearby luxury spa (Hotel Fonteverde mentioned in our hotel guide). Horseback riding or hiking through the Nature Park of Mount Rufeno are additional activities for lovers of the outdoors. Historic cities of Orvieto, Siena, and the hilltowns of Montepulciano, Pienza and Montalcino are all at easy touring distance. *Directions:* From the A1 autostrada, exit at Fabro from the south or Chiusi from the north, traveling towards Sarteano-Cetona, then San Casciano.

LA CROCETTA
Hosts: Cristina & Andrea Leotti
Localita: La Crocetta
San Casciano dei Bagni, (SI) 53040, Italy
Tel: (0578) 58360, Fax: (0578) 58353
Cellphone: (339) 6366336
8 Rooms, Double: €120–€140
Minimum Stay Required: 2 nights
Open: Mar 30 to Nov 12, Credit cards: MC, VS
Other Languages: good English
Region: Tuscany, Michelin Map: 563

Perched atop a hill and enjoying a 360-degree view of perfectly unspoiled landscape, including a stunning medieval castle, sits the Le Radici farmhouse. Ex-urbanite Alfredo carefully chose this peaceful spot in order to offer accommodation to those who truly appreciate nature and the sense of well-being it inspires. The two farmhouses have been restored, maintaining most of the original rustic flavor, and divided into seven double rooms, three suites, and two apartments. The apartments include one or two bedrooms, living room with fireplace, kitchenette, and bathroom. The tastefully appointed rooms in muted colors are adorned by wrought-iron beds and antique furnishings, complemented by wood-beam and brick ceilings. Special attention has been given to landscaping around the immediate property, which includes vineyards and olive groves. The real treat is the absolutely gorgeous "borderless" swimming pool with cascading water, which fits harmoniously into its surroundings. A romantic candlelit dinner showing off Alfredo's passion for cooking is served in the dining room or out on the terrace, using fresh ingredients from the property. The hosts suggest many interesting itineraries in this area, which borders Umbria. One can relax in the thermal waters of San Casciano or venture out to the towns of Orvieto, Todi, or Pienza, among others. *Directions:* From San Casciano follow signs for Le Radici (4 km).

LE RADICI
Host: Alfredo Ferrari
San Casciano dei Bagni, (SI) 53040, Italy
Tel: (0578) 56033 or (338) 5856890
Fax: (0578) 56038
10 Rooms, Double: €150–€250
2 Apartments: €1180–€1450 weekly
Open: Apr to Nov, Credit cards: MC, VS
Other Languages: good English
Region: Tuscany, Michelin Map: 563

Agritourism and bed-and-breakfast-type accommodations are virtually nonexistent in the northern lake district, so coming across the enchanting Villa Simplicitas was a special treat. The pale-yellow country house of Milanese family Castelli, run by sister-in-law Ulla, sits isolated high up in the hills between Lakes Como and Lugano and is surrounded by thick woods. There is a wonderful old-fashioned charm to the place, enhanced by many heirloom turn-of-the-century antiques scattered about the cozy living and dining rooms. Pretty floral fabrics cover sofas and armchairs, in perfect harmony with the soft-yellow walls bordered with stenciled designs. The same warmth is spread among the ten guest bedrooms with their pinewood floors and trompe l'oeil paneled walls, antique beds, and lace doilies adorning dressers. Innovative meals prepared by local chef Maurizio are served either inside or out on the veranda with green-and-white-striped awnings and matching director's chairs. In the evening, impeccably set tables are candlelit for a romantic dinner for two—simply heavenly. *Directions:* From Como head north to Argegno. Turn left, passing through S. Fedele, then just after town at the first bus station, turn left—it is just 2 km up to the house.

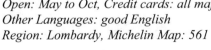

VILLA SIMPLICITAS
Host: Curzio Castelli family
Localita: Simplicitas
San Fedele d'Intelvi, (CO) 22028, Italy
Tel: (031) 831132 (summer) or (02) 460421 (winter)
Fax: (02) 460407
10 Rooms, Double: €100–€150
Open: May to Oct, Credit cards: all major
Other Languages: good English
Region: Lombardy, Michelin Map: 561

Il Casale is a highly efficient and very popular bed and breakfast, thanks to warm and dedicated host, Alessandro, who has combined his extensive hospitality experience with a desire to see his great-grandfather's lovely country property restored properly. Six double rooms and two small apartments including bedroom, kitchen/eating area, and bathroom are all housed within the extended stone farmhouse. Another section is reserved for Alessandro and the family who looks after the wine estate. Access to the guest entrance is through a well-kept garden around the back with a small chapel and lovely views over the soft hills. Main areas include a sitting room and beamed breakfast room with fireplace. The spotless home is appointed with scattered antiques and the very comfortable guestrooms, each with a different color scheme, have new bathrooms and either countryside views or garden or interior patio entrance. Infinite attention to details in both the aesthetics and service offered is given to guests. The entrepreneurial Alessandro has also restored the stone barn and cantina over in the olive grove, Rocca degli Olivi, creating an apartment, five lovely bedrooms with either mansard or vaulted ceilings and gorgeous views, and a breakfast room. An inviting swimming pool is hidden among the olive trees. Plenty of tourist information is on hand. *Directions:* From San Gimignano follow signs for Certaldo for 3 km. Il Casale is on the left and well marked.

❄ ☕ ⚞ 💳 ☎ 🐕 @ W ⏺ P ⏹ 🚭 ≈ 🖼 🏃 🚶 🐎 🍇❦

IL CASALE DEL COTONE
Host: Alessandro Martelli
Localita: Cellole 59, San Gimignano, (SI) 53037, Italy
Tel & Fax: (0577) 943236
Cellphone: (348) 3029091
17 Rooms, Double: €100–€120
3 Suites: €120–€150
2 Apartments: €100–€150 daily
Minimum Stay Required: 3 nights in apartments
Open: all year, Credit cards: all major
Region: Tuscany, Michelin Map: 563

Due to the ever-increasing popularity of the stunning medieval village of San Gimignano, accommodations in the surrounding countryside have flourished. The Casanova is a typical square stone farmhouse with wood shutters and red-tile roof, which you'll grow accustomed to seeing throughout Tuscany. The bed and breakfast's exceptional feature is that it enjoys a privileged view of the towers of San Gimignano, an ancient town referred to as the "Manhattan" of the year 1000. Roberto and his wife Monica, who aim to offer quality accommodation at competitive rates, have the bed and breakfast, adding amenities in rooms such as air conditioning, satellite TV, and telephone, and have also installed a swimming pool. Breakfast is served on the outside patio where guests are immersed in breathtaking scenery, before heading out to visit intriguing San Gimignano and the many surrounding villages. This is an authentic wine-producing farm with eight double rooms with private baths and one apartment for two persons. Country furniture characteristic of the region decorates the rooms, whose original architectural features have been preserved. *Directions:* From San Gimignano take the road toward Volterra. After 2 km, turn left at the sign for Casanova, not Hotel Pescille.

CASANOVA DI PESCILLE
Hosts: Monica & Roberto Fanciullini
Localita: Pescille, San Gimignano, (SI) 53037, Italy
Tel & Fax: (0577) 941902
Cellphone: (347) 1822178
8 Rooms, Double: €100–€105
1 Suite: €115–€125
Open: Mar to Dec, Credit cards: MC, VS
Other Languages: very little English
Region: Tuscany, Michelin Map: 563

Accidentally coming upon the Casolare, tucked away in the unpopulated hills 8 kilometers past medieval San Gimignano, was a delightful surprise. Just before reaching the bed and breakfast, you'll see a half-abandoned stone convent dating back to 1100. The attractive renovated farmhouse, hosted by Andrea, a former art and antiques dealer, and his Spanish wife, Berta, retains all the features characteristic of the original structure. The five double rooms are extremely comfortable and tastefully appointed. Rooms are divided between the two floors of the house, with one being an independent structure poolside. The suites for two to four persons with terrace and living room have been decorated with refined antiques as well. Original watercolor paintings by a local artist adorn an entire wall in the inviting double living room. An extra bonus is the breathtaking swimming pool, with sweeping countryside panorama, surrounded by a manicured lawn, fruit trees, and terracotta pots overflowing with pink geraniums. It provides refreshment after a hot day of sightseeing, while you anticipate another appetizing candlelit meal at dusk under the pergola. Berta is an excellent cook and prepares very special Tuscan menus accompanied by an impressive wine list. This is a truly tranquil haven. *Directions:* From San Gimignano follow signs for Montaione. Staying left at the fork, turn left for Libbiano and take the dirt road to the end.

CASOLARE DI LIBBIANO
Hosts: Berta & Andrea Bucciarelli
Localita: Libbiano 3, San Gimignano, (SI) 53037, Italy
Tel & Fax: (0577) 946002
Cellphone: (349) 8706933
4 Rooms, Double: €110–€130
4 Suites: €130–€170
1 Apartment: €140 daily, €980 weekly
Open: Apr to Nov, Credit cards: all major
Other Languages: good English
Region: Tuscany, Michelin Map: 563

Leaving San Gimignano on the road north towards Pancole-Certaldo, you come across La Fonte, the property of the Bergamasco family run by daughter Maria. This typical Tuscan farmhouse with cupola is surrounded by a nature reserve, vineyards, olive groves, and woods, yet is very close to many major sights and cities. Within the large main house are four fully-equipped apartments with coveted views for longer stays. Three have two bedrooms each with en suite bathrooms and one has one bedroom. Depending on guests' requests, Maria uses the seven bedrooms separately for bed-and-breakfast guests or as four apartments. Maria has enhanced the natural beauty of the home's original features—brick vaulted ceilings and floors—with appropriate country furnishings and smart, colorful fabrics. The cypress-backed swimming pool is nearby, and several patios within the English garden with its extensive lawns offer quiet places for relaxing after touring the many sights of the area. At your fingertips are Volterra, Lucca, the Chianti area, Siena, and many other Tuscan delights. Breakfast can be served outdoors or a pre-ordered tray is brought directly to rooms. *Directions:* 8 km from San Gimignano, 4 km from Certaldo. From Certaldo take the road to San Gimignano. Just as you leave town there is a gas station (ERG) and signs to Pancole and Il Monte. Take the road to Pancole and go for 2 km till you see the sign for La Fonte on the right.

LA FONTE
Host: Maria Bergamasco
Via Canonica 4, San Gimignano, (SI) 53037, Italy
Tel: (0577) 944845, Fax: (0577) 945044
7 Rooms, Double: €125
4 Apartments: €98–€185 daily
Minimum Stay Required: 3 nights
Open: all year, Credit cards: all major
Other Languages: fluent English
Region: Tuscany, Michelin Map: 563

The increasing popularity of this perfectly intact medieval town and the resulting availability of accommodations have made San Gimignano a hub from which tourists fan out to visit nearby, lesser-known treasures such as Volterra, Colle Val d'Elsa, and Monteriggioni. A pleasant, informal stay can be had at the Podere Villuzza, a reader favorite now owned by Salvatore Leanza, his sister Antonella and mother Pina, who recently purchased the 150-year-old stone farmhouse. Chairs are set up in front where visitors can enjoy the view of vineyard-covered hills leading up to the impressive multi-towered town. Common areas include the rustic living room with ceramic-tiled tables and fireplace where guests convene after a day of touring. While Pina prepares meals for guests upon requests, Salvatore produces top-quality wine and olive oil. Six double rooms, on ground and first floors accessed by several different entrances, are furnished in true country style with a mix of wrought-iron beds and antique armoires, complemented by mansard beamed ceilings and stone walls. Rooms have views out over the countryside and town or over hills. For weekly stays there are three small apartments within the house that include a living area and kitchen. A swimming pool is a great bonus for guests. *Directions:* Go through town and follow signs for Certaldo. After 2 km turn right and follow signs for Villuzza.

PODERE VILLUZZA
Host: Salvatore Leanza family
Strada 25, San Gimignano, (SI) 53037, Italy
Tel & Fax: (0577) 940585
6 Rooms, Double: €95–€125
2 Apartments: €750–€1000 weekly
Open: all year, Credit cards: MC, VS
Other Languages: good English
Region: Tuscany, Michelin Map: 563

The countryside around San Gimignano is becoming like the Alto Adige mountain area where practically every house offers some kind of accommodation, and the competition has created bed and breakfasts with high standards of quality and service. Among these, Il Rosolaccio (the local name for the poppies that cover the hill in springtime) is an 18th-century typical Tuscan farmhouse perched high above the road between Certaldo and San Gimignano. As expected, the view over the vineyards and hillsides is absolutely breathtaking. After a 30-year career running a hotel in Rome, Ingrid Music, with her son Steven, bought and very carefully restored the house which, by tradition, was added on to each time someone in the family got married. All the right ingredients are included for a perfectly delightful stay, with tastefully decorated bedrooms and apartments perfectly in tune with the simple beauty of the preserved farmhouse, warm and discreet hospitality, and marvelous views to be enjoyed either poolside or at sunset with a glass of wine. Common areas include the vaulted dining room and cozy upstairs living room with huge open fireplace and family antiques. *Directions:* From San Gimignano follow signs for Certaldo and after 7 km, turn right at the sign up to Il Rosolaccio. From Certaldo drive in the direction of San Gimignano for 5 km and turn left at Rosolaccio.

IL ROSOLACCIO
Hosts: Ingrid & Steven Music
Localita: Capezzano Basso
San Gimignano, (SI) 53037, Italy
Tel: (0577) 944465, Fax: (0577) 944467
Cellphone: (335) 6360715
6 Rooms, Double: €97–€120
6 Apartments: €100–€130 daily, €650–€1200 weekly
Open: Mar to Oct, Credit cards: all major
Other Languages: fluent English, French, German
Region: Tuscany, Michelin Map: 563

La Locanda del Castello is a dreamy place to stay recently opened by Silvana Ravanelli, who took on the ambitious project of restoring part of the village's 13th-century castle (the municipal hall is housed in the other half) and transforming it into charming accommodations and a restaurant. The success she had with her previous, much smaller bed and breakfast in this guide created the desire to offer additional, more upscale rooms. She has a real talent for decorating and each individual room has been thoughtfully appointed with the family's antiques, gorgeous fabrics, and beautiful travertine bathrooms. Most have king-sized beds, double sinks, and generous showers. The golden hue chosen for the rooms' walls harmonize perfectly with the surrounding wheat-covered hillsides dotted with cypresses. The brick-vaulted restaurant, originally the olive press, is accessed through a delightful garden with dining tables right at the historic walls of the castle. The chef adds his own creativity to ancient Tuscan recipes using local percorino cheeses, white truffles, and other fresh local products. San Giovanni is right in the middle of some of Tuscany's most picture-perfect scenery. *Directions:* 35 km south of Siena, exit from autostrada A1 at Bettolle-Sinalunga and follow signs for San Giovanni d'Asso. Stairs from the town's main parking lot lead up to the inn.

LA LOCANDA DEL CASTELLO
Host: Silvana Ravanelli
Piazza Vittorio Emanuele II, 4
San Giovanni d'Asso, (SI) 53020, Italy
Tel: (0577) 802939, Fax: (0577) 802942
Cellphone: (347) 1598450
9 Rooms, Double: €120–€180
Per person half board: €160–€210
Open: all year, Credit cards: all major
Other Languages: good English
Region: Tuscany, Michelin Map: 563

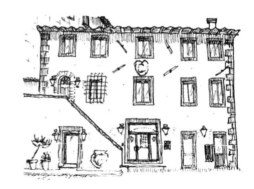

For those seeking a self-catering base for exploring the hilltowns of Tuscany while sojourning in very characteristic accommodation with a rich historical past, the Lucignanello is a sublime choice. Imagine residing in one of the cluster of stone houses that make up the quaint village immersed in the type of picture-perfect, timeless Tuscan landscape seen in Renaissance paintings. The illustrious Piccolomini family still owns the 15th-century property where lovers of Italy can live out a dream. Five two-bedroom houses have been masterfully restored, preserving the original architectural features while ensuring modern facilities. The irregularly shaped interiors are filled with lovely antiques, beautiful tiled bathrooms, and kitchens with travertine counters, and all have large fireplaces. High above the village is a pool set among olive trees with inspiring views. Although breakfast ingredients are supplied, guests are self-sufficient (they find the hamlet's grocery shop and osteria most convenient) but a permanent staff is at their disposal for any suggestions or assistance. A separate five-bedroom farmhouse with private swimming pool is rented out by the week. Country charm exudes from every corner and the ambiance is so authentic you will feel almost Tuscan. *Directions:* From San Quirico go towards Siena, taking the first right to San Giovanni d'Asso. Two km before town, turn right for the 2-km drive to Lucignano d'Asso.

LUCIGNANELLO BANDINI
Host: Angelica Piccolomini Naldi Bandini
Lucignano d'Asso, San Giovanni d'Asso, (SI) 53020, Italy
Tel: (0577) 803068, Fax: (0577) 803082
Cell: (338) 5032004
5 Apartments: €1300–€1800
Minimum Stay Required: 2 nights in low season, 7 in high
Open: all year, Credit cards: all major
Other Languages: English, French, German
Abitare La Storia
Region: Tuscany, Michelin Map: 563

In the countryside on the main road north of Arezzo (16 km) is the Villa Cassia di Baccano, a newly refurbished accommodation within a stately home and 16th century mill next door. The vaulted brick mill is where a buffet breakfast is served and where the reception area is located. Opposite the villa is a lovely borderless swimming pool overlooking a wide open countryside panorama, while the back opens up to face an umbrella pine tree garden. One and two-bedroom apartments within the main building are spread between two floors and are softly appointed with cool white and beige tones in a minimalist style. Wood floors and sleek travertine bathrooms harmonize well with the soothingly simple décor and canopy beds are made up with the finest linens available. All apartments have fully equipped kitchens and the ground floor accommodation includes a patio out in the garden. Rooms looking north have the same open view as that from the pool. Your hostess, Michela, is on hand to suggest itineraries in Arezzo, exploration of the immediate area or over to Chianti just across the tollway. *Directions:* From A1 autostrada, exit at Valdarno and follow for Terranuova and then S. Giustino Valdarno. The Villa Cassia is on this road just before town.

VILLA CASSIA DI BACCANO
Host: Sandro Bartolucci
Via Setteponti Levante, 132
San Giustino Valdarno, (AR) 52024, Italy
Tel: (055) 9772310, Fax: (055) 9772898
10 Apartments: €188–€290 daily
Open: all year, Credit cards: all major
Other Languages: good English
Region: Tuscany, Michelin Map: 563

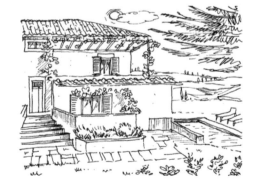

Wine production is nothing new to the Pasqua family, with a personal desire to create a truly exceptional line of wines, Signor Emilio started his own business on the Musella property. He soon reached his goal producing top quality reds, Amarone and Valpolicella Superiore extra virgin olive oil and balsamic vinegar. While he and his daughter Maddalena oversee the farm his gracious wife, Graziella, and son-in-law, Paulo, run the charming B&B. Conveniently located east of Verona, the series of 500-year-old farmhouses, stables and cantina bordering a large lawn and olive trees has been transformed into guest houses, the host's private home, the impressive wine cellars, and a veranda breakfast room. Signora Graziella's sense of hospitality and good taste pervade the cozy (air-conditioned) guestrooms, all of which have been appointed with country furnishings in wood and coordinated fabrics. Past the little swimming pool to the back, guests can hike up the road to the wooded hills and manicured vineyards. In fact everything about the Musella farm from the warm hospitality to the service and room details is attentively cared for. It's a convenient base from which to tour the Veneto region or stay around the farm and enjoy cooking classes and wine tasting lessons. *Directions:* Exit Autostrada A4 at Verona Est and follow for San Martino. At the stop light turn left for Ferrazze/Musella.

MUSELLA-B&B-WINERY
Host: Emilio Pasqua Family
Via Ferrazzette, 2
San Martino Buon Albergo, (VR) 37036, Italy
Tel: (335) 7294627, Fax: (045) 8956287
11 Rooms, Double: €135–€165, 4 Apartments: €200–€280
Minimum Stay Required: 2 nights
Open: Feb 15 to Dec 15, Credit cards: all major
Other Languages: English spoken well
Region: Veneto, Michelin Map: 562

Bordering the region of Veneto and Emilia Romagna is the vast farm property of the Contessa Maria Giustiniani, who runs the agritourism business with the help of her son. Conveniently located on the outskirts of Rovigo, only 15 km from the autostrada exit, you come across the main walled villa and farm complex, now completely abandoned, and shortly thereafter a tree-lined driveway and another group of houses. The horse stables and farmer's quarters have been converted into guestrooms within the main house, while 6 apartments each with two bedrooms, living room and kitchen are divided among four adjacent houses in the garden. The natural red brick of the 500-year old buildings sets off a lush garden with swimming pool. On the main floor past a comfortable sitting area is the rustic dining room where a traditional breakfast and dinner are served. A long, two-story high, arched porch is also a favorite place for outside dining. Upstairs are the air-conditioned guest bedrooms each furnished with family antiques and complimented by sparkling new bathrooms. We particularly like the larger superior doubles and corner bedrooms. Bikes are available and the terrain is flat. Tour Venetian villas, visit Padova and Monselice, or arrange for cooking lessons. *Directions:* Exit autostrada A13 at Boara and follow for Anguillara along river for 10 km to San Martino. The road for Castel Venezze is off to the left.

TENUTA CASTEL VENEZZE
Host: Contessa Maria Giustiniani
Via Fieniletto 420
San Martino di Venezze, (VE) 45030, Italy
Tel & Fax: (0425) 99667, Cellphone: (339) 2436043
13 Rooms, Double: €85–€150
6 Apartments: €690–€1200 weekly
Minimum Stay Required: 2 nights
Open: Apr to Nov, Credit cards: MC, VS
Other Languages: some English
Region: Veneto, Michelin Map: 562

Hidden away from the nearby fashionable beaches of the Emerald Coast of Sardinia is the Ca'La Somara farm where warm hosts Laura and Alberto offer alternative hospitality in nine guestrooms. The 20-acre property stretches up a rocky granite mountainside where the rare Sardinian mules bred here are seen grazing. The bougainvillea-covered one-story main house next door to the owners' quarters has a large, beautiful dining room looking out to a walled, untamed garden and a swimming pool, rare in the area, has a view of the countryside. Rustically decorated in typical Sardinian style, an interior wooden balcony spans the length of the room with colorful hand-woven rugs, baskets, and mule saddles decorating the walls. Guest bedrooms are in a separate house (seven with private bathrooms) and are painted in bright colors with matching bedspreads. A breakfast of homemade breads and cakes is served outdoors under the portico and a superlative vegetarian dinner is available upon request. The hosts' warm and informal hospitality puts guests immediately at ease. The location allows visitors to see two sides of Sardinia: spectacular seaside and inland villages. Many archaeological sites are in the area and activities, such as biking, sailing, diving, horseback riding, and hiking can be arranged. This is a nature lovers' paradise. *Directions:* From Arzachena head for Porto Cervo and turn right for San Pantaleo. After 1 km, turn left for Ca'La Somara.

CA'LA SOMARA
Hosts: Laura & Alberto Lagattolla
San Pantaleo, (SS) 07021, Italy
Tel & Fax: (0789) 98969
Cellphone: (347) 4633087
9 Rooms, Double: €74–€136
Minimum Stay Required: 2 nights
Closed: Nov 15 to Feb 28, Credit cards: none
Other Languages: fluent English, French
Region: Sardinia, Michelin Map: 566

Easily accessed off one of the ancient roads leading from Rome to Florence (Via Cassia), Il Rigo farmhouse sits in its own 600-acre estate. It is ideally located as a base from which to explore the scenic landscapes south of Siena with their sparsely vegetated rolling hills. The large, rectangular stone and brick house dates back 500 years. Its inner courtyard sits on a hill overlooking fascinating vistas stretching to the distant horizons. Within are nine country-style bedrooms on both ground and upper floors, divided by several cozy sitting rooms. Country furnishings such as armoires and wrought-iron beds are very much in harmony with the simple, authentic farmhouse. Breakfast or a light lunch or dinner are served in a spacious dining room on the first floor. Ingredients from the farm include organic grains and beans and, of course, extra virgin olive oil and wine. Hostess Lorenza is an excellent cook and has conducted lessons both here and in the States. The Cipolla's live most of the year in the family palazzo (which has been owned by the family since 1684), Casa dell'Abate Naldi, in the charming village of San Quirico, where four lovely bedrooms with antiques are also available for guests. *Directions:* From San Quirico take the S.S. 2 south for 2 km and turn left at sign for Il Rigo. Continue on dirt road for 3 km up to cypress-lined driveway to the main house.

IL RIGO
Hosts: Vittorio & Lorenza Cipolla
Località: Casabianca
San Quirico d'Orcia, (SI) 53100, Italy
Tel: (0577) 897291, Fax: (0577) 898236
9 Rooms, Double: €105–€115
Open: all year, Credit cards: all major
Other Languages: good English
Region: Tuscany, Michelin Map: 563

Poggio ai Santi has a magnificent view over a green valley down to the distant sea. Francesca has put her heart and soul into the place over the past 20 years with the emphasis being on the comfort and ease of her guests. In order to fulfill the needs of both families and couples she has divided the property into two separate accommodations, conveniently separated by a road. On the left is the Muccheria, two converted farms houses, bi-level family apartments with kitchen facilities, its own swimming pool and play area. On the right is the Poggio ai Santi with the family's stately main house, plus a one-story guest house with five junior-suite-sized rooms, all with independent entrances from the garden. A second guest house with additional suites has just been completed further down the hill. An immediate sense of calm and well-being is invoked by the views, the peaceful ambiance and immaculate rooms appointed in soft earth tones (bedspreads and matching curtains are changed according to season, plus spacious bathrooms with natural stone tiles and rain showers. The pool area is landscaped primarily with aromatic herbs and lavender. Breakfast is served out on the veranda and dinner enjoyed in the restaurant. *Directions:* Exit from the Aurelia freeway S.S.1 at San Vicenzo Sud and drive north to San Vicenzo on the S.S.1 Aurelia for 1 km. Take a right turn for San Carlo and continue for 3 km. Poggio ai Santi is just before San Carlo.

❄ ☕ ✗ ♨ CREDIT ☎ @ W P ⑪ 🚭 ≋ 🖼 ♿ ⚓ 🐴 🍇 ❦

POGGIO AI SANTI
Host: Francesca Vierucci
Via San Bartolo, 100, San Vincenzo, (LI) 57027, Italy
Tel: (0565) 798032, Fax: (0565) 798090
11 Suites: €134–€430
11 Apartments: €400–€1540 weekly
Minimum Stay Required: 3 nights high season, 7 in apts
Open: all year, Credit cards: MC, VS
Other Languages: good English, French, German
Region: Tuscany, Michelin Map: 563

The restored Villa Cefalà is a delightful find conveniently located on the coastline just east of Palermo. The family came back to their ancestral home, dating from 1778, to bring it back to its original splendor, open it up to guests, and oversee the production of organic wine, olive oil and the citrus groves. Cordial and enthusiastic Paola offers her guests accommodation in comfortable apartments, suites and bedrooms, set in four different cottages surrounding the stately, main white villa with its rooftop terrace looking out to the sea. The Limonaia, overlooking the citrus groves, contains 4 well-decorated two-bedroom apartments divided on two floors, complete with living room and kitchenette. Nespolo is a separate 3-bedroom house with sea views. Casetta Rosa and Atrio are separate guesthouses, each containing a lovely 2-bedroom apartment. Oliveto holds four individual bedrooms, all with their own entrance. Wrought-iron canopy beds, country furniture, and country fabric curtains furnish the very pleasant rooms. Dinner is served, upon request, in the rustic dining room in the villa. Airport transfers and laundry services are available. A great location for touring Palermo, Monreale and the northern coastline. *Directions:* 40 km from the Palermo airport and 15 km from the city, take the A19 Palermo-Catania, exiting at Casteldaccia. Follow S.S.113 and at the junction take a left on S.S.113 at sign for Villa. The Villa is on the left side of the road.

VILLA CEFALA
Host: Paola Scaduto Tedesco family
Via S.S. 113, 48, Santa Flavia, Sicily, (PA) 90017, Italy
Tel: (091) 931545 or (349) 5556930, Fax: (091) 941616
10 Rooms, Double: €100–€150
7 Apartments: €140–€150 daily
Minimum Stay Required: 2 nights
Open: all year, Credit cards: all major
Other Languages: good English
Region: Sicily, Michelin Map: 565

Right in the heart of the chic (and expensive) Italian Riviera is a small jewel of a B&B hugging the hillside high above the ports of Portofino and Santa Margherita. The young host, Roberto, has restored almost single-handedly the two small stone farmhouses on a piece of his grandfather's property. Twelve tastefully decorated double rooms are divided between the two houses, each with air conditioning, private bath, some antiques, and lovely panoramic views over the olive trees and fruit orchards and down to the sea. A cozy living room, inviting one to curl up with a book or to converse, gives visitors the feeling of being at the home of friends. In the small, beamed dining room or out in the panoramic terraced garden, breakfast and dinner (featuring local specialties such as the famous fresh pesto sauce) are served and prepared by Roberto while his darling wife, Simona, serves and attends to guests. From Genoa to the marvels of Cinque Terre, the Ligurian coast holds some very special treasures, and the Gnocchi makes a perfect place from which to discover them. Arrival accepted without notice before 1:30 pm or after 5 pm. *Directions:* From Santa Margherita follow signs to Genova/S. Lorenzo uphill for about 4 km to a blue intersection sign. Just after the sign, about 90 meters before the intersection, take the narrow, winding road on the left (red-and-white gate) down to the end.

VILLA GNOCCHI
Hosts: Simona & Roberto Gnocchi
Via Romana 53
Santa Margherita, (GE) 16038, Italy
Tel & Fax: (0185) 283431
Cellphone: (333) 6191898
12 Rooms, Double: €95–€105
Per person half board: €70
Open: mid-Apr to mid-Oct, Credit cards: MC, VS
Other Languages: good English
Region: Liguria, Michelin Map: 561

The Tenuta San Michele, situated at the base of Etna Volcano, consists of 75 acres of vineyards from which the prestigious Murgo wines derives. The combination of mild climate, altitude and terrain offer optimum conditions for this production of ten prestigious blends. Besides reds (Etna Rosso has won many awards) and whites, the line includes spumanti sparkling wines and aquavit. A 200-year-old cellar with reserve barrels sits next to the new one incorporating the latest in modern technology. Within this large wine estate are two houses that offer guest accommodation as eight bedrooms and two apartments. Posed on the top of a hill, views take in looming Etna, over to Taormina and the sea. Rooms are simply appointed without much fanfare, new in feeling, and have the amenities of a hotel. A pool is a welcoming asset after a day of hiking up Etna or touring the vast archaeological site at Piazza Armenina: the Roman Villa Casale with its magnificently preserved mosaics floors. At the restaurant of the Tenuta, where locals flock on weekends, typical recipes of the Etna region are served using ingredients directly from the family's properties, including olive oil, honey, jams, patés, fruits and citrus. This is an authentic taste of Sicily. *Directions:* Exit A18 at Giarre; follow for Santa Venerina on the SP 4 (4 km). In town take Via Vitt Emanuele to Via Martoglio as per signs for the Tenuta. Continue another .5 km, turning right at gate. Located 15 km NW of Catania.

TENUTA SAN MICHELE   **New**
Host: Scammacca family
Via Zafferano 14
Santa Venerina, (CT) 95010, Italy
Tel: (095) 950520, Fax: (095) 954713
8 Rooms, Double: €80–€90
2 Apartments: €120–€170 daily
Open: all year, Credit cards: all major
Other Languages: English, French, Spanish
Region: Sicily, Michelin Map: 565

Situated on the top of Belmonte hill in Sarcedo, a small town north of Palladio's Vicenza, Casa Belmonte offers a splendid view of the Veneto plains below. The 20-acre property of vineyards and olive-groves surrounds the elegant home, a transformed "barchessa" (with its typical annex with arched covered porch) next to the adjacent villa. An expansive manicured lawn and garden leads to the heated swimming pool and garden house with its loft sitting area and veranda where breakfast is served. The six very comfortable guestrooms in the main house have a separate guest entrance and are each sumptuously decorated with rich fabrics, chandeliers, oriental carpets, draperies and antiques and parquet floors. They include amenities such as minibar and air conditioning. The two upper floor rooms enjoy mansard beamed, ceilings. There is also a sauna for guest use and shiatsu massage can be arranged. Mariarosa is a hostess par excellence with an eye for details, pampering her guests and assuring their comfort as well as assisting them with where to go and what to see in towns such as Marostica, Asiago, Bassano del Grappa, and Asolo. *Directions:* From the A4 autostrada, exit at Valdastico which hooks up to the A31. Take the Dueville exit; go left towards Bassano. Continue for 2 km until the sign for Sarcedo. Continue in town, up the hill, and before the church is the entrance gate.

CASA BELMONTE
Host: Mariarosa Arcaro Costa
Via Belmonte 2
Sarcedo, (VI) 36030, Italy
Tel: (0445) 884833, Fax: (0445) 884134
6 Rooms, Double: €180–€220
Open: all year, Credit cards: all major
Other Languages: English spoken well
Region: Veneto, Michelin Map: 562

As more travelers realize how close together destinations of interest throughout Italy are, weekly house rentals to use as a home base for excursions have become more popular. One such ideal base is La Sovana, bordering Tuscany and Umbria and equidistant to Siena, Perugia, Assisi, Arezzo, and many other smaller hilltowns such as Montepulciano, Pienza, and Montalcino—the area where Italy's finest wines are produced. Two stone farmhouses were carefully restored to provide comfortable suites for two to six people. Tastefully decorated with local antique beds and armoires, matching floral bedspreads and curtains, each has a fully equipped kitchenette and eating and living area. Guests can dine by candlelight in the dining room in the main house, whose enormous arched window takes in the expansive view of vineyards, wheat fields, and impeccable landscaping. Giovannella and Giuseppe Olivi, dedicated and amiable hosts, and their two grown children, Riccardo and Francesca, dine with their guests each evening. Potted flowers abound around the pool and Jacuzzi where on Saturday nights a sumptuous barbecue is organized to enable guests to meet one another. Two tennis courts, a small fishing lake, and bikes are available. There are more bi-level suites in a large converted barn in the woods a short walk away from the main farmhouse. *Directions:* Just 2 km from the Chiusi exit of the A1 autostrada. La Sovana is just before Sarteano on the right.

LA SOVANA
Host: Giuseppe Olivi family
Localita: Sovana, Sarteano, (SI) 53047, Italy
Tel: (0578) 274086 or (075) 600197
Fax: (075) 5158098, Cellphone: (335) 7258560
15 Rooms, Double: €182–€210
Minimum Stay Required: 3 nights, 7 in Jul & Aug
Open: Apr 1 to Nov 3, Credit cards: all major
Other Languages: good English
Region: Tuscany, Michelin Map: 563

Tenuta La Bandita is set amid 150 acres of woods, olive groves, orchards, and meadows within a beautifully undisturbed area south of Livorno near the sea. Dino and Daniela, with their former business and hotel experience, bought the estate not too long ago and are in the process of gradually bringing it back to its past splendor. The 17th-century main villa is where most of the guest bedrooms are situated. Their idea was to transform the villa into a bed and breakfast while leaving as much as possible of the original structure and atmosphere of the private residence intact. This was made easier by the fact that the home came with ten furnished bedrooms with bathrooms, situated down one long corridor upstairs. The rooms are appointed with original period furniture, chandeliers, and matching golden brocade drapes and bedspreads. Guests can lounge on the front terrace with wide countryside views or in the gracious arched living and dining room downstairs with gray-stone fireplace and framed portraits. Fifteen additional rooms are divided within two adjacent houses, Gliuliui and La Foresteria, between the villa and swimming pool. *Directions:* Exit from S.S.1 at Donoratico and head for Sassetta/Castagneto for 11 km on a winding mountain road. Take the turnoff left for Larderello/Monteverdi (not Sassetta) for 1 km to the La Bandita property. Pass through the gate and go past the first group of private homes to the villa at the end of the road.

TENUTA LA BANDITA
Hosts: Daniela & Dino Filippi
Via Campagna Nord 30, Sassetta, (LI) 57020, Italy
Tel: (0565) 794224, Fax: (0565) 794350
Cellphone: (328) 1114889
22 Rooms, Double: €100–€190
3 Suites: €170–€220
Minimum Stay Required: 2 nights
Open: Mar 19 to Nov 6, Credit cards: all major
Other Languages: some English, French, German
Region: Tuscany, Michelin Map: 563

Saturnia's thermal waters have been gushing from an underground volcano for over 2,000 years, yet only recently have it and the enchanting surrounding Maremma area become internationally famous, leading to new accommodations springing up. One such is the charming Villa Clodia, once home to nobility, now run by former restaurateur Giancarlo Ghezzi. The villa is a curiosity, seemingly built out of the limestone rock, one side overlooking the street and the other an expansive valley of grapevines and olive trees. Because of its unusual proportions, each room is unique in size and decor. A small winding stairway takes guests up or down to rooms, some of which have been literally carved out of the rock. All bedrooms feature scattered antiques, new bathrooms, and valley views, and a fortunate few boast a terrace. Amenities include air conditioning, TVs, and mini-bars. Breakfast is offered in a sweet, luminous room next to the sitting room. A lush rose garden and fruit orchard surround the inviting star-shaped pool. Advance reservations are a must and weekly stays preferred. *Directions:* From Rome take the Aurelia highway north, turning off to the right at Vulci following signs for Manciano, Montemerano, and Saturnia. Villa Clodia is in the middle of town.

VILLA CLODIA
Host: Giancarlo Ghezzi
Via Italia 43, Saturnia, (GR) 58050, Italy
Tel: (0564) 601212, Fax: (0564) 601305
12 Rooms, Double: €100–€110
1 Suite: €130
Minimum Stay Required: 4 nights
Closed: Jan 9 to Feb 1, Credit cards: VS
Other Languages: good English
Region: Tuscany, Michelin Map: 563

North of the beautifully austere ancient city of Bergamo, at the foothills of the Ortighera mountain range right on the River Brembo is the farm property of young local couple, Cinzia and Ferdy Quarteroni. They bought the stone farmhouse at the edge of thick woods, which dates to 1850, and completely restored it to include four guestrooms, their private quarters, dining rooms, and small store where they sell their home-produced goat cheeses. The cabin-like bedrooms on the two upper floors are simply decorated in tune with the natural features of the house: stone walls, wood-beamed ceilings, and brick floors. Downstairs in the cozy, arched, stone-walled dining room with large fireplace, gregarious Cinzia serves excellent local fare and an ample breakfast with freshly baked cakes and breads. This is a nature lover's paradise where Ferdy sees to the goats and organizes itineraries by mountain bike, horse, or foot while nearby there are several ski resorts. This is a perfect vacation spot for families. *Directions:* From the A4 autostrada exit at Dalmine (35 km), heading north for Villa d'Almè, San Pellegrino, San Giovanni, and Scalvino. Ten km after San Pellegrino, the source of the famous mineral water, park on the right-hand side of road at the agriturismo sign and cross over the footbridge up to the house.

FERDY
Hosts: Cinzia & Ferdy Quarteroni
Scalvino, (BG) 24010, Italy
Tel & Fax: (0345) 82235
4 Rooms, Double: €65–€80
Open: all year, Credit cards: MC, VS
Other Languages: good English
Region: Lombardy, Michelin Map: 561

For those who prefer the intimacy of a small pension, native Salvatore and his amiable Panamanian wife Marisin await you with open arms. The pale-yellow three-story house sits in the quaint town of Scopello with its piazza and three streets. From ancient times this was an important fishing center especially for tuna, and the Tonnara stone fishing station down by the sea still stands as proof. The entrance hall is a combination breakfast and dining room with a sitting area in the corner around the fireplace. A central staircase leads up to guestrooms, a few with balconies facing out to the distant sea. The rooms are simply appointed with light-wood armoires, wrought-iron beds, and crocheted white bedspreads. In the evening after a day at the seaside or touring, you come "home" to a delicious four-course, home-cooked, meal of pasta, fresh fish or meat, vegetables from their garden or salad, and dessert. Olive oil and marmalades are from their own trees. Enthusiastic Marisin spends time chatting with her guests and advising them what to visit in this culturally rich area. "Must sees" include the ancient town of Erice, the ruins of Segesta, Selinunte, and Agrigento. Well-marked hiking trails cover the spectacularly beautiful Zingaro Nature Reserve along the northern coast (one of its kind in Sicily). *Directions:* From Palermo, exit from autostrada A29 at Castellammare and follow signs for Scopello. The Tranchina is just after the bar with outdoor tables.

PENSIONE TRANCHINA
Hosts: Marisin & Salvatore Tranchina
Via A. Diaz 7, Scopello, (TP) 91014, Italy
Tel: (0924) 541099, Fax: (0924) 541232
10 Rooms, Double: €76–€100
Per person half board: €61–€76
Open: all year, Credit cards: all major
Other Languages: fluent English, Spanish
Region: Sicily, Michelin Map: 565

Luciana and Luigi from Rome are pioneers in offering accommodation in Sabino, bringing back to life this lovely property. Gregarious Luciana goes out of her way to see that guests' needs are taken care of and suggests many fascinating local itineraries and events. Accommodation is offered in a variety of apartments divided between the main villa and the well-restored farmhouse with adjacent scenically positioned pool down the hill. Each has one or two bedrooms, bathroom, kitchenette, and eating area, while a double living room with enormous stone fireplace is reserved for all guests. The cozy country decor, with its stenciled borders and mix of family antiques, is the result of Luciana's good taste. Apartments on ground and second floors (some with terraces) take in views of the sweeping valley below. Rooms in the villa are more elegant, with frescoed ceilings, panoramic terraces, and antique furnishings. In addition to producing wine, olive oil, and fruit, Luigi raises horses. On request, everything from interesting hiking tours and courses in Italian and cooking can be arranged besides excellent suggestions on what this upcoming area has to offer. *Directions:* From Rome, leave the A1 at Ponzano Romano/Soratte (a new exit and not marked on maps) after the Fiano exit. Turn right at the next intersection, then left at Forano intersection, continue until the turnoff left for Forano. Before the church, turn right for Selci, then right before town at Via Vallerosa.

VILLA VALLEROSA
Hosts: Luciana Pancera & Luigi Giuseppi
Via di Vallerosa 27, Selci Sabino, (RI) 02040, Italy
Tel & Fax: (0765) 519179
Cellphone: (339) 1226213
7 Apartments: €114–€190 daily, €690–€1075 weekly*
*Apartment rental, no breakfast offered
Minimum Stay Required: 2 nights, 7 in high season
Open: all year, Credit cards: none
Other Languages: good English
Region: Lazio, Michelin Map: 563

The Conte Emo Capodilista estate in the outskirts of Padova offers two types of accommodation in an excellent location for touring all of Veneto. The historic estate of the Count Emo Capodilista consists of a medieval castle, vineyards and working farm plus an intact 17th century villa museum visitable strictly by appointment only. The Count resides in a part of the towering castle overlooking a manicured golf course, while one suite within is reserved for guests. The antique-filled suite consists of a living room with library and family portraits, bedroom and bathroom. The main city road which divides the castle and farm buildings from the hilltop villa, passes the first house where the two most recently restored of the four apartments are located. Next to the offices and wine-tasting room of the major wine producer is the third accommodation, Casa del Prete, a comfortable two-bedroom stone house on two floors with front garden. Number four, Casa di Maria, is just across the way is a large building which originally housed the farmer's quarters and barn. The property is a busy place and ideal for more independent travelers who want to set up base for the week and explore the highlights of Veneto. Here you have everything from a golf course, the spas and thermal baths of the nearby Euganean Hills, Padua, Vicenza and villas of the Brenta Canal. *Directions:* From Tencarola follow for Feriole to the entrance of Castello.

THE CONTE EMO CAPODILISTA ESTATE
Host: Conte Giordano Emo Capodilista
Via Montecchia 16, Selvazzano, (PD) 35030, Italy
Tel: (049) 637294, Fax: (049) 8055826
1 Suite: €250
4 Apartments: €300–€1400 daily
Minimum Stay Required: 2 nights
Open: all year, Credit cards: MC, VS
Other Languages: some English
Region: Veneto, Michelin Map: 562

Siracusa is a fascinating Sicilian city. Its most ancient part, "Ortigia", on a promontory jutting into the sea, is connected to the more modern city by a bridge. The Approdo delle Sirene in a two-story building looking over the harbor is a long-time dream come true for warm and friendly owners Fiorangela and her son, Friedrich. The eight minimalist style guest bedrooms, a few with water views, have air conditioning, television and minibar; each with a different colored bold striped bedspread, and matching tiled bathrooms. The main living room-reception area is cool and modern with parquet floors, white walls and framed nautical maps. What guests rave about most, besides the warm and very helpful hospitality, is breakfast: homemade cakes and breads, served when possible on the panoramic rooftop terrace laden with jasmine and bougainvillea vines and overlooking the sea. Another wonderful feature is the wide choice of itineraries and visits organized by Friedrich: canoe rentals, Greek theater performances, a coastal tour by motorboat. Free bikes are available to explore the immediate city and then there are guided tours of Baroque cities Noto and Modica, as well as more classic ones such as Taormina, Agrigento, or Piazza Armenina. *Directions:* Riva Garibaldi is on the waterfront in the historical center of the city.

L' APPRODO DELLE SIRENE
Host: Friedrich Schmuck
Riva Garibaldi, 15, Siracusa, Sicily, (SR) 96010, Italy
Tel: (0931) 24857, Fax: (0931) 483765
8 Rooms, Double: €90–€125
Open: all year, Credit cards: all major
Other Languages: fluent English
Region: Sicily, Michelin Map: 565

The Limoneto with its family-style hospitality, excellent authentic country meals, simple but comfortable accommodations, and proximity to fascinating Siracusa is an "old favorite" of readers. At just 10 kilometers from the historical center of Siracusa with its Greek and Roman influences, the orange- and olive-grove farm is a perfectly delightful, safe, and economical base from which to explore Sicily's southeastern corner. Adelina, Alceste, and son, Francesco, make guests part of their family. Guestrooms are split between the refurbished barn and part of the main house, all with individual entrances from the exterior. Air-conditioned rooms, some for up to four persons, are new, with pleasant modern decor and spotless bathrooms. Dinner is served in the spacious veranda dining room where locals come for a Sunday meal, overlooking the vast citrus groves. You are welcome into Adelina's kitchen to observe and participate in the making of typical regional meals. The warmth exudes and when the evening is just right and the limoncello flowing, she might even read some poetry. Truly unique is the boat tour on the Ciane river among the Papiro trees of Egyptian origin. *Directions:* From Catania, take the autostrada to Siracusa and exit at Palazzolo (km 152) after a brown sign for the Limoneto B&B. Drive on the S124 and turn left at the first intersection for Canicattini B. At the T-junction turn right again for Canicattini: the house is on the left after 4 km.

LIMONETO
Hosts: Alceste & Adelina Norcia
Via del Platano 3, Siracusa, Sicily, (SR) 96100, Italy
Tel: (0931) 717352, Fax: (0931) 717728
10 Rooms, Double: €90–€120
Minimum Stay Required: 3 nights
Closed: Nov, Credit cards: MC, VS
Region: Sicily, Michelin Map: 565

Situated just outside Siracusa by the Ciane River in the Saline Nature Reserve the Villa dei Papiri, as its name suggests, is surrounded by papyrus. This 200-year-old stone farmhouse and barn have been nicely restored and made into an upscale bed and breakfast with a restaurant. Each of the eight bi-level suites has one or two bedrooms, living area, kitchenette, bathroom and private entrance. Exposed stone walls, wood beamed ceilings and insets of colorful hand-painted ceramic tiles mix well with wrought- iron beds and warm cherry wood floors. Each suite enjoys an outdoor garden area with tables and large umbrellas. Breakfast and other meals are served in the large dining/living room with windows overlooking the palm garden. The expansive property with fifty acres of citrus groves has a Mediterranean garden surrounding the main house lined with enormous palm trees, cypresses and olive groves. Besides visiting the historic center of Siracusa, Ortigia, and the many archaeological treasures surrounding the city (Greek theater, Roman amphitheater, Museum, necropolis), you have the Baroque cities of Noto, Modica and Ragusa as interesting day trips. Horseback riding, golf, canoing and private guides can also be arranged. *Directions:* Exit the Autostrada A18for Siracusa Centro and follow signs Canicattini, then Fonte Ciane to the stone gate of Villa dei Papiri.

※ ■ ✗ ▦ ▲ @ W Ⲩ P ♒ 🏃

VILLA DEI PAPIRI
Host: Christina Bianchi
Via Conrada Cozzo Pantano, Fonte Ciane
Siracusa, (SR) 96100, Italy
Tel & Fax: (0931) 721321
Cellphone: (348) 5121829
8 Rooms, Double: €80–€140
Minimum Stay Required: 3 nights, or €10 supplement
Open: all year, Credit cards: MC, VS
Region: Sicily, Michelin Map: 565

There is a beautiful stretch of coastline on the Adriatic Sea just south of Ancona, dramatically different from the more flat, uninteresting shoreline to the north and south with its modern hotels and condos. The 14th-century quaint stone village of Sirolo sits high above the water on a mountainside looking down to the beaches of the Riviera Conero. Delightful seafood restaurants dot the shore, where you might enjoy a plate of pasta with fresh clams while watching the tide come in. Here Isabella and Giorgio offer seven guestrooms above their highly-rated restaurant with white chairs setting off the natural stone walls. The Locanda, dating to 1300, being actually part of the town's walls and arched entryway, is of great architectural and historical importance. Their bed and breakfast, respecting the original structure, is a true charmer. Comfortable bedrooms, most with sea views, have exposed stone walls and terracotta floors showing off wrought-iron beds with cool white sheets and contrasting gray bedspreads, and antique bedside tables. Amenities include air conditioning, LCD TVs, mini-bars, and newly renovated bathrooms. Isabella's highly praised meals feature fresh seafood dishes. Alternatively nine rooms are available at their new inn, Rocco in Campagna, set in a rose garden, in Conoro Park by the sea. *Directions:* The Rocco sits at the edge of the town of Sirolo, after Portonovo.

LOCANDA ROCCO
Hosts: Isabella & Giorgio Tridenti
Via Torrione 1, Sirolo, (AN) 60020, Italy
Tel & Fax: (071) 9330558
Cellphone: (339) 5205519
7 Rooms, Double: €150–€190
2 Apartments: €700–€800 weekly
Open: all year, Credit cards: MC, VS
Other Languages: some English
Region: Marches, Michelin Map: 563

The fascinating Marches region has been justifiably receiving great press recently as one of Italy's last undiscovered treasures. Certainly one of the most interesting areas from which to begin exploring is that of Monte Conero, which boasts the most spectacular coastline on the Adriatic, with white cliffs plunging into the sea. Here you find many historic villages and churches in scenic countryside, the highest concentration of historic theatres in Italy, and a summer opera festival in Macerata and Pesaro. Just slightly inland is the 80-acre agritourism property of the noble Nembrini Gonzaga family, producers of top-quality Rosso Conero wine and virgin olive oil. Next to the family's elegant 18th-century villa is a restored grain mill converted into guest apartments. An extensive two-story structure of white stone typical of the area, it contains pleasant, practical accommodation for two to five persons consisting of one or two bedrooms, bathroom, and living room with kitchenette. Adjacent to the apartments and surrounded by a large garden is a recently built house with eight very tastefully decorated bedrooms. A wide variety of sports including sailing, golf, hiking on national-park trails overlooking the sea, and horseback riding can all be arranged. *Directions:* Exit the A14 autostrada at Ancona Sud heading for Sirolo-Numana. In Coppo (on most maps), 2 km before Sirolo, turn right on the road opposite the bar and follow the Via Valcastagno up to the property.

❄ ☕ 🚲 💳 ☎ 🐕 🏋 @ W ☨ P ❀ 🖼 ♿ ⚓ 🏃 🚶 🏇 ⛴ 🍷

RELAIS VALCASTAGNO
Host: Francesca Nembrini Gonzaga Family
Via Valcastagno 10, Sirolo, (AN) 60026, Italy
Tel: (071) 7391580, Fax: (071) 7392776
Cellphone: (348) 3399339
8 Rooms, Double: €75–€170
10 Apartments: €285–€895 weekly
Open: all year, Credit cards: all major
Other Languages: fluent English, French
Region: Marches, Michelin Map: 563

The real fascination about the gorgeous Val Gardena mountain resort area is that you can actually ski from one connecting valley to the next and finish up at the end of the day over near Cortina. Siusi is a convenient place to set up camp in any season and the Aquila Nera with its excellent restaurant and amenities of a hotel is steps up from the very economical bed and breakfast choices of the region. The very cordial Mutschlechner family, with a long tradition in the hospitality business, renovated most of the former private home whose origins date back to 1518. A second building was added on, creating additional rooms (and an elevator), which are very fresh with light-wood furnishings and cheerful fabrics. Downstairs common rooms include a luminous sitting area, a stube, a breakfast room completely paneled in wood including floor and ceiling, and a large contemporary dining room where five-course dinners are served based on a combination of Italian and southern Tyrolean recipes. A small swimming pool at the back, plus sauna, steam bath, and free shuttle to the lifts are nice added extras. *Directions:* Turn into the main street of town, Via Santner, and take the first right to Via Laurin.

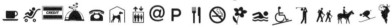

AQUILA NERA (SCHWARZER ADLER)
Host: Mutschlechner family
Via Laurin 7, Siusi allo Sciliar, (BZ) 39040, Italy
Tel: (0471) 706146, Fax: (0471) 706335
21 Rooms, Double: €100–€200*
*Includes breakfast & dinner
Closed: Mar 30 to May 22, Oct 19 to Dec 19
Credit cards: all major
Other Languages: English
Region: Trentino-Alto Adige, Michelin Map: 562

In yet another lesser-known pocket of Tuscany halfway between Siena and the sea is the absolutely stunning 1,000-acre property of the Visconti family. Dating back to the 1400s, in its heyday it was a village in itself, complete with the noble family's main villa, farmers' houses, church, nuns' quarters, oil press, and blacksmith and carpenter's shops. These stone buildings are all attached to the villa in a U-shape formation with a beautiful formal garden within. Terracotta pots with lemon trees and red geraniums give spots of color among the greenery. Vitaliano and Vittoria, whose home has been in the same family since its origins, welcome guests in the restored part of the villa where eight bedrooms with private bathrooms have been created including three large triples. All with beamed ceilings and brick floors, they are simply appointed with beds and armoires, looking out either to the garden or woods at the back. Common areas are the living room with enormous fireplace, the dining room where delectable Tuscan country meals are served (€20), and an upstairs loggia with a panoramic view over the countryside, which seems to take in all of Tuscany. Apartments are available for weekly stays. For those who enjoy spectacular scenery in a very special, historical setting, this is the place. *Directions:* From the Florence-Siena highway exit at Colle Val d'Elsa Sud. Follow signs for Grosseto-Radicondoli-Castelnuova Val di Cecina, then Fattoria Solaio.

FATTORIA SOLAIO
Hosts: Vittoria & Vitaliano Visconti
Solaio–Radicondoli, (SI) 53030, Italy
Tel: (0577) 791029, Fax: (0577) 791015
2 Rooms, Double: €80–€90
3 Suites: €105–€115
4 Apartments: €680–€800 weekly
Minimum Stay Required: 3 nights
Open: Mar to Nov, Credit cards: all major
Other Languages: good English
Region: Tuscany, Michelin Map: 563

Le Sorgive, near Lake Garda, is a vast agritourism property, an oasis that offers a wealth of activities connected with nature and agriculture. Anna and her brother, Vittorio, both passionate advocates for the environment, divide the duties, with Anna operating a large country restaurant, Le Volpi, and a major equestrian center where locals convene, and Vittorio running the hospitality end. The 60 acres are made up of cultivated fields, vineyards, and woods with plenty of farm animals within the triangle of flat countryside between Brescia, Mantova, and Verona. The extensive yellow main house with cupola and arched portico contains the family's private quarters, dining room, and eight well-appointed guestrooms, some with loft beds for two children, spread about the three floors. For longer stays, there are also two lovely apartments. An ample country breakfast is served in the rustic beamed dining room with fireplace. Anna's busy restaurant highlights recipes specifically from the Mantova area, using the variety of organic produce, cheeses, and salamis. Other facilities offered are a fully-equipped gym, swimming pool, and mountain bikes. *Directions:* Exit the A4 autostrada at Sirmione, turn left for Pozzolengo (3 km) and then to Solferino (7 km). Turn left at the first crossroads, then keep to the right towards Castiglione delle Stiviere (1.5 km) until you reach a sign indicating the farm entrance.

LE SORGIVE
Hosts: Vittorio & Adriana Serenelli
Localita: Sorgive, Solferino, (MN) 46040, Italy
Tel: (0376) 854252 or (338) 6113446
Fax: (0376) 855256
8 Rooms, Double: €110–€125
2 Apartments: €900–€1000 weekly
Open: all year, Credit cards: all major
Other Languages: good English
Region: Lombardy, Michelin Map: 561

The Tenuta di Santa Lucia is an agricultural property of nearly 300 acres made up of oak woods, hazelnut orchards, fields of grain, grazing pastures for cows and olive groves. Generations of the Trua family have resided here, near the ancient city of Viterbo for more than 200 years. The current generation, Antonio and Bettina, welcomes guests in the main villa, originally a silk production factory. The six country-style bedrooms, some with exposed brick walls, are furnished with family heirlooms and are provided with smart new bathrooms, air conditioning and Internet connection. Guests often gather in the main living area with its sofas and high-beamed ceilings. Highly praised meals in the dining room restaurant (which is open only on weekends until summer months) are based on the organic products produced by the farm, including wines and olive oil. An elongated swimming pool and whirlpool awaits guests after a day of touring in this culturally rich area. Besides Viterbo with its thermal spas, there are the Renaissance gardens of Villa Lante, Bomarzo park, the Etruscan cities of Tuscania and Tarquinia, and fascinating Civita Bagnoregio. If you prefer your activities nearer to the hotel, cooking and ceramic courses can be arranged. *Directions:* Exit the Autostrada A1 at Orte and take the Orte-Viterbo highway, exiting at Soriano. Follow signs to the town and Tenuta di Santa Lucia.

TENUTA DI SANTA LUCIA
Host: Trua family
SS Ortana km 13,200
Soriano nel Cimino, (VT) 01038, Italy
Tel & Fax: (0761) 759529
Cellphone: (349) 1446956
6 Rooms, Double: €120–€150
Closed: January, Credit cards: all major
Region: Lazio, Michelin Map: 563

The town of Spoleto has gained international fame thanks to the July Due Mondi festival, a month-long series of cultural events including ballet, theater, opera, and concerts with renowned artists, which attracts a worldwide audience. Accommodations are reserved from one year to the next. For the rest of the year, however, Spoleto holds its own along with nearby Assisi, Spello, Todi, and Perugia as an enchanting medieval stone town, rich in its historical past. The 14th-century Palazzo Dragoni, situated on a quiet little street in the heart of the town near the famous cathedral, was completely renovated by the Diotallevi family and offers charming accommodation within 15 bedrooms. Son Roberto manages the property while his parents reside in a section of the palazzo. The spacious bedrooms (larger ones are considered suites) are spread out among the three floors, reached by elevator, and have new bathrooms and many modern amenities including air conditioning. Everything possible has been done to maintain the original architecture and ambiance of a private home, with vaulted and frescoed high ceilings, antique furnishings, Oriental carpets, and Murano chandeliers. The real treat is breakfast served in the glassed-in loggia, taking in splendid views of the tiled rooftops and bell tower of the Duomo. *Directions:* Follow signs for the center of Spoleto, by way of Via P. Bunilli, passing the football field (campo sportivo). Follow white signs for the hotel.

PALAZZO DRAGONI
Host: Roberto Diotallevi Family
Via del Duomo 13, Spoleto, (PG) 06049, Italy
Tel: (0743) 222220, Fax: (0743) 222225
15 Rooms, Double: €125–€150
Open: all year, Credit cards: MC, VS
Other Languages: some English
Region: Umbria, Michelin Map: 563

On the border of Liguria and Piedmont and conveniently located near the Genoa-Milan autostrada sits the hillside property of friendly hosts, Domenico and Rosanna, president of the regional agritourism association. The house is immersed in woods at the end of a long gravel road and is barely visible through the ivy and rose vines that conceal it—a true spectacle in late May. This gives just a hint of one of Rosanna's two passions: cooking and gardening, both of which guests can participate in by taking lessons. Two bedrooms are situated in the main farmhouse dating to 1714 and in Rosanna's family since that time. The apartments with exposed beams are located next door in the converted barn and are all decorated in pleasant country style with antiques and family memorabilia. Guests sit down together "en famille" at a long table to taste one of Rosanna's delectable meals prepared with their own fresh, organically-grown produce from the garden (Domenico's passion). Guests/friends are made to feel right at home in this informal and tranquil atmosphere, where silence and privacy are highly respected and guests become a natural part of the farm's everyday life. A small pool is hidden in lush vegetation just behind the house. *Directions:* Exit the A7 autostrada (Milano-Genova) at Vignole Borbera, following the sign for Stazzano (4 km). Turn right in town at the traffic light and follow the bed and breakfast sign for 2 km on an unpaved road.

LA TRAVERSINA
Hosts: Rosanna & Domenico Varese
Localita: Traversina 109, Stazzano, (AL) 15060, Italy
Tel & Fax: (0143) 61377
Cellphone: (335) 494295
2 Rooms, Double: €88–€110
3 Apartments: €110–€140 daily
Per person half board: €69–€85
Open: all year, Credit cards: all major
Other Languages: English
Region: Piedmont, Michelin Map: 561

Just off the beaten track in the Veneto region, the northern countryside surrounding Treviso offers scenic landscapes, wine roads of prosecco and historic villages such as Conegliano, Vittorio Veneto and Asolo in the foothills of the Dolomites. Here the Lucchetta family have opened a quaint country-style bed and breakfast. The large stone home is divided in half between private and guests' quarters with wood being the primary material in floors, stairs, country furniture and carvings. The other prominent theme is flowers, fresh or dried bouquets, on upholstered chairs, curtains or framed prints and paintings adorn colorful Provencal walls which give names of the bedrooms. Three bedrooms (notice the beautiful bed linens) are on each of the upper floors while a cozy breakfast reception area, and sitting room are reserved for guests on ground floor. The expansive surrounding property includes a swimming pool and picture-perfect organic vegetable garden. A full breakfast is served under the pergola in warmer months and a good restaurant is within walking distance to the home. Friendly host and daughter, Chiara, is happy to assist guests with local itineraries. *Directions:* Exit from the A27 autostrada at Conegliano, follow for Treviso and at Susegana, turn right for Collalto for 5 more km. After passing reaching Via Morgante II, the Maso's gate is on the left hand side of the road.

MASO DI VILLA
Host: Chiara Lucchetta Family
Via Col di Guarda 15
Susegana, (TR) 31058, Italy
Tel: (0438) 841414, Fax: (0438) 981742
6 Rooms, Double: €110–€170
Open: all year, Credit cards: MC, VS
Other Languages: English spoken well
Region: Veneto, Michelin Map: 562

Taormina is on what is referred to as the Amalfi coast of Sicily and, although the historic town is lovely it is very touristy. This of course means that rates are on the high side but, happily, the Villa Schuler is affordable. The villa was converted from a private residence to a hotel by the Schuler family over a century ago and now grandson, Gerardo is at the helm. The pink facade faces out to the Villa Roma and has a large raised terrace with palms and potted flowers. A continental or full breakfast is served either here or in the gazebo where you can enjoy views encompassing the coastline and the peak of the Etna volcano. The hotel offers standard bedrooms and junior suites. All the rooms have air conditioning, satellite TVs, safes, and terraces or balcony often with a sea views.Behind the building is the hotel's botanical garden filled with a profusion of jasmine, bougainvillea, and geraniums. Located in the garden is a secluded two bathroom suite. The garden opens onto the pedestrian main street of town and it is just a short walk to the cable car that takes you down to the beaches, or you can take the hotel shuttle services. For its impeccable service, ideal location and good value, the Villa Schuler is a real winner. *Directions:* Exit at Taormina from the A18 and follow uphill for center and at Piazza Sant'Antonio (post office) follow signs for hotel. They lead you back around and down the one-way Via Roma. Hotel is on left side.

VILLA SCHULER
Host: Gerardo Schuler family
Via Roma 2, Taormina, Sicily, (ME) 98039, Italy
Tel: (0942) 23481, Fax: (0942) 23522
27 Rooms, Double: €107–€190
6 Suites: €152–€250
Minimum Stay Required: 3 nights
Open: Mar to Nov, Credit cards: all major
Other Languages: English, German, French, Spanish
Region: Sicily, Michelin Map: 565

Villa Taormina is exactly the accommodation we searched high and low for in the popular seaside resort town of Taormina. With all the characteristics of an upscale bed and breakfast, its many amenities warrant a four-star-plus rating. Set on a quiet residential street off the main pedestrian-only street in town, the stately white turn-of-the-century residence holds eight very spacious and comfortable guestrooms, two panoramic terraces, several sitting rooms and above all, that marvelous sense of being a pampered guest in a private family home. A cozy reception area adjoins the sitting room and main stairway which leads up to the rooms and suites. All are elegantly appointed with antique pieces, rich fabrics, chandeliers, gilded mirrors and marble floors. A highlight of the stay is the complete buffet breakfast served on the rooftop terrace with stunning sea and Etna volcano views. The home is surrounded by a lush garden with a swimming pool. Besides providing information on local happenings, gracious hostess Signora Rosalie offers extra services such as a shuttle to the beach at Mazzaro, where the hotel has a special area for guests, international newspapers, Internet access, airport transfers and laundry service. *Directions:* 60 km from the Catania airport, exit the A18 highway for Taormina center and take the Monte Tauro tunnel towards Porta Catania. Turn left under the arches and then right on Via Fazzello.

VILLA TAORMINA
Host: Rosalie Gerber
Via Tommaso Fazzello
39, Taormina, (ME) 98039, Italy
Tel: (0942) 620072, Fax: (0942) 623003
8 Rooms, Double: €180–€350
Closed: Nov to Mar, Credit cards: none
Region: Sicily, Michelin Map: 565

The beauty of the Julian Alps is amazing and Prati Oitzinger (named after a local famous mountain climber) is a perfect location to capture glorious views. However, not only its breathtaking setting makes this bed and breakfast so special—it radiates old-fashioned hospitality, country charm, appealing décor, and quality throughout. The property has been in the same family since 1943. It was a farm for 50 years, and then a restaurant was opened. In 2001 the house was totally renovated and four tastefully appointed guestrooms were added, each with a modern bathroom. Marisa Piussi, granddaughter of the original owner, oversees the hotel operation. Her mother Renata is in charge of the kitchen and prepares delicious home-cooked meals. Her father Luciano is passionate about horses and breeds beautiful golden Haflingers that frolic in the nearby meadows. He also has a colorful carriage and, on special occasions, dons his traditional garb and takes guests for a jaunt. Marisa's sister Francesca also loves horses and accompanies guests who wish to ride. If you want a real treat, ask for bedroom 4. In the morning when you awaken, open the curtains and look out your window. The view is one you will always remember—a meadow flowing out to gigantic mountain peaks that seem so close you could almost reach out and touch them. *Directions:* In the countryside outside of town. Ask for detailed directions.

PRATI OITZINGER
Host: Marisa Piussi
Val Saisera, Tarvisio, (UD) 33018, Italy
Tel: (0428) 60224, Fax: (0428) 660449
Cellphone: (333) 2335339
4 Rooms, Double: €75–€85
Closed: May & Nov, Credit cards: none
Other Languages: some English
Region: Friuli-Venezia Giulia, Michelin Map: 562

Halfway between Florence and Siena in the heart of the Chianti region is the Sovigliano farm, restored by a gracious couple from Verona, Claudio Bicego and his wife, Patrizia, and daughter, Claudia. Guests have an independent entrance to the four bedrooms with kitchenette, each very much in keeping with the pure simplicity of this typical farmhouse. Exposed-beam ceilings and worn terracotta floors, antique beds and armoires, and bucolic views make time stand still here. Besides three apartments (two with air conditioning) in a separate farmhouse, there is also a spacious two-bedroom apartment within the house with kitchen and dining area and fireplace. At guests' disposal are a living room, kitchen with country fireplace, TV, large surrounding garden with swimming pool and hydro-jet, exercise trail, and outdoor eating area overlooking the characteristic hills of Chianti. Signor Bicego is actively involved in the production of top Tuscan wines in conjunction with several other wine estates, and also coordinates with other area residents to organize lessons in language, history, and culinary arts with local professors. *Directions:* From Siena, exit the superstrada at San Donato in Poggio; from Florence at Tavarnelle Val di Pesa. Drive through the village of Tavarnelle following the directions to Certaldo-Marcialla. At the end of Tavarnelle, at the fourth traffic circle, veer to the left (blue sign says Magliano), following signs for Sovigliano.

SOVIGLIANO
Hosts: Patrizia & Claudio Bicego
Via Magliano 9
Tavarnelle Val di Pesa, (FI) 50028, Italy
Tel: (055) 8076217, Fax: (055) 8050770
4 Rooms, Double: €130–€190
4 Apartments: €870–€1520 weekly
Minimum Stay Required: 3 nights
Closed: Jan 15 to 31, Credit cards: MC, VS
Other Languages: good English
Region: Tuscany, Michelin Map: 563

With their hearts set on running a bed and breakfast in the Liguria region, the Giani family searched hard and long before finding Giandriale. Set high up in the remote mountains above the coast, the 18th-century stone farmhouse is surrounded by a low range of mountains covered with thick woods as far as the eye can see. Utter silence prevails. There are just two guestrooms within their home and five others plus two apartments in the refurbished stone barn next door, simply decorated with country-style wooden furniture. Guests can relax in one of two comfortable living rooms. Meals are enjoyed in the downstairs dining room with its old-fashioned country stove, which is used occasionally in winter for making polenta. Lucia prepares coffee cakes and jams for breakfast and uses mostly regional recipes in her cooking, taking advantage of their own organic produce. Classic sightseeing destinations in the area include the Riviera (Portofino, Santa Margherita, Chiavari) and the Cinque Terre, 45 minutes away. Nereo can also suggest several interesting off-the-beaten-track itineraries beyond Giandriale. Hiking trails and mountain bikes are available. *Directions:* From autostrada A14, exit at Sestri Levante and follow signs for Casarza Ligure, Castiglione, then, after 2 km and many curves, Missano. After a long tunnel turn right for Tavarone; just before town follow B&B signs for 2.5 km.

GIANDRIALE
Hosts: Lucia Marelli & Nereo Giani
Localita: Giandriale
Tavarone di Maissana, (SP) 19010, Italy
Tel: (0187) 840279, Fax: (0187) 840156
Cellphone: (339) 5324177
7 Rooms, Double: €60–€80
2 Apartments: €40–€60 daily per person
Open: all year, Credit cards: all major
Other Languages: some English
Region: Liguria, Michelin Map: 561

In order to stand out among the crowd of recently opened bed and breakfasts in Italy, many hosts have begun to specialize according to their own personal interests. This is true for enthusiastic and friendly hosts, Alberto and his Brazilian wife Luzia, who opened a gourmet vegetarian bed and breakfast on their isolated 27-acre farm up on a mountain ridge between Perugia and Lake Trasimeno, the first of its kind in Umbria. A 4-kilometer gravel road ends at the panoramic property with its main house, two stone guesthouses, and cultural center where courses on yoga and meditation and ethnic music concerts are held. An informal ambiance prevails and the total respect for nature and tranquility is evident among guests who take hikes in the surrounding woods or read poolside, enjoying both sunrise and sunset over the opposite valleys. The ten neat rooms with independent outside entrances are comfortably decorated with teakwood beds and armoires and the paintings of a reputed artist. The sun-filled dining room is where guests convene for Luzia's and Alberto's famed fare based on strictly organic produce from the farm. So unique is this bed and breakfast that the BBC did a documentary on it, and it has been acclaimed one of the ten best vegetarian destinations in a US magazine. *Directions:* From Perugia follow route 220 for approximately 22 km and turn right before Tavernelle at Colle San Paolo.

COUNTRY HOUSE MONTALI
Hosts: Luzia & Alberto Musacchio
Via Montali 23
Tavernelle di Panicale, (PG) 06068, Italy
Tel: (075) 8350680, Fax: (075) 8350144
10 Rooms, Double: €180–€220*
*Includes breakfast & dinner
Minimum Stay Required: 3 nights
Open: Mar to Oct, Credit cards: MC, VS
Other Languages: good English
Region: Umbria, Michelin Map: 563

The Cinque Terre coastline of southern Liguria bordering Tuscany has earned notable popularity in the past years. Its five quaint stone villages hugging the hillside as it sweeps down to the sea were, until recently, accessible only by boat or by foot and are a delight to explore. Just 40 minutes south of the area right on the Poets Gulf is the adorable seaside town of Tellaro hugging the rock over the sea, where visitors make a point of stopping to have a memorable meal at the Miranda restaurant. Husband-and-wife team Giovanna and Angelo have their own inimitable and ever-varying style of cooking based exclusively on fresh seafood (no meat), which is present in the inexhaustible series of antipasti and pasta plates. Angelo has received plenty of press and praise for these extraordinary dishes. Meals are served in one of the newly renovated dining rooms, pleasantly appointed with scattered antiques. In the same vein are the bedrooms, most with gulf views. Aunt Miranda used to rent them out in the Sixties, and they are now in the capable hands of son, Alessandro. Guests have a cozy living room with fireplace for relaxing. This is an exclusive "residents only" area. If questioned by the local police, declare that you are guest of the Locanda Miranda. Reserve well in advance. *Directions:* Leave the A12 autostrada at Sarzana, following signs for Lerici on route 331. Tellaro is 2.5 km down the coast and the Miranda is on the main road before town.

LOCANDA MIRANDA
Hosts: Angelo & Giovanna Cabani
Via Fiascherino 92, Tellaro, (SP) 19030, Italy
Tel: (0187) 968130 or (0187) 964012
Fax: (0187) 964032, Cellphone: (333) 7073730
7 Rooms, Double: €120
Per person half board: €90
Closed: Jan, Credit cards: all major
Other Languages: fluent English, French
Region: Liguria, Michelin Map: 561

The remote L'Agnata property is truly unique and mystic. After leaving the main road, you follow a seemingly endless country road dense with cork trees and their curious shaved trunks. Never fear—you are delightfully rewarded at last when you come into the world of silence at L'Agnata. You leave your car parked at the entrance near a lake down a ravine and walk up the arbored path to the main 100-year-old ivy-covered house. Host Piero greets guests at the reception house and shows them to their rooms either upstairs in the main stone house where the owners, the De Andre family, reside during the summer months or in the guesthouse at the back across an expansive green lawn. An inviting swimming pool sits at the side of the house and looks perfectly natural with its surrounding large rocks sitting up straight like sculptures. Rooms are well appointed with antiques and warm colors in the rich fabrics and walls. The manicured lawn spreads around both houses and represents the taming of nature while the rest of the 400-acre property is immersed in the more wild and rugged mountain landscapes so typical of Sardinia. In the corner of the magical garden is a little waterfall creating soothing sounds which break the silence. Excellent dishes of this area called Gallura are served in the muraled dining room. *Directions:* From Tempio, follow the S.S.392 towards Oschiri. After 4.5 km turn right for S. Bachisio and take the unpaved road all the way to the end.

L' AGNATA
Host: Ugo Pedrazzini
Localita: L'Agnata
Tempio Pausania, (SS) 07029, Italy
Tel: (079) 671384, Fax: (079) 634125
10 Rooms, Double: €110–€130*
Minimum Stay Required: 3 nights in Aug
*Includes breakfast & dinner
Closed: Nov, Credit cards: all major
Other Languages: some English
Region: Sardinia, Michelin Map: 566

Country tourism has flourished in the last decade, especially in the highly popular region of Tuscany. However, most travelers still flock to the Chianti area, leaving many other parts of Tuscany wide open to discovery. Such is the gorgeous virgin territory of the Valdera Valley between stunning Volterra with its Etruscan origins and Pisa where everything has remained remarkably unspoiled. Affable host Sandro and his family bought a 100-acre farm property here and are restoring the ancient farmhouses piece by piece with guests' comfort foremost in mind. So far, eight neat apartments with one or two bedrooms and five guest bedrooms have been completed within three adjacent stone houses and are tastefully appointed with local antiques. Within one of the houses is the pleasant dining room with large arched windows where breakfast and dinners upon request are served, all prepared by Sandro's mother, who also conducts cooking lessons. Olive oil, wine, fruits, and vegetables all come directly from the farm. There is a beautiful borderless swimming pool and Sandro supplies guests with mountain bikes and a long list of interesting local itineraries. Easy day trips include Florence, Siena, San Gimignano, Lucca, Pisa and Volterra, famous for its alabaster artisans. *Directions:* Il Selvino is located off the main road 439 from Volterra (20 km) between Terricciola and La Sterza at Pieve a Pitti (marked on most maps).

IL SELVINO
Host: Alessandro Sgherri family
Localita: La Sterza, Via Pieve a Pitti 1
Terricciola, (PI) 56030, Italy
Tel: (0587) 670132, Fax: (0587) 670817
Cellphone: (338) 6209229
7 Rooms, Double: €100–€120
8 Apartments: €150–€200 daily
Open: all year, Credit cards: MC, VS
Other Languages: some English
Region: Tuscany, Michelin Map: 563

Since 1830, the remote 12th-century castle and 4,000-acre farm of Titignano have belonged to the noble Corsini family who now offer travelers 15 guestrooms in the main house, a swimming pool, and three apartments in what was originally the farmer's quarters. They are pleasantly decorated with scattered country antiques. Management is in the hands of Monica and Francesca, delightful hostesses who take care of everything from looking after guests to cooking and serving. Meals are shared at a long table in one of the castle's graciously neglected rooms with an enormous gray-stone fireplace sporting the family coat of arms, and lofty ceilings made of the stamped terra-cotta blocks typical of Umbria. Off the dining hall are the spacious bedrooms, each with modernized pink travertine bathrooms and decorated eclectically with unrefined antiques and wrought-iron beds. They have a worn charm about them. Common areas include a living room with bright floral sofas around a fireplace, a game and TV room for children, and a large terrace with a breathtaking, sweeping view covering three regions. Bikes are available for touring the regional park of the River Tiber (part of the property). *Directions:* Leave the Roma-Florence A1 autostrada at Orvieto. Follow signs for Arezzo, turning on route 79 for Prodo. Follow the long winding road for 26 km past Prodo to Titignano. (30 km from Orvieto.)

FATTORIA TITIGNANO
Hosts: Monica Gori & Francesca Marchetti
Localita: Titignano 7
Titignano, (TR) 05010, Italy
Tel: (0763) 308000 or (0763) 308022
Fax: (0763) 308002
15 Rooms, Double: €90
Open: all year, Credit cards: MC, VS
Other Languages: some English, French
Region: Umbria, Michelin Map: 563

Fortunate guests at the fascinating Tenuta di Canonica are assured of an unforgettable stay. Maria and Daniele, with son Michelangelo, have transformed a massive stone tower with foundation dating to the ancient Roman period and adjoining century-old house into a bed and breakfast of dreams. The spacious living room with stone fireplace and vaulted ceiling is reached down a few stairs from the entryway and looks out over the stunning valley down to Lake Corbara. Outstanding medieval architectural features such as stone walls, brick floors, and high, beamed ceilings have been enhanced by Provence-inspired colors. Stairs lead up to the library and bedrooms are divided between the three-story tower and house, respecting the epoch of each: bathrooms in the medieval quarters have gray stone tiles and travertine, while the others have white tile alternating with terracotta pieces. Each tastefully decorated, antique-filled room has some attractive feature, whether it be the more suite-like arrangements with sitting area or the smaller corner rooms with head-spinning views over hills and up to Todi. Common areas include a dining room and large swimming pool with 360-degree views. Cooking classes can also arranged. *Directions:* From Todi take the road for Orvieto, turning right at the sign for Prado/Titignano. After 2 km turn left for Cordigliano and follow the signpost for Tenuta di Canonica to the end of the road (1 km).

TENUTA DI CANONICA
Hosts: Maria & Daniele Fano
Localita: Canonica, Todi, (PG) 06059, Italy
Tel: (075) 8947545, Fax: (075) 8947581
8 Rooms, Double: €150–€185
3 Suites: €195–€235
2 Apartments: €950 weekly
Closed: Dec 1 to Mar 1, Credit cards: MC, VS
Other Languages: good English
Region: Umbria, Michelin Map: 563

Umbria's most international acclaimed wines are without doubt those of Lungarotti, whose 600 acres of vineyards produce a long list of both reds and whites, grappa, and olive oil. Besides a 5 star hotel, the Tre Vaselle, and a wine museum, the family has now branched out to offer accommodation on the farm in the center of their vineyards. At a short distance from Torgiano, the Lungarotti center, the typical elongated stone farmhouse dating to the 1700's has been converted into ten refined country apartments with swimming pool. A separate house at the entrance contains a reception area and breakfast room. Breakfast is served on the terrace overlooking the vines in warmer weather. Your friendly and accommodating hostess (very little English spoken), Gabriella, lives on the property and assists guests. The apartments can sleep from two to six and have living rooms with kitchenette corners, basic white tiled bathrooms and outdoor garden space. A clean country look is achieved with striped cushions on wicker or wrought iron furniture, an occasional antique, painted accents on white walls and Deruta hand-painted hanging plates. For larger groups or families consider renting I Pometo a rustic farmhouse with four bedrooms and a pool. *Directions:* Exit the S.S.3 highway Perugia-Todi at Torgiano. Go past town towards Brufa. After 1.5 km turn left onto the estate.

POGGIO ALLE VIGNE
Host: Chara Lungarotti
Via del Colle, 46, Localita: Montespinello
Torgiano, (PG), Italy
Tel: (075) 982994, Fax: (075) 9887014
10 Apartments: €470–€840 weekly
Open: all year, Credit cards: all major
Other Languages: very little English
Region: Umbria, Michelin Map: 563

This bed and breakfast is right in Torre di Palme, a charming village perched on a flat hilltop overlooking the Adriatic sea and dating back to 1088. You leave your car and walk through the arch of the fortress town with its one main street reaching down to a balcony over the sea. Here Patrizia and Ettore welcome you right into their small home where two upstairs bedrooms are reserved for guests, each with ensuite bathroom. An additional two bedrooms are in the house just across the courtyard. Guests at made to feel at home in the informal and friendly ambiance. Breakfast is served around the family dining room table in the main living room with fireplace, or out in the courtyard. The cozy guestrooms have mansard ceilings, lots of personal items with family photos and one has a wrought-iron bed. The other two rooms, (one with kitchen facilities) have independent entrances and are a bit larger in size. Downstairs, with its own entrance, is the couple's newly opened restaurant serving Ettore's specialties in an intimate stone-walled space with vaulted ceilings, or out on the terrace in summer months. It is certainly a special experience being a , if only temporary, in a medieval village and Patrizia and Ettore's warm welcome make it even more so. Ascoli Piceno, Fermo, Loreto, Monte Conero are all within easy driving distances. *Directions:* From the A14 Autostrada, exit at Porto San Giorgio and follow the signs for Torre di Palme 2 km, in view on the hilltop.

TORRE DI PALME
Host: Patrizia Corradetti
Via Nazario Sauro 2
Torre di Palme, (AP) 63010, Italy
Tel: (0734) 53883
Cellphone: (329) 0589528
4 Rooms, Double: €80
Open: all year, Credit cards: none
Region: Marches, Michelin Map: 563

Returning to his native Italy after running a resort in Mexico, Matteo continues using his expertise in anticipating guest's needs in this latest endeavor at the Lupaia. Finishing touches have been made after a thorough restoration project of the family's vast Tuscan property overlooking the ancient hilltown of Montepulciano. With two stone farmhouses with beamed ceilings and brick floors as a base, and Matteo's mother's flair for details in decorating, each guest room has been given its own distinct character. Bold colors range from celestial blues, chartreuse greens, solar yellows and rusty reds mixed with hot oranges and are found in every single object or piece of furniture cleverly restored by hand. All seven rooms, most with fireplaces, are accessed independently from the outside, each with a terrace or garden. Features such as extra space, extraordinary views, loft beds, kitchen corners and spacious showers are divided among the rooms. Breakfast is served in the garden or in the large dining room with a fireplace. A lovely bi-level pool for simply lounging and taking in the breathtaking scenery has been specially designed to hug the hillside. Cooking classes and wine and cheese tastings are arranged, as well as sumptuous Tuscan fare. With all these marvelous ingredients, you simply cannot go wrong. *Directions:* Exit A1 autostrada at Val di Chiana; pass Torrita; take the turn for Montefollonico. After 2 km turn left; travel 3.5 km to the house.

HOTELITO LUPAIA   **New**
Host: Matteo Murzilli
Località: Lupaia 74
Torrita di Siena, (SI) 53049, Italy
Tel & Fax: (0577) 668028
4 Rooms, Double: €240–€290
2 Suites: €360
Open: all year, Credit cards: all major
Other Languages: English, French
Region: Tuscany, Michelin Map: 563

Just off the busy road that connects the major towns of Umbria—Perugia, Assisi, Spoleto, and Todi—is the elegant country house Giulia, which has been in the Petrucci family since its 14th-century origins. Later additions were built on to the main stone villa, one of which Signora Caterina has opened up to guests. Time seems to have stood still in the six bedrooms, all but one with en suite bathroom, and filled with lovely antique wrought-iron beds, armoires, and period paintings. They are divided among two floors, accessed by a steep stone staircase, the largest having a ceiling fresco depicting the local landscape. Another room with handicapped facilities has been added on the ground floor. Breakfast is served either in the chandeliered dining room upstairs, with Oriental carpets, lace curtains, and a large fireplace, or under the oak trees in the front garden during the warmer months. Part of the barn has been converted into two independent units for up to four persons, including a fully equipped kitchenette. Although the large swimming pool overlooks a rather barren field and the distant main road, it is a welcome respite after a full day of touring, which guests do a lot of from this strategically convenient location. *Directions:* Just off the Perugia-Spoleto route 75 between Trevi and Campello.

CASA GIULIA
Host: Caterina Alessandrini Petrucci
Via Corciano, 1, Trevi, (PG) 06039, Italy
Tel: (0742) 78257, Fax: (0742) 381632
Cellphone: (340) 5186569
6 Rooms, Double: €88–€108
1 Suite: €135–€191
3 Apartments: €52–€108 daily, €420–€860 weekly
Open: all year, Credit cards: all major
Other Languages: some English, French
Region: Umbria, Michelin Map: 563

On the northern shores of Lake Bracciano, 45 kilometers from Rome, is the small town of Trevignano where ex-producer and music director Gianni's home is located a short drive up from town, taking advantage of the high viewpoint over the lake and surrounding countryside. The simpatico host's true passion is cooking and entertaining, and guests are rewarded each day with a superbly prepared full meal based on traditional recipes whose ingredients come from his own organic vegetable garden and accompanied by select wines. Gianni also shares his vast knowledge of Italian cuisine by organizing lessons in his well-equipped kitchen. The six bedrooms on the upper three floors vary in size, from the smaller children's rooms to the master bedroom with hydro-jet tub, air conditioning, TV, stereo, fireplace and terrace with lovely lake views. True coziness and comfort is dedicated to the common areas, which include living rooms with fireplace and grand piano, veranda dining room, garden, and swimming pool. There is also one small apartment for weekly stays with double bedroom and living area with kitchenette for two to four persons. Enjoy the area's historical villages and Viterbo's thermal spas. *Directions:* From Rome's ring highway GRA, take exit 5 for S.S.2 Cassia bis to km 35,100. Leave at the Trevignano exit and drive 11.3 km to Trevignano. Continue through town to km 12.500 and turn right on Via Olivetello before the IP gas station.

CASA PLAZZI
Host: Gianni Plazzi family
Via Olivetello 23, Trevignano
Romano, (RM) 0069, Italy
Tel & Fax: (06) 9997597
Cellphone: (335) 6756290
6 Rooms, Double: €80–€100, 1 Suite: €135
1 Apartment: €500–€600 weekly
Open: all year, Credit cards: none
Other Languages: some English
Region: Lazio, Michelin Map: 563

The Veneto region has so much to offer travelers in art, history, and culture, yet remains terribly weak when it comes to charming bed and breakfasts. This is mainly due to the very strict regulations particular to this region. The Ca'Masieri is a pleasant combination of both hotel and bed and breakfast style accommodation in a country setting. The countryside property has been in the Zarantonello family for three generations and was transformed into a restaurant and inn after Signor Giovanni looked for a creative way to maintain the farm. He and his partner, Angelo, opened the restaurant first, creating an intimate ambiance within three stenciled dining rooms in the main villa. The restaurant gained considerable recognition and the next logical step was to offer a place to stay in the stone farmhouse right next door. These two buildings and the attached barn form a quadrangle, with a gated-in terraced swimming pool. The seven bedrooms are very comfortable with many amenities, though their modern decor contrasts with the country setting. The five new suites in the adjoining wing (former stables) are more in keeping with the general ambiance of the place. Signor Giovanni is also on Vicenza's tourism board and can suggest many itineraries in the area (villas of Palladio etc.). *Directions:* Exit from autostrada A4 at Montecchio and go towards Valdagno. After exactly 10 km enter the town of Trissino and follow signs for Masieri up to the Ca'Masieri.

CA'MASIERI
Hosts: Giovanni Zarantonello & Angelo Vassena
Localita: Masieri, Trissino, (VI) 36070, Italy
Tel: (0445) 490122, Fax: (0445) 490455
12 Rooms, Double: €110–€140
Open: all year, Credit cards: all major
Other Languages: good English
Region: Veneto, Michelin Map: 562

When the Marti family from Rome came across the abandoned castle of Montegualandro 20 years ago, it was love at first sight—only pure passion could have driven them to tackle such an overwhelming project as the entire restoration of the property following original plans. A winding dirt road (1.5 kilometers) leads up to the gates of the walled 9th-century castle. As you enter into the courtyard, the main building and family residence lies to the left and immediately to the right is a cluster of stone dwellings, originally farmers' quarters, with small tower, stable, pottery kiln, dove house, and private chapel. There are four rustic guest apartments, cleverly incorporating all original architectural features. All different, each has a living area with fireplace, very basic kitchen facilities, and bathroom, and is furnished with country-style antiques. A walk up in the turreted walls gives a glimpse of the spectacular view out over olive groves to the lake. An internet point has been set up in the newly restored library. The Martis take special interest in guests' needs, providing a breakfast basket upon arrival, and can also suggest easy day trips. Cortona is just 10 kilometers away. *Directions:* Montegualandro is marked on most maps. Leave the A1-Perugia highway at Tuoro. Take the road 75 bis towards Cortona and Arezzo. After 3 km, at km sign 44,700, follow the signs up to the castle or call from town.

CASTELLO DI MONTEGUALANDRO
Hosts: Franca & Claudio Marti
Loc. Montegualandro 1
Tuoro Sul Trasimeno, (PG) 06069, Italy
Tel & Fax: (075) 8230267
4 Apartments: €700–€800
Minimum Stay Required: 3 nights
Open: all year, Credit cards: none
Other Languages: good English
Region: Umbria, Michelin Map: 563

The area of Lazio north of Rome known as "Tuscia" is rich in Etruscan history, small medieval villages, nature reserves, and three picturesque lakes. It is the homeland of the illustrious and powerful Farnese family whose palazzos and fortresses still stand as monuments of their glorious past. In the heart of this fascinating area not far from the coast is the ancient walled town of Tuscania, completely restored after the dramatic earthquake in 1978. Perla and her Argentine husband José brought back to life one of the buildings right in town, opening its doors as a cozy bed and breakfast and Michelin-star restaurant. A small reception area leads on one side to a lounge and wine bar (over 200 labels) and a courtyard. On the other side you find the cheerful, luminous restaurant with checked drapes and tablecloths, antique armoire, still-life paintings, large windows looking out over the tiled rooftops, and ubiquitous gallo (rooster) motif. Here José works his magic, serving innovative creations using seasonal local produce. (A 10% discount is given to our readers on meals.) Upstairs each very comfortable and appealing carpeted bedroom has its own color scheme in matching floral wallpaper, drapery, and bedspread. They have all amenities including air conditioning and are spacious, with high ceilings and marble bathrooms. Gracious hostess Perla guarantees guests' comfort and assists them in arranging local itineraries. *Directions:* In the center of Tuscania, well marked.

HOTEL AL GALLO
Hosts: Perla Blanzieri & José Pettiti
Via del Gallo 22, Tuscania, (VT) 01017, Italy
Tel: (0761) 443388, Fax: (0761) 443628
Cellphone: (347) 4444293
13 Rooms, Double: €78–€98
Restaurant closed Mon
Open: all year, Credit cards: all major
Other Languages: good English
Region: Lazio, Michelin Map: 563

The Aiola opened its doors to guests several years ago when the Campellis restored the farmers' houses on the wine estate's vast property in Chianti. The family's villa with its ancient origins sits across the street from the guest quarters, almost completely hidden by enormous oak and cypress trees, where the bedrooms, one of which sleeps four persons, all have separate outside entrances. Original architectural features have been preserved and rooms are decorated with wrought-iron beds and antique or reproduction armoires. The vineyards come right up to the house and a wide, open view of the hills is offered to the other side. The barn next door includes common areas such as the breakfast room, where Federica's fresh-baked coffee cakes are served, and a living room. Part of the founding members of the Wine Tourism Association, visits to the cellar and the villa, and wine tasting begin right here at the Aiola. Federica and Enrico aim to make each guest feel special, dedicating much time to suggesting itineraries with maps and making reservations at restaurants, museums, and local concerts. At 12 kilometers from Siena and an easy distance from the highlights of the region, the Aiola serves as an excellent touring base. Total silence reigns here, with only the buzz of cicadas breaking it. *Directions:* From Siena follow route 222, then 102 just past Vagliagli—the Aiola property (well marked) is on this same road.

CASALI DELLA AIOLA
Hosts: Federica & Enrico Campelli
Vagliagli, (SI) 53019, Italy
Tel: (0577) 322797, Fax: (0577) 322509
Cellphone: (335) 7056236
7 Rooms, Double: €95
1 Suite: €120–€140
Open: all year, Credit cards: all major
Other Languages: good English
Region: Tuscany, Michelin Map: 563

It is a pleasure to be able to include such a perfectly efficient, family-run hotel as the Due Fanali, located in a lovely square next to the 12th-century San Simeon church with its original Tintoretto painting. The hotel is housed in a 12th-century palazzo, once part of the church complex. The Feron family had the building restored many years ago to include the sixteen bedrooms (some with smaller "French" double beds) on the top three floors. A small elevator has been added for the convenience of guests. Simply appointed but pleasant guestrooms with occasional antique is the theme throughout including reception area and breakfast room. The quiet ambiance is that of a warm home, accentuated by Oriental carpets and rich-cream draperies. A seating area is set up just outside the front door, however breakfast is taken up in the delightful third-floor veranda, under the open terrace, with its superb view over the square to the Grand Canal. As an alternative to the hotel, there are four independent apartments near San Marco Square, well-decorated and including bedroom, living room with view, kitchenette, and bathroom with hydro-massage tub. A little off the beaten track but with easy reach to vaporetto water bus stop. Hostess Stefania is ever-present for guests, if not across the way in her newly opened deluxe hotel, Ca'Nigra. *Directions:* The hotel is a five-minute walk from the train station or you can take the No. 1 waterbus to the Riva di Biasio stop.

HOTEL AI DUE FANALI
Host: Stefania Stea
Santa Croce 946, Venice, (VE) 30135, Italy
Tel: (041) 718490, Fax: (041) 2448721
16 Rooms, Double: €97–€230
4 Apartments: €200-€388 daily, €2240 weekly
Open: all year, Credit cards: all major
Other Languages: good English
Region: Veneto, Michelin Map: 562

Giuliano Dall'Agnola, managed a hotel in Venice before deciding to open his own. This historic 5th-century building needed total renovation, but it's location was perfect—tucked onto a tiny side street just steps from Piazza San Marco. Don't be put off by the unimpressive gray exterior. The minuscule entry hall is quite simple and a staircase leads to the upper floors (no elevator). But here the surprise awaits: the carpeted rooms, decorated by Marcella, are inviting and offer great quality for such a well-priced hotel in the heart of Venice. All the walls are covered in fabric and enhanced by color-coordinated draperies and bedspreads, while Venetian-style furnishings including painted headboards and Murano glass chandeliers complete the appealing ambiance. The amenities are surprising for a budget hotel. The soundproof rooms are air-conditioned, have direct-dial phones, mini-bars, televisions, and modern bathrooms. Rooms on the top floor have beamed ceilings and balconies, some with views overlooking a small square. Alternative accommodation has been added in three additional bedrooms within the owner's home and an apartment between St. Mark's Square and Ponte Rialto. What makes this intimate hotel so special is the care of its owners who treat guests like visiting friends. *Directions:* San Zaccaria vaporetto stop is on all vaporetto boat lines, including the Alilaguna boats from the airport. The hotel is just 50 meters from the stop.

LOCANDA AL LEON
Hosts: Marcella & Giuliano Dall'Agnola
Castello, Campo St Filippo e Giacomo
Venice, (VE) 30122, Italy
Tel: (041) 2770393, Fax: (041) 5210348
Cellphone: (347) 0766433
14 Rooms, Double: €90–€290, 1 Apartment €150–€300
Minimum Stay Required: 2 nights
Open: all year, Credit cards: MC, VS
Other Languages: good English
Region: Veneto, Michelin Map: 562

The newly renovated Locanda San Barnaba stands out among the many choices of three-star establishments in Venice. The first outstanding feature is its location in a quiet neighborhood just a half-block walk from the vaporetto stop Ca'Rezzonico on the opposite side of the Grand Canal from St. Mark's (not something to be overlooked when lugging baggage through narrow streets and over bridges in Venice!). The intimate hotel in its 16th-century context has the feeling of the private home that it once was—it belonged to the grandfather of hostess Silvia—with each of its 13 guestrooms retaining its individual character. The first floor upstairs boasts a large frescoed former ballroom with stained-glass windows, while nicely appointed air-conditioned bedrooms have antique furnishings, parquet floors and new bathrooms. The superior double rooms, at a slightly higher rate, have the added touch of a frescoed ceiling. A nice buffet breakfast is served in the beamed dining room or in the small walled-in courtyard garden just off the reception area, a rarity in Venice. There is also a rooftop solarium and private dock. Silvia and her amiable staff are always on hand to assist travelers with any needs. *Directions:* Take waterbus No. 1 to the Ca'Rezzonico stop. Directly in front is the Calle del Traghetto where the hotel is located on the left-hand side.

❄ ☕ 🛵 🏧 ☎ 🚭 ⚓ 🚶 ⛵

LOCANDA SAN BARNABA
Host: Silvia Okolicsanyi
Calle del Traghetto 2785-2786, Dorsoduro
Venice, (VE) 30124, Italy
Tel: (041) 2411233, Fax: (041) 2413812
13 Rooms, Double: €120–€220
Open: all year, Credit cards: all major
Other Languages: good English
Region: Veneto, Michelin Map: 562

With admirable determination and family pride, Alessandro and Debora took on the task of renovating and running this historic property, which has been part of the family for three generations. They deserve great credit since they are more concerned with providing warm hospitality and attention to guests' needs than with keeping up with Venice's inflated hotel rates. The spacious and luminous reception area with white travertine floors is a welcome oasis amid the city's more cramped hotels, bustling squares, and crowded narrow streets. Although only a three-minute walk from the Guggenheim collection and Accademia, it has the feeling of being away from the mainstream traffic. The front rooms have water views (higher rate) and all rooms maintain an original flavor with period paintings and personal family objects, parquet floors and matching wood furniture, blue-colored armchairs, new bathrooms, and air conditioning. Four bedrooms have private terraces for a higher rate and other guests enjoy the delightful rooftop terrace. A full buffet breakfast and bar service and meals at La Piscina are offered either in the breakfast room or out on the terrace where you can watch the boats going by. Reserve well in advance. Comfortable suites and apartments are also available in a residential quarter just across the bridge. *Directions:* Take the No. 51 waterbus to Zattere, then follow the quay to the right to the hotel terrace.

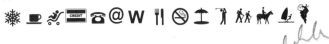

PENSIONE LA CALCINA
Hosts: Debora & Alessandro Szemere
Dorsoduro 780, Venice, (VE) 30123, Italy
Tel: (041) 5206466, Fax: (041) 5227045
27 Rooms, Double: €110–€250
5 Suites: €140–€240
4 Apartments: €161–€239 daily
Open: all year, Credit cards: all major
Other Languages: English, German, French
Region: Veneto, Michelin Map: 562

With just eleven rooms, including three junior suites, paired up throughout the six-floor building (luckily with an elevator), the intimate Santo Stefano was actually the watchtower to an ancient convent. The compact hotel, most recently a private home, is right in the middle of one of Venice's largest squares, leading to St. Mark's on one side and to the bridge for the Accademia on the other. Being close to the busy center, you can observe the Venetians going about their daily business. The hotel is owned by brothers Roberto and Marcello of the Hotel Celio in Rome, who have added fresh decorating touches to bedrooms and reception area. Just beyond is a miniature breakfast room, looking out to an ancient well, for days when the weather does not permit eating out in the front piazza. Touches of elegance in Venetian style follow through in rooms appointed with Barovier and Toso chandeliers, coordinated draperies and bedspreads, and painted antiques with a floral motif. Many amenities are offered including air conditioning. Renovation of all bathrooms included the installation of Jacuzzi and steam baths. Roberto is an experienced and amiable host with a definite aim to please guests. *Directions:* Take waterbus No. 82 to the San Samuele stop or No. 1 to the Accademia stop. Pass over the bridge and go straight into Campo Santo Stefano.

HOTEL SANTO STEFANO
Host: Roberto Quatrini
San Marco 2957, Venice, (VE) 30124, Italy
Tel: (041) 5200166, Fax: (041) 5224460
11 Rooms, Double: €190–€370
Open: all year, Credit cards: all major
Other Languages: good English
Region: Veneto, Michelin Map: 562

With guests' comfort fully in mind, Francesca Adilardi, a native of Rome, acquired and totally renovated a spacious apartment covering two floors of a centuries-old building in the fish market area just across the Rialto bridge. The six charming bedrooms are well distributed between the two floors. Four of them are off the main entrance and dining room where a full breakfast is served. Historic Venetian names have been assigned to individually styled rooms: Doge, Casanova, Turandot, Vivaldi, Goldoni, and Mondo Nuovo. They are all quite spacious and well lit with typical spotted marble or parquet floors, scattered antiques, and the finest of bed linens. Bedspreads come from around the world and give each room a particular personality. The two quaint mansard rooms with exposed beams and skylights have parquet flooring and are somewhat smaller in size. Francesca has obviously enjoyed designing the contemporary styled bathrooms as each is completely different from the next. In a quiet residential area but very close to the action at the market and more touristy area across the famous bridge, this is a top notch B&B. Don't let the gloomy entrance deter you, the main entrance is up a second flight of stairs. *Directions:* Take the vaporetto, or the water taxi to Rialto, Mercato and walk straight ahead passing the fish market. Go over the little bridge, a few meters after you arrive in Calle dei Botteri.

VILLEGGIATURA
Host: Francesca Adilardi
San Polo, Calle dei Botteri 1569
Venice, (VE) 30125, Italy
Tel & Fax: (041) 5244673
Cellphone: (338) 8531264
6 Rooms, Double: €110–€280
Closed: Aug 5 to 25, Credit cards: MC, VS
Other Languages: good English, French, Spanish
Region: Veneto, Michelin Map: 562

The island of Ponza, with its many hotels, expensive restaurants and shops, has traditionally been a favorite resort destination for Romans. By contrast Ventotene island remains today the simple fisherman's village that is always was, almost like a dated film set. The island has a rich history going back to prehistoric periods with archaeological traces (villas and aqueducts) found in civilizations such as the Etruscans, Greeks and Romans. Boats of all types arrive in the small port where colored houses, and outdoor cafés greet you. A steep zigzag ramp leads you up to the main town center. While its sister hotel Mezzatorre sits right on the square, the smaller and more simple Villa Giulia is right around the corner and enjoys a perched position above the sea. Opened as a guest house in 2004, the three-story pink-colored house dates back to the 1700s. Most of the rooms take advantage of the sea views out to Ischia island and the nearby uninhabited Santo Stefano island with its nature and marine reserve. Two loft bedrooms which sleep four persons are great for families. There is also a small breakfast room and sitting area on the ground floor. The owner's restaurant, L'Aragosta, directly down on the beach and set in the rocks, is the best on the island with grilled seafood served on beach front tables. Marvelous. *Directions:* Ferryboats (2 hour) or hydrofoils (50 minutes) depart from Formia to Ventotene.

VILLA GIULIA
Hosts: Renzo & Marisa Aiello
Piazza XX Settembre 2
Ventotene, (LT) 04020, Italy
Tel & Fax: (0771) 854038
Cellphone: (335) 8290099
16 Rooms, Double: €80–€240
Open: Apr to Oct, Credit cards: VS
Other Languages: good English
Region: Lazio, Michelin Map: 563

Just 20 kilometers from the Swiss border, halfway along the shore of Lake Maggiore, at the point where the road curves back down to Verbania, is a farmhouse situated high above the lake (700 meters). It commands a 360-degree view that includes the Alps and Lakes Mergozzo, Monate, Varese, and Maggiore with its miniature Borromeo Islands (accessible by ferryboat). A 5-kilometer long road with many hairpin turns winds its way up to the turn-of-the-last-century house with tower. Energetic and friendly hostess Iside Minotti and her family run the inn and rustic restaurant, which is a busy spot and can get noisy in the summer when locals come up to dine or celebrate an event and take advantage of the cooler air and the spectacular view. Menu ingredients come directly from the vegetable garden and orchards to the kitchen, where sumptuous local specialties are prepared. The 25-acre farm includes riding stables, and the bed and breakfast can also arrange helicopter rides from the property for a breathtakingly scenic tour over the lake, boat excursions, and mountain bike rentals. Nine very basic no-frills bedrooms come in various combinations of twins, triples, and quads, each with a snug shower room. *Directions:* On the outskirts of Verbania, at a major road junction with traffic lights (Pallanza), take Via Azari (also signposted Trobaso) left for 1 km. Go sharp left at the signpost for Monterosso and up 5 km of winding road (I counted 43 hairpin bends).

IL MONTEROSSO
Host: Iside Minotti
Cima Monterosso-C.P. 13, Verbania, (NO) 28922, Italy
Tel: (0323) 556510 or (339) 6985266
Fax: (0323) 519706, Cellphone: (335) 6442859
15 Rooms, Double: €70–€80
Apartments: €300–€700 weekly
Minimum Stay Required: 2 nights
Open: all year, Credit cards: MC, VS
Other Languages: some English, French
Region: Piedmont, Michelin Map: 561

Delightful Verona, with its Romeo and Juliet theme, is decidedly one of Italy's more romantic historic cities and the Domus Nova B&B well matches this magical aura. The distinguished 13th-century gray-white palazzo, renovated in the 16th century, fills one entire side of the ancient square where a statue honoring Dante stands. Guests pass through the enormous center archway, enter by a small side door, and take a little elevator to the top floor where three double bedrooms are found within two apartments. As with a private apartment, you use your own key to enter the attractive drawing room, off which two of the bedrooms are situated and where an elegant breakfast is served complete with silver service and porcelain china. The warm decor of these rooms, all looking out over the splendid square and distant hills through large windows, radiates charm and impeccable taste. Soft, muted tones and stenciled patterns on walls have been taken directly from themes found in the surrounding medieval and baroque buildings. The third room, a double twin, has a balcony looking onto the lively Piazza Erba and its daily market. The spacious rooms are appointed with antiques, Oriental carpets, and fine linens and have lovely marble bathrooms. All these exquisite touches combined with gracious hospitality offer guests an intimate and memorable stay. *Directions:* The Piazza dei Signori is next to Verona's main square, the Piazza Erba, in the heart of the city.

DOMUS NOVA B&B
Host: Giovanni Roberti
Piazza dei Signori 18, Verona, (VR) 37121, Italy
Tel: (045) 8015245, Fax: (045) 8043459
Cellphone: (380) 7071931
3 Rooms, Double: €215–€250
1 Suite: €270–€320
Minimum Stay Required: 2 nights
Open: all year, Credit cards: all major
Other Languages: good English
Region: Veneto, Michelin Map: 562

For years Andrea and Silvia have literally opened their entire home to guests, welcoming and re-welcoming guests to their bed and breakfast. International guests gather together in the evenings out on the patio or in the converted barn for one of Silvia's delightful meals based on fresh vegetables and meats enhanced with their own extra-virgin olive oil. Conversation is never lacking with meals accompanied by La Volpaia's own Chianti (all beverages are included in the half-board rate). Andrea, a native Roman architect and sculptor, bought the wine estate with its 16th-century farmhouse 19 years ago and his pieces in olive wood are displayed in and about the property. The five cozy bedrooms are appointed with antiques, as is the large living room with fireplace. Beyond the patio where meals are served is the spectacular swimming pool with its heavenly views of what can only be described as a truly classic Tuscan landscape. Guests are made to feel immediately right at home in this informal setting and so it is no wonder that many become "regulars" to this idyllic spot so close to the highlights of Tuscany. *Directions:* From the town of Vico d'Elsa follow Via della Villa (on the right) for 2 km, turning left at the wooden signpost for La Volpaia.

LA VOLPAIA
Hosts: Silvia & Andrea Taliaco
Strada di Vico 5-9, Vico d'Elsa, (FI) 50050, Italy
Tel: (055) 8073063, Fax: (055) 8073170
5 Rooms, Double: €100–€150*
Minimum Stay Required: 2 nights
*Includes breakfast, dinner & drinks
Open: all year, Credit cards: none
Other Languages: good English, French
Region: Tuscany, Michelin Map: 563

Villa Verucchio is a small commercial area just inland from the famous beaches of Rimini, the summer playground of young Italians attracted by its nightlife and budget rates. The Tenuta Amalia is a vast property owned by the Savazzi family, divided up into several different businesses, each run individually. Case Rosse is the red farmhouse transformed into a pleasant little bed and breakfast and there are also three different restaurants, vineyards, and a 27-hole golf course created around the family's 18th-century villa. Although it is a bit confusing at first, the bed and breakfast is right on the road leading to the golf club entrance. Partizia Riccardi welcomes guests to the rustic farmhouse, which offers four double bedrooms upstairs and two on the ground floor. Each is appointed individually with country antiques and yellow bedspreads. A separate three-bedroom house nearby offers accommodation for six persons. Breakfast is served either out on the covered porch or in the beamed breakfast room overlooking a small garden and there is a cozy living room with large stone fireplace. From here you have easy access to the beautiful countryside bordering the Marches with such highlights as the independent state of San Marino, San Leo, Santarcangelo and Urbino. *Directions:* From Rimini take the S.S.258 for 12 km to Villa Verucchio and watch for a sign on the right to the Amalia.

TENUTA AMALIA/AGRITURISMO LE CASE ROSSE
Host: Patrizia Riccardi
Via Tenuta Amalia 141
Villa Verucchio, (RN) 47826, Italy
Tel: (0541) 678123, Fax: (0541) 678876
Cellphone: (338) 9354654
7 Rooms, Double: €85
1 House: €190 daily, €1000 weekly
Minimum Stay Required: 2 nights
Open: all year, Credit cards: all major
Other Languages: very little English
Region: Emilia-Romagna, Michelin Map: 562

Ninni Bacchi has done wonders in transforming her family's 300-acre tobacco and grain farm (just on the outskirts of the city) into a very comfortable bed and breakfast in an area that was once the heart of the Etruscan civilization. The Rinaldone is run more like a hotel than a bed and breakfast—arriving guests are warmly received in the luminous, open living room furnished with antiques surrounding a grand fireplace. On hand for guests at reception is cordial manager Sida. Downstairs is the large, arcaded restaurant dating back to the 15th century, where guests can enjoy the typical cuisine of the Lazio region or dine outdoors by the pool. The five bedrooms off the courtyard in the main house have the most character with architectural features intact, while the other five rooms and ten suites are lined up in two cottage-like wings, and are more spacious and modern in decor. A nice job has been done with the landscaping, pleasingly distracting the eye from the rather bland, flat countryside and encroaching commercial area hereabouts. Tennis is available. Guests often visit the nearby thermal spa and visit Viterbo and the gardens of Villa Lanti. Orvieto is 38 km away. *Directions:* From Rome (120 km away) follow signs for Viterbo. Take the Cassia road north of Viterbo for 3 km toward Montefiascone, turning right at the Rinaldone sign.

COUNTRY HOTEL RINALDONE
Host: Ninni Bacchi
Strada Rinaldone, 9-S.S. Cassia km 86
Viterbo, (VT) 01100, Italy
Tel: (0761) 352137, Fax: (0761) 353116
Cellphone: (335) 7479221
20 Rooms, Double: €110–€135
Minimum Stay Required: 2 nights
Open: Apr to Dec, Credit cards: MC, VS
Other Languages: some English
Region: Lazio, Michelin Map: 563

The northern part of the Lazio region holds many intriguing treasures to explore. Besides being less than an hour from Rome, it is the center of Etruscan history, with lakes, nearby seaside, thermal baths, and lovely gardens. Just down the street from the delightful Renaissance gardens of Villa Lante in Bagnaia is the gracious Villa Farinella, a very pleasant bed and breakfast within the 18th-century home of Maurizio and his family. Rita, his mother, lives in a restored farmhouse on the property and has passed her grandfather's ancient home down to her son. In order to revive the home to its original splendor, the bed and breakfast solution was a perfect one. The first floor is entirely dedicated to guests, with four cozy bedrooms entering into one of two spacious living/dining rooms appointed with original antiques and elegant chandeliers. Each quaint bedroom with new bathroom has its own floral theme, which is followed through in color scheme, wallpaper, bedspreads, and curtains. One particularly large room has frescoed vaulted ceilings. On the ground floor, for longer stays, a two-bedroom apartment with kitchen opens out to the garden. You will be delighted with the warm hospitality, historic surroundings, and very reasonable rate. *Directions:* From Viterbo drive towards Bagnaia (directly east) on Viale Trieste to the suburb of La Quercia. Just after the AGIP station turn left on Via Capodistria past houses to the end of the lane.

VILLA FARINELLA
Hosts: Maurizio Makovec & family
Localita: La Quercia, Via Capodistria 14
Viterbo, (VT) 01100, Italy
Tel & Fax: (0761) 344253
Cellphone: (340) 0831848
4 Rooms, Double: €80–€90, 1 Suite: €90–€100
1 Apartment: €100 daily, €600 weekly
Open: all year, Credit cards: none
Other Languages: good English, French
Region: Lazio, Michelin Map: 563

Since agritourism properties are practically nonexistent right along Lake Garda, it is nice to find a variety of alternatives in the scenic countryside a short distance away from its southern tip. Luigi and Emilia thoroughly enjoy opening up their home for guests and actively participate in creating local itineraries and even accompanying guests to the many artistic, cultural, and natural sights of the area. Luigi has a passion for outdoor sports such as cycling and canoing down the Mincio river. The driveway leads to three colorful houses in a row overlooking the swimming pool and surrounding lawn to the front and the fields to the back. The farm produces excellent wine, cheese, honey, and salami. The 200-year-old farmhouse has been completely renovated and has six air-conditioned guestrooms (two are studio spaces with kitchenette) on the upper floors accessed by an iron staircase. They are very clean and new, with reproduction country furniture and some with beamed ceilings. Downstairs in the brick-vaulted dining room, a buffet breakfast is served as well as Emilia's homemade dinners. *Directions:* From the A22 autostrada exit at Mantova Nord and drive towards Brescia, turning off right on S.S.236 for Volta Mantovana. From the center of town there are signs leading to the Corte Onida just on the outskirts.

CORTE ONIDA
Hosts: Luigi & Emilia Crotti family
Loc. Lonida 3
Volta Mantovana, (MN) 46049, Italy
Tel & Fax: (0376) 838137
Cellphone: (348) 3900807
6 Rooms, Double: €56–€74
Apartments: €440–€690 weekly
Minimum Stay Required: 2 nights
Closed: Jan, Credit cards: none
Other Languages: good English
Region: Lombardy, Michelin Map: 561

Places to Stay by Region

Abruzzo
Loreto Aprutino, Magnolie, Le

Aosta Valley
Champoluc, Lo Miete Viei
Entrèves-Courmayeur, Grange, La
Introd, Lo Triolet
Pontboset, Moulin des Aravis, Le
Saint Pierre, Abri, L'
Saint Pierre, Ecureuils, Les

Apulia
Canosa di Puglia, Country House Cefalicchio
Conversano, Masseria Sacerdote
Fasano, Masseria Marzalossa
Galatone, Masseria Lo Prieno
Lecce, Palazzo Personé
Lucera, Elena degli Angeli
Maglie, Tenuta Le Pezzate
Monopoli, Masseria Curatori
Ostuni, Masseria Il Frantoio
Pezze di Greco, Masseria Salamina

Basilicata
Pisticci, San Teodoro Nuovo

Campania
Arola, Villa Giusso

Capri, Minerva, La
Capri, Villa Krupp
Capri, Villa Vuotto
Castellabate, Mola, La
Naples, Albergo Sansevero Degas
Naples, Convento, Hotel Il
Paestum, Seliano
Positano, Casa Cosenza
Positano, Fenice, La
Positano, Villa La Tartana
Positano, Villa Rosa
Pozzuoli, Villa Giulia
Ravello, Villa Maria

Emilia-Romagna
Bologna, Art Hotel Orologio
Brisighella, Palazzo, Il
Castelfranco Emilia, Villa Gaidello
Ferrara, Bagattino, Il
Ostellato, Villa Belfiore
Portico di Romagna, Albergo al Vecchio Convento
Ravenna, Diana, Hotel
Salsomaggiore Terme, Antica Torre
Villa Verucchio, Tenuta Amalia/Agriturismo Le Case Rosse

Friuli-Venezia Giulia
Tarvisio, Prati Oitzinger

Lazio

Amatrice, Villa Sanguigni
Antella–Florence, Villa Il Colle
Bagnoregio, Romantica Pucci, Hotel
Bolsena, Riserva Montebello, La
Casperia, Torretta, La
Coltodino, Santo Pietro
Grotte di Castro, Castello di S. Cristina
Lubriano, Settimo Cielo
Montasola, Montepiano
Orte, Chiocciola, La
Poggio Nativo, Paese delle Meraviglie
Ponza, Casa Giulia Ponza
Ponza, Villa Laetitia
Proceno, Castello di Proceno
Rome, Casa Stefazio
Rome, Due Torri, Hotel
Rome, Fontana, Hotel
Rome, Fontanella Borghese, Hotel
Rome, Locarno, Hotel
Rome, Modigliani, Hotel
Rome, Royal Court, Hotel
Rome, Santa Maria, Hotel
Rome, Villa del Parco, Hotel
Rome, Villa Delros
Rome, Villa Mangili
Rome, Arco de' Tolomei
Rome, Residenza Santa Maria
Selci Sabino, Villa Vallerosa
Soriano nel Cimino, Tenuta di Santa Lucia
Trevignano, Casa Plazzi
Tuscania, Al Gallo, Hotel
Ventotene, Villa Giulia

Viterbo, Country Hotel Rinaldone
Viterbo, Villa Farinella

Liguria

Imperia, Relais San Damian
Monéglia, Abbadia San Giorgio
Santa Margherita, Villa Gnocchi
Tavarone di Maissana, Giandriale
Tellaro, Locanda Miranda

Lombardy

Alzano Lombardo, Cascina Grumello
Besate, Cascina Caremma
Capriolo, Azienda Agricola Ricci Curbastro
Luino, Camin Hotel Colmegna
Mantova, Corte San Girolamo
Milan, Regina, Hotel
Porto Mantovano, Villa Schiarino Lena
San Fedele d'Intelvi, Villa Simplicitas
Scalvino, Ferdy
Solferino, Sorgive, Le
Volta Mantovana, Corte Onida

Marches

Arcevia, Tenuta San Settimio
Castelraimondo, Giardino degli Ulivi, Il
Fano, Relais Villa Giulia
Fermignano, Locanda della Valle Nuova
Fermo, Palazzo Romani Adami
Gagliole, Locanda San Rocco
Monte San Vito, Viadelcampo
Monterado, Castello di Monterado
Osimo, Commenda, La

Recanati, Palazzo dalla Casapiccola
Sirolo, Locanda Rocco
Sirolo, Relais Valcastagno
Torre di Palme, Torre di Palme

Piedmont
Alba, Cascina Reine (Villa La Meridiana)
Barbaresco, Cascina delle Rose
Barolo, Gioco dell'Oca, Il
Candelo, Tenuta La Mandria
Canelli, Luna e i Falo', La
Dogliani, Foresteria dei Poderi
Morra, La, Casa Bambin
Murazzano, Cascina Cichetti
Novi Ligure, Federica, La
Stazzano, Traversina, La
Verbania, Monterosso, Il

Sardinia
Alghero, Porticciolo
Cala di Volpe, Piccolo Golf, Il
Calangianus, Li Licci
Casagliana, Monti Tundu
Padru, Tonino Corda
San Pantaleo, Ca'La Somara
Tempio Pausania, Agnata, L'

Sicily
Buseto Palizzolo, Baglio Fontana
Camporeale, Masseria Pernice
Cassibile, Lady Lusya, Hotel
Fontanasalsa, Baglio Fontanasalsa
Gangi, Villa Raino

Misterbianco, Alcala
Modica, Casa Talìa
Modica, Orangerie, L'
Noto, Monteluce
Petrosino, Baglio Spano
Pettineo, Casa Migliaca
Piazza Armerina, Gigliotto
Santa Flavia, Villa Cefala
Santa Venerina, Tenuta San Michele
Scopello, Pensione Tranchina
Siracusa, Approdo delle Sirene, L'
Siracusa, Limoneto
Siracusa, Villa Dei Papiri
Taormina, Villa Taormina
Taormina, Villa Schuler

Trentino-Alto Adige
Barbian, Bad Dreikirchen
Castelrotto, Tschotscherhof
Ortisei, Digon, Hotel
Ortisei, Uhrerhof, Hotel
Siusi allo Sciliar, Aquila Nera (Schwarzer Adler)

Tuscany
Bagno Vignoni, Locanda del Loggiato, La
Bagnone, Villa Mimosa
Barberino Val d'Elsa, Fattoria Casa Sola
Barberino Val d'Elsa, Paretaio, Il
Bettolle, Locanda La Bandita
Bibbona, Podere Le Mezzelune
Borgo San Lorenzo, Monsignor della Casa
Bucine, Borgo Iesolana
Buonconvento, Ripolina, La

Caldana, Montebelli
Campagnatico, Villa Bellaria
Canonica a Cerreto, Canonica a Cerreto
Capalbio, Ghiaccio Bosco
Castelfiorentino, Boscarecce, Le
Castellina in Chianti, Fattoria Tregole
Castiglione d'Orcia, Castello di Ripa d'Orcia
Civitella in Val di Chiana, Casale Il Caggio
Cortona, Borgo Elena
Cortona, Borgo Il Melone
Feriolo, Casa Palmira
Florence, Antica Dimora Firenze
Florence, Florence Dream Domus
Florence, Botticelli, Hotel
Florence, Hermitage, Hotel
Florence, Orto de'Medici, Hotel
Florence, Silla, Hotel
Florence, In Piazza della Signoria
Florence, Torricella, La
Florence, Antica Dimora Johlea
Florence, Palazzo dal Borgo—Hotel Aprile
Florence, Palazzo Galletti
Florence, Villa Poggio San Felice
Forcoli, Villa Il Torrino
Gaiole in Chianti, Borgo Argenina
Gaiole in Chianti, Castello di Meleto
Gaiole in Chianti, Castello di Tornano
Galluzzo, Fattoressa, La
Greve in Chianti, Casa Mezzuola
Lucca, Alla Corte degli Angeli
Lucca, Romea, La
Macciano, Macciangrosso
Massa Marittima, Tenuta Il Cicalino
Mercatale Val di Pesa, Salvadonica

Montecarlo, Antica Casa dei Rassicurati
Montefiridolfi, Fattoria La Loggia
Montefiridolfi, Fonte de Medici
Montefiridolfi, Macinello
Montefiridolfi, Villa Sant'Andrea
Montemerano, Fontanelle, Le
Montemerano, Villa Acquaviva
Montepulciano, Agnolo, L'
Montepulciano, Relais San Bruno
Monteriggioni, Antico Borgo Poggiarello
Monteroni d'Arbia, Casa Bolsinina
Orbetello Scalo, Grazia
Orbetello Scalo, Casalone, Il
Panzano in Chianti, Fagiolari
Pelago, Doccia, La
Pienza, Traverse, Le
Pisa, Relais dei Fiori
Poggi del Sasso, Castello di Vicarello
Pomino, Fattoria di Petrognano
Prato, Villa Rucellai di Canneto
Radda in Chianti, Locanda, La
Radda in Chianti, Podere Terreno
Radda in Chianti, Podere Val delle Corti
Radda in Chianti, Pornanino
Radicofani, Fattoria La Palazzina
Roccatederighi, Pieve di Caminino
Rosia, Montestigliano
San Casciano dei Bagni, Crocetta, La
San Casciano dei Bagni, Radici, Le
San Gimignano, Casanova di Pescille
San Gimignano, Casolare di Libbiano
San Gimignano, Casale del Cotone, Il
San Gimignano, Rosolaccio, Il
San Gimignano, Fonte, La

San Gimignano, Podere Villuzza
San Giovanni d'Asso, Locanda del Castello, La
San Giovanni d'Asso, Lucignanello Bandini
San Giustino Valdarno, Villa Cassia di Baccano
San Quirico d'Orcia, Rigo, Il
San Vincenzo, Poggio ai Santi
Sarteano, Sovana, La
Sassetta, Tenuta La Bandita
Saturnia, Villa Clodia
Solaio–Radicondoli, Fattoria Solaio
Tavarnelle Val di Pesa, Sovigliano
Terricciola, Selvino, Il
Torrita di Siena, Hotelita La Lupaia
Vagliagli, Casali della Aiola
Vico d'Elsa, Volpaia, La

Umbria
Allerona, I Casali di Monticchio
Assisi, Malvarina
Assisi, Podere La Fornace
Baschi, Pomurlo Vecchio
Bettona, Torre Burchio
Calvi dell'Umbria, Casale San Martino
Castel del Piano, Villa Aureli
Citta della Pieve, Madonna delle Grazie
Deruta, Antica Fattoria del Colle
Ficulle, Casella, La
Fratta Todina, Palazzetta del Vescovo, La
Gualdo Cattaneo, Ghirlanda, La
Gubbio, Casa Branca
Gubbio, Locanda Del Gallo
Lisciano Niccone, Casa San Martino
Loreto—Todi, Castello di Loreto

Montecastello di Vibio, Fattoria di Vibio
Narni, Podere Costa Romana
Orvieto, Locanda Palazzone
Orvieto, Locanda Rosati
Ospedaletto, Borgo Spante
Spoleto, Palazzo Dragoni
Tavernelle di Panicale, Country House Montali
Titignano, Fattoria Titignano
Todi, Tenuta di Canonica
Torgiano, Poggio alle Vigne
Trevi, Casa Giulia
Tuoro Sul Trasimeno, Castello di Montegualandro

Veneto
Abano Terme, Casa Ciriani
Albarea di Venezia, Villa Rizzi Albarea
Barbarano Vicentino, Castello, Il
Cortina d'Ampezzo, Baita Fraina
Cortina d'Ampezzo, Meublè Oasi
Dolo, Villa Goetzen
Follina, Dei Chiostri, Hotel
Gargagnago, Villa Monteleone
Grezzana, Borgo 27
Levada di Piombino Dese, Gargan
Longare, Vescovane, Le
Malcesine, Park Hotel Querceto
Mirano, Villa Mocenigo
Negrar, Magioca, La
San Martino Buon Albergo, Musella-B&B-Winery
San Martino di Venezze, Tenuta Castel Venezze
Sarcedo, Casa Belmonte
Selvazzano, Conte Emo Capodilista Estate, The
Susegana, Maso di Villa

Places to Stay by Region

Index

Index   473

CLARE BROWN was a travel consultant for many years, specializing in planning itineraries using charming small hotels in the countryside, Her expertise is now available to a larger audience—the readers of her daughter Karen's travel guides, When not traveling, Clare and her husband, Bill, divide their time between northern California, Colorado, and Mexico,

NICOLE FRANCHINI was born in Chicago and raised in a bilingual family (her father being Italian), but she has been residing in Italy for many years, Currently living in the countryside of Sabina near Rome with husband, Carlo, and daughters, Livia and Sabina, Nicole runs her own travel consulting business, Hidden Treasures of Italy, which organizes personalized group and individual itineraries, *www,htitaly,com,*

ELISABETTA FRANCHINI, the artist responsible for many of the illustrations in this guide lives in Chicago with her husband, Chris, and their two young children, where she paints predominantly European landscapes and architectural scenes, A Smith College graduate in Art History and French Literature, Elisabetta has exhibited extensively in the past 20 years, *www,elisabettafranchini,com,*

JANN POLLARD, the artist of all the beautiful cover paintings in the Karen Brown series, has studied art since childhood and is well known for her outstanding impressionistic-style watercolors, Jann has received numerous achievment awards and her works are in private and corporate collections internationally, She is also a popular workshop teacher in the United States, Mexico and Europe, *www,jannpollard,com,* Fine art giclée prints of her paintings are available at *www,karenbrown,com,*

Romantik Hotel Laurin, Salò

Romantik Hotels & Restaurants – Arrive, Relax, Enjoy!

At Romantik Hotels & Restaurants we invite you to arrive, relax and enjoy. Among our more than 200 Romantik Hotels you can find historic country inns, opulent estates and elegant city mansions in 11 European countries. We invite you to indulge in regional cuisines, discover award-winning restaurants or simply relax in one of our beautiful spas. We offer true Romantik hospitality, outstanding cuisine and a historic environment steeped in tradition. In Italy over 20 Romantik Hotels & Restaurants are awaiting you. For more information and availability go to www.romantikhotels.com.

Romantik Hotels & Restaurants are about personal service, attention to detail and true hospitality.

ROMANTIK
HOTELS & RESTAURANTS
INTERNATIONAL

We look forward to your visit.
Romantik Hotels & Restaurants GmbH & Co. KG
Hahnstraße 70, 60528 Frankfurt, Germany

Fon: +49 (0) 69/66 12 34-0
Fax: +49 (0) 69/66 12 34-56

info@romantikhotels.com

www.romantikhotels.com.